MARRIAGE AND THE FAMILY

SECOND EDITION

Marcia Lasswell
CALIFORNIA STATE POLYTECHNIC UNIVERSITY, POMONA

Thomas Lasswell
UNIVERSITY OF SOUTHERN CALIFORNIA

WADSWORTH PUBLISHING COMPANY
Belmont, California
A Division of Wadsworth, Inc.

Sociology Editor Sheryl Fullerton
Assistant Editor Liz Clayton
Special Projects Editor Judith McKibben
Editorial Associate Cynthia Haus
Production Editor Vicki Friedberg
Designer Merle Sanderson
Print Buyer Karen Hunt
Copy Editor John Ziemer
Photo Researcher Lindsay Kefauver
Compositor Carlisle Graphics
Cover Merle Sanderson
Cover Calligraphy Elizabeth Lada
Signing Representative Cynthia Berg

About the Cover The overall impression is similar to a family album. The rich texture and colors of the background represent the intricate fabric of marriage, while the visual sensation of movement signifies the change and growth that occur over time in marriages and families. The bright and flowing style of the title conveys the happiness and rewards that marriage and the family can offer.

Printed in the United States of America   34

1 2 3 4 5 6 7 8 9 10—91 90 89 88 87

Library of Congress Cataloging-in-Publication Data

Lasswell, Marcia E.
   Marriage and the family.

   Bibliography: p.
   Includes indexes.
   1. Marriage—United States.   2. Family—United
States.   I. Lasswell, Thomas E.   II. Title.
HQ536.L375 1987   .306.8'0973   86-28149
ISBN 0-534-07584-3

DEDICATION

Without our "tree of life," this book could not have been written.

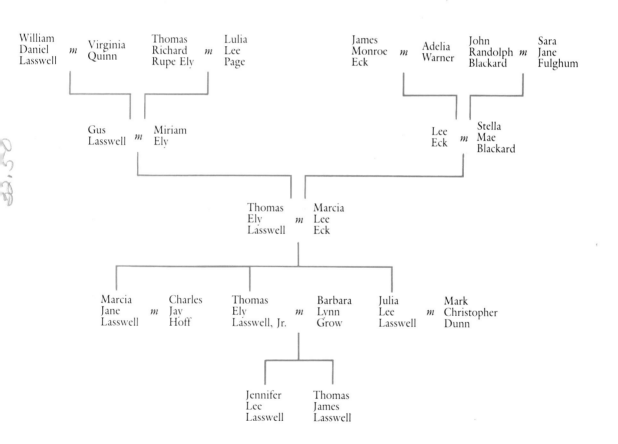

William Daniel Lasswell *m* Virginia Quinn

Thomas Richard Rupe Ely *m* Lulia Lee Page

James Monroe Eck *m* Adelia Warner

John Randolph Blackard *m* Sara Jane Fulghum

Gus Lasswell *m* Miriam Ely

Lee Eck *m* Stella Mae Blackard

Thomas Ely Lasswell *m* Marcia Lee Eck

Marcia Jane Lasswell *m* Charles Jay Hoff

Thomas Ely Lasswell, Jr. *m* Barbara Lynn Grow

Julia Lee Lasswell *m* Mark Christopher Dunn

Jennifer Lee Lasswell

Thomas James Lasswell

BRIEF CONTENTS

Detailed Contents

4 HUMAN SEXUALITY 80

5 SINGLEHOOD AND COHABITATION 114

6 MATE SELECTION AND GETTING MARRIED 144

PHOTOGRAPH CREDITS

PREFACE

There are some things about marriage and the family that do not change. Some form of them is culturally institutionalized in every society, no matter how large or how small, how isolated or how cosmopolitan. Every individual has a concept of what it means to be married and of how one goes about getting married; 95 percent of all Americans will marry at least once during their lifetimes. The average American is spending more years in some form of family living than ever before in our society, or for that matter than the average person at any other time in any society.

Although marriage and the family are here to stay, at least for the foreseeable future, both are constantly changing. The very changes themselves are evidence of the resilience and viability of those social institutions. When we set about to prepare this second edition, we were astonished to discover how much change had occurred since our first edition. Within a few short years there were marked changes in the expectation of life at birth, in the birthrate, in the average age at first marriage of both men and women, in the number of children born out of wedlock, in the acceptability and availability of a variety of forms of contraception, in age-specific divorce rates, and in the likelihood that divorced women would remarry, to mention a few of the many obvious trends in marriage and family patterns.

This book has attempted to assemble the most valid and reliable information available for understanding and explaining the way that people grow up to want to marry and how they choose marriage mates; why problems occur in marital relationships and what has been learned about solving them; how people cope with marital disruption, the aging of their partners and of themselves, the departure of their children, and the death of family members. To the extent that it does these things, it is a book of factual information about marriage and the family. At the same time, it presents these facts with discussions about how they can be useful in everyday life—how to help children learn about sex, how to practice effective family planning, how to prepare for childbirth, how to deal with family finances, how to understand the way that a partner wants to be loved.

One of us is a psychologist, the other a sociologist. We are both social psychologists and marriage, family, and child therapists. Both of us have appointments in academic departments and in clinics; both have private practices. We have experienced more than 36 years of marriage to each other—rearing three children, launching them into marriage and careers, and becoming grandparents.

We have undertaken to introduce our readers to some major theories that apply to marriage and family life as well as to factual information. We think of ourselves as integrationists with respect to family theory rather than as proponents of any one special theory, even though we are both convinced that relationships of any sort must be understood as interpersonal systems, with each individual in any system influencing every other individual within the system.

Key terms that may need definition for readers appear in boldface type where they are first used and are defined in the glossary at the end of the chapter in which they first appear. The appendixes at the end of the book may be included in assigned reading at the pleasure of the instructor.

For those who are interested, a study guide is available from the publisher. Prepared by Tom Gillette and John Wood, it provides self-test questions, review items, key terms, and objectives for each chapter. Gillette and Wood have also prepared an instructor's manual, which offers a bank of questions for test construction. These test items are also available on Micro-Pac, Wadsworth's computerized testing service. For more information contact Helga Newman, Wadsworth Publishing Company, Ten Davis Drive, Belmont, CA 94002, 415-595-2350, or your local Wadsworth sales representative. For instructors who do not have access to a computer, the test items are available from the Wadsworth Teletesting Service (415-593-EXAM).

We gratefully acknowledge the valuable contributions of our colleagues in the field who have supplied us with the research findings on which the book is based. We learned much from our teacher, Harvey J. Locke, who taught us the extreme importance of being critical of the research methods by which information was obtained. We wish to thank our critical reviewers who helped us to sharpen our manuscript: Eleen Baumann, Oregon State University; Cathy Cameron, La-Verne College; Carole Carroll, Middle Tennessee State University; Henry Comby, Tulsa Junior College, Metro Campus; Ross Klein, Iowa State University; James Long, Golden West College; Daniel Schores, Austin College; and Harold Whittington, Temple Junior College.

We are especially appreciative of Sheryl Fullerton's interest in and acquisition of our manuscript for Wadsworth Publishing Company; for the work of Judith McKibben, Special Projects Editor; Vicki Friedberg, Production Editor; Liz Clayton, Assistant Editor; Cindy Haus, Editorial Associate; Merle Sanderson, Designer; and Lindsay Kefauver, who researched the photos for the book. Last of all, but far from least, our special thanks go to Pat Tice, who lived with our demands and frustrations in preparing the original draft of the manuscript and who was always willing to help and to smile when deadlines came, and to Sydney Alter for her aid and encouragement.

Marriage and the Family

At Piggott, Ark., Monday evening, J. A. Northington and Mrs. S. R. Benson were quietly married. Mrs. Benson is a refined and highly respected lady of Gibson. Mr. Northington is one of Campbell's most prominent merchants. The marriage occurred much earlier than first intended, on account of Mr. Northington's housekeeper unexpectedly leaving.

his is a book about some of the experiences of nearly all Americans—experiences that usually involve deep emotions and that most people consider some of the most important in their lives. The reality of these life experiences lies in the beliefs, feelings, and behaviors of those who experience them, as well as in the social and legal meanings given to marriage and the family.

Love, sexual intercourse, commitment, cohabitation, marriage, childbearing, parenting, family, dissolution, and *child custody* are terms for experiences about which most people have strong feelings. Even people who have not had a particular experience often have strong beliefs about how people who do have this experience should behave and feel. This chapter presents an overview of the topics of love, sex, marriage, and the family, including the issues central to our personal and social judgments about them.

MARRIAGE AND THE FAMILY IN THE UNITED STATES

Dunklin Democrat,
Kennett, Missouri,
May 16, 1901

*F*amilies are a prominent feature of every society. Very little happens in people's lives that is not affected by family life and that does not, in turn, affect their own family. Not only are families molded by society into whatever forms are functional, but also families contribute significantly to the success of the society to which they belong. Families prepare future citizens and nurture and sustain adults engaged in the day-to-day business of the society. Sociologists and anthropologists have recently been emphasizing more than ever before that the family is the primary social invention that shapes us into human beings.

Perhaps more than any other feature of the family, its endurance as an institution stands out. This endurance both provides individual family members throughout their lives with a feeling of continuity ("roots") and gives them a sense of leaving a heritage that future generations can use as a similar path for establishing their identities. Each family lives in historical time, not only making its own fate but also being influenced daily in important ways by world events—wars, economic ups and downs, and other less dramatic public occurrences (Elder 1977).

The American belief in the family, demonstrated by the widespread concern for its welfare, as well as for other characteristics of the family—including its problems—is a main subject of this book. We will discuss how the family unit still fulfills basic survival needs for the young, although it has changed from a total institution to a system that focuses primarily on the needs of companionship, love, and intimacy. In a comprehensive review of family life in the United States today, the director of the National Institute of Mental Health said:

> The family gives each newborn its primary nurturing environment, and as time passes, is each child's primary socializing agent, shaping its capacity for personal relations, interpreting and mediating the vast and complex outside world. Beyond these recognized functions we largely take for granted, the family exerts other powerful influences. It can provide us with a continuity of identity throughout our lives—a present network of relatedness, roots into the past, and branches to the future. It is a platform for each member's stages of growth and the intimate arena for learning to recognize and adjust to these stages in others. It has an internal dynamic quality, its functions changing over time according to its members' needs and enduring long after its members have dispersed. Externally the family affects other people and institutions, both as the family unit collectively engages with the world and as its members sally forth, imprinted by their family ways. And the idea of family itself has been extended, providing a unifying function for new combinations of people who choose to call themselves a family. (Pardes 1979, p. 1)

THE STATE OF HEALTH OF MARRIAGE AND THE FAMILY

A cross-section of Americans was asked recently with whom they would spend their time if they had only six months to live. Although the question poses a gloomy thought, the answer gives a vote of confidence to the family: an overwhelming majority chose members of their immediate families (Research and Fore-casts, Inc., 1981).

Such support for the importance of the American family may cause us to wonder about the rumors that the family is in deep trouble, if not dying altogether. For nearly two decades, the press and much of the general public have sounded a pessimistic note about the condition of the American family. Symptoms signifying terminal illness, such as the high divorce rate, violence, intergenerational alienation, sexual freedom outside marriage, have been used by social critics as evidence that an institution with so many problems is doomed (Duberman 1977).

The variety of forms the family currently takes—single-parent families, step-families, dual-paycheck families, communal families, cohabiting families—has been heavily criticized and has been cited as evidence of the breakdown of the American family system. That the same varieties are present (and may always have been present) in other societies has been ignored by alarmists or has been cited by them as evidence of the inferiority of those societies (Bronfenbrenner 1977).

Most serious students of the family believe that the grave concern about the institution of the family arises from the disparity between our idealized notions of the traditional family and the realities of modern life. Today we find multiple family styles in which individual members must attempt to chart their ways in unfamiliar territory. The old rules do not often suit the new lifestyles, but there are no new, uniformly accepted models to guide us toward warmth and intimacy while still al-lowing us to retain individuality. There are currently a great many types of families in the world that seem to function at least somewhat satisfactorily. This apparently has always been true. The standards against which so many critics of current family life measure the family's deterioration seem to be derived from unrealistic ideals rather than from careful observations of historical social reality (Bane 1976b).

We believe that what has been occurring is not the death of the family but rather a powerful struggle by family units to adapt to societal conditions and to the needs of individual family members. The adaptability of the family keeps it alive and is the reason that, no matter what the odds, the family has endured over time and across cultures. Many family-life specialists—and we are among them—believe that the family is thriving. We do not deny that there are serious problems, but we have confidence in the resiliency of contemporary families. Research leaves little question that Americans believe in, support, and depend on the family to fulfill a variety of important needs that society does not meet in any other way (Moroney 1979).

The American family is in a state of change. No one denies this; families have always attempted to adapt to and to maintain continuity in a social world that is constantly changing. There are always pessimists who view any change only from the perspective of a loss of something good. What they view as good often is an idealized version of what has been functional in the past. Frequently emphasis is placed on the sacrifices that must be made when change occurs (Goode 1963). Paradoxically, the capability of families to be flexible, one of their strongest potentials, has been de-nounced by some as a threat to the family's survival. Such critics view **social*** change and the adaptability of social institutions to change as signs of disintegration rather than of strength (Levy 1966). They tend to criticize the innovative methods families

*Terms boldfaced in the text are defined in the glossary at the end of each chapter.

use to cope with reality rather than applaude their creativity. Although pessimists see careers for women as destructive to family life, for example, optimists may applaud the ability of families with working mothers to have better lives than at any time in previous history.

Many view changes positively, as chances for growth and as opportunities to reevaluate social institutions in the light of changing human needs. We are in a state of transition in which **pluralism** is not only becoming more acceptable but is viewed by the majority of social scientists as necessary to our survival (Macklin 1980).

Sociologist Arlene Skolnick (1980, p. 121) has stated the pluralistic view succinctly:

> All forms of the family, by virtue of the fact that they happen to exist, are equally acceptable—from communes and cohabitation to one-parent households, homosexual marriages, and, come to think of it, the nuclear family. What was once labeled "deviant" is now merely "variant." Conflict and change are inherent in social life. If the family is now in a state of flux, such is the nature of resilient institutions; if it is beset by problems, so is life. The family will survive.

The same dire predictions that have been made about the demise of the family have been leveled at the institution of marriage as well. The futurist F. M. Esfandiary (1977, pp. 46–47) has said, "Marriage . . . must go. . . . No variation will work." Certain authors commenting on the American scene have suggested that marriage is an institution in decay (Whitehurst 1975; Packard 1972). There have been many suggestions for improving contemporary marriages, ranging from so-called **trial marriages** to legislation that makes getting married more difficult. And, yet, recent research has shown that, among the many variables studied, the quality of one's marriage is the most powerful predictor of the mental health of married persons (Gove, Hughes, and Style 1983).

Certainly there are many unhappy marriages, and an increasing number of marriages end in divorce. In response to a national poll, 1.7 percent of never-divorced men and 2.8 percent of never-divorced women reported that they were "not too happy." However, 71.3 percent of the men and 70 percent of the women in the sample described themselves as "very happy." The figures for those who had been divorced and remarried indicated slightly less happiness in their current marriages; even so, less than 7 percent reported being "not too happy" (National Opinion Research Center 1973–1975).

Although many marriages end in divorce, in 1979, 85 percent of married men and 88 percent of married women between the ages of 55 and 59 were still married to their first spouse (U.S. Bureau of the Census 1978b, p. 1). Although the increase in life expectancy is largely responsible for these figures, it is also a positive sign that more and more silver and golden wedding anniversaries are being celebrated each year. In 1984, divorced persons represented only 9 percent of the population (although 9 percent is a marked increase over earlier years) (U.S. Bureau of the Census 1985b, p. 2). Evidently not all marriages are in trouble if, as these statistics indicate, the average marriage is lasting longer—only 9 percent report being currently divorced even though divorce is an option—and an overwhelming number of couples report that they are happy in their marriages. Since over 95 percent of all Americans marry at least once and most divorced persons remarry, it seems obvious that Americans overwhelmingly prefer being married to any other lifestyle (Bane 1976a).

CHANGING MARRIAGE AND FAMILY PATTERNS

Many family historians caution that remembrances of the past often are sentimental and idealized. Families have always had hardships, antagonisms, and risks as well as comfort, security, and companionship. Comparing what we have today to an idealized version of what is believed to have occurred in the past inevitably results in a sense that something has gone awry.

Unfortunately, the early history of the American family is not as well documented as one might wish, largely because many of the capabilities of social science to measure long-term cultural changes were not available. In addition, only recently has the field of family history developed to the point that realistic comparisons between families at different points in time can be assessed (Elder 1978). Even the records of such important human milestones as birth, marriage, and divorce have been kept systematically only for the past 30 or 40 years. Much of the information that was not recorded by government agencies or scholarly studies, therefore, had to be gained from deduction, from reported memories of older persons, or from descriptions in the literature of the time. These sources are often inaccurate because people's perceptions have changed over time and also because of the biases of the reporters and writers of history, who were typically white, upper-class, well-educated men. Some experts on family life trace the beginnings of the systematic study of the family to Charles Darwin's 1859 work, *The Origin of Species* (Christensen 1964). In response to Darwin's biological-evolutionary ideas, early studies were large-scale, cross-cultural attempts to find universal laws about marriage and the family.

As the relatively new fields of sociology and marriage and the family developed in the twentieth century, research on social problems and their effects on marriage and the family became the focus of scholars in these two fields. The studies became more and more sophisticated in research techniques and analyses as facts about American family life were collected. Changes were noted by comparing past with present, and trends were forecast for the future.

Functional Changes

The nature of the unifying functions around which individuals come together as families has shifted in the twentieth century. Early definitions of the family often emphasized its utilitarian functions—the economic aspects of the family unit. Even during the first 30 years of this century, and throughout the Depression of the 1930s, the definition of the family was often colored by its practical functions (Burgess, Locke, and Thomes 1963).

Although millions of Americans still live in poverty, and inflation may again be forcing families to focus on economic issues, since the 1940s the major emphasis has been increasingly on the emotional aspects of family life. In her thoughtful discussion of this change, family sociologist Lois Pratt (1976) has commented that families still have difficulty in giving their members all the necessary emotional nourishment but that multifamily forms have developed in an effort to accomplish this task. Although the heavy emotional demands made on each family unit have the potential to create serious problems, most families are motivated by the necessity to do for their members what no other institution can. The forms families take must vary to meet the unique demands of different times and situations, and of the individual members' need to learn to care for themselves and for each other and to have healthy contacts outside the family boundaries. Therefore, not only may one family differ from another, but each family also changes its form over time.

To determine what makes families strong, cohesive, functional support systems for their members, a study was made of 130 families (Stinnett 1978). Six qualities stood out clearly:

1. Most important was the members' *appreciation for one another.* Students of social psychology will recognize at once the important findings of research on affiliation and liking: we like people most who like us; we want to be with those who make us feel good about ourselves and who support rather than criticize us (Backman and Secord 1959). Family members who openly appreciate each other enjoy being together.

2. Because family members enjoyed each other, they *arranged their personal schedules* so that they had time together as a family. Each of the strong families regularly spent time together as a family, although what they did together was by no means routine. They also spent time together spontaneously. Most family members lead busy lives, and each person must make a positive effort to find family time.

3. Strong families are characterized by positive *communication patterns,* as will be discussed in Chapter 7. Positive communication involves openness, genuineness, active listening, respect, interest, and the airing of differences. The important thing is not the quantity of communication—provided there is adequate coverage of concerns and interests—but rather that family members share meaning and agree on the quality of the communication.

4. The well-functioning families provided evidence of strong family feeling and *high family commitment.* Since the family is a small group, small-group research can be used to explain the cohesiveness of strong families. Cohesiveness derives from the belief of members that some of their important needs (being liked and appreciated, for example) are met by belonging and that the group they belong to is a winning team. The presence of these factors induces members to invest time and energy in the family (Shaw 1976, p. 4).

5. Members of strong families felt a sense of a power and a purpose greater than themselves—a *spiritual orientation.* This is not to say that they were necessarily religious or churchgoing people. However, they defined themselves as having values that are generally associated with religion.

6. Finally, these families were able to face their problems and to *deal positively with crises.* They were striking in their adaptive abilities and in the nourishment and care they provided for family members during times of trouble.

Cultural Differences

Some of the most striking examples of changes noted by the twentieth-century sociologists were in popular views of love, marriage, and the family and in the notions of what model has been favored for each. To describe these changes in popular notions

CHAPTER 1

There are many varieties of families and many different family patterns that function well in a society as diversified as the United States'.

accurately, it was—and still is—necessary to consider the many social class and ethnic differences that have always existed in the United States. These differences have been present since the founding of the country; yet many people assume that post–Civil War Americans were **culturally** homogeneous and that the great variation in marriage and the family is of fairly recent origin.

It is true that the years following the Civil War gradually transformed the United States from a largely rural population into an urban, industrialized society. With that transformation came profound changes in attitudes toward the family. Instead of a community of interdependent kin and neighbors, all of whom worked together and paid attention to each other's "business"—blurring the boundaries of home and work—industrialization set the home apart. Families became the source of emotional support; members went outside the home to work or to school. Men's and women's work became more separate; children began to be defined as noncontributing dependents who were not expected to share in earning the family's living. The forms these new families took were, if anything, more varied than those of their predecessors.

One has only to review the evidence to see how unjustified is the assumption that there are or ever have been universal models of love, marriage, and family organization in the United States. One could hardly expect the Irish Catholic immigrant blue-collar worker who came to Boston as late as the turn of the twentieth century to have the same model for his or her marriage and family as the Mississippi-born descendant of a black slave. We know more about differences today because of television and the ease of travel from place to place, but the differences have always been there.

The mosaic of **microcultures** in the United States contains many tiles; the picture is complicated by racial, ethnic, religious, educational, class, and geographical differences that make it difficult for one to shape any general statements about the culture of the society as a whole, particularly with respect to ideals such as love and models for family organization.

The United States has been called a "melting pot," which implies that as immigrants reached its shores they were assimilated into the mainstream. Perhaps this was truer in the early years of the century, but clearly the distinctive lifestyles, values, and norms of more recent immigrants who have come by the thousands to this country have kept much of their cultural identity. Instead of a melting pot, these ethnic populations have helped to create a stew in which each group is recognized as unique. A major way in which certain ethnic groups are set apart is by their family customs.

Even within those family systems that have become assimilated, there are wide differences in approaches to family life. There is no one American way to be a family. Many Asian-Americans, for example, still subscribe to traditional values—duty and obligation to family, respect for patriarchal authority—resulting in more strongly bonded, close family networks. They have fewer divorces and less premarital sex than the majority of other Americans (Suzuki 1980).

Structural Changes

Just as the United States has changed to accommodate diverse cultural patterns of marriage and the family, so have our expectations of relations among family members been modified. Family sociologists have built a strong case for the fact that there has been a widespread shift in the popular conceptualization of the family in the United States. It has been proposed that the family model is generally moving from an *institutional* to a *companionship* one (Burgess, Locke, and Thomes 1963). Although many kinds of changes are described, the emphasis has been on the main shift from the all-encompassing family to one composed of a group of relatively liberated people whose chief ties are affectional. The all-encompassing family was one that prepared its young members for life in society and maintained its social unity through a high degree of economic and functional interdependence of family members. The companionship family, which depends on other institutions for much of this preparation, concentrates instead on nurturance and affection.

Major areas that seem to be changing are ideal patterns related to mate selection, sexual freedom, gender roles in society, romanticism, the degree of mutual interdependence of marriage partners, mixed marriages, and the definitions of masculinity and femininity. Although the differences from the patterns of the past are striking, they are more impressive for the number of people that are affected than for the novelty of the ideas themselves. Because they are documented in literature and films and are openly discussed in classrooms and on television, the changes are highly visible. Thus, even small differences take on significant proportions.

Urbanization

There have been social as well as cultural changes in patterns of love, marriage, and the family; these have resulted from a variety of social events. Data on vital statistics, legislative changes, economics, and population movements are examples of information collected about social change that have had profound implications for family life; much of this information has been carefully recorded.

Among the important social changes noted in the past century are those in the rural-urban distribution of the population. In its early days, the United States was primarily an agricultural nation. Just after World War II, in 1946, almost one-third of the population still lived on farms. By 1979, however, only about 1 family in 28 lived on a farm. Less than half the families in the United States lived in urban areas in 1910; today, over 90 percent of families live in such areas (U.S. Bureau of the Census 1980b, p. 7).

Although the dramatic move away from the farm was not the result of changing ideas about love, marriage, and the family, it certainly had a profound effect on all of these. Many customs that were functional for a satisfactory life on the farm are inappropriate or unsatisfactory for city living. For instance, patterns of mate selection have changed, in part because of the greater mobility of young people (Jacobsen 1959). The physical locations in which courtship, marriage, childbirth, terminal illness, and death occur are drastically different.

Partial employment of both the young and the aged had a very different meaning on the farm 50 years ago from that in contemporary metropolitan centers. Members of the generation moving away from the farm had ingrained in them as children sentiments appropriate to farm life at the time, such as reliance on the family unit to meet most vital needs. Urban children of today, on the other hand, are often exposed to situations in which reliance on the family may be either inappropriate or inefficient.

THE PREINDUSTRIAL FAMILY IN AMERICA

Persons who lived in the American colonies in the seventeenth and early eighteenth centuries made their living primarily from agriculture and a few small-scale businesses. Men, women, and children worked together both inside and outside the home. All family members were productive except infants. If a family did not have enough work for one or more of the children, they were often hired out to other families.

Though husbands controlled the family work and resources, women, who were not viewed as the weaker sex, had a say because they were needed as economic partners. The responsibility for infant-care fell primarily to women, but women were not much more involved in caring for older children than were men because both were too busy working. Children were treated as miniature adults and not as dependents who needed protection. As a result, young children were often neglected and frequently died. The mortality rate for children was high, but the high fertility rates served to keep an adequate number of children to maintain the family labor pool. Children were clearly a financial asset rather than a costly burden because they contributed to the family economy.

Perhaps because such child labor was necessary to the family, a woman's ability to bear children was considered an important part of her value. It was, therefore, considered quite sensible to determine this before marriage. It was common for brides to be pregnant—the families of the couple saw to it that a marriage would take place. Marriage and subsequent childbearing were so important, in fact, that unmarried adults who did not continue to live with their kin or another family were often refused permission to reside in these early colonial communities. Each village was, therefore, made up of families rather than individuals. Village affairs were conducted by men who, as heads of households, were entitled to represent their families. "In colonial America, . . . the term *town fathers* [often] meant just that"—fathers who ran the business of government as well as that of their families (p. 127).

As economic growth became tied to industrialization in the late eighteenth century and through the nineteenth century, families were sustained by productive processes outside the home. Mothers could not as easily work for money when it entailed leaving home to do so. Homemaking and parenting became the work of middle-class women because fathers were away from home to earn money. Only wars changed this. In wartime, mothers found a way, temporarily, to combine mothering and employment when they replaced men in the work force who went to battle. Only recently have women reentered the work world in great numbers, and families are struggling with the balance of employment and parenting. Children are viewed entirely differently in the postindustrial world. Where previously they were important—although poorly cared for—because they were needed in the labor force, today, children are well-cared for although financially unproductive. In effect, families' expectations about parenting, which are based on a one wage-earner model, are not realistic for their current economic needs.

What the future holds is, of course, uncertain. Much is tied to the current economy, but much also is determined by the expectations parents have about who works and who parents.

Source: Adapted from *Women and Men in Society,* 2nd ed., by Charlotte G. O'Kelley and Larry S. Carney. Belmont, CA: Wadsworth, 1986.

Rural children typically do not encounter busy thoroughfares as do city children. Children on farms usually can roam some distance from home quite safely, with the assurance that almost anyone they encounter can help them find their way home if they get lost. In contrast, children in urban environments who wander away from supervision by familiar adults may become lost or encounter dangerous people or situations.

It was not unusual for isolated farm children half a century ago to be acquainted from an early age with the partners that they would eventually marry. Contemporary urbanites, on the other hand, often first meet their future mates when they are adults living alone or apart from their families; sometimes the parents do not even meet before the partners have married. Clearly this is not the result of any conscious effort of the persons involved to make changes in their patterns of love, marriage, and family living. It is instead the result of complex economic and political factors and their effects on human needs and values.

The move from a rural to a more urban life also has had a profound impact on the roles of men and women at work and at home. Men's work has become increasingly separated from the home, and women's work is often both inside and outside the home, depending upon the family's economic needs. If the family needs the income that a wife and mother can produce, she often finds it necessary, though difficult, to combine economic productivity with housework and child care.

Currently, in the United States 59 percent of the married women who are mothers of minor children participate in the labor force, although the majority are employed part-time (U.S. Department of Labor, Bureau of Labor Standards 1985, pp. 155–156). Employed women usually still retain primary responsibility for child care and for some domestic tasks. Because many women must work or want to work, or both, and even though the roles of husband and wife have changed, the practicalities of child rearing have caused many women to delay childbearing and to set a limit of one or two children.

Life Expectancy

The number of years that a person born in a given year can expect to live has changed dramatically since the turn of the century. In 1900, the average person in the United States was expected to live to about age 47. A boy born today in this country can expect to live to about 70 on the average; a girl born today can expect to live more than 80 years (U.S. Bureau of the Census 1977c, p. 1). Even though this change is primarily due to a large drop in infant mortality, the increasing numbers of persons who live beyond their child-rearing years, of men who live until retirement, and of widows have important implications for love, marriage, and family living, as will be discussed in later chapters.

In 1890, half the women who ever married were dead before they were 53 and still had small children living at home when they died (Jacobsen 1959). Some were already widows, of course, since men also died early. Today, half the women who have ever married live to be well over 80. They live to see their own children grown and to have grandchildren and perhaps great-grandchildren. Women outlive their husbands by ten years or more. Such factors, coupled with the migration from farms (where the old may have almost no economic contribution to make to the family), have had a profound impact on the customary ways of life of all family members, old and young alike.

Today, since both men and women usually live for many years after their children leave home, the empty nest poses challenges for many middle-aged married couples, who have to reorganize their lives after their children's departure. The postparental period often gives a couple a new lease on life. They may have more time, more money to spend on themselves, and more opportunity to get to know each other as a couple again. The decrease in child-rearing responsibilities gives them the opportunity for new activities, more leisure time, a job shift, or a host of other pursuits. A new look at postparental adjustments and traditional customs for relating to older family members has been the focus of much research in the past few decades (Streib and Beck 1980).

Changing Marriage Patterns

Throughout the twentieth century, there have been about 10 marriages per year per 1,000 population. Unusual circumstances have occasionally caused departures from this rate, such as the extremely low rate during the Depression of the 1930s (9 per 1,000) and the extremely high rate (12 per 1,000) that peaked in 1946, immediately after World War II (National Center for Health Statistics 1983, p. 3). The actual number of marriages declined until 1977; in 1982, the largest annual number of marriages ever was recorded in the United States (the rate, however was only 10.8 per 1,000 population); the marriage rate has declined each year since, reaching 10.2 per 1,000 in February, 1986 (National Center for Health Statistics 1986, p. 2).

Although the marriage rate has not shown any major long-term trends in the twentieth century, this situation in itself may be remarkable since age distributions have changed considerably during the twentieth century. There have been marked increases both in the fraction of the population past childbearing age and in the number of females who survive from birth to childbearing age. The long-term stability of the marriage rate leads us to suspect, therefore, that there must be changes in the characteristics of the persons who marry. This is borne out by the data, as we shall see.

The median age at first marriage for men in 1890 was slightly over 26 years (see Figure 1.1). This means that approximately half of all men who married were under 26 years of age, and half were over 26. Over the years that followed, the median age of first marriage for men steadily declined, reaching a low of 22.5 years in 1956, a decline of more than 3.5 years from the 1890 figure. Beginning about 1960, a small upward trend began, resulting by 1982 in a median age at first marriage for men of over 25 years.

It is interesting to associate information about age at marriage with the remarkable changes in the median number of years of education. In 1890, since most males went to work rather than to high school, a large fraction of males around the turn of the century had been more or less ready to become self-sufficient (that is, they had finished school and were presumably eligible to be in the labor force, to work on the farm, or to find other kinds of employment) for twelve or more years before they married. In contrast, today's figures show that half the males who marry have been similarly eligible for six years or less. This circumstance is due partly to the later age at which males leave school and partly to their lower median age at marriage. This drastic reduction in the period of independent bachelorhood has many implications for patterns of courtship and marriage, as we will discuss in Chapter 6.

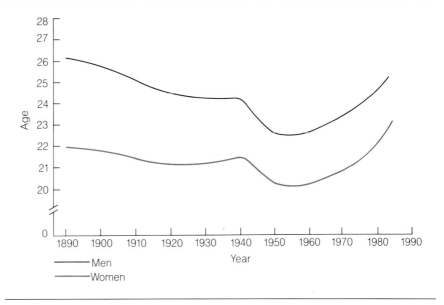

FIGURE 1 · 1
Median Age at First
Marriage by Sex,
1890–1984

Age

Year

——— Men
——— Women

Source: U.S. Bureau of the Census, *Current Population Reports,*
Series P-20, No. 402 (October 1985), p. 2.

Much less change has been observed in the median age of first marriage for women than for men. In 1890, the median age at first marriage for women was 22 years. A slow decline followed, to a low of 20.1 years in 1956, which was followed in turn by a slow rise to 21.0 years in 1973 and 22.0 in 1980. In 1984, the median age at first marriage was about 23.0 for women, an all-time high. The age at marriage for females is slightly higher now than it was a hundred years ago, and there is a slow upward trend. Following our previous logic, we can note that young women a century ago spent seven or eight years working at home or employed outside the home after they had finished school and before they married, whereas today many young women spend only about three years working before marriage, having spent more years in school.

The general implication of these findings for both men and women is that today there is a more immediate transition from the family of one's parents and siblings to the family created with a marriage partner—and thus a much shorter period of self-sufficiency—than there was at the beginning of the twentieth century. This shorter period of self-sufficiency means young people have less time to establish personal identities. The likelihood that a person who marries at a young age will not have established a mature adult identity is believed to be a main factor in the high failure rate of youthful marriages. The recent increase in age at first marriage for both men and women may mark the beginning of a trend toward a longer transition period from dependency on parents until marriage; however, it is still uncertain what this increase means (Rawlings 1978). It does not seem to mean that marriage is going out of style. The fraction of persons aged 40 or over who have never married has been declining steadily and, in 1983, was about 5 percent (U.S. Bureau of the Census 1983b, p. 2).

Changing Birthrates

On average, the first child born to a marriage arrives slightly later than his or her counterpart of a decade ago. At present, about half the firstborn children arrive within seventeen months after marriage. There has been no significant change in the average spacing between the first and second children of women who have only two children. There has, however, been a significant increase in the length of time between the most recent birth to a mother of four or more children and the birth of the preceding child (Rawlings 1978).

The birthrate in the United States has declined since 1800, although during the twentieth century birthrates have fluctuated from 1 birth per year for every 60 people—the all-time low, reached at the peak of the Depression in 1933—to 1 birth per year for every 40 people, a figure reached during the postwar baby boom in 1947. After 1957, when the baby boom ended, the crude birthrate decreased steadily until 1976. Although it has been increasing gradually for the past few years, it appears destined to stay relatively low for the foreseeable future (National Center for Health Statistics 1986, p. 1). Collectively, these data suggest that there is considerably more family planning than there was even a decade ago, especially since much of the recent increase in the birthrate has been accounted for by first births to women over 30 years old. It is significant that the birth control pill was mass-marketed in 1966, providing its users with a more effective means of planning their families.

It is important to note the point made earlier in this chapter that since the population has shifted from rural to urban, parents increasingly find their children are no longer economic assets. In the past it was more costly to raise a large family in the city than it was on the farm. Many believe that economic factors play a most important role in the reduction of the birthrate.

Changing Divorce Patterns

In 1890, there was 1 divorce for every 2,000 people in the population. (U.S. Bureau of the Census 1979a). The divorce rate has increased more or less steadily until the present, when there are about 5 divorces per year for every 1,000 people (National Center for Health Statistics 1986, p. 2). This is higher than the previous peak of 4.3, which occurred immediately after World War II. Divorce is about ten times as common as it was in 1890, but the number of years that the average person remains in his or her first marriage has increased dramatically. Unfortunately, information on abandonment, desertion, and separation without divorce is neither consistent nor reliable; however, it is estimated that these forms of family disruption occur as often as legal divorce and may have occurred even more often in the nineteenth century. Marital disruption overall, however, most often occurs because of the death of one of the partners, even though for younger couples divorce is more likely to end their marriages.

The annual divorce rate published by the National Center of Health Statistics (NCHS) shows that the divorce rate has leveled off after showing a steep rise between 1966 and 1976 (Saluter 1983, p. 4). In 1986, the divorce rate recorded by the NCHS (1986) for the previous twelve months was 5.0 per 1,000 population, down from 5.3 in 1982.

Divorces account for about one-third of the recorded disruption of marriages among whites in the United States today, and they account for about two-thirds of the disruption of marriages among nonwhites. This indicates that most white marriages end with the death of a spouse and most nonwhite marriages end with divorce. The proportion of women between the ages of 30 and 45 who report disrupted marriages is approximately three times as high for the nonwhite population as it is for the white population (U.S. Bureau of the Census 1979a, p. 1). This is thought to represent more an economic factor than a racial or ethnic one. The greatest likelihood of family disruption exists among couples in which the man has not finished high school and has a low income. Interpretations of the implications of the economic factor in divorce are complicated, of course. Not only does low socioeconomic status contribute to a high divorce rate, but divorce is bound to create financial hardship in all but a few families.

Changing Household and Family Size

Between 1970 and 1985, the size of households and the size of families in the United States declined sharply, but the *number* of households increased. In the five-year period from 1980 to 1985, the number of households increased by 1.2 million per year; the number of adults (persons 18 years and older) in those households stayed the same (1.97), but the number of children declined from 0.79 to 0.72, a marked drop since 1970, when there were 1.09 children per household (U.S. Bureau of the Census 1986a, pp. 1–2).

Most households (58 percent) are comprised of married couples and their children, if any. About 14 percent are single-parent families, and 28 percent are nonfamily households, 90 percent of the latter being one-person households. In 1985, there was an average of 2.24 adults per family—but the number of children had declined from 1.34 in 1970 to .98 in 1985 (U.S. Bureau of the Census 1986a, p. 2).

The changing sizes of households and families suggest that living groups are becoming smaller and smaller. While this change is due in part to the fact that more older persons are living alone, there are also more childless families and more single-child families. The effects of this kind of social isolation are not fully understood, but it seems likely that feelings about family life must be different from those in the past.

FAMILY FORMS

Different societies have different types of families, but none is without some form of familial pattern (often called a kinship system) that provides for committed relationships between men and women and between parents and children.

Family sociologists have proposed that what appears to be an almost unlimited variety of families found in different societies of the world actually are different combinations of five basic characteristics seen in all kinship systems (Hess, Markson,

Much of the strength of modern American families lies in the contact across generations, which provides a sense of roots, belonging, and support for members of each generation.

and Stein 1985, p. 259). The first characteristic is how many spouses an individual is permitted at one time—one (**monogamy**) or more (**polygamy**). In some societies only men may have more than one partner (**polygyny**), but in a few societies, women may have more than one husband (**polyandry**).

The second characteristic around which family forms vary is who can marry whom. In Chapter 6, we will discuss the societies in which choices are made by parents in contrast to the method so familiar in the United States of relatively free choice. In societies where parents arrange marriages, the purpose is usually to enhance family status. They attempt to arrange the best bargain they can. It has been suggested that where more freedom of choice prevails, those seeking their own partners are also looking for the best bargain they can find and have developed an elaborate set of dating rituals to aid in finding a mate (Adams 1979).

The third variable affecting family forms is how lineage and family property are transmitted. If through males, the society is considered **partrilineal,** through females, **matrilineal,** and through both parents, **bilineal.** Historically, patrilineality was the most common pattern, especially in agrarian societies. Perhaps this was believed to be a natural order of things since men were considered to be heads of households and legitimate authority figures in their families (**patriarchy**), and it may have seemed that property should belong to them rather than to women. Matrilineality, though not unknown, is not common because it usually appears only in societies where females make the primary economic contributions or where males are absent from the home for long periods of time. Most Western family forms are bilineal, although using the male's name to identify kinship is still a common practice.

The fourth characteristic, where a couple lives, is usually closely related to lineage. A couple that lives with the groom's family is patrilocal, with the bride's family, matrilocal, or in a new location of the couple's own choosing, neolocal. Couples who live with either partner's kin form what is called an **extended family;** those who, with their children, choose a new location of their own form a neolocal or **nuclear**

family. The latter are most likely to have their primary obligation to the marriage tie and to their children, but those who are a part of either side's extended family may have blood relationships as the focus of their obligation.

Finally, an important concern is what the power relationships are within the family. In most societies some form of patriarchy has prevailed. The modern American family tends to be equalitarian in that power differences are reduced between husbands and wives and between parents and children. The United States census defines a *family* as "a group of two persons or more related by birth, marriage, or adoption and residing together" (U.S. Bureau of the Census 1980d, p. 40). Much of the material in this book is based on information gathered by researchers using that definition. Although such a definition permits the collection of general statistics, it tells us nothing about some of the most important features of our own family relationships—how we ought to feel about one another (and how we do feel), how we ought as a family to interact with the rest of society (and how we do interact). In other words, for most of us there is much more to the concept of family than legal marriage, birth or adoption, and common residence. This book is concerned with personal and social feelings and behaviors related to family living, the ways that family rules and roles emerge, common problems families have, and ways of dealing with those problems.

▌ MARRIAGE FORMS

One popular definition of marriage is that it is an institutionalized process whereby given men and women ceremonially begin, and generally maintain, a mutual relationship suitable for the purpose of founding and sustaining a family (Hoult 1969). Some questions may be raised about the applicability of this definition to modern American society.

For many people, marriage seems to be as concerned with the public legitimation of sexual relationships and cohabitation as with the founding and sustenance of a family. A marriage may exist for a number of years both before and after children are a part of it; many people now marry with the intention of remaining childless. However, even if one or both members of a couple are sterile, they may still be subject to both personal and social pressures to represent themselves as married if they intend to live together for a long time. In fact, in all 50 states marriages continue to be valid whether children are born or not; moreover, if children are born, a marriage continues to be valid until it is dissolved by death or divorce, often many years after the children have left the home.

Legal Forms of Marriage

There are two legal forms of marriage in the United States: ceremonial and nonceremonial. A **ceremonial marriage** is one in which the principals state before witnesses that they intend to take one another as marriage partners. Although all states require some form of license in order to register a marriage in the public records, the qualifications for obtaining it differ from state to state (see Chapter 6). Some states require the presence of an authorized officiant; many permit the couple themselves to conduct their ceremony.

In those states providing for **nonceremonial ("common-law") marriages,** the legal status of a marriage can be based on **cohabitation** (living together) and/or **consummation** (engaging in sexual intercourse) over a specified period of time. In such states, having children and establishing other kinds of marital relationships are not required for a marriage to be recognized as legal and valid. In at least one state (Iowa), the courts have ruled that marriage can be established by a couple who are competent to marry (legally of age, not married to someone else, and so forth), simply by their telling witnesses that they are married or by their representing themselves publicly as husband and wife. According to the Constitution of the United States, these marriages must be recognized as legal and valid in all states whenever they are contracted in any state where they are legal. Regardless of where the partners live, common-law marriages can be dissolved only in the same ways that ceremonial marriages are dissolved in the couple's state of residence.

The customs of a society seldom conflict directly with its laws. In other words, laws shape behavior and behavior shapes laws, even in such fundamental areas of our lives as marriage and the family. On the other hand, there have always been minorities in the United States that have codes of beliefs or behaviors that differ from the laws to a greater or lesser extent. For example, the Roman Catholic church may define a marriage as not valid until or unless it has been ceremonially sanctioned according to the church's own prescriptive codes, regardless of the legal status of the couple. Other examples could be drawn from communes, group marriages, and the customs of various religious and cultural groups whose norms for contracting marriage differ to a greater or lesser extent from those of the state in which they occur.

Social Forms of Marriage

In general, we usually think in terms of *mating* or *pairing* when we think of marriage. "Pairing," in particular, suggests a cultural bias—the assumption of monogamy. This concept implies sexual exclusiveness with one's partner, which is not necessarily a requirement for marriage. In fact, an early study by anthropologist George Murdock (1957, p. 686) found that in a world sample of 554 societies, monogamy was the preferred style in only 135. We might be closer to deciding who is married, therefore, by emphasizing the enduring nature of the relationships we observe rather than by looking for monogamous relationships.

Clearly, marriages everywhere must endure or be intended to last through *some* appreciable time span in order to qualify as "real" marriages. This time span must represent a defined period in the human life cycle. Marriage is, therefore, a developmental, enduring (though dynamic) social relationship between two or more people in a social system.

What *kind* of social relationship is marriage? How can an objective observer distinguish marriage from other forms of patterned human social interactions? Four criteria, primarily social in nature (although not entirely lacking in cultural components), may help to characterize marriage:

1. The persons involved expect and usually achieve some form of sexual access to one another for an indefinitely long period, either as a basis for or as a symbol of

their social relationship. If there are exceptions to this generalization, they are considered matters of individual peculiarity rather than of social prescription.

2. The persons involved have an economic relationship, including some understanding about the allocation of their energies and incomes, and an agreement about the communality or exclusiveness of their material goods, services, items for consumption, and real or personal property.

3. The persons involved relate to one another in patterns that are predominantly *symbiotic;* that is, they are mutually supportive and interdependent, with each apparently contributing in some specific (and perhaps also general) ways to the welfare of the other(s).

4. Although they are dynamic and subject to change, the responsibilities and patterned functions of the relationship tend to be stable over an enduring period— a one-day relationship probably would not count unless the persons involved intended it or the effects of it to last longer.

Cultural Forms of Marriage

In addition to these primarily social criteria for a marriage relationship, seven features are usually found in conceptualizations of marriage in the United States that have somewhat stronger cultural overtones.

1. The relationship is **heterosexual.** That is, if the foregoing criteria are applied to persons relating to one another who are of the same sex, most people (and all existing state laws) deny that the systems constitute a marriage.

2. The relationship is monogamous. Although many societies do not concur, this is the only legal pattern in the United States. Only one pair of partners can participate in a marriage at a time; additional relationships are considered to be extramarital, **bigamous** (with one person having two partners), or polygamous (with many partners), by definition. Consequently, group marriages are not legally recognized, nor do most people consider such relationships to be marriages.

3. The relationship is usually thought to be directed toward the establishment of a family, especially through procreation or the adoption (either formal or informal) of children. This assumption may be changing in our society, but it is still the case more often than not.

4. There is a division of tasks in the relationship, with specified (and usually cultural) roles allocated to participants in an organized way.

5. The participants in the relationship "love" each other; or, at least, love was a factor in their selection of each other as mates.

6. The persons involved in a marriage have a common residence. They conceptualize a common dwelling place as "home."

7. Persons with certain kinship (or sometimes other) relationships cannot be partners in a marriage, even though they meet all of the other social criteria. Marriages that are defined as **incestuous** are prohibited by law in every state.

These seven criteria make the conditions for marriage more specific and hence tend to reduce the number of persons conceptualized as being socially married at any given time.

In this book we are concerned with the legal and moral rights and obligations of marriage and the family and with the statistics related to marriage and its termination. Our concerns also are with the feelings and behaviors of people who are involved in marriage and family relationships, and of men and women who pass laws or establish policies that affect marital organization or dissolution.

▌MARRIAGE AND FAMILY RESEARCH AND THEORY

Partly because of concerns about the effects of social change on marriage and the family and partly because the problems noted earlier prompt a general concern, most research in the areas of marriage and the family has been problem oriented. It has been estimated that for every 100 studies investigating families only 1 has been of a positive nature whereas 99 have been concerned with problems (Corfman 1979, p. 1). Marriage and family research has contributed to a better understanding of the family as an enduring unit, although more research on successful marriages and families is needed to complete the picture.

Hundreds of studies have yielded a steady supply of facts. Until relatively recently, in fact, marriage and family research was long on facts but short on **theory.** At first researchers borrowed theories from other disciplines to help interpret the facts derived from marriage and family research. Recently, however, the field of marriage and the family has generated theories of its own in addition to using existing theories to good advantage in explaining contemporary family life and expected trends (Burr 1973). During the past decade, marriage and family theories have become more sophisticated and have expanded to include dozens of "minor" theories in an attempt to interpret findings on subjects that are only peripherally related (Holman and Burr 1980). Throughout this book there will be references to contemporary theories on various phenomena of family life. Although there is no general agreement about which theories offer the best possibilities for explaining family behavior, we have chosen a few to explain certain aspects of marriage and family life.

Theories are statements that attempt to relate and explain ideas and observations—systems that link concepts and facts together. Theories attempt to demonstrate cause and effect and to suggest further areas of research that may make the initial theory more accurate. Frequently, two or more theories appear to be in conflict with each other. More often than not, however, the apparent conflict results from the fact that the theories are approaching a given topic from very different directions. Rather than disagreeing, then, often the theories simply are addressing separate parts of a problem.

With topics as large and diverse as marriage and the family, many theories are probably needed: it is unlikely that any one theory could ever be comprehensive enough to take all factors into consideration. However, the search continues for an "all-purpose general family framework" to unify and consolidate knowledge about marriage and the family (Hill 1966). We are less certain than some of our colleagues that the pursuit of a unified, all-encompassing theory is the most appropriate goal at present, and we are even doubtful that it is now possible to find one theory that is simultaneously broad enough to cover all aspects of marriage and the family and specific enough to be useful (Klein 1979).

Throughout this book we will refer to theories that have been used to explain how people interact in their family relationships. We have selected the major theories as well as a few others that reveal our particular biases. In a recent review of marriage and family theories, Holman and Burr (1980) suggest that there are three kinds of theoretical approaches currently judged to have a major impact on our understanding of issues of marriage and the family. These three approaches are symbolic interaction theory, exchange theory, and general systems theory.

Symbolic Interaction Theory

Many family theorists believe that symbolic interaction may be the most influential theory, because of the number of research projects employing this approach (Klein, Schvaneveldt, and Miller 1977). A distinguishing feature of the interactionist approach is the belief that we acquire a complex assortment of symbols in our minds (words, meanings, gestures—anything that represents an abstract concept) and use these symbols to understand our environment and the people in it, including ourselves. We act, react, and adjust by the use of these symbols—most of which are a part of the environment into which we are born. We are "socialized" to accept and understand the vast array of symbols we use.

Symbolic interaction theory explains mate selection as an evolving process dependent on a person's learning to evaluate potential partners through symbols. It is through symbols that information is gathered and categorized. Choices are then determined by the meanings each person gives to his or her own behavior and to that of others. For example, most persons considering marriage carry in their minds certain expectations about how a husband and a wife should behave. Perhaps from their parents or from friends, or from the media, they have learned how others interpret these married roles. The mere words *husband* or *wife* become symbols that invoke expectations with regard to their own and a partner's future behavior once they are married. In searching for a prospective mate, then, one may look for shared symbolic interpretations. If two people have similar expectations, the likelihood of satisfaction with the way each behaves is increased.

Exchange Theory

Exchange theory has grown in popularity in the past decade. It has been suggested that exchange theory has the potential to be the "grand, all-encompassing" framework that has so far been elusive (Nye 1978). At the risk of oversimplifying a complex theoretical orientation, we can say that exchange theory basically emphasizes the concepts of rewards and costs in any interaction. The sociologist Peter Blau (1964, p. 91) describes exchanges as "voluntary actions of individuals that are motivated by the returns [that the exchanges] are expected to bring and typically do in fact bring from others." People seek rewarding exchanges and attempt to keep the costs lower than the rewards.

Most studies on family decision making have used exchange theory as a basis for explaining how and why decisions are made (Osmond 1978). Each person has certain resources (money, talent, wisdom, affection) that may be used to reward desirable behaviors of others. Such rewards may become sources of power in couples' decision making, for example. Exchange theory has also been widely used as a basis for helping couples in conflict. Much successful marital therapy concentrates on maximizing the rewarding aspects of the relationship for each partner while minimizing the drawbacks (Stuart 1976). Exchange theory has helped scholars understand a variety of marital and family issues in which a clear focus on rewards and costs is evident. Critics of exchange theory point out, however, that not all issues lend themselves to such a clear analysis: many interrelationships appear to be based on highly complicated factors that are often beyond the conscious awareness of the individuals involved (Murstein, Cerreto, and McDonald 1977).

General Systems Theory

General systems theory emphasizes the nature of the family as a system with boundaries that delineate it from elements outside itself. Both the system and the boundaries change constantly as children are born or leave home and as husbands, wives, and children go outside the family to work or to school and bring others into the family through marriage and friendships. Systems theory has been used, for example, to describe the impact on a marriage of the addition of a new member through the birth of the first child (Hobbs and Cole 1976).

The systems approach has gained in popularity immensely in recent years, although critics of systems theory point to the many questions it leaves unanswered and to the lack of documentation of many of the cause-and-effect statements that have been made (Holman and Burr 1980). These criticisms have not dampened enthusiasm for systems theory, however. Those who support this approach—and we are among them—have suggested that general systems theory will continue to develop and grow in importance (Broderick and Smith 1979).

The **circumplex model,** which is compatible with systems theory, has been used to illustrate the hypothesis that the greater the cohesion of family members, the more the family members value belonging and that the more their needs are met by the family and the greater their adaptability, the more successfully the family functions (Olson, Sprenkle, and Russell 1979).

Other Theories

In addition to three major theories described so far, there are three others that have been used frequently and that offer valuable insights into the functioning of marriage and the family: developmental theory, conflict theory, and cognitive theory. We mention these here so that they will be familiar to the reader when they are cited in later chapters.

The six theories presented in this chapter are by no means all the theoretical points of view that have made important contributions to the understanding of marital and family life; rather, they illustrate our own biases. Psychoanalytic theory, for example, has certainly had a strong influence on systems theory, among others. Similarly, social learning theory and the behavioral theories are clearly influential in exchange theory.

Developmental, conflict, and cognitive theories have been used less frequently than the three major ones described earlier; nevertheless, they offer many important explanations about marriage and the family.

Developmental Theory   The life-cycle changes of individuals who marry and have families have been investigated as important factors in marital and family interrelationships and satisfactions (Heiss 1980). Not only are the individual changes seen as important, but it has been proposed that, beyond the importance of the individual changes, changes in the marital life cycle (birth of first child, school entrance of children, departure from home of last child, retirement, and so forth) affect interpersonal issues between family members (Rollins and Cannon 1974).

Almost all textbooks on marriage and the family, including this one, proceed from the topic of courtship to those of love, mate selection, marriage, child rearing, and finally the empty nest and aging. Developmental theory explains each stage of the life cycle as the product of an orderly sequence of preceding events. Such an approach is useful in describing how the life cycle is tied to changes in relationships—both as cause and as effect.

Research investigating variations in marital satisfaction over the life span of married couples uses developmental theory as its basis. There is some evidence that there are certain periods in marriages when marital satisfaction is lower than at other times. One finding that continues to support this point of view is that having small children in the home detracts rather than contributes to marital quality (Spanier and Lewis 1980).

Conflict Theory   This approach has gained in popularity in the past decade as family researchers have attempted to explain marriage and the family in terms of the competing needs of the members who make up the system (Sprey 1979). This theory proposes that the very nature of marriage and the family, which brings together individuals with unique backgrounds and separate needs and desires, provides a setting for conflict in the form of competition, tension, and power struggles. Resolution of the conflict allows for growth and for relationships that are satisfying in new ways. In particular, male-female roles lend themselves to exploration from the perspective of conflict theory. It is argued, for example, that gender-role inequality is based on the differences between the sexes that lead to conflict between men and women (Collins 1971).

Marital decision making has been a major topic for research using the conflict theory. When husband and wife have a disagreement—and conflict theorists believe this is inevitable—the issue arises as to which partner has the power and knows how to use it to get his or her own way. Although decision making is often a cooperative effort instead of a power struggle, when conflict does exist, power and control become relevant concepts.

Cognitive Theory   A central feature of this theoretical approach is that a person's thinking affects not only behavior but also emotions. In many ways, cognitive theory resembles symbolic interactionism because the meaning one attaches to another's behavior as a symbol of that person's intentions determines one's response to that behavior. In other words, what one *believes* to be real is more important in determining one's reactions to an event than is any objective reality (Mahoney 1974).

Phenomenology is a term used to describe the philosophy that one's unique perception of reality is the basis for one's understandings and actions. This approach has been particularly helpful in providing a perspective for marriage and family therapy (Mahoney 1974). Often when couples are suffering marital distress, each partner's version of what has transpired is radically different from the other's. It is not that one or both are being dishonest; instead, each has given such different meanings to what both acknowledge as the facts that their interpretations and consequent reactions may have strayed far from objectivity. If counselors listened to only one of the versions, their advice could easily do more harm than good. By hearing both versions, counselors have a better chance to help couples come to grips with what each partner intended.

Behavior therapy, which is often used with troubled marriages and families, is closely linked to cognitive theory. Both emphasize the translation of behavior and emotions into cognitive terms and the mapping of explicit ways to rethink and hence to change old behaviors.

SUMMARY

1. There has never been only one model for marriage or only one suitable family pattern; currently the models are more varied than ever.

2. Marriage and the family have been affected by several major changes that have occurred in this century, a notable one being the migration from farms to urban areas. Other important changes include that children have become more an economic liability than an asset and that the birthrate has fluctuated with the economy; more women are in the labor force; mate selection has become more a personal choice based on love than a family matter; and the divorce rate has leveled off after a sharp increase beginning about twenty years ago.

3. There are many definitions of marriage and the family—legal, religious, formal, informal—but the most frequently used definitions emphasize the enduring nature of the relationship and the fact that persons living together in marriage and the family form a dynamic social system.

4. Four social criteria help to define marriage:
   a. The persons involved have some agreement about sexual access to each other and to others.
   b. They are economically involved both as an earning and as a consuming unit.
   c. They are mutually supportive of each other's welfare.
   d. The relationship is stable over a period of time; or, at least, the couple intends it to be.

5. In addition to these four general criteria, marriages in the United States are heterosexual, monogamous, and usually directed toward the establishment of a family; they involve task division; they must not involve certain kinship relationships (defined as incest). Further, the partners maintain a common residence and should begin with a basis of love.

6. The health of the family as an institution and family lifestyles today are powerful factors in determining the nature not only of individual family heritages that will be handed down, but also of future society and culture.

7. The current alarm about the poor health of the American family, as measured by high divorce rates, may be inappropriate. Widespread concern about the survival of the family indicates a healthy social interest, however.

8. Although divorce rates have increased over the past century, so has the average number of years that first marriages last. Other severely disruptive family problems, such as infant mortality, abject poverty, and deadly communicable diseases, have declined. We believe there is less misery in families now than in the past.

9. Over the past 50 years, the unifying functions of the American family have shifted from primarily protective, religious, educational, survival, and economic activities to primarily affectional and companionship activities.

10. Both the researcher's and the lay person's concepts of the family include some ideas about what a family does, how it developed its current form, and how it works. These understandings are formally called theories. Currently, the most prominent theories or groups of theories favored by scholars are (1) interactionist theory, (2) exchange theory, and (3) general systems theory.

11. Theories that help explain family structure are (1) developmental theory, (2) conflict theory, and (3) cognitive theory.

GLOSSARY

Bigamy Marriage to two persons at the same time. Bigamy is forbidden by law in all 50 states of the United States. (p. 21)

Bilineal Characterized by tracing descent through both the mother and the father. (p. 18)

Ceremonial marriage A formal declaration in the presence of witnesses of the intention to be spouses. Most states require that ceremonial marriages be registered or licensed to be legally valid. (p. 19)

Circumplex model A model for the measurement and graphic charting of the cohesion and adaptability of family members. (p. 24)

Cohabitation A lifestyle in which two unrelated people live at the same residence. Cohabitation frequently implies a sexual relationship between the persons living together. (p. 20)

Consummation The fulfillment of a marriage through the act of sexual intercourse. (p. 20)

Cultural Referring to ways of believing and behaving that are felt to be right or proper in a social collectivity. Judgments of "right" or "proper" may apply to social behaviors, to ways of thinking and feeling, to symbols, or to technologies. (p. 10)

Extended family A group of persons related by blood, marriage, or adoption that includes more members than a nuclear family—for example, grandparents, aunts, uncles, parents' siblings or their children, or more distant relatives. (p. 18)

Heterosexual Pertaining to different sexes. (p. 21)

Incest Sexual activities between those of such close kinship that laws or customs forbid them to marry or to engage in coitus. (p. 21)

Matrilineal Descent characteristically traced through mothers. (p. 18)

Microculture The shared ideas, feelings, and behaviors of a societal subgroup (such as an ethnic group or a particular family). (p. 10)

Monogamy A form of marriage in which there is one spouse at a time for each person. (p. 18)

Nonceremonial ("common-law") marriage In legal terms, an unregistered or unlicensed relationship that becomes legally recognized as a marriage after a couple cohabits for a specified period. (p. 20)

Nuclear family A married couple and their children who live together. (pp. 18–19)

Patriarchy A family form in which the father (or oldest male relative) is the authority figure. (p. 18)

Patrilineal Descent characteristically traced through fathers. (p. 18)

Phenomenology A point of view that behavior is responsive to an individual's perceptions rather than to objective reality. (p. 26)

Pluralism The belief that reality consists of many kinds of distinct elements with many explanations for those elements. (p. 6)

Polyandry The practice of one woman having two or more husbands. (p. 18)

Polygamy The sanctioned marriage of a person or persons to more than one other person at a time. (p. 18)

Polygyny The practice of one man having two or more wives. (p. 18)

Social Referring to the interactions of two or more persons or to the relationships between them. (p. 5)

Theory A summarizing statement used to explain complex phenomena linked together in such a way as to produce a specific effect or effects. (p. 22)

Trial marriage A tentative or conditional relationship (usually cohabitation) intended to determine whether a formal marriage is desirable. (p. 6)

2

It is true, of course, that the increased activity of women in economic life tends to reduce the differences between male and female roles, but the cause of the alteration in these roles lies also in the decline of the ancient values and the unshackling and unmasking of a masculine hunger for emotional gratifications.

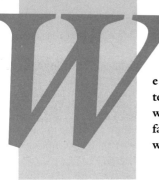

We are born male or female, but we learn to be masculine or feminine. This chapter will explore the differences and similarities between males and females and will consider how we learn sex roles and how those roles affect marriage and the family. To what extent do the differences that exist have a biological basis, and to what extent do they arise from social expectations?

MALE-FEMALE SIMILARITIES AND DIFFERENCES

Jules Henry, *Culture against Man*

*O*ne of the most significant changes in the nature of marriage and the family in the past two decades has been the shift in the roles of men and women. As ideas of what men and women should do and should be have changed, we have had to learn new ways of being together and growing together. There are no easy answers to the challenges involved in balancing the best of the past with the best of the present and future. Men and women often are uncertain what to make of their new options and how to bridge the gap that still exists between traditional models of masculinity and femininity and the ideology of equality. The critical issue for today and for years ahead is sharply defined: "How can women and men successfully come to grips with the changes that are taking place in their roles and relationships and still retain the positive qualities—trust, intimacy, emotional security, mutual respect—that make it possible for them to live together, love together, work together, grow together" (Lasswell and Lobsenz 1983, p. 10)?

Learning **sex** roles is a lifetime project. We come to a relationship with identities that are to a great extent determined by whether we are male or female. Some sociologists call this sense of one's sex a *master trait*. For example, family sociologist James Henslin (1985, p. 142) explains: "No matter what else one is, one is always that plus [a] male or female. One might be rich, for example, but one is always seen as a rich man or a rich woman. One might be old or young, but one is perceived as an old or young man or woman. This social status of masculinity or femininity cuts across all social class, religious, age, racial, cultural, and occupational lines."

All known societies distinguish between men's and women's roles, although there is great variation from one society to another, and within a given society over time, about what is considered masculine or feminine behavior. What may be accepted behavior for men or women in one society may be frowned on in another. Likewise, what is shocking behavior in a society at one historical period may be acceptable within the same society at another time.

LEARNING GENDER ROLES

We can start to understand how we learn **gender** roles with the facts that biology affects behavior and that behavior can also affect biology. This idea is central to what has been called the **biosocial** approach to explaining human behavior and is especially germane to the development of the concepts of masculinity and femininity.

The biosocial approach acknowledges that biological differences between males and females affect the likelihood that sex-appropriate learning will take place later. In other words, biology sets certain limits within which social learning can operate to define masculinity or femininity. Another important fact is that how one views oneself is determined by what one is told about one's behavior. For example, if a boy is active and enjoys rough-and-tumble play, he may be told that he is "all boy." This enters the definition he is forming of himself as a male; he may come to view himself as being judged by masculine standards that differ from those by which girls are judged as feminine. It is not easy to divide these two facts into discrete segments. Each affects the other, and each is vital to our understanding of male-female differences

DESCRIBING THE IDEAL MAN AND THE IDEAL WOMAN

In a poll of 28,000 men and women, the majority of whom were well educated and politically moderate to liberal, the participants were asked to describe the ideal man and the ideal woman, using both personality traits and behaviors as criteria for judgment (Tavris 1978). The ten traits rated the highest for the ideal woman by women themselves and by men are as follows.

IDEAL WOMAN

As Men Describe Her	As Women Describe Her
1. Able to love	1. Able to love
2. Warm	2. Stands up for beliefs
3. Stands up for beliefs	3. Warm
4. Gentle	4. Self- confident
5. Self-confident	5. Gentle
6. Fights to protect family	6. Intelligent
7. Intelligent	7. Fights to protect family
8. Romantic	8. Romantic
9. Soft	9. Sexually faithful
10. Sexually faithful	10. Soft

The descriptions by men and women of an ideal woman are almost identical—over 75 percent of both men and women agree on the first five attributes, and over 55 percent agree on all ten. Other traits and behaviors were mentioned but received many fewer votes. With few exceptions ("self-confident," "intelligent," "stands up for beliefs"), the description does not sound very different from that of the ideal woman of the 1950s or 1960s. Only 41 percent of the men and 60 percent of the women mentioned being successful at their work as a criterion for being "ideal."

The ideal man was also described by women and by men themselves.

IDEAL MAN

As Women Describe Him	As Men Describe Him
1. Able to love	1. Able to love
2. Stands up for beliefs	2. Stands up for beliefs
3. Warm	3. Self-confident
4. Self- confident	4. Fights to protect family
5. Gentle	5. Intelligent
6. Intelligent	6. Warm
7. Fights to protect family	7. Gentle
8. Successful at work	8. Successful at work
9. Romantic	9. Romantic

The men's and women's lists for the ideal man not only are very similar to each other but also are surprisingly close to the lists for the ideal woman. Those polled evidently value almost the same attributes in both men and women.

and similarities that are at the core of sexual interaction, marriage, reproduction, and gender roles in our society.

Every society has some norms that differentiate ways of behaving for men from those for women and tasks considered appropriate for each sex. Collectively these differences in appropriate behaviors and tasks become gender roles that are assigned and assumed. In every society, as a part of their growing-up process, children are taught directly what they are expected to do as "good" boys or girls.

As **sexologists** Gagnon and Henderson (1985, p. 147) remind us: "The decision whether to rear a child as a male or a female is probably the most significant labeling experience that the youngster will receive. The vigor of play, the frequency of mother-child as opposed to father-child interaction, and the tolerance of aggression in the male but not the female infant and child all contribute to the development of the self, defined as masculine or feminine. During the years after the child learns to talk, the build-up of gender identity continues."

We are born male or female, but we learn concepts of masculinity and femininity just as we learn other cultural definitions. Such learning begins in ways that parents may be unaware of fostering in their children. For instance, research shows that girl babies are picked up more quickly when they cry than are boy babies, even though newborn males in fact cry more and sleep less than female babies (Korner 1974). Boys are held as much as girls, but they are held differently and are played with more boisterously than are girls. Although too young to label such differential treatment as "how boys are treated" or "how girls are treated," children may come to consider the distinction made by their parents as familiar and normal.

Small children watch their parents closely and often model their behaviors on those of the same-sex parent. Their attitudes about what is good and what is bad are reinforced by the rewards and punishments that are attached to their behaviors. Parents and teachers pay more attention to boys when they are aggressive, whereas girls are rewarded for being sweet, looking pretty, and keeping quiet. They may be told that "little girls don't (or can't) do that," a statement that reinforces their dependency. Eventually children develop a concept of what it means to be a socially approved male or female child in our society.

The learning experiences that ultimately lead to the development of gender-role behavior come under the collective heading of **socialization,** the process by which children learn to interact effectively with others in their society. In this process children learn to anticipate the probable responses of others to their behaviors. These typically differ according to their genders and ages. For example, most parents expect that small children will cry from time to time when they are hurt or upset. Expectations are that crying will decrease as children get older, but boys are generally expected to control this behavior earlier. In addition to direct teaching, the principal methods of socialization for sex roles are imitation and identification.

Imitation

Children are great imitators of parents, peers, adults in the community, and media figures. They observe much more closely and carefully than adults may realize. They adopt a bit from one source and a bit from another, mixing and matching until they form a style of their own. Children can often be seen playing at roles as though they were trying

Watching admired adults and wanting to behave as they do is basic to the way children learn gender roles.

on what it is like to be a fire fighter, an angry neighbor, a nurturant, or a busy parent. They are very selective about whom they imitate, and research has identified some of the variables that influence them in choosing models (Bandura 1971).

Reward and punishment are among the most important and perhaps least complicated factors influencing which observed behaviors children will imitate. Children are more likely to imitate behavior that is rewarded and to avoid behavior that elicits punishment. When parents reward what they consider sex-appropriate modeling and punish what they consider inappropriate imitation, children learn quickly what is expected. If, for example, a little boy imitates his mother by putting red polish on his nails, he may get a negative reaction that quickly lets him know that his parents consider this modeling behavior inappropriate for him, although the same behavior in his sister may be approved or at least tolerated.

Reward and punishment have another equally important effect on children's behavior. When children observe others whose actions are either rewarded or punished, they are more likely to imitate those who receive rewards. (Bandura 1965). There is also a good deal of evidence that children are most likely to imitate those with whom they have positive relationships. Thus a child is much more likely to model him- or herself on a parent, a teacher, or a coach, for instance, if the adult in question is accepting, warm, and supportive. (Kagan 1964).

Other studies have shown that children are well aware of which adults have the power to reward and to punish and are much more likely to imitate an adult in such a position. The parent who is dominant in the home is more often imitated than the less dominant parent. When the parent seen as powerful is also warm and supportive, the likelihood of his or her being imitated is increased even more. (Hetherington and Frankie 1967).

Several experts on gender-role typing have proposed that children more frequently choose to imitate those with whom they feel a similarity or a kindred spirit.

One of the most influential similarities seems to be sameness of sex—males imitate other males and females imitate other females (Lynn 1969). In practice this usually means that boys imitate their fathers and girls model themselves after their mothers. Thus, the maximum amount of imitation should be facilitated by a warm, supportive parent of the same sex who is also seen as the purveyor of rewards or punishments. There is considerable evidence suggesting that this is the case. Since fathers are viewed as more powerful in many families, it can be anticipated that boys will be likely to imitate their fathers and that girls will be likely to imitate both parents to some extent. As it now is, girls are less likely to be teased, shamed, or punished for imitating their fathers than are boys for imitating their mothers.

It appears that parental attitudes and parental treatment of children are more often closely related to children's learning of masculine or feminine traits than are the actual masculine or feminine behaviors of the parents whom the children imitate (Kohlberg 1969). For instance, a father who himself might not fit the stereotyped notion of masculine might still insist that his son conform to standards the father deems masculine. Studies have indicated that fathers have stronger influences than mothers on whether their daughters develop highly feminine traits (Sears, Rau, and Alpert 1965). Although girls imitate their mothers, fathers appear to be the most insistent parents in expecting gender-typed behavior of children of both sexes (Hetherington 1972).

Studies have found that, when there is no father in the home, there can be effects on the psychosexual development of both boys and girls different from those evident in father-intact homes. Father-absent boys have been shown to identify more with their mothers or to have a confused gender-role identity unless there has been another male adult with whom to identify (Biller 1970).

Girls are less affected by father absence in their early years, but differences show up in adolescence when father-absent girls display attitudes toward males that differ from those of girls whose fathers have been present (Hetherington 1972). Girls whose fathers were absent because of divorce sought more attention and praise from males and were more often described as "boy crazy," whereas those whose fathers had died tended to avoid males. Therefore, the parents' presence in the home and their sex-role definitions and behaviors become crucial to the ways children learn to behave. The more traditional the parents, for instance, the more the children may use this behavior as a model and grow up believing that this is the right way to be.

In the United States, "traditional" gender-role behavior varies greatly between different ethnic, religious, and social-class constituencies. Puerto Rican, Mexican, Japanese, and African family traditions can be very different from each other and from those of other ethnic entities; so are Mormon, Orthodox Jewish, Buddhist, and Unitarian traditions; so are the customs of Boston "Brahmins," Dallas suburbanites, and St. Louis ghetto residents (Hess 1970).

Identification

Most theorists distinguish between imitation and a more complex process called **identification.** The term *identification* has been used to connote a variety of processes, including the child's belief that he or she actually possesses some of the same characteristics as the one being imitated. In a review of the literature on identification, it has been noted how often the term is used interchangeably with *imitation*. Among those who distinguish between the terms, there is sometimes disagreement on just how they differ (Bandura 1969). Most definitions agree that identification is a broader concept but that imitation plays a central role in the identification process.

Freud's theory of identification (which changed throughout his career) has been very influential in defining gender identity. Freud believed that children develop strong emotional bondings with and dependencies on nurturant parents. Their dependency makes them want to be as close as possible to their caretakers; as a result, they attempt to take on various personality characteristics of one or more of these adults (Freud 1949). For example, a girl who is told how much she resembles her mother physically and in her mannerisms may want to become even more like her mother in opinions and emotional behavior. In time, she may begin to respond as her mother does to similar events. She is no longer simply imitating her mother; she now has taken the behavior as her own.

Many aspects of Freud's theory have been criticized, although the basic notion that children often incorporate traits of their parents (particularly of same-sex parents) finds little disagreement. Whether identification and imitation are too closely related to require differentiation may be an academic argument better left to those who want to pursue it. For our purposes, each is seen as a process by which children learn gender identity and sex-appropriate behavior.

Gender-Role Models

In explaining the process in which children come to understand how to play appropriate gender roles, it is important to acknowledge a distinction between the gender-role model of parents and the gender-role model of peers. An adolescent male, for instance, may see his father as a responsible, hard-working authority figure and disciplinarian but may rarely see him in the masculine role defined by the adolescent's peers—sexually potent, physically strong, attractive to females, competitive, and athletic. Likewise, the gender-role model an adolescent female gets from her peers is quite different from the model supplied by her mother. The adolescent female is likely to see her peers anticipating a role of sexiness and romanticism—quite the opposite of the model, emphasizing nurturance, understanding, and success, that she learns from her middle-aged mother. The notion of the sexy, romantic female is reinforced by the mass media and usually is restricted to those who are well below middle age.

The impact of peers has been demonstrated in research from early childhood to adolescence. Three-year-olds in nursery schools have been observed to reinforce each other for gender-appropriate behavior. In one study boys criticized and ostracized other boys whom they judged not to be behaving appropriately (Fagot 1974). In another study adolescent boys who, as a result of early childhood experiences, appeared to have confused or weak gender identification in many instances showed exaggerated masculinity in an effort to conform to the model of a "real man" described by their adolescent peers (Bandura and Walters 1959).

Sex-Typed Behavior

People in most societies have used the obvious sex differences as a rationale for defining the concepts of masculinity and femininity as complete opposites. Some authorities have claimed that a division of labor between the sexes is natural because of the physical differences between men and women. They have pointed out that men are

Fathers are taking a more active role in the day-to-day care of their children than at any other time in the history of the American family.

better suited to physical labor and combat because they are, in general, bigger and stronger than women. Women, who have the unique biological capability to bear and nurse children, have been given the task of caring for the children they bear. Since the responsibilities assigned to women are better accomplished in a safe and stable environment, it has been functional for them to combine home care with child care. The factors of size and strength in men and of pregnancy and lactation in women thus have been reasoned to be basic to the division of labor. As a result, these authorities have pointed out, every society throughout history has organized men's and women's work around these differences.

Although we make fewer distinctions today between the behaviors considered appropriate for one sex or the other, it is slow and arduous to swim against the tide of so many years of tradition. In most societies throughout history, women have tended the home (with forays into the fields for food gathering); men have built houses, gone hunting to bring home meat for the table, and defended the family against attack.

In the past, children typically grew up expecting women to do the work compatible with child care—homemaking and food production—and men to perform tasks that took them outside the home for prolonged periods, even if they were significantly involved with their children when they were at home. Boys and girls are brought up surrounded by the traditions and customs of their parents. Their early training and the examples of adult behavior they observe reflect these customs.

Gradual Changes in Roles

Modifications in the ways young children are socialized are most likely to occur as a result of changes in the roles of adults. Lifestyles in the United States have changed in response to economic changes and have in turn led to adaptive changes in family

Many women in their childbearing years have begun to challenge the traditional notion that homemaking and child rearing are primarily a woman's responsibility while a man's is to provide financially for his family.

life. Very gradually, there have come to be fewer distinctions between the behaviors considered appropriate for each sex.

For example, it is now relatively acceptable for men to feed infants. The development of mechanical refrigeration for safer storage of milk, of pasteurization, of vulcanization (for the manufacture of acceptable artificial nipples) combined with advances in the sciences of hygiene and nutrition made it possible to feed infants satisfactorily without depending on a nursing mother or wet nurse. There was undoubtedly a lag of a few years during which both men and women thought it was odd or peculiar for a man to want to feed an infant or for a woman to want a man to do so. Now, however, most members of both sexes are quite comfortable with the idea of a man feeding a baby, even though this represents a reversal of a long-standing pattern.

Similarly, there is now a greater acceptance of women working outside the home and of men performing a greater share of home and child care than in the past. These changes signal shifts in popular attitudes about masculinity and femininity. Thus, although some hospitals still issue blue name bracelets to boy babies and pink ones to girls, and although members of each sex begin to be treated differently almost immediately, the capabilities of the two sexes are now increasingly seen as similar as a result of cultural, economic, and social changes and technological developments.

The acceptance of changes in female and male roles seems to be increasing among the American people at all social and economic levels. It was once commonly accepted that basic role changes begin among more highly educated persons and trickle down very slowly to those with less education. If it was ever true, however, that only highly educated persons tended to break with traditional sex roles, it is no longer so.

Changes in sex-role behavior in the United States have been gradual. Even though today the average woman is likely to bear children over only a relatively short part of her life, many Americans still cling to the notion that a woman's role is basically that of mother and a man's primarily that of provider. In the past, opinion polls made this very clear: as late as the mid-1970s, 75 percent of respondents still supported the idea that "it's up to the man to be the main provider in the family," and 82 percent believed "a woman with small children should go to work only if the money is really needed" (Yankelovich, Skelly, and White, Inc., 1977, pp. 68–69). These sentiments seem to have changed as much as they have primarily because married women with small children and the growing number of single mothers really need the money their labor can earn. As more and more mothers enter the labor force for this reason, public opinion reflects more tolerance of those who choose to work outside the home primarily because they want to do so.

SEX, GENDER, AND SEX PREFERENCE

The extent to which the observed differences between men and women arise from genetic factors as opposed to social learning is a complicated and still controversial question. In order to discuss male and female roles more easily, we will examine three aspects of sexual identity. The term *sex* refers to the biological state of being male or female, *gender* and *gender role* describe one's self-concept and social presentation as male or female, and **sex preference,** sometimes called sexual orientation, refers to one's choice of opposite- or same-sex partners. The designation of these three categories allows us to see where they overlap and how easy it is to confuse one with another or to assume that if one is present, then the other two must invariably also be present.

One's sex is determined by the coincidence of many qualities. To determine sex, "one must assay the following conditions: **chromosomes,** external **genitalia,** internal genitalia (for example, uterus, prostate), hormonal states, and secondary sex characteristics. (It seems likely that in the future another criterion will be added: brain systems.)" (Stoller 1968, p. 9). Not until 1976 did scientific discoveries unravel the puzzle of how germ cells cause a human embryo to differentiate the male sex organs from those of the female (Wachtel 1978). It is now clear that sex develops on the basis of prenatally programmed genetic processes in the central nervous system and in hormonal function. These processes program differentiation of the internal reproductive anatomy and the external genitalia.

Nearly everyone is assigned to a sex immediately upon birth. This assignment is universally made on the basis of the appearance of the external genital organs. A baby's sex is announced at once; no one would think of waiting for a microscopic examination of a baby's chromosomes before saying "It's a girl!" or "It's a boy!" From that moment on, the child's social experiences and self-concept will be profoundly affected by the announced sex. At **puberty** the hormonal system mobilizes to develop secondary sex characteristics, such as body hair, voice changes, and breast development.

Gender

> Gender is a term that has psychological or cultural rather than biological connotations. If the proper terms for sex are "male" and "female," the corresponding terms for gender are "masculine" and "feminine"; these latter may be quite independent of (biological) sex. Gender is the amount of masculinity or femininity found in a person, and, obviously, while there are mixtures of both in virtually all humans, the normal male has a preponderance of masculinity and the normal female a preponderance of femininity. (Stoller 1968, p. 9)

American children and adults alike assess persons' genders in everyday interaction by their behaviors and appearances. The ways in which they dress, talk, posture their bodies, groom themselves, and relate to others are all evidence of people's genders. The overt behavior one displays in society is one's *gender role*.

The hormones from the fetal testes and ovaries have important effects on gender. They play a major role in programming **neural** pathways in the brain that will eventually direct the behavior of the individual through his or her lifetime. These hormones do not necessarily preordain behavior but do appear to predispose certain behavioral patterns. Research is currently proliferating rapidly in an attempt to determine just what brain differences result from the variation in hormones and whether these biological differences are programmed in such a way that they resist alteration through later learning. There are intriguing questions about the existence of biological differences that create a "male" or "female" brain and make certain types of behavior more likely in one sex or the other (Bardwick 1971; Weintraub 1981).

GENDER ROLES AT WORK IN PLAY BEHAVIOR

Boys and girls not only are *offered* different toys and games by their parents but by the time they are four years old boys and girls have learned to *prefer* different ones. Until recently, toy manufacturers always showed what they considered to be sex-appropriate play advertisements for their products—boys playing with trucks or girls playing with dolls, for example. While such sex-stereotyped advertising still exists, more and more toy companies are aware that children learn much about sex-role behavior from their play, and as a result, they are careful not to push sex-role stereotypes.

Parents and relatives buy most of the $5 billion worth of toys sold each year. Even though toy manufacturers may do less sex-stereotyped advertising, parents still purchase toys selectively for their children according to the child's gender. Consider the following:

- Almost 100 percent of the lifelike baby dolls that wet and drink from a bottle are purchased for girls.
- Doll clothes, dollhouses, doll furniture, and household toys are almost exclusively bought for girls.
- Guns and toys that simulate war are purchased almost exclusively for boys.
- Approximately 85 percent of chemistry sets and a majority of other scientific toys and kits are purchased for boys.

One problem is that adults buy toys that they remember enjoying as children, when the toy business was predominantly sexist. They also like to buy toys that most resemble real-life objects, and these are often sex-typed. Since toys and how children play with them are important to how children learn about the world around them, the toy-buying habits of adults seem to need to change to give children less sexist views of the way they fit into society.

Children learn a gender identity at an early age, and few question the gender to which they were assigned at birth (Money, Rucker, and Weideking 1980). Even a very young child can become visibly upset by being referred to as a member of the opposite sex. Besides knowing their own genders, children also learn early to assign others in their environment to their correct genders. At first they may use superficial clues like clothing or hairstyle, but they eventually become more sophisticated in such identification.

One's self-image as male or as female develops as a result of comparing one's own body and behavior with those of others; interacting with others who also distinguish maleness from femaleness; and learning from teachers, books, the mass media, and other sources. In this way a cognitive bridge is formed from sex assignment that is biologically determined to gender identification that is learned.

Transsexual persons represent exceptions to the rule of acceptance of one's assigned sex and the development of gender identity. Such persons feel that they have the body of one sex but the mind (or the "soul") of the other—"women trapped in the bodies of men" or vice versa. They often seek hormonal and surgical treatment to align the two conflicting definitions of themselves. In the past 25 years, thousands of such transformations have taken place, although they continue to be medically, psychologically, and legally controversial.

Children begin play activity at an early age. Play is critical in many respects for social and personality development. Play is considered by many child psychologists to be children's "work."

Many transsexual persons, such as Renee Richards, have sought hormonal and surgical treatment to physically change their gender identity.

Males who wish to become females can take estrogen to stimulate breast growth and to feminize their bodies in other ways. Surgery can be performed to enlarge breasts, to remove the testes and penis, and to create an artificial vagina. It is not yet possible to construct a penis that will erect naturally or testes that produce sperm; for females who wish to become males, however, these organs can be simulated for the sake of appearance, and the breasts can be removed. When clothed appropriately, a person of either sex can then attempt to pass for a member of the other sex. Sometimes size of feet and hands or height seems unusual, but seldom beyond the limits of variation within each sex.

The term **transvestism** has been used to describe the occurrence of cross-dressing (primarily that of males who dress as females). Not even a small percentage of those who enjoy dressing as members of the opposite sex can be construed as transsexual, although most transsexual persons have cross-dressed prior to surgery, and many report feeling quite comfortable in the clothing of the opposite sex. For women in the United States, dressing in male clothing is so common and so acceptable that it is not thought of as transvestism. In fact, it is often fashionable for women to emulate masculine dress, although in many localities "masquerading" as women is a crime for which men can be prosecuted.

Sex Preference

Just as one's sex and one's gender identity are not always perfectly matched, sometimes one's gender role and *sex preference* may not correlate, either. Sex preference refers to the individual's preference for partners in sexual activities. In this society it has generally been considered normal and natural for people to prefer **heterosexual** partners for sexual interaction—that is, for men to be attracted to women and for women to be attracted to men. Yet historical and cross-cultural accounts tell us that preference for sexual activity with partners of one's own sex—**homosexuality**—is well known in all societies.

Ancient Greek society recognized that members of the same sex might be sexually attracted to each other, although the approved pattern was that of **bisexuality:** being attracted to members of one's own sex exclusively was not accepted as natural (Hale 1970). The assumption of bisexuality allowed for sexual intimacy with both one's own and the opposite sex. It was from writings of the female Greek poet Sappho, who lived with other women on the island of Lesbos and left accounts of their sexual intimacies, that the term **lesbian** is derived.

Even though bisexual and homosexual activity may have been widely accepted throughout history, in recent times this behavior has generally not been accepted in the United States. Until very recently in this country, a man or woman whose sexual preference was not exclusively for the opposite sex was thought to have a personality disorder. As a result, many men and women who may have engaged in (or may have thought about engaging in) a sexual act with a person of the same sex were made to feel that they were abnormal. Not until 1975 did the American Psychiatric Association take such behavior out of the category of mental disorder. As far back as 1948, Kinsey found that 1 in every 3 males in his study had had one or more homosexual experiences in adolescence and that approximately 1 in 20 had had such an encounter as an adult (Kinsey, Pomeroy, and Martin 1948). In a comparable study of women in 1953, up to 6 percent reported a homosexual experience (Gagnon and Simon 1968). These numbers represent a high proportion of men and women who may have been left with guilt and anxiety.

Most current research indicates that although there are some men and women who deny ever having thoughts of or actual sexual experiences with partners of their own sex—in other words, who are 100 percent heterosexual—such persons are clearly not in the majority. On the other hand, the same may be said of those few who only think of and engage in sexual activities with those of their own sex—who are 100 percent homosexual. Instead, sexual preference can more realistically be viewed as potentially changing over time for most normal men and women, who may have thoughts or experiences of same-sex interests at some point in their lives.

A study of persons with homosexual and heterosexual preferences found that most of those who identify themselves as homosexual reported that they had also experienced heterosexual intercourse; approximately one-fourth of them stated that it had occurred within a year of the interview (Bell and Weinberg 1978). Not only might the same individual change behaviorally over time—from same-sex play in prepuberty to heterosexual or bisexual behavior as an adult—but the strength of the preference also can vary from person to person. For instance, one who may feel very attracted to a person of the same sex or who fantasizes about a same-sex partner may never act on those feelings. On the other hand, the person who may have little overall attraction to members of his or her own sex may engage in homosexual behavior occasionally because willing opposite-sex partners are not available.

It appears that sexual preference does not always fall neatly into two discrete categories—heterosexual or homosexual—but instead that most men and women have their own unique thoughts, feelings, and behaviors that lie somewhere between these two preferences and that may change with time and with the situation. *Most* people exhibit heterosexual behavior *most* of the time, but we cannot say clearly whether most prefer that behavior because social (and even legal) sanctions against any other behavior have been enforced. Until 1978, for instance, "homosexuals" routinely were denied military or government service; even in 1980, two women out of a total of eight who were tried by the Navy were discharged because it was claimed that their lesbian activities were interfering with their duties. In 1981, a United States congressman was forced to resign his office after it was reported that he had performed a homosexual act. No one asked whether that was his exclusive sexual preference or inquired how homosexual activity disqualified him for his work.

Identified homosexuals are still the object of public ridicule and prejudice. Religious groups have usually condemned same-sex preference and have used as their rationale the argument that such behavior undermines the family unit. Until recently, a single parent who admitted homosexuality was usually deprived of the right to have custody of his or her children even if such a person had established a stable home by living with another person. The courts considered such a person incapable of providing a "proper" home.

Although there may be a growing tolerance and acceptance in the United States of an individual's right to his or her sexual preference, it will probably be a long time before men and women with anything other than an exclusively heterosexual preference will feel entirely comfortable and free of the stigmas that have prevailed in our society.

The debate continues over whether one's sexual preference is primarily learned or is at least partially, if not mostly, due to biological causes. Those who hold the biological point of view believe that prenatal hormonal brain effects hold the key to homosexuality (Dorner et al. 1975). The hormones of puberty are not believed to be the deciding factors in sexual preference, although early research concentrated on these hormones probably because sexual preference first becomes an issue at puberty.

Most research leans toward the explanation that sexual preference is learned; more research is needed, however. The case for learned behavior stems from studies indicating that homosexual behavior as viewed in different societies has a visibly strong cultural influence. It seems to be influenced by peer groups and by the responses to the individual with same-sex preference by his or her family. Most studies on homosexuality indicate that the first such experience occurs at a relatively early age. Studies have shown that the boys and girls involved are less physically interested in the opposite sex during adolescence and have received less information about sexual interaction from their parents and peers (Saghir and Robins 1973).

Other, less direct arguments for the position that sexual preferences are learned are built on the fact that human sexuality—especially female interest in sexual activities—is less controlled by hormones than is that of other animals. The fact that many nonhuman female animals are sexually receptive only during a part of the estrous cycle (when they are often aggressive as well) but human females are capable of being sexually aroused at almost any time is cited as evidence that hormones play a different role in humans from that in animals.

HOW GENDER ROLES MOLD OUR LIVES

Regardless of the theoretical bent of those concerned with socialization for gender roles, there does appear to be agreement that as gender roles develop, each individual will adopt a multifaceted self-concept. The gender role is not only multifaceted but also subject to change both over time and according to the particular situations in which behaviors take place. There is also a great deal of variation from one society to another with respect to what is considered appropriate for each gender.

In Margaret Mead's early studies of three societies in New Guinea, she found one society, the Tchambule, in which men's roles very much resembled those of women in the rest of the world (1961, p. 935). In Madagascar, the Vakinankarata women are assigned the role of the dominant members of society and handle all community transactions, and the men enact roles more similar to the stereotyped patterns for females in our society (Money and Rucker 1975, p. 83). Men are trained to be passive and dependent on dominant women; those who are gentle and polite are highly regarded.

Anthropologists have noted the central roles women have traditionally held as income providers. Women in the !Kung tribe of the Kalahari desert exercise a striking degree of autonomy and are the mainstay of the tribe's economy (Shostak 1981).

In the United States, there is great variation in how men and women of different ethnic, religious, and social-class backgrounds enact gender roles. The possibilities for both men and women today are more diverse than at any time in the past. Yet, tradition and stereotypes rarely fail to leave their marks. In most people's minds, there is no question about which behaviors belong to each sex. The following are descriptions of two individuals; it should not be difficult to guess their gender.

> J. is an engineering student who is now attending a prestigious technological institute on the East Coast. J.'s parents knew from the time J. was a toddler that the child had mechanical ability since favorite toys were always ones that could be taken apart and put back together. As J. progressed in school, favorite sub-

jects were math and physics. All was not work, however; there were also honors in football and baseball. J. decided to work on a construction crew in the summer to keep fit for sports during the school year. Now that college studies are so time-consuming, J. is worried that life is going to be more work than play.

L. is a major in foods and nutrition. As a small child, L. always liked to be in the kitchen, helping to cook. Petite and very attractive, L. receives much attention from the opposite sex. Working with children, teaching them crafts and games, has occupied L.'s summers. All these activities have been voluntary, following a family tradition of helping out with charities and groups that cannot afford to hire such services. L. also works on Saturdays as a volunteer in the local hospital, reading to patients and running errands for them.

There is little doubt for most readers that J. is a male and L. is a female. Of course, some girls do grow up to be engineers and do work on construction crews. Even in the 1980s, however, this is still the exception rather than the rule. Even less likely is that a male would be described as petite or would have spent his early years following his mother around or helping her fix dinner. There are still enough differences between the ways males and females behave that such distinctions are not difficult to make.

Gender Roles in Marriage

The notion that many gender-role differences reflect a polarity between kinds of family responsibilities is widely accepted. Talcott Parsons and Robert Bales (1955) characterize these polarities as *instrumental* and *expressive*. Men traditionally have been thought to be the representatives of the family in the community and the world of work, and women have been considered the nurturers of the family, tending to its members' physical and emotional needs. Therefore, men managed their families' economic interests through having access to the exchange of assets outside the family. Women, on the other hand, controlled men's access to affection, sex, and nurturance. The polarity hypothesis implies that if men were powerful and dominant agents of the family in its interface with the world, then women could not be. Similarly, if women were dominant in controlling the affectional resources of the family, then men could not be.

In the Parsons and Bales theoretical model, men could gain power in the family by withholding (or threatening to withhold) money; women could gain power by withholding (or threatening to withhold) sex. At present, court decisions and state laws are much more likely to restrict men's power in this model than women's. Recent decisions and recently passed laws generally support a wife's right to withhold sex from her husband but deny a husband's right to withhold financial support from his wife.

A perspective on marital gender roles that differs from the structural view of polarities taken by Parsons and Bales—a perspective that is reminiscent of conflict theory—is the more functionalist view of a marriage as a *system* based on gender roles that complement each other. From such a perspective, the system can be said to have survived because a man and a woman living together believe that the way they enact their roles expresses their values and enables them to achieve their goals. If each partner believes that both instrumental activities (exchange of assets with the outside

The revision of gender stereotypes has allowed many women to enter the labor force in areas that previously have been closed to them.

world) and expressive activities (affectional satisfactions within the family) are important, then their gender roles should evolve in a direction that maximizes this achievement.

In the three decades since the Parsons-Bales position was announced, gender roles have changed considerably. In particular, a good deal of attention has been paid to changes in the roles of women. There have been many shifts in the positions women hold and in how men view women, women view men, and both view themselves. Psychologists Grace Baruch and Rosalind Barnett note that Parsons's description of marriage was that it "consisted of two separate, fenced-off territories in which husband and wife had completely different functions. One of this model's many inadequacies was that it did not take into account the emotional capacities of men and ignored the fact that women were constantly using their instrumental capabilities in the home" (Baruch, Barnett, and Rivers 1983, p. 61).

Female Roles

Some have called the 1980s the decade of women. If nothing else, the increase in the number of middle-class women who are working outside the home has forced some revision of gender stereotypes. Changes have occurred both in the work place and in home life. Women have slowly begun to realize that as childbearing and child rearing require a smaller proportion of their lives, they as well as men can be responsible for extrafamily economic activities.

Many women who are in their child-rearing years also work outside the home to help support the family unit. As a result, middle-class women have been reexamining gender roles, and some are beginning to challenge the traditional notions of femininity that they have been socialized to believe—especially those that suggest that homemaking and child rearing are primarily a woman's obligation, whereas earning a living is the province of males.

A recent survey of family-relations professionals indicated that they consider the shift in women's roles and the greater involvement of women in extrafamily activities among the most significant changes ever to affect the American family. Typical of the comments about the impact of women's changing gender roles were: "Influence of the women's movement encouraging growth of women leads to discontent with the status quo when it is seen as oppressive"; "More women are ready to be independent"; and "Women in their relationships have become much more demanding" (*Marriage and Divorce Today* 1980).

When women change their definitions of femininity and of sex-role behavior, men also change, and vice versa. There are no signs that men and women today are any less involved with each other than in the past; thus, changes affecting one sex must necessarily lead to changes for the other. Some observers of men's reactions to the "new woman" have noted that some men find it difficult to accept the changing definitions of femininity and even more difficult to adjust to women's new roles.

Male Roles

Men who have taken their responsibilities of supporting a wife and children seriously and have worked long hours to this end have understandably resented being labeled "male chauvinist pigs." Many were at least somewhat confused by the demand that they denounce the "masculine" roles taught to them by their parents and adopt "feminine" roles taught (often painfully) to be inappropriate for them. The demands of the traditional male role, involving sole responsibility for earning a living, made some men wonder whether they would be shirking their moral responsibility if they transferred part of the financial burden of supporting their families to their wives in return for a chance to spend more time with their children.

"Men's liberation" has become a popular topic in recent years as men and women have begun to change their gender roles. Special issues of professional journals have been devoted to examining changing male roles critically and sensitively (Pleck and Brannon 1978; Skovholt, Gormally, Schauble, and Davis 1978; Lewis and Pleck 1979). Research provides evidence that the American male is in transition—partly clinging to the values and behaviors learned from his parents and peers and partly adjusting to new values, with some men changing and others holding tenaciously to traditionalism. Sam Julty (1979, p. 21) has proposed that men's roles currently fall into one of three general patterns:

1. The *traditionalist* feels most comfortable when the differences between masculinity and femininity are clear. He may be upset with women who wish to deny him what he sees as his morally imperative role and puzzled by men who accept traditional feminine roles.
2. The *liberal* tries to respect both old and new values. He is likely to favor equal rights for women. However, he sometimes has difficulty dealing with his emotions over changes that affect him personally—the feeling that he is inadequate if his wife earns more than he does, for instance, or the feeling that he is risking his job security (and indeed at the present time he may well be) if he stays at home with a sick child as often as does his working wife.

3. The *changing man* has a strong sense of equality and attempts to eliminate destructive sex-role stereotyping. Sometimes he has been active in consciousness-raising groups of men who discuss men's concerns, issues of sexism, and the challenge involved in changing their definitions of masculinity.

Betty Friedan, whose book *The Feminine Mystique* became legendary in the 1960s, recently stated:

> I believe that American men are at the edge of a tidal wave of change—a change in their very identity as men. This is a quiet movement, a shifting in direction . . . a searching for new values, a struggling with basic questions that each man seems to be going through alone. At the same time, he continues the outward motions that always have defined men's lives, making it (or struggling to make it) at the office, the plant, the ball park—making it with women—getting married—having children—yet he senses that something is happening with men, something large and historic, and he wants to be a part of it. He carries the baby in his back pack, shops at the supermarket on Saturdays, with a certain showing-off quality. (Friedan 1980, p. 23)

There are few role models on which men and women can pattern new ways of relating to each other. Both at home and at work, men and women are concerned about the effect of their new roles on conventional standards of masculinity and femininity. Sometimes the strains may seem more numerous than the satisfactions during the transition from old roles to new ones.

We believe that the changes in gender roles are evolving slowly enough that, although many men and women have some private doubts about the "rightness" of alternative gender-role behaviors, they are finding constructive ways to adjust. The changes taking place are exposing them to unexplored parts of themselves that offer the potential for expansion and greater fulfillment—but, of course, at a price. People often resist change because it leads to uncertainty. The old ways, even when they are undesirable, are at least familiar, whereas the prospect of the unknown can produce anxiety. Changes of the magnitude currently expected of men and women do not occur quickly or without some pain. However, social organization is emergent—that is, it is always changing toward an ordering of behavior that grows out of the flow of human interaction.

SUMMARY

1. The behavior that results from cultural beliefs and concepts of masculinity or femininity based on observable physical differences between males and females gives rise to different gender roles for men and women.
2. Children are normally taught directly how to behave according to their sex. They also imitate others of their same gender with whom they relate positively.
3. Socialization is the process by which children learn how to interact effectively with others in their society; gender-appropriate behavior is a major focus of this process.

4. Children learn about gender roles from their peers as well as from adults. Peers become particularly influential during adolescence in defining appropriate sexual behavior.
5. Each person is born genetically male or female. This is called one's biological sex.
6. Sex assignment is made at birth on the basis of the appearance of the external genitalia.
7. Hormones from the fetal testes and ovaries play a major role in brain development; their effects appear to predispose males and females to certain differences in behavior and attitudes.
8. Gender identification is the self-image that a biological male or a biological female develops normally as a result of sex assignment.
9. Transsexual persons do not develop a gender identification that matches their original sex assignments. Technically, they are persons who undergo surgery to alter their genitalia so that they more closely resemble members of the opposite sex.
10. Sex preference may be for sexual interaction with the opposite sex (heterosexuality), with the same sex (homosexuality), or with both sexes (bisexuality).
11. Current research indicates that few people have always been either 100 percent homosexual or 100 percent heterosexual. Many have had at least some limited experience (usually in early sex play) with persons of both sexes.
12. Hypotheses about the determination of sexual preference have focused primarily on learning. There is also some speculation that homosexuality may be partially caused by the effect of certain hormones on the fetal brain.
13. In our society males and females have been socialized to believe that masculinity and femininity are polar opposites in definition. The presence of traits of one automatically has meant the exclusion of traits of the other.
14. In this century, there have been trends toward more egalitarian ideas about gender roles. Middle-class women's roles have changed most noticeably, but because women and men are so involved with each other, men's roles have had to change in order to keep pace.
15. Women's liberation and men's liberation have caused confusion and uncertainty about the new roles and about how men and women can be expected to relate to each other.
16. Both men and women need time to accept change and to adjust to new styles of masculinity and femininity.

GLOSSARY

Biosocial Dealing with both biological and social phenomena simultaneously; sometimes refers to social effects attributed to biological causes. (p. 32)

Bisexuality Sexual attraction to members of both sexes. Bisexual persons may alternate between male partners and female partners or may seek mixed-group sex. (p. 44)

Chromosomes Bodies in the nucleus of reproductive cells that carry the genes for heredity. (p. 41)

Gender The knowledge and awareness, whether conscious or unconscious, that one belongs to one sex and not to the other. (p. 32)

Genitalia The organs of reproduction, especially those that are external; the penis-testicles-prostate system in human males and the vulva-vagina-uterus-ovaries system in human females. (p. 41)

Heterosexuality The preference for sex partners of the opposite sex. (p. 44)

Homosexuality The preference for sex partners of one's own sex. (p. 44)

Identification The process by which a person, often a child, incorporates certain behaviors or characteristics of another person, often a parent, and makes them a part of his or her personality. (p. 36)

Lesbian A woman whose sexual preference is for other women. (p. 41)

Neural Pertaining to nerves. (p. 41)

Puberty The beginning of biological sexual maturity, when the capability of creating or supporting a pregnancy develops and secondary sex characteristics (for instance, pubic hairs, breasts, beards) begin to appear. (p. 41)

Sex The biological state of being male or female. (p. 32)

Sexologist One who specializes in the study of sexual behavior, particularly that of humans. (p. 34)

Sex preference (orientation) One's preference for a sexual partner (either same sex, opposite sex, or bisexual). (p. 40)

Socialization The process by which persons learn to interact effectively with others in their society. (p. 34)

Transsexual A genetically male or genetically female person who, at odds with his or her own sex, believes that he or she is mentally and emotionally of the opposite sex. (p. 42)

Transvestism The practice of dressing in clothing of the opposite sex, especially for the purpose of attaining sexual excitement. (p. 44)

As there are as many minds as there are heads, so there are as many
kinds of love as there are hearts.

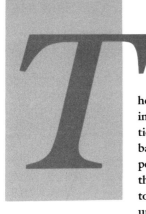

There is no question that from childhood on people are more attracted to some individuals than to others. Social psychologists have been intrigued by the questions of just what causes attraction—or rejection—and why some relationships based on attraction persist, whereas others fade. Exchange theorists agree that people are attracted to those from whom they feel they gain something and reject those who seem to cost them more. Gains and costs are not always easy factors to measure objectively, however, since each person may have his or her own unique needs and standards. Research shows that most people feel rewarded by those who are similar to themselves, who like them, who meet their needs, who make them comfortable, and who match their self-judgments.

Human beings are born with a potential to be loved and to love. Throughout one's lifetime, love is a much sought-after source of personal happiness. In the United States, it is the basis for those intimate relationships that determine the nature of marriage and the family. In the past, love has been considered a mystery with no place in the world of scientific inquiry. Most informal analyses of love have been far from objective and have asked such questions as "How

ATTRACTION AND LOVE

much do you love me?" or "How *long* will you love me?" In the 1970s, however, social scientists began to inquire about the processes and definitions of love: how it begins, how it grows, how it functions, and how and why it ends. Such researchers believe that any emotion that can bring so much joy and so much sorrow to so many people needs to be better understood.

Leo Tolstoy,
Anna Karenina

eorge Bernard Shaw (1960) once commented that love is an overemphasis on the difference between one person and all others. Once we have discovered that all people are not alike, we begin to have different feelings about different individuals. We feel "better," "happier," or "more powerful" in the presence of some people than in the presence of others. We wish to spend more time with some and less time (or perhaps none at all) with others. We can actually sense changes in our bodies when particular people are near us. If those sensations are unpleasant, they can be called **antipathy**; but if they are pleasant and make us want to be near the other person more often, they can be called *attraction*. Since at some point relationships involve attraction between two people, it is important to understand this phenomenon.

ATTRACTION

There have been countless studies of the reasons that partners are attracted to each other. Among the most widely quoted is one based on "equity theory"; this study by Elaine Walster and William Walster (1978, p. 135) encompasses four basic propositions:

1. We seek pleasure rather than pain.
2. However, we have to be able to give pleasure in order to receive it. The more we give, the more we receive.
3. We are most comfortable when there is a fair balance between what we give and what we receive. Having less than we deserve makes us resentful.
4. If the giving and the receiving are out of balance, we will work to restore a balance, either actually or in fantasy, or we will end the relationship.

Walster and Walster found that couples whose relationships were more equitable were happier and more content with each other. Happy lovers were similar on a remarkable number of traits, such as physical attractiveness, popularity, emotional and physical well-being, although a plus in one area could offset a minus in another. For instance, a physically attractive person might not be hampered by lack of money, whereas one with neither good looks nor wealth might have to make up in other areas or settle for a partner with the same total social value. This theory is a variation of social exchange theory, which says, in effect, that one can predict which persons might fall in love by knowing what they have to offer each other.

A research psychologist who favors exchange theory is Bernard I. Murstein (1971b). He believes that we are attracted to those who offer the best combination of rewards for the most reasonable cost. If the satisfaction is mutual, the relationship continues. Murstein has proposed a three-stage process by which attraction and love develop. First, there is the *stimulus* stage, in which physical appearance plays a large role. The second stage, termed *value comparison*, occurs when the couple tests their "fit" for each other. The third phase is that of compatible *ideal self* and *ideal other* images. These ideal images refer to expectations of how partners will feel, think, and behave. When all three phases are experienced successfully, romance can blossom.

Exchange theory has offered one of the most popular explanations of the process of falling in love with particular individuals. One criticism of the theory is that not all people are as logical and as able to evaluate themselves and others as exchange theory implies. Some relationships even seem to be based on altruism (unselfish love), which is concerned only with giving, not with receiving. The idea of mutually rewarding relationships is well entrenched, however, and there is more than a kernel of truth in it.

Sensing Others

Most people observe others for many of their waking hours. As people-watchers they size up others by observing physical features and behaviors and, if they are close enough, by listening to what people say and how they say it. They listen not only to language—the accents, pitch, rhythm, and content of things spoken—but also to sighs, wheezes, coughs, and giggles. If they are closer still, they may smell the other person, too, although in American society they learn not to say much about people's odors.

Touching is another way to gain information. Touching may occur in the form of a handshake or may imply intimacy and the existence or wish for some kind of relationship. The temperature and moisture of the skin, the soft or calloused texture of hands, even the locations on the person's body where he or she feels comfortable being touched—all provide information about a person.

Visual (seeing) and auditory (hearing) sensations involve far less intimate contact with another person than do tactile (touching) or olfactory (smelling) sensations. Uninteresting or negative visual or auditory impressions usually discourage people from getting close enough ever to use the other senses for attraction.

Only a person's physical characteristics and actions can actually be observed, of course. Everything else one person believes about another derives from memories of experiences with that person or with someone like him or her, beliefs about "that kind of person," or an identification with the person ("I know how he feels" or "I can understand why she did that").

Usually, one thinks of a person as a complete, self-contained being. However, the meaning we give to our observations depends largely on our own beliefs and feelings about people in general (or about people similar to the one we are observing). To be *attracted* to a person (or repelled), then, is a function of one's own mind as much as of the physical characteristics or behaviors of that person. "Beauty is in the eye of the beholder" is not an idle phrase (Wilson and Nias, 1976).

We learn who attracts through our socialization, which is the ongoing process of establishing ways of relating to others. A child usually begins the process of socialization within the family to which he or she is born. Of course, one cannot choose one's family members, with their particular ways of relating to one another and to persons outside the family. No child is asked whether he or she would like parents who are rich or poor, black or brown, residents of Chicago or Pocatello. Consequently, until later in life there is no alternative to learning the ways of the family to which one is born. Often these family patterns become deeply ingrained from early childhood and resist new learning later in life.

In families, young children learn various behaviors, such as making special kinds of sounds to affect the behaviors of others. Eventually they learn a language with which to communicate. Children also learn what others do when they smile or frown or hit or hide or kiss or cuddle. At the same time children are also experiencing *feelings* about those with whom such interactions take place. These feelings, although not directly observable themselves, are often inferred by others from children's behaviors.

Feelings toward others, such as love and hate or anger and comfort, seem to be so natural that we rarely analyze the ways in which they were learned as responses to particular people in particular situations. Furthermore, because it is easier to deal with a consistent and orderly world than with one in which definitions change from day to day (or even from minute to minute), people tend to generalize or stereotype their feelings toward particular others or groups of others. Whatever form this takes— "I love blonds," or "I hate women"—an overgeneralized feeling toward an entire category of people often leads to ineffective or inappropriate behaviors. Clearly, *all* members of any category are not going to be identical.

As misleading or ineffective as stereotyped beliefs may be, the behaviors based on them are nonetheless very real. Inaccurate generalizations about racial, religious, or social-class categories often are responsible for blind spots in perceiving others. These blind spots may be the basis for rejection of some people, but they can also work in the opposite fashion to form the basis for attraction.

Sociologists Edwin Sutherland and Donald Cressey (1960) proposed that the influence another person has on one's feelings and behavior is determined by the frequency, duration, intensity, and priority of social contacts with that particular person. Since most of us are with our mothers and fathers over a long period of time, have strong feelings toward them, and place those relationships ahead of others in importance, parents are very influential in early socialization.

By the time children begin school, they have been socialized to have definite ideas about certain types of people. Sociologists say that children normally develop degrees of *social distance* toward whole categories of people (strangers, old people, children, boys, girls, teachers, racial or religious categories, nurses, police officers, and so forth) as well as toward particular individuals. Social distance varies from a minimum ("social nearness"), to a maximum ("social farness") (Bogardus 1959, pp. 7–13).

Social nearness is expressed as a feeling of sympathetically understanding others, liking them, being comfortable with them, or loving them. Social farness is felt as being uncomfortable with particular people, disliking them, believing that it is impossible to understand them, or even hating them. Children usually accept their feelings of nearness or farness as valid without giving any thought to how they originated. It is well documented that adults do the same.

Human Hungers

Most studies of attraction have focused on the attributes of attractive persons. However, the idea of attractiveness necessarily involves two or more people; one cannot be attractive without being attractive *to* someone. The need to be attractive to someone has been called a *human hunger* (Berne 1970).

Why does a person hunger for interaction and relationships with other people? What kinds of stresses can best be reduced through interaction with another person? Obviously, tiny human fetuses need another human body to grow in (even "test-tube babies" need someone to provide care for them if they are to exist for long). This is a survival need, just as air, water, and nutrients are for all humans.

Touch conveys many messages concerning caring and intimacy. Persons who have grown up in a touching environment seem never to grow too old to crave this contact.

Human interaction is a survival need for the first few years of life. Although it is not humane to conduct isolation experiments on children to see what will happen to them, nearly all the evidence from observation of cases of "natural" isolation suggests that infants who lack adequate interaction may develop a condition called **marasmus,** as a result of which they become sickly and may even die. If they survive, they may fail to develop many "human" characteristics (Davis 1947). In famous nonhuman experiments, Psychologist Harry Harlow (1962) and his associates demonstrated that even though young monkeys may not die from lack of interaction with other monkeys, they will not want to mate (or, if mating is forced on them, they usually relate poorly to their own babies).

Do human adults also need contact with other humans? No one really knows how long an adult can survive in isolation in a comfortable environment with adequate nutrition and freedom from illness or accident. Admiral Richard E. Byrd (1938), a pioneer explorer of the Antarctic, wrote in his diary that after 75 days of isolation he no longer knew whether he was sane or insane. One of the concerns about space travel is the possible effects of long periods of isolation on astronauts. Most adults—even those who enjoy brief periods of time alone—have a limit to how much time they can spend without human contact. Some experiments report that each person has a unique threshold beyond which isolation becomes intolerable (Zuckerman et al. 1962).

Psychiatrist Eric Berne (1970) has concluded that five "human hungers" are inherent in all normal people. These help to explain the need for affiliation.

1. *Stimulus hunger:* the need for sensations to which the body can respond. Laboratory studies of sensory deprivation show that being immersed in water at 98.6 degrees Fahrenheit in a dark, soundproof place quickly produces disorientation in human subjects.

2. *Recognition hunger:* the need to have one's identity affirmed (or at least positively responded to) by another person. Studies of the **serial invalidation** of a child's self-concept indicate that this is a likely cause of mental illness (Sze 1975).

3. *Contact hunger:* the need to touch or be touched by another person. So far, the few experimental studies of this need have been inconclusive because ethical and practical considerations make this a difficult area to study. We believe, however, that for many persons the need to be touched can be nearly as great as the need for food and is certainly as important as recognition is for others. This need seems to depend on whether one was raised in an environment in which touching was welcome. There appear to be touchers and nontouchers. Touchers seem to have this hunger, whereas nontouchers may fail to comprehend its importance. Sometimes, however, nontouchers who are given permission to touch others in a safe environment such as a therapy group may overcome any antipathy they may feel, at least to the extent of being more comfortable in the presence of people who are touching each other.

4. *Sexual hunger:* the need for sexual contact. The emotional context of sexual intercourse in our society makes it virtually impossible to do laboratory studies to confirm or deny the validity of this concept. Certainly many humans go for long periods of time—even a lifetime—without sexual contact. Symbolic substitutes may be so personal that generalization is impossible or so well concealed (even from the persons who employ such substitutes) that they are inaccessible for objective study.

5. *Incident hunger:* the need for "something to happen." *Happenings* may be personally defined: what is a happening for one person may be an ordinary experience for another. The exciting event may be getting a driver's license, discovering a new planet, having the new boy or girl in school smile at you, or seeing an old friend. Little research on incident hunger has been performed, but it is clear that such a hunger exists.

One explanation for the greater attractiveness to a person of some individuals is that people may believe that certain persons (or perhaps one certain person) can reduce the stress of all or most of these hungers. In infancy, that person is usually the mother. A mother's reliability in reducing stress leads her child to believe that she is a very strong person who can make everything all right. Her reliable appearance in stressful situations and her manifest concern for reducing her child's stresses are conceptualized by the child as her commitment to him or her (Berne 1970). The degree of reliability and commitment a child perceives determines the child's trust in the mother. According to this explanation, attraction is the identification of that special person one can trust to relieve the stresses of one's human hungers. Because people define attractive qualities according to their own childhood experiences, being attracted is thought to be partly subconscious on the part of the attracted one.

There is no doubt that we use certain filters in determining who is attractive. For instance, quite a bit of research has been done on the relationship of beauty to attraction. Psychologists Glenn Wilson and David Nias (1976, p. 1) comment, "In the course of being introduced, we are frequently so absorbed with the person's looks that we forget to register their names." There seems to be considerable general agreement on who is good-looking in photographs. Two studies have shown good consistency on rankings of the relative beauty of women whose photographs were published in newspapers (Iliffe 1960; Udry 1971).

The notion that "beauty is in the eye of the beholder" or that personality is more important than **physiognomy** in judgments of good looks seems to hold only after a person has had some experience with the one being judged. Even a brief direct experience with a person may alter an initial attraction based on physical beauty. Wilson and Nias point out that when judges see beauty contestants "walk, talk, sniff, blink and smile," their agreement is less consistent. (Wilson and Nias 1976).

The observation that campus beauty queens chosen by student election seem to be objectively less beautiful in small institutions than in large ones probably does not mean that the most beautiful women go to the largest schools. It is likely, instead, that in small schools the meaning of "beauty" is affected by personal interaction.

Most current research ties physical attractiveness to a host of other positive traits attributed to the person who is good-looking. To paraphrase Sappho, "What is beautiful must also be good." One recent study found that good-looking people are considered more competent and that those questioned made guesses about their abilities to do things that had virtually no intrinsic relation to beauty or ugliness—such as piloting a plane (Webster and Driskell 1983).

What people hear can also be a positive source of attraction, even quite apart from the spoken message. Devices have been developed for altering tape-recorded voices in such a way that the speaker's voice qualities are retained but the content of the message is unintelligible. Studies using such devices have indicated that the voice qualities alone conveyed to a listener whether he or she was liked or disliked, even when the words themselves could not be understood. One such study concluded that a person's tone of voice might be a better indicator of his or her like or dislike for another than a verbal statement (Rubin 1973).

T. H. Pear (1955), a noted British psychologist who did extensive research in England on listeners' reactions to radio voices, remarked that "social intimacy or distance, friendliness or enmity, interest or boredom . . . are usually expressed by an appropriate speech-melody, . . . by the way in which the voice goes 'up and down.'" Theodor Hendrik Van de Velde (1957, p. 94), a medical sex researcher, was almost lyrical on the same point:

> The sexual impulse is far more often powerfully stirred by the intensely personal medium of the human voice; of a special voice.
>   The tone color of a voice, and the intonation of a single word—and it may be a word with no special meaning or association in itself—may excite incredible intensity of desire.

A negative factor related to language behavior was reported by Havelock Ellis:

> One of my fellow passengers—another teacher, if I remember rightly—improved the occasion by flirting with a girl he had become acquainted with on the boat and sat with his arm around her for several hours; toward night, having evidently thus acquired all the satisfaction he desired, he generously introduced her, unasked, to me . . . and left us alone. We walked once or twice up and down the deck, and she remarked to me by way of opening the conversation: "Ain't the moon lovely?" Such a feeling of loathing rose up within me that in a few moments after briefly responding I said it was time to go below and wished her good night. (Brecher 1971, p. 45)

Odors, too, play a positive role in attraction. Setting aside for the moment the current discussion of whether humans have **pheromones** (attractive odors given off by animals during periods of sexual receptivity), there do appear to be attractive—and repulsive—scents to breath, hair, and perspiration, although Van de Velde (1957, pp. 27–28) labeled these *idiosyncratic*—that is, differing widely in different individuals. "Cases in which the odor of perspiration is attractive from the first are relatively rare, but they exist." He believed that the abilities to perceive individual differences of this kind "are less numerous in the Western-Atlantic civilizations than among Orientals and in the tropics."

Desmond Morris (1971, p. 35) commented:

> Every human body is constantly sending out signals to its social companions. Some of these signals invite intimate social contact and others repel it. Unless we are accidentally thrown against someone's body, we never touch one another until we have first carefully read the signs. . . . We can often sum up a social situation in a split second. . . . This does not imply carelessness; it simply means that the computers inside our skulls are brilliant at making rapid, almost instantaneous calculations concerning the appearance and mood of all the many individuals we encounter during our waking hours. The hundreds of separate signals coming from the details of their shape, size, colour, sound, smell, posture, movement and expression, crowd at lightning speed into our specialized sense organs, the social computer whirrs into action, and out comes the answer, to touch or not to touch.

Inferences from Behaviors

Since another person's feelings and thoughts cannot be observed in the same fashion as can actual behavior, they are usually inferred from observed behaviors or physical conditions. When a person says, "I like you," or "I love you," the one he or she is addressing must decide whether to doubt or to trust the accuracy of that statement. The decision may be based on previous experience with the speaker, on observations of his or her behaviors, or on a general tendency of the listener to believe or to doubt what people (or certain kinds of people) say. There is no way for the listener to observe the speaker's *liking*. Only behavior associated with liking can be observed.

Recently, social psychologists have been interested in how attraction to others is affected by the observer's interpretations of others' behaviors and by expectations of how others will behave. Social psychologists Harold Kelley and John Thibaut (1978) have developed a theory of attraction based on one person's **attribution** to another of behaviors and traits. Attribution is defined as an assumption that a person's behavior is attributable either to his or her will or to certain external conditions. The attribution made determines appropriate response behavior. If Harry attributes Hildegarde's attraction to him as a result of her rational will, he may respond differently to her from the way he would respond if he attributed it to Hildegarde's mother's manipulation of her.

It is suggested that some history of experience with a person may improve the accuracy of one's expectations, although attribution does not actually require such experience. One may experience liking—or even love—at first sight. It is not unusual for people to judge the character of others on the basis of a single observation. Once this has been done, even though the judgment may be inaccurate, a system of inter-action develops between the two people based on the assumptions of each about the other. If their mutual responses lead them to be comfortable with their self-concepts and their predictions, the system will function for them, and they probably will maintain their relationship. If not, they will experience disillusionment. This helps to account for the couples who decide after one meeting that they are in love, marry, and actually do live happily ever after. It also accounts in part for the high divorce rate among such couples.

Inferences about the other's attributes also include predictions about how the other person feels or what he or she believes. Again, this may or may not be based on a history of actual experiences and observations. Psychologists Ellen Berscheid and Elaine Walster (1978) believe that attraction occurs when others are believed to (1) like us; (2) have the same views that we do on social, economic, and political matters; and (3) furnish emotional support to us if we are lonely, fearful, or under stress. In fact, what an individual believes to be true is usually much more powerful for determining his or her behavior than any objective measure of the situation or the other person is likely to be.

We know that there is not only some general agreement about what is attractive—whether it is physical or behavioral—but also individual tastes that may be shared by few, if any, others. These unique tastes may be about specific characteristics no matter who exhibits them. For instance, one may believe that slender people have better self-concepts or that blonds have more fun. On the other hand, an idiosyncratic notion of what is attractive is specific to one person. A friend of ours who dislikes beards fell in love with a man who has a glorious one. When questioned, she said that on him it is attractive but that she still generally prefers clean-shaven men.

Most of the actions and traits that attract us to another person are attributed to choices that the other person makes more or less voluntarily. However, one fascinating research finding is that if a photograph of a young woman is retouched so that the pupils of her eyes appear to be larger, she will be rated by most men as more attractive than in the unretouched photograph (Hess 1965). Although humans have little or no control over the dilation of their pupils, the pupils have been shown to respond to excitement in general by enlarging. Thus larger pupils seem to suggest interest or excitement (presumably about the observer). The thought of this is attractive, even though the person's pupils may have enlarged because of stress or tension (Rubin 1973, p. 37). Dilated pupils and slightly moist eyes have been symbols of love for a long time. In the first century B.C., the Roman poet Catullus described his beloved as "cow-eyed," an expression that loses something in the translation to twentieth-century English.

The system of mutual attraction seems to be circular; that is, knowing that a person is attracted to us usually makes that person seem more attractive to us than we had previously noted. One's behavior usually reflects that fact, and the other person responds accordingly, thus generating another round of attraction. Research

---

ADOLESCENCE: GOTTA RING, GOTTA CAR?

The key to popularity for high school men is still making the grade on the playing field rather than in the classroom. For women, it's being in the right clique, while athletics continues to be nowheresville. That's what researchers at Southern Illinois University found when they surveyed 600 high school students from six states.

It's brawn over brain as far as what high school women think makes men popular, more so today than in a similar 1976 study. Women rated being an athlete as the leading criterion for men's popularity, followed by being "in the leading crowd," coming from the right family, having a nice car and getting high grades.

Men agreed with the women on the first two factors of men's popularity—athletics and being in the leading crowd—but differed thereafter. They rated being a leader in activities next, followed by having high grades and coming from the right family. This order remains unchanged from a similar 1961 study.

In ranking high school women's popularity, both men and women placed being in the leading crowd first.

For men, high grades came next, followed by coming from the right family, being an athlete and having a nice car. After being in the in crowd, women placed being a leader in activities, being a cheerleader, having high grades and being an athlete. Coming from the right family placed dead last.

The students were also asked what they wished most to be remembered for. "Given a choice between 'brilliant student,' 'athletic star' and 'most popular,' 43 percent of the women surveyed selected 'brilliant student,' 40 percent selected 'most popular' and only 17 percent selected 'athletic star,' " the researchers say.

"In contrast, when men answered the question, 37 percent selected 'athletic star,' 34 percent selected 'brilliant student' and 29 percent selected 'most popular.' "

The study appeared in *Sociology of Sport Journal* (Vol. 2, No. 2).

Source: Vincent Bozzi, *Psychology Today,* May 1986. Copyright ©
1986 APA. Reprinted by permission of *Psychology Today* magazine.

has shown that a person who appears to grow increasingly attracted to another becomes even more attractive to that person than does one who was highly attracted right from the start. The concept of *gain* in attractiveness evidently works positively, causing us to find a person increasingly attracted to us more attractive to us also (Aronson 1980).

It is possible that, because of this "gain phenomenon," strangers and new acquaintances may always be more attractive to some people than are old friends and lovers. People for whom this is true seem to change partners frequently and to be seeking someone new and—they believe—more rewarding. For most persons, this is not the case, however. Aronson explains the continued attraction necessary in enduring relationships by the fact that the long-term relationships that generate the greatest attraction between two partners are those that have ups and downs: the occasional bad times make the good times look more attractive. Such a system minimizes the threat of a new person stepping in to lure a partner away. Couples we know who have been through many ups and downs together have reported that they find quite enough novelty with each other to keep life interesting and to ensure that their relationship remains alive.

Self-Concept

A number of studies report an association between one's degree of self-esteem and the tendency to find others more or less attractive. A study of the psychological factors involved in attraction reported that persons with low self-esteem are less likely than their counterparts with high self-esteem to demand that their partners meet their ideals for what is attractive (Murstein 1971b). In other words, it seems that one's self-esteem influences who seems to be a realistic choice. For someone with low self-esteem, a highly attractive person may seem out of reach.

Social psychologists report that some people choose not to associate with others who upset their self-concepts (Snyder, Tanke, and Berscheid 1981). A man who believes he is good-looking, for example, will be less likely to be attracted to (or to interact with) a woman who seems to act as though he is not good-looking than to a woman who seems to confirm his self-concept. A woman who is confident in her ability to succeed in her chosen career will be unlikely to be attracted to people who imply that she will not succeed or to those who do not view her success in a career as a valuable trait.

The reasons that certain individuals are attracted to each other continue to prompt more questions than answers. However, social psychologists have begun to put the pieces of the puzzle together. The search is an important one for students of marriage and the family because each couple that eventually marries begins some-place on the continuum of mutual attraction. For some, attraction is instantaneous, whereas for others it may develop slowly over months or even years. Not all attraction leads to permanent relationships, of course, so we must search further to learn why some find love and eventually choose each other for mates.

LOVE

Do you remember the first time you gave any serious thought to the meaning of love? As a youngster you may have carved entwined hearts on a tree or scrawled them on a notebook. For many of you, the words "I love you" flowed easily during high school dating experiences, but for others the sentiment was unspoken or virtually unknown.

We can remember as teenagers talking about love with our peers and wondering how we would know when it happened. At times we felt certain that what we were feeling was love—only to decide, in light of the broken romance, that it was just "infatuation." Occasional discussion with adults elicited a series of homilies about not letting the heart rule the head. A married cousin, perhaps speaking from experience, advised, "Never date anyone you wouldn't consider marrying." The point was clear: one might fall in love with someone with whom marriage was inappropriate. Parental words of wisdom ranged from "It's as easy to fall in love with a rich person as a poor one" to "Don't worry about it. When love hits, you'll know it." None of this advice seemed very helpful. Even so, we all knew that whatever love was, it was *very* serious.

Popular songs, films, and novels were just as confusing. Literature classes exposed us to the peculiarities of love as experienced, for example, by Dante and Beatrice—the love that inspired Dante's *Divine Comedy*. As a child, Dante saw Beatrice once and never recovered from the passion he felt. He married someone else and had seven children, but in his poems he mentions only Beatrice.

Love in Antiquity

In the fifth century B.C., Plato explained his theory of why people fall in love. In his *Symposium,* Plato proposed that there were once three categories of humans—men, women, and hermaphrodites. In a rage, the god Zeus, who was armed with thunder and lightning, cut all mortals in half. Today, we sometimes hear someone say, "Without the one I love, I am only half a person."

Plato believed that love comes to us when we meet our other half. A man needs a woman; a woman needs a man; hermaphrodites likewise seek those who match them in such a way that they become whole.

Homosexual love was considered as natural in Plato's time as love between men and women. In fact, Plato seemed to favor homosexual attachments, although his definition of love has more to do with the essence of beauty and goodness within each person than with sex. This emphasis on mind and heart led to the concept of **platonic love,** a term that has been used throughout the ages to denote love that does not involve sex.

In Roman, as in Greek times, marriage was commonly arranged and institutionalized as a procreative union—often a way of merging the estates or political power of families by producing common heirs. Love was not considered essential; the linkage of families by property and power was more important than romance. This notion was perpetuated through medieval times, particularly among the nobility. We know little of the customs of the powerless and propertyless because they usually went unrecorded (Money 1983). There are records indicating that some girls were abducted from their families to avoid having to pay the high bride prices that were then customary. However, stealing a bride was often an economic move rather than a romantic one.

Romantic Love

Sometime between the tenth and twelfth centuries in Europe, platonic love and sexual love merged in the concept of *romantic love.*

Troubadours of southern France began to sing love songs that are thought to have been derived from poetry of ancient Greece. The love of which they sang was typically unfulfilled because the two lovers had already been promised to others deemed suitable by their families. Occasionally, there was a happy ending, but for hundreds of years romance was not viewed as likely to be a part of married life. Instead, romantic love occurred mostly outside of marriage and often at a distance. The idea of romance lived on, however, and led eventually to the Romantic movement in the nineteenth century.

In his excellent treatment of the history of love, family sociologist Ira Reiss (1980, p. 121), speculates about the reasons for the rise in romantic love at this particular time in history:

> Surely it was in part the rediscovery of the Greek and Roman writings; in part, a reaction to the brutality of the age; in part a reaction to the scarcity of noblewomen in castles with many bachelor knights; and in part, perhaps an antichurch reaction. But whatever the causes were, the romantic love development of those centuries led to a tender, sexual relationship between men and women.

Male-female friendships are more frequently found between single persons, although a growing number of well-educated married men and married women in careers also report platonic relationships.

. . . This is a very important historical event if we are to understand present-day love and sexual customs.

Platonic Love and Friendship

So powerful was the sexual component of romantic love that the notion of platonic love was nearly lost as a meaningful concept. The idea of a close, caring, nonsexual, loving relationship between two people who have the potential to become sexual with each other seems to many an impossibility. To many, the intimacy achieved in such relationships is inevitably a precursor of a sexual relationship. In fact, the word *intimate* has come to suggest "sexually involved."

A search of current marriage and family texts turns up scant mention of platonic relationships. Yet, countless men and women have experienced a close "brotherly-sisterly" type of love. Adolescents frequently have best friends of the opposite sex who serve an important function of helping to bridge the gap to understanding of how each sex thinks, feels, and behaves. Many young adults have intimacies with colleagues, neighbors, old friends, and even apartment-mates of the opposite sex without romantic or sexual involvement.

In a recent study on friendship, sociologist Lillian Rubin (1985) interviewed 400 men and women who reported that, though highly valued, friendships across the gender line usually are "special purpose" friendships. In other words, these platonic relationships had built-in limitations determined by whether either or both of the friends were single, unmarried but cohabiting, or married. Few married or cohabiting persons had close friends of the opposite sex (those who did were more likely to be well-educated professionals), whereas single men and women frequently had cross-gender relationships that were close and nonsexual.

It is clear that platonic relationships do exist, but it is also clear that these are not generally considered the material from which "normal" marriages spring in the United States today, and indeed increasingly throughout the world. Some variation of romantic love that includes sex is considered necessary for a couple to marry. At the same time, much of society disapproves of close cross-sex relationships for married persons, no matter how platonic.

Defining Love

Today, the results of virtually every research study and poll tell us that nine out of every ten Americans consider love the most essential foundation of a happy relationship (Hinkle and Sporakowski 1975). Indeed, when love is *not* the stated reason that two people decide to form an intimate relationship, the usual reaction is disapproval. For instance, marrying for security or because one is lonely is not considered healthy by most Americans. Love is the basis on which one is expected to make a major life decision. As Marcia Lasswell and Norman Lobsenz wrote in *Styles of Loving* (1980, p. 2):

> If we do not have it, we want it. If we have it, we want more of it, or a different version of it, or a different partner with whom to share it. If our love is unrequited, we are miserable. If we have it and then lose it, we seek to recapture it. Even those who admit to never having experienced love at all still agree that it does, indeed, exist. And they, too, hope to find it.

By the end of adolescence most of us have experienced something we called love. Before people marry, they may claim to have been in and out of love several times. Males usually claim to have been in love more times than females do. One study of this phenomenon suggested that females tend to see only the current love as "real love" and to regard past loves as "infatuations." Males on the other hand, are more likely to describe all serious involvements as "being in love" (Kephart 1967).

Everyone agrees that love is a feeling about another person. However, some people resist trying to understand what the feeling means to those who have it, others are confused about its meaning, and still others have concluded that the meaning is so personal that people cannot communicate about it.

In his presidential address to the American Psychological Association, Harry Harlow (1958), whose pioneering work with primates we noted above, defended his studies of loving behavior:

> Love is a wondrous state, deep, tender and reassuring. Because of its intimate and personal nature it is regarded by some as an improper topic for experimental research. But, whatever our personal feelings may be, our assigned mission as psychologists is to analyze all facets of human and animal behavior into their component variables. So far as love or affection is concerned, psychologists have failed their mission. The little we know about love does not transcend simple observation and the little we write about it has been written better by poets and novelists.

Nearly ten years after Harlow, sociologist William Kephart was still lamenting the absence of research on love. In 1967, Kephart wrote, "It is strange that in a

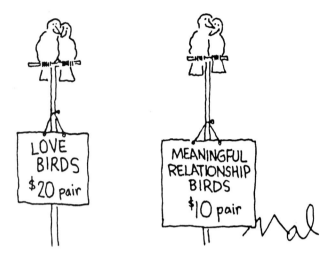

Source: From *The Wall Street Journal,* May 10, 1982. Reprinted by permission of Cartoon Features Syndicate.

society in which romantic love presumably serves as a basis for marriage, love itself has been largely rejected as a topic for serious study" (p. 470).

Yale psychologist Robert Sternberg (1985, p. 60) expressed this same sentiment recently: "With a national divorce rate approaching 50 percent and actually exceeding this figure in some locales, it is more important than ever that we understand what love is, what leads to its maintenance and what leads to its demise."

RESEARCH ON LOVE

At the same time that Kephart's article was published, love was being studied in at least a dozen locations in the United States, Canada, and England. Such research tended either to involve attempts to separate love from similar emotions (such as liking, physical attraction, or infatuation) or to identify the common elements in the definition of love used by couples who said they were in love. Almost all the research was based on the assumption that there was one *true* definition of love that people who were *really* in love shared and that whatever else they might experience was something other than love.

Zick Rubin's report (1973) that lovers gaze into each other's eyes more than nonlovers do was a step toward cataloging the attributes of love. Rubin is best known, however, for his research studies that distinguished loving from liking. His efforts were not free of frustration. He remarked that "setting out to devise measures of love is like setting out to prepare a gourmet dish with a thousand different recipes but no pots and pans." Despite the obstacles, he devised scales to measure two attitudes: the Romantic Love Scale and the Liking Scale. He tested these scales on students at the

University of Michigan in 1968 and 1969. The relatively simple tests proved capable of distinguishing the two concepts quite clearly. His subjects evidently knew the difference between liking and loving.

Rubin stated that, of all that he learned about liking and loving, perhaps the most important fact was that each has as much to do with what people *think* as with how they feel. In other words, sentiments consist of both feelings, or **affect,** and thoughts, or **cognition,** so that the process of falling in love is to some extent a cognitive one.

Other researchers through the last two decades have continued to refine the differences between liking and loving. Recently, Psychologists Michael Todd and Keith Davis (1985) have suggested that love relationships differ from even the best of friendships along several important dimensions. Love relationships are characterized by higher degrees of exclusiveness, sexual desire, and fascination. In addition, those in love show a greater depth of caring for and enjoyment of the loved one. All is not rosy, however, because love relationships differ from friendships in terms of their potential for distress, conflict, and mutual criticism.

Several important studies on love began to appear in the 1970s, including five that have become the basis for our understanding of the nature of love. The theories about love developed from these studies are wheel theory, limerance theory, physical attraction theory, styles of loving theory, and the cognitive approach.

Wheel Theory

Sociologist Ira Reiss began his studies on love earlier than most of the researchers discussed in this section. He labeled his overall conception of how love develops the "wheel theory" (1980, p. 129). He proposed that love involves four major processes: (1) *rapport*—the extent to which two people feel at ease with each other; (2) *self-revelation*—the extent that each partner feels free to be open with the other; (3) *mutual dependence*—the way both rely on each other; (4) *need fulfillment*—the ability of each to meet the other's needs. These are interdependent, and the growth or reduction of any one of them affects all of the others. Reiss places them in a circle or wheel (Figure 3.1), indicating that the wheel will move forward or backward depending on the weight of each quadrant. Love increases with the flow from one process to the next.

Limerence

Another scholar who began research on love in the 1970s was University of Bridgeport psychologist Dorothy Tennov (1979). She has been particularly interested in romantic love—especially the sort that distresses otherwise normal people. She found that more than half of her subjects had been depressed at one time or another over a love affair and that many had even considered suicide. (She also noted that significant numbers of her respondents had never experienced the trauma connected with love at all.) She coined the term **limerence** to describe the extreme highs and deep lows that accompany love for so many and that begin, as the French say, with a *coup de foudre* ("thunderbolt"). Limerence is an emotion of enormous intensity and is characterized by:

FIGURE 3 • 1
Wheel Theory
of Reiss

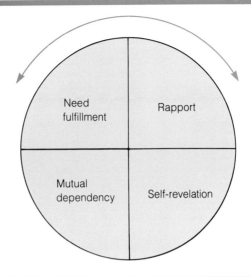

Source: From *Family Systems in America,* 3rd ed., by Ira L. Reiss. Copyright © 1980 by Holt, Rinehart and Winston; 1976 by The Dryden Press, a division of Holt, Rinehart and Winston; and 1971 by Holt, Rinehart and Winston, Inc. Reprinted by permission of Holt, Rinehart and Winston.

- Intrusive thinking about the lover
- Acute longing for him or her to reciprocate
- Mood swings in response to the lover's action—"walking on air" when things are good, "heartache" when there are troubles
- Blindness to the possibility that anyone but the lover exists as someone to love
- Unsettling shyness or clumsiness around the lover because of fear of rejection
- Preoccupation with and sensitivity to any act or thought (real or imagined) of the lover's, to the point of letting other interests slide
- Inability to see any flaws in the lover and overemphasis on his or her strengths

Limerence appears to have four dimensions that define its nature: (1) the speed of onset, (2) its intensity, (3) whether it is reciprocated, and (4) its duration. It is possible, therefore, to have onset be sudden (love at first sight) or more gradual; intensity can vary from overwhelming to somewhat milder; it can be one-sided or mutual; and it can be brief or long-standing.

We know little about who is likely to experience one pattern or the other; however, Tennov's research has led others to explore this question. Some seem to experience limerence at early ages (crushes) and with some degree of frequency throughout life. Money (1983, p. 311) has defined a phenomenon that he labels "ultraertia" to describe those who seem "unable to exist with a sense of well-being unless they reiterate the experience of limerent pair-bonding in periodic love affairs." For others, limerence may not occur until later in life—unfortunately for some, after they are married. We often have heard a man or woman account for an extramarital affair by saying, "I never knew before now what it is to be *really* in love." In still others, limerence appears never to occur. Money (1983, p. 311) has called this phenomenon "limerent inertia."

Those who experience limerence describe extreme highs and deep lows that accompany love; they have little ability to see any flaws in the loved one.

At times, two people are perfectly matched along the four dimensions of limerence. But when the attachment is not reciprocal, the syndrome called "love sickness" frequently results. Physiologists M. R. Liebowitz and D. F. Klein (1979) have linked being lovesick to one of the brain's neurotransmitters (phenylethylamine), which appears to play a part in such emotions as sadness and depression.

Still others who are limerent appear to be unusually affected by feelings of jealousy. Such jealousy may be mutual or one-sided, low-grade or acute; it may even be violent. Trouble seems to abound for many limerents; for a variety of reasons, they tend to personalize all their partners' actions as stop-or-go signals. Thus, a limerent person's actions are reactions. If he or she does not realize that many people never experience such intense feelings and that a partner's less extreme actions may reflect a different way of loving, love can be a miserable experience.

Sometimes after a romance has ended, one of the pair suffers from "love addiction." Such persons appear to have withdrawal symptoms, such as illness and an inability to eat, sleep, or work. Their urgent need to see, talk to, or touch the ex-lover resembles a drug addict's need for a fix. Such contact feels good for the moment but results in increased pain when the withdrawal begins again (cf. Peele 1975).

Physical Attraction

In Wales in 1977, at the International Conference on Love and Attraction, a group of people interested in love research met to compare their results. British psychologists Glenn Wilson and David Nias (1976) along with Bernard Murstein (1971b), a professor of psychology at Connecticut College, emphasized physical attractiveness as an important preliminary to falling in love. Although they acknowledged that beauty is in the eye of the beholder, they pointed out that there is considerable general agreement about who is or is not physically attractive.

In Wilson and Nias's model for falling in love, mutually held, similar attitudes that eventually serve to reinforce and sustain the initial attraction gradually unfold. An important mutual attitude, Wilson and Nias emphasized, is sexual attraction—the "chemistry of love." Although many studies carefully separate love from physical attraction, these psychologists believe that both sex and love are enmeshed in a total "eligibility score" that people assign to their potential partners.

Murstein (1971b) added to the notion of the "eligibility score" that each individual has insight into his or her own level of attractiveness. In other words, men and women rate themselves on a scale of attractiveness, which they then use to determine who might be interested in them. While others may not always agree with the estimate, the belief in one's degree of attractiveness seems to be a powerful force in whether one allows love to develop with certain others. For example, if one feels unattractive, attention from a very attractive person might be rejected as insincere.

Styles of Loving

Sociologist John Alan Lee (1973) has produced a comprehensive typology of love. He devised a scale for identifying a subject's "style of loving" based on the extent to which the person associated different meanings of love with particular feelings, thoughts, and actions. He distinguished eight different meanings commonly used by lovers. Using the analogy of a color wheel, he suggested that just as all colors are derived from the three primary colors—red, blue, and yellow—so the several types of love derive from three primary ones:

1. *Eros:* romantic, sexual, sensual love, characterized by love at first sight
2. *Ludus:* a playful, challenging, nonpossessive kind of love
3. *Storge:* a comfortable, affectionate, slow-to-develop but intimate kind of love

In addition, Lee proposed three secondary types of love that are often mixed in varying degrees with either eros, ludus, or storge: *mania* (a possessive, jealous, and stressful love reminiscent of Tennov's "limerence"); *agape* (an unselfish, altruistic love); and *pragma* (a logical and sensible love). Lee added two commonly seen combinations—*storgic ludus* and *ludic eros*—for a total of eight different types of love.

Cognitive Aspects of Love

Our own work was influenced by our growing recognition that, along with most other social scientists, we had uncritically accepted the popular notion that there was one, true, universal concept of love that had not been clearly defined. We began examining the kinds of conflict that occurred when a couple used a common word—love—to talk about different conclusions and behaviors.

We were especially interested in the definitions—the cognitive aspects—of love. We were also aware of a physiological component, ranging from changes in heart rate, skin temperature, breathing rate, blood pressure, and pupil dilation to scores of reported sensations such as "butterflies in the stomach" and "stars in the eyes." However, we knew from the work of psychologist Stanley Schachter (1964) and his colleagues that physiological reactions during one emotion can look deceptively like those of any other. That is, people who display similar physical symptoms might be experiencing fear, anger, excitement, or love. Surprisingly, two people—both of them experiencing an emotion that they call love—might manifest very different symptoms.

In a pilot study, we instructed our subjects to imagine an experience that made them angry (or to recall a real one). We measured their bodily reactions by using **biofeedback** equipment, which gave us information on their heartbeat, skin temperature, blood pressure, and heightened skin resistance compared with corresponding measures in a normal state. After a rest interval, we repeated the measurements, asking the subjects to imagine or recall both a fearsome time and an experience of love. The results confirmed those of Schachter and indicated that a subject's definition of love made no reliable difference in his or her biofeedback reactions; those with nearly identical definitions often showed very different bodily symptoms (Lasswell, Lasswell, and Goodman 1976). In other words, our bodies tell us that we are experiencing some kind of emotion, but we use our minds to label it.

In Appendix B, we describe the six definitions of love that emerged from our research. Also included in Appendix B is the self-test that we used and that readers can employ to determine their own definitions.

Research on love continues on many fronts—sociological, psychological, and physiological. Most studies agree that love is a combination of emotions unique to each individual. Perhaps the most important variable in the success of a loving relationship is how each person wants to be loved compared with how his or her partner feels. The closer a lover matches one's expectations and desires, the greater the satisfaction.

FAMILY AND PEER EFFECTS ON LOVE
Family Influence

The potential for loving and being loved is believed to exist from the moment we are born. The way our needs are met from the very beginning either conveys or fails to convey that love is an emotion flowing from parent to child.

At first an infant is intensely attracted to anyone who fulfills his or her needs. The noted psychiatrist Martha Mahler and her associates have proposed that, for the first few months after birth, the baby and mother (or other principal caretaker) are linked as one social-psychological unit (Mahler, Pine, and Bergman 1975). The infant's world revolves around interaction with this person, and the baby perceives the caretaker's world as centering on her or his limited orb. This perception is motivated by the child's need for survival; it is also the earliest form of love.

A baby's evident contentment when its needs have been met is pleasing to its parents. In that sense, the infant is a source of love for the parents as well as a receiver of parental love. This interaction sets the stage for one definition of love: the desire to be close to another who meets our needs. Mahler suggests that true emotional attachment develops by the age of five to six months. When babies of that age are near their parents, they reach out, touch, smile, and make contented sounds. These gestures and body rhythms are the early language of love.

As soon as a baby can crawl and move away from its parents—as well as toward them—a certain amount of separation comes under the child's control. Until then, the parents have been the ones to leave and return. Separation may distress the infant until he or she begins to make some of the choices about how much togetherness there will be.

Even some adults feel fearful of abandonment. One theory holds that such people never bridged the gap between the early dependence necessary for survival in childhood and the assurance that a certain amount of separation is both necessary and desirable. Such awareness is generally considered a significant step toward mature love (Lax, Bach, and Burland 1980).

An adult who has never learned to be comfortable when separated from a caretaker finds it impossible to choose a partner from any perspective other than that of a dependent, needy child. We often see whining, clinging children who seem panicky at the thought of any separation from their parents. As marriage counselors, we see similar behavior in many persons who are adults chronologically but who never learned that it is not catastrophic to be alone for a while. As children they somehow failed to make the transition from dependency to a sense of security when separated from their parents. One reason for this failure may have been that the parents were emotionally distant, making it virtually impossible for the child to feel secure. Another possibility is that the parents bound the child too closely, never allowing him or her to develop independence.

Most children do manage to become secure in the belief that love does not vanish when loved ones are out of sight. At first the child needs love substitutes while parents are away: a favorite sitter, a doll, or a pet. As adults we sometimes carry love substitutes when we are away from loved ones: a picture, a letter, a ring. These are reminders that love is constant. They help us learn that separation is as important an aspect of love as is the initial bonding (Erikson 1963). Learning to be apart teaches the valuable lesson that one can be intimate and yet retain a sense of self.

Overprotectiveness—too much love—is damaging in much the same way as is too little love. Overprotective parents usually convey the idea that life is filled with hazards with which a child cannot hope to cope alone. Such an attitude often has a lasting effect, producing an adult who does not trust his or her capacity to be alone. With either too much or too little attention, a child can grow into an adult who finds it difficult to be independent and who frequently exhibits extreme emotional neediness. Such persons often seek a love that will fulfill their infantile yearnings—a partner who will satisfy all needs. The search is rarely fruitful, and the result is constant fear of being alone and helpless.

Much has been written concerning the different paths that men and women take from infancy to adulthood in learning to love and be loved. Most researchers agree that the differences begin when parents begin to socialize boys and girls in distinct ways as well as when a boy is forced to disengage from his mother's world to identify with his father's masculine patterns. Girls, on the other hand, continue to identify with the same person to whom they have been bonded since infancy—the mother, who for most infants is the first and most consistent caretaker.

Lillian Rubin (1985, p. 97) has written: "To protect against the pain wrought by this radical shift in his internal world, the boy builds a set of defenses that will serve him, for good or for ill, for the rest of his life. This is the beginning of the development of ego boundaries so characteristic of men—boundaries that are fixed and firm, that circumscribe not only his relationships with others but his connection to his inner emotional life as well." Girls and women typically are more open to

Children learn how to love by seeing loving behavior between their parents and by experiencing being loved by their parents.

intimacy and the sharing of thoughts and feelings. By the end of childhood, their friendship patterns are already quite different—"boys travel in bunches" to share activities, girls travel in pairs to share secrets (Lever 1978).

And yet, as Rubin (1985, p. 100) reminds us, despite a man's efforts "to stand apart, to keep himself tightly under emotional control, in adulthood, he's caught between his hunger to recapture the repressed part of himself and his guardedness." Men so frequently look to women to help them resolve this dilemma that, for a great many men, their closest relationships are with women, not with other men (S. Miller 1983).

Another important influence in learning to love—other than how we are loved by our parents—is how our parents love each other. Children are keen observers and often learn more from watching what others do than from hearing what others say. Some parents are very loving to each other in front of their children. Others make no display of affection at all. There may be ample love in such undemonstrative marriages, but children are left to pick up indirect and often vague clues. Children, after all, cannot observe parents' feelings—only their behaviors. Love is a learned emotion, and it is best learned when a child has early opportunities to see loving behavior modeled directly.

Beginning about age four to six, children imitate adult relationships almost as if rehearsing through play for their later roles. Such play may include weddings, parenting, and other domestic scenes, including sexual exploration. Adults' reactions to such play ranges from amusement to punishment. In our society, teasing children about boyfriends or girlfriends and taboos on sexual rehearsal usually combine to cause children either to stop such play or to be secretive about it by the time of middle childhood (ages seven to twelve). This does not mean, however, that they stop observing and learning from adults and somewhat older children.

In *love-poor* families, children neither see loving behavior between their parents nor experience sufficient love themselves. There are some striking similarities among such families. They tend to act as though loving behavior is unimportant and to emphasize material possessions as substitutes for relationships. Children from such families are far more likely to grow into adults who prize money as the avenue to happiness than are those who grow up in families that share and display love openly.

Children from love-poor families often comment that their parents provided everything material they ever wanted but that they never got the parents' time, attention, and affection. As a result, these children learn to ask for more and more things to substitute for the love that has not been forthcoming. As adults, they may even try to avoid situations and relationships in which love might be found. Many do not seem to know how to love.

In sharp contrast to love-poor children are those whose families, though financially poor, were rich in love, or those whose families gave love freely in addition to providing material resources. To be without love would be incomprehensible to such children. Material items could never compare with the love they received. Clearly, then, parents exert a powerful influence on how children learn to love and on what they expect from those they love and those who love them.

Peer Influence

By the time children reach the age of six, peers begin to exert an increasingly important influence on their thoughts and emotions. Harry Stack Sullivan (1953), an early and prominent psychotherapist, believed that the years of middle childhood provide children with experiences with others of the same age and sex that are invaluable to their later development of loving behavior. Sharing secrets with nonfamily peers, whether about sexual knowledge and activities or discoveries about the reality of Santa Claus or the Easter Bunny, provides new experiences with commitment and trust.

Sullivan was a **neo-Freudian** who considered the period of same-sex friendships as one during which sexual feelings were quiet and children had no thoughts of love. Early literature in the field of child psychology emphasized that this is a time during which boys ignore girls and vice versa or they tease (but are repelled by) members of the opposite sex. This may be true in part, but more recent observations have indicated that children from six to twelve do have active thoughts and feelings of love for those of the opposite sex (Broderick 1966a).

Boyfriends and girlfriends are not at all uncommon in elementary school. Passing love notes in school, gossiping about who likes whom, and playing kissing games are commonplace activities. In his extensive studies of childhood romances, family sociologist Carlfred Broderick (1966a) found that nine out of ten of the children he observed had sweethearts whom they claimed to love. His studies seem to indicate that at least a large percentage of children do not have a sexually quiet period. What a young child means by saying he or she loves someone may be different from what an adult would mean. But whatever children felt, "they behaved for all the world as if they had crushes on each other" (Broderick and Rowe 1968).

So important is the learning about love that takes place throughout childhood that John Money (1983), noted authority on love and sex, has proposed that children are as predisposed neurologically to incorporate patterns of love as they are preprogrammed to learn their native language. He calls the developing patterns mental lovemaps.

Perhaps the greatest peer influences on concepts of love occur during adolescence. As the young person's autonomy within the family grows, the influence of peers outside the home increases. Most young people begin to attend mixed-sex parties—often as couples—by the beginning of the teenage years. Most have fallen "seriously" in love by the end of adolescence (Simon and Gagnon 1967).

The eminent child psychiatrist Erik Erikson (1968) believed that the teenage years are crucial for learning how to love and to be intimate with persons outside the family system. "Where a youth does not accomplish such intimate relationships with others—and I would add, with his own inner resources—he may settle for highly stereotyped interpersonal relations and come to retain a deep sense of isolation." Adults who did not learn how to achieve intimacy with peers during adolescence may find it difficult to care for or be close to another person. If Erikson is right, parents who prohibit or unnecessarily delay dating during the teens may be doing a real disservice to their children.

All in all, by the end of adolescence and the beginning of young adulthood, we come to recognize love as a basic element of meaningful relationships. Each person has developed his or her own unique definition of love. The definition may be incomplete since future experiences undoubtedly will change that understanding. However, current research suggests that elements of our early definitions of love run as threads throughout our lives (Hatkoff and Lasswell 1977).

The persistence of early definitions of love may well account for the romantic experiences of couples in their later years who, having met and fallen in love, can be as starry-eyed as they were in their youth. It is probable that they are adding years to their lives as well. Being with someone you love and who loves you correlates positively with longevity and an absence of heart disease (Lynch 1977, p. 197). No matter how we define love, and whether our notions of love change with time, there is nearly universal agreement about its importance in our lives.

SUMMARY

1. Attraction can be one-sided, but one-sided attractions are unlikely to develop into enduring relationships. Relationships come from mutual attraction that reinforces each partner in a variety of ways. Mutual attraction is believed to result from the belief of each partner that the other satisfies certain human hungers.
2. Exchange theory and equity theory are popular explanations for attraction. A relationship that both partners consider a fair exchange is more likely to continue than one in which either partner feels he or she is giving very much more than the other.
3. Proponents of attribution theory hold that attraction is determined by one's inferences about another's behavior. If those inferences create a positive picture, attraction is more likely.
4. How attraction to others is affected by one's self-judgment has been the subject of considerable investigation. It appears that the self-concept influences each person's choices of friends and lovers.
5. Despite the acknowledged importance of love, it has defied serious study by social scientists until very recently. A few studies began in the 1960s, but only in the 1970s did love research come into its own.
6. Definitions of love range from those that call it a learned response to those that describe love as a dependent, addictive clinging to another person who holds promise of meeting one's needs.

7. In an attempt to bring more objectivity to the study of such a complex emotion, a number of love scales have been developed. Most emphasize an intensity of feeling that must be present for love to be felt and the ascription of certain unique attributes to the loved one. It is clear that loving and liking are two distinct phenomena.

8. In an effort to avoid sticking to only one definition of love (which seemed artificial to many of those objectively exploring love), it has been proposed that there are several basic definitions used in various combinations to account for differences in both behavior and reported feelings of those in love.

9. Love is the basis for marriage in much of the world today, although romantic love as a basis for an enduring relationship is a concept that emerged relatively recently.

10. Learning to love and to be loved begins at birth. Parents teach love directly and serve as models of loving behavior for children. It has been said that we learn to love through the way we remember having been loved.

11. Siblings and peers are influential in helping children form a definition of love. All during childhood, boys and girls are aware of the idea of love, both from interacting with each other and from their interpretations of adults' behaviors. They play house, show affection to each other, and have crushes on each other.

12. By adolescence most young people have experienced feelings that they call love. Teenage dating facilitates this developmental task, which is a necessary part of learning how to be close and, ultimately, how to achieve intimacy.

13. Each person, through unique experiences, develops his or her own definition of love, which is of great importance for intimate relationships, marriage, and family life.

GLOSSARY

Affect A feeling or emotion. (p. 70)

Antipathy A dislike of or aversion to an object, person, or idea. (p. 56)

Attribution The assignment of motivations, emotions, and attitudes to others to explain their behaviors. (p. 62)

Biofeedback A process by which internal biological states are reported by instruments. An example is the use of an EEG (electroencephalograph) to measure brain waves. (p. 74)

Cognition Feelings and knowledges. (p. 70)

Limerence A term coined to describe the intense emotional highs and lows that sometimes accompany the state of being in love. (p. 70)

Marasmus A progressive emaciation found in infants, associated with the lack of consistent positive responses from parent or parent-surrogate figures. (p. 59)

Neo-Freudian A modernized version of Freudian theory that uses an approach combining the concept of the unconscious, one's childhood experiences, and one's conscious functioning in the present. (p. 77)

Pheromones Chemical substances exuded by animals that give off odors that elicit sexual responses from others of the same species. (p. 62)

Physiognomy The face of a person or object, especially when it is used to make judgments of characteristics not visible. (p. 61)

Platonic love A love relationship in which no overt sexual behavior and no erotic components are present. (p. 66)

Serial invalidation A condition that exists when one or both parents continually judge a child's behavior as wrong or inappropriate or when the child interprets their behavior as such a judgment. (p. 60)

Sex is by no means everything. It varies, as a matter of fact, from only as high as 78 percent of everything to a low of 3.1 percent of everything. The norm in a sane, healthy person should be between 18 and 24 percent.

Human sexuality is both an individual and a social matter. In every society children are taught how to view their sexuality and how to behave sexually. This socialization takes place in precisely the same way as does learning about any other important aspect of children's lives—through direct teaching from adults and peers, through observation and imitation, and through personal experience. As a result, children grow up with a blend of accurate and inaccurate information. However, as adults, we keep learning about our sexual selves and about our partners. Early influences affect adult attitudes and behaviors—sometimes in limiting ways. Warm, loving experiences often can help us overcome earlier misconceptions and enable us to achieve new levels of sexual understanding and enjoyment.

HUMAN SEXUALITY

James Thurber and E. B. White, *Is Sex Necessary?*

*O*ver half a century ago, Mark Twain (1962, p. 23) wrote: "Adam and Eve entered the world naked and unashamed—naked and pure-minded; and no descendant of theirs has ever entered it otherwise. All have entered it naked, unashamed, and clean in mind. They have entered it modest. They had to acquire immodesty and a soiled mind; there was no other way to get it."

Twain's commentary points to the kinds of sentiments and assumptions that children learn—and that adults have grown up with—about sex and eroticism. Sentiments are learned in many ways—by modeling on others with whom a person is trying to identify, by very precise indoctrination, and by conditioning. Often they are learned through emotional responses to the behaviors of important others—parents, family, and close friends. Everyone brings sentiments to social interaction, and sexual interaction is no exception.

HOW CHILDREN LEARN ABOUT SEX

Both children and adults may associate—often in confusing ways—the notion of sex with other ideas. These include ideas about excretion, reproduction, and social **taboos** related to sex.

1. *Ideas, terms, and behaviors associated with excretion:* the first association many children make with their genitals is that they are the point of exit of urine for males and near the point of exit for females. In teaching bathroom hygiene, adults do not always make clear to children whether it is the sex organs themselves or their excretory products that are "dirty." When an adult tells a child that it is important to keep his or her genitals concealed from public view, the child usually associates them with excretion and concludes that they are, at the very least, unattractive or obscene and, if not actually shameful, so provoking that they may cause trouble.

Sometimes adults who fail to mature sexually continue to find something sexy or **erotic** about urination. However, adults are usually able to distinguish clearly between the eliminatory and the sexual functions and erotic feelings of their genitals.

2. *The reproductive process:* technically, the human reproductive process is a sexual one; that is, it begins when a female sex cell is fertilized by a male sex cell. This fertilization may or may not be the result of an encounter that is erotic for both a male and a female: one does not have to enjoy **sexual intercourse** to become pregnant. Sex education, particularly in elementary school, is likely to be concerned exclusively with reproduction (and usually the menstrual cycle), leading children to believe erroneously that **coitus** always causes conception or that grown-ups have intercourse only in order to conceive.

Four- or five-year-olds may comprehend very well the erotic properties of their sex organs, even to the point of recognizing differences between the erotic quality of sex play for boys and for girls (Bernstein 1976). Children may also know that a baby grows in its mother's abdomen, that it makes its exit from her body by means of a "special passage," and that it originates there because the father puts "seeds" in the mother; but from such a description children are unlikely to perceive reproduction as very "sexy" (Bernstein and Cowan 1975). Children may believe that coitus between their parents is a solemn ritual, occurring once for each baby and totally unrelated to the excitement of their own secret games and sensations.

Actually few adults are excited sexually by thoughts of reproduction. They may make sentimental associations between childbirth and sexual arousal, but for most people these sentiments are very different. If the reproductive organs (the uterus, the **prostate gland,** and so forth) seem sexy to an adult, it is because they are associated with the notion of two persons giving each other pleasure by joining their sex organs. That is the distinctive theme of erotic sex as opposed to reproductive sex.

It is true that, when **contraception** was less effective than it is now, coitus usually resulted in pregnancy sooner or later. However, the confusion of erotic sex with reproduction has affected the sexual attitudes of many people.

3. *Social taboos:* social taboos of one sort or another have somehow come to have a sexual connotation, emotionally at least, for some people—and often especially for young children. Nudity, the visibility of underwear, being in the bedroom of a nonfamily person of the opposite gender, seeing or hearing "obscene" words, even whispering secrets, may produce genital responses. Perhaps it is when they are forbidden that such acts become associated with sexuality. The use of inanimate objects (most often underclothing, a lock of hair, stockings, shoes, or gloves) to attain sexual gratification is called **fetishism.**

Sexiness may be confused with elimination, **menstruation,** reproduction, fetishes, or taboos. Sex education as conceptualized in this book, however, has nothing to do with excretory behavior; it is not focused exclusively on reproduction; and it is in a completely different category from social taboos and deviation.

Role of Peers

Several studies have been conducted to determine the ages and the sources that are the best for imparting sex education and other kinds of information about sexuality to young people (Thornburg 1970; McCary and McCary 1977). Generally, the data indicate that young people are most interested in sex education between the ages of twelve and fifteen years and that **peers** are their most frequent source of information (S. McCary 1978).

The sex education provided by peers is very different from the lessons taught by parents. Children have a lore and a language passed on from child to child in songs, games, and rhymes. They use words that are taboo around adults, and early learn certain sexual terminology common to the peer group.

An important function of children's sex lore is that it establishes a special language and a set of shared sentiments distinct from those of the family of origin. Children form bonds of trust (reinforced by secrecy) and learn to respect affiliations of their own choosing as opposed to those thrust on them. Parents are sometimes astonished to learn that their children are telling the same jokes and using the same words that they used at that age, and children wonder why their parents already know the punch lines. It is clear that children pass on this lore to other children quite independently of the adult society.

Children use at least half a dozen explicit and unmistakable terms to describe coitus, as well as dozens of euphemisms that convey the idea adequately. Euphemisms range from "screw" or "scrump" to "make love" or "do it," just as poets "pluck blossoms," "touch souls," or "become one." Children readily acquire taboo terms at such an early age that most cannot remember where they first heard them. By the end of the fourth grade, any child who does not know what these words mean is thought by his or her peers to be either poorly enculturated or else overprotected by parents.

Two additional ideas have usually been conveyed: first, "nice" girls and boys must not be caught "doing it" by adults; but, second, "it" is a very exciting thing to do. This relieves parents and teachers of several painful chores. They do not need to tell children who are ten or older that sexual intercourse exists: the children already know. They do not need to tell children that sexual intercourse among children is subject to the disapproval of adults: the children already know. They do not need to tell children that sexual activities can be exciting: the children have already learned this (unless they have somehow been so conditioned that they are repelled by the idea, which happens rarely to boys but occasionally to girls).

Peers can share certain notions and feelings about sex, but they often lack the necessary knowledge to provide complete and accurate information. They may fail to make the conceptual distinctions between sex itself and elimination, reproduction, taboos, and other notions. They often exaggerate the social humiliation and parental anger that will result if sexual activities are discovered. Some teenage girls may even commit suicide because they believe that the disgrace of the disclosure of sexual activities or pregnancy will be too much to face.

Role of Adults

Through casual behaviors and conversations, parents can make it clear that they have a warm and physical relationship. Sex therapist William Masters (1976) has said that the best sex education a child can receive is to see Dad give Mom a pat on her fanny and to see her smile and enjoy it. Adults can make clear in informal conversations that sex is a normal, pleasurable, mutual activity. Parents and teachers can convey many bits of information to children in order to guide, enlighten, or make them feel more comfortable with their own sexual propensities or activities. Accepting children's discussions about sex and sexual behaviors as appropriate family conversation keeps the door open for questions. Replacing misinformation received from peers and other sources with factual information discussed in an open and relaxed manner can help young people grow up with healthy attitudes toward sex.

A number of factors, however, may interfere with this communication process. For example, American society, among others, has many cultural, religious, and legal rules that define appropriate adult-child communication and interaction. Second, different child and family experts recommend conflicting child-rearing methods. Third, to some, parent-child discussion of sexuality borders on violation of incest taboos. Fourth, the words needed for discussion may be forbidden for a child to use. Finally,

A child comes to have healthy thoughts and feelings about his or her body through the responses of important others—particularly parents.

it may seem simplest to parents and teachers to deny or even punish any sexual or erotic interests, communications, or behaviors by children.

Taboos on discussions of sexual or erotic behaviors during adolescence and preadolescence can be carried forward into adulthood and may prevent establishment of satisfactory sexual relations (Kaplan 1979, p. 89). Several substantial studies support this belief. A report by a congressional commission indicates the mentally unhealthy outcome of severe restriction of children's erotic interests (The Report of the Commission on Obscenity and Pornography 1970, p. 277). Another study shows that the overwhelming majority of persons imprisoned for sex crimes were reared in families that did not discuss sexual behaviors (Gebhard 1965, pp. 470–472). Still another landmark study blames repression of children's sexual interests for failures in treatment of sexual disorders (Masters and Johnson 1970, pp. 175–176, 222–229).

Communication about sexual topics may be difficult for some families. However, research findings suggest that open family acceptance and discussion of children's interests in erotic and sexual matters may be important for children's future mental health, marital adjustment, and social behaviors (Rogers 1982, pp. 92bb–92cc).

Sex is usually an emotional issue. Since the parent-child relationship is an emotional one, it is likely that some parents cannot comfortably undertake the total sex education of their children, just as physicians cannot undertake the total medical care of their own children. Few parents had completely unbiased sex training as children, which may make their role as objective sex educators more difficult with their own children. They certainly can provide support, add factual information, and share their own values about sex. If, however, their own information is inadequate or inaccurate or their personal biases interfere with their objectivity, it may well be that the overall task can be carried out better by a detached, qualified professional over a reasonable period of time, preferably beginning in early elementary school years. To meet the needs of these families and to offer reinforcement for those families in which parents provide quality sex education, a well-planned curriculum taught by specially trained teachers should be a goal for all educational systems. Unfortunately, just as the quality of sex education in the family varies, so does the quality of programs offered outside the home.

What Children Need to Know

What, then, can a child be taught about sex before puberty? Both words and actions can help to convey the conceptual distinctions discussed earlier in this chapter. Ideas, terms, and behaviors associated with excretion, reproduction, menstruation, and other areas often confused with erotic sexuality can be clarified and distinguished from sex and related to sex appropriately.

Parents and teachers can point out that many diseases are contracted by sexual contact with other persons and that a child who suspects that he or she has contracted a disease should get immediate treatment. **Sexually transmitted diseases** are a serious health problem—just as many other communicable diseases are—to be avoided and, if contracted, to be treated by medical professionals.

Children should learn that it is unfair for an individual to engage in any sexual behavior with another person when that person is unwilling or is ignorant of what is taking place. This approach may help a child to define appropriate sexual behavior and to respond more rationally and calmly to sexual aggression. Emphasizing mutuality and responsibility in sexual activity may go a long way toward teaching morality and the ethical notion that exploitation is what is obscene—not sex itself.

Parents and teachers can convey the idea that erotic, sexual feelings are normal and healthy and that young people are not alone in having them—so do toddlers, adults, and grandparents. They can mention that erections of the penis are normal and that erections can occur from just thinking about sex or even for no apparent reason. This information seems fairly obvious; yet many boys grow up with feelings of guilt about their erections, and many girls are misinformed on this subject. Many otherwise sophisticated women believe that erections are under a man's voluntary control and that a man can either produce one at will or keep himself from doing so.

Girls, too, can be assured that their feelings of sexual arousal are normal. They should know that sexual excitement causes wetness of their genitals and that this wetness is not urine but rather a clean secretion that indicates they are growing up. This secretion, rather than menstrual fluid, is more nearly analogous to a boy's first **preejaculatory fluid** heralding the beginning of adolescence. Boys and girls can be taught to wash their sex organs, along with the rest of their bodies, when they bathe. Parents can explain that sex organs are no dirtier than any other parts of the body. They can point out that, in a normally healthy person, secretions from sexual organs are less likely than other body products (for example, saliva or feces) to contain bacteria (Gadpaille 1975).

Girls may imagine that males urinate into females during intercourse and may be relieved to learn that this is not so. This common carry-over from the early childhood confusion about the use of the penis both as an excretory organ and as a sexual organ, if not cleared up satisfactorily, may cause a young woman to dread contact with a penis.

Although most children begin sexual self-stimulation at a very early age, their feelings about it are often determined by the attitudes of peers and of their parents. Unless there are stringent religious objections, parents and teachers can offer supportive counseling to aid children in accepting this activity as normal. Very young girls and boys frequently touch their genitals or **masturbate** simply because it feels good. It may be embarrassing to their parents or to others if it is done in public, but it is harmless to the child unless it is made an emotional issue. As a normal child grows older, this behavior may disappear for several years. After puberty, however, masturbation in solitude often returns and is a lifelong activity for most individuals (Diamond and Karlen 1980, pp. 171–187).

Although children of both sexes are capable of achieving **orgasm** before puberty, relatively few do. Self-stimulation without orgasm is likely to be intermittent in both sexes before puberty. Once a child achieves orgasm, however, masturbation normally becomes regular and frequent unless repressive instruction by peers and elders has led to guilt feelings.

There may be occasion to explain to a child that one cannot use up one's sexual capacity and that, if anything, regular sexual activity tends to prolong one's effective sexual life span. Much has been said about "excessive masturbation" without defining "excessive." Such phrases sometimes reflect a fear that masturbation causes one to lose energy or to become a victim of uncontrollable sexual desire, but more often such statements have moralistic overtones. Adults can help put masturbation in a sensible perspective for children and to reassure young people that it is physically

TEACHING KIDS ABOUT SEX

Most teen-agers know it isn't true that if a girl jumps up and down after sex she'll shake out the sperm and not get pregnant.

Some teen-agers aren't sure, however, if it's true that a girl never gets pregnant the first time. Nor are some teen-age girls quite clear on whether sex is a good way to clear up problem pimples.

Those are a couple reasons why there are [1.2 million] teen pregnancies a year . . . nationwide.

These figures indicate that a lot of sex misinformation is bandied about the schoolyard.

Undoubtedly, the sexual misinformation doesn't come solely from teen-age boys hoping to overcome the resistance of high school lasses. It can come from locker room jokes, advertisements, television and movies.

To prepare teen-agers for the responsibility of sex, marriage and parent-hood, schools are offering sex education classes.

But according to Planned Parenthood, parents still bear the main responsi-bility for teaching kids about sex.

And to help kids and parents bridge the communication gap, Planned Par-enthood has . . . published a guide called "Let's Talk About . . . S-E-X . . . for peo-ple 9 to 12 and their parents." . . .

At the onset of puberty, between ages 9 and 12, children finally are open to parental discussions about sex, . . . although they may start asking pointed ques-tions long before.

"The way in which a child has been raised from birth, the way the parents caressed him and talked to him, will influence whether the child will approach sex in an open and positive way," said Hugh Anwyl, executive director of Planned Par-enthood, Los Angeles.

"It may be up to the parent to initiate a discussion about sex in a roundabout way, if a direct discussion seems to cause the child embarrassment," Anwyl said.

According to the guide authored by Sam Gitchel and Lorri Foster, as chil-dren progress through adolescence, talking about sex may become more difficult for them. It is normal for adolescents to want more privacy and distance from their families.

But if there is an established pattern in the family of discussing emotions and problems it is much more likely to continue into adolescence, the authors say.

If preadolescents don't ask questions, it may be because parents uncon-sciously have communicated the idea that sex is a taboo subject, Anwyl said.

"Parents can show it's OK to talk about sexual issues by talking about them with the spouse at the dinner table, when children are around. They can comment on sex-related events in everyday life, such as a pregnant friend, or somebody getting a vasectomy," Anwyl said.

In sex education, either at home or at school, maintaining the child's self-esteem is essential, said Jackie Goldberg, a Los Angeles school board member who has campaigned for sex education as part of the regular curriculum. "Adults often are uncomfortable talking about the subject with kids, but kids are so happy to find an adult they can talk to about sex. . . .

"It is also important to communicate family attitudes, values and beliefs, but they should be differentiated from facts," said Ruth Rich, instructional special-ist for health education for the Los Angeles Unified School District.

"For instance, parents should explain both the contraceptive alternatives to children when they have reached the maturity level to understand the informa-tion, as well as the family values regarding their use.

"Children also have to be taught how to say no to uncomfortable touch-ing," Rich said.

Parents must be the role models, and help children become self-assured enough to resist peer pressure that might persuade them into self-destructive be-havior, Rich said.

Source: Phil Garlington, "Teaching Kids about Sex," *Los Angeles Herald Examiner,* October 6, 1985, p. A-2. Reprinted by permission.

harmless. Some religious groups still consider self-stimulation a sin; children who are taught this will face a continuing dilemma of reconciling their religious upbringing with the frequent urge to masturbate.

Often children know how a baby is conceived long before they realize that not all sex is for procreation. Children should know that there is not always a one-to-one relationship between sexual intercourse and pregnancy and that their parents or other adults have intercourse fairly regularly with no desire for pregnancy. As a corollary of this principle, children may be told about contraception as a typical practice of those who want to have intercourse without having babies. Parents or teachers might add that contraception is a special blessing for people who wish to plan the size or timing of their family—an advantage that people of past generations lacked. Again, certain religious groups view contraception as sinful.

Children can be told that it is not uncommon for unmarried women to become pregnant, even though contraceptives are easily obtainable. Such a conversation might lead to a discussion of the reasons for and the possible outcomes of such a pregnancy. Parents can point out that once a couple begins having sexual intercourse, it is sometimes difficult for them to discontinue without ending their relationship entirely. This should be offered as an observation, not a threat.

Planned Parenthood publishes a guide called *Let's Talk about SEX: For People 9 to 12 and Their Parents* (see box at left). Among other information, it suggests that parents avoid

- Teasing children about their changing bodies and feelings and permitting others to do so.
- Making harsh judgments about other people's sex lives. This can hamper further discussion.
- Joking too much about sex. Sometimes a little humor can relieve embarrassment, but if parents always talk about sex in a joking fashion, children may believe that their parents do not appreciate the depth or beauty that sexual experiences may have.
- Passing on feelings or sentiments that arise because they are having sexual problems that are distressing or creating anxieties, or because they view all sexual behavior as sinful or bad or even unpleasant.

ADOLESCENT SEXUAL BEHAVIOR

Sexual behavior is far more than genital involvement. It is determined as much by one's perceptions—which in turn are heavily influenced by social learning—as by one's physiology. At the onset of adolescence, hormonal changes cause a new awareness of the body, but each young person's personal definition of what those changes mean in terms of sexuality can differ enormously from that of others.

The first experience of simultaneous orgasm and **ejaculation**—inevitable in normal pubescent males—can hardly go unnoticed. In most young males, it adds a new and pleasurable dimension to any existing notions about sexuality. Almost without exception, orgasm becomes a rewarding experience. As social learning theory predicts it tends to be repeated.

For females, the hormonal changes at puberty do not inevitably bring the rewarding experience of orgasm. In fact, puberty often has little to do with a young female's understanding of her sexuality. The increased awareness of her capability of becoming pregnant may, in fact, have negative effects or, at best, lead to conflicting perceptions about sexual experiences (Kitzinger 1983, pp. 177–186). Many women report being so anxious about pregnancy that they do not enjoy sex or may even have a strong aversion to it. For most young females, sexual activity seems to be motivated more by social learning than by hormonal changes. It is not surprising that adolescents of both genders frequently assume that sex is something that males *do* to females. Young males generally seem to learn the pleasures of sex earlier than females and to spend considerable time fantasizing about finding a female willing to share this experience.

About five times as many boys as girls are reported to engage in sexual experimentation during early adolescence (Reevy 1973). The reasons for this double standard are not entirely clear. Experts do not agree whether boys and girls act differently because they have learned different feelings about sex—feelings of rightness or wrongness, for example. It is possible that boys' testosterone levels are more nearly constant than are girls' estrogen levels, which are cyclic, and that the levels of these hormones are directly related to tension that can be satisfactorily relieved only by orgasm. It may be that the constant sexual tension of boys is comparable to that experienced by girls for only a few days each month. The evidence either way is far from conclusive; however, it does appear that in humans social and cultural constraints on sexual behavior are more powerful than hormonal ones.

Same-Sex Peer Activity

In the contemporary United States, it is not unusual for adolescent boys to have a history of sexual activities with other boys. They often engage in genital exhibition and examination, mutual masturbation, and other forms of sexual behavior, usually in the company of same-sex peers and sometimes in the presence of girls. This activity is usually secret. Some males report having to perform sexual exhibitions as a condition of membership in boys' clubs or gangs. Sex organs may be measured; the number of ejaculations produced in a fixed time or the number produced without losing an erection may be carefully counted. Although such activities are unquestionably erotic, they are not indications of any proclivity toward homosexuality. They can best be described as a combination of playing and learning one's sexual potential. They are usually boisterous rather than passionate, "fun" rather than "serious" (Sorensen 1973).

Cliques of early adolescent girls may talk about sexual behavior and circulate books on the subject, but they reportedly engage in less same-sex erotic play than do boys. Exhibition and mutual examination of genitalia may be the extent of sex play. Many adult women have never seen female genitalia—not even their own in a mirror. Breast exhibition is a different matter, however. Early adolescent girls seem to be just as aware of the breast development and dimensions of the members of their own clique as boys are of the penis size and growth of pubic hair of the members of theirs.

Kinsey reported that the homosexual behavior that does occur between early adolescent girls involves for the most part kissing and general body contact; genital techniques come later, if at all (Kinsey et al. 1953). Although there may be some boisterousness in breast play comparable to that of boys' penis play, girls' homosexual genital contacts, when they do occur, seem to be "serious" rather than "fun" and perhaps more predictive of adult homosexuality than the penis play of boys.

According to Kinsey, older women who have had homosexual contact report that adolescent homosexual activity was more satisfying than coitus, whereas older men report the opposite. Kinsey noted that women with a history of early homosexual experience usually report an intention to engage in homosexual activity again but that men do not.

As the all-male clique disappears into the heterosexual crowd around or before mid-adolescence, patterns of same-sex activity among boys disappear except among the relatively small fraction of males who will continue homosexual or bisexual behavior in adulthood. The data for females are not as clear, but it appears that the fraction engaging in active homosexual behavior—always reported as smaller than the fraction for men—continues to increase until well into middle age (West 1968).

By late adolescence, most males regard their earlier homosexual behavior as a developmental phenomenon, consider it childish, and are not disturbed by whatever recollections they have not forgotten or repressed. It should be noted, especially in view of the extensive work done by Broderick and others, that most male sex play with other males during early adolescence is accompanied by joking, conversation, recounting of experiences, plans for the future, and fantasies about heterosexual activities with particular girls or with girls in general. Thus, although the behavior is homosexual, the **ideation** is heterosexual (Broderick 1966b, pp. 18–24).

Cross-Sex Peer Activity

Most studies on cross-sex activity report that the number of boys engaging in various forms of heterosexual activity during adolescence greatly exceeds the corresponding number of girls (Diamond and Karlen 1980, pp. 171–187). The number of boys reporting that they engage in sex play with girls during adolescence is from five to seven times as great as the number of girls who report engaging in sex play with boys. This discrepancy might be reconciled—incorrectly—by the simple explanation that those adolescent girls who do engage in sexual behavior with boys are very active and each has, on the average, contact with five to seven times as many boys as boys on the average have with girls. However, in all studies, the average adolescent girl who has engaged in heterosexual sex behavior reports contact with fewer boys than the number of girls with whom the average boy reports contact. Nor does frequency of contact help to solve the dilemma; on the contrary, girls typically report less frequency of heterosexual contact than boys. Our own notion is that boys may tend to exaggerate and girls may tend to underreport what they actually do. In addition, males may define certain activities as sexual that females overlook. Noticing that her partner has an erection when they are dancing close may very well not have the same meaning to a female as it does to the male who is experiencing intense excitement.

When a boy experiences an orgasm while engaging in any activity with a girl, it is immediately clear to him that the experience was a sexual one, regardless of how the girl may interpret it. Most men and boys can recall their first orgasms in some

The heterosexual crowd begins to appear around midadolescence creating a good deal of concern about sexual approaches and limits.

detail. Male orgasm is a definitive event; there is no question whether or not it has occurred. A male's criterion for defining an experience as sexual is reasonably stable from his first orgasm on.

Girls who report that they are currently in love tend to discount their earlier experiences as "not really love" more often than do boys (Kephart 1967). Thus, it is possible that, as girls progress to more effective and more satisfactory sex experiences with boys, they tend to discount their earlier experiences as being somehow less than sexual. On the other hand, girls—especially those age sixteen or over—are likely to be introduced to sexual activity by males who are older than they are. This prevailing norm should result in a higher, rather than a lower, rate of sexual activity for adolescent girls than for adolescent boys.

Girls are more likely to have many heterosexual contacts before they ever achieve orgasm. Of sexually active women aged nineteen or younger, 51 percent have reported no experience with orgasm (Bell and Coughey 1980). Even though each contact might have been clearly defined as sexual in the girl's mind at the time, her later experience of orgasm might call for a redefinition of her criteria. If orgasm did not occur, she might, on reflection, be likely to redefine the earlier experience as not truly sexual. Thus, it is entirely possible that an adolescent boy may perceive an encounter as sexual because he achieved an orgasm, whereas his female partner may not consider the same contact overtly sexual, especially when she recalls it after she has become more experienced sexually.

At least until mid-adolescence, the sexual activities of boys might more accurately be described as exploratory ventures, with a twofold purpose: to find out how girls are constructed anatomically and how they function physiologically and to determine the extent of permissiveness of particular girls.

The cross-sex activities of adolescents leave little question of the existence of a double standard at this age. A boy may use sexual exploitation to enhance his self-esteem and self-confidence in an area that is almost totally free from parental interference. Perhaps the most he is told is to be careful about pregnancy and disease. This freedom is probably an important developmental stage in the establishment of a male's sexual identity. The gratification that comes from establishing a social relationship free of parental domination may be new to him and may not have been achieved very often in other areas.

Adolescent girls are more likely to transfer a wider range of sexual attitudes from their parents or other restrictive adults to themselves. Most young women are monitored more closely by their parents and are given more admonishments about their sexual reputations than are males. A girl learns that she must make and enforce her decision about how far to let a particular boy go. She may consider it a tribute to her attractiveness if she can achieve and maintain the interest of boys while denying them access to sexual privileges, although in fact her shyness about exhibiting her body or her inexperience may be a greater factor. The ultimate decisions that she must make when she is alone with boys are hers, but they may be strongly influenced by her parents and her peers. For her, too, learning to manage her heterosexual activities is an important task in the development of a sense of adequacy and self-sufficiency.

Because the average boy in the United States discovers orgasm at an earlier age than the average girl does, boys' reasons for wanting to engage in coitus may be somewhat different from those of girls. For the adolescent boy, experiencing orgasm during coitus often is a goal in itself, although it may also signify both a social accomplishment and an affirmation of his masculinity. For the adolescent girl, it is often a means to achieve a different goal—to satisfy her curiosity; to please the boy; to show that she is grown up; or to prove that she is sexier, warmer, or more of a woman than her competitors. For most adolescent boys and girls—at least at the conscious level—conceiving a child has little or nothing to do with their motivations for having coitus. Whether they wish to propagate the human race or not, boys are apparently more likely to anticipate physical rewards in coitus, and girls more typically to anticipate social rewards.

Once a male has established a pattern of mutual sexual behavior leading to orgasm on his part, he is less likely to be interested in a relationship with a partner who permits him less intimacy. Similarly, females are unlikely to regress from the level of intimacy they achieved in young adulthood, tending instead to resume the maximum intimacy permitted with a former partner shortly after committing themselves to a long-term relationship with a new partner. Both males and females, once they have had pleasurable intercourse, rarely stop seeking such sexual experience in later relationships.

In a society with many inhibitory sanctions, adolescents who are experiencing active levels of sexual interest often feel caught between their urges and adult values. As one observer of this conflict remarked:

> To whatever extent a youngster has been molded by middle-class values, he is "damned if he does and damned if doesn't." There is the double burden of attempting to suppress his increasingly urgent sexual desires and the weight of guilt when he almost inevitably fails to do so. Where the attitudes of middle-class culture have determined a child's rearing, they make healthy adolescent use of any sexual outlet very nearly impossible. (Gadpaille 1975, pp. 268–269)

Phillip Sarrel, co-director of the Yale Sex Counseling Service and an associate professor in the Yale University School of Medicine, has, however, reported a noticeable trend toward conservatism among college students since 1977. It has been increasingly clear, Sarrel (1984, p. 17) says, that remaining virginal through the college years is more personally and socially acceptable than it was a decade earlier.

Masturbation

Awareness of the importance of masturbation usually precedes adolescence. Ordinarily, it begins when a boy or girl realizes that touching his or her genitals produces unique sensations. Boys who have not experienced the sensations of masturbation directly—by handling their genitals during bathing, by exploring their own body with their hands, or by allowing someone else to manipulate them—will almost certainly learn about it from their peers by the time they reach puberty.

Masturbation is reportedly much less common among females than males (Gagnon 1977, p. 160). Kinsey, in his extensive reports on human sexuality, estimated that by the time of marriage the average male has experienced slightly over 1,500 orgasms, with about 330 of those occurring during intercourse (Kinsey, Pomeroy, and Martin 1948). He estimated that the average female, at marriage, had experienced a total of 223 orgasms, with only 39 of them occurring during coitus (Kinsey et al. 1953). As discussed earlier, the sexual activity of boys, whether coital or mastubatory, is probably more closely related to the number of orgasms they have than is the sexual activity of girls.

Acknowledging that the Kinsey data on female masturbation agreed closely with their observations in the 1970s, Lorna Sarrel and Phillip Sarrel (1984, p. 17) observed that about 70 percent to 80 percent of college women say that they masturbate. More college women today accept the idea that masturbation is healthy. In 1970, 66 percent of them agreed with the statement "Masturbation is acceptable when the objective is simply the attainment of sensory enjoyment." By the 1980s, more than 82 percent agreed.

It is unrealistic to think that a person who has begun masturbating will stop voluntarily without some replacement activity, particularly once he or she has achieved orgasm in this way. There seems to be no satisfying substitute for orgasms, which provide a unique kind of pleasurable satisfaction. Since every physically and mentally healthy adolescent has the physical equipment necessary to produce orgasms, the only likely reason that girls report a lower incidence than do boys is either that fewer of them have learned how to induce orgasm or that girls have learned stronger taboos about masturbating or about admitting it. As the sexual double standard declines, girls may feel freer to report such activity, and their frequency of self-stimulation and orgasm may more closely approximate that of boys.

The end of frequent masturbation seems to be closely tied to the beginning of coitus, although those who have active sex lives do continue self-stimulation. Research has indicated that nearly all males continue to masturbate throughout their lifetime, even though the incidence is highest in adolescence and early adulthood. Women, too, both married and unmarried, feel that masturbation is a positive aspect of their lives (DeMartino 1974). Those with the highest feelings of self-esteem and with high sex drives are more likely to masturbate (Abramson 1973, p. 139).

LEGAL INSTITUTIONS AND LAW ENFORCEMENT AGENCIES

Some sexual behaviors involving children and adolescents are subject to legal regulation. Not only does every state in the United States recognize this in specific statutes, but also law enforcement agencies commonly are empowered to warn, cite, and arrest persons for a number of sexual behaviors under statutes of a more general nature.

"Contributing to the delinquency of a minor," juvenile delinquency, public indecency, vagrancy, loitering, and a wide variety of other offenses named in state or local laws are sometimes defined broadly. In practice, police officers who seek out or apprehend offenders (or ignore them) define their actual meaning, often according to their personal moral judgments. For instance, a child enticing another child to go swimming in the nude in a country stream might be apprehended by a police officer on the grounds of any of the above-named offenses (one of the authors attended precisely such a hearing in juvenile court). On the other hand, an officer coming across a male having intercourse with a seventeen-year-old female (a felony in all but three states) on a public beach (an additional violation) may simply look the other way, especially if the woman's age is doubtful and she appears to be consenting.

In some jurisdictions, precisely defined sexual behaviors of adolescents may be specifically forbidden by statute. In other states, probation departments or juvenile courts are permitted to inquire into the sexual activities of juveniles and to take steps toward the prevention of any sexual behavior patterns that they consider improper or harmful. Such supervision terminates as early as age sixteen in some jurisdictions and as late as age eighteen in others. Although these age distinctions may appear arbitrary since they do not seem to take into consideration the different rates of individual development, legal codes universally regard chronological age as appropriate for determining the acceptability of a wide variety of sexual behaviors.

SEXUAL SENSATIONS

The state of knowing something is the result of brain activity. However, responses to many kinds of bodily stimuli do not pass through the brain in the same way other sensations do. Some sensations that may be identified as sexual do not. Stimuli to nerve endings in various parts of the human body may produce responses in both primary sex organs (penis, clitoris) and secondary sex organs (those that are not consciously associated with sex, such as nipple or ear lobe, but that may nevertheless be defined as sexual). An infant's penis or clitoris may become erect when it is stroked or when a stream of water plays on it. Even though the infant cannot *think* about what his or her nerve endings are sensing or interpret these sensations as sexual, they still cause a sexual reaction.

In contrast to unwilled and unknowing reactions of the sex organs to stimuli, humans also may interpret as sexual any stimuli (memories, fantasies, sights, sounds, scents, touches, and tastes) that produce erections of the penis, clitoris, and perhaps nipples, as well as lubrication of the vagina or secretion of preejaculatory fluids. Areas of the body that are associated with sexual responses are called **erogenous** zones. Although some of these connections are **subcortical**—that is, they do not have to be interpreted as sexual by the brain in order for the response to occur—most of them do involve either awareness or conditioning. The context of an interaction is important to the interpretation of sensations as sexual (Gagnon 1977, p. 130). For example, a woman may react differently to a pelvic examination by a gynecologist and to genital caresses in intimate situations, in terms of physical responses such as clitoral erection and lubrication, although the parts of the body touched or pressed may be the same.

There are also individual and cultural differences in the interpretation of sensations as sexual. One woman may find that nursing her baby stimulates strong genital responses; another may report that she cannot stand to have her partner touch her breasts during the months she is nursing her baby because "he's invading the baby's territory; my breasts are not to be used for sexual approaches then." Kinsey reported that better-educated persons typically are much more likely to interpret oral stimuli (French kissing, **cunnilingus, fellatio**) as sexually arousing than are less well-educated persons—undoubtedly a cultural difference (Kinsey et al. 1953).

Sexual arousal in human beings varies not only from person to person, but also from one time to another and from one situation to another with the same person. Some women have heightened sexual responses about the time of ovulation, others during menstrual periods, and some during the period between these events (Greenblatt and McNamara 1976). It seems unlikely that such differences are genetic.

One of the main reasons that enduring sexual relationships seem to be preferable to one-night stands is that maximum satisfaction in sexual activities depends in part on getting to know what pleases one's partner. What "turns a person on" seems to grow out of personal experiences and usually seems natural to that person. Guessing what someone will find sexually stimulating is probably less satisfactory than having experienced that person in a variety of contexts and having had open communication with him or her over an extended period of time.

THE PROCESS OF ORGASM

Once a decision has been made to engage in sexual activities and erection of the **penis** or **clitoris** has occurred, continued stimulation leads to the establishment of a "plateau" level of sexual tension (Masters and Johnson 1966, pp. 4–6). At this plateau level, the sex organs have reached certain recognizable physical conditions (see Appendix A). The ridge (the **corona**) that separates the head of a penis from its shaft usually increases in circumference, as does the head itself (although in some men this may not happen at all and in others it may occur only sometimes). The outer third of the **vagina** (the inner sheath of a woman's sex organ, which is not usually visible) decreases in size, becoming "tighter"; its diameter shrinks to perhaps as much as 50 percent of what it is in the relaxed state.

As sexual stimulation continues during the plateau, males secrete anywhere from two drops to a cubic centimeter of glandular fluid, which, although it is not **semen,** may contain some **spermatozoa.** In the plateau phase, interior "sweating" of the vagina diminishes, but secretions begin from glands in the **vulva** (the outer, visible part of a woman's sex organs). Near the end of the plateau phase, the clitoris appears to go upward and backward, and the little lips within the vulva turn bright red (in women who have never borne children) or a deeper burgundy color (in women who have). Once this change in color has occurred, continued stimulation of the clitoris will produce orgasm.

In males, the plateau phase ends when orgasm begins. The man feels a sudden contraction of the internal sex organs, which is a signal to him that an ejaculation will begin within two or three seconds and is no longer under his control. At this "point of no return," he is likely to make a forward thrust and "freeze," pausing briefly until involuntary contractions of his prostate (an internal gland that spurts out most of the fluid in an ejaculation) begin.

At the conclusion of this "period of inevitability," two or three strong contractions occur through the major pelvic organs at intervals of approximately eight-tenths of a second, followed by a series of lesser contractions at progressively longer intervals. The first strong contraction causes the ejaculation to begin. The peak of pleasure for a male probably comes just before and during this first spurt of semen, although the ejaculation may continue through several contractions.

Normally, the release of tension in the muscles and the relief of congestion in the sex organs of the ejaculating male is so great that his penis quickly becomes flaccid. He experiences such total relaxation that he may soon drift into sleep or lie still for several minutes in a trancelike state. Occasionally, however, particularly among the relatively young, a man may be able to maintain his erection and return to a plateau level immediately.

Masters and Johnson (1966, p. 213) documented the case of one male subject who experienced three ejaculations within ten minutes from the beginning of sexual stimulation. Normally, however, even in young men, the resolution of tension is so complete and so relaxing that a satisfactory erection will not be regained for at least twenty minutes.

The female orgasmic experience differs from that of the male in several ways. First, the two- or three-second freeze between the plateau phase and the onset of the contractions of the uterus, which constitutes the beginning of orgasm, is not present. In fact, for a female to experience complete release, it may be essential for her to have continued rhythmic stimulation, not just until the orgasm has begun but until it is quite advanced, if not finished.

For females, orgasm begins with anywhere from four to eight contractions of the uterus accompanied by squeezes of the outer third of the vagina at intervals of eight-tenths of a second, followed by three to four contractions of diminishing intensity at irregular intervals. Like males, females also experience two to four contractions of the **anus** at the same eight-tenths-of-a-second interval.

Resolution of muscle tension and pelvic congestion occurs more slowly in females than in males, requiring up to several minutes after orgasm. No doubt it is partly because of this difference that women can experience orgasm several times during coitus. If stimulation continues, some women are capable of achieving *status orgasmus* lasting from 20 seconds to as much as 60 seconds, during which they experience either rapidly recurring orgasms or a single long, continuous orgasmic episode (Masters and Johnson 1966, p. 131).

Orgasm provides a fast and satisfying resolution of the muscle tension and congestion that results from sexual stimulation. If orgasm is not achieved, the length of time required for resolution is roughly proportional to the length of time that stimulation has continued. In both sexes, frequent stimulation without orgasm may lead to discomfort and even to chronic inflammation and pain as a result of unrelieved congestion.

Females report that the orgasms achieved through masturbation often are more intense than those experienced through intercourse. Some report that they alleviate menstrual or premenstrual symptoms (backaches, cramps) by self-stimulation (Masters and Johnson 1966, p. 125).

The experience of orgasm is exquisite. Having once experienced it, people generally desire any subsequent strong sexual stimulation to continue to orgasm if circumstances permit and may remain tense until the sexual stress is relieved. This tendency may seem to be considerably stronger in men, possibly because it usually has been effectively reinforced by "wet dreams" if no other outlet intervenes. Because male and female sentiments and socialization patterns are different, it may be difficult for a woman who has never experienced orgasm in any way to understand the attraction that coitus holds for most males or females who *have* experienced orgasm.

It is often difficult for those who have established an orgasmic response pattern to discontinue sexual activities altogether for any appreciable period of time. Losing a partner, for whatever reason, with whom one has established a pattern of orgasmic release may be particularly difficult. For those who have never learned to achieve orgasm through self-stimulation, the discomfort may be even greater.

Sexual Fantasies

Whether stimuli are considered erotic depends on the interpretation given to them. This interpretation in turn depends on individual experiences and includes "imagining"—constructing a context of ideas about situations that do not actually exist and including these in the interpretation of what does actually exist. The point at which interpretation becomes fantasy may be much less precise than the terms suggest. It is clear, however, that the most important sex organ in the human body is the brain and that how one thinks about sex can greatly enhance one's experiences.

Those who are making their first sexual approaches to each other have some interpretation of the meaning of that behavior as well as some images or fantasies about the behaviors that will follow, even though they have not yet occurred. How they feel at the moment—anxious, joyous, frightened, content, sexually stimulated—depends to a great extent on their expectations of events that have not yet occurred.

Few people feel at any given moment that they have all the qualities, possessions, or relationships they would like. Nearly all persons find that inadequacies, rules, frustrations, or powerful people stand between them and their hearts' desires. A small boy can sometimes escape the reality of his powerlessness by visualizing himself as a powerful person such as a professional football player; a little girl can blot out her musical ineptitude by imagining herself up on the podium conducting the New York Philharmonic. An adult can respond to current needs or frustrations by fantasizing about past achievements, about potential capabilities or attributes, or about personal goals that may or may not be possible: wealth, power, love, sexual attractiveness, potency, and fulfillment, to name a few.

Probably few adults feel as powerful or as attractive as they would like. For most men and women, the prospect of being able to exert power over others is exhilarating; the prospect of being desired sexually by attractive persons is itself sexually arousing. The fear of defeat or rejection that may be present in the real world can be set aside in the world of fantasy.

For the most part, men's sexual fantasies involve freedom from restrictive rules about sexual behavior, which they often see, consciously or unconsciously, as having been set down by their mothers and other women (Friday 1980, pp. 11, 45–48). Men tend to fantasize that they are free to choose their own sexual activities and their own sexual partners, although a very small minority are stimulated by fantasies of being enslaved or humiliated by a woman (Stein 1974, pp. 243–265). Men also seem to fantasize about actual persons whom they know or have seen or heard about.

Women are likely to fantasize about faceless persons, mysterious strangers, fictional characters, or other unattainable individuals (Kitzinger 1983, p. 8). This double standard of fantasy is probably related to the widespread notion in our society that women "give" sexual favors and that men who receive them should see themselves as specially privileged or chosen over other men to receive these valuable gifts. Women, on the other hand, have often felt more special when they felt wanted sexually by many men than when they were wanted by only one man.

Although women's fantasies (which, according to Nancy Friday, are often the strongest foreplay of all) have the same basic quality as those of men, they seem much more likely to involve power than freedom (Friday 1973, p. 45). Many women fantasize being overpowered by men or other women who force them into sexual acts; others fantasize that they are the powerful persons—that either their aggressive behavior or their irresistible seductiveness commands others to carry out their sexual wishes.

Since no one can foretell the future, most persons fantasize to some extent whenever they base their behaviors on what they believe is going to happen. If the prospects are happy, they feel good; if bad, they feel depressed. Most people have spent many years fantasizing about what certain sexual experiences will (or would) be like. Even when they are engaging in sexual activities, they may be comparing reality with anticipation—but the anticipation may already have been defined in part by their ideas of what the mysterious reality will be like. In a 1984 interview, David Barlow, director of the Sexuality Research Program at the State University of New York at Albany, was quoted as stating that most people have about 7 or 8 sexual fantasies per day, although the range is from none to more than 40 (Goleman 1984, p. 1).

No one knows exactly what another person is feeling, let alone what another person will feel. Fantasies about what other persons are feeling help to establish what one's own feelings will be. For example, fantasizing that one's partner is having sex out of a sense of obligation or only to satisfy a selfish desire is certainly possible but is not very exciting. On the other hand, fantasizing that one's partner is having sex because one is special and attractive, even irresistible, can be sexually stimulating.

Researchers at the Masters and Johnson Institute studying fantasies of both heterosexual and homosexual adults concluded that one's sexual preference is not defined by the content of one's fantasies. (See Table 4.1 for their findings of the most frequent sexual fantasies of both heterosexual and homosexual men and women.) Perhaps most surprising is the frequency with which both men and women reported fantasies involving force. Such fantasies do not mean, of course, that the fantasizers would enjoy acting out such behaviors in real life (Schwartz and Masters 1984).

Because sexual behavior is intimate and private, there is no need to be judged by other people's standards or realities. If a couple wishes to imagine during their

	Heterosexual Men	Heterosexual Women
TABLE 4 • 1 Common Sexual Fantasies (most frequent, listed in order of occurrence)	1. Replacement of established partner 2. Forced sexual encounters with woman 3. Observing sexual activity 4. Sexual encounters with men 5. Group sex	1. Replacement of established partner 2. Forced sexual encounters with man 3. Observing sexual activity 4. Idyllic encounters with unknown men 5. Sexual encounters with women
	Homosexual Men	**Homosexual Women**
	1. Images of male anatomy 2. Forced sexual encounters with men 3. Sexual encounters with women 4. Idyllic encounters with unknown men 5. Group sex	1. Forced sexual encounters with women 2. Idyllic encounters with established partner 3. Sexual encounters with men 4. Memories of past sexual experiences 5. Sadistic imagery

Source: Mark Schwartz and William Masters, "The Masters and Johnson Treatment Program for Dissatisfied Homosexual Men," *American Journal of Psychiatry* (February 1984), pp. 173–181. Copyright 1984, the American Psychiatric Association. Reprinted by permission.

sexual activities that they are in a pine forest, on a desert island, or in the tenth or the thirtieth century, or that they are Romeo and Juliet, they need answer to no one else.

SEXUAL SCRIPTS

A **script** is a set of directions that actors follow to convey the writer's story or message. It includes the words and actions that create a mood and enact a story line. Nearly everyone has a script or scripts that define his or her sexual character to others. This is usually conceptualized as the way to behave in order to achieve certain outcomes. People who have very different sexual scripts may not be able to establish an enduring relationship.

Of course, having the same script does not mean that the actors play the same roles in a relationship; rather, in most scripts the roles are complementary or reciprocal. *Complementary roles* are demonstrated when each actor enacts a role that fills in the parts that are not enacted by the other(s). *Reciprocal roles* are enacted when each actor's role is developed through an ongoing response to that of the other(s).

Let us suppose that Jane's sexual script, which she has constructed from communication with parents and friends and from the mass media, defines sexual intercourse as necessary for making babies and for fulfilling her needs to be a mother, but as something personal and private, never to be mentioned to others—especially not to her parents or children—and not to be entered into lightly, since babymaking is a serious matter. She sees her vagina as being constructed as it is in order to enable sperm to be deposited to fertilize her egg cells and to permit the birth of her babies when they come to term. She views the complementary function of her husband as providing sperm to fertilize her egg cells. The role of her breasts is to provide milk for her babies. Jane's sexual script could have been written by students in a sixth-grade sex education course in many schools.

Karen's sexual script is very different from Jane's. Karen views sexual intercourse as a natural step in growth toward intimacy. People who are attracted to each other enjoy physical contact with each other. A person who holds your hand likes you and wants to be your friend. If he kisses you, he wants to establish some sort of relationship. If he has intercourse with you, he wants that relationship to be special and intimate. For Karen, pregnancy and marriage are separate issues from sexuality.

Laurie's sexual script is different from either Jane's or Karen's. Laurie enjoys experiencing orgasms. Although she can achieve orgasms by herself, she enjoys them more when they are produced by a skilled and willing partner. She intends to marry and to have babies but does not see marriage and conception as the primary goals of sexual activity. Sex should be gratifying for its own sake; relationships and babies might as well be associated with good sex as with poor or mediocre sex.

Diana has still a fourth sexual script. To Diana sexual intercourse is a gift (or perhaps a sacrifice) that she gives to someone in exchange for love or commitment. It has nothing to do with babies, intimacy, or pleasure—although all of these may result. Sexual intercourse is something you do because your partner wants or expects it. If you love him, you will give it to him.

John's sexual script is complementary to Jane's. He defines sexual intercourse as necessary for making babies to continue his family name and heritage. His dating is strictly social, and he has carefully avoided any sexual involvement or commitment lest it interfere with his educational and career plans. He sees a professional education at a good university as necessary for the career that he plans to have. He believes that marriage is out of the question until he has established himself in a position with a promising future. Until then he will relieve his sexual tensions by secret masturbation. He plans to marry a sexually inexperienced woman, somewhat younger than himself, from a "good" family who has been to a "good" college for two or more years, who will be a homemaker and a "good" mother. He expects to live near his parents in a suburb of the city in which he was born. Whether his future wife will be a responsive and exciting sex partner is of such secondary concern to him that he is quite willing to accept whatever level of sexual interest and behavior she offers. He has not given the matter much thought, but he assumes that "good" husbands do not make many sexual demands and that they probably stop having intercourse soon after their wives become pregnant and do not resume it until about the time the baby is weaned.

Kevin's sexual script is different from John's. Kevin engaged in secret sex play with first one neighborhood girl and then another from the age of ten on. Seduction is a way of life for him. He believes that any girl who expects him to go steady with her should be willing to have intercourse with him regularly. If women are willing to have sex with him, they should be responsible for avoiding pregnancy; if one of them becomes pregnant because she failed to take the proper precautions, it is not his responsibility. If she does not want to have a baby out of wedlock, she should arrange for an abortion; if she insists on having the baby, she can either rear it herself or put it out for adoption. Marriage is out of the question for Kevin until he finds the "right woman." He thinks it is convenient to live with an attractive woman for a year or so to share expenses and provide regular access to sex, but marriage would probably spoil such a good friendship.

Larry's sexual script is that all forms of sex are good as long as they do not involve commitment. One of his rules is never to have three successive dates with the same woman. He hangs out in singles' bars, and if he fails to score there, he knows the telephone numbers of a few call girls and the locations of some massage parlors where he can depend on sex for pay. He gets antsy without some form of sexual release two or three times a week, but marriage is not for him. He hopes to remain single unless some woman traps him.

David believes that true love can happen only once in a lifetime. He fell in love with Diana when they were juniors in high school. They started having intercourse the summer after they began to go steady. David believes that they should marry as soon as possible, preferably before a pregnancy occurs, even though neither of them has a job that pays enough for them to rent a place of their own. They can live with the parents of one or the other until they find good jobs, but he cannot consider giving up their almost daily intercourse, and it is inconvenient and uncomfortable to be unable to share a bed every night. Their sex and the love that it expresses are more important than anything else and he will undergo almost any hardship in order to continue them.

Of course, these scripts are oversimplified. Not only are there other sexual scripts, but also most persons have some elements of more than one such script (Gagnon 1977, pp. 5–20). Scripts mediate between us and our social context. They tell us how to interpret the behavior of others and how to structure our own behaviors meaningfully and properly. Our scripts tell us how to make interaction turn out right and what to do when things are not going as we wish.

Scripts may change through time, but they seldom change rapidly once adulthood has been reached. Most people seem to believe that the sexual script of all "normal" people either is the same as theirs or ought to be; therefore, it is not unusual for a couple to fail to recognize the source of discord in their relationship as the incompatibility of their scripts. A skilled counselor or therapist usually can spot such incompatibilities quickly and can confront the couple with the need to resolve their differences in order to reduce the discord.

When an adult couple or group engages in behaviors that they jointly perceive as sexual, what does it mean to them or about them? What does it say about two people that they have slept in the same bed overnight? For that matter, what does it mean if two adult men are seen embracing each other and kissing each other's lips? What does it mean if an adult married to someone else is invited to have sexual intercourse?

These questions have almost as many answers as there are people to answer them because there are almost as many sexual scripts as there are people. For one person, in one situation, intercourse means permanent bonding. For another it means rebellion; for a third, conquest; for still another, defilement. Sexual intercourse may be an affirmation of gender, of adulthood, of relationship status. It may mean reaching for immortality through producing children; it may mean fun and games; it may mean security and contentment; it may mean restoring one's soul.

Whatever sexual intercourse means to particular persons, it is usually a landmark event. People do not ordinarily forget whether they have had sexual intercourse with particular others, regardless of the circumstances. Intercourse is also a matter of social interest and concern, as is evident from the number of laws about it and the amount of gossip it generates. At times it seems that the significance of sexual intercourse is exaggerated beyond reason. Relationships lasting half a century or more have been generated by it, and others lasting equally long have been dissolved because of it. People may be disgusted—or enthralled—to learn that two people are making love.

Whatever sexual intercourse may mean, we can conclude that it is one of life's most significant activities for most people. Whether that significance is rationally justifiable is beside the point, both for individual mental health and for the comfortable functioning of marital and family systems.

▌ SEXUAL PREFERENCES

Virtually all adults have sexual impulses. People may express this by saying that they need "outlets," or seek "sexual peace," or are trying to gratify an "urge" or a "drive." However they are viewed, such sexual impulses must be channeled into patterns that not only are satisfying to the individuals but also do not cause stress within the society. Deciding whether to gratify these urges, either along or in interaction with another person or persons, may result in a consistent pattern of sexual activity or may depend entirely on the opportunities present in a particular situation.

What is considered a "sexual opportunity" differs considerably from one person to another. Some choices and opportunities are defined consciously; often the chooser sees them as his or her "natural" preferences and believes that few other satisfying possibilities exist for himself or herself.

Celibacy

Celibacy is a state in which one does not engage in sexual activities with any other person. Usually the choice is conscious. Sometimes the term is used to denote a person's choice not to marry (usually for philosophical or religious reasons), but that choice may or may not have any connotations for sexual activities.

Celibate persons, such as priests and nuns, may take vows declaring that they do not intend to provoke in themselves any genital sexual sensations or even to have thoughts of doing such things. Many celibate persons do not condemn sex as bad or wrong for everyone but aspire to channel their own sexual energies into activities and thoughts that are more valuable to them. If they are successful, their sexual glands and other organs eventually may atrophy—shrivel or become incapable of functioning—making their aspirations easier to achieve.

Celibacy may also mean that one confines one's sexual gratification to self-stimulation. This can be either a moral choice—a feeling that it is not right to engage in sex with another person—or a result of social ineptitude, shyness, or a poor self-concept. Celibacy is sometimes forced on people by their acceptance of the idea that physical disfigurements somehow disqualify them sexually; by their feeling that they have nothing worthwhile to offer any partner; or by their expectation of being so inept sexually that their partners would laugh at them or would be unsatisfied. Celibacy may also result from lack of available partners and may be long- or short-term. Men living in prisons or mining or lumber camps without access to women may be celibate for varying periods of time.

Obviously, the happiest celibates are likely to be those who have made a conscious choice to forgo sexual activity, thus gaining from that abstinence some more valuable reward. Such persons, if deprived of that choice, would be deprived of their right to human dignity.

Heterosexuality

The most common form of sexual preference in the United States at present, at least among adults, is generally believed to be heterosexuality. Most people consider "proper" only those sexual activities that take place between a male and female.

Sentiments about the correctness of heterosexuality are often so powerful that those who have them react strongly to any sexual attraction they may feel to persons of the same sex. Many men and women immediately deny or repress any hint of sexual feeling toward a person of their own sex. Such people may scrupulously avoid behaviors that might be construed as homosexual and ridicule or punish persons who appear to have homosexual inclinations.

Virtually all kinds of erotic behaviors can be acted out both homosexually and heterosexually. Coitus, however, is exclusive to heterosexual couples since it is defined as the union that occurs when one person's penis is placed inside another person's vagina. For many people this is considered to be the ultimate sexual act—both in degree of intimacy and as an expression of love.

Because intercourse has such significance, it has a great deal of anxiety and surplus meaning attached to it, both by couples who are contemplating intercourse and by those who have been engaging in it for years. The refusal of a partner to engage in sexual activities of any sort is easily interpreted as rejection. Sometimes people are unwilling to urge their partners toward coitus in particular because the potential for feeling rejected threatens to destroy their self-esteem.

Homosexuality

Homosexual sex preference means that one prefers to engage in sexual activities with other persons of the same sex. Depending on how one defines *sexual behavior,* one might conclude that homosexual behaviors are if anything more "normal" during preadolescence than are heterosexual behaviors. Social psychologist Michael Storms (1982) has theorized that children who reach puberty earlier than their peers are more likely to develop homosexual preferences. It may be that a homosexual developmental phase is necessary for the emergence of a comfortable heterosexual preference later on.

Even though the American Psychiatric Association ceased listing homosexuality as a psychological disorder in 1973, there has continued to be a great deal of social

prejudice and discrimination against adults known to engage in homosexual activities and, indeed, even against those merely suspected of homosexuality, often on insubstantial grounds. This has been particularly true for men.

The prejudice against females who may be engaging in homosexual behaviors has usually been less vehement than that against males. One can only speculate about the reasons for this, but it has been suggested that the idea of two women holding hands, being otherwise affectionate to each other, or even living together has never had the same connotation as does similar behavior between two men. In our society, women are allowed a wider range of physical contact with other women than men are with other men. In addition, women who choose other women as sexual partners usually have no more than one or two such partners. Men who choose other men as partners sometimes have many partners and may therefore call more attention to their sexual activities than do women (Hunt 1974b, p. 317).

The gay rights movement has successfully combated some of the discrimination against persons who engage in homosexual behaviors or who express such preferences. California, for example, has passed a state law prohibiting job discrimination on grounds of sexual preference. With a few exceptions, when laws or policies that discriminate on grounds of sexual preference have been challenged in court, they have been repealed or annulled; even so, there is still a considerable amount of social prejudice (Humphreys 1972).

Bisexuality

Since sexual behaviors are transitory—that is, individual sex acts do not last forever—one might engage in homosexual behaviors on some occasions and in heterosexual behaviors on others, just as some preadolescents do. Although this is popularly called *bisexuality,* that term suggests an enduring personality trait that may not exist. It is entirely conceivable, for example, that some men and women may during their lifetime have warm erotic relationships both with those of the same sex and with those of the opposite sex at different times or, perhaps, even at the same time.

Our avoidance of the words *homosexuals, heterosexuals,* and *bisexuals* as substantive nouns is in part an effort to avoid labeling *persons* and thereby legitimizing their treatment in some discriminatory way, on the basis of limited behaviors. People are *sexual,* and their sexual *behaviors* may be heterosexual, homosexual, or bisexual. Not everyone agrees with this distinction, however; there are those who identify themselves as "straight" or "gay" or "lesbian."

There are people who claim a true bisexual identity, although the definition of this is not completely clear. Some young people seem to have been influenced by media figures—rock stars, actors, and writers—who are self-proclaimed bisexuals (Kopkind 1973). Some bars that once were exclusively gay now try to attract patrons who dance with persons of either sex (*Newsweek* May 27, 1974, p. 90). Many of those who identify themselves as bisexual seem to believe that this somehow represents more liberated behavior than does exclusive heterosexuality or homosexuality (Warren and Ponse 1979).

Society's view of bisexuality is varied. Some people may consider that participation in any homosexual act automatically categorizes the individuals involved as homosexual, regardless of their heterosexual activities. Those engaging in bisexual behaviors may become subjected to the same prejudices and discrimination as are those with homosexual preferences, sometimes because of the discovery of a single incident. On the other hand, some may consider a few homosexual activities as merely a transient phase in a heterosexual individual's sexual life. Bisexuality may also be considered a unique and separate sexual preference for some individuals. Very few people report anything like an equal balance of same-sex partners. Should this happen, however, it may stimulate attitudes toward such persons different in some respects from society's attitudes toward either heterosexuality or homosexuality.

TYPES OF SEXUAL RELATIONSHIPS

The term *relationship* usually implies a repeated interaction over an appreciable period of time, with some ordering of behavior by the two or more people involved. Casual sexual events do not necessarily constitute social relationships since they imply only the briefest or most superficial ordering of behavior. In fact, the essence of casual sex may lie in the avoidance of commitment, ordering, or consistency. Such behavior may represent a desire not to be committed and may simply be an experiential outlet or an anonymous release of sexual tension.

Establishments exist in which one may engage in sex with strangers. Some have darkened rooms so that the persons never see each other clearly. There may be a rule against using last names, or people may elect to use fictitious names. Some people choose to have sex with strangers whom they will never see again so that there can be no further involvement. However, few people are content to rely solely on casual sex for any extended period of time. This is too lonely and too unpredictable a life for most people. It can be risky because it increases the likelihood of contracting sexually transmitted diseases—especially **acquired immune deficiency syndrome**

(AIDS), which strikes mainly, but not exclusively, males engaging in homosexual behaviors (Taulbee 1983, p. 324; Franklin 1984, p. 260)—or of meeting with physical danger. Many people deliberately choose a short-term emotional-sexual involvement because they want to avoid a premature commitment but are not content with casual sex. They may believe that all friendships have the potential for sexual contact but that circumstances can either encourage sexual involvement or, just as easily, terminate sexual involvement.

Monogamous Relationships

At the opposite end of the scale from casual sex is the *monogamous relationship*. Such relationships usually function as marriages. The concept of marriage in our society assumes an enduring and mutually consenting sexual relationship. In fact, in some states a marriage is not valid until the couple has consummated it (that is, engaged in coitus).

Monogamy literally means "one mating." It can be interpreted to mean having only one sexual partner during one's marriage or having one primary sexual relationship over any long period of time. Many people practice each of these interpretations, and many more hold one or the other as personal ideals.

There are no convincing data on the number of persons in the United States who have sexual intercourse with one and only one partner during their entire lifetimes, including the periods before marriage and after widowhood. The conclusions of both Kinsey (1953) and Hunt (1974b) suggest that the number of such persons is greater than less carefully chosen samples have indicated. Most research indicates that around half of the population has only their spouse as a sexual partner during marriage but that the number who have had more than one partner before, during, and after marriage is increasing (DeLamater and MacCorquodale 1979).

The sexual expectations and activities in a monogamous relationship are normally in a constant but gradual state of change. The sexual peak for men (in terms of *potential* frequency of orgasm) occurs in the late teens, whereas the sexual peak for women (in terms of *actual* frequency of orgasm) occurs in the early thirties. Thus, one would expect the greatest frequency of mutual sexual activity to occur somewhere between these two peaks. This usually occurs in the first few years of most marriages (Reiss 1980, pp. 272–279).

It is more difficult both to collect and to interpret information on *satisfaction* with sexual behaviors over the span of a marriage than to collect data on the frequency of intercourse. The quality of sexual activities should improve steadily over the course of a marriage. As couples overcome inhibitions and learn new and more effective skills in sexual communication and in sexual behaviors, at least the potential for increased satisfaction exists.

One of the most thorough of recent studies of marital sexuality supplied evidence that there is a high correlation between the degree of marital closeness and the quality of a couple's sex lives with each other. Researcher Morton Hunt's (1974) work generally confirmed the essential sexuality of Americans and showed trends toward wider acceptance and enjoyment of sexual activities that had in the past been considered deviant. For example, over three-fourths of all married couples reported engaging in oral sex.

Most marriage experts agree that mutual satisfaction in a couple's sex life is a powerful factor in overall marital adjustment. Conversely, couples who report sexual maladjustment may have more general problems in their marriages.

Extramarital Sex

Probably more has been written on the subject of coitus with persons other than marriage partners than on almost any other aspect of marital sex. The major reasons for engaging in **extramarital sex** seem to be a desire for variety and for the enjoyment of intimate friendships with others than the spouse (Yablonsky 1979). An "inadequate sex life at home" and "other serious problems in the marriage" are rather low on the list of reasons. In fact, 80 percent of the middle-class men reporting extramarital sex in Yablonsky's study said that their sex life with their wife was "good" or "excellent," and an additional 14 percent reported that sex life at home was "fair." Other research, however, has indicated that those who have affairs rate marital sex lower than those who do not (Maykovich 1976). Those who have extramarital affairs may bias their replies according to what they want the interviewer to believe or in order to justify their own feelings about their behavior.

A few marriages have incorporated understandings between the spouses sanctioning extramarital sexual activities, which often include short-term relationships or "affairs." In one study, about half the married men reported extramarital sexual experience. The wives of nearly a third of these men knew about it. In 20 percent of the cases, the men told their wives; in 3 percent, the wives found out by other means; and in about 8 percent, there was a prior understanding that extramarital sex was permissible in the marriage (Yablonsky 1979).

Of those who eventually divorce, extramarital sex typically begins early in the marriage. Half of those in one study reported that extramarital relationships began in the first year of marriage. For those who did not divorce, the average duration of the marriage before the advent of extramarital sex was between six and seven years (Hunt 1974b).

Although discussions with friends and interviewers about extramarital affairs appears to be much more open than 40 years ago when Kinsey did his studies, Hunt (1974b, p. 270) notes that "our data indicate that there is still a great emphasis on secrecy, based on the clear recognition that such extramarital acts will be perceived by the spouse as disloyalty, partial abandonment, and a repudiation of marital love." Only one-fifth of both men and women engaging in extramarital intercourse believed that their spouses knew about it, and Hunt concluded that the "liberated" younger married people were just as secretive as older men and women.

The debate over whether a middle-class person can have an extramarital affair and a healthy marriage at the same time continues. A spokesman for one point of view says that the long-term affair in particular is a form of neurotic behavior and a reflection of the immaturity of the persons so engaged (Strean 1980). This point of view emphasizes the frustrations, disappointments, and expectations of the man or woman involved in a long-term affair. Another viewpoint is represented by psychologist Warren Gadpaille (1975, pp. 371–372):

> The most interesting question of all may well be whether or not extramarital intercourse is normal. I must answer with a somewhat qualified yes. It is normal

in that sexually monogamous permanent marriage places an unnatural restriction upon the human animal's biologically normal desire and capacity for sexual variety. . . . It is equally true that any specific instance of infidelity may have its roots not in normal human tendencies, but in every kind and level of intrapsychic and interpersonal immaturity or emotional disorder. The existence of inappropriate motivations similarly cannot justify a blanket condemnation of sex outside an existing marriage.

Whether particular extramarital relationships are healthy or neurotic, it seems clear that the incidence of such affairs is rising, particularly among younger middle-class couples. Some reasons offered for the increase are that life expectancy is increasing; that our society has become more mobile and urban; and that there are more middle-class women in the labor market, which maximizes extramarital opportunities for them as well as for men. Last, but certainly not least, is the existence of effective birth control methods, which permit the separation of sex from reproduction (Sprey 1972a).

Although it is impossible to determine the exact percentage of men and women who have extramarital sex, a conservative study reported that about 45 percent of husbands and about 35 percent of wives have one such encounter or more (Pietropinto and Simenauer 1977). The Kinsey and Hunt studies show much higher figures. Other studies show that the first instance of sex outside marriage is occurring at a younger age for both men and women and that few stop after just one instance (Bell, Turner, and Rosen 1975; Maykovich 1976).

It is clear that one of the major problems in research on extramarital sex is classifying all such incidences as belonging to one category. In fact, the variety of reasons for such behavior, as well as the range of marital agreements and degrees of marital secrecy, result in many meanings for sex outside marriage. "Open marriage," for instance, is a relationship in which fidelity is defined not as sexual exclusivity but, rather, as unconditional commitment to one's mate. There is open respect for the spouse's judgments and behaviors, including his or her own and the partner's extramarital sexual relationships (Knapp and Whitehurst 1977). There can be little doubt that open respect for the spouse's judgment sets up an entirely different climate from one in which there are feelings of betrayal of trust.

SUMMARY

1. Children often confuse attitudes about sex with other ideas based on generalizations that have an emotional quality. For many children, sex and reproduction are paired so completely that for years children may not know that making babies is not the only motivation for coitus.

2. Children learn about sex as they learn about everything else that is emotional—through direct teaching, imitation, and experience. Peers are a common source of (often inaccurate) sex information for young people. They also learn from adults—both parents and other teachers—who can convey either that sex is normal and healthy or that is is sinful and dirty. Most parents probably convey both messages from time to time. Parents may have their own biases and, in addition, may be so

emotionally involved with their children that they find it difficult, if not impossible, to be the sole providers of sex education.

3. Many of the sexual attitudes of young people are formed in early discussions and experimentation with their peers. About five times as many boys as girls are reported to engage in social sexual behaviors before adolescence—much of it with same-sex peers.

4. By mid- to late adolescence, heterosexual relationships are the rule. Girls still report less frequent encounters, fewer partners, and fewer orgasms than do boys. This is largely due to differences between socialization patterns for males and those for females; early sexual activity is more widely accepted for males. In addition, females may typically underreport their activities, whereas males may overreport. Much of this early activity is noncoital.

5. Masturbation normally begins in adolescence or early adulthood and continues throughout life for most men and women.

6. Laws and law enforcement policies affect young people's sexual behaviors.

7. The context of an interaction often determines whether or not one interprets one's sensations as sexual. There are both individual and cultural differences in how people interpret sensations; these vary not only from person to person but also from one time to another with the same person.

8. Orgasm is the release of muscle tension and the relief of congestion in the genitals and pelvis. Those who have experienced orgasm are very likely in future encounters to want to follow sexual stimulation to an orgasmic experience.

9. Sexual fantasies enhance most individuals' sexual encounters. Men's fantasies differ somewhat from those of women, but members of both sexes find them to be powerful arousal mechanisms.

10. Sexual scripts—what people think must be said and done—are usually both complementary and reciprocal. Scripts change over time, but some of their elements may be so fixed that two individuals with conflicting scripts can find difficulty resolving their expectations. Whatever *sex* means to a particular person, establishing a sexual relationship is usually a landmark event.

11. Celibacy is a state in which one refrains from engaging in sexual intercourse. Often celibates choose abstinence for religious reasons, and it is seen as a way of channeling sexual energies into valuable thoughts or activities more valuable to them. Some celibates believe that self-stimulation is acceptable, but not mutual sexual interaction.

12. Heterosexuality, homosexuality, and bisexuality are identified as sexual preferences. Heterosexuality is the most frequent preference and is considered "normal" by most persons. Homosexuality and bisexuality are subject to less social stigmatization now than previously, although in the United States today there is still a widespread repressive attitude toward these variations of sexuality.

13. Casual sex and short-term relationships are both prevalent forms of sexual encounters. The most openly acceptable form of social sex, however, is married monogamy. It is perhaps more of an ideal than an actuality for many reasons, however, since many have had sexual relations with other partners before and after they were married, and still others have sex with partners other than their mates while they are married.

14. Extramarital sex ranges from that which may be agreed on in open marriages, where there is spousal acceptance, to disapproved sex that is sometimes cited as the reason for dissolving a marriage relationship. One study estimates conservatively that approximately 45 percent of husbands and 35 percent of wives have at least one such encounter. Other studies show much higher figures. The numbers seem to be increasing somewhat, especially among younger persons.

GLOSSARY

Acquired immune deficiency syndrome (AIDS) A contagious disease, believed to spread by exchange of bodily fluids, which destroys the body's immune system. It is believed to be fatal. Currently, 40 percent of diagnosed cases have died. (pp. 106–107)

Anus The opening at the outer end of the lower intestine through which feces leave one's body. (p. 97)

Celibacy Abstinence from sexual activities with another; sometimes used to denote the state of remaining unmarried. (p. 103)

Clitoris A small erectile organ in the vulva that is usually highly sensitive to sexual stimulation. (p. 96)

Coitus Specifically, insertion of the penis into the vagina; it does not include other sexual acts (for example, homosexual behaviors). (p. 82)

Contraception The practice of attempting to prevent pregnancy; a contraceptive is any device or procedure intentionally used to prevent or minimize the chances of conception or of the implantation of a fertilized ovum in the uterus. (p. 83)

Corona The ridge on the penis at the base of the glans. (p. 96)

Cunnilingus Oral stimulation of the female genitals. (p. 96)

Ejaculation The rhythmic ejection of semen through the penis. (p. 89)

Erogenous Pertaining to those feelings, thoughts, and sensations that produce sexual arousal. (p. 95)

Erotic Sexually arousing. (p. 82)

Extramarital sex Sexual relations by a married person with someone other than his or her spouse. (p. 108)

Fellatio Oral stimulation of the male genitals. (p. 96)

Fetishism The use of inanimate objects (most often underclothing, stockings, shoes, gloves, or a lock of hair) to attain sexual gratification. (p. 83)

Ideation The process of forming ideas or thoughts about issues, people, or objects. (p. 91)

Masturbation Stimulation of the genital organs usually by stroking with fingers, hands, or hand-held objects, but sometimes by pressing the genitalia against surfaces or by directing a stream of water on the penis or clitoris. (p. 87)

Menstruation The monthly sloughing of the endometrium or lining of the uterus, which normally occurs when no fertilized egg has been implanted. (p. 83)

Orgasm Sexual climax in which sexual tension reaches a peak and is reduced in a series of extremely pleasurable rhythmic contractions. (p. 87)

Peers Persons of equal status; they may be the same age or sex, of the same educational level or social class, for example. (p. 83)

Penis The male organ of copulation and urination. (p. 96)

Preejaculatory fluid A cleansing, acid-neutralizing glandular fluid secreted from the penis in response to stimuli. (p. 87)

Prostate gland The male gland that supplies much of the seminal fluid and produces some hormones. (p. 83)

Script Preconceived ways to behave and expectations of the behaviors of others that together explain to the subject how life goes. (p. 100)

Semen The fluid that carries sperm cells. (p. 96)

Sexual intercourse Sexual interaction; may denote oral, anal, or homosexual activities as well as coitus, but always involves at least two persons and the genital organs of at least one. (p. 82)

Sexually transmitted disease Diseases such as gonorrhea, syphilis, genital herpes (*Herpes simplex* II), AIDS, chlamydia, and many others that are acquired by contact of the genitals with infected persons; a refinement of the older term *venereal disease*. (p. 86)

Spermatozoa Male reproductive cells. (p. 96)

Subcortical Characteristic of that part of the brain, below the cerebral cortex and above the midbrain, that is particularly involved with emotions. (p. 95)

Taboo Behavior, thoughts, or feelings that are believed to be forbidden and punishable by social sanctions or metaphysical forces. (p. 82)

Vagina The internal female organ that receives the penis during coitus, serves as a passageway for menstrual fluids, and is the canal through which babies pass at birth. It connects the vulva with the uterus. (p. 96)

Vulva External female genitalia. (p. 96)

5

I never wanted to get married. The last thing I wanted was infinite security, and to be
the place an arrow shoots off from. I wanted change and excitement and to shoot off in
all directions myself, like the colored arrows from a Fourth of July rocket.

The young single population in the United States increased by 1.2 million between 1970 and 1980 but declined by 402,000 between 1980 and 1985. Roughly 40 percent of women and 50 percent of men between the ages of 15 and 40 have never married; a few will never marry at all; some will marry and divorce; some will be widowed.

There is probably no such thing as a "singles lifestyle" because the population of unmarried persons at any given time is so diverse. Attitudes and behaviors with respect to unmarried sex have changed greatly over the past few decades, with about two-thirds of Americans accepting unmarried sex for males and over half believing that it is also permissible for females. If couples have an affectional bond, and especially if they are planning to marry, most persons now agree that it is likely that the couple will engage in coitus. Most of those who live together do so for very short periods of time, subsequently either separating or marrying each other. Thus for some couples, cohabitation seems to be part of the courtship system, a way of postponing marriage for the time being. Eventu-

SINGLEHOOD AND COHABITATION

ally, however, virtually all persons marry at least once; cohabitation shows no signs of taking the place of marriage.

Sylvia Plath,
The Bell Jar

*S*ince 1970 an interesting change in single life has developed in the United States. The proportion of people who are single has gradually increased. Singlehood, of course, is not a new phenomenon; periods of being single have always been permissible—adolescence, early adulthood, and a period of time following the divorce or death of a spouse. Moreover, in many societies there have been periods of low marriage rates. In Australia during the European settlement, for example, an extreme shortage of women caused a higher rate of single persons than at present (Stolk 1981). In the United States, the westward movement was heavily male, and some of the same patterns of singlehood found in Australia existed.

In times of war there often have been imbalances due to the high death rate of men of marriageable age. As we will discuss later in this chapter, "baby booms" create an imbalance in societies in which males are customarily older than the females they marry. In general, however, the male-female balance has usually been favorable for finding a mate. In the past, when a man or woman remained unmarried past an age that parents and friends deemed appropriate, the judgment was sometimes made that no one wanted to marry him or her. Even today few people intend never to marry, although some predict that 10 percent of those currently in their early twenties will stay single. Of those who are now over 40 years of age, only 5 percent have never married (U.S. Bureau of the Census 1985b, p. 2).

▌ THE CHOICE TO BE SINGLE

In March 1984, approximately 26 percent of the population of the United States fifteen years of age or older had never married—although most of them probably will. Nearly a fourth of those who had been married were currently single due to widowhood, divorce, separation, or other reasons (U.S. Bureau of the Census 1985b, p. 9). (Figure 5.1 shows the percentage of the U.S. population aged 20–54 that never married, from 1890–1984.) Although most persons eventually marry—in 1984, 96 percent of women and 95 percent of men had married before they were 65 years old—an increasingly large fraction of American adults spend a significant amount of time single before, between, or after marriages. A disproportionately large number of these persons are black women, and a disproportionately large number of those are the heads of single-parent families. Being single does not necessarily mean being childless.*

Racial differences in the proportion of men and women who live alone are remarkable. A 1981 census report comments:

> Among people 45 to 64 years old in 1979, the majority of men (83 percent) and women (72 percent) lived with their spouses. . . . In addition, far greater proportions of White men and women lived with their spouses than was true of Black men and women . . . ; Black women were three times as likely as White women to maintain families with no husband present (28 percent versus 9 percent).

*Proportionately, over three times as many black families as white were one-parent families (U.S. Bureau of the Census 1985a, p. 1).

FIGURE 5 · 1
Percent of U.S.
Population Aged
20–24 That Never
Married, by Sex and
Age Group, 1890–
1984

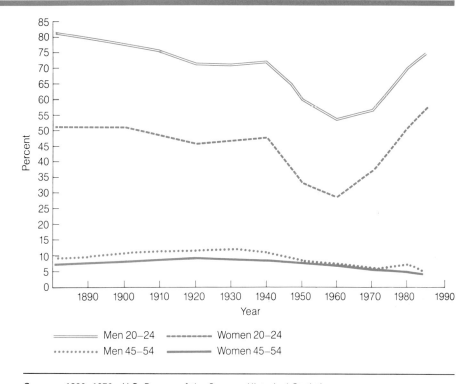

Sources: 1890–1970—U.S. Bureau of the Census, *Historical Statistics of the United States, Colonial Times to 1970, Part 1, Bicentennial Edition,* Series A (1975), cols. 160–171; 1980—U.S. Bureau of the Census, "Marital Status and Living Arrangements, March 1980," *Current Population Reports,* Series P-20, No. 365 (October 1981); 1984—U.S. Bureau of the Census, "Marital Status and Living Arrangements, March 1984," *Current Population Reports,* Series P-20, No. 399 (July 1985).

Blacks 45 to 64 years old, especially men, were less likely to live in a family than Whites in this age group; 23 percent of Black men did not live in a family, while only 9 percent of White men did not live in a family. The percentages for Black and White women were 21 and 14 percent, respectively. (U.S. Bureau of the Census 1981d, pp. 3–4)

Middle-aged white men are much more likely to be married and living with their spouses than middle-aged black men (85.3 percent versus 61.9 percent), five times less likely to be separated, three times less likely to be widowed, and less than half as likely to be divorced. Black women, on the other hand, are more likely than white women to be single. The single life is much more typically a black than a white lifestyle.

More research on singlehood is needed to understand all the variables determining why persons remain, or voluntarily become, single, but several studies indicate that many variables combine to explain it (Stein 1978; Spreitzer and Riley 1974). Other studies attempt to define the different types of single lifestyles, exploring the ways that single people manage their lives (Barkas 1980; Stein 1976).

Increase of Singlehood

One interesting reason offered by some for the increase in singlehood is that sex roles have changed—in particular, the life options of middle-class women have expanded, as have opportunities for education and employment. One study reported that during the 1960s not only did the women's movement change many women's views of marriage, but also of the 13.8 million new jobs that were created, two-thirds were classified by employers as "women's jobs" (Bird 1972). Not coincidentally, between 1970 and 1985, there was a 90 percent increase in the number of single-person households. A large number of these represented independent women working and living alone before marriage, between marriages, or instead of marrying, although the number of men living alone has also more than doubled between 1970 and 1985 (U.S. Bureau of the Census 1985d, pp. 3, 9).

Along with greater economic opportunities for women have come ideas of liberation from stereotyped roles for both men and women—roles that may have hampered freedom and personal goals. In one survey, single men and women, asked why they chose to remain single, frequently mentioned career opportunities, freedom for change and mobility, and psychological and social autonomy (Stein 1978).

The options that greater economic independence has brought to women, along with the desires of both men and women for autonomy, have led to more critical examination of marriage. Not only may singlehood be growing more attractive, but also, for some persons, being married may have become less attractive. Many young persons report disillusionment about their parents' marriages and wonder whether marriage is worth giving up their freedom. In one study, half of the single men interviewed reported that their parents had unhappy marriages (Knupfer, Clark, and Room 1966). Many divorced persons are so disenchanted with the idea of marriage that they vow never to marry again. A considerable number of these disillusioned persons nevertheless do marry or remarry, but a few never do.

One significant result of greater choice for women and a more critical examination of marriage is the increase in age at which men and women first marry. Since 1956, the median age at first marriage has risen from 20.1 to 23.0 in 1984 for women and from 22.5 to 25.4 in 1984 for men (U.S. Bureau of the Census 1985b, p. 1). This increase has led some observers of the single world to conclude that the single lifestyle is nothing more than a temporary state for most men and women, the only real change being that more years are spent in this lifestyle than was previously the case.

The high divorce rate has also contributed to the population of singles. The time interval between divorce and remarriage has increased, with the result that twice as many divorced persons have not yet remarried as had a decade ago.

What population experts have called the "marriage squeeze" has also contributed to the growing numbers of singles. The post–World War II baby boom, which lasted from 1946 to 1957, followed a wartime period during which many fewer children were born. Thus, when those born in 1946 reached marrying age, a problem developed. Since women in the United States usually marry men two to three years older than they are, those born in the first two to three years of the baby boom found that the number of potential mates was much smaller than the number looking. When the first baby-boom women reached the age of twenty, there were not enough 22-year-old men for them to marry.

Those who advocate the single life report such advantages as freedom and independence to pursue career goals.

Many women born in these early postwar years had to choose between postponing marriage or remaining single indefinitely. Of course, some of them voluntarily opted for singlehood. Those born from 1946 to 1949 reached the average age of marriage during the late 1960s and early 1970s, just as the women's movement began to peak and employment opportunities for women increased. Another phenomenon of the 1960s was the development of the birth control pill, which helped to remove the fear of pregnancy for those single women who chose to have active sex lives. All these factors helped account for the rising number of single women.

Demographers believed that, as the years passed, the surplus of women of marriageable age would level off and that the rising number of single persons was therefore a temporary phenomenon. However, the leveling off took long enough that it merged with still another marriage squeeze. This time, there was a shortage of available women, and there were too many men who were looking for wives. When males born during the last three years of the baby boom (1954–1957) reached marrying age in the late 1970s, they found that there were fewer females from whom to choose because the fertility rate had begun to drop in 1958 and there were, therefore, fewer females two to three years younger than they were (Heer and Grossbard-Schectman 1981).

The Social Acceptance of Singles

As the number of single persons has grown, so has society's acceptance of them. This is true not only because of the increasing number of other singles with whom to associate but also because being single has become more socially approved. Young singles have become a social force to be reckoned with. Advertisers appeal to the young singles market because singles spend more than married persons on entertainment, travel, au-

SINGLEHOOD AND COHABITATION   *119*

	Pushes from Marriage	Pulls toward Singlehood
TABLE 5 · 1 Pushes from Marriage and Pulls toward Being Single	Restrictions within relationships: suffocating one-to-one relationships Feeling trapped Obstacles to self-development Boredom, unhappiness, anger Role playing and conformity to expectations Poor communication with mate Sexual frustration Lack of friends, isolation, loneliness Limited mobility and availability of new experiences	Career opportunities Variety of experiences and plurality of roles Self-sufficiency Psychological and social autonomy Exciting lifestyle Mobility and freedom to change Sustaining friendships Sexual availability Recreational autonomy Freedom to refuse or to resign from unappealing work

tomobiles, clothes, and accessories. It was reported in 1974 that young single women spent over one-third more money on clothes than young married women did and that almost half the Porsches sold were bought by young singles (*US News & World Report* October 7, 1974, pp. 54ff.). The existence of 26 million young singles—67 million of all ages—has given rise to apartments for singles, singles' bars and clubs, singles' vacations, and singles' magazines. The old notion of the lonely, socially isolated spinster or bachelor has given way in the media to a picture of the carefree life of the swinging singles. Although in fact only a small percentage of singles live this "good life," the image has been well enough publicized to suggest an attractive alternative to marriage for millions of persons. A recent study of 3,000 single men and women aged 20 to 55, concluded that "single life is a mixed bag, an ambivalent, bittersweet, confused and sometimes desperate medley of experiences" (Simenauer and Carroll 1982).

The experiences of singles indicate that friendship networks form a primary source of social support and take the place of marriage and parenthood (Adams 1976). Single people seem to have different types of friendships from most married people. Intimate relationships may be same sex or opposite sex, sexual or nonsexual (Simenauer and Carroll 1982). One single professional has written of her friendships: "It has struck me more than once that the way I describe my friendships—I can't live without them—is the way my mother described her marriage" (Spake 1984, p. 48).

Those who are single have a variety of viewpoints about the advantages and disadvantages of singlehood. Many report being lonely and bored, but others report advantages in terms of privacy, independence, and excitement. Table 5.1 contrasts the reported negative features of being married (pushes) with the positive features about being single (pulls) (Stein 1978, p. 68). The chief issue that seems to underlie the pushes and pulls is control—control over one's activities, one's time, one's associates, one's assets, and one's sexual objectives.

A recent study of over 900 mothers and daughters based on an eighteen-year intergenerational research project indicated that attitudes toward remaining single have changed not only for young people but for their parents as well. When asked how much it would bother them if they never married, only 25 percent of the young

As the number of single persons has increased, the ease and acceptability of single lifestyles has also grown, and a new picture of a carefree life for singles has become a dominant theme.

people said they would be greatly upset, and another 25 percent said they would mind only a little. More than 40 percent of their mothers said they would not be bothered at all, and only 10 percent said they would be greatly troubled (Thornton and Freedman 1982).

SINGLE LIFESTYLES

As we have noted, the popular view of swinging singlehood is a distortion. Although such a carefree life may be possible for many men and women, this simplistic view does not fit the countless varieties of persons who are unmarried at any given point in their lives. Young singles who are merely postponing marriage, previously married men and women who have custody of one or more children, and older singles who have been divorced or widowed present very different pictures. Being single in a small town may be nothing like being single in New York City, Chicago, or Dallas. Affluent singles may avail themselves of the good life, but those barely getting by financially live very differently. Millions of single persons spend every penny they earn just to have a decent standard of living. Expenses per person are usually greater for a single worker than for a married worker. Although two cannot live as cheaply as one, two generally can live as cheaply as 1.7 (Stein 1984).

Types of Lifestyles

Perhaps among the most important factors for understanding the various lifestyles of singles are whether singlehood is voluntary or involuntary and at what age a person is single. For example, voluntarily choosing to be single for several years before marrying has become a respected and applauded attitude among family-life experts, many parents, and young people themselves (see Lasswell 1974). However, after a certain age—usually around 30—pressure to marry may come from parents, friends, and even subtly from employers. Friends may begin to arrange meetings between "eligible" singles; parents may wonder aloud whether their son or daughter is "seeing anyone"; and employers may have second thoughts about promoting single persons to responsible positions (Jacoby 1975).

It is unlikely that all single persons fall into the same category whether they are studied from the perspective of the circumstances in which they find themselves or from the perspective of their reasons for being unmarried. Peter Stein (1978, pp. 12–14) devised an elaborate scheme for distinguishing among categories of singles for his extensive study:

Temporary Voluntary Singlehood

1. Young persons who have never been married and who are postponing marriage indefinitely
2. Recently divorced or widowed persons who need time to be single but want a mate again eventually
3. Older never-marrieds who have decided that if the right person comes along, they would marry, but who are not actively looking
4. Cohabitors who will eventually marry either each other or someone else

Temporary Involuntary Singlehood

1. Young persons who have never been married but who are actively seeking a mate
2. Divorced or widowed persons or single parents who are lonely and want to remarry soon

Permanent Voluntary Singlehood

1. Cohabitors who never intend to have a ceremonial marriage
2. Formerly married persons who believe that once was enough
3. Those who have taken religious vows not to marry
4. Never-married persons of all ages who have no intention ever to marry

Permanent Involuntary Singlehood

1. Older, widowed, divorced, or never-married persons—most frequently women—who wanted to marry or remarry but have had no opportunities and have become reconciled to their single state
2. Never-married persons who are handicapped in some way that has made them unavailable or undesirable as marriage partners (for example, those who are mentally retarded or grossly physically impaired)

In contrast to Stein's typology, sociologist Robert Staples (1981) set up a simpler set of four categories of unmarried adults for a study of black singles:

1. *Free-floating:* childless, under 45, unattached, variety of partners; colloquially referred to as "swinging singles."

2. *Open-couple:* attached principally to one person but with enough freedom to encompass friendships or romantic liaisons with others.
3. *Closed-couple:* attached exclusively without living together—possibly engaged.
4. *De facto married:* living together in a committed relationship. Long-term de facto relationships are rare because most such couples eventually either marry or break up.

In an in-depth study of never-married, college-educated men and women over the age of 30, M. A. Schwartz (1976) described six lifestyle patterns:

1. *Professional:* these persons organized their lives around their work and identified strongly with their occupational roles. Most of their time and energy was spent in career-related activities.
2. *Social:* individuals in this category had involved social lives and many personal relationships. They often enjoyed their work, but their friends clearly held first priority. They were "joiners" or pursued hobbies that put them in frequent contact with people. Family often played an important role in their lives as well.
3. *Individualistic:* those with this lifestyle focused their attention on self-growth. They emphasized the joys of freedom and privacy. They liked living alone and having to answer to no one for their time. They pursued hobbies, took classes for self-improvement, and enjoyed reading and other solitary pursuits.
4. *Activist:* this group centered their lives around the community and political causes. They did not get involved for the social contacts nearly as much as for the sake of the issues. Their work was important, but most of their time and energy was devoted to working for what they considered a better world.
5. *Passive:* these were the loners who spent their free time at home alone or in solitary pursuits such as shopping or attending movies. They showed the least initiative of any of the six groups in shaping their lives creatively. They also had the most negative outlooks on life.
6. *Supportive:* persons falling into this pattern filled their lives by giving service to others. Few persons reported this lifestyle, but the women in this category reported that they were highly satisfied with their lives.

These three typologies are quite different; sociology students may wish to speculate how their differences might lead to differences in the conclusions of studies using them.

It is obvious from the research on single lifestyles that there is great variety. Some people live alone, some live with roommates or with their families of orientation (parents or other kin). Some want to marry eventually; others plan never to marry; still others cohabit in a semimarried state. Some are affluent; others barely get by financially. Some are young, but many are middle-aged or old. Some are parents; some are grandparents; many are childless. One thing is certain, however: single persons are members of a rapidly growing minority group. They are as individual as members of any other minority, but they face problems common to any group of persons who voluntarily or involuntarily occupies a minority status. Certain discriminatory attitudes and practices are still common, but as their numbers grow, singlehood

It has been suggested that single women have an easier time with the domestic side of life than do single men.

not only should assume a more attractive status but also should generate its own social support systems to combat the social stigma that being single has often carried.

Gender Differences

Researchers have noted an important difference in single lifestyles between men and women. Virtually every study has indicated that single women get along better without men than single men get along without women (Campbell 1975). Single women of all ages are less lonely, have fewer mental health and adjustment problems, and are happier (Gove and Tudor 1973; Campbell 1975, p. 38). A significantly larger percentage of single women (61.2 percent) than married women (50.2 percent) are in the labor force, but a significantly smaller percentage of single men (70.7 percent) are in the labor force than married men (81.0 percent) (U.S. Bureau of the Census 1981a). Single women also report a higher degree of satisfaction with their work than do single men.

One explanation for the fact that single women seem to adjust better is that women seem more adept than men at establishing and maintaining close friendships with members of both sexes. Women seem to experience less profoundly the loneliness and alienation experienced by many men (Pleck 1975a). It has also been suggested that single men have more difficulty coping with mundane tasks of life: shopping, cleaning, cooking, ironing (Davis and Phillip 1977). On the other hand, it is possible that fewer men experience as much anxiety over the outcome of such tasks as women, possibly because they lacked models for such during childhood or because they were told repeatedly that males do not perform these tasks well.

Some family-life experts have proposed that childless single women get along so well precisely because they are free from domestic roles and from having to adjust their lives to the demands of husbands and children. They are, therefore, able to develop their potential for growth (Gove 1972). The results of several studies suggest that women may profit from marriage much less than men do (Bernard 1973).

Another possible explanation is that men who do not marry may be the rejected ones, whereas women may be choosing to stay single. This explanation for differences between unmarried men and women had been proposed by sociologist Jessie Bernard (1973, p. 18), who coined the term **marriage gradient** to describe the tendency of lower- and middle-class females to marry men higher in economic and social status than they are, whereas middle-class men obviously do just the opposite. Thus women of high status and high achievement have a smaller pool from whom to choose and are therefore more likely to remain single. At the same time, men of low status and low achievement are not chosen. According to Bernard, (p. 4): "As the marriageable men drop out of the single population, those who are left show up worse and worse as compared with their feminine counterparts, so that [by] ages forty-five to fifty-four, the gap between them is a veritable chasm."

Other studies, however, have noted that for younger men and women the differences in adjustment between the sexes is less pronounced, although, as one researcher says, "the truth is that there are more carefree spinsters and anxious bachelors (Campbell 1975, p. 38). Nonetheless, single men and women both report good and not-so-good sides to the single life. As an article on singlehood reported:

> Living alone is an obscure blend of joys and terrors. I have never been able to decide whether I love it or hate it, nor have I ever known whether I actually chose to live alone or simply wound up there by default. . . . For myself, I know that I have a very active, independent life, good friends, am successful in my work and travel a lot, that I would never go to a singles bar, never have a computer date or even go skiing in the hope of meeting someone interesting. The life I lead suits my character. And yet—like most people—sometimes I wonder. (Bengis 1973)

SINGLEHOOD AND SEX

With a growing number of adults being single at certain stages in their lives—and some remaining single for extended periods or for a lifetime—unmarried sex has become an accepted fact for more and more persons. The later men and women marry—or the longer they remain single between marriages—the more likely they are to become sexually involved. By definition, those who never marry only have pre-marital sex. By society's standards, unmarried sex is very different for a 47-year-old, never-married person from that for a 17-year-old. As single persons leave the teen years, more sexual experience and a history of more sexual partners are the rule. However, the reality is far from the picture of general promiscuity often drawn by the media or lamented by those who fear that changing sexual values mean a serious decline in the nation's moral standards (Francoeur 1972).

The National Centers for Disease Control estimated that in 1983, 42 percent of never-married American females aged 15 to 19 years had had sex (*Los Angeles Herald Examiner,* May 17, 1985, p. A-11). The Alan Guttmacher Institute's 1983 survey of American women revealed that most never-married women between the ages of 20 and 29 years have had sex at some time. Seventy percent had had sex in the six months preceding the survey and 53 percent within four weeks preceding the interview (Tanfer and Horn 1985). A study commissioned by the National Institute of Child Health and Human Development reported in 1986 that of single women in their twenties, one in six habitually engages in coitus without contraceptives and that 40 percent had aborted their first pregnancy (*Los Angeles Herald Examiner,* June 2, 1986, p. A-14).

Sexual activity for singles who have previously been married is much more wide-spread than for young unmarrieds. Research indicated that of divorced persons under the age of 55, all the men interviewed and 90 percent of the women were sexually active, usually having several partners in a year (Hunt 1974b, p. 154). In another study, 82 percent of the divorced women reportedly had engaged in sex during the first year after their divorce (Gebhard 1971). However, sometime after that first year, most divorced persons seemed to tire of sexual experimentation and settle into more intimate relationships (Weiss 1975, p. 154). Although attitudes toward sex before and between marriages appear to have become much more permissive in recent years, the patterns of unmarried sex still appear to be operating largely "within the framework of long-held cultural values of intimacy and love" (Hunt 1974b, p. 154).

Standards of Unmarried Sex

Approval—or even acceptance—of new sexual standards is far from unanimous, however. Religion plays an important part in molding more conservative attitudes for countless men and women. Small towns, rural communities, and entire regions may hold far less permissive opinions about sexual behavior for unmarried persons (Zelnik and Kantner 1977). From a survey of the research on sexual attitudes and sexual behavior, four standards for unmarried sex have been proposed (Reiss 1980).

1. *Abstinence:* restraint from nonmarital intercourse. In most cases this attitude is based on a religious, moral belief that sex outside marriage is sinful. Many fundamentalist religious organizations support this viewpoint, as do many conservative parents who cannot bring themselves to condone in today's young people what was forbidden in their own youth (Williams 1977).

For several years from the mid-1960s to the early 1980s, many teenage women reported the same kind of social embarrassment that many men have felt for a long time—the stigma of still being virgins by the time they finished high school. Very recently, however, this pressure appears to be lessening. Many young men and women now view abstinence as an expression of free choice rather than as a religious or moral imperative. Virtually no research exists on those who voluntarily become celibate for long periods of time, although interviews with these persons suggest some information about their motives. Reasons vary considerably, but a common motivation is the need to shift one's energy and creativity to work, to self-assessment, and to an evaluation of relationships generally (Sandler, Myerson, and Kinder 1980).

2. *The double standard:* the idea that premarital intercourse is always more acceptable for males than for females. This standard was supported by approximately one-quarter of the college students interviewed in the 1960s (Reiss 1967). Older men and women seem to favor the double standard more than younger persons do, although in general all age groups are shifting noticeably away from the belief that males should be allowed more sexual freedom than females (Zelnik and Kantner 1977). A variation on the double standard that has surfaced in the past two decades is that it is less acceptable for females to have several partners than for males to do so. That is, it is acceptable for women to have nonmarital sex only with a person with whom they are in love or whom they plan to marry, but males are not limited in this fashion (Udry, Bauman, and Morris 1975).

3. *Permissiveness with affection:* the double standard does not apply here; instead, the "right" or "wrong" of unmarried sex is tied to whether two people love each other (or at least are in a stable and caring relationship). This is not a new standard by any means; couples who are seriously involved with each other have always received less condemnation for unmarried sex—especially if they eventually marry (Queen and Habenstein 1974).

4. *Permissiveness with or without affection:* if two people are so inclined, then nothing more is needed to make sex acceptable. In other words, the decision should be mutual but need not (although it may) reflect love or even a stable relationship. Of those who hold this standard, some still may place a greater value on sex with affection. In our society more men than women are thought to hold this standard, but in other societies women, too, may engage in unmarried sex as freely as men do (Marshall 1971).

Those who specialize in working with divorced, widowed, separated, and never-married men and women believe that sex is often a major source of frustration in a single person's life (Edwards and Hoover 1974). For the most part, this frustration is the result of sheer unpredictability. As one book for singles says:

> Overall singles complain that there isn't enough sex when they want it or more rarely, that there is an abundance available when they can't handle it. For most singles, it is either feast or famine. Though there may be long periods at the bare subsistence level, the sex life of singles lacks the predictability associated with marriage. And it is anything but the copulation cornucopia associated with the popular image of the swinging single. (Edwards and Hoover 1974, p. 164)

Common Sexual Problems

The double standard still seems to linger among many single people. Women complain that men do not want a serious relationship but instead rush them into one that is sexual. Furthermore, they often note that men abandon the relationship soon after it has become sexual. Men, on the other hand, claim that women lead them on by indicating that they are interested in them as sexual partners and then refuse to become involved on that level. Some men have difficulty with what they call "aggressive women" who make the first moves.

Some women complain that the growing equality of males and females in the marketplace does not extend to the bedroom. In the not-too-distant past, only men were sanctioned to be sexually assertive, and many men and women are still having problems finding a new standard. Psychologist Marie Edwards, who runs groups for single persons, says:

> Women's liberation notwithstanding, traditional role playing cannot be reversed overnight. Since sex roles are no longer defined as they were just a few years ago, there is confusion for everyone. With traditional courtship patterns changing—a less extended pursuit, less clearly defined rules, the dropping of coyness and game playing—we often find men and women equally confused and uncertain. (Edwards and Hoover 1974, p. 175)

Because of the obvious physical hazards of having a variety of sex partners, most singles prefer to settle for a companion who also limits his or her sexual contact to a carefully chosen few. The incurability of **herpes,** the deadliness of AIDS for both males and females, and the damages of **gonorrhea** and **chlamydia** to the female reproductive system should be sufficiently dramatic to discourage casual sexual interaction with strangers. Even so, the Centers for Disease Control in Atlanta estimate that 15,000 new cases of AIDS will be reported in the United States in 1986, as will half a million new cases of herpes, just under two million cases of gonorrhea, and nearly five million cases of chlamydia (*Newsweek,* April 21, 1986, pp. 70–71).

Even though giving birth to a child out of wedlock seems to be less of a social disgrace than it was in the past, most unmarried heterosexual persons still consider pregnancy a state to be avoided—especially if they do not know their partner well. Apart from the social embarrassment, pregnancies and even abortions are expensive. The emotional and financial investment of rearing a child is great, and a person who is unable, for whatever reason, to make a similar investment in a relationship with a partner may be incapable of such a commitment to a baby, especially if neither parent wants it.

In addition to venereal disease and pregnancy, another major concern of the unmarried is the problem of where and when to have sex. "Your place or mine?" has become a cliché, but singles often speak of the impact of family, roommates, and neighbors who may not approve of an overnight visit. Getting up to go home in the middle of the night is not usually a good solution. If the relationship is not exclusive, couples may worry that another lover will call or drop in. Single parents with custody of their children usually do not like to be away from them overnight very often, and most will not have an overnight guest when their children are at home. Motels and hotels often have connotations that unmarried men and women dislike. Especially for older unmarried persons, parking in a car is unacceptable; for many younger singles as well, the dangers involved in being in an isolated area at night have become too great. Meeting for afternoon trysts, borrowing a friend's apartment, and taking advantage of weekends when the children are visiting the noncustodial parents have become modes of maintaining a sexual relationship.

Despite all these difficulties, unmarried sex is a growing phenomenon. Not only have sexual values and sexual behavior been changing, especially among the unmarried, but the liberal trend is expected to continue in the future as well (Safilios-Rothschild 1977). More unmarried men and women are likely to experience sexual intercourse and to begin at a younger age. During the 1970s, there was a 30 percent increase in women under the age of nineteen who engaged in coitus, with the average age for the first experience declining about four months during this decade (from 16.5 to 16.1) (Zelnik and Kanter 1977). Sexual equality is expected to continue to increase, as is the belief that sex and procreation are separate issues. As one family sociologist has stated, "Sexuality will no longer be the primary resource to be used in negotiations toward commitment and marriage, but rather as an expression of emotions to be enjoyed" (Safilios-Rothschild 1977, p. 117).

COHABITATION

Cohabitation is the term usually used to refer to unrelated adults who are living together and presumably having sexual relations but are not married to each other. Although the concept is reasonably clear, it is not as easy as it might seem to learn the extent of the practice. After reporting that about two million households consisted of two unrelated persons in 1979, the U.S. Census Bureau (1980b, p. 20) commented:

> In addition to a certain number of what are generally termed "unmarried couples," these multimember nonfamily households include unrelated adults sharing a dwelling to reduce their individual housing expenses, two widows who are not related but are living together for companionship, or a landlord/landlady with several persons living in their home as roomers.

Offsetting the effect of counting persons who are merely roommates, however, is the failure to count the unknown number of persons who maintain separate living quarters but who have an enduring sexual relationship, perhaps spending several days or nights a week together in a marriagelike relationship. They may appear in the census as householders living alone or with their families. The phenomenon of "living apart together" seems to be a growing one. The best estimate is that approximately 2 million unmarried couples were living together in 1985, three times the estimated number in 1970 but about the same as the number for the preceding six years (U.S. Bureau of the Census 1985d, p. 1). The Census Bureau calls such cohabiting persons "POSSLQS": persons of the opposite sex sharing living quarters. Not only does the U.S. Census Bureau have difficulty estimating just how many unmarried persons cohabit, but those doing research on such couples have even greater difficulty defining just what the term implies. A survey of the literature found that there were over twenty definitions in use, which varied around such factors as how long a couple must live together to be classified as cohabiting; how many days and nights of the week they must sleep in the same household to qualify; and perhaps most important, whether or not the couple considered themselves cohabitors (Cole 1977).

The most controversial of the questions posed by those who have searched for a definition of *cohabiting couple* is how long a man and a woman must live together in order to qualify. Some have suggested six months (Clayton and Voss 1977). Several research studies have used the number of nights per week over a continuous period of time as their criterion (Macklin 1978). It is likely that this definition of cohabitation includes some persons who consider themselves merely roommates and excludes many who consider that they are living together after only a few days because they intend their relationship to continue.

Counting numbers of couples who meet the specifications set (unrelated, opposite sex, not legally married to each other, sharing a bedroom for a specified number of nights over a specified period of time) has resulted in the labeling of a numerically small proportion of all two-person households as cohabiting. This figure was placed at less than 4 percent in 1985 (U.S. Bureau of the Census 1985d, p. 3).

A study made several years ago found that 18 percent of young men aged 20 to 30 had cohabited for six months or more (Clayton and Voss 1977). The extensive survey by the National Institute of Child Health and Development reported in 1986 that a third of the single women in their twenties had lived with a man at some time (*Los Angeles Herald Examiner*, June 2, 1986, p. A-14). Research has been carried out in all regions of the United States; the percentages are comparable from region to region (Bower and Christopherson 1977).

About half of all cohabiting couples have never been married, but over 90 percent of college students living together plan to marry someone (if not their current partner) at some time in the future (Bower and Christopherson 1977). For them, cohabitation seems to be part of courtship. The other half of all males and females who are cohabiting have been married previously or are married but separated (Macklin 1978, p. 907). Seventy-five percent of cohabiting couples have no other persons in their households, but a growing number of single parents with custody of their children are choosing this lifestyle (U.S. Bureau of the Census 1980a, pp. 3–5). In addition, more senior citizens are cohabiting—almost one-third of cohabiting couples are over 55—seeking companionship without merging their financial assets or diminishing any retirement benefits that might be affected by marriage (U.S. Bureau of the Census 1980a, pp. 3–5).

Reasons for Cohabiting

The rapidly growing popularity of living together has been the subject of much speculation. Possible explanations range from the high cost of living to the increased availability of reliable contraceptives, both of which seem well documented (Macklin 1978, p. 16; Makepeace 1975).

One of the most thoroughly discussed explanations for the dramatic increase in cohabitation deals with the gradual liberalization of sexual attitudes. Traditional values with respect to virginity and waiting until marriage for sexual involvement have slowly been giving way to a widespread belief that being in love—especially with an intent to marry—justifies sex outside marriage (Glenn and Weaver 1979). In addition, adherence to the double standard condoning sex outside marriage for males but not for females has diminished considerably during the last two decades. Previously, most women believed (often correctly) that men did not want to marry a woman who had experienced sex before marriage. Since according to current estimates approximately two-thirds of American women have had intercourse by the average age of first marriage for women in the United States, that old admonition clearly has lost most of its meaning (DeLamater and MacCorquodale 1979).

"Honey, look who I ran into downtown—Bob Phelps, my old college roommate."

Drawing by W. Miller; © 1979 The New Yorker Magazine, Inc.

As social attitudes concerning sexual involvement between two persons who love each other have changed, more permissive sexual attitudes have also begun to include those who have limited commitment to each other. As values concerning sex outside marriage have changed, so has acceptance of unmarried persons living together (Bower and Christopherson 1977). Several studies have indicated that among the college population there is a generally supportive attitude toward cohabitation and, in fact, that college students may actually encourage each other to do so (Macklin 1978).

Styles of Cohabiting

Among cohabiting couples, there appears to be a wide range of commitment. Research has identified several types of cohabiting couples, ranging from those who are together for a few weeks to those who maintain a permanent cohabiting arrangement as an alternative to marriage. The following types of couples have been identified:

1. *Short-term relationships:* often these couples are young and are looking for a sexual experience. One study reported that 82 percent of males and 67 percent of females under age 20 reported that their longest period of cohabitation was less than three months. Of those 21 or 22 years of age, 63 percent of the males and 48 percent of the females reported a three-month maximum (Peterman, Ridley, and Anderson 1974). Because of the large number of such short-term relationships, the rates of those who have "ever cohabited" are much higher than any estimate of those who are currently living together (Macklin 1978).

2. *Longer-term love relationships:* these are primarily couples who have never been married. They have a definite degree of commitment to each other but are not ready to marry each other—or anyone else—in the foreseeable future. It is estimated that slightly over half of all cohabiting couples fall into this category (Macklin 1980, p. 907). In this sense, cohabitation has the effect of delaying marriage. In Sweden most individuals cohabit before eventually marrying someone. There, cohabitation is a step in the courtship process; many believe that something similar may be happening in the United States as the average age at first marriage rises. The Swedish sociologist Jan Trost (1979) has suggested that this kind of cohabitation in the United States is much more like the going-steady aspect of courtship in Sweden.

3. *Trial marriage:* a growing number of couples who have previously been divorced, and still others who have previously cohabited with one or more partners, state that they first want to live with any person they may eventually marry (Jacques and Chason 1979). In this sense cohabitation is a variation of the engagement period, although there may be no public announcement of the intention to marry. It is estimated that between 10 and 20 percent fall into this category (Macklin 1978).

4. *Permanent alternatives to marriage:* since very few persons never marry, it is unlikely that more than 1 or 2 percent of all cohabiting couples fall into this category. Virtually all cohabitation either terminates or moves into legal marriage (Clayton and Voss 1977). One major distinction between this type of cohabitation and all other forms is that the idea of having children is accepted (Macklin 1978). Another important difference is that the family and friends of the couple in this category are likely to be supportive of the relationship (Reiss, 1980, pp. 106–107). In many states the legal system eventually recognizes such unions as nonceremonial marriages or common-law marriages.

In reviewing the research and talking to couples who were living together at the time, a study named four patterns of living together (Peterman, Riley, and Anderson 1974):

1. *"Linus blanket":* sometimes couples decide to live together because they are insecure and dependent. Many young persons who have recently left their families but who are not yet ready to live alone drift (or rush) into cohabitation in order to have someone to lean on. Pregnancy, parental pressure, or fear of abandonment may push such couples into marriage. Usually, however, these relationships end when one or both partners grow strong enough to move on. If one partner remains insecure and dependent while the other grows more secure, the one who no longer needs a "security blanket" may feel used or trapped.

2. *Emancipation:* some young persons seem to use cohabitation to make a statement of their adult status and sexual freedom to their parents. Those in this category usually had a history of several short-term cohabiting relationships. The research turned up many females with this motivation who came from a very traditional, strict moral upbringing (a large number of Catholics were in this group). They seemed to be seeking a way to break out of their early patterns but tended to become so guilt stricken or to face so much parental disapproval that they broke off the relationship.

3. *Convenience:* some obviously exploitative cohabiting relationships were found, in which one or both partners were meeting selfish needs at the other's expense. The usual pattern was one in which the male openly acknowledged that he was in the relationship primarily for sex and often to have domestic tasks done for him. Females often hoped for eventual marriage but sometimes traded their services for financial support. In some cases women were seen as supplying sex and homemaking because the males were their emotional security blankets. Since social exchange theory states that inequitable relationships will not endure for long, one must assume that relationships of this type will not last unless both partners are fulfilling some of their important needs (Walster, Walster, and Traupmann 1978).

4. *Testing:* relationships in this category are often labeled *trial marriage*. They usually begin with an established commitment and are set up for the purpose of determining whether living together confirms a couple's decision to marry. Couples who choose *not* to marry as a result of having lived intimately with each other usually report that it was a beneficial experience and that they are wiser for having done so.

Some studies have reported that cohabiting respondents indicated that they would not consider marriage without first having lived with the prospective partner. They described their relationship primarily as preparation for marriage (Lewis et al. 1977).

Characteristics of Cohabiting Couples

Most research on the differences between individuals who choose cohabitation and those who do not has used college-age subjects as the sample. Since nearly two-thirds of the cohabiting couples are older than this age group, it is obvious that the following information presents an incomplete picture. The median age of cohabiting men is 41.4 years, over 24 years younger than the median age of cohabiting women (65.5 years). More than a quarter of cohabiting women are over 75 years old (U.S. Bureau of the Census 1985d, p. 3).

As is true of married couples, most unmarried cohabiting adults live with someone of the same race, nearly the same educational attainment, and in the same general age group. There are approximately equal numbers of never-married and formerly married women who cohabit, but the majority of men who cohabit have previously been married (Spanier 1983).

In general, those who cohabit are fairly representative in many ways of other persons of similar ages. They tend to label themselves as more flexible and more liberal about life than they believe others to be, but the only objective evidence of this comes from some of their personal habits. For instance, they use marijuana and other drugs more often than noncohabitants (Henze and Hudson 1974). They have had a greater variety of sex partners and report less guilt about their sexual behavior than do noncohabitants (Markowski, Croake, and Keller 1978). They report that they are not rigid about sex roles—cohabiting males are more emotionally supportive than noncohabiting males, and females who cohabit are more assertive than those who do not (Macklin 1978). In addition, cohabiting couples report lower incidences of religious affiliation, although they perceive themselves as having many beliefs of a religious nature (Peterman, Ridley, and Anderson 1974).

A recent study has indicated that couples who live together before marriage have less formal weddings, with fewer guests, and are less likely to go on honeymoons (Risman et al. 1981). The couples interviewed reported that, while they were living together, their parents had pressured them either to marry or to quit living together. Another interesting finding was that for cohabiting couples who eventually marry each other, there was a shorter time between their first date and their decision to marry than for noncohabiting couples who marry. It is an open question whether this occurred because of parental pressure or because the cohabiting couples were more serious early in their relationship.

Couples who cohabit usually have friends who are also living together (Macklin 1978). They report an openness of communication and an ease in establishing intimate relationships. One researcher sums up the profile of those who cohabit: "In general, those who take the opportunity to live together have no religious reasons not to, are comfortable engaging in nontraditional behavior, have had considerable interpersonal experience, and want to increase the amount of time spent with the partner because they feel happier when with the partner (Knox 1979, p. 210).

In spite of perceiving themselves as more liberal in nearly every way, most cohabiting couples nonetheless adhere as closely to the traditional division of labor as do their married counterparts (Blumstein and Schwartz 1983). For instance, even more cohabiting females wash the dishes than do married females; the likelihood of responsibility for cooking and menu planning is nearly the same for cohabiting as for married females. The percentages of cohabiting males and married males who cut the lawn, take out the trash, and clean the garage are very similar. As with married couples, more cohabiting females than males are responsible for dusting, vacuuming, and doing the laundry (Stafford, Backman, and DiBona 1977). Perhaps this is because the research has centered primarily on young couples who are still fresh from parental homes with their traditional role models. It would be interesting to determine whether older cohabiting couples follow the same patterns and whether those young couples who stay together evolve into more egalitarian relationships over time.

An interesting finding concerns the difference in male and female views of the meaning of their cohabitation. For younger, previously unmarried couples, the meaning seems to be significantly different. Males view living together rather pragmatically (Jackson 1983). Although fond of their partners, men often report practical reasons for cohabiting. Women, on the other hand, defined their cohabitation as a step toward a stable, long-term relationship.

There is very little research on cohabiting divorced persons when one or both have custody of children from former marriages. Family therapists report that this is a growing phenomenon, even though a search of the literature leaves the distinct impression that it is rare. There was a time—rather recently, in fact—when a custodial parent risked losing his or her children if any sexual involvement could be proved. However, times have changed; the census reports that in 1984, about 30 percent of the unmarried-couple households contained children under the age of fifteen (U.S. Bureau of the Census 1985b, p. 7).

What little information there is on the plight of the "almost stepparent" is mostly about men who have custody and the women (usually childless) who move in with them (Keshet and Rosenthal 1978). In such homes, there are many aspects of role reversal, with the father's child-care and home responsibilities being equally important to, or more important than, his relationship with his lover.

Homosexual Cohabitation

In recent years cohabiting homosexual persons have been more open about their relationships. Many not only live together openly but also consider themselves "married." Some have marriage ceremonies similar to those performed for heterosexual couples. One of the main differences between such unions and heterosexual marriages, of course, is that homosexual marriages are not legally recognized. This creates a situation for homosexual couples nearly identical to that of unmarried heterosexuals who live together on a committed basis. There has been increasing research on same-sex intimate relationships as a type of family form. The studies have shown that there is a growing acceptance of stable couple units within the homosexual community (Jones and Bates 1978; Tanner 1978).

In both Berkeley and West Hollywood, California, unmarried "domestic partners," including homosexual partners, may legally file for a "domestic partnership"—much as they would if they were obtaining a marriage license. City employees who establish such partnerships receive benefits such as medical and other insurance coverage that married employees receive.

In a recent study of homosexual couples, it was determined that nearly all those interviewed were involved in an exclusive relationship that had lasted over a year and were currently leading satisfying personal lives (Bell and Weinberg 1979). Very few differences existed between homosexual couples as a group and heterosexual couples (not all of whom cohabited in either category). Caring for one another and relational adjustment were very similar for the two groups (Lee 1976).

Most homosexual couples are childless, but not all. One or both partners in a lesbian couple often have custody of children from a previous heterosexual union (Silverstein 1977). It is less common for a gay father to have custody of his children and to live in a "marriage" with another man, but this phenomenon may become less unusual as the numbers of both gay couples and custodial fathers increase (Hitchens 1979–1980).

There has been little research on how children fare in a home with a gay parent and a gay "stepparent." In counseling such families, however, we have found that children generally adjust as well as the adults do to their lifestyle. In other words, if the parents are comfortable with their lives, the children adjust well. These families have many of the same problems as other stepfamilies. In addition, however, they have certain other social adjustments to make that may be generated by the attitudes of their peers and of other community members. They may be subjected to teasing, criticism, or in some instances, ostracism. In many respects, the treatment of gay families resembles the treatment received by families of unmarried cohabitants in some very conservative communities (Voeller and Walters 1978).

Cohabiting and Marital Success

There is still no definitive answer to the question of whether cohabitation before marriage increases a couple's chances for success in marriage. Cohabitors who eventually marry each other usually report that living together was beneficial, although little objective evidence exists that they have better marriages than those who did not cohabit

(Jacques and Chason 1979). There is some evidence that the transition to marriage is less stressful for couples who have previously lived together, and as a consequence, the first few months of marriage may be smoother (Watson 1983, p. 139).

A recent study of couples married from 12 to 24 months who had lived together prior to their marriage showed that they rated their marriages as less satisfactory than did a comparison sample of couples who had not lived together before they married (DeMaris and Leslie 1984). Some of this was due to differences in the characteristics of the two samples—such as religion and sex-role traditionalism—but even when the authors controlled for those differences, the effect still was in the direction of lower satisfaction, especially for wives.

Cohabitation appears to be chosen by couples who are less traditional and who may have more difficulty adapting to the role expectations of conventional marriage. It may be that cohabitation itself is not detrimental to marital satisfaction but that the types of people who choose to cohabit are less likely to report high satisfaction after they are married.

Ending the Relationship

As noted, there is a high breakup rate for cohabiting couples. It is quite likely that those that break up are the ones in which one or both partners were not seriously committed or were using living together as a way to avoid commitment (Hill, Rubin, and Peplau 1976). Research that centered primarily on those who enter cohabitation as trial marriage and who marry ceremonially later might show a rate of success that was better than average. However, the factors involved in making marriages work are so complex that it seems doubtful that cohabitation would ever be the deciding factor. Perhaps the greatest benefit cohabitation affords the success of marriages in general is that it keeps some persons from marrying each other at an early age, having children, and later divorcing. As one study concluded: "The best divorce you get is the one you get before you get married" (Hill, Rubin, and Peplau 1976, p. 165).

Breakup of cohabiting couples is not necessarily free of the pain and other stresses associated with divorce, however. For those who are highly committed, the breakup often resembles a divorce in its emotional aspects. This is especially true for couples who may have lived together for several years, making a home together and, in some instances, having a child together.

There are important legal differences between being married and cohabiting, of course. Research in both the United States and Sweden has indicated, for one thing, that commitment is greater in marriage (Budd 1976; Trost 1975). Not only have married couples publicly announced their commitment, but also they have the recognition of family and friends of their intention to make a life together.

Cohabitation and the Law

Legally, of course, there are major differences between married and unmarried co-habitation. Statutes and case law related to cohabitation in the United States vary from state to state and among jurisdictions within states. Although most statutes and court decisions involve the distribution of property when cohabitants separate or when one of them dies, cohabitation itself is illegal in ten states: Arizona, Idaho,

Couples who live together without being legally married are found in nearly every society. However, cohabitation does not always occur for the same reasons in different societies. Cohabitation is usually found in societies in which intimate relationships are left to the couple's discretion; neither government nor other groups such as religious ones have much, if anything, to say about the practice in such countries.

In Denmark, for example, hundreds of couples are involved in "paperless marriages." These relationships may be as permanent as a legal marriage would be. However, women keep their own names and hold their own property. Should children be born, they will use their mother's surname, and she will have legal custody of the children. Some men in Denmark who cohabit in this fashion feel they would be better protected legally if they were married. They would then have rights over their children and legal ways to divide possessions should the marriage end. "Being legally married would not change anything while we are together," one Danish man explained. "We wouldn't love each other more nor be any more secure. It's if the relationship *ends* that having legal status is important."

In many Middle-Eastern countries, women who commit adultery are guilty of a criminal offense. There is, therefore, nothing comparable to cohabitation on a large scale as there is in much of Western Europe and the United States. However, in Iran, there is a custom of "temporary marriage," which permits males to live with women without legally marrying them if the man's wife is ill, pregnant, or is for some other reason, unavailable for sex. If an Iranian man wanted to marry such a woman legally, he could since polygyny is practiced. Usually, however, women who enter "temporary marriages" do so out of financial need and are not considered suitable wives.

Cohabitation is sometimes affected by the male-female ratio. In the People's Republic of China, for example, wives are highly valued because there is currently a shortage of women. There are very low rates of premarital and extramarital sex. Marriages are usually arranged by the parents, and parents of unmarried women protect their daughters' reputations so they will be able to marry well. Parents would never condone living together because traditional, conservative values still prevail. Because there is a shortage of women, men compete for them, and marriage is one way to ensure that they have won.

In Russia, on the other hand, there is a shortage of men, and as a result, there seems to be no urgency for men to marry. Many women cannot marry since there are not enough men to go around. Often they live with single men, who change partners frequently, or even with married men on a "sometime" basis.

In most Latin cultures, both parents and religion place great value on female virginity and chastity. However, free, consensual cohabitation is not uncommon between nonvirginal women and either married or unmarried men. Also, because divorce is made very difficult in Latin countries, desertion is quite common. Since no legal marriage can take place without a divorce, many of those who have deserted their legal spouses cohabit.

Illinois, Massachusetts, Michigan, Mississippi, New Mexico, North Dakota, Virginia, and West Virginia. If one of the cohabitors is married to someone else, cohabitation is illegal in Alabama and South Carolina (*Pomona* [CA] *Progress Bulletin,* May 22, 1986, p. 33). The laws are not enforced with great regularity, but some states provide for a penalty of six months' imprisonment and a $500 fine (Macklin 1978, p. 300). Until recently, unmarried cohabitors had no legal obligations to each other. When they split up, they could both go their own ways, she taking her television set and

The case between actor Lee Marvin (right) and Michelle Triola Marvin (far right)—unmarried cohabitors—over her rights to "palimony" support after their separation brought to the attention of cohabiting couples the need to understand the laws of their states.

he taking his stereo. However, several recent court decisions have changed the obligations and the property ownership of cohabiting persons dramatically (Myricks 1980). These decisions have opened the way for legal enforcement of certain agreements made between unmarried cohabitants.

At present in ten states, an ex-spouse may be excused from paying part or all of support or alimony awarded to an ex-partner who is cohabiting with another person (*Pomona* [CA] *Progress Bulletin,* May 22, 1986, p. 33). Laws and policies about the cohabitation of same-sex persons have been developed in a few jurisdictions, for example Berkeley and West Los Angeles, California, but we were unable to find any systematic collection of them. Many states solve legal problems related to cohabitation by declaring cohabitants legally married under certain conditions, usually but not always related to the period of time that they have cohabited.

A landmark case involved actor Lee Marvin and Michelle Triola, a woman who lived with him for seven years and who took his last name, becoming known as Michelle Marvin. After they separated, Lee Marvin supported her for nearly two years. When the support ceased, Michelle Marvin sued, claiming that Lee Marvin had promised to support her for life and to share his earnings with her if she would drop her career as an entertainer and live with him. During the seven years they lived together (during a part of which he was still married), they purchased no joint property and filed separate income tax returns. This later became an issue in the case because Lee Marvin's attorneys claimed that this indicated that he meant to keep his assets separate. Michelle Marvin was eventually awarded $104,000 in 1979 as compensation for the years that her career was set aside and as a fund to help her financially while she reestablished herself ("Marvin v. Marvin" 1979, p. 3109). Although the decision did not award her either lifetime support or a share of Lee Marvin's earnings, she was the first unmarried person to win "equitable relief" similar to that offered to married

persons by alimony. The term **palimony** was coined to describe this award, and since then several other cases have been decided in a similar fashion (Myricks 1980). In 1981, a California appellate court overturned the ruling, denying the award in the process. Michelle Marvin's attorneys appealed once more, and a decision was given that the couple had a contract agreement for Michelle Marvin's services that was separate from the couple's voluntary living arrangements. In other words, California still did not recognize nonceremonial marriage but did acknowledge contracts between two unmarried persons who live together.

Couples who cohabit are well advised to understand the laws of their states. Many lawyers advise unmarried cohabiting couples to draw up a contract specifying exactly how they want to agree on property and earnings. There can be a contract *not* to share or a contract *to* share. Lawyers often suggest:

1. Couples should list the major items each brought to the relationship.
2. Any property acquired while living together should belong to whoever paid for it, unless each partner's proportionate share of ownership has been spelled out at the time of purchase.
3. Any agreements to share earnings or property while living together or in the future should be put in writing.
4. Couples should keep separate bank accounts and credit cards and should keep names as they were before living together.
5. If large investments—for example, a condominium or a house—are made jointly, both names should be on the deed or mortgage, and it should be stated clearly what happens to the property in case of a breakup. This advice is also applicable when the couple signs a rental or lease agreement (Macovsky 1979).

Cohabiting couples also face other important differences from married couples with respect to insurance and taxes. Automobile insurers, for instance, consider even a long-term cohabiting couple as two single persons. Not only does each partner pay premiums higher than those married couples would pay, but cohabiting couples also do not qualify for the discount usually given for a second family car. Health insurance plans cover the couple as though each were single, denying them the lower rate a spouse enjoys. In fact, one unmarried partner may not even include the other as a dependent, but each must have his or her own coverage. In case of death of one partner, employee survivors' benefits often are payable only to spouses (Macovsky 1979).

The way taxes are levied on two unmarried cohabitors can be more advantageous than for married couples if each has large deductions and both are employed. However, if one stays at home, in the nineteen states in which cohabitation is a crime, that partner does not qualify as a dependent (as a spouse or other relative would).

In his book, *Oh Promise Me but Put It in Writing,* civil lawyer Paul Ashley (1978) recommends legal agreements such as joint ownership agreements, partnerships, and other types of contracts whether or not the couples live in states where cohabitation is legal. He cautions couples in states where they are breaking the laws by living together to avoid mentioning this fact in their contracts, but encourages them nonetheless to have a "proper agreement."

SUMMARY

1. There has been a gradual increase in the number of men and women who are choosing to remain single for long periods of their lives. Most eventually marry or have been married.
2. Sex roles have been changing. In particular, women have more life options than ever before. With greater economic opportunities for women has come a degree of liberation from stereotyped sex roles for both men and women. Not only is being single growing more attractive, but also marriage is increasingly seen as restrictive, especially for those who have been married.
3. Demographers have called attention to the "marriage squeeze" brought about by the two cycles of rising and falling fertility rates in the United States. This has resulted in later marriages for many persons.
4. There is no one "single" lifestyle; instead, there are probably as many as there are single persons. Two major factors seem most important in determining how singles live, however: age and whether singlehood is voluntary or involuntary.
5. Women seem to fare better in singlehood than do men. Some family-life experts suggest that women profit less from marriage than men do. Another explanation is that men who do not marry may be the rejected ones, whereas women may more often choose to remain unmarried. The concept of the "marriage gradient" has been proposed to explain this phenomenon. Females tend to marry upward and males downward in terms of various measures of status. Consequently, when the most eligible men are taken, women of higher status have so few partners to choose from that they often opt to remain single.
6. Unmarried sex has come to be accepted by more and more persons, especially by those who delay marriage for several years beyond the average age at which their

peers marry. Sex between marriages also has become the rule rather than the exception. However, most unmarried persons who engage in coitus have only one or two partners in the space of a year and thus are far from promiscuous.

7. Approval of and participation in unmarried sex is far from universal, however. There are still those who favor abstinence and those who choose long-term celibacy.

8. A variation of the double standard is still widely held in the United States. Even though women are gaining sexual equality with men in many ways, the notion that casual sex is less acceptable for women than for men is still common.

9. Few men or women condone sexual permissiveness without some kind of relationship. Even those who feel that the sole prerequisite of coitus is mutual agreement between the individuals involved often believe that sex with affection is very different from (if not necessarily better than) sex without affection.

10. Unmarried sex has its problems—sexually transmitted diseases, pregnancy, unavailability of a propitious time and place for the encounter—but despite the difficulties, it is a growing phenomenon and is expected to continue to increase in the next decades.

11. Although it is impossible to get an accurate count of the number of unmarried persons who cohabit, there is agreement that the numbers have grown dramatically in recent years among both young never-married persons and those who have been divorced or widowed. Beyond the problem of determining the numbers accurately, it also has been difficult to define *cohabitation* precisely.

12. About half of all cohabiting couples have never been married, but over 90 percent of young persons who cohabit plan to marry someone eventually. Thus, cohabitation is not taking the place of marriage but appears instead to be part of the courtship process for many, as well as a way of delaying marriage.

13. One major reason that cohabitation has grown in popularity is that sexual values have changed, making it less important for couples to marry before they engage in coitus. As these attitudes have come to be shared by large numbers of single persons, social attitudes about living together have also changed among a sizable portion of the population.

14. Many levels of commitment are found in cohabiting couples, ranging from minimal commitment to an intention to live together for a lifetime. In general, those who cohabit are fairly representative of other persons of similar ages.

15. Homosexual "marriages" have grown more frequent in recent years and are another form of unmarried cohabitation because they are not recognized as legal in any state. Most homosexual couples are childless, but some have custody of children from a previous heterosexual union. This type of home may become more common in the future.

16. There is a high breakup rate for cohabiting couples, perhaps because many are not highly committed to the relationship from the beginning. There is still no definitive answer to the question of whether living together helps a future marriage between the two persons involved.

17. Couples who live together must face certain legal problems. Lawyers advise unmarried cohabiting couples to draw up a contract specifying exactly how they want to agree on division of property and earnings.

GLOSSARY

Chlamydia A widespread bacterial disease that attacks the female reproductive system. Although carried and transmissible by members of both sexes, its effects are most serious and most painful in women; it can result in pelvic inflammation, ectopic pregnancy, miscarriage, and sterility. Chlamydia is transmitted by sexual contact. It can be cured quickly and inexpensively by antibiotics if treated promptly. (p. 128)

Gonorrhea A bacterial disease causing inflammation of the genital organs. An acute infection is obvious and painful in males, but may be difficult to detect in females. It can cause sterility in females and blindness in babies delivered vaginally to an infected mother. It can be cured if treated promptly. (p. 128)

Herpes simplex II An infection caused by a virus, characterized by open lesions on the genital organs. It is caused by contact of the genitalia with infected mucous surfaces. It can cause death and mental retardation in babies delivered vaginally to a mother in an acute stage of the disease. There is as yet no known cure. (p. 128)

Marriage gradient A term coined to describe the tendency of lower- and middle-class women to marry men of higher social and economic status than they. (p. 125)

Palimony Court order to pay a former cohabitant support, civil damages, or a share of community property earned during the period of cohabitation, based on proof of intent to establish a household even though no valid marriage existed. (p. 139)

6

Sometimes I think people were meant to be strangers. Not to get to know one another,
not to get close enough to damage the heart made older by each new encounter.
But then, someone comes along and changes all that.

Even though in general there may be less pressure on young Americans to marry than there was in the past, marriage is still a life-course experience that nearly all people expect to have sooner or later. Very few persons (probably less than 5 percent of the population) live alone or with a member of their families of origin all their lives. The increase in the number of couples living together without marrying has not seemed to decrease significantly the number who eventually marry. Cohabitation may delay marriage, but ultimately nearly everyone walks down the aisle—a growing number more than once. Some are looking for "that special person" or a "marriage made in heaven." Others are just looking for *someone* and seek the best prospect through work, church, friends, dating bureaus, or even newspaper advertisements. Family specialists are interested in the process of mate selection and in the ways that people successfully move from singlehood to marriage or to unmarried cohabitation.

MATE SELECTION AND GETTING MARRIED

*C*hoosing a marriage partner is a serious business. In many parts of the world it involves an agreement of the families of both prospective partners and sometimes religious and community leaders. At the other extreme, some partners make their choice in what appears to be an impetuous manner, involving very little deliberation and no consultation with parents or other kin.

The way people pair off for marriage is usually determined by the way they were socialized. Sociologists point out that no matter how couples ultimately make their decision to marry, they follow social dictates prescribed by their societal norms. Even elopement follows a pattern that has existed in Western societies for many centuries.

There are mating patterns in many societies that seem quite strange to Americans. Such patterns not only are different across cultures but may vary at different periods of history in any given society. A look at these different patterns, historically and cross-culturally, sheds light on how we have come to adopt the ways that are popular in the United States.

■ MATE SELECTION CROSS-CULTURALLY

In eighteenth-century America, the early settlers sometimes sent across the Atlantic for unseen brides and met them for the first time when they arrived at the dock. Selections, although sometimes made by family members, might also be made by a ship's officer, who would deliver a marriageable woman for the price of her passage. In the nineteenth and early twentieth centuries, Chinese laborers in the United States ordered brides from the Orient from agencies that distributed pictures of prospective mates. Even today, Orthodox Jews in particular may seek the help of a "marriage broker"—either a professional or a nonprofessional—to help find a suitable marriage partner.

In other parts of the world, arranged marriages still occur. In Turkey, for instance, a study reported that in 1975 three-quarters of the marriages were arranged by the families or their designated intermediaries (Fox 1975). In other areas the arrangement may be largely ceremonial, but couples are far from having the kind of free choice taken for granted in the United States. In Japan, half of the marriages are arranged either by families or by matchmakers. Young people may have a veto over parents' choices for them, but few defy their parents by marrying someone of whom the parents disapprove. The Japanese have even enlisted the computer to help find suitable mates for those of marriageable age. The large firm Mitsubishi runs such a service for its employees and for friends and relatives of employees. Over 25,000 marriages have resulted from the use of its computer (*Singapore Straits Times,* August 29, 1983, p. 1).

In the urban centers of Ghana, personal choice has grown in importance, but there is ample evidence that parental consent still is sought and given in choosing marriage partners in much of the country (Oppong 1981). A South African black man never proposes directly but sends an aunt or uncle to intercede for him. Mexican men usually go with their parents and sometimes a priest to ask the woman's parents formally for her hand in marriage. In Russian or Albanian communities, the man's parents almost always go to the woman's home to discuss the marriage proposal with her parents.

In general, the trend for the world as a whole over the past ten years has been toward more self-determination for couples in choosing their mates. The rate of movement toward freer choices seems to be related to industrialization and, in particular, to the growing role of middle-class women in subsistence-level or higher-income production (Adams 1979). In his review of the literature on mate selection in the 1970s, psychologist Bernard Murstein (1980, p. 779) concludes:

> It can be speculated that, cross-culturally, the absence of economic means for the woman leads to early marriage and little individual freedom. The possibility of working leads women to avoid arranged marriages, enhances the possibility of love matches, and may slightly diminish the marriage rate.

Although it is often difficult for contemporary Americans to understand, historically "love matches" have had very little to do with the choice of a life partner in much of the world. Most Americans firmly believe that it would be miserable, possibly tragic, perhaps even immoral, to enter into a life partnership without being in love. Yet in many present-day societies and in some cultural groups, getting married simply because one is in love is considered frivolous at best (Goode 1959).

Although the marriage of Edward VIII of England to Wallis Warfield Simpson in the 1930s delighted the hearts of romantics because he gave up the throne for the woman he loved, others (including his own family and especially the Queen Mother) saw his behavior as weak and irresponsible. In their opinion, anyone who thought that marriage should be based on love alone was insufficiently wise and mature to be king of England, especially when the woman involved had no royal ancestry and was divorced. "Love," for them, could not possibly compensate for these flaws. Whether Prince Charles and Princess Diana have changed the royal perception of love versus duty must be left to history to determine.

As young persons have moved away from the direct influence of their parents in choosing their mates, the trend has been away from practical criteria for selecting a partner and toward more emotional criteria and a greater concern with love as the basis for a lifelong commitment.

Although it may seem that in the United States we have as much free choice as possible to fall in love and choose a mate, there continue to be restrictions and factors that predetermine our choices. There are "automatic disqualifications" or filters for mate selection that occur upon acquaintance—or even before. These reduce the pool of possible eligible mates (Winch 1958). Thus, whether marriage partners are chosen by parents, family, or the participants themselves, there is a social context within which the choice is made.

DIFFERENTIAL ASSOCIATION

Everyone spends more time with some persons than with others. This is known as **differential association** and is one of the important determinants of who will be part of the potential pool of mates for a given person. Differential association occurs for a number of reasons. One is simply that of physical availability or **propinquity.** A child is likely to spend less time with a playmate who lives a mile away than with one who lives next door. We associate more with our schoolmates or co-workers than with persons who live and work far away. Several studies have shown that the geographic accessibility of an attractive potential partner may make a big difference in whether a relationship persists (Saegert, Swap, and Zajonc 1973).

Geographic accessibility, however, although necessary, is by no means sufficient. We may never become friends with our next-door neighbors or with some of our co-workers. Another important factor in differential association, therefore, is the amount of time people spend together. Some of this is not so much the result of mutual attraction as it is of **functional involvement.** For instance, members of the same household usually find it more efficient to eat their meals in the same place and at the same time, to take vacations together, to visit relatives and friends together, and even to do some household chores together. People who go to the same school, work in the same place, attend the same church, or do the same type of volunteer work have to spend some time together in order to achieve their goals.

Propinquity, or nearness of physical location, and functional involvement are components of mate selection that play a powerful role in providing or denying the opportunity for selection to occur. Most people get together in one of the ways mentioned here, although some resort to dating services or advertisements to meet those whose paths they might otherwise not cross. Even the advertisements in a magazine such as *Intro,* however, typically indicate either the area in which the persons placing the notices live or the area in which they wish to meet people. Most people find enough attractive persons nearby or through their activities to make voluntary friendships or to choose special friends and lovers.

NEGATIVE AND POSITIVE FACTORS IN MATE SELECTION

Although there is general agreement on some of the factors involved in bringing two people together as a couple—propinquity and functional involvement, for instance—there are many other variables in attraction that are harder to explain. Obviously, one does not establish a relationship with every person of a suitable age who lives nearby or with every person with whom one is functionally involved. Neither does one establish a relationship with every sexually attractive person one encounters.

Negative Factors

The pool of prospective partners is always reduced by factors that are often beyond our control—historical, cultural, social, and physiological features. Those factors that reduce the population from which one selects are called *negative factors* in selection. They determine those persons who may not be (or at least have little probability of being) chosen as partners. Since, as already noted, propinquity brings people together, geographic distance is thus a negative factor. A woman in Coos Bay, Oregon, is not likely to develop a love relationship with a person in Ullapool, Scotland, simply because she is unlikely to know that such a person even exists. A Northern Irish

Prince Andrew and Sarah Ferguson (shown here before their wedding) illustrate the concept of homogomy— marrying one's own kind. In real life, the wealthy prince seldom marries the poor shopkeeper's daughter but instead chooses a bride whose background is similar to his own.

Protestant may be unlikely to fall in love with a Northern Irish Catholic—not because of geographic distance but because of the historical struggle between Catholics and Protestants in Northern Ireland. Similarly, negative factors may restrict the field of eligible persons by ruling out prison or mental hospital inmates, slum dwellers, college professors, vegetarians, "liberated women," or just about any category of persons about whom one might say "I wouldn't (or couldn't) marry . . ."

Homogamy   The sum of the negative factors in partner selection leads to a condition called **homogamy**—the tendency of persons to select as mates those who have several significant characteristics similar to their own. There is a common belief that people voluntarily seek out those who are like themselves. Sometimes this may be true, but it seems more likely that the choices of persons who are similar on the variables usually studied—social class, race, religion, educational background, and so forth—are the result of the failure of people to be attracted by those who are very different from themselves. In other words, they screen out persons dissimilar in some negatively significant way rather than looking consciously for those who are similar.

A Protestant male from Northern Ireland does not choose a particular mate simply *because* she is Protestant—after all, there are many Protestants from whom to choose. What is important to him is to avoid marrying a Catholic. He does not choose his mate *because* she is near his age but because she is neither "too old" nor "too young." He does not choose her *because* she is of his social class but because she is neither a snob nor a slob (unless he is either a snob or a slob).

Exogamy and Endogamy　Regulation of the potential pool of partners whom we do meet is accomplished by a variety of other factors that determine who is and who is not eligible for marriage. Two fairly common social regulations are **exogamy** and **endogamy.** Exogamy rules out large numbers of persons from the field of eligibles by requiring that mates be chosen from outside specified groups of people. For instance, in some tribal societies marrying a member of one's own clan or tribe may be prohibited. The best-known exogamy rule is that no legal marriages are allowed between persons who are close kin (incest) or who are of the same sex (homosexual). Endogamy, on the other hand, disqualifies those who are not within a certain set of boundaries that are socially acceptable.

Race is as good an example as any of endogamy. Although a few persons do choose mates who are of a different race, the majority do not do so. Interracial marriage accounts for only about 3 percent of all marriages in the United States (Spanier 1983). In a decision handed down on June 12, 1967, the U.S. Supreme Court ruled that laws prohibiting interracial marriage were unconstitutional. Before that date, 40 states had such laws at one time or another. In spite of the change in the laws, however, in many communities informal sanctions still operate to cause members of certain racial groups to marry only within these groups.

Interracial marriages are increasing, however. From 1970 to 1980, the number of black-white marriages more than doubled (mostly black men marrying white women), and yet, over 95 percent of both black men and women marry in their own group, as do approximately 70 percent of Asians. Only American Indians marry outside their group in large numbers—about 55 percent do, mostly to whites (Alba 1985, p. 3).

Interethnic marriage is now so common that only one out of four American-born whites marries someone of exactly the same ethnic ancestry. Ethnic intermarriage varies according to age and region, a study by New York demographer Richard Alba (1985) reported. Younger people have a higher out-marriage rate than did their parents; the rate in the South is lower than elsewhere.

Studies of intermarriage involving those with Spanish surnames document a wide variation in the rate of intermarriage, depending on the state or county under consideration. In California, a 55 percent rate of intermarriage was found (Shoen, Nelson, and Collins 1978). Other research indicates that the increase in Chicano exogamy has generally been slow in more rural areas and in border counties where a larger pool of partners of the same ethnicity is available (Murguia and Cazares 1982).

Interreligious marriage is another example of the principles of exogamy and endogamy. There has been an increase in religiously mixed couples since 1957, indicating a strong continuing trend toward secularization of the institution of marriage (Glenn 1982). Jews seem to be an exception, although there is a large amount of switching of religion and moving away from religion in anticipation of marriage or immediately afterward (Farber and Gordon 1982).

All kinds of prejudices and antipathies lead to automatic disqualification of persons from consideration as partners for a long-term intimate relationship. Many disqualifications are based on some personal characteristic, ranging from sexual orientation and religion to tastes in clothing and language habits. As discussed previously, disqualifying all but a few in this way tends to have the effect of homogamy or similarity between those who finally choose each other. In other words, homogamy arises not from positive selection of those who are similar as much as from lack of interest in or sympathetic understanding of whole categories of people.

This interreligious marriage illustrates the trend in the United States toward free choice of partner based on compatibility, love, and secular factors rather than on religious background.

One of the most important disqualifiers of potential partners is age. Although most persons prefer to choose marriage partners within a range of ages near their own, social pressures may be brought to bear on persons who "rob the cradle," "marry their mothers," or "find a father figure." There are no statutory upper limits to the ages of persons wishing to marry, but every state has statutes, or "age of consent" laws, prohibiting persons below specified ages from marrying (see Table 6.2 on p. 160).

It has been customary in most societies for the husband to be older than the wife. Most likely this is because women have traditionally been viewed as dependent on men, who were expected to be responsible for and to assume authority over them. Also, since a main objective of marriage was to produce children, men had to be prepared to support a family soon after marrying. One would suppose that with changes in men's and women's roles, the ages at first marriage would no longer show that males are older. In fact, there has been a gradual decrease in the age gap at first marriage since 1890, when the average difference was 4 years. By 1930, the gap had dropped to 3 years and by 1950 to 2.5 years; it remained fairly constant until 1974, when the difference narrowed to 2 years. However, in 1975 it returned to 2.5 years, where it has since remained with only minor fluctuations. The age at first marriage in 1984 was 25.4 years for men and 23.0 years for women, or 2.4 years difference (U.S. Bureau of the Census 1985b, p. 1). Old traditions are slow to fade, it seems, regardless of role change.

Kinship is another negative selective factor for most people with respect to partnership attraction. As with age of consent laws, every state has laws prohibiting incest. Typically, incest laws prohibit marriage to or sexual relations with ancestors, descendants, brothers, sisters, uncles, aunts, nephews, and nieces. Some states include first cousins as well as many specific other relationships (half-brother, steprelative, and so forth). These taboos are so ingrained that the thought of dating someone who falls into one of these categories does not even occur to most people. They would quickly dismiss the thought even if they felt such an attraction. Such laws do not always prevent involvement, however, and there are exceptions to all of these general attitudes. Again, as with age of consent, laws cannot prevent attraction but can provide punishment for behaviors resulting from attraction. Incest laws probably reflect usual patterns of attraction rather than determining them.

Interactive Disqualifications   Other ways in which endogamy regulates mate selection involve the system of interaction—the flow of responses—that develops between two persons. We tend to exclude those who do not interact well with us and to include those whose behaviors are congruous with our expectations. This kind of disqualification—often expressed as "we just can't get along" or more often as "I just don't like him"—may reflect a simple lack of social skills on the part of the evaluator, chiefly in the area of communication but also often in a lack of **empathy**—an understanding of how another person feels. Lack of empathy is closely related to limited experiences and produces communication problems, including complaints that "he doesn't respect my feelings" or, more dramatically, "she doesn't treat me like a human being!" and is likely to disqualify the nonempathic person as a potential partner.

Interactional disqualification occurs when people cannot communicate well. When they cannot share their feelings and meanings, each has to guess who the other is. The result is that each has a mental picture of the other that sooner or later will be inconsistent with the other's actual behavior. When that happens, expectations are not met and disappointment occurs. Although communication and empathy are never perfect, if they contribute to too many disappointments, they make it unpleasant to maintain a relationship.

Another kind of interactive disqualifier has been reported in some recent research showing that sex drive and sex interest are also assortatively selected. In other words, engaged couples have significantly greater agreement on their respective needs for sex than do others who are dating (Centers 1975). Murstein (1980, p. 789), suggests that by 1990 marital choice may well be influenced more by such dynamic aspects of interpersonal relations than by the traditional sociocultural disqualifiers, such as race, religion, and social class.

Positive Factors

Positive factors are those that motivate one to choose another in order to gain some value or goal or to enhance one's self-concept or general feeling of well-being, often expressed as, "I want to marry someone who . . ." Positive factors seem more likely to change through one's life cycle than do negative factors. At 18 a woman may be attracted to a good dancer, at 28 to a high achiever, at 58 to a good companion. She may always find all these qualities desirable, but her priorities may shift.

Balance Theory   A basic theory of *homogamy* is Fritz Heider's *balance theory* (1958). Generally, balance theory maintains that less stress is produced when one selects a partner who has the same beliefs, thoughts, and feelings about other persons, ideas, and events. People tend to like and to feel comfortable with others who think and feel as they do. They may have less to argue about, as well as more in common to talk about and enjoy together.

Suppose that one of Darleen's main satisfactions in life comes from knowing that she is intellectually capable and that she takes particular pride in her excellent academic record. While she is talking with Daniel and Joe at a college orientation meeting, Daniel remarks that he hopes he can make an "A" in his English course because he plans to try to get into one of the best graduate schools. Joe laughs at him and says that he (Joe) is not going to waste his time going to graduate school but intends to get out of college as soon as possible and become a salesman. All things being equal (which they never quite seem to be), according to Heider's balance theory, Darleen will like the academically motivated Daniel better than she likes Joe. She will say that she and Daniel have "more in common."

Being "too tall" or "too short," having a "bad temper" or a prison record, having children by another partner—all these are reasons that some people are disqualified as mates. A moment's reflection or a little research will reveal that such persons usually are chosen as mates by someone; we know of no hard data demonstrating that such choices are any less happy in the long run than others. The fact is simply that each person has a set of judgments about who is a suitable mate, and most of us tend to be as choosy as we dare. Murstein (1980, p. 786) believes that we may more often *settle for* than *choose* a partner: "... only individuals with numerous interpersonal assets and few liabilities really *choose* each other. Those with fewer assets and more liabilities often *settle* for each other."

Assortativeness   Research on mate selection consistently shows strong evidence that automatic disqualification is a force that moves those who are similar toward each other (Trost 1967). The term **assortativeness** is often used in the literature to describe how traits or persons are distributed into similar groups or varieties. Assortativeness is well documented as a factor in mate selection in such categories as age, education, intelligence, socioeconomic status, race, and (to a somewhat lesser extent) ethnic background and religion. In addition, personality traits also have been shown to lend themselves to assortativeness. For example, similar traits such as kindness or intelligence draw potential mates to each other (Buss 1985).

It is possible that college admissions offices are among the most effective matchmakers in the United States. They screen for academic ability, give men and women of equal educational background an opportunity to meet each other, and provide a pool of eligible persons of similar age and socioeconomic backgrounds from whom to choose (or for whom to settle).

It is interesting how often marriage partners are from the same social class. Although one study has reported that upper-class women "marry down" in socioeconomic class more often than men do, interclass marriage in the United States has been shown to be quite infrequent (Glenn, Ross, and Tully 1974). The high degree of consistency of the social classes of marriage partners is hardly surprising, considering that social class is significantly related to education, occupation, values, attitudes, and goals. Two people with so much in common are much more likely to like each other and to want to spend time together: they speak the same language.

THEORIES OF MATE SELECTION

Social scientists have long been interested in why two people choose each other to marry. Theories have developed around the basic notion that in a society where there is relatively free choice to pick a mate, factors that influence who eventually is selected depend greatly on partners' mutual estimates of interpersonal assets and liabilities.

While there is need for more research in mate selection to add to existing information, there are some existing theories that partially explain how and why choices are made. Perhaps there will never be one grand unifying theory but instead several well-tested ones. Each may answer some of the many questions concerning mate selection.

Exchange Theory

Exchange theory may be the most widely accepted explanation of interpersonal attraction (Nye 1979). Chapter 3 described part of Murstein's stimulus-value-role theory of general attraction. This is an exchange theory that posits that "in a relatively free choice situation, attraction and interaction depend on the exchange of value of the assets and liabilities that each of the parties brings to the situation" (Murstein 1980, p. 785). This theory holds that the basis for a continuing relationship between two partners is that each believes he or she will get as much or more from the relationship as it will cost. Exchange theory was not developed as a mate-selection theory, but it has interesting implications for understanding the way in which two people choose each other as mates. Since the theory implies that those who are looking for mates all have the same idea—to maximize their chances for a rewarding marriage—partners more often than not wind up being quite equal in their abilities to reward one another (Scanzoni 1979a). Those who believe they have a good deal to offer will choose someone who also has resources or traits that seem valuable. In other words, each person compares his or her assets and liabilities with those of a potential partner. Anyone above or below this *comparison level of exchange* is likely to be disqualified (Thibaut and Kelley 1959).

Equity Theory

A variation on exchange theory in explaining mate selection has been described as *equity theory* (Walster, Walster, and Traupmann 1978). In simple terms, equity is fairness. Most people believe it is most fair to get benefits from a relationship in proportion to what they give to the relationship. Giving to a partner may be measured in ways that are complex (Blau 1964), and fairness is not the same as equality. For instance, an agreement that each partner will spend the same number of dollars on apartment rent may seem unfair if one partner's income is much lower than the other's even though both work an equal number of hours. It is just as uncomfortable to feel one is shortchanging one's partner as to feel one is being shortchanged; indeed the partner with the better deal may develop contempt for the other. Equity theory stresses that one is attracted by a fair deal rather than by a profitable exchange.

Fairness is partly psychological. For example, a campus beauty who dates the football captain may feel that the value of her prettiness should be judged by its scarcity and that the relationship is equitable because football captains are also scarce. He, on the other hand, may feel that the value of becoming football captain should be judged by the amount of time and effort necessary to attain the position and that, since being pretty requires little effort for her, she should contribute something more than her looks to make the relationship equitable.

Even though the analogy of the market is often used to explain exchange theory, neither exchange theory nor equity theory should be understood in terms of objective monetary values alone. More often in interpersonal relations, intangibles like thought and effort are the primary considerations. For example, a person may feel that a handknit sweater either is or is not an equitable exchange for an expensive watch. If the person who knitted the sweater spent hours working on it but believes that the person who bought the watch spent no more than fifteen minutes picking it out and perhaps charged it to a parent, the knitter may feel that the inequitable exchange (in terms of energy, care, and time spent) lessens the attractiveness of both the watch and the watch-giver.

In equity theory, as described by Walster, Walster, and Traupmann (1978), persons feel attracted to others from whom they get as much as they give. As a corollary, we propose that at least for some persons the getting is no more important for attraction than equity of the *giving* on both sides.

It has been suggested that the values involved in judging equity may include physical attractiveness, mental health, physical health, family background, family solidity, and popularity (Hall and Hall 1979). One can easily expand that list by adding items such as career expectations, potential income, political and religious status, sexual skill, and a host of other personal values.

Complementary Needs Theory

Family sociologist Robert Winch (1958) and others have explored attraction as a relationship between two (or possibly more) persons who could be said to have needs that the other *complements*. Although most theories of mate selection propose that each partner believes his or her functioning in the relationship is dependent on the other's behavior, few make this as clear as Winch does in his concept of "complementary needs" in mate selection.

Winch, as well as his followers and his critics, has tended to limit his discussions to the attractiveness of complementary personality needs. He described two types of complementarity. In the first type, known as "Type I complementarity," a person with high needs in certain areas is attracted to a person with few needs in the *same* areas. For example, consider Gary, who has a tremendous need to talk constantly, and Geraldine, to whom he is attracted, at least in part because she rarely feels the need to talk at all, thus giving Gary the opportunity to do almost all the talking when they are together. It pleases Geraldine that Gary talks enough for both of them. An example of Type I complementarity is that of the couple with one member who has hands large enough to grip and unscrew pickle jar lids while the other has hands small enough to reach inside the jar when it is opened. The result: both can enjoy the pickles!

"Type II complementarity" occurs when people are attracted to each other because each has *different* needs that the other can satisfy. This can be illustrated by the case of Fred and Frieda. Fred loves to eat, and Frieda needs to be appreciated. She also loves to cook (as most good cooks do), and Fred hates to cook. When they get together, their mutual needs ensure a satisfying time. Frieda cooks for Fred, who in turn gives her the appreciation she needs.

If the notion of complementarity seems to be contradictory to the theory of homogamy, it is probably because both have been overgeneralized. Most couples are likely to consist of two persons who are homogamous in several census-listed characteristics but complementary in many idiosyncratic ones. They may be alike in educational, religious, and family-income backgrounds, for instance, but have complementary differences in certain areas of interpersonal, intimate behavior. They may be alike racially (homogamous) but of opposite, mutually gratifying sexual orientation (one is turned on by female sexuality, the other by male, and thus they are complementary). The roles played by two marital partners may be influenced by the fact that the two are very similar in consumer values, recreational interests, and economic goals, and also by their complementarity. As the old nursery rhyme puts it, "Jack Sprat could eat no fat; His wife could eat no lean; And so between the greedy pair, They licked the platter clean!"

So far, the possibility that complementarity is the main factor in mate selection for most people has not been demonstrated empirically. Complementarity is clearly neither the only process nor even the most important process involved in choosing a mate, but it does account for some kinds of attraction.

Psychodynamic Theory

Childhood interaction with one's parents or other family members is thought to affect mate selection because it is believed that a person searches for a partner who will help him or her to reenact earlier emotional experiences. Some have suggested that a woman looks for a man similar to her father and that a man seeks a wife who resembles his mother (Freud 1927). The song lyric "I want a girl just like the girl who married dear old Dad" reflects this belief. There is little current research to support this contention, however, although one study has shown that mothers' images often influence the marital choices of both their sons and their daughters (Aron et al. 1974).

Psychodynamic influences include such explanations of mate choice as **imprinting**—an emotional attachment developed in the early months of life to persons with particular physical characteristics—which is reputed to cause a search for a mate whose physical appearance is just right. Studies of *birth order* are another attempt to find answers to why certain persons choose each other to marry (Toman 1969). Birth order refers to whether one is the firstborn, second, last, or only child. Some well-done studies have failed to support the original research (Birtchnell and Mayhew 1977), and still others have shown that size of the family may have a more pronounced effect on personality than does birth order (Hayes 1981). Other studies, however, support the notion that birth order does affect not only the way one perceives others but also other personality and behavior patterns (Forer and Still 1976).

It has been suggested that an only child may be at a disadvantage in marriage because he or she has never experienced competition in intimate relationships and may also have an exaggerated sense of importance in relationships. According to the birth-order theory, the oldest brother in a family of sons should get along better with men than with women. His aggressiveness and need to control suggest that his happiest choice of mate would be a woman who functions in a subservient manner.

FIGURE 6 · 1
Filtering Process in
Mate Selection

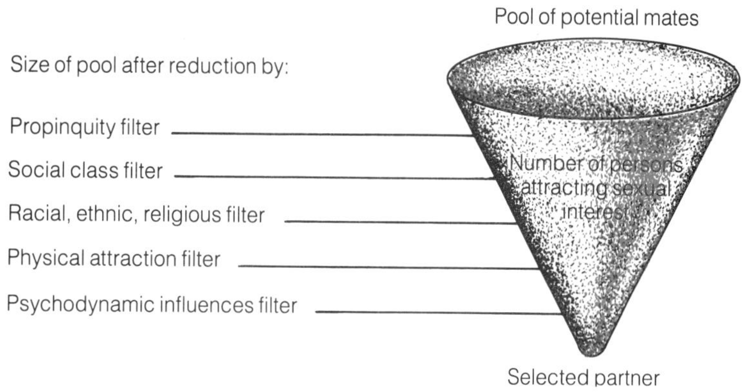

Size of pool after reduction by:

Pool of potential mates

Propinquity filter _____

Social class filter _____

Racial, ethnic, religious filter _____

Physical attraction filter _____

Psychodynamic influences filter _____

Number of persons attracting sexual interest

Selected partner

Source: David Klimek, *Beneath Mate Selection and Marriage: The Unconscious Motives in Human Pairing* (New York: Van Nostrand Reinhold, 1979), p. 13. Used by permission.

The youngest son in a family with all male children was reported to be imaginative but shy and awkward around females. His most compatible partner thus ought to be an oldest sister of brothers, provided that she is nurturant and capable (Toman 1969).

Such analyses can also be made for the oldest brother of sisters, the youngest brother of sisters, the oldest sister of sisters, and so on. The general conclusion is that people have better chances of happiness in relationships when they choose partners who allow them to enact the roles that they learned in their families of origin and that they are therefore presumably attracted to such persons more often than chance would dictate (Forer and Still 1976).

Although birth-order theory, which may in some instances be relevant to how men and women choose each other for marriage partners, is appealing, its general application is still questioned. Perhaps the statement of two researchers who have done exhaustive work on birth order sums up the implications of birth-order theory: "In marriage consider yourself and your partner as unique people, partially molded and trained in special ways of relating to others by the accident of your birth position" (Forer and Still 1976, p. 286).

Process Theory

Mate selection is clearly a process of choice determined by a complex assortment of social and psychological factors that both restrict and enhance choice. Figure 6.1 shows David Klimek's conceptualization of the hierarchy of filters used to sort through all potential mates to the final choice of a partner. The filtering process has been called a "funnel" because the initially large number of possible partners is reduced by each filter until only a few eligibles remain for the final choice. Since two people are engaged in the same selection process, Broderick has called it "the double funnel" (Broderick, personal communication, May 1981).

Process theories insist that there can be no single-principle approach but that instead there are many factors that determine marital choice (Lewis 1972; Centers

WHAT MAKES LOVE GROW?

Every married couple has a story to tell about how they met and began the path that eventually led to their wedding. We have been collectors of these stories over the years and have heard some interesting ones. Some partners do not agree when they met, which is no surprise to us because we don't tell the same story either. One of us insists that the meeting occurred weeks before the other remembers that it did.

Some couples grow up next door to each other or have known each other for years before they gradually come to realize that they love each other more than just as good friends. Others meet in the supermarket, in class, at work, at the beach, or through a dating service. Still others have unusual and even quite dramatic meetings. One of our favorite stories is told by a friend:

> I was walking down the street one summer evening and saw a girl I had never seen before sitting on her porch reading a book. Something—some force—made me stop. I introduced myself and said, "You don't know who I am or anything about me, but I have a feeling you and I are going to be married." To this day I have no idea what made me say that. She laughed and said, "That's impossible because I'm already engaged." "Break it off," I replied. And do you know, three weeks later she did, and in another month we were married; just as I had said we would be.

Not everyone has such a romantic beginning. There are those who do not like each other at first meeting—some even report an extreme dislike for each other. Social psychologist Elliot Aronson (1972, pp. 262–266) was interested enough in how dislike eventually turns to love that he developed the gain-loss theory to account for this phenomenon. His theory suggests that winning someone over from an initial negative opinion has a greater impact on one's own positive feelings for that person than if the other person had started initially from a favorable position.

There appears to be no one formula that always works to move from a first meeting to an intimate relationship. Some people hardly notice each other in the beginning but seem to grow to like each other. Some have an instantaneous attraction—even "love at first sight"—that results in marriage. Others dislike each other at first but overcome their negative feelings. No doubt there are many couples where one partner feels one way while the other has a very different reaction. Certainly, being calculating and manipulative is not encouraged.

What does appear to work for those who wish to grow closer to another is to provide that other person with an avenue by which he or she can gain self-esteem within the relationship. This does not mean being completely nice to each other all the time. An occasional negative feeling along with the positive ones acts as proof of authenticity since no one honestly feels nice all of the time. We agree with Aronson (1972, p. 270) who believes that what makes love grow is "the ability of individuals to communicate a wide range of feelings to each other under appropriate circumstances and in ways that reflect their caring." By so doing two people will be less likely to take each other for granted, and their relationship should avoid boredom while at the same time, providing relatively high feelings of gain for each partner.

1975). Deciding whom to marry is a complicated matter for most persons, one that may vary not only from individual to individual but also for the same person over his or her life cycle. There is an increasing need for further research on the many variables involved in mate selection and on how men and women move from single-hood to marriage or unmarried cohabitation.

	Year	Women	Men
TABLE 6 • 1	1790	21.0	24.0
Age at First Marriage	1890	22.0	26.1
	1920	21.2	24.6
	1940	21.5	24.3
	1950	20.3	22.8
	1956	20.1	22.5
	1960	20.3	22.8
	1970	20.8	23.2
	1980	22.0	24.7
	1984	23.0	25.4

Sources: 1790–1960—B. Wilson, "First Marriages: United States," National Center for Health Statistics, Series 20, No. 35 (September 1979); 1970–1984—U.S. Bureau of the Census, *Current Population Reports,* Series P-20, No. 399 (July 1985), p. 1.

LIFE CYCLE AND MATE SELECTION

There is a relationship between one's location in the life cycle and the probability that one will choose a partner and settle down. The usual statistic collected and reported to reflect this is the average age at first marriage. In the United States in 1984, the median age at first marriage for men was 25.4 years and for women 23.0 years. These figures show that both men and women are about three years older at first marriage than they were in 1956, when the median age at first marriage was the lowest since statistics have been available for comparison (see Table 6.1).

The age at first marriage has been rising slightly for the past decade, and there is reason to believe that it will continue to rise slowly for the next few years. Age at first marriage fluctuates with a number of factors, such as the economy, liberalization of attitudes toward premarital sex, and changes in sex roles for both women and men. It is a common myth that in the early years of the United States couples married much younger than they do now. Actually, the age at first marriage in 1790, 24 for men and 21 for women, was only slightly less than it is now. The lowest ages at first marriage occurred during the two decades following World War II.

Age at Marriage

Every state has a legal minimum age for marriage. Parental consent or court approval may authorize exceptions to those minimums. The laws defining minimum ages are probably based primarily on cultural beliefs, but they also have many intricate associations with the personal needs and capabilities of adolescents as well as with the social and economic organization of the states in which they have been enacted. For example, an old Iowa statute provided that persons under the age of 21 could not legally be sold any alcoholic beverages—unless the person was a married female, in which case there was no minimum age.

	Age with Consent		Age without Consent	
State	**Men**	**Women**	**Men**	**Women**
Alabama	14	14	18	18
Alaska	16	16	18	18
Arizona	16*	16	18	18
Arkansas	17	16*	18	18
California	18*	18*	18	18
Colorado	16	16	18	18
Connecticut	16	16*	18	18
Delaware	18	16*	18	18
District of Columbia	16	16	18	18
Florida	16	16	18	18
Georgia	16	16	18	18
Hawaii	16	16	18	18
Idaho	16	16	18	18
Illinois	16	16	18	18
Indiana	17*	17*	18	18
Iowa	16*	16*	18	18
Kansas	14	12	18	18
Kentucky	18*	18*	18	18
Louisiana	18*	16*	18	18
Maine	16*	16*	18	18
Maryland	16	16	18	18
Massachusetts	†	†	18	18
Michigan	18	16	18	18
Minnesota	—	16*	18	18
Mississippi	17	15	21	21
Missouri	15	15	18	18

TABLE 6 • 2
Marriage Age with and without Parental/Court Consent, 1985

(continued)

Presumably, for an Iowa woman, being old enough to be married was a more important criterion for being considered old enough to drink alcohol than attaining a specific chronological age. At the time that the Iowa statute was passed, the minimum age for marriage for women was sixteen years, but under "special conditions" it could be as low as twelve years. Almost certainly the "special conditions" in the minds of the legislature meant pregnancy. The logic apparently was that any woman who was old enough to become pregnant was old enough to marry legally and old enough to drink alcoholic beverages. In Kansas, New Jersey, and Rhode Island, the legal age for females to marry with consent is twelve years; in New Hampshire it is thirteen; and in several other states, fourteen (see Table 6.2).

The logic that being old enough to create a pregnancy means being old enough to marry has not been applied as widely to males. Currently in most states the minimum

CHAPTER 6

TABLE 6 • 2
(continued)

State	Age with Consent		Age without Consent	
	Men	Women	Men	Women
Montana	15	15	18	18
Nebraska	17	17	18	18
Nevada	16	16	18	18
New Hampshire	14*	13*	18	18
New Jersey	—	12	18	18
New Mexico	16	16	18	18
New York	16	14	18	18
North Carolina	16	16	18	18
North Dakota	16	16	18	18
Ohio	18	16	18	18
Oklahoma	16	16	18	18
Oregon	17	17	18	18
Pennsylvania	16	16	18	18
Rhode Island	14	12	18	18
South Carolina	14	12	18	18
South Dakota	16	16	18	18
Tennessee	16	16	18	18
Texas	14	14	18	18
Utah	14	14	18	18
Vermont	18	16	18	18
Virginia	16	16	18	18
Washington	17	17	18	18
West Virginia	†	16*	18	16
Wisconsin	16	16	18	18
Wyoming	16	16	18	18
Puerto Rico	18	16	21	21
Virgin Islands	16	14	18	18

Sources: William E. Mariano, Council on Marriage Relations, Inc.,
110 E. 42nd St., New York 10017. Data as of January 1, 1983; *The
World Almanac and Book of Facts, 1986,* New York: Newspaper
Enterprise Association, Inc., 1985.

*Minimum can be reduced with consent of parents/court.
†If under eighteen, consent of parents and court.

legal age is eighteen for both males and females, but until the advent of equal rights legislation, the minimum age for men was often higher than that for women.

The doctrine underlying the enactment of minimum-age-for-marriage statutes was undoubtedly concern about the capacity of the applicants to undertake the economic responsibility for support of the household, the couple, and their probable children. At the time the first of these laws was passed, there was no federal support for welfare programs. The misery created by the marriage of young people and their propagation of societal dependents was obvious to all.

The responsibilities of men and women in nineteenth- and early twentieth-century marriages were assumed to be different. An adequate male was one who could provide an income; maintain the family's real property; protect the family from external perils; and represent the family in civic, political, and economic matters. An adequate female was one who could bear and rear children, maintain the system of interpersonal relations within the family, run a smoothly functioning household, maintain the family's standards of cleanliness and health, generally accept responsibility for the manners and morals of herself and her children, and be the family's social secretary and social leader. Although the marital responsibilities of women seem as heavy as those of men, it appears that those who made the laws believed that women could handle the role of wife at an earlier age than men could take on the role of husband. Perhaps the uncertain longevity of the parents of even an early teenager made legislators doubly anxious about her support in the event of the then irrevocable physical reality of her pregnancy.

Legislators must have recognized, consciously or unconsciously, that before a certain point in the development of the life cycle a child cannot carry out the traditional marital roles, even if they are fully understood, and that therefore the right to make the decision to marry before that point should be withheld. In states that permit marriage at an earlier age with parental consent, the implication is that either the parents are able to determine whether an individual child is sufficiently mature to marry or the parents will assume some of the child's marital responsibilities because the child is a minor.

A recent study of age at first marriage and its effect on marital stability suggests that age at marriage is a very significant predictor of marital instability (Booth and Edwards 1985). Although teenage marriages are at great risk of divorce, marriages that occur in the late twenties or after have a greater chance of instability during their first seven years than do marriages contracted in the early twenties. However, the interpersonal problems of later marriages differ from those of teenage marriages. In general, the research supports the notion that staying single for a long period of adulthood is associated with a strong sense of self-sufficiency. Standards, values, and habits may be more firmly entrenched so that being flexible may be more difficult. It is also possible that those who wed somewhat past the average age may possess certain traits that kept them from being chosen earlier. These same traits may make them more susceptible to marital instability.

Those who marry early seem to suffer primarily from a lack of the knowledge and skills needed to perform their roles adequately. They find the most difficulty in sustaining intimacy and in carrying out marital obligations, both of which are core elements in marital adjustment. So well-documented is the belief that early marriage sets up a high risk for divorce that early age at marriage is the single best predictor of divorce (Bumpass and Sweet 1972).

Several questions come to mind concerning age requirements for marriage: Are the laws specifying minimum ages for marriage more or less necessary than they were in the past? Is it any of the state's business whether people are sufficiently mature to be good companions, affectionate partners, and adequate parents? If so, below what age should people be deprived of the right to marry? The evidence is mixed and is nearly all probabilistic. That is, the probability that age at marriage affects the outcome of the

Couples who marry in their teens—and especially those who become parents almost immediately—may not have time to bond as a couple before they are diverted to parenthood.

quality of the marriage is based not on a clearly established cutoff point that applies to all persons, but rather on the odds that marriage after a given age will endure.

Some first marriages at any given age last until one partner dies, but the fraction that endures increases with each year up until both bride and groom are in their late twenties. And those figures tell us only about endurance of the marriage. So far, there are few procedures for collecting direct, objective evidence on the degree of companionship and affection experienced by people who marry at various ages; however, there is some indirect evidence that sheds light on the subject. For example, in 1979 half the divorces granted to women were awarded to women no older than 27 (Glick 1980).

Since a divorce is likely to be preceded by a period of separation and a required **interlocutory period,** it can fairly safely be estimated that most women who ever divorce will have experienced some kind of marital unhappiness by the age of 25. From this, it can be concluded that the proportion of women who are not going to stay married is probabilistically greater for those who marry before age 24 (allowing a year for unhappiness to surface). Although many persons do remain in unhappy marriages, it appears that those women who marry before they are 24 years old run a greater risk of having a short marriage than those who marry at age 28 or later.

Divorce rates are lowest for both men and women who marry for the first time at age 28 or later. The chances for a stable marriage increase as both partners reach the age of 30 and then the rates level off. Waiting beyond 30 to marry does not increase the probability of avoiding divorce significantly, even though marital instability is heightened during the first seven years of marriage for those in their late twenties but not yet past 50.

Couples who desire children have reason not to wait much beyond ages 30 to 35 to marry if they want to have children before the risk factor of late pregnancy becomes an issue. This knowledge has led to the conclusion that the maximum likelihood of success in companionship, affection, and procreation in marriage exists when marriage occurs between the ages of 28 and 34 (allowing a year for conception if one child is planned), between 28 and 32 if two children are planned, and between 28 and 30 if three children are planned. If no children are desired, the age of the couple for parenthood obviously is not a consideration (Lasswell 1974).

Personal values differ, of course. If having a large number of children is more important than affection and companionship with one's mate, earlier marriage may be indicated. If childbearing is not a value, then marriage at any time after 28 holds the greatest promise of lasting until the death of one of the partners.

On the average, men marry women two to three years younger than themselves. This most likely reflects the expectations that men's responsibilities for earning a living and providing for a family are better carried out when they are older. On the other hand, since the average woman lives several years longer than the average man, women who marry men who are older than they are can expect their later years to be spent as widows. From this standpoint, the argument can easily be made that men should be younger than their wives so that both partners are likely to spend fewer lonely years at life's end.

On the average, an additional year could be added to the length of the marriage for each year the husband is younger than his wife. It has been found that men who marry older women also stay married to them longer on the average than men who marry younger women (Burgess, Locke, and Thomes 1971). This is probably less a magic formula than an insight into the personalities of the participants. Since their age pattern is contrary to popular practice, the participants in an older woman–younger man marriage must value their personal relationship more than conformity to custom. In other words, their motivation to be married to each other may be greater than (or at least different from) that of those who follow the usual pattern. Whatever the explanation, empirically, marriages are less likely to end in divorce if the bridegroom is younger than the bride than if the reverse is true. If a man values a long marriage, he might do well to marry an older woman some time after his twenty-eighth birthday.

Sex and Age Considerations

Because we live in a complex social world in which sexual behaviors are subject to many social and internal controls, there are some issues that should be thought through carefully by those who consider deferring marriage until age 28. For instance, there is research indicating that the earlier in life a woman becomes orgasmic, the longer and more active her sex life will be (Kinsey et al. 1969, p. 265.). If it is morally important to a woman to remain virginal until her marriage, then waiting until age 28 to marry may well foreshadow a shorter, and perhaps less active sex life.

Various solutions to the dilemma of evaluating "best age to initiate sexual activity" as opposed to "best age to marry" have been proposed. It has sometimes been recommended that there should be a trial, nonprocreational marriage that would be legally distinct from a more permanent, childbearing marriage (Lindsey 1927; Mead 1966). Such a trial marriage would have legal sanction but would not involve the same property, support, and inheritance provisions that characterize traditional marriages; therefore, it could be more easily dissolved. It would also be a marriage without children. Although social and personal acceptance cannot be legislated, those who propose such a plan believe that public acceptance probably would follow.

The formalization of a new legal status may actually be unnecessary. Although the relative percentage of such couples is still low, social acceptance of cohabitation is increasing, with two-and-a-half times as many couples reporting that arrangement at the end of the 1970s as at the beginning of that decade (U.S. Bureau of the Census 1985b, p. 7). For couples under 25, the increase was eightfold. In fact, it has been reported that the primary change in courtship behavior in the 1970s was in the number of unmarried couples who were living together (Macklin 1980).

In 1984 over half of those living together as unmarried couples had never been married. Cohabitation is not meant to replace marriage, although it does have the effect of delaying marriage. Over 90 percent of cohabiting college students reported that they intend to marry eventually—if not the current partner, then someone else (Bower and Christopherson 1977).

Increasing acceptance of sex before and between marriages and particularly of unmarried couples cohabiting may be cause for distress among persons with traditional views of sexual behavior. It would be a mistake for us to insist that there is one right or one wrong point of view about sexual behavior outside marriage because of the differing and sometimes highly emotional sentiments of contemporary potential marriage patterns. Nevertheless, delaying marriage until the late twenties does seem predictive of greater success in marriage. Early sexual interest and activity (including self-stimulation) do seem predictive of a fuller and better lifetime of sexual adjustment. To delay both marriage and sexual activity creates a set of conditions very different from those that result from marrying early to legitimize sexual activity or delaying marriage but being sexually active premaritally.

Social Maturity

Regardless of chronological age, some persons are always going to be more or less socially immature. Some eighteen-year-olds may be more ready for the commitment and the responsibilities of marriage than are others in their mid-twenties. At any given chronological age, a socially immature person often denies that there will be any problems in a close personal relationship such as marriage or believes that someone or something will prevent them or solve them if they do occur. The most painfully immature are those who plan to escape the problems and responsibilities they face in their parental families by getting married. Many socially immature people marry to get away from home. Many, unrealistically, believe that getting married will solve their problems or that they will have more freedom and less responsibility than in their families of origin. A study of 22,652 members of the high school class of 1972 compared those who married young with those who did not. Those who married early frequently came from homes in which they experienced harsh discipline, poverty, or undue responsibility. These and other factors often led young couples to marry early so they could escape their home environments (Lasswell 1983).

More common than those who are running away from intolerable home situations, we believe, are those socially and emotionally immature young people who marry as one way to break away from their dependency on their parents. They almost seem to believe that two socially immature persons together can help each other grow up. Of course, this does occur sometimes. On the other hand, they may make unrealistic demands on each other, which neither is capable of fulfilling. Not infrequently these demands border on the expectation that the mate will function as a "good parent" or will give unconditional love and support in the face of any problem that should arise. Greater effort may be expended in trying to change each other to meet these demands, with disappointment and disillusionment as frequent results. Many experts are convinced that the high divorce rate among such young couples can often be traced to social immaturity (Lewis and Spanier 1979).

Ideally, marriage partners in our society should be two adults who are physically, socially, and psychologically capable of modifying their individualities into mutually acceptable patterns that will bring them more joys than sorrows in their lifelong relationship with each other. The ability to be social adults is probably more widespread among 22-year-olds than among 18-year-olds and is almost certainly more widespread among 28-year-olds than among 22-year-olds. Nevertheless, chronological age is far from a perfect index.

The meshing of personal identities into marriage and family life is a characteristic of social adulthood. Confidence in one's personal ability to overcome reasonable problems is also characteristic of adulthood. Although social adults typically have concerns and even doubts about how any new undertaking will work out, such awareness also typically helps them cope with marriage and family problems. They know there will be problems, but they also believe that they will find solutions.

Young people are often advised to try living independently on self-produced incomes for at least a year before marrying—worthwhile advice in most cases. One rarely hears married couples complain that they waited too long before they decided to marry. In fact, considering the research data on the optimum time to marry for the greatest success of a marriage in terms of both stability and reported satisfaction, many couples probably marry for the first time five to ten years before they are ready to achieve their most satisfying and longest-lasting relationship. In 1984, almost half of all American men and two-thirds of all American women who had married did so (U.S. Bureau of the Census 1985b, p. 2). Thirty percent of women and 15 percent of men had married by the end of their teens. In many instances, had they waited, they would not have ended up marrying the person they did.

THE TRANSITION FROM CHOICE TO COMMITMENT

It is probably safe to say that for most people an ideal relationship is envisioned as one in which the persons involved are strong, have good self-concepts, perceive each other accurately, communicate freely and well, and feel secure in their relationship because each knows that they are together because they both want to be together. Such an ideal would satisfy virtually everyone except perhaps the rare person who would wonder if he or she could merit a partner who sounds almost too good to live with.

Relationships that measure up to this ideal are uncommon. However, the number of persons who want to believe that theirs is one of them is much larger than the number who will admit—even to each other—that it is perfectly all right for their relationship not to meet those high standards all the time in every respect (Schulman 1970).

A person can mentally construct an idealized picture of another and can identify with it even though it is not based on direct experience with that person. This is a problem in human relations for young people who are thinking about marriage. Sociologist Marion Schulman (1970) found that women are more likely to idealize their partners than are men.

The idealization of sexual and marital partners is not different in its effects from any other kind of idealization. The greater the element of fantasy in the mental image of a lover, the greater the probability that expectations will not be met. Young persons who compare their own marriages with idealized pictures of marriage (perhaps drawn from conversations with unmarried friends, movies, or television) can expect to find many of their expectations invalid. Although idealization of marriage is a normal developmental phase, young persons are likely to experience considerable stress when their ideals cannot be met. This may be true even if the sentiments on which they have based their fantasies have been learned from their parents in childhood.

Why do people supply "facts" they cannot possibly know from any direct source to fill in blanks about others? To begin with, the very basis for thinking is recognizing objects as alike and putting them into categories that are usually represented by words. Because the actual information used to place an object or a person in a category is almost never sufficient to meet our actual needs for information, we generalize about the category from special cases we have known or sometimes from learned prejudice. Most of us come to believe that a very few clues about a person predict much more than they do. When we are right, it is efficient to believe this. When we are wrong, we may *make* it efficient by avoiding interaction with those who do not fit our **stereotypes.** That may be easier than giving up the stereotypes.

Some popular stereotypes are that beautiful women are more skillful sexually than plain women or that effeminate men prefer homosexual activities to heterosexual activities. The idealization of a prospective partner is much like stereotyping. Once one has become committed to another as a choice of mate, there is a strong desire to believe that one's choice was a good one. It becomes necessary, then, to reassure oneself of this by expecting any untested qualities of the partner to be "good." In the case of persons who had fantasized finding "Mr. Wonderful" or "the girl of my dreams," much of the stereotype was already prepared, waiting to be triggered by a few cues. Persons who are highly romantic often report that they had very precise images of what their lovers would be like before they ever saw them (Lasswell and Lasswell 1976).

Like stereotyping, idealization of a loved one may create a self-fulfilling prophecy. Sociologist Charles Horton Cooley (1902) observed that people tend to behave in accord with the expectations they believe others have of them. If a person stays in a relationship very long, he or she will either begin to take on some characteristics the other person expects or will become uncomfortable in the relationship and perhaps end it. The peak of the idealization period usually comes in the early stages of commitment, or the "engagement" period. This is a very happy time for most couples. The partners are thinking positively about each other, mutually reinforcing their self-esteem.

Research indicates that idealization and expectations about partners are closely related to the definition given to a relationship by them (Schulman 1970). For example, as one partner changes from boyfriend or girlfriend to fiancé or fiancée or to cohabitant or mate, both his or her expectations and the partner's behavior also change. We have only to listen to those couples who say that the day they were married, they both changed. No doubt, they did change—not only in behavior but also in the expectations that each held for how the other would behave in this new role.

As with all stereotypes, expectations are not always fulfilled when one person idealizes another. Usually by the second year of a relationship, unless the expectations of partners have come to match their behaviors to an appreciable degree, the relationship may be in for serious trouble. Most idealizations involve such high expectations that almost no one could measure up to them. Since a sufficient number of Americans marry persons with whom they have an idealized relationship, it is not surprising to find that the divorce rate peaks around the third year after marriage (National Center for Health Statistics 1978).

More will be said about disillusionment after marriage in Chapter 13. At this point, disillusionment should be mentioned as a phase in the life cycle of a relationship that is moving in the direction of a choice of long-term partners. If disillusionment arises early, it will probably lead to the termination of the relationship before it has really begun. There are said to be three major reasons for breaking up: boredom, differences in interests, and the desire to be independent. Breaking up is rarely a mutual decision: 87 percent of the men and 85 percent of the women involved say that one person initiated the termination of the relationship (Hill, Rubin, and Peplau 1976). All three of the reasons given are major ingredients in and reactions to disillusionment.

Disillusionment is the direct result of idealization. It occurs when one partner's behavior fails to meet the other's expectations or when the relationship itself fails to fulfill some idealized image. Some degree of disillusionment seems inescapable since no one can have completely accurate expectations for the future. It is for this reason that many persons who date long enough to get to know each other do not progress to engagement and that many who do become engaged never go on to be married.

COMMITMENT TO A RELATIONSHIP

To give a very brief and generalized definition, *commitment* refers to a person's persistent willingness to be loyal to another and to give time and energy to achieve the goals of their relationship (Schrader 1980). The process of moving from attraction to commitment in a relationship is called *courtship*. Courtship is an old-fashioned word that describes a process of great concern to contemporary family-life experts. In connection with commitment, it has a special meaning. In important ways, courtship is the pursuit of commitment from and to a loved one.

The psychological and sociological literature has identified five characteristics of commitment, although research has shown that most people do not analyze their own commitments but see them as a single characteristic. The elements described in the literature and reported in a recent study by sociologist Sandra Schrader (1980, pp. 90–92) are:

1. Dedication to continuing the relationship
2. Rejection of competing or alternative relationships
3. Limitation of one's personal activities to conform to the perceived social expectations for a committed couple or group
4. Personal feelings of attachment
5. Willingness to accept the behavioral norms that grow as the relationship develops

A committed person gives time and energy to keeping the relationship going; does not get involved in other relationships that reduce the time, energy, or attention required for this primary relationship; gives up selfish activities so that others define him or her as committed; wishes to be physically close to the partner much of the time; and wants to work out patterns of behavior that are mutually satisfactory.

Commitment can be measured by three basic standards: duration, intensity, and priority. Duration refers to the length of time that one is willing to give unreserved love and support to another. Many people think of the length of a relationship as the most important sign of commitment, but the length of time that two people are together does not necessarily define the quality of the relationship or show real dedication to each other.

A second dimension of commitment is intensity—the strength of feeling and the depth of caring that each partner is prepared to invest in the other. Just as some long-term relationships may have only a minimal emotional investment, some short-term relationships are emotionally intense and satisfying.

A third standard for measuring commitment is the priority one gives to the relationship. This is calculated not only in the quantity of time and energy expended but also in the quality of a couple's mutual involvement. Giving a relationship priority over other relationships means that concern for it takes precedence over concern for other relationships.

Schrader (1980, p. 95) found that whether or not a couple believes they are committed to each other is more predictive of how long the relationship will last than any other variable that she studied, including the acceptance of their relationship by others, the couple's agreement on the definition of their relationship, or their homogamy.

In her studies of commitment, Schrader found that men tend to believe that their partners define their commitment in the same way they do themselves—that is, that their partners want to be involved in a relationship that is fun, provides good companionship, and respects the freedom of each partner (the right to make good decisions on his or her own). She found, however, that men are incorrect in this assumption. In fact, women define commitment primarily as sexual exclusiveness and dedication to the duration of the relationship. Unlike men, however, most women are aware that they define commitment differently from their partners.

Males tend to feel that their partners ought to show their commitment to a relationship by moving toward increased willingness to share and enjoy sex. Although females are fully aware that males have such expectations, their own commitment is actually to permanence of the relationship, with the intimacy of sex either irrelevant or of secondary significance. Schrader (1980, p. 118) contends that "it is the women who are primarily pushing for a binding, exclusive, and committed relationship. They, more than the men, are holding to the traditional sex role ideology."

Commitment was defined somewhat differently in another recent study (Risman et al. 1981). Cohabiting and noncohabiting couples were asked to predict the probability of their marrying their current partners. Their predictions were then matched with whether or not the partners actually did marry within the period of the study. Women who were cohabiting estimated the probability of eventually marrying their current partners as somewhat greater than did men, apparently suggesting a stronger link between commitment and permanence of the relationship for women than for men.

Interestingly, cohabiting women saw themselves as at a greater power disadvantage in their relationships than did women who were "going together" with men but not cohabiting. The authors said, ". . . it may be easier for noncohabiting couples to achieve . . . an egalitarian relationship, than it is for cohabiting or married couples" (Risman et al. 1981, p. 79).

What about those who seem unable either to give or accept commitment? Psychologically, commitment implies being responsible for and to another person. Some people simply do not want to accept such a challenge, perhaps for selfish reasons, but our experience tells us that most people who shy away from commitment lack the maturity to handle that kind of assignment. Psychologists call this a "fear of commitment" and believe that the trouble frequently lies in low self-esteem (Lasswell and Lobsenz 1983, p. 31). Such persons have learned to be emotionally elusive rather than to risk rejection—which those with poor self-concepts seem to anticipate.

Engagement

Engagement to marry is still a customary preliminary to marriage in most of the world and is a public statement of commitment. Four concepts of betrothal have been described: Mediterranean, Nordic, Amerafrican, and contemporary American (Money 1980). In the Mediterranean tradition, sexual access is viewed as an exclusive right of marriage partners. Coitus or the public statement of the intention to engage in sex is the moral equivalent of intention to marry since coitus is not only improper but also socially disgraceful for women if it is not accompanied by marriage or at least by a promise of marriage. The Mediterranean tradition incorporates the double standard, however; premarital sex is considered permissible for men. **Betrothal**—a promise to marry—is a necessary prerequisite of indicating a desire for sex for a "socially acceptable" female. The Mediterranean concept of betrothal was prevalent in the United States in the late nineteenth and early twentieth centuries and continues today in some more traditional sections of the country and among some groups.

In the Nordic tradition, sex between unmarried persons is neither disgraceful nor improper but is viewed as a natural developmental expression of normal falling in love. However, it is usually considered improper for a couple to become parents without at least an intent to marry. In the Nordic tradition, the discovery of pregnancy rather than the intent to have coitus is the appropriate occasion for betrothal. The Nordic tradition is apparent in the Scottish pattern of **handfasting** and the American colonial tradition of *bundling*. The seeming intimacy of both these customs seems almost shocking for their times until we realize that they had great significance for their societies. Bundling, for instance, was a courtship practice in the eighteenth century in which a couple would lie fully clothed, bundled in blankets (ostensibly to keep warm as well as to keep the young man from a chilly horseback ride home late at night). Often a board, as well as blankets and clothing, separated them; some parents added extra insurance by insisting that the young woman's legs be tied together. It is likely that another important purpose of bundling was to induce the couple to marry in order to legitimize any sexual arousal they might feel (Calhoun 1960).

Money (1983) describes "the Amerafrican legacy" in the United States as an absence of betrothal practice. The Africans brought to the United States as slaves came from so many different cultural backgrounds that there was no uniformity among them in betrothal or marriage practices. Further, the practice of slavery, the occasional separation of partners by sale, and the reputed practice of matings arranged to produce genetically superior slave stock are widely believed to be responsible for the general absence of betrothal. Neither coitus nor pregnancy indicated the propriety of a commitment on the part of either partner. Because of the absence of restrictions on coitus and the potential material value to the owner of each child, pregnancies began to occur soon after puberty. Children born to any slave woman were the property of her owner and were typically reared by slaves who were too old to do heavy labor.

The contemporary betrothal patterns that have developed in the United States (but that still meet some resistance among more conservative members of the population) tend to be variations on the Nordic pattern rather than on the Mediterranean or Amerafrican patterns. The chief difference from the Nordic pattern is that births may be prevented by contraception or abortion by the partners. No public recognition of betrothal is necessary for initiating coitus or even for creating a pregnancy. Money (1980) feels that this concept of voluntary betrothal on grounds of commitment to a partner relationship (rather than a parent-child relationship) may eventually result in more mature patterns of mate selection, fewer divorces, and hence better homes for children, owing to the removal of the necessity to marry because of pregnancy or to legitimize sexual involvement.

It is interesting to look back in early editions of textbooks on marriage and the family to note the treatment of the topic of engagement. Compared with a few paragraphs (or no mention at all) in current works, those of 30 or 40 years ago treated the subject extensively. They viewed engagement as a period for evaluating the relationship, uncovering potential problems, and learning to become more effective partners. Nearly 40 years ago one of the leading textbooks began a chapter on engagement this way: "An engagement is a happy situation because it is one of the few in which both sides feel they have won something. Man is the only animal to provide such a period. All other animals follow courtship with immediate mating" (Magoun 1948, p. 227).

Still another volume had two chapters—one on engagement and one on broken engagements—noting that a third to a half of engagements terminated short of marriage (Landis 1955). Although some things remain as true today as several decades ago, the importance of engagements appears to have diminished.

As an announcement of betrothal, formal engagement has been slowly disappearing from the American scene. Exceptions are found in certain regions of the

Premarital counseling can make couples aware of potential problem areas as well as provide help in communicating and resolving conflicts.

country and in some upper- and upper-middle-class populations where engagement may function as much to reserve a date for the public celebration of a formal wedding as to indicate the nature of the current relationship between the partners. It is not a reliable indicator of whether the couple is having sexual relations or of whether a pregnancy has occurred, and hardly anyone expects it to be. (A substantial, though not particularly vocal, fraction of brides and grooms still follows the Mediterranean pattern of virginity until marriage, but this is generally considered a matter of personal preference rather than of social pressure.)

We noted in Chapter 5 that the number of never-marrieds who choose to live together has been growing steadily (currently 3–4 percent of the population). It is estimated that 10 to 20 percent of these couples view their cohabitation as a trial marriage or a variation of the engagement period (Macklin 1980). Since the traditional purpose of engagement was to allow the couple time to come to know each other more intimately, it makes sense that couples who live together would not see the reasoning for a formal engagement.

Those who do choose formal engagement frequently make a public announcement, and almost always the couple becomes more involved with their families at least for a time. Often the suitor gives a ring to his fiancée. It has been suggested that many couples may have avoided becoming formally engaged in recent years because of the high price of diamonds, the traditional gem for engagement rings. A diamond merchant told us recently that most sales of diamond engagement rings are to older couples entering second or third marriages or to couples of upper socio-economic status.

A growing number of engaged couples are availing themselves of premarital programs offered through religious organizations, schools, or marriage therapists. The success of such programs is still being evaluated; some scholars believe that there is not yet enough evidence to ascertain whether they are successful (Bagarozzi and

Rauen 1983). Others report confidence in the success of such programs, indicating that they increase the number of satisfying marriages (Riley et al. 1984).

A five-year study in Canada compared engaged couples who had participated in a communications-training and conflict-resolution program to a control group of engaged couples who had not (Bader, Riddle, and Sinclair 1981). It found that after five years program participants were less likely to have engaged in destructive conflict with each other than were nonparticipants. Participants were also more likely to seek professional assistance for solving problems. Presumably those who had experienced professional guidance were convinced that it helped.

As a result of the Canadian study, many programs have been developed using the following format: (1) before marriage—four sessions on communication in marriage, family background, finances, and sexuality; (2) after six months to a year of marriage—three sessions on changing roles in marriage, resolving conflicts, and building a better relationship. Since each year 200,000 marriages end prior to the couples' second anniversary, the development of such programs takes on even greater significance.

Premarital inventories have been developed to help engaged couples to identify strengths and weaknesses unique to their own relationship. The Locke-Wallace Inventory was an early instrument used by countless young couples planning to marry (Locke and Wallace 1959, pp. 251–255). Such tests point out potential problem areas and serve as points for discussion for the engaged couple.

Assessment techniques for predicting success in marriage have continually improved, and far more systematic and objective measures of both personal and relationship issues for couples are currently possible. One of the most recent premarital inventories is the Pre-Marital Personal and Relationship Evaluation (PREPARE) (Olson, Fourier, and Druckerman 1982). This evaluation has been tested on thousands of engaged couples and provides information on areas of agreement or disagreement on such topics as sex, finances, leisure activities, family, friends, role expectations, and religion. In addition, there is a measure of idealism—to reveal whether engaged couples have such idealistic views of marriage that their scores must be adjusted accordingly.

The Wedding

The wedding vows that a couple make represent a public statement—and one with great legal significance—of their mutual commitment to their enduring relationship. Regardless of cynical comments that the high divorce rate reflects a lack of commitment, it seems unlikely that very many persons actually enter into marriage without the intention of staying married. The very act of cohabiting out of wedlock is testimony to the seriousness with which people view the transition to being married.

The married state is of major social and psychological significance to the partners themselves, to their families and associates, and even to government and other agencies. For example, income tax legislation has often discriminated against married persons when both are employed. Court policy is still being hammered out over the propriety of spouses testifying in court cases involving each other. The most profound effect of ceremonial marriage, however, is surely on the partners themselves.

Weddings, including wedding vows, are the public statements that two persons make of their intention to be husband and wife to each other and of their desire for social sanction of this decision. Some weddings are very private, with only the necessary officiant and witnesses present, but others are elaborate affairs with hundreds of guests. Many weddings are casual, nonreligious ceremonies; however, it has been estimated that three-fourths of weddings do have a religious base to them—that is, they are performed in a house of religious worship and/or the one who officiates is a minister, priest, or rabbi (Benson 1971).

Despite the facts that fewer brides and bridegrooms have had traditional courtships and engagements, that some have lived together, and that many are sexually involved with each other, when the time comes to make a legal, public statement, most couples become somewhat traditional. Many have weddings that are not unlike those of their parents and grandparents (Seligson 1973). One study reports that couples become traditional for their wedding because they realize the solemnity of adding a new family unit to society and intend to take their new roles seriously (Blumberg and Paul 1975).

Friends and relatives usually view a wedding as a happy occasion for the couple and give not only their good wishes but also gifts to help the pair furnish their home together. Figures gathered from bridal magazine surveys and from related business sources reveal that 40 percent of jewelers' business comes from wedding-related purchases: rings, attendants' gifts, silver, china, and crystal. One out of eight dollars spent on home furnishings and appliances is spent by engaged couples, newlyweds, or those buying gifts for them. Over $1 billion each year is spent on other wedding-related items such as clothing, cosmetics, and luggage, with nearly as much spent on honeymoon travel (Gagnon and Greenblat 1978).

Wedding rituals have been of particular interest to family historians. The original meaning of certain rituals is not always clear, but it is fascinating to know that parts of even the most modern wedding ceremonies may have roots in ancient times. Candles or torches, for example, not only served to light the bridal party's way when daylight turned to evening while the festivities continued, but there are records that candles were used to symbolize the enduring flame of love (Lacey 1969). In Christian marriages, one large candle was used to signify the presence of God and the couple lit small individual tapers from the larger one. A more common recent practice is for each of the partners to light a single candle with which they jointly light a third one; then they extinguish their individual candles to symbolize the end of their singlehood and the beginning of their unity in marriage.

Flowers, too, have always been a part of weddings. An olive or myrtle wreath worn by a bride has been used to symbolize her virtue. In the Victorian age, the garland became a bouquet. Eventually flowers were chosen for their special meaning, with orange blossoms and baby's breath becoming popular as symbols of fruitfulness and fertility—ironically sometimes the last thing a modern bride and groom want (Eichler 1924).

The bridal dress and veil have special significance. The white color of the wedding gown was a symbol of the bride's virginity. The veil is symbolic in Christian, Jewish, Moslem, and Hindu weddings. Originally, it was probably meant to protect against evil spirits and to give the "blushing bride" privacy from stares. Revealing her face to her groom and the guests after the vows indicated her status as a married woman (Thompson 1932). This has traditionally been followed by a kiss to seal the vows.

CHAPTER 6

The ring may be the most ancient and widely used symbol. The circle symbolizes never-ending love, the gold or platinum represents nontarnishing love, and the diamond was thought to ward off temptation as well as to stand for innocence (Thompson 1932). Wearing the wedding ring on the third finger of the left hand is believed to have originated with the notion that the left hand denotes submission and obedience and the third finger had an artery leading directly to the heart (Chesser 1980).

The date for a wedding has traditional roots and varies from society to society. Marriages are seasonal in the United States, with most occurring from June to December. June is the most popular month; August and December are also popular. Autumn is the most popular season for weddings in Japan; in Taiwan fortune-tellers may be consulted to determine the lucky month, day, and even the hour for the ceremony.

After the wedding vows are spoken, whether they are read from the Book of Common Prayer, the Koran, or whether they are words composed by the couple themselves, the legal documents are filed and the relationship is formalized and can be broken only by death or a court action. In all of the United States, marriage is recognized as valid only between those over a certain age who are not already married, who are considered capable of making a legal contract, and who are of opposite sex. Homosexuals may have a wedding ritual (and many committed homosexual couples do have such a ceremony and consider themselves married), but they are not married in the eyes of the law. Should they dissolve their relationship, no legal documents of divorce or **annulment** are required.

The statutory requirements for marriage vary from state to state. The statutory definition of marriage spells out the rights and obligations of each partner. Couples may, if they wish, make additional informal or formal agreements with each other. Some couples draw up special agreements in legal documents, which, if properly witnessed and filed, are valid as long as they do not in any way violate the laws or policies of the state in which the couple is married. For example, a contract that spells out conditions under which a couple might be divorced would not usually be valid, since the spirit of marriage is not well served by anticipating divorce. In other words, public policy, which fixes the privileges and obligations of marital life, must not be subverted by individual contracts. More than a dozen states, however, uphold **prenuptial** or **antenuptial** agreements provided they are fair and equitable to both partners. The American Bar Association offers a 57-page booklet to help couples understand the complexities of such contracts, *Law and Marriage: Your Legal Guide* (ABA Order Fulfillment, 1155 E. 60th St., Chicago, IL 60637).

A kind of contract now allowable, but formerly not so, is one that might cover where the couple will live. Most states automatically used to change a woman's legal residence to that of her husband; if she lived in North Dakota all her life but married a Texan, she automatically became a Texan, too, regardless of where she lived. When California had such a law designating a wife's legal domicile as her husband's legal residence, an acquaintance of ours who had always lived in California met and married a fellow student while at the University of California. Her husband was from Illinois, and she immediately was reclassified as a resident of that state, thus losing her claim to the much lower university tuition for California residents. A wife had to list her residence as her husband's; not to do so was considered desertion and thus constituted grounds for divorce. When travel was slow and difficult, when there was little or no option about family planning, and when men were legally charged with the total financial support of their wives and families, these laws were both sensible and necessary for the maintenance of marriages and families. As they became less meaningful, they were repealed. Of course, there is some lag in the legislative process (and probably wisely so), but the U.S. system of separation of legislative, judicial, and executive powers is probably the most effective way of eliminating the injustices of such antiquated legislation until it is repealed.

Still another example of a customary understanding between marriage partners involves the name change that most women make. There is no statutory requirement that a woman take her husband's last name, but many couples never discuss other possibilities. A few women keep their maiden names; some couples use a hyphenated name. Most follow the traditional pattern of both husband and wife using the husband's last name.

A growing number of couples have agreements that are permissible in the state in which they are drawn and that deal with certain financial arrangements, child care, the education or religious training of children, household management, career decisions, and other issues that may be troublesome areas later if left to chance but that are not regulated by law. Of course, such contracts can always be renegotiated. Questions may be raised about appropriate penalties for broken marriage contracts if the partners are unwilling to renegotiate. Is a broken marriage agreement grounds for a civil suit? If so, how can damages be assessed? Should injunctions be ordered for violations of private marriage agreements? Is divorce an appropriate action when a contract concerning household management, career decisions, or child care is broken? It seems that prenuptial agreements can cover almost anything, but some of the provisions do not carry legal weight since courts of law are reluctant to interfere in everyday marital matters. In practice, the American Bar booklet says, a prenuptial agreement becomes legally enforceable only when a couple seeks divorce or one of the spouses dies. The court does not, for example, enforce decisions about how household tasks are divided, even if they appear in a couple's contract.

Perhaps in the future contracts will be used more than they are currently. For now, most couples do not bother with formal agreements. Those who do often cannot depend on support from the courts should the contract be broken.

SUMMARY

1. Choosing one's mate is a rather recent phenomenon. In the past ten years, however, the trend throughout the world seems to be in the direction of the independence of choice that Americans take for granted, leading to the growth of love as a basis for mate selection.
2. Homogamy—the tendency for persons in a relationship to be alike in many respects—is probably achieved more by elimination of certain persons than by seeking out those who possess particular characteristics. Whatever the reason, partners who are drawn to each other usually have common characteristics such as race, religion, and social class. There is a greater tendency to marry within socially defined boundaries (endogamy) than without (exogamy).

CHAPTER 6

3. *Positive factors* are those that draw one to another person. These may change over the life cycle as one's interests and values change. What attracts us to another person is ordinarily a behavior or trait that he or she has chosen, although it may be a behavior that is determined at an unconscious level.

4. There are certain automatic disqualifications employed in mate selection, some of which occur even before one meets a potential mate. Some of these are based on prejudice and others on various practical considerations. Factors of age, race, religion, ethnicity, and socioeconomic status are among those used as filters.

5. There are interactive disqualifications as well for mate selection. These depend on the system of interaction between two persons rather than on individual attributes. Empathy and ability to communicate, as well as sexual compatibility, are important factors in determining mate selection.

6. Exchange theory applies the logic of the marketplace to mate selection. People try to get equal value—or perhaps a bargain—when they "invest" themselves in a relationship, and they expect their chosen partners to seek an equal or profitable "return."

7. Equity theory emphasizes that the values in exchange are not necessarily perceived identically by the partners, so that *equity* is not necessarily the same as *equal exchange*. Personal values rather than market values determine what constitutes a profit.

8. Complementary needs theory maintains that people choose partners who are either low in needs in which they themselves are high (or vice versa) or who have different needs that can be satisfied by their chosen partners.

9. Similarity of chosen partners to opposite-sex parent and complementariness of birth order are examples of psychodynamics in partner selection.

10. Process theories stress that mate selection is a process determined by a complicated array of social and psychological factors. They hold that there can be no single-principle approach to mate choice but that a multivariate approach is necessary.

11. The age at first marriage for both men and women has been rising in recent years and is expected to continue to rise for at least the next decade.

12. Every state has a minimum age for legal marriage, ranging from a low of 12 years for females (with court and parental consent) to a high of 21 years for both sexes (parental and court consent not required).

13. Divorce rates drop off sharply for both men and women whose first marriage occurs in their late twenties. If the number of children desired is taken into consideration, later marriages have better chances to succeed than do earlier marriages.

14. Some authorities have recommended more than one form of legal marriage to provide for the different needs and values of each of the partners. However, the present system actually functions quite well because cohabitation serves informally in such a capacity for some couples.

15. Courtship is the process of moving from attraction to commitment in a relationship. Five characteristics of commitment have been identified, although most couples tend to see their commitments as a single characteristic. A couple's belief that they are committed is more highly predictive of the length of the relationship than any other factors involved.

16. Betrothal, or engagement, is a customary and public statement of commitment. Expectations concerning betrothal differ in various societies, ranging from those who expect the partners (and especially the bride-to-be) to be virginal to those who consider marriage necessary only when couples want to have a child.

17. Formal engagement as a preliminary to marriage appears to be declining somewhat in the United states. Some believe that cohabitation before marriage is being substituted for engagement by many couples.

18. The wedding is an even more definite statement of commitment—both socially and legally. Despite the informality of the courtship process among a growing number of couples, today's couples have weddings that are still usually traditional and often not unlike those of their parents and their grandparents.

19. Marriage implies both legal and extralegal contracts that vary from state to state. The extralegal ones vary also from couple to couple.

GLOSSARY

Annulment A court order declaring that what was assumed to be a marriage is not legal or valid. Typical grounds for annulment are that the participants were not competent to marry, that one person deceived the other or the licensing authority about an important fact, and so on. (p. 175).

Assortativeness The probability that particular persons select friends or mates from particular population categories or aggregates; the notion that one does not have an equal likelihood of marrying everyone in a population. (p. 153)

Betrothal The mutual promise partners make to marry each other or to live as husband and wife at some future time; often used synonymously with the word *engagement* in the United States. (p. 170)

Differential association The concept that a given person will associate with only a relatively small number of others and that relationships with those persons will vary in frequency, duration, priority, and intensity. (p. 147)

Empathy The quality of *understanding* how another thinks or feels; differs from *sympathy*, which is feeling what another feels. (p. 152)

Endogamy The practice of marrying within socially defined boundaries such as within particular religious or racial groups. (p. 150)

Exogamy The practice of marrying outside specific social boundaries such as kin groups. (p. 150)

Functional involvement Social contact resulting from the organization of people's individual activities, such as that arising from common work space or needs to obtain information, goods, or services by one person from others. (p. 148)

Handfasting A woman's consent to engage in coitus with a man on the stated condition that he will marry her if she bears his child ("will ye marry me if it takes?"). In Scotland the marriage did not always take place until after the birth of the child (or sometimes after the birth of several children), but the man's commitment to marry was socially acknowledged. (p. 171)

Homogamy Similarity of objective characteristics (social class, education, race, ethnic group, religion, interests, values, and so forth) between partners selected. (p. 149)

Imprinting A learning mechanism, highly resistant to modification and occurring at critical periods soon after birth, by which a newborn animal forms a bond to its species. Imprinting is critical to later species-specific behavior. (p. 156)

Interactional disqualification The process in which certain individuals are judged unsuitable for further association because their interaction is uncomfortable or counterproductive in some way. (p. 152)

Interlocutory period A legally required waiting period between the time a divorce action is filed and the time the divorce can become final. (p. 163)

Prenuptial or antenuptial Pertaining to any acts or contracts between two betrothed persons prior to their marriage; also used to describe anything pertaining to a couple before they marry. (p. 175)

Propinquity Geographical or physical nearness. (p. 148)

Psychodynamic Referring to the constantly changing psychological system underlying human behavior; the explanation of feelings or behaviors on the basis of a person's interpretation of his or her experiences, especially early life experiences.(p. 156)

Stereotype A belief that all the people who have a given characteristic are alike in a much broader set of characteristics. (p. 167)

7

Two may talk together under the same roof for many years, yet never really meet;
and two others at first speech are old friends.

As two individuals enter a marriage and begin to share their lives, their psychological, social, and cultural differences are blended in a way that makes their marriage unique. In the past, couples usually had the roles of husband and wife spelled out clearly. Today's couples have more choices and for this reason, are more likely to have a marriage tailored to their unique needs, desires, and expectations. Communication is central to the way that couples learn to live harmoniously with each other. As two partners communicate, they share a system of interaction that changes as they progress through the stages of the life cycle, sharing emotions, children, good times, and troubled times.

Self-Awareness and Communication in Marriage

Mary Catherwood
"Marianson," *MacKinac
and Lake Stories*

*A*nd they lived happily ever after is the positive and romanticized view of life after the wedding. The transition to marriage is expected to be a happy one. For most couples, fortunately, it is—although usually not without some turbulence along the way. The negotiations necessary to blend two individuals into a couple almost certainly pose some basic dilemmas and create some problems.

Every marriage consists of two unique individuals. Each brings to the relationship a history of experiences, memories, and ways of behaving. Unique personalities have been formed since birth and have been influenced by genetic, physiological, psychological, social, and cultural factors. Sometimes these uniquenesses are difficult to blend in a way that allows for each person's opinions and feelings to be accommodated. To be able to express ideas and feelings and to hear another's messages are the heart of the communication process.

It is no wonder that communication in marriage has received a great deal of attention as an important determinant of how two people get along. In fact, studies of marital adjustment have indicated that "quality communication is central to a quality marriage" (Montgomery 1981). And, we might add, the quality of the marriage is important to the quality of communication. When two people feel content with their relationship, they are more likely to be receptive to each other's messages. "Warm feelings give rise to tolerance for imperfection, a margin for error that allows each person to give the other the benefit of the doubt, to increase trust, to reduce suspicion, to take less seriously words spoken in anger" (Lasswell and Lobsenz 1983, p. 69). Although there is probably no *perfect* communication, some guidelines to quality communication have been gleaned from several research studies and from family therapists (Miller, Corrales, and Wackman 1975; Satir 1964).

SENDING AND RECEIVING MESSAGES

Those who study communication patterns and skills—particularly in marriages and other intimate relationships—believe that all behavior communicates a message. Nonverbal actions such as withdrawal and silence send messages just as surely as words do. The statement "One cannot *not* communicate" suggests that a perceiver may attach a meaning to any behavior, including silence or hesitation.

Sending a message is not a simple exercise in which one person conveys what he or she intends to convey openly and clearly to a listener who not only hears but understands. Instead, both the sender and the receiver process the message through several physical and psychological media. The sense organs, postures, motions, memories, feelings, and relative statuses all play parts in inducing and eliciting ideas in our minds.

Sometimes the intent of a message may be explicit and clear in the mind of the sender, but often it is only implicit and perhaps ambiguous in comparison with the spoken words. For example, one partner may say, "You always say the right words to make a person feel good." This could be a sincere compliment, or if said sarcastically, it could be a cutting comment.

Meanings implied by and inferred from a message are often more important than the actual words or gestures. The simple message "I love you" not only has different meanings to different persons, but its meaning may change through time for one person as a result of experience. Although intense interaction with another person over a long period of time helps achieve shared meaning, it is no guarantee that two people always understand each other. A lengthy relationship may even stand in the way of consensus, if, for example, one partner clings to a meaning that was shared by both ten years earlier while the other has developed a new and different meaning for the same symbol.

"Talking about talking" is the way many family therapists describe the need to discuss meaning behind words or nonverbal behavior. The term **metacommunication** refers to the messages that are implicit in overt statements or questions (Watzlawick, Beavin, and Jackson 1967). Behind the actual words may be an intent or a meaning not obvious to the listener. Two people who communicate well have learned to read each other's implicit messages by developing the ability to understand, for example, a tone of voice, a body posture, or a choice of words that conveys the precise definition or intensity of the interchange.

Confusion is the typical symptom of misunderstanding and can, from this perspective, be a useful step in the communication process. It signals that the partners are conscious of something awry and of possible differences in understanding. This awareness is better than the assumption that an incorrectly understood message is understood, which can lead to inappropriate action. Studies have shown that couples who are more satisfied with their relationship with each other are better able to make the adjustments necessary to cut through confusion and misunderstandings. They more frequently feel understood by their mates because they know how to get their messages across (Navron 1967; Orthner 1976).

Messages usually convey both content and intent. The content may give factual information, for example, but the intent may be to get the receiver to take some action. A wife who says to her husband, "This house seems chilly to me," may be asking her husband to close the windows or to build a fire in the fireplace. The intent may not be clear to her husband; or, if he does not want to get up, he may choose not to understand the covert message. The intent of a message often is vague and may even conflict with the content. People often mean something different from what their words convey.

Most communication experts believe that the essential element in clear and honest communication is not only the actual words but also the feelings and the intent of the messages. In other words, it is not only what two people say to each other, it is also how and why they say it. Couples in an intimate relationship attach personal meanings to both verbal and nonverbal behavior based on their experiences before as well as after they met. These meanings may be quite independent of social and cultural meanings.

The language with which a couple speaks to each other is symbolic of their experiences individually and their interactions; it provides a pool of meaning from which only they may draw. They may speak without words—with only a glance, a smile, or a shrug of the shoulders. When two people have the same style (or recognize each other's meaning if it is different), it increases their comfort in the relationship and builds a foundation of security. It feels good to be understood.

Although both are important, it is not so much a matter of what is discussed or even of how much a couple talk that can make or break a relationship. Instead, it is how they communicate.

Elements of Communication

Open and clear communication between two people in a relationship depends on several qualities. Each person brings to the relationship a personal history of communication. Patterns and skills of expression and listening are established early in life. These early experiences and still later ones build on our basic patterns of expression and listening in such a way that they affect our openness, honesty, ability to trust, empathy, and listening skills.

Openness

One of the most important factors in quality communication is the degree of openness between the two partners. The amount of self-disclosure and genuineness in an intimate relationship has been shown to have a significant effect on the levels of satisfaction that the partners feel with their relationship (Altman and Taylor 1973). In general, the more open partners are with each other, the greater their satisfaction. The openness must be mutual, however. If only one partner offers personal and private information and the other does not (and perhaps is not even receptive to such disclosures), the relationship is not enhanced.

Openness allows others to get to know a person's likes, dislikes, thoughts, and feelings. It is basic to interpersonal understanding. The mutual understanding and awareness that partners have of themselves and their partners are essential ingredients in marital satisfaction (Witkin and Rose 1978). Openness is determined by a variety of factors, but perhaps the most basic is each partner's level of self-awareness.

Self-Awareness Self-awareness affects communication in two important ways: to *say* what one means implies that one *knows* what one means. Otherwise the information given is misleading. Self-understanding is so basic to knowing what one means that it hardly needs elaborating. It is surprising, however, how many people speak with authority from a very confused inner perspective.

A serious barrier to being open is insecurity. Insecurity is often based on a fear of displeasing a loved one or of being rejected. When self-understanding promotes a level of inner security, unrealistic notions of having to please others or else face rejection are diminished. Good communication requires that we understand what we are saying, how we are saying it, and, perhaps most important, why we are saying it.

We have said that our communication history is rooted in our early years. No one remembers the early months of life clearly, but our minds and bodies accomplished a great deal prior to our earliest memories. Much of that affects our later lives and our ability to be good communicators. From the moment of birth, we experience thoughts and particularly feelings that we store but do not understand. For instance, we may have had feelings about our mothers long before we had any cognitive concept of "mother." Even in adulthood one may have a physiological reaction to the physical presence of one's mother without rational or intellectual insight into these feelings. Despite an apparent lack of understanding of what is happening to them, very young children grow in awareness of themselves as unique and separate from others. This awareness is the beginning of the development of one's **self-concept,** which is at the root of all attempts to communicate.

Self-Esteem   We all have mental pictures of ourselves. Part of these pictures deal with specific traits—the color of our eyes, our intelligence, and so forth. We also have global estimates of ourselves by which we compare our sense of overall worth or **self-esteem** with that of others. We have feelings about our specific traits: "I hate being shy," or "It makes me feel good to know that I am intelligent."

People like to think that their behaviors are in harmony with their evaluation of themselves. People seem to feel uncomfortable when their traits or behaviors—or, especially, others' reactions to them—do not match their picture of themselves. Being put down by others—especially by those one loves—is painful; being highly overestimated by others can be embarrassing.

Self-Sufficiency   The identity and feelings of self-sufficiency of adults are important determinants of how they live and love and express themselves. Any relationships into which two adults enter can be no healthier than the two "selves" involved. Erik Erikson (1968, pp. 217–220), who has written extensively on the concept of the "self"—recognizing that each person has many facets that correspond to the various relationships and situations that he or she meets in a lifetime—says:

> What the "I" reflects on when it sees or contemplates the body, the personality, and the roles to which it is attached for life—not knowing where it was before or will be after—are the various selves which make up their composite self. There are constant and often shock-like transitions between these selves: consider the nude-body self in the dark or suddenly exposed in the light; consider the clothed self among friends or in the company of higher-ups or lower-downs; consider the just-awakened drowsy self or the one stepping refreshed out of the surf or the one overcome by retching and fainting; the body-self in sexual excitement or in a rage; the competent self and the impotent one; the one on horseback, the one in the dentist's chair, and the one chained and tortured—by men who say "I." It takes, indeed, a healthy personality for the "I" to be able to speak out of all of these conditions in such a way that at any given moment it can testify to a reasonably coherent self.

Others who have attempted to define the self focus on a "core-self" that remains essentially the same over time and that gives stability and continuity to an individual's personality. This core has been referred to by sociologist Ralph Turner (1976) as the "true self"—a subjectively held sense that people have of who and what they really are.

Adulthood has been described as that stage of a person's life in which he or she has achieved a sense of self-sufficiency. This includes the ability to be one's own person, to function on one's own, and to enjoy the experience of autonomy. Marital therapists believe that this sense of identity is a vital ingredient in whether an individual is successful in his or her intimate relationships (Zerof 1978; Lasswell and Lobsenz 1976). Psychologist Laura Singer says:

> In the early stages of marriage, couples inevitably discover certain things that can be very distressing. I often hear the dismayed reactions of people the first time they realize that they and their partners are separate individuals. Being dissimilar creates anxiety, and it usually stems from the unconscious sense that, "If we love each other, we should be the same. And if we're different, then something's wrong. Maybe we don't love each other. (Singer and Stern 1980, p. 36)

Until the sense of identity and the feeling of being able to depend on oneself develop, it is unlikely that a man or woman is capable of a truly intimate adult relationship. Until there is a sense of being separate and self-sufficient, there are barriers to the kind of intimacy that successful, sustained relationships need. Each act of communicating—of revealing or protecting the self—is affected by a sense of self-sufficiency.

The barriers to being close to another are usually left over from childhood. As children, we are necessarily dependent and, consequently, extraordinarily vulnerable. This vulnerability often subjects children to fears of abandonment by those on whom they must depend. In adults the fear of abandonment may surface from time to time and, if allowed to become too important, may interfere in relationships. Excessive demands on others for a total fusion with them hinder or prevent true intimacy and open communication.

The yearning for total unity with another is a distorted concept that many people attach to the notions of love and marriage. Psychologists believe that the desire to "be as one" with a loved one is an attempt by those who have not achieved comfortable separation from their parents to relive the dependency, security, and warmth of the early mother-child relationship, if it was a good one. If it was not, then it is urgent for the new partner to replace feelings of rejection and neglect with feelings of security and to search for what is missing in the new relationship. Either way, the expectations of how a partner will fulfill needs, wants, and expectations are unrealistic and may severely strain the relationship. Striving to be one denies the individuality of both partners and confuses the notion of intimacy with that of too much "togetherness" or sameness (McGoldrick 1980).

For most children, a time comes when they—as young adults—separate themselves from their parents and establish their autonomy. This is a gradual process marked by adolescent struggle to redefine boundaries of the self and to discover ways to live separately from parents. This period is marked by intervals of distancing that alternate with returns for emotional and financial refueling. At the end of this period, the adult personality emerges as a product of the successes and failures of childhood and adolescence.

The adult personality is characterized by greater security and integration and a readiness to establish intimacy with others that includes a willingness to be open with thoughts and feelings. As one study on adult identity concludes:

> People must first begin to feel more secure in their identities; they then become able to establish *intimacy* with themselves (in their inner lives) and with others.

This is the case both in friendship and eventually in a love-based mutually satisfying sexual relationship. In addition to establishing a mutually satisfying sexual relationship, the issues in establishing intimacy with another person involve learning to share financial goals, ideas, friends, and emotions. It is the successful establishment of this sharing that enables one to achieve intimacy. When people cannot enter wholly into an intimate relationship because of the fear of losing their identities, they may develop a sense of isolation. (Gernstein and Papen-Daniel 1981, p. 2)

Unfortunately, some persons never have the chance to develop a sense of separateness. Those who marry young—in their teens or early twenties—often move directly from dependence on their parents to dependence on a partner who may also be less than autonomous. Neither of them may have had time to learn to be independent. Once married, each may cling to the other, full of anxiety about being alone and giving the other room to be alone. The other may begin to feel trapped, as though he or she missed some freedom that it is now too late to capture.

Some newly married persons experience a feeling of having been "engulfed." There is a terror that vulnerability and total togetherness mean a surrender of the budding self. The very word *surrender* can cause acute anxiety in a man or woman who lacks a solid sense of identity. For such a person, the only way to survive seems to be to resist intimacy out of the fear of being swallowed up. If both partners fear being engulfed by each other's needs and desires for closeness, they may view each other alternately as demanding or clinging and then as emotionally and physically distant. If only one partner avoids the vulnerability of intimacy, the other often experiences a chasing game—the more frustrated and distressed he or she becomes, the more the other runs away. A frequent complaint in marriage is that one partner feels he or she is constantly asking for more openness and sharing while the other retreats.

The fear of being engulfed and the fear of abandonment may seem at first glance to be opposites, but both actually stem from the same lack of inner self-confidence and sense of identity. Both are the result of a fear of true intimacy—one that intimacy will devour the insecure "self," and the other that the vulnerability that accompanies intimacy is a possible prelude to abandonment. Both feelings point to the fact that one cannot be intimate with another person unless one is secure enough to risk vulnerability. To communicate openly implies that one is willing to share in a way that may leave one vulnerable.

Fears of vulnerability adversely affect the ability to communicate in those who have a poorly defined sense of self. Psychiatrist William Meisner (1978, p. 47) has said of such individuals:

The poorly defined self establishes a relationship of dependence upon the other which tends to have a life and death quality. It is as though life and existence depend on the attachment to the important other. Often this attachment has a quality of hostile dependence to it, the "can't live with you, can't live without you" syndrome which is so familiar to clinicians.

As the person with a well differentiated and individuated identity enters into a relationship, he/she is able to enter into, share, and participate freely in the emotional life that takes place between and around the marital partners.

Honesty

An important aspect of quality communication is, of course, *honesty*. We have already stressed that, for good communication to exist, not only must one know what one feels and thinks, but the information must be believable to one's partner. Honesty helps clarify feelings, avert misunderstandings, and dissipate resentments. With so much emphasis on full and free communication as the basis for a satisfying relationship, it is easy to see how total honesty has come to be seen as a worthy goal.

How much one reveals must likewise be measured against how much one's partner reveals. Research indicates that an imbalance in levels of honesty between partners results in a lower level of marital adjustment. Regardless of the amount of self-disclosure exchanged, partners who are similarly open and honest are more satisfied than partners with a marked discrepancy in openness between them (Davidson, Balswick, and Halverson 1983).

There are times, however, when telling the total truth may not be in the best interests of the relationship. Frankness may be a mask for hostility or for a need to unload one's fears or guilt or to seek reassurance for one's own opinions. In short, there may be such a thing as too much honesty—the kind that can cause conflicts and harm relationships. Family therapist Paul Watzlawick put it well when he said, "A large part of communication consists in knowing what one is not supposed to say, not supposed to think, not supposed to see, not supposed to hear" (Wilder 1978, p. 41).

In a study made some years ago, couples reported that they felt the biggest difference between good and bad communication was whether a partner said things that would be better left unsaid (Levinger and Senn 1967). Honesty appears to be a two-way street, involving both the giving and the seeking of information but not the frankness that is intended to hurt or to bolster oneself at the other's expense. The problem for each partner is to be sensitive to occasions when frankness may hurt rather than help.

Family therapist Richard Stuart (1976) uses the concept of "measured honesty" to describe the balance between honesty and frankness-for-the-sake-of-being-frank. He cautions couples first to ask themselves whether what they have to say will be *constructive* to the relationship and, second, whether it is *necessary* to a better understanding between them.

In every successful relationship some things probably go unsaid in the interest of getting along more harmoniously. Criticism usually falls into this category. Successful married couples have usually learned to use criticism sparingly and never to hide behind "This is for your own good." Although the intent of criticism may be to help one's partner, it often is read as disapproval or even rejection. Apparent disapproval can lead to feelings of alienation and lack of support rather than to a sense that the criticism was for one's own good. The implications of feeling rejected have been documented by family therapists who link **disconfirmation** and feelings of alienation with disturbances in marriages and families (Watzlawick, Beavin, and Jackson 1967).

Advice about honesty from marital therapists can be summarized as follows (Lasswell and Lobsenz 1979c, p. 69):

- Before you volunteer information or respond to a question, ask yourself: Is what I am about to say really true? Is it useful for the other person to know it? Will there be a more appropriate time and place to make this statement? Am I saying this to put myself "one up"?
- Be as certain as you can about the other person's emotional capacity to handle a frank answer or comment. In general, someone who is unwilling to level with you is unlikely to want you to respond frankly to him or her. At certain times or in certain situations, a person may be more sensitive or vulnerable than at other times.
- Be sensitive to the other person's values, and talk about matters you know are important to him or her with particular accuracy, gentleness, and tact.

One of the barriers to honesty in communication is that sometimes honesty hurts and, in the effort to be kind, one may not tell the truth. It is true that, as surely as disapproval is correlated with unhappiness in marriage, endorsement and acceptance are correlated with happiness and satisfaction in the relationship (Clarke 1973). This is not to imply that approval always works for healthy marital functioning. For example, approval that is not honestly felt—perhaps given to avoid an argument or for fear of hurting the partner's feelings—may set up an atmosphere of disconfirmation. Honest approval says, "You are right" or "I like you." Disconfirmation communicates, "You cannot handle what I might say" or even "You do not exist" (Watzlawick, Beavin, and Jackson 1967). What is perhaps most important for quality communication and for marital satisfaction is that both partners agree on the defintions each holds about the other and about the relationship, whether approving or disapproving. For communication to be a quality experience, it is vital to have what one is, what one thinks, what one feels, what one does, and what one says confirmed by another. Experts on marriage emphasize that the amount of agreement about each other's good qualities couples have is predictive of their degree of intimacy (Sprenkle and Olson 1978; Fisher and Sprenkle 1978).

Having partners agree with each one's own self-concept and behavior is called **mutual validation.** It is a singularly important aspect of positive human interaction and of individual psychological well-being. Studies of communication indicate that marriages in which there are mutual validations have more realistic expectations and better communication (Levinger and Senn 1967). As reported in one survey of marital communication, mutual validation "permeates all segments of the partners' lives together. It determines their style in managing such stock marital concerns as conflict, ... decision making, ... and affiliation" (Montgomery 1981, p. 28). When two people feel confident that their partners see them in the same ways that they see themselves, responses to each other are bound to be more appropriate and communication more open.

Trust

As we have suggested, intimacy and vulnerability are indispensable conditions in openness and honesty in communication. Trust, which is essential to intimacy and vulnerability, is largely based on how honest two people are with each other.

Many psychologists think that the ability to trust begins early in life when children must depend on others for their very survival. As a result of these early experiences—good or bad—and of other life experiences as we grow older, men and women enter relationships with varying abilities to let themselves trust. This leads to the conclusion that trust is measured not just by a partner's trustworthiness but by how each individual can or cannot allow himself or herself to be trusting.

Most couples entering into a commitment to marriage have some measure of trust for each other. Yet, it is quite common to see two people who trust each other in the routines of daily living and working together become defensive in areas where caring and love are involved. Nowhere do we see this more clearly than in their attempts to communicate ideas and feelings that really matter.

There are some important conditions that promote lack of trust and consequent defensiveness when two people attempt to communicate. One, in particular, is conveying by words, gestures, or tone of voice that a negative judgment is being made, especially when blame is likely to be assigned to the communicator. Such judgments often include making an inference about the communicator's motivations, feelings, and thoughts. These inferences are then treated as factual, and any further effort to explain may be detoured to a misunderstanding, a fight, or a cold silence. It is quite frequently the case that the evaluator conveys a superior, "one-up" stance that arouses defensiveness in his or her partner as a self-protective mechanism. To feel put down or inadequate is hardly conducive to open communication.

In some instances, the defensiveness and lack of trust seem to be the result of one partner's feeling at a verbal disadvantage when trying to express ideas or feelings to the other. Some people are more articulate, and they need to be sensitive to the effect this may have on a less verbal partner. Although women are usually thought to be the most verbal, studies have indicated that men tend to dominate conversations, interrupt, and change the subject more than do the women to whom they are talking. Yet men seldom do this to each other (Zimmerman and West 1975). Today's more assertive women may resist this pattern more than did women in the more traditional mold.

Another major reason for a lack of trust is that some senders are worried that their messages will be used against them. They may believe that their partner will use shared information to control future discussions or to manipulate future events. Believing that our listener has a selfish strategy or that our words may come back to haunt us can easily turn an attempt to communicate into defensive game playing or shut down communication entirely. To facilitate trust in communication, a listener needs to convey sincere, non-self-serving interest in what others are saying. Mutual supportiveness rather than self-interest conveys an attitude that "we are on the same team." Research also shows that when each partner listens to the thoughts and feelings of the other without judging, blaming, or giving unsolicited criticism or advice, couples can, at least most of the time, decrease defensiveness and promote a trusting atmosphere for good communication (Indvik and Fitzpatrick 1982).

Empathy

Empathy results from the ability to listen actively and attentively. In a survey of therapists, it was reported that listening and being empathic and receptive to a partner's messages are vital to good communication and are important determinants of

Taking the time to talk and to listen empathically and to develop a unique communication style increases comfort in the relationship and builds a foundation of security.

marital satisfaction (Fisher and Sprenkle 1978). Empathy is the ability to identify with another's emotional state even when one does not actually share those same feelings. There may be no more difficult assignment than this in a couple's efforts to communicate with each other. We will discuss how empathy plays a role in all of marital life throughout the rest of the book. Here we focus on why males and females often have difficulty imagining being in each other's shoes.

Men and women sometimes seem to operate on different wavelengths. For instance, several research studies have found that the two sexes have quite different ways of speaking and writing—that the same words frequently connote different concepts to each. Women tend to use more nouns and descriptive adjectives in their conversations; men tend to use more verbs that convey movement and action (Maccoby and Jacklin 1974).

Studies have shown that even at a very early age, boys are more interested in objects and in seeing how things work than are girls. When very young, boys demonstrate spatial orientation, depth perception, and a sense of direction superior to the analogous capabilities of girls (McGuinness and Pribram 1979). Their interests change the way they perceive the world and the way they communicate about what they perceive. On the other hand, young girls seem attuned to human relations from their earliest months of life. They smile earlier (some studies report that females smile more throughout their lives), talk earlier, and pay more attention to people than do boys. They learn early to rely on social cues and, as their verbal ability develops, seem more aware than boys of verbal behavior in others.

Men are presumably more articulate about facts than they are about emotions. As marital therapists, we see one problem that bears on this so often that it merits mention. When a boy grows up and marries, he may handle his more "feminine" emotions with stoicism, silence, repression—what has been called the "stiff-upper-lip" attitude. This may puzzle his wife, who as a woman may feel free to cry when

COMMUNICATION ABOUT EMOTIONS

A great deal has been written and said about how important it is for men to be able to express their emotions. However, men often complain that when they do so, it seems to upset women. Recently, this issue became a lively topic of discussion in a class on changing sex roles. One male student reported that his wife said that he comes on too strong and that when he pounds the table in anger or cries, it makes her frightened. Yet, she urges him to share his worries and feelings with her. "She says she can't stand to see me so upset," he told the class. "So I am not sure how to behave."

"I know how she feels," a young woman quickly responded. "Sometimes when my boyfriend gets really upset, I leave the room. We finally figured out that he and I express our feelings very differently, and I don't know how to respond to him when he tells me how he feels. I have even thought he was angry with me when he wasn't at all. One time I asked him to help me hang some curtains, and when he dropped the screwdriver he acted furious. I thought it was because I had asked him to do something for me that he didn't want to do. He did get angry with me then because he said I always take his feelings so personally. He was only upset at his clumsiness."

The responses of women to men who cried in front of them were more puzzling to most of the men than the reactions they received to their "anger." Most of the women in the class acknowledged that it was much easier for them to deal with another women's tears than with a man's.

It is quite possible that some men have adjusted to the idea of expressing their emotions more than the women in their lives have. When women ask for nontraditional behavior from men and then have trouble accepting it, they place men in the classical double bind: "Damned if you do, and damned if you don't." Both men and women have to work with patience and sensitivity to develop new communication patterns to meet changing sex roles.

Here are some steps for allowing one another to communicate emotions effectively:

1. Try to watch for signs that your partner may want to (or need to) express his or her feelings. Clues may be unexplained silence, physical withdrawal, irritability, or even unusual eating, drinking, or spending patterns. Any upsetting or exciting event may also cause an emotional buildup and a need to talk about feelings.
2. Sit down in a private setting, facing each other and perhaps holding hands or touching each other in some way, to facilitate more open expression of feelings.
3. Listen attentively and without interrupting. Do *not* say "You shouldn't feel that way," and do not belittle the other person's feelings in any way.
4. Do not overreact or sympathize in a patronizing way. Joining the other person's feelings by becoming as hurt or angry as he or she is can be discouraging. Sharing with another is positive, but outdoing them is not helpful.
5. Do not use what is shared as a weapon later on, and never gossip to others about the confidences with which you have been entrusted.

she is upset and to acknowledge her feelings more openly, as she has done since her girlhood. She often complains that in her relationships with men there is little sharing of feelings. Thus, many women report that men not only fail to share feelings but also seem distressed when women exhibit emotions. On the other hand, the same women may be distressed at their partners' exhibitions of "masculine" feelings—anger and sexual assertiveness, for example—and their verbal and physical expressions. The extent to which these respective gender-related feelings are the result of structural

FEIFFER

MAN TALKS. WOMAN LISTENS.

WOMAN FALLS IN LOVE WITH MAN AND HIS TALK.

MAN AND WOMAN MARRY.

WOMAN TALKS. SHE HAS BECOME "WIFE."

MAN DOESN'T TALK; MAN DOESN'T LISTEN. HE HAS BECOME "HUSBAND."

TRIBAL RITE.

brain differences in the two sexes or of enculturation is currently a matter of debate in some circles. Whatever the case, it seems clear that there are gender differences in feeling-based behaviors and possibly in the learned definitions of feelings themselves that affect the ability of males and females to empathize with each other.

To facilitate empathy and mutual understanding, both partners must recognize and be empathic to their uniqueness as men and women. Each partner must be able to take the role of the other and to *control the flow of communication* to produce constructive results. In other words, quality communication requires "marriage partners to control their communication rather than letting their communication control them" (Montgomery 1981, p. 28).

Listening

Listening is an active process, one that requires concentration. Unless both partners listen actively to each other, there can be no dialogue. Listening also requires that one be able to give "feedback" on what has been said. That is, the listener should be able to sum up what the speaker has just said to the satisfaction of both. A study of couples with communication difficulties reported that the most frequent problem was that neither partner really listened to the other (Schauble and Hill 1976). Common faults in listening are interrupting constantly, not paying attention, hearing only the parts that one wants to hear, picking out points to debate rather than waiting for the complete message, and becoming so emotional that concentration is blocked (Kelly 1977).

Because listening is often poor, *misinterpretation* is common. Misinterpretation, of course, is just as often the result of the way the message is sent as of the way it is received. Quality communication, then, depends equally on each partner's capacity to send and receive information.

Listening with empathy means that one tries to put oneself in another person's shoes and to understand what he or she is feeling. Several research studies have pointed to the positive effect that empathic listening has on marital communication (Scheff 1967; Schulman 1974). Empathic listening shows a genuine interest and concern for what others mean: an empathic listener usually has to get beyond words or gestures to discover the intent of the message. To be an empathic listener, one must examine one's own assumptions and avoid attributing one's personal meanings to what another says without trying to discover the other's *intended* meanings.

Listening and giving appropriate feedback are particularly difficult for most couples when emotions are running high. Maintaining one's emotional balance while listening is a special and demanding skill. In recent years, there was a popular notion that venting emotions freely was the best way to get marital discord out in the open. With the emotional atmosphere cleared—the theory held—a couple could begin to deal with the real issues. Some couples have found that this works, but most experts believe that the dangers of aggressive confrontation may prove more counterproductive than helpful. Instead, they counsel cooling off first and then discussing (Lasswell and Lobsenz, 1976).

Styles of Communication

It has been suggested that the ability to establish and sustain a smooth and easy pattern of interaction is the essential element of quality communication (Argyle 1969). Couples develop rules governing their dialogues that may make communication either more or less effective. Eventually the rules shape predictable and stable patterns. Such patterns are the result of the couple's continued interaction and are related to their reported level of marital satisfaction. If the rules encourage open communication, the satisfaction level is high. If the rules impede communication, the satisfaction level is affected negatively (Jackson 1977).

It may seem strange that couples frequently develop and sustain unworkable patterns of communication. It is true, however, that oftentimes both partners participate willingly and consistently in some or all of the following communication rules, all of which can cause problems:

1. They interrupt each other so that the speaker is sidetracked.
2. They fail to complete their messages, leaving the listener with an inadequate understanding.
3. They are vague, sometimes purposely, as in "You really upset me last night, but I'd rather not talk about it," when the listener is unaware of the upset.
4. They make impersonal statements in the third person by talking about "some people" instead of "you," "mother," "Mary," or "I."
5. They overgeneralize by using terms such as "always," "never," "men don't . . . ," "women like to . . . ," or "older people can't. . . ."
6. They evoke emotional responses when asking for or giving information.

Drawing by Levin; © 1978 The New Yorker Magazine, Inc.

7. They complain about the other's attributes or past behaviors rather than dealing with the issue at hand.
8. They grow silent or leave the area to avoid hearing new information that they fear will be threatening to them in some way. (This differs from leaving when the same information is being repeated over and over.)

Several inventories have been developed to assess marital communication patterns and behaviors. Perhaps the best known is the Marital Communication Inventory (MCI), which uses 46 questions to yield information concerning regard, empathy, self-disclosure, discussion, aversive communication (that is, communication that causes the listener to withdraw because it is painful), and conflict management (Bienvenu 1978). The degree of regard or general supportiveness each partner feels for and from the other seems especially important for marital adjustment and may be the key to other aspects measured by this inventory. Without positive regard, there is some question of how empathy can be experienced; how safe self-disclosure can be; or how discussion leading to conflict resolution can be maintained without each partner resorting to aversive techniques (Schumm et al. 1983).

One analysis of basic communication styles among couples described three types: complementary, symmetrical, and parallel (Scoresby 1977). It is believed that although most couples may use all three, there is a tendency for each to favor one of these modes of communication.

In the complementary communication style, each partner plays counterpoint to the other. For example, one may be verbal and expressive, and the other quiet and self-contained. If each were as talkative or as quiet as the other, their pattern would be symmetrical. A symmetrical pattern is often seen in couples who compete with each other for center stage, each trying to outtalk the other. This may be their way of trying to influence each other or to win arguments. Members of silent couples, too, may use the silence to maximize their control of the situation.

The third style, parallel communication, is more flexible and emphasizes situational adaptability. When one partner needs to talk, the other listens. In another situation, the roles may be reversed. Those who adopt this as a favored pattern communicate in a manner that seems most appropriate for the particular situation. This quality is believed to be important to marital satisfaction; flexibility in both style and content is a factor in what couples consider good communication (Gilbert 1976).

Four styles, or levels, of communication different from those described above give another way to classify communication. Each has a characteristic set of intentions behind it (Zerin and Zerin 1980).

1. *Style I:* a casual, chatty conversation that is meant to keep things light and friendly. Many couples use this style to check in with each other at the end of the day or to talk sociably over breakfast or dinner. Often there is little content and few feelings are involved.
2. *Style II:* the intention of this style is to persuade or to give directions. Conversation is punctuated with the words *should* and *ought*. This style often is judgmental, blaming, and filled with unsolicited advice about how the other might behave differently. Often this style is high in emotional content.
3. *Style III:* this style is often speculative and explores alternatives. Many questions are asked in a search for thoughts and feelings; the implication is that others will ask questions too. Unlike Style II, which has *the* answers, Style III is searching.
4. *Style IV:* this style emphasizes sharing of thoughts. Compared with Style III, less tentativeness and more personal statements are involved. A problem-solving approach is evident, which is explicit, responsive, accepting, and aware—based on listening to the other.

Style IV is viewed as the most fruitful for the development and maintenance of a compatible relationship because this style allows two people to resolve differences. In this type of interchange, couples share feelings and emotions and reveal their perceptions of themselves.

Another communication-style typology also defines four communication styles: controlling, conventional, speculative, and contactful (Hawkins, Weisberg, and Ray 1977).

1. *Controlling:* persons who exhibit this style discourage any disagreement and seek to have their own way. Often they show little awareness of their partner's opinions; even if they do, being right and winning is more important to them than affection or having a good relationship. Power in all decisions and issues is paramount for a person who is classified as controlling. Implicit is lack of trust of the partner's judgment or capabilities, or sometimes lack of respect for the partner's personal dignity.
2. *Conventional:* this style is similar to Style I or Style II described earlier. Those who communicate in this manner give the appearance of talking, but the topics

are superficial and do not risk exploring issues that may be emotional or controversial.

3. *Speculative:* this type involves exploration of issues and openness to new ideas. This kind of person, however, is unable to self-disclose readily and may spend a good deal of time asking questions of the partner to avoid talking about himself or herself.

4. *Contactful:* persons who exhibit this style not only are interested in their partners' viewpoints but are also self-revealing. They are similar to Style IV communicators mentioned earlier in that they emphasize sharing of thoughts. This type, followed by the speculative style, was ranked as the most positive communication style in the research that defined these four types.

Some couples seem to start out with a similarity of communication style. This may, in fact, have been an important reason that they were drawn together in the first place. Other successful couples have had to work at developing a good communication style because they have not always understood each other. Some couples seem to expect little communication with each other and are not disappointed by its lack. Others discuss everything and would be unhappy any other way. Dissatisfaction evidently is experienced only when expectations are not met (Komarovsky 1964). Good marital communication, then, is based on mutuality and shared understandings that allow couples to experience intimacy and security with each other. Communication expert Barbara Montgomery (1981, p. 27) believes that this process is necessary to each couple's definition of marriage:

> Within the marital dyad spouses are constantly sharing information about their individual conceptualizations of the relationship and then negotiating a mutually acceptable relationship definition. This process of collaboration results in a "custom-made" definition of marriage that is unique to the individuals involved.

SEXUAL COMMUNICATION

Communication occurs whenever two or more people arrive at the conclusion that they have achieved the same idea or the same feelings about an idea as a result of their interaction. Of course, no one can ever know whether two persons' ideas and feelings are really the same because there is no way to observe another person's ideas or feelings directly. All that can be observed directly are behaviors or bodily changes believed to result from ideas and feelings—what a person says, what he or she does, what happens to his or her body. Some words, an action, a blush, or a tear give clues to another's thoughts and feelings.

Sexual communication is a special kind of communication between partners. It differs from personal sexual satisfaction, although the latter may facilitate good communication and also may be facilitated by it. For people with a high degree of sympathetic understanding about their mutual sexual activities, intimacy and love may be more effectively communicated by actions than by words.

Obstacles to Open Communication

Some couples who report that they communicate well in other areas of their lives may find talking about sex troublesome. Many couples seem hesitant to comment on a partner's sexual behavior and equally reticent to speak of their own desires. It seems paradoxical that in a time of liberated sexuality, many couples find that talking about their own or their partner's sexual behavior, needs, and desires is troublesome, but this is frequently so. Probably the risk of rejection, which could be devastating to anyone who needs to feel attractive—or even adequate—is too great at times for persons to express their sexual thoughts to a partner that they do not want to lose.

There are several major obstacles to constructive sexual communication. One of the most common is embarrassment. Embarrassment is rooted in inhibitions often learned as a child in a family where talk about sex elicited embarrassed silence—or sometimes reproof or even punishment—from parents. Sex is a powerful, attractive drive in the minds and bodies of most men and women. If this were not so, the human species would have died out long ago. Sex is also symbolic and reflects values not only of each partner but of their relationship in general. Most partners believe that talk of sex between them must affirm, support, and make each feel loved and accepted. Uniquenesses or suggestions for improvements may be viewed as risky. Marital and sex therapists find that overcoming this insecurity about one's sexual acceptance is the first step toward better sex talk—and toward better sex (Lasswell and Lobsenz 1983).

Like all other kinds of intimacy, sexual intimacy rests on a foundation of mutually honest communication. However, another obstacle to good sexual communication is fear of such honesty. Many partners fear that frankness often will be interpreted as personal criticism; indeed, it is not uncommon for a person to precede a highly destructive remark with "I know you want me to be perfectly honest with you." This fear is not without justification since many males' sexual assertiveness has met with resistance, censure, or even punishment at some time in the past. As a result, many couples continue to endure less than satisfactory sex rather than to risk any conversation about it.

We can only speculate that problems in sexual communication may pose special problems because of the emotional content of such messages and because in our society "sex talk" was not present in most families of origin. Serious inhibitions and a great deal of sensitivity often surround such issues.

It may be difficult for some women to understand the penetration of another person's body as a loving act, even though the same women can accept a growing fetus within them with a loving feeling. It may be difficult for some men to understand the wish to be penetrated and impregnated as loving. It is probably easier for both men and women to understand the giving and receiving of pleasure in orgasm as loving behavior. It is often easier, therefore, for a couple to feel in touch with one another about sexual behaviors that lead to mutual satisfaction from day to day than to agree on whether or not there are differences between the deep underlying sexual urges of men and women.

Improving Sexual Communication

Suggestions for improving sexual communication fall into two general categories: ways partners can ask for what they want and ways each can find out what the other wants. Expressing one's own needs and desires is best accomplished by positive and loving comments rather than by critical ones. By not shifting the responsibility to the other, one partner can minimize the chances of making the other partner defensive. Saying "Touch me here" rather than "Don't touch me there" is not only specific but noncritical. Making specific statements about one's own sensations and feelings may elicit more information from a partner than asking questions about the partner's sensations. Checking out nonverbal clues such as voice tones and body movements can provide additional information. The essence of sexual communication is to make oneself and one's partner as comfortable as possible about sex talk. Defensiveness is a sure way to cut off constructive sexual communication.

Specifically, how do those in close relationships go about asking for what they want and finding out what the other wants in order to increase sexual intimacy? Four important areas common to all quality communication are also, we believe, crucial for sexual communication: signals, meanings, feelings, and roles.

Signals *Signals* vary in clarity and accuracy. Verbal communication is at its best when words are clearly spoken and used with shared meaning. Nonverbal communication is most successful when touches can be felt, sighs can be heard, and frowns or smiles can be seen. Only half the responsibility lies with the one who signals. The intended receiver must also be listening, watching, paying attention, and recognizing the significance of the signals.

Getting signals straight may be the easiest step in communication in most situations; however, in highly emotional sexual interaction, although crucial, it is not always simple: many people will not ask such questions as "What did you say?" or "Did you touch me there on purpose?" or "Did you pull away just now?" To confirm, deny, or elaborate on signals appears to be difficult for many persons. Some couples seem to believe that they should intuitively know what the signals mean and that clarification should be unnecessary. Often, however, partners do not read each other very well. In working with couples, we have found that most can improve their sexual communication by learning to understand each other's signals. The assumption that one person naturally understands the other's signals is frequently a source of sexual difficulty (Bell and Lobsenz 1977).

Meanings As discussed earlier, *meanings* behind words or gestures must be mutually understood to facilitate good communication. This principle is equally true in sexual communication. What meaning is intended when a woman slips her hand inside a man's shirt or when she straightens his necktie? What meaning is intended when a man takes a shower and shaves before going to bed? Are the meanings the same for both persons?

One couple reported that they had difficulty understanding each other's signals until the husband figured out that when his wife said, "I'm going to bed now. Are you going to be long?" she meant she was interested in sex and wished he would turn off the television set and come to bed with her. He had never caught her meaning before and had always interpreted her question as meaning that she was tired and hoped he would not stay up too late or disturb her sleep when he finally did come to bed. Meanwhile, she had been feeling rejected.

Exploration of meanings sometimes reveals hidden agenda; the outcome is not always desirable. In the previous example, the woman might actually have been tired;

if her husband had followed her to bed in hopes of having sex, she might have considered him just as insensitive for not knowing that she really meant to go to sleep.

Feelings   *Feelings* almost always accompany a couple's sexual behavior with each other. Two people who can be open with each other about their feelings usually gain useful information for increasing sympathetic understanding and for facilitating sexual communication. In general, listening to another's description of his or her feelings and granting that person the right to have those feelings, whether they are agreeable or not, encourage sexual intimacy.

Occasionally one partner or both may have negative feelings about their sexual life with each other. As painful as it is to talk about these matters, keeping silent is often a greater barrier to improvement. Dishonesty blocks intimacy whenever it makes it difficult or impossible for partners to develop shared meaning. Feelings are not always logical, but they are real nonetheless. They often can be traced to the sexual scripts that each partner brings into the relationship. Talking about them often puts them in a perspective that can enable the couple to deal with them. Unspoken, they remain troublesome.

Roles   Finally, a part of sexual communication involves a consensus about the *roles* taken by the persons involved. A person making a sexual statement or gesture is assuming the existence of some kind of relationship with the partner. By assuming a role, one necessarily projects a reciprocal role on the person with whom one is interacting. For example, a woman who believes that men should always be the initiators of sex may be dissapointed when her partner does not initiate sex. But having defined her role as one who waits to be asked and his role as one who initiates, she will not make any suggestion herself.

Consciousness of the role one is taking is vital to good sexual communication. It is also necessary to let one's partner know what is expected and to determine his or her own consciousness of that role. If one's partner does not wish to play out the role, a mutually acceptable one can often be negotiated. Sexual relationships can involve the roles of "teacher," "learner," "critic," "judge," "nurturer," "adventurer," "martyr," and so forth—and a long list of ways that each role can be played.

Each role demands that one's role partner enact the reciprocal role if communication is to be achieved. Being a teacher is senseless if there is no learner; being a critic is futile if no one is open to criticism; being a judge is meaningless if there is no one on trial. Being aware of the role one takes in communication makes it easier to discover what role one is demanding the other take and therefore to adjust one's messages accordingly.

An index of good sexual communication is a mutual feeling of closeness and intimacy. The cues between two people may be subtle—just a touch or a word—but easily responded to. Sexual communication may well permeate all aspects of a couple's life together (Scoresby 1977).

Sexual communication is one of the most intimate and often one of the most difficult kinds of interaction between couples. Sexual signals and their meanings are often vague, yet highly emotional. Awareness of the roles taken by and hence assigned to sexual partners plays an important part in sexual communication.

There are bound to be times of conflict in every enduring relationship. Arguing may help clear the air, but it is only preliminary to the final stage of conflict resolution, which is negotiation of differences.

Resolving Differences

One stress in relationships lies in the naturalness—if not inevitability—of disagreement. This is stressful because the ideal of communicating freely and well sometimes is accompanied by another idea—that open disagreement is "bad." Most people acquired this sentiment from unsettling childhood experiences with others (usually parents) who were angry with them. Since children are often punished for acting out their anger, particularly if the anger is directed toward parents, it is an easy step to believing that disagreement is bad.

Free and unguarded communication therefore seems risky because it might lead to disagreement and conflict; it might hurt feelings or damage the relationship. The less secure one feels, the more risk there appears to be in open communication.

Some people may consciously believe that one way to reduce threats to a relationship is to avoid accurate and meaningful communication. Unfortunately, this tactic tends to lessen communication and to make misperception more likely. The result is a vicious circle in which personal stress and insecurity in the relationship increase, making the relationship more insecure than ever.

One way of denying conflict or disagreement is to assume that one's partner shares one's important values, beliefs, or ideas about right and wrong. The partner is idealized as a good person who wants to do good things, just as one is and does oneself, so disagreement cannot exist. When the partner eventually and inevitably behaves differently, the idealizer may respond with anger and feel betrayed. Since no two people are identical, it is unrealistic to expect any other person to have exactly the same goals, values, morals, and tastes as oneself. Thus, idealization is doomed from the start, although it is still a major factor in some persons' choice of marriage partner.

One of the most important aspects of marital communication is how couples resolve their differences. Happily married couples have been found to use ways that are different from those of unhappily married couples. The latter use a great deal of "cross-complaining." This sets up a chain of negative responses that can easily escalate to a real fight or, instead, sidetrack the discussion. Each partner typically becomes defensive and responds in accordance with that defensiveness rather than to the partner's messages. Both frequently come away from the argument feeling misunderstood.

Happily married couples, on the other hand, do not get locked into defensive attitudes that prevent them from listening to each other's side. They listen carefully and sympathetically, although not necessarily with agreement. They argue no less vigorously for their own beliefs, but they do not get stuck before they get to the negotiating stage of resolving problems. Happily married couples are more likely to listen for the intent of the message as well as to the overt content (Gottman 1979).

Every marriage has conflicts from time to time. Most couples have developed methods to resolve them; if this were not so, the divorce rate would likely be higher. Conflict is so much a recognized phenomenon in relationships that many family experts use conflict theory to explain much of marital interaction (Sprey 1979). Conflict theory proposes that it is impossible for two persons who are products of unique experiences (one having been treated as a male and one as a female while growing up, for instance) to live together without having their uniquenesses clash from time to time. It is through the resolution of these disagreements that growth in the relationship is believed to occur. Many marital therapists encourage couples to bring disagreements into the open so that they can experience the growth that comes from resolving them rather than simply avoid a fight (Charney 1974).

The amount of conflict varies from couple to couple, of course, and the amount that a given couple experiences may vary from period to period during the marital life cycle. In other words, some couples may argue throughout a lifetime as an accepted part of their interaction—they may even expect to disagree almost daily. Some even appear to enjoy a good argument and have developed a pattern of fighting unique to their marriage. Couples who develop this pattern of interaction have been described as "conflict-habituated" by some experts who believe these partners have a habituated need to do psychological battle with each other (Cuber and Harroff 1963). Other couples may go along smoothly for periods of time but have cycles in which they disagree much more than usual. These usually are periods of change in one or both partners that make it necessary to confront certain troublesome issues between them. Some marital therapists believe that change by one partner and the other partner's resistance to that change is the basis for much marital conflict.

Change and Conflict

Two kinds of personal change have been recognized in the literature (Watzlawick, Weakland, and Fisch 1974). There is change that arises out of the natural stages of life. Such change comes gradually and seems to fit sensibly into normal life-cycle

patterns. People marry and have children, children grow and adults mature, relationships deepen and fade away—these changes we can accept and understand. They are likely to occur for both partners over generally the same period of time, and couples can usually deal with such transitions together—or at least have a degree of understanding about what is going on so that they are able to weather the other's "natural" disruptions (Lasswell and Lobsenz 1978b). Sometimes these changes cause disagreements, but for the most part they seem to cause far less disruption than does the next variety.

A second kind of change seems to occur abruptly and unpredictably. Forces may have been at work for a long time to cause such change, but it often appears sudden and puzzling to both partners. For example, one partner may suddenly announce that he or she has resigned from a job. The idea may have been fermenting for weeks, or it may have been an impulsive action. To the partner who is caught off guard, it may be not only a surprise but a disruptive one at that. This variety of change is often cause for conflict in a marriage.

Even changes that both partners agree are desirable may disrupt their marriage equilibrium (Terkelson 1980). Such changes usually require transformation of attitudes toward the initiating partner's new status or new behavior. There may be a sense of discontinuity, strangeness, and frustration. Some such changes provoke anger, anxiety, confusion, or even a feeling of betrayal. Such changes frequently call for extensive alterations in the relationship and are therefore understandably unsettling.

The partner who makes an unexpected change forces a change on his or her partner. For example, many former homemakers who enter the labor force and become enthusiastic about their jobs make changes in their marriages that cause resentment and confusion on the part of their husbands. Systems theory explains that when one partner in a system changes his or her behavior, the other partner must change in reaction (Broderick and Smith 1979). For many persons, having to change in order to accommodate another's behavior is distressing, and their resistance is the basic element in the conflict that results.

Another kind of conflict involving change in relationships is the desire of one partner for the other to change. Conflicts in a marriage often are reduced to blaming the partner. Criticism of one partner by the other becomes a weapon; the clear message delivered is "If only *you* would change, there would be no problem." Criticism and blame are much less effective in negotiating change in another than are respecting the other's dignity, stating one's own position, and patiently focusing on the interpersonal problem rather than the other's "wrongness."

People do not usually resist change just because they are innately stubborn. Most persons are more comfortable with stable (that is, unchanging) relationships because they feel more secure in being able to predict the effects of their own behaviors in the relationship; they know how the other is likely to respond to what they do. Changes create the risk of unpredictable responses and hence of having to redefine the other's intentions. Changes require reorganization. Changes heighten insecurities. On the other hand, complete stability in a relationship is impossible because people, situations, and even the world about us are in constant change.

Marital and family therapists are familiar with resistance to change and with the difficulties, in particular, of adjusting to what appears to be a sudden change in one family member. It is this difficulty with "evolving"—or being stuck in an outmoded way of reacting to a changed partner—that is at the heart of many marital problems. As one family therapist has written, ". . . the task of therapy should be to make available . . . the power inherent in all living systems: the ability to transcend the stuckness and move to a different stage" (Hoffman 1980, p. 55).

Most couples do not need marital therapy to accomplish the adjustments or "transcend the stuckness" involving their own and their partner's changes throughout the life cycle. Couples usually learn that communicating about the motives for the change and reassurance about its outcomes go a long way toward making it easier to understand what is happening. It is inevitable that two people will change. How each person adjusts to change becomes crucial to the success of their relationship.

In recent years, behavior modification has become a popular method for teaching couples to change their own and each other's behaviors through the use of rewards for desired behaviors (Jacobsen and Margolin 1979). A husband may, for example, exchange an act his wife desires for a change he is requesting from her. For instance, he may agree to build shelves to store her papers and books if she will agree to keep the desk they share uncluttered. A contract such as this can prove useful in achieving specific changes, and most couples agree that it is more pleasant than criticism.

Family therapists have suggested three important steps involved in negotiating change (Lasswell and Lobsenz 1979a):

1. *Communication:* talking honestly about the behavior in question and the changes desired is important. Who seeks the change, why the other values stability, and what goals the change would achieve need to be understood by both.
2. *Specific goals:* the partner who is asking the other to change can facilitate an understanding by being specific about what he or she wants the other to do. This includes spelling out the advantages of making the change.

Drawing by Geo. Price; © 1986 The New Yorker Magazine, Inc.

3. *Request behavior change only:* negotiating for change in what another *does* is far easier than trying to get him or her to modify feelings or even thoughts. In other words, one partner can ask the other to behave in a particular fashion but it is ridiculous to demand that he or she enjoy it.

Roles in Couple Conflict

It has been suggested that how a couple relates to each other during their disagreements is directly related to the roles each plays in their interpersonal system (Kantor 1980). Four roles or "parts" frequently observed are (1) a *mover*, the partner who defines or initiates an action; (2) a *follower*, who agrees with, supports, or continues the action; (3) an *opposer*, who challenges or goes against the action; and (4) a *bystander*, who watches what happens but who remains detached. A couple may, for example, be composed of a mover and a follower, who coexist very peacefully and have little conflict. A couple consisting of one mover and one opposer, however, may have a great deal of disagreement. A bystander may remain aloof from a mover, causing frustration. A bystander also may offer an opposer no one to oppose. Two followers, two bystanders, or a follower and a bystander married to each other may well become stuck in the decision-making or problem-solving processes.

Family-systems theorists believe that a marriage without a mover would be dull; a marriage in which neither partner ever follows cannot reach its goals; a marriage without opposers learns nothing new from within; and a marriage in which bystanding never occurs is likely to repeat unsuccessful problem-solving patterns. The flexibility of the partners in learning to play each of the four roles when appropriate is believed to be an important index of how well the couple functions in resolving conflicts.

An individual who is stuck in one of the four roles in a couple system—for example, one who is always an opposer or always a follower—limits his or her mate's options to change roles. If one always opposes *any* suggestions—no matter what their merit—or always complies with *all* suggestions—no matter how inappropriate—the couple's ability to adjust to a changing system is seriously impaired.

Many couples develop what may be called a *ritual impasse,* in which they typically become stuck at the same point in every effort to solve problems (Kantor 1980). The stuck bystander, for example, might always mask any disagreement by predictably refusing to become involved. In that example, the ritual of withdrawal effectively terminates the problem-solving process and creates an unrecognized impasse, no matter how serious the issue.

A set of attitudes that have been labeled **reality-oriented** and **defense-oriented** may be used to designate characteristic responses of persons to couple conflict. A reality-oriented person habitually directs his or her inputs to a conflict toward understanding and solving the underlying disagreement. A defense-oriented person habitually attempts to reduce the discomfort, tension, or disagreement by explaining behavior that appears to be causing it (Coleman 1979).

Although defending one's position or behavior may reduce personal tension, it is rarely useful in solving problems—especially marital problems—and can sometimes heighten conflict.

Typical defensive behaviors include, among others:

1. *Rationalization:* giving reasons for one's behavior that make the action taken sound logical, but that have been made up after the fact
2. *Intellectualization:* moving the focus to a discussion of higher principles of ethics, aesthetics, or philosophy and away from the concrete behavior
3. *Denial:* insisting that what apparently happened did not happen at all, that perhaps it was misperceived
4. *Suppression:* "forgetting" an agreement or a contract previously made on the issue
5. *Pollyannaism:* insisting that no matter how painful the situation may be, it is surely all for some future good or benefit

Most defense-oriented persons form distinctive defensive patterns that they use whenever anxiety is high, as it often is in a conflict situation. However, defense-oriented behavior usually blocks the resolution of conflicts simply because defenses typically distort or deny reality—just as the user intends them to do. As long as one partner avoids reality, effective problem solving cannot take place, and serious erosion of a relationship may develop.

Conflicts are sometimes masked by what the psychiatrist Eric Berne (1967) has called marital *games*. These games are used to sidestep real issues. Each partner in a game defends his or her position—usually a "basic truth" about the way things really *ought* to be done (what Berne calls a *script*)—while manipulating the other into a "wrong" position. Marital games take many forms—for example, "See what you've made me do!" or "Look how hard I was trying!" The common feature of games is that they distort the real issues that the couple may need to resolve in order to reduce conflict.

Reality-oriented persons may not always have solutions for their conflicts, of course; but when couples can keep their problems in focus, they stand a much better chance of discovering their areas of difference and working out a solution. Problem solving is impossible unless the problem can first be identified. Mutual agreement that a problem exists, what the problem is, and that each partner contributes to it by responding to some wish or need of her or his own may be the three most important steps to the marital challenge of conflict resolution (Lasswell and Lobsenz 1976, p. 22).

Responding to Conflict

Conflict emerges in a variety of forms, ranging from minor irritations to serious and often complicated issues. Many couples, after a fight, have trouble remembering what was the original issue. If they do remember, the issue often seems rather trivial in retrospect. The tensions couples experience often are not so much the result of major differences between them as of comparatively minor day-to-day irritations. Marital therapists probably hear as many complaints about trivial faults—leaving a messy bathroom or letting the gas tank run dry in the car—as they do about more serious problems such as infidelity and lack of trust (Lasswell and Lobsenz 1978a).

Minor irritations are often symptomatic of more serious underlying problems. One study of married couples found that when couples are experiencing stress in their relationship, they tend to find fault with each other and to interpret each other's actions and words more negatively than was intended by the mate (Gottman, Markman, and Notarius 1977). Minor irritations also have a way of escalating into major conflicts; they may accumulate until they affect a couple's basic relationship. Even when the partners do not mention their irritations, an undercurrent of anger or disappointment can easily create a distance between them that erodes the relationship.

Couples can find an endless variety of things to disagree on. Virtually anything can become a problem (Klein and Hill 1979). In particular, couples who are engaged in a struggle over the balance of power between them can usually find an arena for disagreement. However, even couples who usually agree and who have little or no power struggle between them are bound at times to have differences between them that are important enought to fight for.

Disagreements often bear a direct relationship to the stage of the marriage. Young couples may fight over differences in how they accomplish household tasks or over who will make certain decisions. Couples married longer may have children over whom to disagree, and outside interests provide the fuel for many a heated argument.

As couples grow older and children leave, the possibility of more time alone together and renewed intimacy may be the cause for conflict as couples attempt to readjust their lives.

Some marital therapists stress that under the right circumstances fights can be productive and can bring partners closer together rather than pushing them apart (Bach and Wyden 1970). Psychologists George Bach and Ronald Deutsch (1974) have prescribed several suggestions for how to make a fight fair and productive:

1. Be specific about your complaints and ask for a reasonable change that will make things better. Confine yourself to one issue at a time.
2. Make sure both you and your partner understand by asking for and giving feedback. Be open to your own and to your partner's feelings. Never assume you know what your partner means.
3. Be fair. Dont' tell your partner what he or she should know, feel, or do. Don't label or make sweeping judgments or use sarcasm.
4. Stay with the here and now and do not overload your partner with old grievances or unrelated complaints.
5. Always consider compromise. There is never a single winner in an honest argument between partners. Remember you are a team, not adversaries. Try to be empathic with your partner's viewpoint. There is always more than one good way to proceed.

SUMMARY

1. Every marriage is composed of two individuals who are unique genetically, physiologically, psychologically, socially, and culturally. One's concept of one's uniqueness constitutes the "self." The relating of two unique "selves" and communication between them form the transition from singlehood to marriage.
2. Communication is essential to a good marriage. The information one communicates and the security one feels in self-relevation are important factors in the degree of openness there is in communication.
3. All verbal and nonverbal behavior communicates some message. The intent of a message may be explicit and clear, but often it is implicit and ambiguous. *Metacommunication* refers to the meaning behind a message; meaning is not always conveyed by the actual words. Quality communication encompasses not only the actual spoken words but also the feelings behind the message and its intent.
4. Essential elements in good communication are openness, honesty, trust, empathy, and listening. *Openness* refers to the amount of self-disclosure, genuineness, and acceptance one brings to a relationship. An individual's self-awareness, self-esteem, and self-sufficiency all contribute to the degree of openness to oneself and one's partner.
5. *Honesty* helps to communicate and clarify feelings in a relationship, although frankness must be balanced by sensitivity. *Trust,* which is learned early in life, involves mutual support rather than self-interest.
6. *Empathy* is the ability to identify with another's emotional state. *Listening* not only involves concentrating on what is being said, but also requires that one give feedback on what has been said.

7. The styles, or patterns, that partners develop to communicate with each other are governed by certain rules unique to each couple. What is important is that couples establish, share, and sustain clear styles of interaction.

8. Sexual communication may be expressed through actions as well as words. Obstacles to communication may include the risk of rejection, embarrassment, the fear of criticizing one's partner, and defensiveness.

9. Sexual communication can be improved by giving clear verbal and nonverbal *signals;* establishing consistent *meanings* behind words or gestures; listening to and accepting one another's *feelings;* and enacting reciprocal and complementary sexual *roles.*

10. Conflicts are a natural phenomenon of marriage. How couples deal with their differences is one of the most important aspects of marital communication. If handled constructively, conflicts may open the way for growth.

11. Change is one of the major reasons for conflict. Some changes are gradual and seem sensible as adjustments to normal life-cycle patterns. Other changes occur unpredictably and abruptly, often causing conflict in a marriage.

12. Family therapists have suggested three steps in negotiating change: communicating honestly about the behavior in question; setting specific goals about the change desired; and requesting a change in the actual behavior rather than in feelings.

13. Marriage partners often learn particular roles in dealing with each other during conflict. If they are not flexible in playing roles that are appropriate and constructive for problem solving, they may find themselves in an impasse.

14. Conflict emerges in a variety of ways, over major issues and minor irritations. Couples who are engaged in a power struggle may disagree on an almost unlimited number of issues. Learning constructive approaches to conflict resolution is one of the major challenges in marriage and may also be one of its most difficult obligations.

GLOSSARY

Defense-oriented Pertaining to behaviors, thoughts, or feelings that deny or distort reality for the purpose of reducing personal anxiety. (p. 206)

Disconfirmation Denial of or attack on a person's self-perception by another. (p. 188)

Metacommunication The messages behind actual spoken or written words; nonverbal behavior that may convey different meanings or may emphasize overt messages. (p. 183)

Mutual validation The condition that exists when two people support each other's values, behaviors, or self-concepts. (p. 189)

Reality-oriented Pertaining to a condition in which an individual perceives his or her environment in substantially the same way that it is objectively measured or is seen by most other persons. (p. 206)

Self-concept The mental picture one has of oneself; the feelings, attitudes, and values that each individual has with respect to his or her own behaviors, abilities, and worth. (p. 185)

Self-esteem The worth one places on oneself, usually based on comparisons with others or with some idealized self. (p. 185)

8

But one of the attributes of love, like art, is to bring harmony and order out of chaos, to
introduce meaning and affect where before there was none, to give rhythmic variations,
highs and lows, to a landscape that was previously flat.

*I*t is through sharing that a marriage stands or falls. Sharing love, companionship, decisions, goals, and time together are essential to maintaining feelings of closeness. Adapting to the inevitable changes while maintaining the stability necessary for commitment is a great challenge for every married couple. Meeting individual needs as well as working toward mutual goals is a part of establishing and maintaining a couple's identity. All couples form a system of interaction that serves as a "trademark" of their marriage—their unique marriage style. Certain patterns develop in every successful marriage in the course of day-to-day living. Decisions are made, power struggles overcome, problems solved. Most couples want to make an already good marriage even better or to improve a marriage that is floundering. Skills, insights, and confidence are ingredients for a more effective and more rewarding relationship.

MARRIAGE AND ITS CHALLENGES

Molly Haskell, *From Reverence to Rape*

*I*n our experience and that of many other marital specialists, the quality of married life—adjustment, happiness, and satisfaction—is related directly to husbands' and wives' abilities to be flexible in their marital roles. This includes adaptability both in their rules for living together and in their goals as they respond to changing life situations while simultaneously maintaining the stability of their marriages. A balance between stability and flexibility appears necessary for marital development (Olson, Sprenkle, and Russell 1979).

All married couples face certain basic challenges in their relationships. These challenges are not unique to marriage: any long-term, close relationship (such as those of business partners or of parents and children) must develop patterns of interaction that allow for change and growth. However, few relationships last as long as the average marriage or have the intimacy and range of common ground that marriages have. For this reason, meeting the basic challenges that we will describe in this chapter is central to the quality of marriage.

Couples differ greatly in how they respond to the challenges of marriage. Some couples react only slightly to a major life event, others feel the impact briefly and then recover, and still others never seem to reorganize effectively. Family sociologist Wesley Burr (1973) has questioned the emphasis on life's transitional events as the cause of marital challenges. He suggests that since change is common to nearly all couples, the established *strategies* that couples use to manage changes in their lives may be more important than the *changes* that create the challenge.

Couples with a greater ability to modify their habits and roles stand a far better chance of avoiding the turbulence that may be caused by inevitable changes. As will be seen in Chapter 13, many couples run into serious difficulties with each other, and many marriages end in legal dissolution. Other couples live together as roommates in a caring but sexless relationship. Some perpetuate a "cold war." These deviations from the American dream are often a result of the way couples respond to several basic challenges in their partnership.

THE MARRIAGE PARTNERSHIP

A number of studies have focused on the qualities found in good marriages. We have discussed good communication, intimacy and closeness, sexuality, honesty, and trust, all of which are necessary to satisfying relationships. Other aspects of marriage are also important and basic and must somehow be accommodated by every married couple. Basic to good marriages is forming a partnership in which teamwork is emphasized. When confronted with their inability to work as a team, one couple we know said they should have realized this right after their wedding when they were redecorating their apartment. "You should have seen us trying to hang wallpaper together," the husband said. "It was a disaster." If two people can't cooperate on such tasks as wallpapering or cooking a meal, they may have trouble learning to work as partners in more complicated life events.

Forming a partnership in marriage and working as a team involves mutual *interdependence*. Each partner's behavior has implications for the other's complex and interesting ways. At the most fundamental level, interdependence requires two people to coordinate a host of individual needs, wants, and expectations—some of which may be in competition—through a process of mutual give-and-take.

Coordinating Individual Needs

A *need,* by definition, is something a person must have to stay healthy and sane. It is necessary and compelling. As noted in Chapter 3 on love and attraction, all human beings share basic physical needs: air, food, water, rest, and elimination. In addition, every individual has personal emotional needs. Some are common to nearly everyone, while others are unique. Recognition—having one's self-image validated by others— is thought to be an almost universal need, for example. To be accepted by those who matter and to receive affection and to be loved and cared for—are also basic needs for nearly everyone. Needs that are less widely shared may originate from the different genetic or physiological backgrounds of a particular individual or from psychological, social, or cultural differences between his or her experience and that of others. As a result, what may be indispensable for one person may be less urgent for another. For example, some individuals need a certain amount of privacy or room to be alone with their thoughts and activities. They run out of "emotional space" and need time for themselves. Without room to recoup on a regular basis, they become upset and depressed and function very poorly.

Carlfred Broderick (1979a, p. 23) has observed that "as emotional space approaches zero, one's repertoire of social responses is reduced to two: fighting or running." Some people do not need to be alone much at all, and some even find it stressful to be alone. The latter eagerly seek out company and often have little understanding of those who must have blocks of time by themselves to function adequately. As with so many other issues couples face, how much privacy each needs must be defined, and some provision for it made—perhaps a compromise if their needs are very different.

Some needs can be met independently—eating, sleeping, being free to make decisions—but some can be met only by another person. Affection, emotional support, and companionship require not only another person but a very special one at that. Reliance on another to meet such needs is the basis for dependency. The more one person has to have from a particular other, the greater the dependency. We have found that a great many couples are drawn to each other—and often stay together—because they become so mutually dependent that they believe that they could not survive apart. This may not be a problem if their relationship is generally a good one. Occasionally, however, couples are bound in mutual misery by their dependency. Each is afraid to let the other go.

Each individual brings his or her own set of needs to a relationship and hopes that a chosen partner will help to satisfy at least some of these needs. The amount of satisfaction a relationship brings is determined by (1) how well both partners meet each other's needs and (2) how much freedom their relationship allows both of them to meet their own needs. Self-analysis—finding out what one's needs actually are— is an important part of an individual's search for his or her self-image. The psychologist Abraham Maslow (1971) has proposed that needs can be identified by focusing on whether the absence of something in an individual's life causes a chronic feeling of dissatisfaction, anxiety, or deprivation. Satisfied persons are believed not to experience this kind of craving. Those who are not content in the deepest human needs—love, for example, or respect—may be frustrated, constantly seeking fulfillment, or may become defeated. Many of the disappointments registered in relationships stem from beliefs that needs that *ought* to be met by one's partner are not being met. Even the most loving partners may fail to meet each other's needs either because these needs have never been clearly defined or because one partner or both are unable to meet them.

Acknowledging Wants and Expectations

Although needs are basic and necessary to physical and psychological well-being, wants or desires represent a longing for something beyond fulfillment of needs. To be able to distinguish needs from wants is a significant step in self-analysis but often a rather difficult one. Because wants are often intense in nature, implying a strong motivation to attain the desired object or condition, they are frequently interpreted as essential to an individual's well-being and happiness.

Confusing needs and wants is a common failing. In therapy sessions, we often hear statements such as "I need to earn more money to feel successful," or "I need my husband to be more sexual with me," or "She needs me to tell her that I think she's beautiful." In each case, it is doubtful whether "need" is the real issue; more likely, needs are being confused with wants. Just as with needs, each person brings to a relationship his or her own desires in life, and the health of the relationship may well depend largely on how well one's desires are met by the other. This is not to suggest that anyone ever gets everything he or she desires, but rather that a person's wishes must be acknowledged as an integral part of the self.

Not only do persons often fail to clarify to themselves the difference between their wants and their needs, but they often fail to understand their partners' distinctions. One partner may project his or her own classification onto the other, believing that it is correct or proper for everyone. For instance, a husband who *needs* validation of his sexual attractiveness to maintain his self-esteem may be treated by his wife as if that need were merely a selfish wish. The same wife may *need* new experiences for personal growth in order to maintain her self-esteem only to have her husband treat her need to grow as a selfish wish—perhaps an improper or frivolous one at that.

Along with everyone's needs and wants, there are also expectations about how others will behave, about one's own behavior in a given situation, and about the likely progress of each relationship. To have an expectation is to count on something happening (or to assume that something will not happen). Expectations are products of past experiences, values, goals, and dreams. They range from modest to monumental, from realistic to unrealistic. Unmet expectations are a common source of stress and frequently result in feelings of disappointment, hurt, and anger.

Psychologists use the term *scripts* as a label for the patterns of expectations that individuals carry with them into each relationship (Berne 1961; Warren 1972). When the relationship is a marriage, the scripts are often based on the marriages of the partners' parents. Broderick (1979a, p. 71) points out that a marriage script may be based on the marriage of parents "even when the parental marriage style is consciously rejected in favor of a different kind of relationship. We may indeed achieve much of what we aim for; yet the parental model has a habit of sneaking up in the most unexpected places."

Family therapist Leonard Friedman has devised an effective way to enlighten couples who do not realize how greatly their expectations are affected by their parents' marriages (Pearce and Friedman 1980). Each partner is encouraged to imagine a marriage between the father of one and the mother of the other. Through exploration of how these two people might get along in this fantasized marriage and what it would be like to be a child in such a home, scripts often become more obvious. Often each spouse comes to a much better understanding of the other when he or she has gained insight into the other's script and into the influence of each set of parents.

Certain issues may be so basic to each person's script and, therefore, to his or her expectations for marriage that one of them may jeopardize the marital commitment. Marital therapist Richard Stuart (1976) calls these central issues **core symbols.** What may be a core symbol to one partner may seem relatively unimportant to another. For instance, Stuart cites the wearing of a wedding ring as a core symbol of marriage to countless men and women. Many would never consider removing the ring for any purpose short of terminating the marriage once it has been put on during the wedding ceremony. Others, however, remove their wedding rings with no thought of violating their commitments; some even have more than one wedding ring and may wear them interchangeably or may not wear a ring at all or only on special occasions. None of these patterns of behavior is objectively more right or wrong than any of the others. However, core symbols are seldom viewed objectively. If two people feel very differently about such a basic issue, conflict that is not readily resolved can easily arise.

Expectations are often fantasies that others will behave in ways that they have never agreed to do or that they may even be unaware are expected of them. These fantasies may attempt to minimize differences between the partners that one or both of those in a relationship do not want to accept. By expecting certain behaviors and then registering disappointment when they do not occur, a person may hope to ensure that, next time, the anticipated action will actually take place. Expectations may even be translated into demands that the partner change to fit the spouse's fantasy.

Some persons believe that marriage will change their partners in specific ways—often to resemble *their* parents or some ideal couple. Such beliefs may be reinforced by platitudes, such as "She'll settle down once she's married." The expectations that flirting, or drinking, or selfishness, or gambling, or workaholism, or any other characteristic of a partner will change automatically and effortlessly during a wedding ceremony are, of course, fantasy. People will change, but a wedding alone is not a good predictor of the kind, direction, or degree of change.

Many of the conflicts that arise in the first months of marriage can be traced to one partner's or both partners' expectations of what marriage should or should not be. Most couples do not share a uniform set of expectations. Consequently, both partners may have many unfulfilled expectations, which are likely to lead to marital disillusionment. Sometimes partners fix their expectations of each other during their courtship period. Often each partner has put a best foot forward to attract the other before marriage, and it is impossible to maintain that unnatural posture permanently. Once married, they may relax, believing that courtship behavior is no longer necessary or even appropriate. Untidy habits reappear, little courtesies disappear.

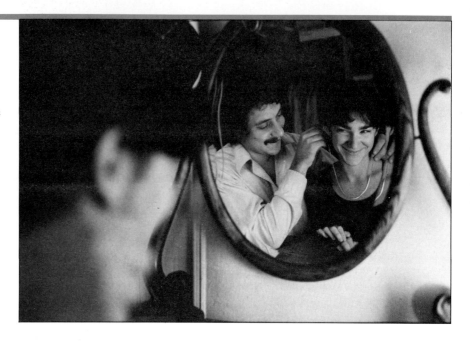

Once married, couples need to continue the special attentions that first attracted them to each other. Much disillusionment occurs in new marriages when partners change once they are married.

Because of idealization, we may not see the loved one as clearly during courtship as we do when we settle into day-to-day existence with him or her. Unless the couple has lived together (and often not even then), there may be considerable disillusionment when both partners exhibit daily living habits (not picking up clothes, leaving wet towels on the floor, and so forth). These behaviors do not meet expectations that the two persons may have of married life.

The phrase "The honeymoon is over" acknowledges the unrealistic belief that one has married an individual with few faults (or that he or she will quickly change those behaviors that are annoying). The "real" selves of both partners come into focus and may not be accepted readily by either of them. A tug-of-war to get one partner to change to fit the other's expectations often ensues. Unfortunately, some couples never get beyond this struggle; when they are unsuccessful in molding each other into a "suitable" pattern, they begin to think of divorce. The highest percentage of divorces occurs during the first few years after marriage (U.S. Bureau of the Census 1976, p. 15). Many divorce experts attribute this in large measure to the many unfulfilled expectations of the couple (Singer and Stern 1980).

Sometimes partners go into a relationship without fully understanding their own expectations. They somehow expect their partners to be mind readers who can figure it all out. If communication between them is difficult, expectations may not come out in the open until a residue of hurt, disgust, or anger has been built up. Such feelings, which are usually clues to unfulfilled expectations, can serve as paths to understanding when they do arise. For example, if one feels hurt or disappointed by a partner's behavior, there usually was an expectation that something different "should" have occurred. The question "What did I expect?" followed by "Did my partner know what I expected?" and "Did my partner agree with my expectation?" often points to a misunderstanding or to a disagreement about appropriate behavior. Partners often prove to be poor at mind reading, and once they discover each other's expectations, they may lack the resources **to meet** them should they want to do so. A great deal of conflict might be avoided if partners discussed their preconceived notions of marital expectations early on in their relationship.

Setting Mutual Goals

With the current emphasis on individual growth and satisfaction, marriage is no longer identified as an institution into which men and women must mold themselves. Instead, marriage is seen as a union that enables partners to meet their needs. Thus a good and satisfying marriage allows for enough freedom and enough separateness for each partner to grow and to pursue his or her own goals in life. In this respect, marriage is no different from any other relationship—whether with a friend or with a group in which one is involved. Social psychologists report that we place greater value on a relationship or a group that facilitates meeting our goals. On the other hand, when a relationship such as a marriage, or a group such as a family, limits our freedom, we tend to become dissatisfied (Cartwright 1968). In other words, if a marriage is to be rewarding, it must not severely inhibit either partner's need fulfillment or growth.

We rather routinely ask couples in marital therapy "If you could be doing anything you want, anywhere you want, with anyone you want, how would you like your life to be five years from now?" This apparent exercise in fantasy can be useful in revealing potential goals. More important, if each partner's "five-year plan" includes the spouse, this is one of the best predictors that a relationship will continue to thrive. Partners whose individual plans include the other have set themselves up for *mutual interdependence* (Deutsch 1949). They need each other in order to accomplish their goals.

Individual and Mutual Goals   One of the most important tasks of any two persons in a partnership or of members of a group (such as a family) is linking individual goals with mutual goals (Shaw 1976). If good marriages provide room for the attainment of individual goals, then it is equally important that there be enough closeness and cooperation to allow couples to achieve mutual goals. The lack of mutual goals is often a warning sign that a marriage is in serious trouble. Research indicates that working cooperatively as a team toward mutual goals leads to greater feelings of attraction to each other (Lott and Lott 1965). Evidently, everyone likes to be on a smoothly operating team that is getting the job done. Cooperative behavior is rewarding in and of itself since it moves the couple toward their desired goals. As partners aid each other, make constructive suggestions, and share the load, they come to value each other more.

Differentiating individual goals from mutual goals is not always as easy as it may seem at first. Early analyses proposed that mutual goals are merely composites of the individual goals of the two partners (Shaw 1976). It soon became obvious, however, that one partner's goals not only may differ from the other's but also may actually conflict. For example, a husband may wish to save money for a new car, but his wife may want to spend money now for landscaping the yard. This is an example of a conflict between a long-range goal and an immediate goal as well as an example of a conflict between goals: saving for one means that the other is denied.

Mutual marital goals that are a composite of each partner's individual goals are made possible by a cooperative effort to include what each partner desires when possible so that a mutual goal is the end result. Individual goals that do not become mutual continue to influence each partner's behavior and often may be achieved simultaneously with joint endeavors. The degree to which both mutual and individual goals can be achieved by the same activities helps to determine how satisfying a marriage becomes (Stuart 1980).

Early studies on social psychology were instrumental in showing how two persons become interdependent by developing mutual goals (Deutsch 1949). These studies found that when one of a pair completed a task that both wanted done, it affected the other partner as if he or she had completed it. In other words, once a couple establishes mutual goals, completing them (even if only one partner actually performs the task) has the same effect as if both had accomplished a personal goal.

It is easy for some couples to identify their mutual goals because they have discussed and agreed on them. Saving to buy a home, building a business, or planning for a special vacation are frequent joint marital ventures. However, many couples, if asked to list their mutual goals, would be at a loss to reply. They may never have thought about articulating their goals. Couples vary greatly in the extent to which they are aware of their mutual goals, and some seem truly to have none. Research has indicated that those couples who are aware of and can articulate their goals show greater interdependence between the partners (Raven and Rubin 1976).

Variations between married couples are found in the extent to which they accept stated marital goals. Disagreement is particularly common in marriages with many goals because the question of priority frequently arises. When two people cannot agree about which goal takes priority, there is the risk of a power struggle and of diminishing cooperation. If, for example, a couple has agreed that they both want to save for a new car and also want to buy new furniture, they can be said to have two mutual goals. However, since both goals require the same resources for fulfillment, it is essential that the couple agree on priority as well. If buying the car is a top priority for one partner but buying furniture ranks higher with the other, the stage is set for the transformation of mutual goals into two personal goals. This sets up a competitive situation that undermines interdependence (Deutsch 1973). When both partners accept a goal, accord it the same level of priority, and work toward it together (even though one partner may be more responsible for its achievement than the other), interdependence and satisfaction are maximized.

Cooperation versus Competition in Marriage   A *cooperative relationship* has been defined as one in which the goals of the participants are so linked that either partner can attain his or her goal if, and only if, the other also attains his or hers (Deutsch 1973). For example, a newly married couple might mutually desire to buy a condominium that is more expensive than either partner could afford alone. Both must agree to work and to contribute to the cost of the condominium. Neither of them can reach this goal without working cooperatively toward it. Competition, on the other hand, results when goals are linked in such a way that one partner can reach his or her goals only if the other does not. For example, if one partner wishes to go to Hawaii for vacation and the other wants to use the vacation money for investment, the one who "wins" does so at the other's expense.

Cooperation is not defined only in terms of shared goals, however. Although working toward a joint goal is obviously of primary importance in cooperation, the *means* by which couples go about reaching their goals are also important. In fact, as marital therapists we probably hear as much disagreement about the means to the goals as we do about the goals themselves. It is not unusual for two persons to fail to reach a goal that both want very much because they cannot agree on how to get there. Husbands and wives may agree, for instance, that they want their children to be well behaved or to do well in school, but may argue about how to achieve these goals. Agreement on ways to achieve shared goals is vital to the cooperative effort because in a cooperative marriage each partner must facilitate the other's contribution. Without agreement, this is not possible.

There are several ways in which couples disagree about means to ends. They often attempt to duplicate each other's efforts because one does not like the way the other performs. If they have agreed that one will cook the dinner while the other sets the table, for example, each may instead attempt to redo what the other has done or may criticize the other's efforts. Both behaviors often can lead to breakdown in cooperation. The simplest solution for this type of disagreement is to agree that the person assigned the task sets the standards for it. If the other wishes to set the standards, the other can ask to do the task.

Sometimes unequal participation in working toward a goal is perceived, so that one partner may believe that the other does not want the end result as much. Problems occur when both partners agree on a goal, but one is seen by the other as giving it only halfhearted effort. Although it is true that a mutual goal, when reached, is rewarding to both spouses, the spouse who believes that he or she did more than his or her share of the work to obtain it may feel a lack of support and be less willing to repeat the effort.

Studies comparing the means by which couples work together with the extent to which they agree on their goals reveal that the most satisfactory relationships occur when couples *share* ways of getting to goals. It is even more important that they *agree* on where they are going (Deutsch 1973). As long as two people do not work against each other by setting up a competitive situation, it is possible for them to work independently or to pursue their mutual goals quite differently and still work out a satisfactory solution. If, for example, two people decide to redecorate a room in their home, not only might they work independently at different tasks (the husband may paint, the wife may sand the floor), but they also could have very different approaches to their work (he working ten hours each day over the weekend, she doing a little bit every evening for several weeks).

Cooperative behavior appears to be facilitated when partners communicate their intentions to each other—usually, the more they communicate, the greater the co-operation (Voissem and Sistrunk 1971). Married couples with a history of successful communication have been shown to cooperate more on joint ventures assigned to them in research projects than do couples who have no such history (Schoeninger and Wood 1969). Although laboratory research is far different from studying couples working together at home in real-life situations, the importance of communication for facilitating goals seems to be a well-established fact. Our experience, and that of many other marital therapists, is that helping couples increase and improve their communication with each other leads to less competitive and selfish behavior and to more cooperative and considerate interaction.

Other research has indicated that cooperation often hinges on the *trust* two people feel for each other (Wrightsman 1966). A frequent complaint in troubled marriages is that one partner has failed to be there for the other at a time when cooperation was necessary. Many couples complain, for example, that their cooperative interaction breaks down during a crisis. They seem unable to give each other the support both need to make and implement constructive decisions. Trust between marital partners, at the simplest level, may be the antidote to most power struggles and competitive relationships that hinge on being right or winning.

MARRIAGE STYLES

When two unique human beings marry, they form a system of interaction with each other based on how they communicate, what their expectations are, and how they behave in relationship to each other. The development of such an interactional system involves establishing patterns relating to dependence and independence; setting boundaries for friends, relatives, and other outsiders; managing change in their lives; and dividing and performing tasks (Aldous 1977). Their system of relating may bring out either the best or the worst both in each other and in themselves. They may get along with each other very differently from the way they relate to others because of the intensity and the meaning of their relationship. We often counsel couples who are successful in all their other social endeavors but are failing with each other. They are puzzled by their behavior with each other since they behave in such distressing ways with no one else. Clearly, marriage brings out behaviors that are unique to the relationship.

Family therapist David Kantor (1980) believes that each relationship has its own behavioral repertoires or patterns of actions and reactions that are "steering mechanisms" for the relationship. He describes these as *strategies* developed specifically for each marriage or for each family system. The strategies are called on for decision making, problem solving, and crisis resolution—for living and working together. Kantor refers to the particular configuration that each couple or each family works out as its *signature*. No two marriages (and no two families) are ever exactly alike. One task of each couple and of each family is to tailor their own unique patterns and style of being together.

Compatibility is an important factor in the way members of a system work out their agreements. Compatibility is measured by the efficiency with which those who make up a system such as a marriage or a family interact. Values, interests, behaviors, and other facets of their individual styles of living must be accommodated. The more mutually acceptable the behaviors of people are, the more compatible they are said to be. Many couples start out and remain in considerable agreement, but other couples may grow either more alike or more different from each other as time passes. Perfect agreement is largely unattainable, of course, and might be dull if it were achieved. However, a fairly high level of compatibility is a major source of satisfaction in marriage and family living. Those whose relationships are burdened with marked differences in their philosophies about important areas of living together report considerably less satisfaction and marital happiness (Chadwick, Albrecht, and Kunz 1976).

Learning to live harmoniously and intimately with another person for a lifetime, sharing in all facets of life—finances, emotions, sex, children, illness, criteria for assessing success and failure—is perhaps the most challenging task we ever face. One of the leading family sociologists in the United States has said: "The most popular—

and the roughest—contact sport in the country is not professional football; it is marriage" (Broderick 1979a, p. 13). Although this statement may sound a bit grim, many couples who have struggled through problems of marital adjustment—successfully or unsuccessfully—may nod in agreement.

The difficulties of marital adjustment and of working out a marital lifestyle are compounded by the fact that most marriage partners do not know each other as well as they believed they did when they got married. In one study of couples in both successful and unsuccessful marriages, it was reported that virtually everyone interviewed had faced at least one postnuptial revelation about his or her spouse's habits or personality that came as a surprise. Usually there were several such revelations. Often these surprises would have been fairly obvious had both partners had their eyes open a little wider. But being in love caused them to see selectively and even to disregard or mislabel what they saw. "The end result," the authors state, "is that, in varying degrees, everyone marries a stranger" (Marshall and Marshall 1980).

Our own bias is that not much can be done to ensure that two people who marry will know all that they need to know about each other in order to adjust right from the start. Even if they do, both will change with time, experience, maturity, and certainly with the addition of children. Just about the time two people feel comfortable and settled, something changes in one or both of them or in the external environment that affects their definitions of themselves, their partners, or their relationship.

The essence of compatible marriage styles is not only acceptance of the habits and personality traits of partners but also the ability to be flexible and to accommodate to change. As the life span increases, more years will be spent in marriages. About half of all North American men alive today are expected to live to be over 70. If they are married in their early twenties to women a year or two younger than they, their expectation of life together could be 50 years or more. Any photograph album records the physical differences between couples in their early twenties and those same persons in their early seventies. Personality changes are developed just as gradually as wrinkles and gray hair, but these cannot be caught by a camera and frozen at two moments in time. Common sense tells us that we cannot expect to act and think the same when we are constantly changing physically and encountering new experiences. What this means is that couples cannot realistically expect to develop one style of being married that will work at every phase of the life cycle.

Marital Stages

A great deal of research has suggested that adults go through "stages" just as children do: the venturesome but trying twenties, the occupationally oriented and family-building thirties, the "middle-age crises" of the forties and fifties, and the adjustment to retirement and the end-of-life adjustments that come in later years (Gould 1978; Levinson et al. 1978). When two people are married, these adult stages affect each partner just as much as do the external happenings in their lives.

In addition, family sociologists have suggested that marriages also have "stages" that together form what is termed the *marital life cycle* (Rollins and Feldman 1970). These are not likely to be developmental in the same way that individual life-cycle changes are but are accounted for by life-course events. A review of the existing information on the marital life cycle reveals that stages appear to be caused in three separate but intertwined areas of a couple's life: (1) changes in the parental role; (2) changes in the economic state—both earning and consumption; and (3) changes in roles played outside the family (Menaghan 1983).

Three events in particular illustrate the impact of changes in parental roles on the marital life cycle: birth of the first child; adolescence of the child(ren); and departure of the last child from the family home. (See Chapter 11 for further discussion of parental roles.) The birth of the first child produces the most impact, presumably because this child forces the couple to add the new roles of mother and father to their already existing identity as a couple. Parents frequently report a marked decline in the amount of time spent with each other after the birth of the first child (Campbell 1975).

During the period of their children's adolescence, parents may feel especially insecure about their parenting; morale in the marriage frequently seems to drop. The final event is when the last child leaves and the "empty nest" signals the end of an era of parental activities (Menaghan 1983). Husbands' satisfaction with marriage increases at this point; wives' satisfaction decreases slightly at the beginning of this period but rises again just before retirement (Rollins and Feldman 1970).

Changes in the economic state of a couple occur according to their education, their occupation, and the number and spacing of their children. Two stages in the marital life cycle seem especially vulnerable to economic stresses—the early years and the retirement years—and are only loosely, if at all, related to burdens of supporting a family. Low income at any period during the life cycle can have a damaging effect on the quality of a couple's life.

Changes in roles played outside the family also vary with the marital life cycle. One of the most pervasive of recent influences on marriage has been the number of women returning to the work place after staying at home with small children for several years. For many this change is welcome; for others the strain may be more than the already stressed marriage can stand.

Couples married 20 to 25 years often note a role change, as well, that coincides with the "mid-life crisis." Those at mid-life assess their power in the world outside marriage as they face the question of whether their goals and ideals have been or will be met. This is a time when egos may suffer and physical signs of aging appear. To reestablish a feeling of being desirable, some men and women have extramarital affairs. The cyclic pattern of intimacy in the marriage often is at a low point, and divorces are not uncommon (DeFrank-Lynch 1982).

Research has indicated that regardless of family life-cycle stage, men tend to be more satisfied with their marriages than women (Ryne 1981). However, the same factors—satisfaction with love, interests, friendship, sex, time together and with children, help at home, friends, and in-laws—are the factors important to their assessments. In other words, judgments of marital quality differ in degree rather than in kind.

The impact of life-cycle stages is important for an understanding of marital lifestyles and interaction patterns. There are ups and downs—biological, emotional, and psychological cycles—within each stage in all marriages, regardless of differences in economic or social backgrounds, education, personality, or habits of the couples. Certain stages of marriage are subject to potential difficulties no matter how the partners feel about each other (Lasswell and Lobsenz 1976). The couple's flexibility in adjusting to each other's changes, to changes brought about by the marital life cycle, and to changes in the external environment is the key to much of the success of the marriage.

Marital Adjustment

The concept of marital adjustment implies that two individuals have learned to accommodate each other's needs, wants, and expectations. We believe that marital adjustment means achieving a good degree of comfort in the relationship through mutual give-and-take. This is not to imply that adjustment termed is an absolute state; rather, it is an ongoing process.

A few notable research projects have examined couples judged to be well adjusted to married life. These studies report that many variables have positive effects on marital adjustment and satisfaction. Exchanges of love—however a couple manages to do this effectively—are especially important (Ammons and Stinnett 1980; Bohannan 1984). Couples almost always agree that factors related to loving behavior such as respect, competence in role behavior, helpfulness, and sharing also are important (Rettig and Bubolz 1983).

Other studies point to the amount of spousal interaction and time spent in joint activity as consistently correlating with marital adjustment. However, interaction may be defined as a cause as well as a consequence of marital quality (White 1983).

The outstanding finding of the studies on good marital adjustment is that there are many models of marriage that seem to work well. In one early study, over 400 prominent people described their marriages in depth to the researchers. From the data, five separate successful marriage styles were delineated (Cuber and Harroff 1965):

1. *Devitalized*: a placid match involving little if any conflict but also little if any passion. Whatever zest there was in the early years of the marriage seems to have faded, but the couples do not seem to miss it.
2. *Conflict-habituated*: characterized by a great deal of fighting, which, however, was tolerated well by the couple, if not actually enjoyed.
3. *Passive-congenial*: a comfortable and convenient match with each partner involved as much or more outside the marriage as in it.
4. *Total*: characterized by constant togetherness and intensely shared mutual interests.
5. *Vital*: highly involved but not locked into restrictive togetherness. Couples give each other more room for personal growth than in the "total" marriage.

The first three styles—devitalized, conflict-habituated, and passive-congenial—were categorized as *utilitarian* types. Couples considered representative of these three types judged their marriages to be good, functional ones. These marriages were often successful because the couples were allowed to meet mutually important goals: raising children, maintaining a certain standard of living, attaining a desired social status, and otherwise meeting their requirements for adult living.

The "total" and "vital" marriages were termed *intrinsic* marriages. These marriages were marked by the personal involvements the partners had with each other. Partners shared many activities and had deep feelings for each other. The primary

Among variables associated with marital satisfaction are sharing activities that are mutually enjoyed and spending time as a couple, which allows communication to occur.

focus in life was on each other. Cuber and Harroff found fewer intrinsic marriages than utilitarian ones and concluded from their research that the norm for successful marriage in the United States is that the relationship be comfortable, functional, and of low intensity. Evidently, the kind of involvement necessary for intrinsic marriages is too great for most couples to sustain while they are busy building careers and raising families. As Cuber and Harroff (1965, p. 142) comment: "People who live in this way place enormous stress on the personal relation—strains that are not present in the utilitarian marriage."

Virtually all scholars who have engaged in research on successful relationships have approached the study of marital quality by acknowledging that there are a variety of models that work and that are considered successful by the couples interviewed. Most such studies have used as departure points the traditional marriage on the one hand and the egalitarian marriage on the other (Scanzoni 1975; Forisha 1978). The types of marriages that fall near the *traditional* end of the scale tend to emphasize time-honored roles and expectations of husbands and wives that are more in keeping with the traditional sex roles. Division of responsibilities provides that the husband be the principal provider and the wife the principal homemaker and child rearer. Most studies indicate that the more traditional the marriage, the more the husband is obligated to define the roles and is expected to be dominant, brighter, better educated, and somewhat older (Stuckert 1963).

Studies of marriages leaning toward the *egalitarian* model show that emphases are on communication, shared tasks, closeness, privacy, and caring (Forisha 1978). These marriages are considered successful by those in them when there is comfortable personal interaction and when the emotional well-being of the partners is being met. Individual growth is also an important variable in the happiness of couples who are in more egalitarian marriages (Pratt 1972).

The results of a recent study indicate that the secret to marital quality and marital adjustment is not so much what model of marriage a couple chooses, but whether they agree on what influences satisfaction. Couples found to have the lowest evaluation of marital quality were those with a traditional husband and a "modern" wife (Bowen and Orthner 1983).

It appears that the quality of marriages—no matter what the style—is highly correlated with how much agreement the husbands and wives have about their roles (Bernard 1973). "Role fit" necessarily rests on how partners see both their own and each other's roles. Total agreement is not essential; most experts agree that good marriages leave room for individual differences. It is seen as vital, however, that there be a plan for resolving conflict (Lewis and Spanier 1979).

Marital Adjustment Scales

Over the past 40 years, more than a dozen major inventories have been devised to measure marital adjustment (Burgess and Cottrell 1939; Locke 1951). Sophisticated statistical methods and computer capabilities gradually improved the adjustment inventories so that more variables can be considered and the interaction of those variables can be studied. As a result, it is now generally agreed that social, cultural, and personal variables are associated with marital adjustment in a complex variety of ways (Blood and Wolfe 1960; Nye and McLaughlin 1976). Even so, the complexity of the relationship, the speed and variability of social change, and the richness of human experiences make valid findings difficult to obtain.

As noted above, mutual validation, shared meanings in communication, and compatibility increase marital adjustment. One marital adjustment factor implied by these qualities is being comfortable with one's partner. A scale assessing the degrees of "feeling comfortable" determined that six factors were basic to comfort in a relationship (Haun and Stinnett 1974):

1. *Empathy*: the ability to put oneself in another's shoes, to try to understand how he or she might feel
2. *Spontaneity*: being able to be oneself without having to be guarded or otherwise inhibited
3. *Trust*: being able to count on each other and to know that honesty prevails
4. *Interest-care*: feeling loved and loving, cared for and caring, interested in and interesting to one's partner
5. *Respect*: having a high regard for and a belief in the other's integrity and right to be unique
6. *Critical-hostility*: a negative factor in feeling comfortable, indicating that individuality is not appreciated or respected

Almost all marital inventory scales have attempted to ascertain the current state of the relationship by asking the partners to rate their happiness, satisfaction, or adjustment on a variety of factors. In recent years, however, researchers have begun to measure *factors* that are believed to contribute to the ongoing process of marital adjustment rather than to make a simple judgment of the quality of the current state. One measure was designed to assess the quality of marriages and of the relationships of couples who may not necessarily be legally married but who live together (Spanier 1976).

Graham Spanier, the author of the scale, states that the success of couples in adjusting to each other may be viewed in two distinct ways: (1) as a process that must be studied over the life of the relationship or (2) as a qualitative evaluation at any given period in which couples analyze their marriages. The latter approach is like taking a snapshot of a couple's compatibility at any point in time. The process approach allows a relationship to be viewed both at a particular time and as a predictive measure of the probability of future adjustment. Such factors as adaptability, communication, interpersonal tensions, and affectional expression are thought to be parts of the process of the marital life cycle that are not as likely to change from one time to another as are reports of whether the partners are currently happy and/or satisfied with their relationship.

The Spanier Dyadic Adjustment Scale is shown in Figure 8.1 (see p. 228). In addition to using this scale to measure adjustment and to speculate about future adjustment, it may be interesting for a couple to complete it and compare how much they agree on each of the 32 items. The scale has a possible total score of 151 points. Spanier studied married and divorced persons and reported a mean (average) score of 114.8 for married persons and 70.7 for divorced persons.

The Marital Satisfaction Inventory (MSI) is another respected assessment tool developed to understand how partners' attitudes and beliefs regarding specific areas of their relationship enhance or detract from satisfaction (Snyder 1981). It includes a measurement for assessing the distress in an individual's life that is not specific to the marriage. Some people are anxious and have general ways of responding that, although they affect the marriage, are directly the result of outside sources or of a general personality trait.

A recent addition to marital adjustment scales has been the ENRICH Inventory, which has been used successfully with thousands of couples (Olson, Fourier, and Druckerman 1982). The inventory assists couples by emphasizing their marital strengths and isolating the most troublesome areas. A couple's scores are compared to national averages to highlight similarities and differences in such categories as personality issues, communication, conflict resolution, children, family and friends, equalitarian roles, religious orientation, marital cohesion, and marital adaptability.

DECISION-MAKING CHALLENGES

Most couples eventually develop one or more decision-making patterns, but these are often neither mutually satisfying nor particularly efficient. In fact, often these methods are self-defeating for the partners and may lead to open conflict. For example, one partner may make a decision without consulting the other, even though the other partner is affected by the decision. Financial disagreements can often be traced to one partner's expenditures that deplete the family budget while the other partner worries about how to pay the bills.

Decision making is one of the key day-to-day challenges of being married; yet many couples are not quite sure how they reach decisions or why they sometimes have trouble coming to an agreement. This is not surprising because most parents do not teach decision making to their children directly. In fact, parents' discussions about important decisions are often so carefully screened from children that they learn little about the process by observation. Research has indicated that sometimes couples do not even agree with each other on who makes their decisions, let alone on how they are made (Ross and Mirowsky 1984).

A flawed pattern for making decisions is actually based on *not* making decisions. *Decidophobia* is a word coined to describe avoidance of decisions until someone else— an outsider such as a relative, a lawyer, an employer, or even a police officer—makes the decision instead. Defaulting on decisions frequently creates a crisis, and some couples seem to live from crisis to crisis precisely for this reason. Essentially, "deciding by default" often reflects a fear of making choices on the part of one or both partners. One partner may defer to the other, or they may juggle the choice between them out of apathy or unwillingness even to discuss it.

Some persons who cannot make decisions are obsessed with the possibility of being wrong. They are so fearful of criticism or failure that they literally get stuck at the point of decision. It is one thing to choose not to take any action in order to wait for further developments, but quite another to hope for the best while taking no action.

Power in Decision Making

Family experts report that the power balance between the partners is a key factor in how couples make decisions. The study of marital power and decision-making patterns has been the subject of much research, beginning with a study of 900 couples published in 1960 (Blood and Wolfe 1960). Decisions such as which car to buy, where to vacation, and how to set up household budgets were analyzed. It was discovered that the partner with the most resources—earning power, education, information—made most of the decisions. The *resource theory of family power*, as it was termed, took into account many different kinds of resources: skills, social status, physical attractiveness, and other assets. The theory postulated that when one partner perceived the other as being more in control because of these resources, he or she usually gave in on decisions.

Traditionally women were more financially dependent and were seen by some as deferring to men because men had more power by virtue of their earning ability. Thus, the extent of a man's power was proportional to his wife's need for money. The upheaval in sex roles has changed this dependent state for millions of women; however, researchers continue to be interested in just how power and dependency affect decision making in marriage (Hiller 1984; Rank 1982). To the extent that men are dependent on their wives for nurturance, heterosexual affection, and sexual gratification, these are powerful resources for wives. It is interesting that the movement for the redistribution of family resources has focused almost entirely on diminishing the traditional power of husbands by enabling wives to develop resources outside the family; little or no attention has been given to ways in which an equitable and congenial balance of power might be maintained.

More recent studies of power and its relation to decision making have added to the resource theory by suggesting that possible bases for power might include what the couple consider an appropriate authority structure between husbands and wives (McDonald 1977). There are various cultural definitions of who has or should have decision-making power. For example, certain religious doctrines designate husbands

FIGURE 8 • 1

Dyadic Adjustment
Scale

Most persons have disagreements in their relationships. Please indicate below the approximate extent of agreement or disagreement between you and your partner for each item on the following list.

	Always Agree	Almost Always Agree	Occa-sionally Disagree	Fre-quently Disagree	Almost Always Disagree	Always Disagree
1. Handling family finances	5	4	3	2	1	0
2. Matters of recreation	5	4	3	2	1	0
3. Religious matters	5	4	3	2	1	0
4. Demonstrations of affection	5	4	3	2	1	0
5. Friends	5	4	3	2	1	0
6. Sex relations	5	4	3	2	1	0
7. Conventionality (correct or proper behavior)	5	4	3	2	1	0
8. Philosophy of life	5	4	3	2	1	0
9. Ways of dealing with parents or in-laws	5	4	3	2	1	0
10. Aims, goals, and things believed important	5	4	3	2	1	0
11. Amount of time spent together	5	4	3	2	1	0
12. Making major decisions	5	4	3	2	1	0
13. Household tasks	5	4	3	2	1	0
14. Leisure time interests and activities	5	4	3	2	1	0
15. Career decisions	5	4	3	2	1	0

	All the Time	Most of the Time	More Often Than Not	Occa-sionally	Rarely	Never
16. How often do you discuss or have you considered divorce, separation, or terminating your relationship?	0	1	2	3	4	5
17. How often do you or your mate leave the house after a fight?	0	1	2	3	4	5
18. In general, how often do you think that things between you and your partner are going well?	5	4	3	2	1	0
19. Do you confide in your mate?	5	4	3	2	1	0
20. Do you ever regret that you married (*or lived together*)?	0	1	2	3	4	5
21. How often do you and your partner quarrel?	0	1	2	3	4	5
22. How often do you and your mate "get on each other's nerves?"	0	1	2	3	4	5

FIGURE 8 • 1
(continued)

	Every Day	Almost Every Day	Occa- sionally	Rarely	Never
23. Do you kiss your mate?	4	3	2	1	0

	All of Them	Most of Them	Some of Them	Very Few of Them	None of Them
24. Do you and your mate engage in outside interests together?	4	3	2	1	0

How often would you say the following events occur between you and your mate?

	Never	Less Than Once a Month	Once or Twice a Month	Once or Twice a Week	Once a Day	More Often
25. Have a stimulating exchange of ideas	0	1	2	3	4	5
26. Laugh together	0	1	2	3	4	5
27. Calmly discuss something	0	1	2	3	4	5
28. Work together on a project	0	1	2	3	4	5

These are some things about which couples sometimes agree and sometimes disagree. Indicate if either item below caused differences of opinions or were problems in your relationship during the past few weeks. (Check yes or no)

	Yes	No	
29.	0	1	Being too tired for sex.
30.	0	1	Not showing love.

31. The dots on the following line represent different degrees of happiness in your relationship. The middle point, "happy," represents the degree of happiness of most relationships. Please circle the dot which best describes the degree of happiness, all things considered, of your relationship.

0	1	2	3	4	5	6
.	.	.	.	.	.	.
Extremely Unhappy	Fairly Unhappy	A Little Unhappy	Happy	Very Happy	Extremely Happy	Perfect

32. Which of the following statements best describes how you feel about the future of your relationship?

    5   I want desperately for my relationship to succeed, and *would go to almost any length* to see that it does.
    4   I want very much for my relationship to succeed, and *will do all I can* to see that it does.
    3   I want very much for my relationship to succeed, and *will do my fair share* to see that it does.
    2   It would be nice if my relationship succeeded, but *I can't do much more than I am doing* now to help it succeed.
    1   It would be nice if it succeeded, but *I refuse to do any more than I am doing* now to keep the relationship going.
    0   My relationship can never succeed, and *there is no more that I can do* to keep the relationship going.

Source: Graham B. Spanier, "Measuring Dyadic Adjustment," *Journal of Marriage and the Family* 38 (February 1976), pp. 15–28. Copyrighted 1976 by the National Council on Family Relations. Reprinted by permission.

Drawing by Ziegler; © 1980 The New Yorker Magazine, Inc.

as the final authorities in any major or contested decisions. Decision-making patterns in several racial or ethnic groups have also been studied. For example, the stereotype of the "black family matriarchy" has been shown to lack validity; a pattern of equality in decision making is more often the rule. In fact, black middle-class couples more often share power than do white middle-class couples (Willie and Greenblatt 1978).

In addition to the effect of resources on the power balance and decision making in marriage, several studies have explored the techniques couples employ in their attempts to negotiate with each other or to gain control of the decision-making process (Scanzoni and Polonko 1980). These techniques include assertiveness, manipulation, persuasion, and a variety of other direct and indirect acts that influence the course of couples' decision-making patterns. One of the favored definitions of scholars who study the power balance between individuals in relationships is that *power* is the ability to produce intended effects on others. Thus power is viewed as a process rather than as a residual characteristic (Blalock and Wilken 1979).

Many couples find that their marital happiness is eroded when they reach decisions on the basis of power. The partner who feels coerced or manipulated and who typically gives in can easily become frustrated and resentful. Couples who habitually deal with decisions on a win-or-lose basis often discover that winning a marital conflict can be an illusion. The victory can easily turn into an ultimate loss for both when angry and hurt feelings develop between the partners. The marriage is reduced to a power struggle as winning becomes more important for each partner than having a good relationship. Many couples who seek marital therapy are locked into just such conflicts. They argue over everything from household duties to their sex lives.

Power does not always have to involve conflict but, in fact, often functions to keep conflict at a minimum. The use of resources or techniques, for example, may be a way for husbands and wives to provide definitions of situations for each other or to utilize their knowledge or expertise to solve problems (Sprey 1972b). If a wife convinces her husband that she knows best how to handle a particular situation, her husband may, in fact, feel relieved that she has taken the matter into her own hands.

In addition to the resources and techniques used in deciding who decides, it is important to look at decision outcomes. In other words, it is a question not only of how the decision is made and of whether one or the other "wins," but also of who decides which partner will ultimately carry out the decision. In a study of couples to determine which partner implemented decisions and which delegated authority, two types of power were distinguished: **orchestration power** and **implementation power** (Safilios-Rothschild 1976).

In orchestration power, a particular family member is understood by the whole family to have the responsibility for interpreting the family's general goals and the nature of its interface with the larger society. Ordinarily, orchestration power is ascribed by unspoken consensus. In making decisions each family member considers this leader's probable response to his or her behaviors. The person with orchestration power is the ultimate authority in allocating the duties and privileges of family members. In exercising that authority, she or he designates the responsibilities of each family member and is assumed to have the right—or duty—to control the rewards (or punishments) for the behaviors of each.

Implementation power is the right of a family member to decide how (or sometimes when) to carry out a designated duty or responsibility. For example, a wife who is the keeper of the family budget may decide that the family will take a vacation and that they can afford to spend $1,000 on it. She may then say, "Since your father has only two weeks a year for vacation, it is only fair that he decide when and where we will go, whether we will drive or go by public transportation, and how long we should stay." In this instance, the wife clearly has assumed orchestration power and the husband has been delegated implementation power.

Constantina Safilios-Rothschild, the noted family sociologist who originated the terms, proposed (1976) that orchestration power within a marital couple is most frequently held by the partner with the most resources. In an earlier publication, Safilios-Rothschild (1967) suggested a "relative love and need theory," which posited that the degree to which one spouse loves and needs the other may be the most crucial variable in understanding power between a husband and wife. Especially important was the factor of being "more in love." The spouse who reported being more in love was found to have less orchestration power, whereas those partners who believed that they were equally in love shared major decisions in the marriage. Women who had lower levels of economic resources were often able to gain in orchestration power when their husbands were the ones more in love. It was as though they exchanged love for the right to make many of the major decisions.

Exchange theory has been used to explain the bargaining power derived from controlling resources by using the concepts of costs and rewards. Partners attempt to maintain a basic equality of what they give to and receive from each other. Since there are individual differences in what each needs and what each gives, the value that each partner places on what is given or received determines whether a balance is struck. In addition, needs vary between partners. Some are more self-reliant; others are more dependent, as we have already noted.

Recent research seems to indicate that there is more to how husbands and wives make decisions than who controls the most resources and what each partner has learned about who should or should not make decisions (McDonald 1980). For one thing, as more women are earning a more equal share of the family income, their decision-making power has increased to the point that they often have *more* impact than they previously did on decisions (McDonald 1980). It has been suggested that women who earn as much as their husbands are likely to be as well educated, as intelligent, and in possession of as many or more personal skills and competencies; therefore, they may move into a position of greater power than their husbands. Some studies also point to the increased marital power currently being achieved by women as a major factor in divorce (Pearson and Hendrix 1979).

Earlier studies suggested that marital satisfaction is greater in families in which women do not have greater marital power than their husbands (Kolb and Straus 1974). A recent large and comprehensive study of couples came to much the same conclusion, indicating that earnings still largely determine the balance of power and that most married men are not happy when they do not have that power (Blumstein and Schwartz 1983).

Of course, since many, if not all, couples have different hierarchies of values, power contests are significant to them in only those areas in which each believes it is important to control the other's behavior (and when they disagree on the appropriate behavior). It is unlikely that any partner has—or even wants—*total* control over *all* of a partner's behaviors or all decisions. Most studies seem to focus on power in major expenditures, recreational decisions, housekeeping, or infant care; those may or may not be the only (or even the highest priority) values in a given family.

It cannot be concluded that men are unhappy if they are not dominant or that women prefer to be stronger. Although either conclusion may be true for some couples, it is more likely that, when couples get into power struggles, certain dissatisfactions are already present and that the resources of affection, nurturance, income, or personal skills make it possible for one partner to gain a more powerful position.

A frequently mentioned explanation for the greater marital content sometimes found in husband-dominated marriages is that such marriages often fit a learned notion of the traditional pattern that couples may have seen modeled by their own parents. However, not all research agrees that husband-dominated marriages have the highest satisfaction (Corrales 1975). A study of over 2,000 men and women indicated that 63 percent of the respondents preferred an equal sharing of power (*Connecticut Mutual Life Report on American Values in the 80s* 1981). The fact that couples who share marital power are likely to report high marital satisfaction reflects an important principle of decision making.

Strategies of Decision Making

Considerable research has indicated that when all parties affected by a decision have a part in making the decision, they are usually more satisfied with the outcome (Wilson 1978). These findings probably reflect that such couples have achieved a cooperative relationship. It has been shown that in such relationships tasks and family roles are less traditionally assigned and are more often shared (Richmond 1976).

No one formula for decision making can work for all couples. Some husbands and wives delegate decision areas so that each partner has his or her own territory. These different "spheres of interest" may be divided traditionally, according to "men's work" and "women's work," or according to interest, expertise, or qualifications unique to each couple (Scanzoni 1979b).

Sharing in family decisions has been shown to result in greater satisfaction with the decisions to be made.

Two couples we have counseled illustrate the spheres of interest approach. In each of the marriages, the wife was a bookkeeper for a large corporation. In one instance, the husband insisted on taking care of the checkbook and record keeping even though his wife was more skilled, and his wife concurred because in each family of orientation the father had played that role. The other couple had the same arrangement, but in this case the wife asked to be relieved of the task because she spent over 40 hours a week keeping books and said she would rather do some other task instead.

Many couples have concluded that not every decision needs to be a joint one or even agreed on by both partners. There is merit, for instance, in keeping a portion of one's life separate *within* the unity of the relationship. Some matters that affect the partners individually are resolved by each person independently, whereas those decisions having an impact on both members are made jointly. What one couple might consider suitable for an individual decision, another couple might want to decide together (Cromwell and Olson 1975). Some couples agree that all major decisions will be made jointly (provided they can agree on just which ones are major). Usually both partners consider major decisions as those about place of residence; earning, spending, and saving money; children, friends, and relatives; and sex, although not necessarily in this order.

Decision-making patterns and power balances frequently change over the marital life cycle. For example, many marriages begin as egalitarian relationships, with both partners earning their livings and sharing domestic tasks. With the birth of children, roles may become specialized—the wife/mother may decide household/child matters, and the husband/father may decide matters about family financial support and future security. As mentioned earlier, some experts believe that such specialization tips the balance of power in the husband's favor and so gives husbands more of a role in major decision making (Gillespie 1971). Later, when the children are older, wives may return to the labor market and find that they no longer have the interest or time to make all the household decisions. Once again contributing to the family income, they also may want a larger voice in other major decisions, including financial ones.

Marriage counselors often are called on to help couples correct faulty decision-making patterns or to change from one pattern that may have functioned well during a preceding period of their lives to a new one that fits their changed statuses. Restructuring decision-making processes usually involves the following steps: (1) exploring why the present method is not working; (2) sorting out which decision areas each partner believes are major and which minor; (3) deciding which decisions are to be made jointly; (4) examining the effectiveness of following through with decisions, including who implements them; and (5) developing a variety of techniques to be used depending on the situation, rather than getting locked into one set pattern (see Lasswell and Lobsenz 1979b).

In addition to these guidelines, couples can draw on the well-known, orderly sequence of steps in making decisions developed in business management and by social psychologists (Bales and Strodtbeck 1951; pp. 485–95; Aldous 1971; Tallman 1970).

1. *Define the issue to be decided.* Usually one partner brings an issue to the other's attention, although sometimes both are aware that something needs attention. The issues may, of course, be problems, but not all decisions involve conflict— often there are pleasant decisions to be made too.
2. *Gather relevant information and discuss the facts.* This step includes several major issues. Perhaps as important as getting the objective data about the issue (if not more important) is determining how each partner feels about this issue. In other words, it is essential not only to discuss the facts but also to take the other person's feelings, priorities, and values into consideration in reaching a mutual decision. It has been shown that decisions made by considering only objective facts but omitting feelings are more likely to be regretted later (Hall and Hall 1979).

3. *Explore alternative decisions and select one.* Sometimes, when the issue is fully understood and each partner has had the opportunity to be heard, the decision is easy to reach. Sometimes, however, the decision is not what either person would have chosen if left to his or her own devices but, rather, a compromise that both can live with.

4. *Spell out whatever action is needed to implement the decision.* This step is important in preventing the partners from working at cross-purposes. This may also include setting a future time to check progress to be certain that the plan is working and does not need to be amended. Some couples also set a timetable for taking action on the decision.

The follow-through is as important as the decision, of course. Many couples make a good decision and map a strategy for it but find that their downfall is that no one actually carries out what they agreed to do. Getting things accomplished and feeling good about it seem to be powerful ingredients in most successful relationships.

TIME MANAGEMENT CHALLENGES

Still another major challenge to couples in adjusting to each other over a lifetime together lies in finding time both for each other and for themselves as individuals, while balancing busy schedules with heavy demands from outsiders. "Time to talk or to be quiet, time to play together or to work side by side, time for sex, time for solitude, time to be a spouse, parent, lover, but also time to be one's self—all these 'times' are vital ingredients of marriage" (Lasswell and Lobsenz 1976, p. 202).

In a recent study of American couples, sociologists Philip Blumstein and Pepper Schwartz (1983) noted that husbands and wives who spend too much time apart in the beginning years of marriage are more likely to break up. In some cases, spending large amounts of time at work or attending to relatives, friends, or hobbies may have been just a symptom of not enjoying each other's company. Keeping too busy to spend time with a mate often is a way of avoiding intimacy. In that case, the difficulty is not one of time management but of a deeper level of conflict in the marriage. One of the important clues to a troubled marriage is when one or both partners begin to withdraw from contact (Weiss 1975).

Most studies of time management in marriage support the notion that marital satisfaction depends largely on the quality of time spent together (rather than on the quantity) and on whether the partners agree on how their time is allocated (Pepitone-Rockwell 1980). For example, there are countless couples who spend every evening together but who complain of being bored with each other or who may feel lonely and alienated. Other couples spend much less actual time together but find their moments rewarding. One partner may believe that "time together" includes time spent reading or independently watching television, but the other may count only time spent together while interacting in some enjoyable activity.

Major interferences with quality time together as a couple come from many sources. When both partners fill their days with too much activity, shared or otherwise, they may find that tension and fatigue undermine their enjoyment of each other. Couples frequently give their best efforts and energies to their work, to children, or

LEISURE-TIME MANAGEMENT

Most couples find that working and taking care of household duties often do not allow much time for anything else. It is, of course, important for couples to establish routines to accomplish all that needs doing. When children come along, they must be integrated into already busy schedules, and sometimes husbands and wives feel that there is very little time to relax or have fun. Couples often report guilt about time and money spent on leisure pursuits even though mental health professionals emphasize that every life should be balanced. Working all the time can be stressful to one's mental and physical well-being.

Leisure activity acts as a stress-reducer by giving one control over one's own time. Time away from the structure and responsibility of everyday cares is important. Being able to spontaneously choose what to do or what not to do provides a needed break. Weekends, holidays, and vacations offer opportunities for highly-scheduled people to decide for themselves how they will manage their time, provided they do not create even more stress by poor planning.

Following are some of the major ways that poor planning can ruin leisure time and some tips on how to avoid such pitfalls:

- Some people manage to turn play into work. They go at whatever they do with such intensity and speed that they have managed little rest or change of pace. It is well to remember that play is what one does for fun with no other goal in mind. Some people, for example, play at tennis or fishing, others work at it because their goal is to win or compete.
- On weekends and vacations, many families report tension just from being together 24 hours a day. Because work, school, and other outside activities take up so much time, family members often see very little of each other during the work week. Being confined in an automobile or a camping tent on vacation leaves little room for privacy and no place to get away when nerves get frazzled. Parents will probably need a breather from the children from time to time and from each other as well.
- Some families who have problems look to a vacation to bring everyone closer together. They want every activity to be shared. It's as though they want to make up for lost time and to heal all rifts. Not everyone may enjoy the same activities or want to eat at exactly the same time. It is being in control of one's own time that is, after all, the stress-reliever not forcing all participants into one routine.
- Reentry at the end of the leisure-time break is often poorly planned too. There is a certain amount of stress in changing back to one's workday self. Coming home very late the night before going back to work or school usually does not give ample time to shift gears. Some people come home from vacation very tired and need at least some time to read the mail and get a good nights' sleep.
- Reentry also may mean paying the bills for the vacation. Keeping within one's budget can help keep stress from developing. Remember, too, that the most expensive leisure activity isn't necessarily the most fun.

to outsiders. Home may become a refuge from outside pressures—a place to relax—with the result that the partner gets what is left over—perhaps only a nervous and exhausted mate.

For those couples who do want to spend more quality time together but are caught by other demands such as work, children, and friends, the dilemma of how to carve out that time for themselves becomes a central issue. On top of these demands come what family sociologist Arlene Skolnick (1973, p. 213) describes as "the horde of seemingly irrelevant trivia—missing buttons, lost keys, dental appointments, PTA

The birth of a couple's first child forces the couple to add the new roles of mother and father to their existing roles of husband and wife, which usually results in a significant decline in time spent alone together.

meetings, broken washing machines—that determine the time, energy, and moods" a couple have to give to each other.

In working with couples who present time management as a problem in their marriages, we have found a number of techniques useful for helping them satisfy the essential claims of outsiders while still finding time for themselves as couples.

1. *Find out exactly how time is spent.* Many couples have only a vague idea of how each day is spent. Keeping a fairly detailed log for at least two weeks may reveal several extended telephone conversations that could have been shorter or unnecessary errands that could have been consolidated. Some couples discover that by finding exactly where their time goes, they can make constructive changes that help erase their time problem.

2. *Compare calendars.* Two busy people can easily discover that when one has free time, the other does not. Although it may seem peculiar to try to schedule time to be together rather than let it happen spontaneously, the fact is that otherwise they may never find time for themselves as a couple. It may help for them to think of these calendar comparisons as a way of making sure they do not make individual schedules that *prohibit* them from having time together.

3. *Learn to say "no."* There may come a time in the overcommitted lives of any couple when they must face the fact that if they take on one more obligation, it will mean that something else must go undone. Too often what is sacrificed is time either with a partner or alone. Often spouses and children are asked to be tolerant so that outsiders can be served. Most people find it difficult to turn down invitations or other kinds of requests until they realize that they are giving other people higher priority than those at home.

Every marriage needs nurturance and quality attention if both partners are to be satisfied with their relationship. Although time spent together may not be the most important ingredient in a happy marriage, it is perhaps the base on which the other factors must rest. It is very difficult to become intimate companions, love each other, make joint decisions, and reach mutual goals without spending sufficient time in interaction to accomplish these tasks.

All happy couples do not manage their time alike, so there is no single formula. However, most satisfying relationships have a common characteristic: the two people enjoy being together. Paramount to this shared enjoyment is a quality of playfulness and humor that transcends the complexities and problems of everyday life. Research on play and marital adjustment indicates that intimate playfulness seems to help couples keep a balance between too much distance and too much intensity (Cole 1982). Playfulness and humor also serve to defuse conflict and to cement the bonds between the partners.

H. V. Dicks (1967), a British psychiatrist, has stated that play in marriage can serve as a kind of therapy because human beings play with each other only in an atmosphere that they perceive as safe and relaxed and where they can feel free to be spontaneous without loss of dignity. Sharing a sense of humor has been cited frequently as an important bond in marriage. Couples report that humor is an implicit statement that values are shared and that you are in tune with your partner (Betcher 1981).

SUMMARY

1. Since no two people are identical, each partner brings individual needs, desires, and expectations to their relationship. The amount of satisfaction in a relationship is determined by how well both partners meet each other's needs and by how well the relationship allows each of them to meet his or her own needs.
2. Expectations often are unknown unless one's partner fails to measure up. Hurt, anger, and disappointment are often clues that expectations have not been met. Some expectations are known to one partner but not to the other. Since most human beings are poor mind readers, unfulfilled expectations are common. Expectations are often unrealistic since they are based on idealization of oneself, of one's partner, or of married life.
3. Couples whose marriages give them room to meet their individual goals place greater value on their marriages. When each partner facilitates the other's plans, they have what is termed *mutual interdependence*.
4. Good marriages must find ways to link individual goals to the mutual goals of the partners. Research indicates that working cooperatively as a team toward mutual goals leads to greater attraction between partners and to greater satisfaction with their marriage.
5. Cooperation is also defined in terms of the means by which couples seek their goals. Not only must there be mutual interdependence in goals, but there must also be interdependence in the means of achieving goals.
6. Cooperation often hinges on communication. The more couples communicate, the more they facilitate cooperation.

7. Each marital relationship develops its own style based on unique behavioral patterns and the partners' reactions to one another. They develop strategies for problem solving, decision making, and living and working together.

8. Learning to live harmoniously with someone else is a measure of compatibility with that person. Marital adjustment is significantly correlated with a couple's compatibility. Learning to mesh individual traits is an ongoing process in marriage because rarely do two people know each other totally when they marry. Even if total knowledge were possible, people still change over the life cycle, making adjustment a dynamic process that continues throughout the marriage.

9. Studies of successful marriages indicate that there are many styles that work well. The quality of marriages—no matter what their style—seems to be highly correlated with how much agreement the husbands and wives have about their roles.

10. Many marital adjustment scales have been developed over the years to measure couples' satisfaction with their relationship. Most inventories determine the current state of the marriage, but recent attempts have focused on those facets of marriage that are believed to carry over from one stage of the life cycle to the next.

11. Flexibility in marital roles—which includes adaptability in rules and goals—is essential in dealing with the changes that are inevitable during the marital life cycle. The need for partners to differ and to accommodate each other's growth are sources of challenge to every long-term relationship.

12. Decision making is one of the most important challenges facing couples as they attempt to work out mutually agreeable and efficient ways of living together compatibly. Family experts report that the perceived power balance between the partners is a key factor in the decision-making patterns that each couple characteristically develops.

13. The resource theory proposes that the partner perceived as having the most resources has the most authority to decide how the couple will live. Resources may be financial or may relate to skills, personality traits, self-confidence, or love and sex.

14. Techniques that couples use to negotiate with each other, such as assertiveness, manipulation, and persuasion, affect the decision-making process. Power, therefore, lies not only in resources but also in the ability to use these techniques.

15. Time management is another challenge that can enhance a marital relationship or, if handled poorly, can create serious feelings of distance and alieination between the partners. Most studies of the time that couples spend together emphasize the quality of the time rather than the quantity. However, the quantity must be sufficient to satisfy both partners in a reasonable fashion.

16. Major interferences with quality time for couples come from too many activities, the demands of work and other activities, and children, family, friends, and others. Busy couples should compare calendars and schedule time for themselves as they do for others. This may entail giving their marriage a higher priority than many of the activities or persons that previously may have taken precedence.

17. Play and humor are important ingredients in marital satisfaction and a desire to spend time with one's partner. Such sharing implies that the two partners are able to share values in a relaxed and spontaneous way.

Glossary

Compatibility The ability to exist together in harmony as measured by the efficiency with which those who live together accommodate each other's values, interests, behaviors, and other facets of their individual styles of living. (p. 220)

Core symbols Words, behaviors, or objects that have such powerful meanings to those involved in a relationship that their use or abuse may be interpreted as a crisis in the relationship (for example, putting on or taking off a wedding ring; sleeping in the same bed or in separate beds or rooms; denying coitus to a partner or having coitus with someone else). (p. 215)

Implementation power The right or responsibility of a person to whom tasks are delegated to make the decisions necessary for carrying out those tasks. (p. 231)

Orchestration power The right or responsibility of a delegated person to decide who will carry out organizational tasks so that the necessary activities to achieve family goals are effectively articulated. (p. 231)

9

Many will still decide, for all sorts of personally valid reasons, that parenthood is not for them, but others, remembering their own joyful childhoods, will be eager to participate in such an experience again, as parent now instead of child.

Throughout most of the world for most of human history, women have been expected to be either pregnant or nursing babies from adolescence until menopause. Civilization brought with it a restrictive morality about childbearing, although before the Christian era ways of enjoying sexual intercourse without causing pregnancy were devised. Motives for limiting the number of pregnancies began to change in the nineteenth century. Since that time contraceptive procedures have advanced technologically with growing speed.

This chapter deals with the contraceptive methods currently in use, their advantages, their drawbacks, and their relative effectiveness. It also deals with abortion as a means of limiting births, the methods by which abortions are carried out, and their effects. Finally, there is a section on the remedies for involuntary childlessness.

FAMILY PLANNING AND BIRTH CONTROL

Bernice Lott

*U*ndoubtedly early humans saw pregnancy as a normal developmental event for women, occurring first in adolescence and recurring until menopause (or, in most cases, until death, since relatively few females lived to reach menopause). As civilizations aged, ruling classes in particular controlled lines of descent by restricting sexual access to their women, demanding virginity at marriage (or concubinage) and prohibiting extramarital sexual activity for women. This evolving social system made it desirable for members of both sexes to find ways to have sexual intercourse without causing pregnancy.

In some societies pregnancy was believed to be caused by a spirit that entered a woman's body; in others it was believed to result from exposure to the wind or from eating some special food or potion. Even where the association of sexual intercourse with subsequent pregnancy was known, its nature was not always well understood. Some explanations centered around the phase of the moon or the tides. Some societies believed that each time a member of the group died, another was created. (Stannard 1970). Others believed that males exuded microscopically small human beings in their semen and that these grew to birth size in women's wombs.

THE HISTORY OF CONTRACEPTIVE METHODS

Contraception has a fascinating history. In ancient times, when a woman wished to prevent or to postpone pregnancy, she had a choice of several methods. Women were advised to place feathers or small sponges in their vaginas to absorb the sperm or to use hollowed-out lemon or pomegranate halves to cover the cervix. Some women believed that they could prevent conception by jumping up and down after the man had ejaculated or by holding their breath during orgasm (Himes 1963).

The notorious lover Casanova viewed contraception as a way to avoid the social responsibilities of pregnancy and devised methods to protect men from unwanted paternity. He used animal-skin condoms tied with a ribbon and recommended the use of a gold ball inserted in the vagina. In 1798 Thomas Malthus suggested abstinence from premarital intercourse, followed by late marriage, as a birth control plan. He reportedly never engaged in coitus until he married at age 40.

The issue of birth control has caused much social conflict. In the United States in 1873, opponents of birth control successfully persuaded Congress to pass the Comstock Law (named for the secretary of the New York Society for the Suppression of Vice), which made it unlawful to disseminate birth control devices or information about them through the mail. Many states enacted further legislation that forbade the sale or dispensing of such devices by doctors or druggists or in any store. These laws were in force in many areas of the United States until very recently. Not until 1966 was the last state law banning the sale of contraceptives repealed.

In 1915 Margaret Sanger (who coined the term *birth control*) in the United States and Marie Stopes in England began attempts to overturn the Comstock laws. Applying skills she had learned in England, Sanger opened a birth control clinic. She published a newsletter and initiated research aimed at developing reliable methods

Margaret Sanger was a pioneer in programs to help women whose health was jeopardized by pregnancy or who lacked the resources to care for children. She also believed that women were entitled to the right to prevent unwanted pregnancies.

of controlling fertility. Sanger went to jail for her efforts, which were aimed primarily at helping women whose health was threatened by pregnancy or who lacked the resources or the strength to care for more children (Bullough and Bullough 1977).

Until Stopes and Sanger began their activities on behalf of women, men had generally taken the initiative in contraception, usually as a way of enjoying sexual intercourse while reducing the probability of the social or financial responsibilities of fathering a child. Stopes and Sanger introduced the idea that women as well as men were entitled to the right to prevent pregnancy. However, they were probably more concerned with women's health and financial welfare than with their right to enjoy sex whenever they chose.

Slowly, over the years, laws and sentiments about contraception have been changing—but the controversy has not totally ended. Until 1979, the sale of contraceptives was illegal in Ireland; a law passed in that year legalized the sale of contraceptives to married couples but only with a doctor's prescription (Blanche 1985). Many American Catholics, including some members of the clergy, are beginning to question the banning of contraceptives; it is a matter of record that the majority of Catholic women use some form of birth control. In a speech delivered before the United States National Conference of Catholic Bishops in September 1980, Archbishop John Quinn said that in view of published studies reporting that 76.5 percent of American Roman Catholic women were practicing birth control and that 71 percent of Catholic priests in the United States did not believe that birth control is immoral, a new church doctrine of "responsible parenthood" was needed (*Los Angeles Times,* September 29, 1980, Part 1, p. 1). The Vatican almost immediately denounced this position, however, and the conflict continues.

Even today, some people oppose making contraceptives available to sexually active unmarried teenagers. Opponents of free access to contraception believe that allowing teenagers access to contraceptives encourages premarital sexual activity. Still others believe that sex outside of marriage is a sin and that sinners should be punished by having to live with their mistakes—any resulting pregnancy, any resulting social disgrace, any financial burden. However, the burden of babies born to teenagers is not only individual but societal.

Whether people wish to remain childless while enjoying an active sex life or simply wish to plan the timing of their pregnancies, most want a reliable contraceptive procedure. Although the average woman is fecund for approximately three decades and theoretically ovulates once every lunar month (13 times a year or, on average, 390 times in her life), it is unlikely that she would want as many children as she is capable of having. Even more unlikely is the notion that a man might want to fertilize as many ova as he is capable of doing since, theoretically, he could provide the sperm to impregnate many women every day.

FERTILITY

As a result of improved nutrition, better methods of refrigeration, better maternal and infant care, and better control of contagious diseases, the survival rate of babies and the prolongation of life caused an unprecedented population boom in the twentieth century (see Figure 9.1). In the United States this coincided with the movement of the bulk of the population from family farms to urban industrial areas. Dependent children no longer contributed to the family economy but instead became a severe financial drain. The limitation of reproduction became necessary for economic survival in many families.

A substantial fraction of the adult population—including members of virtually all religious, racial, and ethnic groups—practices some form of birth control, primarily for personal rather than ideological reasons. "A majority of women exposed to the risk of pregnancy in the developed countries of Asia, North America and Europe are currently using contraception" (U.S. Bureau of the Census 1983c, p. 2). As contraceptive use has spread, for the first time in history it has become possible for most persons to choose when to have a child, how many to have, or whether to have any at all. The result has been that many countries that formerly had burdensome birth rates have been able to curb the growth of their population.

Singapore, Mexico, and the People's Republic of China have successful official policies encouraging the limitation of family size. The highest fertility rates in the world are found in African countries; the lowest rates of childbearing are found in the European nations and in North America. For teenagers from fifteen to nineteen years old, the highest rates are found in Africa, Latin America, and the Caribbean (100 to 200 births per 1,000 women per year); the lowest rate is in Japan (4 per 1,000 women per year) (U.S. Bureau of the Census 1983c, p. 2).

As a result of the use of contraceptives and abortion, the United States is now near or even below **zero population growth**, meaning that the average woman is having 2.1 or fewer children who will grow to be old enough to replace themselves in the population pool. A low of 1.8 was reached in 1976 (Hoult, Henze, and Hudson 1978, p. 396). Considering that 5 percent of married couples will have no children and another 5 percent of women will remain unmarried and probably childless, our population size may even begin to decrease, although probably not until well into the twenty-first century.

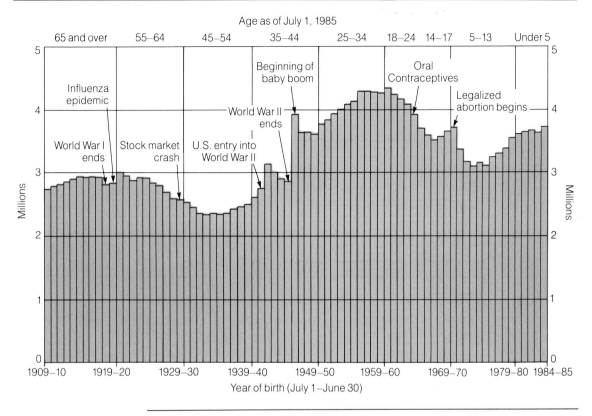

Age as of July 1, 1985

FIGURE 9 • 1

Number of Births by Year, 1910–1985, and Relationship to 1985 Age Groups

Source: U.S. Bureau of the Census, *Current Population Reports,* Series P-25, No. 985 (April 1986).

The fertility rate for 1976 was the lowest for the United States in recorded history; the 1978 rate was the second lowest (see Figure 9.2). The rate for women age 40 to 49 increased by about 9 percent in 1979. (U.S. Bureau of Census 1981a, p. 19). Postponement of childbearing is credited for the increase in birth to older women. Births to women age 30 and over as a percent of total births has been increasing steadily since 1974 (see Figure 9.3). In 1983, 19 percent of the women age 30–44 had their first baby; they were more highly educated, more likely to be employed in a professional occupation, and had higher incomes on the average than their counterparts age 18–29 (U.S. Bureau of the Census 1984d, pp. 1–2). In 1984, the only age group whose fertility had increased since 1980 was women age 30–34 (U.S. Bureau of the Census 1985c, p. 1).

As they near the age of 35, many American women believe that their time to reproduce is running out. They are aware of research showing more maternal and infant deaths and more birth defects when older women conceive. The risk factor for the most frequently diagnosed defect, Down's Syndrome, is 1 in 1,500 live births for mothers under age 30 but 1 in 130 for mothers between the ages of 40 and 45 and 1 in 20 for

FIGURE 9 • 2
Total Fertility Rate,
1920–1983

Source: U.S. Bureau of the Census, *Current Population Reports,*
Series P-23, No. 145 (September 1985).

women over 45 (Whelan 1975, pp. 171–173). Consequently, women aged 30–34 who have postponed having children may decide they cannot safely wait any longer.

Out-of-Wedlock Births

In the United States, there is a distinction made between children born to married women and those born to unmarried women; in other countries no legal distinction is made. In Sweden, for instance, the notion of **illegitimacy** is not an important one, especially in matters of support or inheritance from the biological father as well as from the mother (Linner 1976). In 1975 the European Convention on the Status of Children Born out of Wedlock suggested that the concept of illegitimacy be dropped. The point was made that children born to a married woman are not considered illegitimate even if a man other than her husband is the biological father. The question became, "Why is the child of an unmarried woman singled out for discrimination?" (Eekelaar 1980).

The United States is beginning to shift away from legal distinctions between legitimate and illegitimate births. One reason for this may be that a growing number of single women are freely choosing to bear children. In 1950 only 4.0 percent of all

FIGURE 9 · 3
Births to Women 30
and Over as a Percent
of All Births, 1970–
1982

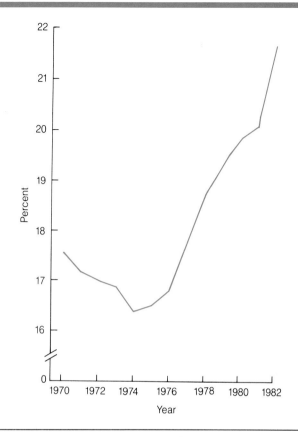

Source: U.S. Bureau of the Census, *Current Population Reports,*
Series P-23, No. 145 (September 1985).

women who had a child were unmarried (see Figure 9.4) compared to seventeen
percent of all women who had a child between 1980 and 1984. These are sometimes
somewhat older women who decide not to marry but who nonetheless want to be
mothers. Some are formerly married women who bear children while they are between
marriages. In 1970, "about 11 percent of twice-married women had given birth
between separation and divorce, with an additional 14 percent having a birth between
divorce and remarriage" (Rindfuss and Bumpass 1977, p. 518).

Although earlier data are often incomplete and unreliable, in 1940 there were
only 17 illegitimate births recorded in the United States for every 1,000 unmarried
women over 25 years of age. By 1977 that figure had more than tripled, to 57 for every
1,000 unmarried women over 25 (National Center for Health Statistics 1979a, p. 19).
In 1982, never-married white women aged 25 to 34 had given birth to 148 children
per 1,000 women, and never-married black women in the same age bracket had given
birth to 1,490 children per 1,000 women (U.S. Bureau of the Census 1984e, pp. 34,
36). Since nearly all women over 25 have knowledge of the use of contraceptives, it is
believed that a large number of the conceptions may be deliberate. An older woman
choosing to have a child even though she is single presents quite a different picture of
illegitimacy from that of a teenager who gets pregnant intentionally or unintentionally.

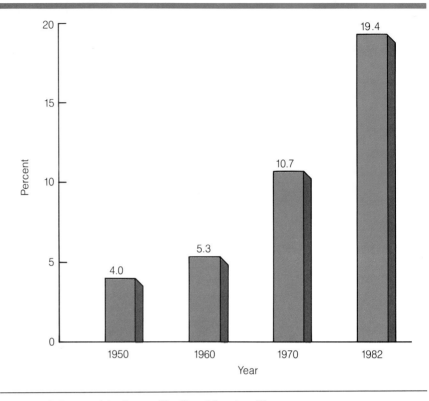

Source: U.S. Bureau of the Census, "Fertility of American Women: June 1982," *Current Population Reports,* Series 20, No. 387 (1982), pp. 1–12.

Sixty-nine percent of women maintaining one-parent households in the United States in 1984 were divorced or never married; the proportion that were black was more than three times the proportion that were white. Fifty-nine percent of all black family groups with children under the age of eighteen were living with only one parent in 1984, 94 percent of them with their mothers (U.S. Bureau of the Census, 1985a, pp. 1–5).

Teenage Contraception and Pregnancy

Teenagers account for nearly 50 percent of all out-of-wedlock births in the United States. The U.S. teenage birthrate of 96 births per 1,000 teenagers is among the highest for developed countries. The Alan Guttmacher Institute found that the rates in England and Canada were under half the U.S. rate per 1,000 girls aged fifteen to nineteen; the rate was 43 per 1,000 in France, 35 per 1,000 in Sweden, and 14 per 1,000 in the Netherlands (Mall 1985, p. 27). The same institute reported the U.S. rate as 52 per 1,000 in 1981, only four years earlier (Mecklenburg and Thompson 1983, p. 21).

Seventy-five percent of first births to white teenagers fifteen to seventeen years old between 1977 and 1982 were either born or conceived before marriage, as were

99 percent in the comparable age category of black teenagers (U.S. Bureau of the Census, 1984e, p. 1). An unplanned birth can make a very young mother and her baby vulnerable to economic, social, and psychological problems. In 1985, families that resulted from teenage pregnancy cost U.S. tax payers $16.6 billion (Goodman 1986).

In an important work on family planning, Arthur Campbell (1968) stated:

> The girl who has an illegitimate child at the age of sixteen suddenly has 90 percent of her life's script written for her. She will probably drop out of school, even if someone else in her family helps to take care of the baby. She will probably not be able to find a steady job that pays enough to provide for herself and her child; she may feel impelled to marry someone she might not otherwise have chosen. Her life choices are few, and most of them are bad. Had she been able to delay the first child, her prospects might have been quite different assuming that she would have had opportunities to continue her education, improve her vocational skills, find a job, marry someone she wanted to marry, and have a child when she and her husband were ready for it.

A wealth of research has attempted to explain why the fifteen- to nineteen-year-old age group has such a high rate of illegitimacy. One factor is that females are sexually active at an earlier age than ever before. By age nineteen, 55 percent of all females report experiencing intercourse (Zelnik and Kantner 1977). It is unlikely that sexually active teenagers will be married: only 24 percent under the age of nineteen have ever been married; less than 3 percent under the age of seventeen have ever been married (U.S. Bureau of the Census 1979b, p. 2). Therefore, any children conceived by sexually active females in this age category are likely to be born out of wedlock. As a result of better diets and a general increase in health, American girls today begin to menstruate nearly a year earlier than their grandmothers did, indicating the possibility of earlier pregnancy.

There are two other important factors in teenage pregnancies. First, teenagers are likely to be less well informed about both reproduction and contraception than are older persons. This situation seems to be improving somewhat as more sex education courses are being offered in high schools. Unfortunately, many of these focus on reproduction—on how babies grow in the uterus rather than on why they get there in the first place. In the 1976 National Survey of Young Women, 70 percent of the single fifteen- to nineteen-year-old females reported that they had taken such a course and that it had included instruction about the menstrual cycle and pregnancy (Zelnik 1979). Our impression, however, is that the necessity for the use of contraceptives if pregnancy is to be avoided is often underemphasized in such courses and that the necessary social skills for discussing contraceptive use with a partner are likely to be totally ignored as a topic.

A second factor accounting for the current number of teenage pregnancies is that learning about contraception in a classroom is a far cry from purchasing and correctly using such devices. Particularly when they first begin sexual activity, many young women report that they resist the idea of going on a date "prepared" since this eliminates spontaneity and causes them to feel calculating. Of those who do want to use contraceptives, many report that they are embarrassed to buy them or to ask a physician for them.

Fortunately, at least 26 states either have opened or are planning to open health clinics in public schools (115 as of 1985), offering, among other health and social services, the dispensation of birth-control information and devices. Such clinics have been operating in high schools in Dallas and Saint Paul since the mid-1970s. Parental approval has been reported as near 100 percent in the schools. There is no evidence of any increase in sexual activity in the schools. Although 115 is a small fraction of the 25,000 high schools in the United States, the estimated $125 per year per student that it costs to operate such a clinic may be sufficiently appealing to taxpayers to encourage a steady growth of the movement (Dryfoos 1985, p. 104). The cost of supporting to adulthood one child born out of wedlock to a welfare recipient has been estimated at $80,000.

Two national studies have determined that many teenagers are sexually active for as long as a year before they begin to use any kind of contraception (Zelnik and Kantner 1979). As young women get older, there is an increase in their use of contraceptives. There has been a significant change from 1971, when the first of the National Survey of Young Women studies was done, to 1976, when the second one occurred (see Table 9.1).

The American Public Health Association has indicated that the age of first intercourse is related to current use of contraceptives. Those age fifteen or younger when they first have intercourse are significantly less reliable users than persons who are older at first intercourse (Cvetkovich et al. 1978, pp. 231–36).

Shah and Zelnik (1981) have studied the effects of parental and peer influence on the use of contraceptives by unmarried fifteen- to nineteen-year-old women. They report:

> The premarital pregnancy experience of young women by parent and peer influence is consistent with their contraceptive use status. Black women with views like their parents' [who condone premarital pregnancy] have the highest rate (50 percent) of premarital pregnancy. This group also has the highest proportion (52 percent) of those who never use contraception. White women with views like their parents' [who do not condone premarital pregnancy] have the lowest rate of premarital pregnancy (22 percent); this group also has the lowest proportion of women who have had unprotected intercourse. The association between parent and peer influence among whites is not surprising; those influenced by parents are less likely to have a premarital pregnancy than those influenced by friends.

The increased knowledge and use of contraceptives by teenagers is encouraging to those who would like to see teenage pregnancy rates drop. It should follow that the availability of contraceptives will lead to a decrease in the number of children born to women who are not yet ready to be mothers. However, this has not been the case. Although some of the more than 500,000 births a year to unwed mothers in the United States may have been planned, it is safe to say that the majority probably were not.

Ninety-four percent of single mothers elect to keep their babies (Fosburgh 1977). In their extensive study of premarital pregnancy, Zelnik and Kantner (1978) reported that 9 percent of those women fifteen to nineteen years old who became pregnant married shortly after their baby was born. Eighty-five percent of teenaged unwed mothers spent a longer period of time as single parents.

One study reported that one year after their baby was born, 75 percent of the young mothers reported that they were responsible for its care. The figure dropped to 60 percent after two years and to less than 50 percent in a subsequent follow-up. After

	Age	1971	1976
	15	30%	52%
	16	38	56
	17	45	63
	18	47	70
	19	55	69

TABLE 9 • 1
Percentage of Sexually
Active Women Using
Contraceptives

Source: M. Zelnik and J. Kantner, "Sexual and Contraceptive Experience of Young Unmarried Women in the United States, 1976 and 1971," *Family Planning Perspectives* 9 (March–April 1977), p. 62. Reprinted with permission from the authors and *Family Planning Perspectives,* Volume 9, Number 2, 1977.

one year, nearly 20 percent of the mothers had lost contact with the fathers; after five years, 37 percent of the fathers had not been heard from for over a year. The main source of assistance the young mother had was her own family (Furstenberg 1976b, p. 174). Many schools now have classes for pregnant teenagers to help them deal with their complex problems and the difficulties that face them. The state of Illinois has a special program called Parents Too Soon to help and support teenage mothers, funded by $12 million in federal grants (*Pomona* [CA] *Progress Bulletin*, May 3, 1984, p. 33).

Eventually, most teenage mothers marry someone. It may be that the most serious drawbacks to an illegitimate pregnancy are short term. In the long run, with the help of their families, many young women manage to overcome some of the negative personal consequences of premature motherhood.

WHY PEOPLE HAVE CHILDREN

The reasons for creating pregnancies differ from person to person. Couples who are deliberately trying to produce a pregnancy do so for a variety of reasons, and indeed any person, married or not, may have unique reasons for wishing to become a parent.

It has been found that first-birth probabilities change as factors such as war, inflation, or unemployment rates change and as a woman's age increases (Rindfuss, Morgan, and Swicegood 1984). Although these may be neither necessary nor sufficient reasons to create a pregnancy, they have been found to be related to whatever reasons people have.

The factors most predictive of whether a woman will have additional children are her present age and the number of children she already has. The number of children that the average 22-year-old woman will have depends on how many she has already had by that age. The younger she is and the more children she has already had, the more she will have later (U.S. Bureau of the Census 1985g, p. 1).

Unintended or even unwanted pregnancies may occur simply because a male or female or both together have a compelling urge to have sexual intercourse. They need not have any enduring relationship; in fact, the compelling urge may be acted out in prostitution or rape between total strangers. The pregnancies resulting from such acts produce children just as surely as ones for which the parents have planned for years. There is no way of knowing how many babies are born simply because a sexual encounter was so overpowering that one or both of the participants were not really concerned with the consequences. The Emory University Family Planning Program issued a report stating that of every 100 sexually active women who left the consequences of intercourse to chance, 90 actually became pregnant in the course of one year (Knox 1979, p. 412).

The Commission on Population Growth (1972, p. 163) reported that 44 percent of all births to married women in the United States between 1966 and 1970 were unplanned. It can be assumed that these babies were conceived because having intercourse was valuable to the couples—or at least to one of them—for whatever reason, and that there were varying degrees of concern (either positive or negative) about whether a pregnancy would result. It is frequently reported that "acts of God," ranging from blackouts to blizzards, often confront couples with unanticipated opportunities to engage in coitus (or more cynically put, limit the opportunities to do much of anything else), with a resulting increase in the number of births about nine months later.

Studies of motives for having children have revealed that nine basic values are often reported as important reasons for conceiving children (Hoffman and Hoffman 1973; Rapoport et al. 1980, pp. 139–140):

1. To prove that one is an adult
2. To have some personal expansion of oneself and perhaps of one's ancestors that will last beyond one's own lifetime
3. To satisfy certain standards set by one's family or religion
4. To create an intimate, affectionate living group larger than the couple alone
5. To experience the adventures of childbearing and child rearing
6. To create a new person
7. To have someone to take care of who is dependent and can be molded
8. To demonstrate that one can accomplish something that others long to do
9. To have another family member to share in the family's work and to count on in old age

The fact that these motives are often cited does not mean that they are valid. In fact, research has shown that at least some of them are not (Keith 1983). A review and modification of this list may suggest further rational motives that many persons actually have or at least are aware of having. Although a wish to have children that is separate from the wish to have sexual intercourse may not qualify as an urge or a drive, there does seem to exist in some persons a longing to have one's own children that has no rational component. Many couples may well ask why they must have a reason—they just want to have children, and it is not a decision they spend a great deal of time debating.

VOLUNTARY CHILDLESSNESS

Although many couples are deciding to have children, a slowly growing number are currently childless. Until relatively recently, if a woman did not bear children, it was assumed that she could not. Those few who chose to announce bravely that their state was voluntary were often subjected to harsh judgments about their mental health or their lack of femininity. Kinder friends or relatives might have tried to make them see the error of the decision.

The effectiveness of the considerable social and emotional pressure that was often applied is evident in surveys made by the Bureau of the Census that asked women how many children they planned to have. During the 21-year period from 1946 to 1967, only about 3 percent of American women said that they expected to be childless (U.S. Bureau of the Census 1977a). In the 1920s and 1930s the figure had been much higher: about 20 percent of the women surveyed expected to remain childless; however, many of those may simply have been acknowledging their own or their husbands' infertility. With improvements in diet, general health, and medical care (especially treatment for infertility and the acceptability of artificial insemination), more women knew they would be able to conceive if they wished to, and that may have accounted for some of the change.

Once involuntary childlessness decreased, the number of women who remained childless dropped from 20 percent to 5 percent, where it stayed until the "baby boom" that followed World War II (1946–1957). As families were reunited after the war, there seemed to be an urge to get the country "back to normal." Most couples evidently wished to have children: part of normality, evidently, was "nest building" and filling the nest with babies.

The trend toward large families lasted until 1957, but the general idea of having some children continued to be popular for another decade. Not until the birth control pill was mass-marketed in 1966–1967 was there a marked gain in the number of women who wanted no children at all. Even then, the increase was only enough to bring the percentage back to 9 percent.

As recently as 1973, a Gallup poll found that only 1 percent of the population believed that being childless was preferable or that childless couples had a better life (Blake 1979). It may be that many of those who are childless at any given time are either involuntarily so or will change their minds eventually. Since 1976 there has been little change in the number of young married women who expect to remain childless. A recent census report shows that the figure is now about 6.4 percent for women aged 25 to 29 (U.S. Bureau of the Census 1984e, p. 4).

Educational attainment is related to the proportions of women who expect to remain childless. Expectation of childlessness is most common among women who have attended college, less common among high school graduates, and still less common among those who have dropped out of school (see Table 9.2).

Related to the figures on education and childlessness is the fact that women who are (or intend to be) successful in careers for which education has prepared them are those who are least likely to want children (U.S. Bureau of the Census 1979c, p. 27; 1984e, p. 19). At the same time, school- and/or college-age women who have babies are surely less likely to continue in school than those who do not, regardless of whether the pregnancy was intentional or unintentional.

Married white women are somewhat more likely to remain childless if they are college educated than are married black women (9.1 percent of white women compared with 6.9 percent of black women). Although the same bulletin did not report 1982 data for other racial and ethnic groups, a report issued on women of Spanish origin in Los Angeles would lead us to believe that the proportion remaining childless would be significantly lower. Women of Spanish origin have a much higher fertility

	Education	1976	1982	Change 1976–1982
College				
	5 years +	14.3%	10.6%	−3.7%
	4 years	7.5%	8.2%	+0.7%
	1–3 years	7.3%	7.9%	+0.6%
	High school graduate	4.9%	6.1%	+1.2%
	Non–high school graduate	2.6%	3.9%	+1.3%
	Total (18–34 years of age)	14,940,000	15,299,000	+359,000

TABLE 9 · 2
Married Women Who Expect to Remain Childless

Sources: 1976—U.S. Bureau of the Census, *Current Population Reports,* Series P-20, No. 341 (1977), p. 27; 1982—Series P-20, No. 387 (1984), p. 19.

rate than American women as a whole. This is attributed to their desires for larger families rather than to the failure of their family-planning efforts, which have been found to have the same rate of success for them as for other American women (Sabagh 1980).

Deciding to Remain Childless

Researchers have addressed several questions about people who decide not to have children. In recent years well over a hundred studies have addressed themselves to (1) how couples make the decision to remain childless; (2) when they make this decision; (3) whether it is a mutual decision or one more heavily influenced by the wife or husband; and (4) how couples who aspire to childlessness compare in terms of marital satisfaction with couples who decide to have children (Veevers 1979).

It has already been mentioned that women who are contemplating lifelong careers are among the foremost advocates of voluntary childlessness. It appears from this that couples' decisions would be dominated by women since it is women who are most affected by having to balance their children with their jobs. Most of the research on this topic has indicated that, indeed, wives are much more likely to make the decision in nearly all instances. One study found that half the husbands who agreed not to have children admitted that if their wives should change and want a baby, they would agree (Nason and Poloma 1976). Not one of the wives said that a change of heart by her husband would affect her feelings on the subject.

It is very possible that the general finding that women have the greatest influence in the decision of whether to have children would not hold for some populations if separate data were compiled. The data for college-educated women, upper-socioeconomic-class wives, those with formal religious ties, and those with careers are not known; women in some of these categories may be more strongly influenced by what their husbands want.

According to one study of childless couples, most of them talked about whether to have children for months or even years before they made their decisions; most reported a minimum of two to three years (Nason and Poloma 1976). Further, most of the couples studied reported that the decision was made after their marriage, not before, and attributed it primarily to the wife's employment and the couple's subsequent commitment to a childless lifestyle. Having more time for each other as a couple and enjoying travel and leisure time together were important considerations. In another study, 29 percent of those replying to the question of why they were remaining childless mentioned feeling that they would not be good parents or that they did not like children (Silka and Kiesler 1977).

A recent study has identified some women who make the decision to remain childless relatively early in their lives, long before they marry (Houseknecht 1979b). These women were compared with women who made the decision after marriage. Significant differences in family background between women in the two categories were found. Those who decided early to remain childless had been socialized to accept more autonomy and were more likely to describe themselves as independent of social pressures. In addition, they were high achievers and had surrounded themselves with a support group of other achievers who approved of their choice to remain childless. This study refutes the notion that social pressure always aims to get women to decide to have children. Women who prefer not to have children also seek each other out for support (Houseknecht 1977).

Marital Satisfaction

Most of the research comparing the degree of marital satisfaction of childless couples with that of those who do have children has reported that children often have a negative effect on marriages (Houseknecht 1979a). However, rarely have the reasons behind the childlessness been considered. Marital satisfaction may be more closely related to whether couples who want children have them and those who do not want children do not have them than to the mere presence or absence of children (Ryder 1973).

In a carefully designed study that distinguished the marital adjustment of voluntarily childless women from that of women who were postponing conception or who were involuntarily childless, a small but significant trend toward greater adjustment was found for those women who intentionally chose not to have children (Houseknecht 1979a). The fact that the difference was not large has led to speculation that the major factor in marital satisfaction may not be having or not having a child but, rather, that childless couples often have more resources, more time to be together, and more flexibility in their schedules. This points to the need for more research to control for the factors of education, employment, religion, and resources including money, household help, and family support.

It is reasonable to assume that populations who do not value large families, who are well educated, and who have access to effective means of contraception will have lower reproductive rates than their counterparts in other groups. In 1979 the average family with a college-educated head under 45 years of age had 1.95 children under 18 years of age; their grammar-school-educated counterparts had 2.49 children (U.S. Bureau of the Census 1980b, p. 81). Whether this is due to a positive wish to have more children on the part of less well educated persons, to lack of knowledge about or access to contraceptives, or simply to indifference about birth control probably varies from couple to couple, if not from person to person.

Most men and women who use contraceptives do so because they want to have a specific number of children or to have them at certain intervals. Very few use contraceptives for the purpose of remaining childless throughout their lifetimes. Today, only one married woman in twenty dies or reaches menopause without ever having been pregnant; in 1790, one in three never gave birth. The number has declined steadily over the years and is continuing to do so as a result of much higher marriage rates, improvement in the general health of the population, and better methods of increasing fertility. Therefore, even though substantially more couples are choosing to be childless—citing overpopulation or their personal wishes not to be parents as reasons—the decrease in involuntary childlessness has more than offset these numbers. Consequently, the total number of childless couples remains low. So, however, does the number of those who have very large families.

Although most women have at least one child, millions of women are postponing the births of their first children. In the last ten years the number of women under the age of 30 who are still childless but who eventually want children has increased dramatically. A variety of explanations have been offered, but the most likely is that women have occupational goals to achieve before they become mothers and that financial conditions for most young couples necessitate that they have two incomes for several years if they are to be able to afford a family.

BIRTH CONTROL

Birth control is used to decrease the probability that coitus will result in pregnancy or to influence the likelihood that pregnancy will occur at a particular time. Considerations of whether and when to become pregnant involve such issues as the ages of the parents, their financial security, religious and family pressures or customs, the career stages of each partner, the number (if any) of previous children (of this or previous marriages), and even the kind of neighborhood or housing in which the prospective parents currently live.

The physical health of both mothers and children is believed to be adversely affected by pregnancies that are spaced more closely than two years apart (*Family Planning Perspectives* 1975). An increasing number of couples recognize this fact and also wish to give themselves a breather between children for reasons of finances and fatigue. Twenty-seven percent of couples now wait more than five years after marriage to begin to have children (as opposed to only 15 percent ten years ago), and couples are waiting three or more years on the average between births (U.S. Bureau of the Census 1984c, pp. 7–8). It is impossible to determine definitely how many of these shifts represent changes in the values of particular persons, how many represent changes in knowledge about and proper use of contraceptives, and how many represent changes related to other factors such as economic or housing problems.

The picture in the United States currently is one of relative contraceptive freedom, with 92 percent of married women who do not want to become pregnant (including the 27 percent who have chosen sterilization) using some form of contraception (Reiss 1980). Teenagers are currently legally free to receive contraceptive advice without parental consent. Some physicians reportedly still refuse to give contraceptive assistance to unmarried teenagers because of their own personal religious or moral beliefs. Planned Parenthood clinics across the United States, however, give advice and make referrals for any person who needs them, possibly recognizing that the younger the potential parent, the more urgent the need.

The last stronghold of opposition to freely available contraceptives seems to center around the issue of who pays for them. Many taxpayers resent subsidizing birth control clinics and contraceptives for those who cannot pay. The logic seems to be that making such help available provides an easy way out of the risk of pregnancy at the taxpayers' expense and perhaps encourages illicit sexual activity. Ironically, it is likely to be those who can least afford to support children who are prohibited from securing contraceptives by their inability to pay for them. Instead of paying for birth control clinics and contraceptives, taxpayers may well end up paying for prenatal care, childbirth, and eighteen years of support for each out-of-wedlock child.

It is interesting to note that those who wish to prevent any pregnancy, if they are well informed, have a higher success rate than do those who are delaying birth or spacing children (Vaughn et al. 1977). This is evidence of the importance of motivation in the use and success of contraceptives.

In their analysis of contraceptive use, Milton Diamond and Arno Karlen (1980, p. 400) give three rules, to which we have added a fourth:

1. Any method is better than none.
2. Two methods combined are better than one.
3. No method is perfect: all have failures or side effects.
4. Always provide for *your own* contraception, no matter what your partner does, if you want to be absolutely certain that precautions are being taken.

We added the fourth rule because we believe it eliminates any tendency to blame one's partner for a contraceptive failure; because, ironically, people may engage in sexual intercourse and yet feel embarrassed about discussing contraception; because all too often people *assume* that their partners "know enough to be on the Pill," or "know enough to withdraw before ejaculation" without checking their assumptions; because the best way to be sure of the quality of contraceptives is to buy them yourself after an informed discussion; and, most of all, because we believe that people who are old enough to be risking pregnancy are old enough to take full personal responsibility for any and all of their behaviors, including the decisions they make and the choice of persons whose advice they take.

With these thoughts in mind, we turn to a discussion of the various methods of contraception.

Chemical Contraceptives

Chemicals are used for contraception in two ways: (1) to stop the production of eggs (as with the birth control pill) and (2) to create a destructive environment for sperm (as with spermicides). It is estimated that one-third of all women of childbearing age in the United States use oral contraceptives. About 80 million women around the world are users ("Oral Contraceptives" 1979). The popularity of "the Pill" has been based on its effectiveness (among those who use it exactly as directed, fewer than 2 percent become pregnant each year) and on the fact that taking contraceptive pills is independent of the sex act and thus does not interfere with spontaneity.

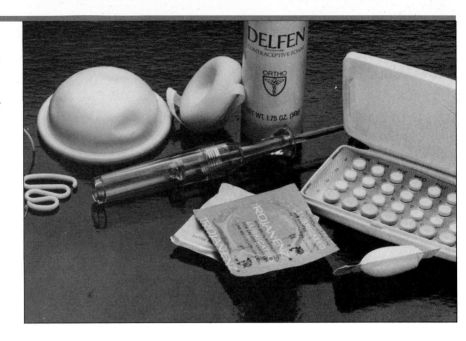

*Contraceptive methods
include the diaphragm,
the sponge, foam, the
Pill, suppository foam,
condoms, and the IUD.*

Contraceptive Pills   The Pill works to prevent ovulation by increasing hormones (combinations of estrogens and **progesterones**) to the levels found in pregnancy. It also acts to thicken the mucous plug in the **cervix**, which inhibits sperm penetration, and to change the lining of the uterus so that even if the first two effects fail, a fertilized egg is not likely to implant. As extra benefits, some women find that menstrual irregularity, cramps, heavy flow, and premenstrual tension are diminished or eliminated by the use of oral contraceptives.

There has been a decline in use of many varieties of the Pill, although it is still the most popular nonpermanent contraceptive method (Ford 1978). This drop is almost certainly due to exaggeration of the side effects of oral contraceptive use. The contraceptive pill causes changes in body chemistry and, consequently, affects nearly all the organs of a woman's body. The risk of heart disease varies with the kind of pill used (see Table 9.3). Authorities disagree on whether there is an increased risk of cancer (Crane 1986a). Serious complications are rare, however, and the risks to most women from oral contraceptives are much lower than the risks from pregnancy and childbirth. Dr. Luella Klein, President of the American College of Obstetricians and Gynecologists, reported that there were 5 pill-related deaths per 100,000 women using it, compared to 10 deaths per 100,000 women who give birth. Klein added that the death rate for non-smoking pill users under 40 is less than 1 per 100,000, or one-tenth the risk of death due to pregnancy (Cimons 1985a).

One recent study reported by Nancy Lee of the Centers for Disease Control suggests that if birth control pills are used *prior to* menopause, estrogen replacement *after* menopause might cut the chance of having at least one kind of cancer by more than half (Rowand 1984a). On the other hand, a study reported in the April 19, 1985, *Journal of the American Medical Association* showed that although the Pill decreases risks of **pelvic inflammatory disease** (PID) caused by gonorrhea, it may actually increase the amount of PID caused by chlamydia. Twelve of fourteen pub-

TABLE 9 · 3
Birth Control Pills and Heart Disease Risk

| | Lowest Risk | | |
Trade Name	Manufacturer	Trade Name	Manufacturer
Ovcon-50	Mead Johnson	Ovcon-35	Mead Johnson
Norinyl 1 + 50	Syntex	Norinyl 1 + 35	Syntex
Ortho-Novum 1/50	Ortho	Ortho-Novum 1/35	Ortho
Brevicon	Syntex	Ortho-Novum 10/11	Ortho
Modicon	Ortho		

| | Highest Risk | | |
Trade Name	Manufacturer	Trade Name	Manufacturer
Ovulen	Searle	Ovral	Wyeth
Enovid-E	Searle	Norlestrin 2.5/50	Parke Davis
Ortho-Novum 2 mg	Ortho	Norlestrin 1/50	Parke Davis
Norinyl 2 mg	Syntex	Demulen 1/35	Searle
Ortho-Novum 1/80	Ortho	Lo/Ovral	Wyeth
Norinyl 1 + 80	Syntex	Loestrin 1.5/30	Parke Davis
Enovid 5 mg	Searle	Nordette	Wyeth
Demulen	Searle	Loestrin 1/20	Parke Davis

Source: The Medical Letter on Drugs and Therapeutics; adapted from *Los Angeles Times,* August 9, 1983, Part V, p. 1.

Note: Entries are ranked starting with the highest dosage of estrogen. While certain basic brand names appear on both lists, many pill manufacturers offer several different formula versions of the same brand of contraceptive, and there are significant differences in dosage of estrogen and progestin within brands.

lished studies have reported that the incidence of chlamydia has increased two to three times among oral contraceptive users (Bennett 1985). Ironically, antibiotics—the quick cure for chlamydia—may render oral contraceptives less effective than they normally are.

A "minipill" has been developed that does not aim at stopping ovulation but does slow down the rate of movement of eggs in the fallopian tubes. It also thickens the mucous plug to inhibit sperm entry at the cervix. Since this pill contains no estrogen (which some studies suggest is related to cancer and blood clots), risks are minimized. The contraceptive ability of the minipill is as good as that of the older varieties, although some women experience irregular menstruation and more may develop infections with this type of contraceptive pill.

Newer than the minipill, "triphasic pills"—a series of three kinds of pills taken in a sequence to simulate the hormonal changes that one goes through during a normal menstrual cycle—have received the recommendation of Planned Parenthood for new pill users (Crane 1986b). Unfortunately, however, it is clear that no pill has yet been developed that is both effective and free of all complications. Pills are, after all, medication; any medication may produce undesirable effects and must be medically managed (Boston Women's Health Book Collective 1976).

Use of the so-called morning-after pill is infrequent in the United States. An injection or a three- to seven-day series of pills containing high levels of artificial estrogen speeds up the progress of the ovum to the uterus so that it arrives before the lining of the uterus is prepared for implantation. These high estrogen doses are a shock to the system, however, and many women report unpleasant effects, such as nausea. More seriously, the artificial estrogen (diethylstilbestrol, or DES) has been linked to the presence of cell abnormalities in the cervixes of daughters of women who have been given this drug to prevent miscarriages. The sons of such women also often show testicular abnormalities (Stewart et al. 1979).

Spermicides   Spermicides are the second major type of chemical contraception. These have a history that dates back at least as far as the ancient Greeks, who inserted vinegar or lemon juice mixed with honey into the vagina to destroy sperm. Dried pigeon, elephant, or crocodile dung soaked in sour milk has also had wide usage over the years in various societies. Various other acids—including boric acid and even fruit beverages—have been used since an acid environment is not healthful for sperm.

Men have coated their penises with pastes containing an acid combined with cedarwood oil, fig pulp, and other such exotic substances in an effort to kill their sperm. One of the recently developed spermicides based on these earlier techniques is widely used in Switzerland. It can be used either by men (on the penis) or by women (in the vagina). It is a postage-stamp-sized filament called C-film that is melted readily by body heat and is an effective spermicide (Julty 1979).

The best-known commercially produced spermicides are sponges, jellies, creams, foams, and suppositories inserted into the vagina shortly before intercourse. Although these are less effective than oral contraceptives, they provide protection when they are used according to instructions and renewed for each act of intercourse. To be highly effective, most of these must be used in conjunction with a condom or a diaphragm. A few persons may have mild allergies to particular brands. Some couples complain that some of them cause more lubrication than they want, although others consider the additional lubrication an advantage. In addition, some spermicides may incidentally afford protection against various venereal diseases and vaginal infections. They are not designed as prophylactics, however, and one should never assume that they provide adequate protection against contracting syphilis, gonorrhea, or herpes from infected persons.

Although douches have been notably ineffective for contraception in the past, research is now being done on a douche that contains no hormones but alters mucus secretions in the cervix, preventing the entry of sperm into the uterus during much of the ovulatory cycle (*Los Angeles Herald Examiner*, February 14, 1983, p. D-8).

Barrier Contraceptives

Diaphragm   At one time the most popular contraceptive was the *vaginal occlusive diaphragm* used with a spermicide. Commonly called simply "the diaphragm," this thin rubber sheet is surrounded by a flexible spring. When diametrically opposite points on the circular spring are held together, the diaphragm (ideally well-coated with a spermicide) can be inserted quickly and easily through the outer opening of the vagina. Once past the muscular entrance, the spring resumes its circular shape, with the supple vaginal sheath adapting to its configuration. When there is nothing in it, the vagina has no empty space within its periphery; it is completely collapsed. When the dome-like diaphragm is tucked up behind the pubic bone in front, the cervix is beyond the rubber barrier; sperm ejaculated against the front of the diaphragm would have to journey through the spermicidal jelly and around the perimeter that is snug against the vagina to reach the entrance to the uterus. Statistics demonstrate that few sperm ever make it.

Because the measurements of women differ, the size of a diaphragm should be selected by a trained health-care professional. Because women's measurements typically change with weight gain or loss, pelvic surgery, childbirth, and sexual activity, the fit should be checked at least once a year routinely, immediately following any of the changes described above, and a few weeks after beginning coitus for the first time.

In the 1940s and 1950s about one-third of American couples practicing birth control favored the diaphragm for contraception. Its popularity began to wane when other successful methods became available that did not have to be used just before or during the sex act (oral contraceptives and the intrauterine device, or IUD, for example). Recently, however, use of the diaphragm has increased as reports of adverse effects have raised serious questions about the newer methods. Studies have shown that, properly used, a diaphragm plus a spermicide is very nearly as effective as the best oral contraceptives (Hatcher et al. 1978).

Cervical Cap   A device that is very popular in Europe and is somewhat similar to the diaphragm is the *cervical cap*. It is smaller than the diaphragm and fits directly over the cervix, held there by suction. Certain varieties can remain in place at all times except during menstruation, although others must be removed every two or three days to prevent irritation. A recent model has been developed with a one-way valve that allows menstrual fluids to flow out but prevents sperm from entering (Julty 1979). Although hollowed-out lemon halves were used as cervical caps in the Roman Empire, the cervical cap is currently considered "experimental" by the U.S. Food and Drug Administration and is not widely available in the United States because of restrictions by that agency.

Condom   The *condom* ("rubber," "safe") has been in wide use since it was first developed after the mid-nineteenth-century invention of vulcanizing rubber (which also made the diaphragm possible). Earlier, men had covered their penises with skin from animal intestines, fish skin, or linen (Himes 1963; Kitzinger 1983). Currently, condoms are the most popular contraceptive method in Japan, Sweden, and England. They are marketed in a variety of textures, colors, and shapes; however, most women report that they cannot feel the textures, and all four of the dyes reported to be in use are prohibited by the Food and Drug Administration—the black dye actually contains known carcinogens. The safest for all concerned is the reservoir-end, plain, uncolored condom ("Forum International" 1980, pp. 6–7).

It is estimated that 15 to 20 percent of American couples (compared with 79 percent of Japanese couples) use condoms to prevent pregnancy (Levin 1976; Cohn 1982). As with the Pill and the diaphragm, if condoms are properly used, the success rate is high. Proper use includes (1) putting the condom on before there is *any* contact of penis with vulva or vagina; (2) making sure there is no air between penis and condom, but a little space to receive semen at the end; (3) making sure that the vagina is well lubricated, preferably with natural fluids and *never* with any petroleum product (hydrocarbons disintegrate rubber); and (4) being careful to withdraw the condom while the open end is still at the base of the penis, especially if the penis has become flaccid after ejaculation. The overall pregnancy rate of couples using condoms is only 1 or 2 percent a year after the first year. Experience in using them is important; the pregnancy rate during the first twelve months of use is 10 to 20 percent (Cohn 1982).

Some men object to condoms because a loss of sensitivity is caused by the covering. Other men report that they are able to maintain an erection longer before orgasm because of the decreased sensitivity, which may be appreciated by women who are slow to reach orgasm or who wish to have several orgasms during coitus. This points to a recognized fact about contraceptives—that each person must decide for himself or herself just what suits best.

One of the major advantages of the use of the condom for the male is that he can be more certain that protection actually exists. As one unmarried male told us: "I am never sure when a woman says she is on the Pill that she remembers to take it every day. Sometimes diaphragms might not fit right or get dislodged. I know I put the sheath on right and I can check to see whether it comes out still in place."

Besides being highly effective in preventing pregnancy, properly used condoms are the most effective method of preventing the spread of venereal diseases. Herpes II (which is now epidemic in the United States) has no known cure. The incidence of herpes in newborn babies has risen from 2.6 per 100,000 in 1969 to 11.9 per 100,000 in 1981 in an observed region, which is believed to parallel the incidence in adults (*Science News*, December 31, 1983, p. 413). The use of the condom for protection against this and other venereal diseases may be its most important function. Texas pioneered legislation making it a criminal offense punishable by a $1,000 fine and/or six months' imprisonment to give another person herpes. Unfortunately, some carriers of genital herpes may be asymptomatic and unaware that they have it (*Science News*, June 28, 1986, p. 410).

The Journal of the American Medical Association reported that up to 30 percent of **spontaneous abortions** may be the result of herpes infections (Morse 1984a). One-third of newborns afflicted with herpes die from it; another one-fourth suffer brain damage (*Science News*, December 31, 1983, p. 413).

A final and considerable advantage of condoms is that they can be very inexpensive and are readily available. There is no research indicating that expensive condoms are any more effective than inexpensive ones. Pharmacies and drugstores sell them without prescription. Any brand will fit, and they are usually accompanied by instructions for their use. When the advantages and disadvantages of methods of contraception—especially for unmarried persons—are weighed, the condom usually ranks high. For those who have infrequent or unexpected sexual contacts, especially with new or different partners, the condom seems unexcelled.

Intrauterine Device The *intrauterine device* (IUD) became widely available in the 1960s, although the idea of putting a foreign body in the uterus to discourage pregnancy dates back centuries. Items of glass, ivory, ebony, gold, or platinum have been used; Hippocrates described such devices over 2,000 years ago. It is well known that camel drivers who were concerned that their animals not become pregnant on long trips across the desert inserted pebbles into the camels' uterine cavities.

No one is absolutely certain why intrauterine devices work, although there are some widely held theories. A popular explanation is that the foreign body causes a constant mild irritation of the lining of the uterus (the **endometrium**), rallying white blood cells, which destroy sperm. Special types of modern plastic IUDs work in additional ways. The copper wire used to wrap one model is believed to change the chemical balance of the uterus in such a way as to foil implantation. Another model is treated with progestins, which are slowly released in the uterus, affecting implantation of ova and increasing the mucous plug of the cervix as a barrier to sperm entry.

The IUD is highly effective in preventing pregnancy. It is now the leading contraceptive method in many countries of the world. It is estimated that approximately five million women in the United States are users, although recently many have grown skeptical because of the incidence of infection, which sometimes leaves scar tissue that can block the fallopian tubes; heavy menstrual bleeding; and increased likelihood of anemia, doubling the user's risk of subsequent infertility (May 1983).

The risk of PID, a major cause of infertility among women, is increased by use of intrauterine contraceptive devices. Women using an IUD are generally at a ninefold greater risk of getting PID than are women using other forms of birth control, researchers reported in the August 12, 1983, *Journal of the American Medical Association*. Women using the Saf-T-Coil are at 24 times greater risk, Lippes Loop users at 13 times greater risk, and copper IUD users at 7 times greater risk (*Science News*, August 20, 1983, p. 127).

IUD users are 2.6 times more likely than other women to be infertile. It is estimated that about 88,000 women in the United States are sterile as a result of using IUDs. However, many women in the study had used the Dalkon Shield; those using this device were 6.8 times more likely to be infertile than a control group of nonusers. The Dalkon Shield and the TATUM-T are no longer marketed. The risk of using copper-containing IUDs is only 1.3 times greater for users than for nonusers (Silberner 1985a). However, in 1986 one of the leading copper-containing IUDs was removed from the market. Under some conditions, the risks of using the IUD may be lower than the alternative of pregnancy. Unfortunately, threats of litigation may eventually end its manufacture, at least for sale in the United States (*International Journal of Childbirth Education*, May 1986, pp. 33, 41).

Surgical Intervention: Sterilization

The word *sterilization* is not a neutral one to many people. For some it threatens the very essence of their self-concepts as males or females. For others, it may be controversial from a social or a religious perspective. There is evidence of involuntary sterilization of persons on welfare, prisoners, and minority-group members who did not understand that they had a choice about whether or not to be sterilized (Dreifus 1975). The first recorded intentional surgical sterilization in the United States was performed in 1897 on a woman who was judged mentally deranged and who already had several children. In that same year vasectomies were given to prison inmates in Illinois.

The Department of Health and Human Services has attempted to prevent any future injustices such as those that have occurred in involuntary sterilizations by issuing guidelines that forbid sterilization of any patient in a federally assisted medical program who has not received complete information in a language that he or she clearly understands. In addition, there is a mandatory 30-day waiting period between the time the person signs the consent form and the date of the operation. No doubt some sterilization still occurs that is not truly voluntary; however, with heightened public awareness, the amount of such action seems to be diminishing.

The religious objections to sterilization have remained fairly constant over the years. The major argument is that any means of controlling pregnancy other than abstinence or the rhythm method is against the will of God unless the sterilization occurs as a by-product of surgery for other purposes. For instance, a papal encyclical of the Catholic church in 1968 approved hysterectomies as necessary for certain gynecological reasons and therefore sanctioned the resulting sterilization as well.

Some arguments against sterilization have come from members of the medical professions, who in many cases have set themselves up as judges of whether a man or woman has a right to be sterilized. Such criteria as age, number of children, and marital status (persons under 25 with no children and unmarried persons have been routinely turned down by many physicians) have been used as factors to restrict such surgery. Successful lawsuits have been brought, and currently sterilization is rarely refused (except in Utah, where the law requires that medical necessity must be proved) (Westhoff and Jones 1977).

In spite of opposition in some quarters, sterilization is now the most popular form of contraception in many countries for those couples who have already had their desired number of children. Recent figures indicate that among women using contraception, voluntary sterilization was used by 27 percent of married women 15 to 44 years old in the United States. Voluntary sterilization was used to an even greater extent in many countries in Asia and Latin America (U.S. Bureau of the Census, 1983c, p. 2).

A sample of sterilized American couples revealed that the poorer their assessment of their communication, the more likely that the wife, rather than the husband, would be the partner to be sterilized. That pattern was found to be more characteristic of couples in which the wife was not employed outside the home than among couples where the wife worked (Bean et al. 1983).

Vasectomy The usual procedure for male sterilization is called **vasectomy**. The physician cuts and ties off the tube (*vas deferens*) that carries sperm from each of the testicles. Between 400,000 and 500,000 such operations are performed in the United States each year (Parachini 1984). A vasectomy affects only the delivery of sperm, not their production nor the production of male hormones. After vasectomy, sperm produced are resorbed into the bloodstream rather than being ejaculated with the seminal fluid (which continues to be produced by the prostate and other glands). Since the production of androgens is not affected, neither interest in sexual activity nor secondary sex characteristics should be changed. This surgery is considered minor; it is usually performed in a doctor's office with the patient under a local anesthetic; discomfort is usually not great, although there are rare exceptions ("Forum International" 1981). Most physicians recommend the resumption of normal sexual activity, using contraceptives, in two weeks.

The success rate for preventing pregnancy by vasectomy is almost perfect. Any pregnancies following surgery usually are due to the resumption of intercourse before the seminal fluid has had time to clear itself of sperm left between the ligation and the end of the penis at the time of surgery. Ejaculate usually is sperm-free after approximately fifteen ejaculations (or in six weeks or so) but must be checked microscopically to be certain that this is so.

Vasectomy is generally considered a permanent sterilization since attempts to reconnect the vas deferens, though fairly successful with new microsurgery techniques, do not necessarily result in resumption of fertility. Pregnancy rates for the partners of previously vasectomized men in the United States who have had reversals have been reported in some 27 studies at figures ranging from 16 to 85 percent, with most between 35 and 50 percent (*Sydney Sunday Telegraph*, September 23, 1984, p. 7).

Five years after having a vasectomy, a man is likely to have developed **antibodies** that prevent fertilization of eggs with his sperm (Parachini 1984, p. 1). So far, although special treatment of the sperm has made fertilization possible, most of these fertilized eggs fail to implant in the uterus (Morse 1984b).

Earlier beliefs that vasectomies resulted in long-range health problems have been dispelled. An extensive study has found that vasectomized men tend to have lower mortality and morbidity rates than nonvasectomized men (see Table 9.4).

Female Sterilization   More than 600,000 women undergo surgical sterilization in the United States each year. Sterilization for women (**tubal ligation**) is more complicated than vasectomy since the tubes that must be severed and tied are less accessible than the male's vas deferens. One tubal ligation procedure closely approximates the simplicity of the vasectomy, however, and its popularity has been growing. This process, called a *minilaparotomy*, usually is performed on an outpatient basis, under only local anesthesia in most instances. The procedure involves two small incisions near the pubic hair line, which make the fallopian tubes accessible to be tied or cut.

Many physicians use an instrument called a *laparoscope*, which they insert through an abdominal incision (often at the navel so that no scar shows) both to see the instrument at work internally and to perform the operation. This procedure is called *laparoscopy* and, since the incision is so small, has been referred to popularly as "band-aid" surgery.

An older and more traditional method is performed in the hospital under general anesthesia because a larger incision is made in the abdomen and the process (*laparotomy*) is considered major surgery. Women who are obese or who have a history of pelvic infections or certain other health problems are candidates for this procedure rather than for the simpler ones.

Both the *laparoscopy* and the *laparotomy* can be performed through the vagina. This is less commonly done but is favored by some women since it leaves no visible scars.

Tubal ligation works by interfering with the progress of eggs, which cannot pass through the fallopian tubes after such surgery. It has no other known physical effects. The eggs disintegrate and are absorbed by the body. It is generally considered permanent sterilization, although the minilaparotomy is believed to have some potential for reversibility (Hatcher et al. 1978).

An alternative to sterilization, called Ovabloc, is now being tested by the U.S. Food and Drug Administration. In this procedure, liquid silicone is injected into the fallopian tubes; the liquid contains a hardening agent that causes it to gel into a rubberlike substance in a few seconds. The procedure requires no hospitalization, no anesthesia, and no incision and takes about 45 minutes. Should a pregnancy be desired

TABLE 9 • 4
Incidence of Disease
or Death among
Vasectomized and
Nonvasectomized Men

	Vasectomized Men	Nonvasectomized Men
Death	212	326
Asthma	71	71
Heart attack	244	321
Angina pectoris	325	400
Stroke	37	40
Hepatitis	82	70
Diabetes	141	200
Rheumatoid arthritis	32	43
Cancer	133	181
Impotence	162	155

Source: National Institute of Child Health and Human Development, data cited in *Los Angeles Times,* February 17, 1984, Part V, p. 1.

Note: Tabulated for 10,590 pairs of men matched statistically so the only significant difference between members of each pair was that one man had had a vasectomy and the other had not. Deaths and reports of illness were rare, primarily because the vast majority of the research subjects were under 50 and most were under 40.

later, the Ovabloc can be removed by pulling on a hook implanted in its end (*Science News,* July 17, 1982, p. 41; Berry 1983).

A **hysterectomy** (removal of the uterus) is not routinely used for sterilization purposes because it is major surgery and necessitates a long recovery period. However, since large numbers of women need such surgery for other gynecological problems (it is the third most common female operation), it is also a source of sterilization for these women (Diamond and Karlen 1980, p. 419). Hysterectomy often has negative effects; Masters and Johnson (1966) report that the uterus is important for a woman's orgasmic response and should never be removed unless it is absolutely necessary. Nevertheless, thousands of women make good recoveries. Since ethical physicians perform hysterectomy only to alleviate serious problems, the complications are usually not as bad as the original complaints were. The resulting sterilization is usually seen as a bonus for a woman who wants no more children.

Psychologically, some persons report feeling better as a result of sterilization. This is attributed to the lack of worry about unwanted pregnancy and a feeling of freedom from the constraints of other types of contraception. On the other hand, some men and women are bothered by the removal of the ability to reproduce. Those who associate their masculinity or femininity with their fertility may report a decreased interest in sex once they realize that this fertility is gone. In a recent study of 200 men who had had successful vasectomies, 1 percent regretted that they could father no more children, and 3 percent reported "sexual problems." However, 8 percent reported that their sexual performance was more satisfactory than before the surgery. The majority reported no regrets and no changes in their sexual performance or satisfaction ("Forum International" 1981).

CHAPTER 9

Other Techniques

Other contraceptive techniques include the *rhythm method*, which has been widely used, with varying success, depending on the knowledge and regularity of the female's menstrual cycle. The rhythm method is the only method of birth control officially sanctioned by the Roman Catholic church and some other religions. Others use it because they dislike ingesting chemicals or using devices that are not "natural." Generally this has not been a very reliable method because a woman is unlikely to ovulate at exactly the same time each month for a variety of reasons, including emotional and physical stresses. It has been estimated that two-thirds of all women are too irregular in their menstrual cycles to depend on this method (Brayer, Chiazze, and Duffy 1969). In addition, many women are either uninformed or careless about keeping track of when they are in a fertile period. Even when women keep accurate records, some experts believe that there is no absolutely safe period—not even during menstruation. This is true because some women seem to be "reflex ovulators" who ovulate at odd times as a result of high levels of excitement or anxiety (J. McCary 1978). For women (and partners, too) who enjoy frequent or spontaneous intercourse, reliance on the rhythm method alone has the serious disadvantage of several sequential days' abstinence from coitus. This is especially distressing for persons who restrict their sexual interaction to coitus exclusively.

Recent modifications and implementations designed to enhance the rhythm method's effectiveness have resulted in improvements. One development involves the use of the basal body temperature to gauge the time of ovulation. Twelve to 24 hours before ovulation, the body temperature drops slightly; rises again as soon as ovulation has occurred. A clock/microprocessor called Rite Time is available to assist in analyzing these data daily (Kitzinger 1983, pp. 193–194). Another improvement in the rhythm method requires that a woman learn to detect changes in the mucous discharge from her cervix. That discharge becomes clear and slippery (rather like raw egg white) when she ovulates. Some women experience recognizable breast tenderness and a special ovulatory pain called *Mittelschmerz* (cramps in the middle of the month). Devices have been developed to measure the viscosity of the mucus, to give accurate temperature readouts, and to measure changes in body rhythms that accompany ovulation (Seaman and Seaman 1977). The Ovix Fertility Computer is available to store and analyze these data (Kitzinger 1983, pp. 193–194). None of these procedures (called "sympto-thermal" and "natural family planning") should be attempted without competent professional guidance, however, unless the persons involved are prepared to accept the responsibility for a pregnancy.

When properly used, the new devices simplify record keeping and reduce human error. They may make the rhythm method more reliable than it was in the past. Some recent studies have indicated that effectiveness rates for the rhythm method are at an all-time high of 89 percent (Sandler, Myerson, and Kinder 1980, p. 110).

A problem with the rhythm method that has received little attention is that there is considerable variation in the length of viability of male sperm. Part of the sperm's vitality is associated with the chemical conditions present in the female reproductive tract, but part of it is inherent in the spermatozoa themselves. Although most sperm die within two or three days in the reproductive tract, live sperm have been recovered as much as seven days after they were deposited (J. A. Zimmerman, personal communication, October 1984). Most rhythm computations allow no more than four days in estimating the probable occurrence of ovulation. If even three days were allowed for the life of the sperm and four days allowed for error in estimating when ovulation might occur, then intercourse would need to be limited to the first nine and the last ten days of a 28-day menstrual cycle. Couples who do not have intercourse during menstruation would be restricted by an additional three to seven days.

Withdrawal (coitus interruptus) is an old and relatively widely used but not very effective method of preventing pregnancy. Part of the problem with coitus interruptus is that it is difficult for many men to exert the necessary control to withdraw when orgasm is imminent. The greatest trap, however, is that the preejaculatory fluid easily can contain enough sperm to cause fertilization.

Hyperthermia—the application of heat to the testicles—has long been thought to kill sperm. Shepherds reportedly have decreased the size of their herds by wrapping the rams' testes in pouches to keep them unusually warm in order to destroy the sperm. Some fertility experts have speculated that men's tight-fitting underwear and

(continued)

SEXUAL PRACTICES MAY CHANGE IN FUTURE

- Amusement or theme parks geared to sexual pleasure of all kinds.
- Super-psychic sex—lovers separated by vast distances will be able to engage in sex by means of advanced methods of telepathy.
- Sex under zero gravity conditions such as exist in outer space. Weightlessness would enable lovers to move far more freely than is possible on Earth. Future newlyweds might honeymoon on the moon to experience the low gravity environment there.
- Laser holography will make it possible to create extremely realistic scenes for sexual pleasure—a room filled with animated 3-D pin-ups, for example.
- Intercourse may be regarded as an archaic method of obtaining sexual pleasure when compared to such exotic methods as electrical stimulation of the brain, which could produce sexual pleasure without involving sexual acts.

Implications for Morality

Sex under these conditions would have little relationship to present-day morality. How will people react to these developments? We can't know for sure. But history may hold some clues.

As human societies developed, serious problems inevitably occurred when people engaged in sex without any restraints. There is little the ancient Romans and other peoples failed to try at one time or another. So rules developed concerning when, where and with whom a person could engage in sex. The concept of marriage minimized the conflicts that resulted from unregulated sex.

All of the future sexual possibilities might not seem immoral under today's standards. For example, handicapped, mentally retarded, aged or sexually unattractive people would be able to have rich sexual lives. Use of electrical stimulation of the brain, producing sexual pleasure without overt sexual acts, could provide a non-sinful way for people to have pleasure and might dissuade perverts from molesting other humans.

But if ordinary sex becomes simply another Brand X in TV commercials of the future, one of the greatest supports for marriage and family life will have been removed.

Source: Edward Cornish, *Los Angeles Times*, March 8, 1985, Part V, p. 2. Edward Cornish, President, World Future Society, is the author of the nationally syndicated feature *Your Changing World*. This column is reprinted through the courtesy of Sun Features Inc. © 1985.

pants may keep their testes so warm that they act to kill sperm. Hot baths and saunas may interfere temporarily with sperm life, but most experts do not advise hyperthermia as a primary means of birth control.

Experimental Contraceptives

Some contemporary researchers are investigating the use of ultrasonic waves as a hyperthermic contraceptive procedure (Crooks and Baur 1980, p. 519). This research is based on the knowledge that in rare cases of undescended testicles, sperm are less likely to mature because of the higher temperatures that exist where they are housed in the abdomen. Descended testicles hang outside the body, where the temperature is lower, and that fosters sperm development. It is also known that extremely high fevers over a long period of time often cause temporary—if not permanent—sterility, as in some cases of mumps.

Some chemical contraceptives banned for use in the United States, usually because they have not yet been tested thoroughly enough to satisfy the Food and Drug Administration, are widely used in other countries. One of these is Depo Provera, an injection of progestin given to women that lasts for three months. Although they are unlikely to be available in the United States for some time to come, safety trials have been completed on antipregnancy vaccines in six cities in India, according to G. P. Talwar, director of the National Institute of Immunology at Jawaharlal University (*Science News*, June 7, 1986, p. 365). Subcutaneous implants for women of time-released capsules of progesterone that remain effective for as long as seven years are also being tested and are used outside the United States (Mayfield 1982).

A morning-after injection based on the hormone HCG (human chorionic gonadotropin), which may have fewer undesirable effects than other morning-after drugs, is being studied in Canada. When modified HCG is injected soon after conception, it prevents implantation of fertilized ova or terminates a recently implanted embryo (*Science News*, July 20, 1983, p. 74). Kitzinger (1983, p. 194) mentions another alternative, particularly effective if two or three days pass after coitus: insertion of an IUD. With such a procedure, there is no way of knowing whether a pregnancy has occurred. However, as with all female-used contraceptives, there are some risks to the woman's health.

Birth control pills for males have been tested and are in use in other parts of the world, often on an experimental basis. These pills are reported to produce such undesirable effects (impaired liver function, cardiovascular problems) that they are not recommended by the World Health Organization. However, recent reports are encouraging, and acceptable male birth control pills may be developed in the future.

Gossypol, a substance made from cottonseed, has been found to interfere with sperm development (Pollie 1982). However, one-third of the persons using this Chinese-developed male contraceptive suffered from fatigue, anorexia, reduced libido, muscle weakness, or potassium loss, and one-fifth remained infertile for a long period (Kitzinger 1983, p. 195). Other experimenters are attempting to produce antibodies to sperm like those that develop in many men after vasectomy (Morse 1984b, p. 258).

Ecbelatericin, in tablet form, has been reported to cause a sharp temporary decrease in the number and mobility of sperm cells when taken orally by men. The effect is said to begin in a half hour and last for eight to twelve hours. As of mid-1986, it had not been approved or even tested by the U.S. Food and Drug Administration (Nordwind 1983).

A salve containing testosterone and estradiol is believed to suppress sperm production when rubbed on the skin of males. After twelve years of experimentation with male Rhesus monkeys, Larry Ewing, a scientist at Johns Hopkins University, is applying to the FDA for approval to conduct clinical tests on humans (Steinberg 1983, p. 117).

No method of birth control—surgical, chemical, barrier, or rhythm—is completely effective (see Table 9.5). *Total abstinence* is the only completely safe, reliable method of contraception. Temporary abstinence is widely used, particularly during periods of presumed fertility. Sexual play can take the place of coitus at these times. However, many of those who use abstinence as a means of contraception do so because

TABLE 9 · 5

First-Year Failure
Rates of Birth Control
Methods

Method	Lowest Observed Failure Rate*	Failure Rate in Typical Users†
Tubal ligation	0.04	0.04
Vasectomy	0.15	0.15
Injectable progestin	0.25	0.25
Combined birth control pill	0.5	2
Progestin-only pill	1	2.5
IUD	1.5	4
Condom	2	10
Diaphragm (with spermicide)	2	13
Cervical cap	2	13
Foam, cream, jelly, and vaginal suppository	3–5	15
Coitus interruptus	16	23
Fertility awareness techniques (basal body temperature, mucus method, calendar, and "rhythm")	2–20	20–30
Douche	—	40
Chance (no method of birth control)	90	90

Source: Contraceptive Technology, 1982–83: R. A. Hatcher, M.D., and G. K. Stewart, M.D. Used with permission of R. A. Hatcher.

Note: Many of the failure rates in the second column of this paper (failure rates in typical users) were derived from "Contraceptive Failure among Women in the United States, 1970–1973"; B. Vaughn, J. Trussell, J. Menken, and E. Jones, Family Planning Perspectives 8:81–86, 1976.

*Designed to complete the sentence, "Of 100 women who start out the year using a given method and who use it correctly and consistently, the lowest observed failure rate has been ———."

†Designed to complete the sentence, "Of 100 typical users who start out the year employing a given method, the number who will be pregnant by the end of the year will be ———."

their religion prohibits any other means. Those same persons may find that certain alternative forms of sexual activity (oral sex, anal sex, or masturbation) are forbidden to them.

Lawrence Severy, at the University of Florida, has studied birth control preferences and found that:

- Men worried more about the health effects of contraceptives on their wives than their wives did.
- Women disliked condoms and diaphragms more than their husbands did.
- Three-quarters of older couples prefer sterilization.
- Three-quarters of younger couples (under age 35) prefer (1) the pill, (2) the diaphragm, and (3) condoms over sterilization.
- The criteria for choosing contraceptives were, in order
  1. Effectiveness
  2. Danger to health of user

3. Ease of discontinuing to become pregnant
4. Danger to health of unborn child
5. Convenience (Horn 1984, p. 14)

INDUCED ABORTION

Half or more of all pregnancies are unplanned, and it is estimated that about 30 or 40 percent of those who do not want any children (or who do not want a child at the time they conceive) will seek an **induced abortion** (Forrest, Tietze, and Sullivan 1978).

Legal Status

Whether a healthy woman has a right to end her pregnancy may well be the most controversial topic in the marriage and family field today. In a 1972 Gallup poll, 64 percent of the respondents supported the notion that a pregnant woman and her physician should determine whether she could have an abortion. In 1973, the Supreme Court handed down a decision in the case of *Roe* v. *Wade* that reflected the sentiment of a growing number of people in the United States that women have a right to choose whether to bear the children they have conceived. Courts have, however, consistently denied fathers' efforts to gain an equal right, regardless of whether the couple were currently married (King 1982).

The 1973 Supreme Court decision decriminalized abortion and allowed a pregnancy to be terminated by qualified medical personnel. It was believed that as a result of this decision the complications and possible deaths of women undergoing such procedures could be kept to an absolute minimum. Although the sentiment of the majority still seemed to be that preventing undesired pregnancy in the first place was far preferable to terminating one already begun, the decision seemed to be necessary to safeguard the health of millions of women who were resorting to illegal abortions.

Hardly had the decriminalization of induced abortion been announced, however, when "pro-life" groups across the country voiced objections, arguing for the rights of unborn children to live. These groups cited both legal and religious reasons for their opposition to abortion; those favoring legalization of abortions stressed economic, social, and mental health reasons that women should not be forced to bear unwanted children.

In the years since 1973 the voices for and against induced abortion have not been silent. Laws have been passed, and new laws have overturned previous ones. Recently there has been conflict over who will pay for the abortions for women who want them but cannot afford them, particularly those on welfare. In keeping with a 1977 Supreme Court ruling, Medicaid, the program that provides combined state and federal medical payments for low-income persons, has ceased payment for induced abortion. Before that, Medicaid paid for nearly one-third of all abortions following the decriminalization ruling in 1973. Under the later ruling, exceptions are made if a woman's health is in jeopardy as a result of pregnancy or if her pregnancy is the result of incest or rape.

States are funding fewer and fewer abortions since the federal courts have established a minimum use of Medicaid funds for such purposes. Many feared that the result would be that women would either resort once more to "back-alley" abortions or continue their pregnancies and, often, ultimately end up living on tax-supported welfare for themselves and their dependent children. However, these fears seem to be unfounded, since illegal abortions have remained low in number and the number of abortions performed in states where funding is available is about the same as the number performed in states where funding is not available.

Certain religious groups strongly oppose induced abortion. The Catholic church is an interesting case in point. Until 1869 abortion was permissible by Catholic canon law for the first 90 days for a female fetus or 40 days for a male, at which time the soul was thought to enter the fetus. (It is not clear how the sex of the unborn child was determined; this is a rather recently developed technique.) However, in 1869 Pope Pius IX took the position that all abortion is murder; and for more than a hundred years, this has been the Catholic position (Sandler, Myerson, and Kinder 1980, p. 119).

The Mormon church also maintains that induced abortion is a sin: "As a church we oppose legalized, nontherapeutic abortions. . . . We consider such actions among the most grievous of sins. As in other areas, we receive some helpful counsel from modern scripture in which we are instructed not to kill, 'nor do anything like unto it' " (Christensen 1979, p. 4).

Statistics on the number of induced abortions and characteristics of the women who have them have been kept only since 1969, when enough states had adopted liberalized laws to allow for relevant data collection. For earlier periods, there are only estimates of the number of abortions, except for the few legal ones performed (when the mother's life was clearly in danger from the pregnancy or the pregnancy was due to rape or incest). The estimate was that a million illegal abortions occurred every year before 1973 (Hatcher et al. 1978).

In 1977, 1,270,000 legal abortions were performed—a small increase over the previous estimated number of illegal abortions but one that signified a large change in the quality of care. Approximately 75 percent of the legal induced abortions involved unmarried (including divorced and widowed) women, with two-thirds of the women being under the age of 24. Teenagers accounted for 400,000 abortions (Hatcher et al. 1978).

Abortion is now the most common surgical procedure in the United States—in fact, in the world. The variety of techniques used to terminate a pregnancy are reasonably standard in modern societies. In some Asian and European countries abortion is much more prevalent than in the United States. In Hungary there is about one abortion for every two live births. Czechoslovakia, Poland, Romania, Denmark, and Singapore all have higher rates than does the United States. Bulgaria has about nine abortions for every ten live births. Cuba has the highest rate of abortions of any country for women aged 15 to 44 (Forrest, Tietze, and Sullivan 1978; U.S. Bureau of the Census 1983c, p. 2).

Reasons for Induced Abortion

The decision to have an induced abortion is usually motivated by such practical considerations as finances, job and educational goals, age, and the lack of support of the father and of family and friends. Reasons most frequently given are (1) "I am not married" (34 percent); (2) "I cannot afford a child now" (31.5 percent); (3) "A child would interfere with my education" (22 percent); (4) "I feel unable to cope with a child now" (22 percent); (5) "I have enough children already" (16 percent); and (6) "I think I am too young to have a child" (14 percent). Most women asked gave more than one reason (Diamond et al. 1973).

Women from all backgrounds and of all ages seek induced abortions—women who are married or unmarried; Catholic, Jewish, or Protestant; black or white—and 15 percent of them have more than one abortion (Steinhoff et al. 1979).

When induced abortions were illegal, women were cautioned that repeated abortions might create serious problems in later pregnancies. Repeated terminations were associated with later low-birth-weight infants, spontaneous abortions, and premature deliveries. However, the risks were considerably reduced when the legalization of abortion made back-alley abortions almost a thing of the past. It has been reported that some women have had as many as twenty abortions under careful medical care without known problems resulting. However, recent research indicates that although some of the risks have been lowered in multiple abortions, they still may damage the uterus and interfere with later implantations, making spontaneous abortions more likely. Repeated abortion does not seem a desirable alternative to contraception for these and many other reasons.

The great majority of women who decide to have abortions do so as soon as their pregnancies are confirmed. One study reported that nearly 10 percent had decided even before they became pregnant that if pregnancy did occur, they would certainly terminate it (Diamond et al. 1973). Most women who have had abortions say that they made the right decision; follow-up studies consistently show that most of them continue to feel that their decisions were correct (Osofsky, Osofsky, and Rajan 1973). Even so, others are troubled by their abortions at the time, and some have regrets later, especially if fertility problems occur.

An exception to early decisions about abortion is found in the case of women who have had **amniocentesis** or **chorionic villi biopsy** (CVB). Amniocentesis is a procedure in which cells drawn from the amniotic sac surrounding the fetus are collected and examined. Careful analysis of the cells can detect damage to the fetus caused by such events as German measles in the mother, as well as major chromosomal and other types of genetic abnormalities. Amniocentesis cannot be performed successfully until after the fourteenth week of pregnancy, and the most valid results cannot be obtained until the seventeenth week. CVB can be performed as early as seven weeks into pregnancy, and the results can be interpreted in a few hours as compared to two or more weeks for amniocentesis. A CVB can screen for virtually every disorder detectable by amniocentesis; it cannot detect spina bifida. (There is a newly developed test that *can* detect spina bifida.) The cost for a CVB is about the same as amniocentesis. Relatively few U.S. hospitals offered CVB in 1986, partly out of concern for the chance of triggering spontaneous abortion at such an early date. The procedure has been used in China and Russia for more than a decade (Parachini 1983; Rovner 1984; *Science News*, June 9, 1984, p. 358).

Learning that there are no likely defects can be tremendously reassuring to a couple who have been in doubt. If there is a great risk or certainty that the fetus will have a serious birth defect, many couples may decide to have an induced abortion. CVB has the advantage of allowing a first trimester induction; amniocentesis may dangerously approach the third trimester and fetal viability—the time at which a baby would survive if delivered.

CHAPTER 9

Abortion Induction

For those who believe that having an induced abortion is preferable to having an unwanted child, the first indication for abortion is confirmation of the suspected pregnancy. Once a menstrual period has been missed, this may be accomplished by pregnancy tests given as early as the time of the first missed period.

There are home pregnancy tests on the market that a woman can use one week to ten days after a missed menstrual period, with a repeat test a week later as an added precaution, to determine whether she needs to consult a physician. A study at Marquette University found that in three of the most widely used home tests (which cost between $7 and $15), error rates ranged between 11 percent and 54 percent. However, an earlier study found that women using home pregnancy tests failed to follow directions nearly a third of the time. Even a minor deviation in the procedure can lead to a false reading (Parachini 1986, p. 1).

False negative results from pregnancy tests (indications that a woman is not pregnant when in fact she is) are common in the early stages of pregnancy; consequently, many physicians wait until the second menstrual period is missed before performing a test for pregnancy. By this time the woman is six to eight weeks pregnant.

Recently tests have been developed to check for the presence of HCG (a hormone produced by the **placenta**) in the blood. As soon as the placenta begins to grow, this substance, which shows up in the blood first and in the urine a bit later, can give an accurate reading of a pregnancy. Accurate assessment of pregnancy by these methods can come within the month following conception. For women who do not want to be mothers, this is usually a time of high anxiety, during which they must decide whether to terminate the pregnancy.

If a decision is made to have an induced abortion within the first few weeks after conception, there is ample time for the most commonly used technique—*vacuum aspiration*. (See Figure 9.5 for a summary of procedures.) This method is used from seven to twelve weeks after the most recent menstrual period and is usually performed in a clinic on an outpatient basis. A local anesthetic may be used because there is some discomfort, but the operation is relatively simple. The duration of the procedure is usually no more than fifteen minutes, although preexamination, counseling, and a stay in the clinic for several hours to be certain that there are no complications may take the better part of a day. Any anesthesia affects the mind-body system; some time may be needed to restore comfortable functioning as well as to discharge the emotions heightened by the pregnancy. Usually a few days' time suffices.

The procedure for abortion by vacuum aspiration is to dilate the **cervical os** gradually, either by a series of graduated dilators or by use of *laminaria digitate* (a seaweed stem), which works to draw moisture from the cervix and thereby to pull the os open gently. A tube is inserted into the uterus, and the contents are withdrawn by suction.

In one method of inducing abortion, a curette (curved scraper) may be inserted into the uterus following dilation and the contents removed by scraping them loose. This is called *curettage*; it is also a common operation for women who are not pregnant but who have some need for treatment because of menstrual difficulties or infection. The operation is widely known as D&C (for dilation and curettage) and usually calls for a general anesthetic.

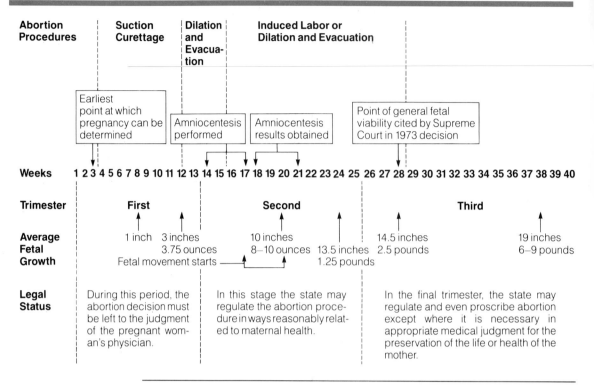

Abortion Procedures	Suction Curettage	Dilation and Evacuation	Induced Labor or Dilation and Evacuation

Earliest point at which pregnancy can be determined

Amniocentesis performed

Amniocentesis results obtained

Point of general fetal viability cited by Supreme Court in 1973 decision

Weeks 1 2 3 4 5 6 7 8 9 10 11 12 13 14 15 16 17 18 19 20 21 22 23 24 25 26 27 28 29 30 31 32 33 34 35 36 37 38 39 40

Trimester First · Second · Third

Average Fetal Growth
1 inch   3 inches
        3.75 ounces
Fetal movement starts
10 inches
8–10 ounces 13.5 inches 1.25 pounds
14.5 inches 2.5 pounds
19 inches 6–9 pounds

Legal Status

During this period, the abortion decision must be left to the judgment of the pregnant woman's physician.

In this stage the state may regulate the abortion procedure in ways reasonably related to maternal health.

In the final trimester, the state may regulate and even proscribe abortion except where it is necessary in appropriate medical judgment for the preservation of the life or health of the mother.

FIGURE 9 • 5

Induced Abortion Procedures

Source: Philip Hager, ''Medical Gains Stir Debate on Abortion Ruling,'' *Los Angeles Times,* September 9, 1985, Part I, p. 12. Data from Centers for Disease Control and National Abortion Rights Action League.

After the twelfth week of pregnancy abortion becomes much more complicated. The walls of the uterus have become increasingly thin, soft, and spongy. They can be perforated more easily; inserting objects into the uterus is more likely to cause damage. Also, as the fetus grows larger, suction removal becomes less and less possible. From the twelfth to the sixteenth weeks, however, some physicians will perform what is termed *dilation and evacuation* surgery, which takes longer than the other procedures described and is done under general anesthesia in a hospital. This method uses both vacuum and curettage.

Generally, between the twelfth and the twenty-sixth week (some physicians will not perform abortions after the twenty-fourth week), the safest method for terminating pregnancy is inducing a kind of premature labor and forcing delivery. The further along the pregnancy, of course, the more like a full-term birth the procedure is. Women who choose abortion following amniocentesis at the seventeenth week will undergo this process. There are two accepted methods used in these later pregnancies. One is to remove an amount of the amniotic fluid from around the fetus with a syringe, replacing it with a saline solution. The uterus will react to the saline solution by contracting and will expel the fetus and placenta within a day of the procedure.

An alternative method of inducing a late abortion is to insert a hormonal substance called **prostaglandin** into the amniotic sac, either by injection or in the form of suppositories. This procedure usually causes expulsion of the fetus to occur more quickly than does the saline injection; however, many women complain that they suffer side effects such as diarrhea and vomiting. Both the saline solution and prostaglandins cause the painful contractions associated with birth, which may last from eight to fifteen hours (Stewart et al. 1979). Experimentation with prostaglandins for self-induced home abortions in the first seven weeks of pregnancy is currently being done in Sweden. The first 100 women who used the Swedish procedure were adjudged to have had safe—though painful—experiences (*Los Angeles Times*, October 27, 1982, Part V, p. 3).

Eugene Sandberg (1976), a professor of gynecology and obstetrics, comments: "Abortion, although undesirable, is sufficiently inexpensive and safe to be accepted as a legitimate escape from an undesirable situation and, in many minds, is not an undue price to pay if sensual gambles fail." But women who have been through an abortion usually do not want to repeat the experience. Only a small proportion of women have subsequent abortions; it is probable that they have learned that abortion is not to be taken lightly and that contraception is a far better way to postpone motherhood until the time is right.

INVOLUNTARY CHILDLESSNESS

Since there are more couples in college attuned to preventing conception than concerned with being unable to bear children, it is understandable that the distress caused by infertility has often been overlooked in textbooks. But infertility can put stress on the strongest marriages. It is estimated that at least 15 percent of American women aged 15 to 44 cannot conceive; for many such persons this is a deep disappointment. Some have no hope of ever being able to conceive—a condition called sterility. Others have low fertility—a condition that may lend itself to treatment. Success in treating low fertility has increased from 50 percent in the 1960s to about 70 percent today (Culverwell 1983).

The cure for low fertility is sometimes as simple as learning new coital techniques. Certain positions in coitus increase the likelihood of fertilization. The man above, face-to-face position is particularly recommended, especially if the woman raises her hips after her partner's ejaculation so that the semen stays inside. A rear-entry position with the woman on her knees and elbows is also highly effective.

An occasional cause of infertility is timing. Although women usually ovulate thirteen times a year, it is easily possible for a couple to miss each occasion, especially if one of them has low sexual interest or vitality that results in infrequent coitus. Couples who have coitus fewer than three times a week may need to use basal body temperature charts to pinpoint the time of ovulation. Such charts may also show lack of ovulation, which can often be remedied by the use of drugs such as Clomid or Pergonal. Human chorionic gonadotropin can be used to control the timing of ovum development (*Science News*, February 4, 1984, p. 72).

Infertility in Women

Some infertility problems in women are very serious and difficult to treat. Others have quite simple causes and solutions. Obesity is associated with a problem called polycystic ovarian disease, which prevents ovulation. Affected women sometimes begin to ovulate simply by losing weight (*Science News*, July 23, 1983, p. 59). Exercise may also affect fertility. Women who are joggers, runners, or dancers may have insufficient body fat to produce needed estrogen; they need to gain fat to become pregnant. Stress, as most women know, can suppress ovulation (*Time*, September 10, 1984, p. 50); the obvious therapy is to reduce stress.

Those with more serious infertility problems must seek medical help and sometimes even surgery to find a cure. Both sterility and low fertility have a variety of causes, including hormonal imbalances, infections or other types of illnesses, anatomical defects, anemia, and even psychological stress. In current practice, diagnosis of the cause can be made 95 percent of the time (*Time*, September 10, 1984, p. 50).

The incidence of infertility in women aged 20 to 24 increased from 3.6 percent in 1965 to 10.6 percent in 1982 (Cimons 1985b). Some authorities on infertility believe that fertility problems are on the increase as a result of the use of modern methods of birth control and of the epidemic rise in venereal disease, which can lead to blockage of the fallopian tubes. Herpes virus is thought to be responsible for a high percentage of repetitive spontaneous abortions.

The birth control pill is believed to stop ovulation permanently in some women with a history of irregular menstrual periods and ovulation problems. The chemicals in these pills are known to depress the fertility hormones that are released by the pituitary gland, and the suspicion is that this effect may be permanent even though use of the Pill is discontinued.

Chlamydia, gonorrhea, and the IUD (intrauterine device) have been cited as causes of pelvic infection and tubal blockage in many women. Both of these are causes of infertility; women are believed to have a problem in 80 percent of infertile couples.

It is estimated that since 1970 well over a million women have suffered from acute pelvic infections. By 1986, nearly 300,000 women were hospitalized annually with PID, and over 2.5 million PID-related visits were being made to outpatient providers per year (Cimons 1986). Of that number, nearly one-quarter either are already sterile or have had their fallopian tubes damaged to such an extent from the infections that they stand almost no chance of getting pregnant. The fallopian tubes may become so scarred that they can no longer function to transport eggs from the ovaries. In many cases the tubes are completely blocked by scar tissue that was laid down as a result of infections. Microsurgery can solve minor problems of scar tissue about 70 percent of the time (*Time*, September 10, 1984, p. 48).

Infertility in Men

In men (who have a problem in 40 percent of infertile marriages), fertility problems are usually due to some deficiency either in the sperm count or in sperm activity. A healthy sperm count is between 60 and 100 million sperm per cubic centimeter, with 60 percent of these being observably active (Crawley et al. 1973, p. 218). **In vitro fertilization**, however, has good chances for success with only 50,000 sperm (*Time*, September 10, 1984, p. 52).

In a long-range study of men conducted over the past 50 years in the United States, it has been discovered that sperm counts are dropping. In 1929 the median count was over 90 million per cubic centimeter; in 1974 the median count had dropped to 65 million; and in the most recent study (in 1979), the median was 60 million, or just at the low edge of normal. Twenty-three percent of the subjects had sperm densities of 20 million or less, a level generally agreed on as a functional definition of sterility.

Although it is not clear just why the sperm count is dropping, Ralph C. Dougherty (1979), a chemist who reported this research at the meetings of the American Chemical Society, has said: "It is possible that toxic substances in the environment may be partially responsible for this apparent shift. The chemicals enter the body through the food chain where they usually accumulate in fatty tissue."

A variety of factors have been suggested for the decline in sperm count. At an international conference in Jerusalem in 1980, Paolo Parisi, a geneticist at the Mendel Institute in Rome, suggested that industrial pollutants, especially pesticides, may be what is damaging sperm and noted that the effect is worldwide (Rodgers 1980). Research done with laboratory animals in Bulgaria found that exposure to loud noise (100 decibels) for a period of one year resulted in sterility in 80 percent of the animals (*Sexual Medicine Today*, May 1979, p. 17). It may well be that as industrialization and resulting environmental pollution increase, sperm counts in males will continue to decrease. Tobacco and alcohol continue to take their toll. As previously mentioned, some fertility experts report that they have had good results in increasing male fertility by getting men to change to loose underclothing and pants. Close-fitting underwear and jeans interfere with the natural process that drops the testes automatically away from the body when they become too warm for sperm to stay healthy (Kitzinger 1983, p. 197).

Treatment for Infertility

The choice of whether or not to have a child is taken for granted by a majority of couples. When that choice is removed by sterility or diminished by low fertility, the realization can be a painful one. Couples usually consult a physician who evaluates the cause of the problem and attempts to correct matters when possible. A series of tests may be indicated, usually beginning with the male since his sperm count is fairly easy to determine from a specimen of his ejaculate. A widely used assessment technique employs multiple-exposure photography, which provides quick information about the number of sperm, the percentage of them that are motile, and their velocity. If the count is low or if the sperm are less active than normal, various remedies can be tried. One option is to determine as exactly as possible the time that the woman ovulates and to plan intercourse to coincide. The male will be advised to refrain from ejaculation for 48 hours beforehand so that as many sperm will be available as possible. Sometimes, the administration of Clomid will increase sperm count.

In cases in which it is determined that the woman is fertile but her partner's sperm count is low, his semen may be collected and saved by freezing it over a period of many ejaculations. Ultimately, it may be thawed and made into a concentrate that can be used by placing it directly into the uterus during the woman's time of ovulation. This process is one of the means of artificial insemination and is called AIH (which stands for "artificial insemination husband") if the husband's semen is used.

Artificial insemination is becoming increasingly accepted as a technique to enable couples with low fertility to have children. A controversial form of artificial insemination uses a donor other than the husband as the source of sperm (AID, for "artificial insemination donor"). When the husband is sterile, this is an option that allows his wife to conceive and to bear a child in a normal fashion. Although he is not the biological father, he is of course the parent in every other way—just as he would be with an adopted infant. A variation of this procedure involves mixing the husband's semen with that of a donor.

A few religions prohibit artificial insemination generally, although they may allow some variations. The Roman Catholic church, for example, has approved what it calls "assisted insemination," which involves marital intercourse followed by the use of an instrument that pushes the semen into the cervix.

Legal and Moral Issues

Since the birth of Louise Brown—the first child born as a result of in vitro fertilization—in July 1978, procedures for creating pregnancies have advanced rapidly. Over 1,000 babies have been born in more than 200 in-vitro fertilization (IVF) clinics around the world; embryos have been transferred from one woman to another; sperm removed from the testicles of a man with blocked tubes have been "capacitated" so that they can fertilize an ovum; a prematurely menopausal woman has given birth to a son conceived in vitro by her husband's sperm and a donor's ovum; women have received embryo implants conceived by AID from their husbands in other women's reproductive tracts; a way of "harvesting" ova without surgery has been invented; over a hundred couples have engaged surrogate mothers to carry and give birth to babies conceived by AID from the husband of the couple; embryos have been frozen to be implanted later and babies have been born of such frozen embryos.

A variety of legal and moral issues have arisen from both actual and hypothetical situations growing out of solutions to problems of infertility. Can a clinic offering AID deny that service to a woman because she is not married? "No," said a Michigan court. Is the man married to a woman who has conceived by AID the legal father of her resulting baby? If he consented to the procedure, he is, say the laws of half of all U.S. states—but not the other half.

Who determines the disposition of a dead man's previously frozen sperm? His widow, said a French court, granting her the right to have herself inseminated with it after his death. What does one do with the frozen embryos conceived by AID in vitro for a couple who are now both dead? Australia is uncertain at this writing. In the event that such an embryo were implanted in another woman, would a resulting child be an heir to the couple who arranged for its conception? "Fortunately, that hasn't happened," said Justice Austin Asche of Melbourne. "I don't feel at all comfortable with the knowledge that a married man has impregnated a surrogate mother by coitus rather than by AID," said Dr. Stuart Purvis-Smith of Sydney. "It's socially and morally improper, regardless of any legal decision." And these are just a sample of the first few questions that have already arisen.

Should the social parents of a child born with donor or surrogate assistance conceal that information from the child? From their friends and relatives? Is conception a "privileged communication" that may not be subject to legal or judicial inquiry? Does a donor or surrogate have an obligation to support a child born with his or her assistance should the social parents be unable to do so? What about inheritance rights in either direction? These and many other thorny issues have begun to arise. There

"Baby Louise" Brown, the first ever "test-tube" baby, is shown here in 1979 at the age of fourteen months.

are probably many more opinions than there are issues (see Goulder 1985, p. 8; Andrews 1984; and Walters and Singer 1982).

Emotional Reactions to Infertility

It has been estimated that about half the childless couples who seek medical aid eventually will have children. For those who must accept their infertility, there can be many strong emotional reactions. Couples who have spent months preoccupied with temperature charts and ovulation schedules in an attempt to have intercourse at exactly the right moment and who have endured repeated tests may understandably respond angrily to the innocent query from friends, "When are you going to have a baby?"

The discovery of sterility often sets up what has been called the "infertility syndrome" by David Rosenfeld, professor of obstetrics and gynecology at Cornell Medical College, who has counseled hundreds of infertile couples. The syndrome is the "emotional trauma couples experience during the process of establishing their infertility and then the gradual, painful task of accepting it and incorporating this unwanted reality into their lives" (Cipriano 1980). Such couples pass through a series of predictable emotional stages:

1. *Denial:* they say, "It's really not happening. We're probably just not having sex enough."
2. *Self-blame:* they accuse themselves, asking, "What did I do to make this happen? Is God punishing me?"
3. *Communication gap:* husband and wife don't admit to each other that there is a problem. It is very difficult for one or the other to say, "Hey, there's something wrong. Let's see a doctor."
4. *Anger and depression:* when infertility is confirmed, the partners experience tremendous anger, alternating with depression. They are angry with everyone—themselves, their spouses, and their physicians.

Adoption

One option for sterile couples who want to stay married and rear their own children is adoption. This may not be easy; traditionally there have been far fewer desirable infants available for adoption than prospective adoptive parents. This ratio is becoming even less favorable because of the widespread use of contraceptives, the availability of abortion, and the fact that single mothers often keep their babies.

Public and private agencies provide state-regulated systems for adoption. These agencies employ screening processes that provide the best assurance possible that a baby will be placed in a home that is appropriate. However, the procedure is necessarily a lengthy one, and prospective parents may face a very long waiting period even though the process has been modified considerably in recent years to make it less arduous. The waiting time at Catholic Charities in 1984 was seven years (*Time*, September 10, 1984, p. 46).

In an attempt to hasten the time when a child will be available for them, many couples turn to private placement. In such cases they often know little if anything about the child's natural parents; nor have they undergone a preplacement investigation of themselves as potential parents. Often an intermediary between the biological mother and the adoptive parents—a physician, an attorney, a friend, or a relative—makes the arrangements. This is illegal in some states, however, and is prohibited in still others if any money has changed hands (Podolski 1975).

Because children who are matched to the adoptive parents in terms of racial, ethnic, religious, and educational background of the natural parents are in such short supply, more and more couples are adopting children who are very different from them, are older than the infant they originally desired, are handicapped in some way, or for some other reason are classified as "hard to place." Such children must wait for adoption, and although statistics are inexact, it is estimated that there are about 100,000 of them at any given time (Katz and Gallagher 1976).

Although it has been generally accepted by both scholars and adoption agencies that an adopted child's behavior is the result of social learning, new research findings in Sweden, Denmark, and the United States suggest that genetic effects on behavior can no longer be disregarded (Bower 1984). These findings may make adoption an even more difficult decision for many.

SUMMARY

1. It is more possible now than at any previous time in history for people to control the conception of children.
2. Although there has been a long-term decline in fertility rates in the United States, there has been an upward trend since 1976, especially among women aged 30–34.
3. There has been a sharp rise in recent years in the number of births to unmarried women over half of whom are teenagers. A half million babies are born to unwed mothers each year, and 94 percent of their mothers keep them.
4. Although more sex education courses are being offered in high schools, they tend to focus on the physiology of menstruation and reproduction rather than on contraception and the social skills needed to avoid unwanted pregnancies. Although an increasing number of sexually active teenagers are using contraceptives, nearly one-third do not.
5. Pregnancies normally result from acts of coitus. Intercourse may occur because of its intrinsic value to one or both members of a couple or because it is intended to achieve some other value, including causing a pregnancy.
6. As recently as 1970, about nine out of every twenty births to married women were unplanned. The motives for having babies intentionally are varied and often complex.
7. Voluntary childlessness by means other than abstention from coitus is relatively recent as a widespread practice. In 1984 only about one married American woman in sixteen wanted to be childless, down from one in five during the 1920s and 1930s.
8. The decision of married couples to have or not to have children is almost always made by wives. Decisions frequently involve work and career choices.
9. Birth control is used to permit coitus with a minimal risk of pregnancy. The goal may be for a couple to remain childless, or it may be to control the time or spacing of births.
10. Chemical contraceptives are used either to inhibit the production of ova or to destroy sperm. Contraceptive pills are the most effective and douching is the least effective of these.
11. Barrier devices such as diaphragms, condoms, and cervical caps block sperm from reaching ova. Interuterine devices inhibit implantation of fertilized ova.
12. Sterilization is surgical intervention that prevents conception without interfering with the capacity to have coitus. The process is usually carried out by vasectomy in males and by tubal ligation in females.
13. The rhythm method dictates that partners avoid sexual intercourse at times when conception is likely. Coitus interruptus is intended to prevent spermatozoa from being deposited in the female genital tract by withdrawing the penis from the vagina during intercourse so that ejaculation occurs outside the female. Abstinence is refraining from having intercourse and is widely used on a periodic basis for contraception.

14. The right of a healthy woman to interrupt her pregnancy legally through induced abortion was upheld by the United States Supreme Court in 1973. A Supreme Court ruling in 1977 held that federal funds may not be used to pay for voluntary induced abortions except in cases of incest, rape, or undue risk to the woman. Well over a million legal abortions are performed each year; unmarried women account for approximately three-quarters of them, and teenagers figure in about one-third. A small number of abortions are performed because a fetal defect has been determined by amniocentesis or CVB.

15. Some religious and "right-to-life" groups have strong opposition to induced abortions. Catholic and Mormon authorities hold that abortion is a sin.

16. Early abortions are most often performed by vacuum aspirations; an alternate method is dilation and curettage. Later abortions are performed by dilation and evacuation; still later ones by the injection of a saline solution or prostaglandins.

17. Involuntary childlessness results from sterility or low fertility, both of which have a variety of causes, including hormonal imbalances, infections, psychological stress, and anatomical defects. There is a growing rate of infertility among women. The sperm count of American men has been dropping for the last 50 years, a phenomenon that many believe to be a prime consideration in many cases of low fertility.

18. Artificial insemination (using either the husband's semen or that of a donor) may be used to facilitate pregnancy. Although this has been a controversial topic, it is gaining in acceptability in the United States.

19. In vitro fertilization makes it possible to implant an already fertilized egg into a woman's uterus and have her carry it to full term. This method resulted in the birth of the first "test-tube" baby in 1978.

20. About half the couples seeking medical aid for childlessness are actually helped. In some of these couples, at least one partner is sterile. For these with low fertility 70 percent are helped. Of those who do not conceive, many choose to adopt a child, although infants available for adoption are far fewer than couples who wish to adopt.

GLOSSARY

Abortion, induced Surgical removal of an embryo or fetus. (p. 274)

Abortion, spontaneous Unintended expulsion of an embryo or fetus prior to viability. (p. 264)

Amniocentesis A technique for checking cells in the amniotic fluid to determine the state of the fetus, especially with respect to potential birth defects. (p. 276)

Antibody A substance found in the blood that destroys particular kinds of cells or that counteracts the growth of foreign bodies. (p. 267)

Cervical os The opening in the cervix connecting the uterus with the vagina. (p. 277)

Cervix The neck of the uterus, which protrudes into the inner end of the vagina. (p. 260)

Chorionic villi biopsy A sampling of rudimentary placental processes intended to predict potential birth defects. (p. 276)

Endometrium The lining of the uterus, which thickens with tissue and blood each month in preparation for the implantation of a fertilized ovum. (p. 265)

Hysterectomy The surgical removal of the uterus. (p. 268)

Illegitimacy The state of having been born to an unmarried woman. (p. 248)

In vitro fertilization Fertilization of an ovum "in glass," that is, outside the body. (p. 280)

Pelvic inflammatory disease (PID) An inflammation of women's internal reproductive organs that can lead to infertility. (p. 260)

Placenta The organ, attached to the umbilical cord of the fetus, that provides for the exchange through the uterine wall of nutrients to and waste material from the fetus. (p. 270)

Progesterones Female hormones secreted by the ovaries to prepare the uterus for the implantation of a fertilized ovum. (p. 260)

Prostaglandin A drug that can stimulate a fertilized ovum to be released with the menstrual flow any time from conception to one month after conception. (p. 279)

Tubal ligation A procedure in which the fallopian tubes are cut, cauterized, and/or tied off to prevent the passage of ova to the uterus or sperm to the ova. (p. 267)

Vasectomy A process in which the two tubes (the *vasa deferentia*) that normally carry sperm from the testes to the seminal vesicles are cut and tied to prevent the passage of the sperm through the penis. (p. 266)

Zero population growth A term used to describe a birthrate that is at or below a population's replacement level—one baby (or fewer) born for each person who dies. (p. 246)

10

The value of marriage is not that adults produce children
but that children produce adults.

The birth of a child transforms a married couple into a family. Although today couples have more choice than in the past about becoming parents, very few remain childless. Family-life studies have given special attention to the birth of the first child, which is seen as having more impact on the parents than do subsequent additions to the family. Not only are both pregnancy and birth brand-new experiences with the firstborn child, but also the couple's familiar way of life becomes that of a three-person system that is infinitely more complex.

Couples are much better prepared for pregnancy and childbirth than they are for taking the baby home to begin family life. With the firstborn, this transition can often be difficult as new parents attempt to balance demands on their time, energy, and financial resources. A family system—mother, father, and children—may change over time but does not end. Parents are parents forever; even if their marriage does not endure, they almost always have lifetime contact with each other through their children.

PREGNANCY, BIRTH, AND TRANSITION TO PARENTHOOD

Peter De Vries

*T*he birth of a child still seems miraculous. The sense of wonder has not been destroyed by scientific knowledge of conception, pregnancy, and birth. For parents, the addition of a child leads to important changes. Until recently, however, research into the dynamics of these personal and interpersonal changes had not kept pace with that into the physical aspects of conception, pregnancy, and birth.

Recent studies have begun to shed some light on the important psychological and emotional effects of the emergence of a new family system. Initially the research explored various dimensions of motherhood, reflecting the traditional attitude of both men and women that pregnancy and birth are a woman's domain. Studies have found that the decision to have children is affected by length of time since marriage, the socio-historical period, and the woman's age (Rindfuss, Morgan, and Swicegood 1984, p. 359). Gradually researchers have inquired into the impact of parents on children and, finally, have focused on the effects of having children on fathers, marital relationships, siblings, stepparents and stepchildren, and grandparents.

Each stage in the emergence of new human beings has a social and psychological significance for family members, whose lives are being altered by the addition of new persons to their families. The birth of the first child has received special attention because it is credited with having greater impact on the parents than do subsequent births. It has been described as a "period of 'metamorphosis' when a two-person group suddenly changes into a three-person one" (Blehar 1980a, p. 144). It requires that new parents make major adjustments; it is influenced by and influences the woman's career path, the couple's accumulation of assets, their housing, and the risks of marital disruption (Rindfuss, Morgan, and Swicegood 1984, p. 359). Success or failure in making these adjustments may set the stage for meeting the challenges of childbearing and the quality of later family life.

Even though couples today are more successful in preventing conception than in the past, most ultimately will have one or more children. More than ever before, married women who become pregnant are likely to have planned their pregnancies. Approximately two-thirds of women are married at the time their children are conceived, and an even larger fraction (83 percent) are married when their children are born (U.S. Bureau of the Census 1985c, p. 1). For most couples there is a relatively short interval between marriage and the birth of their first child, although couples are waiting longer now than in the past. Of couples who marry before conceiving a child, 42 percent have their first child within three years of marriage, 43 percent within three to five years, and 15 percent after more than five years (U.S. Bureau of the Census 1978a).

REASONS FOR HAVING CHILDREN

Leland Foster Wood, theologian and sociologist, and distinguished gynecologist Robert Latou Dickinson (1948, p. 86) wrote:

> The joys and responsibilities of parenthood enrich family experience and bring the particular couple into the endless process of renewal and ongoing of all the interests and values of the race. The world is constantly being fashioned and re-

fashioned in its homes. To say that the social virtues of tenderness, responsibility, sympathy and devotion have their spots in parental experience is true and important, but pale compared with the radiant joy that parents have in the renewal of themselves and their love in children. In the family plan therefore children should have a central place. It is better to spend money for children than for "nice things" or an expensive manner of living.

The sentiments expressed by Wood and Dickinson are still widespread in American society today. Virtually all religious denominations agree with them formally, and some see the procreation of children as expected.

Men and women want children for various reasons. There have been many investigations into the motivations for having children. One study that asked unmarried, childless women who stated a preference for children why they wanted to be mothers found that three reasons were rated equal in importance (Gerson 1978, p. 153):

1. They wanted to experience the honesty and freshness of children.
2. They wanted to participate in the miracle of birth.
3. They thought they could be a good parent.

The last of these seemed related to other findings of the same study showing that positive memories of the young woman's own childhood and of her parents' loving care were important variables in determining whether she wanted children.

To give love, to enjoy children, and to be a good parent are generally conceded to be positive motivations. Unfortunately, other frequently mentioned reasons are at best questionable motivations for becoming parents. Couples often mention pressure from outsiders—perhaps their own parents want a grandchild or an heir to carry on the family name or aspirations. Sometimes the pressure comes from members of organizations that define having children as a moral obligation. Some men and women report that they want to have children because all their friends are having babies. Still others hope that a baby will improve a troubled marriage or relationship or be proof of virility or femininity. They may believe that a child of their own will fill a need for companionship or love or will keep them from loneliness now or in old age.

FINANCIAL ASPECTS OF CHILDBEARING

One of the chief anxieties in deciding whether to have children and, if so, how many, is financial. Couples are increasingly worried about the cost of living and the expense of providing for a family. Figures from the United States Department of Agriculture indicate that the average costs of rearing a welfare-supported child to the age of eighteen are about $80,000. Estimates of the costs for privately supported children range around $100,000. Unless totally supported by public welfare, many express concern about fees for prenatal medical care, hospitalization, and delivery of a child. Some of the costs to parents paying wholly or partially from their own resources for having a baby and supporting it for its first year are:

- Mother's maternity wardrobe
- Mother's prenatal care, delivery fee, hospital or birth center bill for normal delivery, and postpartum hospitalization (or additional costs of alternative home care)

- Baby's hospitalization
- Pediatrician's hospital visits, regular well-baby checks, required immunizations, sick visits, medications
- Baby's clothing, bedding, linens, diapers (or diaper service)
- Nursery furnishings: bassinet, crib, bathtub, stroller, highchair, chest, car-seat, infant carrier, toys
- Baby's food and vitamins
- Supplies: bottles, swabs, tissues, powder, baby soap, oil
- Baby-sitters or day care

It is clear that *someone* must spend at least $5,000 (in 1986 dollars) in the childbearing year for each baby. Although a great deal more than this may be spent, the total can be cut if:

- Parents shop for their maternity care; some hospitals and birth centers offer one-, two-, or three-day maternity packages for postpartum care for mother and baby.
- "Hand-me-downs" are available for maternity and baby clothing, bedding and equipment.
- Parents take advantage of "garage sales" and furniture exchanges in equipping the nursery.
- The baby is breastfed for a portion or all of the first year and parents learn to make their own baby food.
- Families receive gifts of supplies or services from friends and relatives.
- Parents investigate early the options for babysitting co-ops, job sharing, part-time resumption of work for the mother (or father), or the possibility of bringing the baby to work for a few weeks or months.
- Parents have jobs with maternity and/or paternity leave benefits.
- Parents participate in infant car-seat rental programs, which are available through many hospitals, especially in states where state law requires the use of infant and child auto-safety restraints.

Of course, medical and hospital insurance helps immeasurably. Although the Pregnancy Discrimination Act of 1979 mandates that health plans for employed persons must offer maternity benefits, partial coverage or coverage for uncomplicated births only is the rule (Lichtendorf and Gillis 1979). Some medical plans cover expenses only if the insurance was in force before the pregnancy began. Others pay only for complications that arise during the pregnancy. Still others pay only what the insurance company deems a "reasonable and proper" charge, which may be much less than the actual cost.

Insurance coverage for the newborn is variable. Some policies cover the baby only *after* an initial waiting period (usually the period when most expenses for newborn care are incurred). Others cover the baby only for the first 30 days of life. Still others offer coverage only for complications. Many policies specify a deductible amount before coverage begins. Because of gaps in insurance coverage, many parents still must make sizable expenditures for medical care during the childbearing years. It is not uncommon for them to have relatively poor information about their insurance coverage.

Even small children can experience the first levels of understanding about birth and can be part of the parents' joy of anticipation.

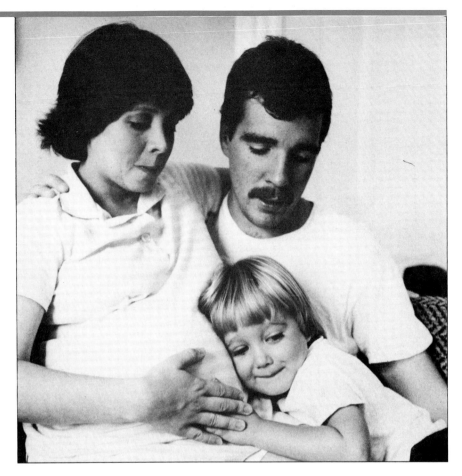

The costs for those on welfare who become pregnant are covered by tax-supported government programs. Welfare expenditures of as much as $15,000 for the support and care of an unwed mother and her baby for three years beginning with the discovery of her pregnancy were reported in 1982 (*Los Angeles Times*, October 8, 1982, Part II, p. 5), and there is reason to believe that they are substantially more now.

CONCEPTION

Anne Bernstein (1976), a social scientist, has asked children, "How do people get babies?" She finds that children go through six basic levels of understanding about birth and sex. The first level is common to those under five years of age: "You go to the hospital to get one." The second level, which shows confusion about "constructing" a baby, is common to children in kindergarten and the first grade. They believe that babies are manufactured somewhere before they are ready to be picked up at the hospital. Level three shows some understanding of growth inside the mother as a result of a "seed" being placed there by the father.

However, the facts of reproduction are not clear to most children until level four, which reflects an understanding of sperm, eggs, and penile penetration. Level five is marked by a more complete understanding of the process of conception and of how the fetus grows and is born. The sixth level, which occurs sometime around the age of twelve, shows the influence of reading and teaching and of responses to children's questions about cause and effect.

By age twelve most children have a fairly clear picture, which persists until they learn more of the details as teenagers or young adults (Bernstein and Cowan 1975). Much, of course, depends on the accuracy of the information children originally receive. Unfortunately, some of the adults who answer children's questions have misguided notions themselves. Other children obtain much of their information about reproduction from their peers, who may or may not give them accurate information. Many children at level six, therefore, have a clear but not necessarily totally accurate picture.

By early adolescence most children begin to have their inaccurate ideas about pregnancy and birth corrected by knowledgeable adults. Many schools teach courses or units on reproduction. The quality of instruction has steadily improved over the past decade, so that most young people are learning that every cell in the body contains 23 pairs of chromosomes, which hold genetic information carried by the genes. Young adults also generally know that when the **sperm** cell of the male and the **ovum** (egg cell) of the female unite, they combine their sets of chromosomes (see Figure 10.1).

Adult understanding of conception involves the knowledge that a sperm cell has a head that contains *chromosomes,* a neck and a midsection that seem to guide the movement that is energized by a whiplike tail propelling the sperm forward after ejaculation. Sperm are produced in the testicles and are carried in glandular fluid called *semen*—the Latin word for seed—through the penis by muscular contractions during ejaculation. The tube through which semen is ejaculated (the urethra) is the same tube through which urine passes; however, when a man's penis becomes erect, the processes that cause it to get hard automatically block off any urine input. A more detailed discussion of the male reproductive anatomy and physiology appears in Appendix A.

Semen collects from the **seminal vesicles,** the **bulbourethral glands,** and the prostate gland. Each contributes substances necessary to the strength and motility of the sperm. The prostate, for instance, gives the seminal fluid its milky color and its characteristic odor; it provides nourishment for the sperm with acid phosphatase. In cases of rape, it is the remains of acid phosphatase that constitute evidence of intercourse (Diamond and Karlen 1980, p. 368).

The bulbourethral glands release the cleansing and lubricating fluid that collects on the tip of the penis during sexual excitement. Because this fluid is alkaline, it helps sperm survive during ejaculation by neutralizing the otherwise acid environment of the urethra.

The clear preejaculate fluid sometimes has enough sperm in it, either from the swelling seminal vesicles or from an earlier ejaculation, to cause pregnancy. This may happen when a couple have touched penis to vagina in foreplay but have believed they were safe from impregnation since actual ejaculation had not taken place. Sperm in the clear fluid can travel through a lubricated vagina, the cervix, and the uterus, into a fallopian tube to reach an ovum and fertilize it. Since sperm can easily reach a fallopian tube in a short time, it is impossible to stop them by douching if they

CHAPTER 10

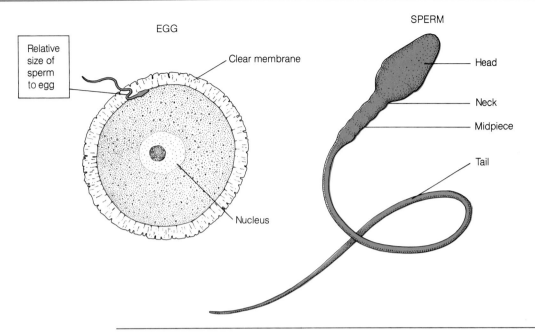

FIGURE 10 • 1
Sperm Cell and
Egg Cell

have reached the uterus. If an egg is waiting in the tube, fertilization may indeed take place.

During each cycle any eggs released move in fluid through a fallopian tube to the uterus. If an egg is not fertilized during the approximately three-day journey through the tube, the uterine wall (which has been preparing for the implantation of the fertilized egg), sloughs off about two weeks after ovulation and leaves the body as menstrual flow.

What keeps pregnancy from occurring more frequently than it does in healthy, fertile women who are sexually active is that their ovulations theoretically happen only once a month. However, irregular ovulation (more or less often than once a month) or a complete lack of ovulation affects the likelihood of pregnancy. Women may be anovulatory (releasing no eggs) for a time. It is also possible for women to ovulate twice or even more often in a month from one or both ovaries. Fraternal twins and other multiple births of nonidentical babies are conceived in just that way—if a woman is having daily intercourse without contraception, there are always plenty of spermatozoa to fertilize as many ova as are present. In fact, a typical ejaculation contains thousands of times as many spermatozoa as would be needed to fertilize all the eggs that any woman could produce in a lifetime.

The released egg (or eggs) is viable for only a few days before it disintegrates. The next month the entire process begins again. Women have some 400,000 primitive eggs (**oogonia**) present in their ovaries at birth. These lie dormant until puberty, when hormones begin the maturation process for the eggs one by one. Only about 400 will ever become mature enough to be released.

FIGURE 10 • 2

The process of con-
ception is depicted.
Released from an
ovary, the ovum en-
ters the fallopian tube
where it is fertilized
by a single sperm.
The cells of the fertil-
ized ovum repeatedly
divide as it moves
into the uterus. The
ovum develops into a
hollow base of cells
(blastocyst) and im-
plants in the endome-
trium. The elapsed
time from ovulation
to implantation is
about seven days.

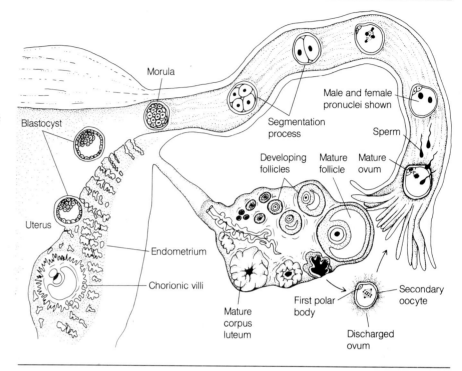

If fertilization does take place, cell division begins about twelve hours after the sperm has penetrated the egg (see Figure 10.2). Cell division continues as the fertilized egg—now called a **zygote**—travels to the uterus. Already, genetic materials have determined just what this baby will be like, including what sex it is.

Human cells can be classified as body cells or germ cells. The body cells are the living "building blocks" of which body tissues are constructed and by which they are maintained. The germ cells are the sperm and ova that are stored and/or produced in the gonads. The nucleus of every normal human cell contains 46 chromosomes (23 pairs), each containing groups of genes that instruct the cells how to grow into tissues.

Two chromosomes in each cell carry the genes that direct the reproduction of germ cells and the development of sex organs and sex-linked characteristics. In females these two chromosomes are similar and are called X chromosomes. In males the two chromosomes are different; one is like the X chromosome in females, but the other—called Y—is uniquely male.

Soon after the union of a sperm and an ovum, the cell nuclei merge, following a complex process that has already separated each pair of chromosomes; 23 chromosomes from the sperm pair up with the corresponding 23 from the ovum to form a new set of 46 necessary for human growth and development.

No matter which of the original pair of sex chromosomes from the ovum splits off and joins with the sex chromosome supplied by the sperm, it will surely be an X— ova have no Y chromosomes. There is almost (but actually not quite) a 50–50 chance that the X chromosome from the sperm will join the X from the ovum. If that happens, the new conception is instantly programmed to develop with female body cells and

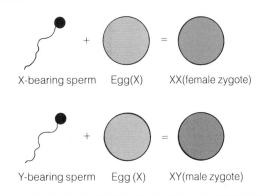

FIGURE 10 • 3
Father Determines Sex of Child
Egg cells contain two X chromosomes and no Y chromosomes. Sperm cells contain one X chromosome and one Y chromosome. Therefore, the sperm determines whether the conceptus will have XX or XY chromosomes in its nucleus.

X-bearing sperm + Egg(X) = XX(female zygote)

Y-bearing sperm + Egg (X) = XY(male zygote)

female sex cells. If the sperm's Y chromosome joins the ovum's X, an XY pair—the male program for growth and development—is established (see Figure 10.3).

Thus a child's genetic sex is set at fertilization. For every 100 females conceived, there will be between 120 and 150 males, although only about 104 will actually be carried to full term and born alive.

Men are capable of producing mature sperm soon after puberty and can have a reproductive life of over 70 years. Theoretically, men can father an almost limitless number of children in a lifetime—possibly even thousands without considering the possibility of artificial insemination.

The earlier a girl begins to menstruate, the sooner she will begin to ovulate every month. Thus girls who menstruate before the age of twelve will be ovulating during half of their cycles within a year; girls who first menstruate between their twelfth and thirteenth birthdays will not be ovulating during half of their cycles for an average of three years; when menstruation begins later than age thirteen, the 50–50 frequency will not be reached for four and a half years (Vihko and Apter 1983). Women are normally fertile until after menopause, which begins between 45 and 50 years of age on the average. They may ovulate irregularly at the end of their menstrual lives as well as at the beginning. Women of menopausal age should not rule out the possibility of pregnancy until they have gone for at least one year without a menstrual period. Theoretically, then, a woman might be able to supply a maximum of 550 mature ova for in vitro fertilization but not more than about 40 for normal pregnancies.

The *Guinness Book of World Records* lists a Peruvian girl as the youngest person whose child bearing has been documented (five years, eight months). In the United States, the Bureau of the Census's gross population statistics often posit that the fertile years of a female's life are, on the average, 15 to 44. Women younger than 15 and older than 44 sometimes, however, give birth.

PREGNANCY

Once conception has occurred and there is awareness of the pregnancy (especially the first pregnancy), the lives of the expectant parents begin to change. Their adjustment depends on a variety of factors—whether the pregnancy was planned; their physical and mental health; their financial circumstances; their ages; and, most important, the expectant parents' mutual support and/or the support of significant others such as their families of origin and their close friends.

Expectant Fathers

Traditionally, both men and women have treated pregnancy as a woman's experience even though men are usually intensely emotionally involved with the children they father—as projections of themselves or their dreams, as heirs, or even as adversaries. Traditionally, men were to be supportive of their partners during pregnancy but were not expected, unlike women, to let the experience disrupt their careers. This pattern is changing rapidly; in fact, many employers are now granting paternity leaves (Brazelton 1981, p. 191), which permit the father to be intimately involved with the baby and the child's mother during the immediate postpartum period. In some dual-career families, when maternity/paternity leaves end, some couples opt for the wives to return to their jobs while the husbands assume responsibility for full-time child care.

Jokes are often made about men who are jealous of the attention pregnant women receive. Not infrequently expectant fathers show symptoms of pregnancy such as morning sickness, weight gain, or backache. Some become depressed and share the "baby blues" after the delivery. These symptoms constitute the "pregnant-husband syndrome." Some estimates are that nearly half of all expectant fathers experience some physical or emotional symptom of pregnancy (Davenport 1977). The syndrome is ritualized in some societies where husbands even take to their beds and "experience" birth in the belief that they will lure evil spirits away from the mother (Meigs 1976). This practice is termed **couvade** (Cogan and Hinz 1982).

However unusual (or even amusing) we may find the idea of couvade, child psychologists tell us that a father-to-be who is completely involved with his mate in a pregnancy is more likely to be an involved father. Today's expectant fathers are more likely to become involved before birth than were their fathers through reading about the experience of pregnancy and fetal development, sharing in prenatal care, listening to the baby's heartbeat, talking about (and even to) the baby, participating in childbirth education classes, "nesting"—making practical preparations for the baby's arrival, such as painting or making furniture or toys—and baby-sitting for friends or relatives (Heinowitz 1982).

When an expectant father takes part in preparations for the birth (as in childbirth education classes) and participates in prenatal care and in the birth itself, he is likely to enjoy fathering more and to do a better job of it. Many fathers spend as much of their time alone with infants in touching, talking to, and looking at the babies as do the mothers (Trause, Kennell, and Klaus 1978). This is especially true when there has been a **cesarean delivery** (Cain et al. 1984).

In the Hopkins Study, a pioneering piece of research on couples having their first child, it was reported that fathers who had been present in the delivery room had very positive feelings about the experience. Furthermore, if a man reported that he had been deeply involved and interested in his wife's pregnancy, he was more likely to become an active parent to the baby (holding the infant, for example, or picking up a crying baby). There was also a correlation between how much husbands shared in housework during a pregnancy and how much they held and diapered their babies

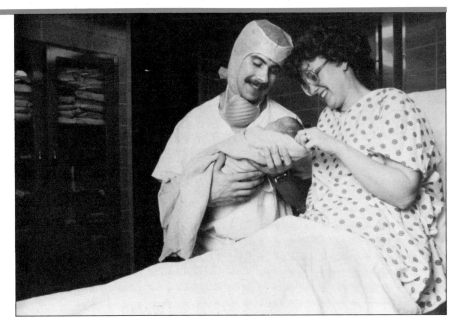

Research has demonstrated the importance to both parents and the newborn of the initial period of attachment that results from allowing the new mother and father to touch and talk to their baby from the moment of birth.

(Doering and Entwisle 1977). There is an encouraging trend toward more involvement of fathers in pregnancy and childbirth; the change is welcomed by most women, and, for those who experience it, it seems bound to change the emotional nature of pregnancy and childbirth for both parents and to have an effect on later family life.

It will always be impossible for an expectant father to experience pregnancy in a physical sense. Listening to the heartbeat or perhaps viewing the fetus during an ultrasound procedure or feeling it move and kick are often the limits of a father's physical experience of his child before birth. This limit to a father's capacity to sense the physical being of his unborn child 24 hours a day may inhibit either parent or both parents from conceptualizing the fetus as just as much the father's as the mother's. The father may unwittingly fail to make attempts to get to know the unborn child.

Recent work by a number of researchers has demonstrated clearly the unique physical and emotional bonding that can occur prenatally between both mother and father and their unborn child. Psychotherapist Thomas E. Dunn (1984, p. 22) uses the term *fetal entrainment* to describe the connection that can exist between both parents and their unborn baby. He encourages communication between parents and their babies during pregnancy as a means of strengthening the family relationship and minimizing the stress that can result from the addition of the child.

Gestation

The average duration of a pregnancy is a little over nine calendar months, or 280 days, from conception. For most women this is the equivalent of ten menstrual cycles. Obstetricians consider a pregnancy to be **40 weeks** of **gestation,** counting from the first day of the woman's last normal menstrual period until birth. The baby's birthday can most easily be estimated by subtracting three months from the first day of the mother's last period and adding ten days. However, only 5 percent of all babies are born on their due dates, and two weeks either side of the estimated date of delivery is considered normal. Most babies are born no more than two to three weeks past their due date, or 41 to 42 weeks of gestation. On the other end of the range, some babies are born as much as three months early, at around 28 weeks. These babies usually require long-term intensive care, and their chances of survival are much less than those of full-term babies.

Pregnancy is divided for convenience into three periods (trimesters), each lasting slightly over thirteen weeks. For many women the first trimester is well along before they know for sure they are pregnant. About 20 percent of pregnant women continue to have some periodic vaginal bleeding, which they may believe to be menstruation; they do not have the clue most women use—a missed menstrual period—to alert them to their pregnancy. Some do not have (or may not notice) other first-trimester changes, such as breast swelling and tenderness, increased frequency of urination, unusual drowsiness or tiredness, or nausea. They may not notice the darkening of the area around the nipple (areola) or Montgomery's tubercles (like big goose bumps in that area). They may attribute any unusual sleepiness and fatigue to overwork or to illness. Most women, however, do notice one or more of the clues; urine or blood tests can confirm their pregnancy as early as the day of the missed menses. It is usually six weeks or more from the beginning of a woman's last period before a physician can confirm her pregnancy by ultrasound or pelvic examination.

Although there are a number of do-it-yourself home pregnancy tests on the market, at least two studies—one at the University of Cincinnati in 1982, and one at Marquette University in 1986—have found that the results are often of questionable accuracy; however, the Cincinnati study reported that the women who used the tests failed to follow directions nearly a third of the time. The U.S. Food and Drug Administration found much lower inaccuracy rates in their laboratory tests of the kits, suggesting that it is not the kits but the users that introduce the errors (Parachini 1986).

The First Trimester

The fertilized ovum (zygote) undergoes cell division and passes into the uterus, where after approximately three days it implants on the uterine wall. Researchers from the National Cancer Institute believe that a special biochemical immunosuppressive agent active at this very early stage prevents the mother's body from rejecting the zygote, which is, in effect, the same as a graft, half of which comes from the father (Silberner 1985b). It is now called an **embryo** and begins to grow at a steady rate, supported by life-giving tissues centered in the placenta (see Figure 10.4). The placenta, connecting the uterine wall to the embryo by the **umbilical cord,** exchanges nutrients and oxygen for the waste products of the embryo. (The placenta is expelled soon after birth.)

During the first trimester, the head, nervous system, internal organs, skeleton, and limbs of the embryo are formed. By the end of eight weeks of pregnancy the embryo takes on a human appearance, and from this time until delivery it is called a **fetus.** It is during this important developmental period that many potential birth defects can be caused by drugs taken by the mother, by her exposure to radiation, or by transmission of some viruses or contagious diseases.

FIGURE 10 • 4

Growth of Human
Embryo and Fetus
from 14 Days to 15
Weeks (Shown
Slightly Smaller Than
Life Size)

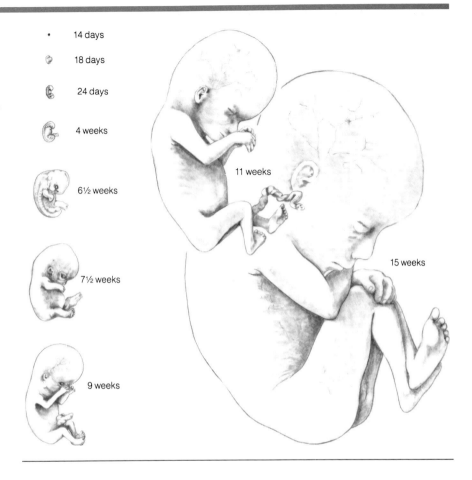

14 days

18 days

24 days

4 weeks

6½ weeks

7½ weeks

9 weeks

11 weeks

15 weeks

Since anything in the bloodstream of a pregnant woman crosses the placenta into the fetus, women who might be pregnant should guard against ingestion of potentially dangerous substances and exposure to infectious diseases or to environmental hazards such as radiation or air pollutants. The likelihood of harmful effects is small (only 3.5 percent of babies are born seriously damaged), but simple precautions by each pregnant woman can increase her chances of having a healthy baby.

Tobacco smoking by an expectant mother does affect the development of her baby. Nicotine and carbon monoxide from cigarette smoke pass into her bloodstream and through the placenta into the baby's. Nicotine constricts the placental blood vessels, impairing the heart rate, nutrient transfer, blood pressure, oxygen supply, and acid balance in the unborn child (Kretzschmar 1978). The effects are increased rates of prematurity, low birth weight, placental separation, stillbirth, and miscarriage.

The effects of maternal smoking continue after birth. The babies of mothers who smoke have a higher death rate in the first month of life and suffer from twice as many respiratory problems during the first year of life. It is also possible, if findings from animal research can be extrapolated to humans, that children of mothers who smoke during pregnancy may have possible memory, learning, and behavioral deficits that may continue into adulthood (Fechter 1984, p. 384).

Recent research points to the ongoing problems related to "passive smoking"—that is, health problems associated with continuous exposure to someone else's smoke. The significantly higher incidence of respiratory problems among children who live with smokers has serious implications for the habits of fathers who smoke as well as for mothers who resume smoking after pregnancy is over (Rowand 1984b).

Caffeine (which is present in coffee, cola drinks, cocoa, and chocolate) and theophylline (which is found in tea) are both stimulants that pass through the placenta to the fetus. Although they have not been shown conclusively to cause serious damage to the fetus, moderate intake at most during pregnancy is suggested as a precautionary measure (*International Journal of Childbirth Education,* May 1986, p. 33).

Birth abnormalities associated with heavy alcohol consumption ("fetal alcohol syndrome") are the third most frequent cause of mental retardation in the United States (Wisconsin Association on Alcoholism and Other Drug Abuse 1984). Even expectant mothers whose alcohol consumption is less cannot consider their babies immune from the potential effects of alcohol. Lesser amounts of alcohol ingestion during pregnancy have been associated by various researchers with other types of malformations, lowered weight for placentas and babies at birth, and such behavioral effects as decreased alertness, increased jitteriness, and sleep and feeding difficulties (Scott 1984, p. 1). How much alcohol is safe during pregnancy? The risk of growth retardation among babies of pregnant women who have one to two drinks per day is reportedly significant (Mills et al. 1984).

It seems clear in light of the available information that pregnant women should stop all alcohol consumption once they suspect that they may be pregnant. In fact, animal studies in England and the United States have shown that chromosomal abnormalities—which are associated with about half of human spontaneous abortions—indicate potential danger to the zygote from as little as a single episode of heavy drinking near the time of conception (J. Miller 1983). To be on the safe side, a woman trying to get pregnant should avoid alcohol; conversely, a woman drinking heavily should avoid coitus without contraception whether she wishes to become pregnant or not.

Any woman who suspects that she is pregnant is advised to check with her health care provider before taking *any* prescription *or* over-the-counter medications. Once the pregnancy is confirmed and she is under medical care, she will be told to avoid all drugs (unless specifically approved), to avoid unnecessary radiation (including X rays), and to be extra conscientious in diet, rest, exercise, and hygiene to maximize her and her baby's health.

There has been a recent tendency to urge exercise as both a cure for many physical problems and a prevention for many. Although a number of studies have reported no increase in infant illnesses or deaths resulting from the expectant mother's physical exercise, others report that vigorous exercise may lead to low birth weight and early delivery. The *ICEA Review* (May 1986, p. 33) concludes:

> Vigorous exercise programs during pregnancy cannot be given an unequivocal "green light." Although many physically fit women will undoubtedly be able to continue (and benefit by) physically demanding training programs during pregnancy, such decisions should be made on a case-by-case basis in consultation with the prenatal care provider.

Pregnant woman should avoid or, where necessary, minimize exposure to contagious diseases. Rubella (German measles), if contracted during the first three months of pregnancy, can cause serious birth defects. Most women, however, have either been immunized against rubella as a child or have had the disease at some time. Exposure to rubella, or to other diseases such as chicken pox, poses no threat to the fetus if the mother is immune. It is important that pregnant women report exposure to other diseases to their health care provider, especially herpes, syphillis, gonorrhea, or chlamydia.

Diabetes occasionally results from hormonal changes during pregnancy. About 90 percent of the cases can be treated with dietary changes; 10 percent require medication. Johns Hopkins University recommends screening all pregnant women over 24 years old for the possibility (*Science News*, May 18, 1985, p. 312).

It is probably prudent for a pregnant woman to avoid contact with potentially toxic fumes of either a household or industrial nature. The effects on the pregnancy and the fetus cannot always be determined, but avoiding exposure eliminates any possible risks.

A number of medical procedures may also carry some risk for the fetus. In such instances the risks must be weighed against the benefits in deciding whether to undergo the procedure. X rays, for example, cannot be guaranteed to be safe for the unborn child. It is best, therefore, to avoid any nonessential X ray (such as routine dental X rays) until after the pregnancy. Amniocentesis or chorionic villi biopsy (CVB) may be indicated where the risk of birth defects is significant or to assess fetal maturity or in cases of Rh sensitization. But because they are invasive techniques that involve penetration of the sterile environment of the uterus, they are not options solely for the purpose of determining the sex of the fetus.

CVB may replace amniocentesis as a test for genetic defects. CVB involves passing a catheter through the woman's cervix to take a small sample of tissue. Indications are that this test is as safe as amniocentesis, but additional years of testing will be necessary to establish its safety completely (*Science News*, August 20, 1983, p. 116).

The use of diagnostic ultrasound as an obstetrical procedure has increased markedly since 1970. There is considerable debate concerning the risks and benefits of what has in some places become a routine procedure. As an alternative to X ray, ultrasound allows the fetus to be "seen", which is both diagnostically useful and, at the same time, exciting for the parents. Although questions of long-term safety have not yet been answered, there are specific instances in which the potential risks would seem to outweigh the benefits; these would include ultrasounds done merely to see the baby move or to determine the baby's sex. On the other hand, there may be specific medical indications for ultrasound examination: fetal size that does not correspond with the woman's dates, suspected fetal or placental abnormalities, multiple pregnancy, miscarriage, pelvic masses, or abnormal position of the baby, for example (*ICEA News*, May 1983, pp. 1–7).

Psychological Problems   By the end of the first trimester, most women feel well and have begun to work through some of the early feelings of depression or anxiety they may have had. For all women, being pregnant creates ambivalence and takes getting used to. A woman may have to contend with drowsiness or morning sickness or both. The pregnancy may have been unplanned, or the mother-to-be may have doubts about the effects of the pregnancy on her career, about how she will manage as a mother, or about how the baby will affect her relationship with the baby's father.

Part of a woman's anxiety may be related to how the father-to-be is adjusting to pregnancy and to the prospect of parenthood. For him, too, the early weeks of pregnancy may be a time of adjustment. He may be expected to provide physical support (ranging from assuming some of the expectant mother's usual tasks to exercising with her) during a time when the mother-to-be is coping with uncomfortable body changes, as well as emotional support to help her deal with her pregnancy-related anxieties. At the same time, he may be having difficulty coping with his own pregnancy adjustment—anticipating with some apprehension his new role as father, his added long-term responsibilities, and increased pressures on his time and energies.

The couple may notice a change in their sexual relationship during the first trimester. Although this is often attributed to the nausea, drowsiness, hormonal changes, and other physical symptoms of the early part of pregnancy, it may be influenced just as greatly by the emotional changes and anxieties that the couple is experiencing. Couples should expect decreases in sexual enjoyment, coital frequency, and female orgasm as pregnancy progresses. In early pregnancy, women who have not previously given birth report a greater frequency of orgasm than women who have. Overall sexual satisfaction has been found to be significantly higher for women who are not unhappy about being pregnant. Possible consequences of restrictions on sexual expression are extramarital liaisons by the husband and the emotional isolation of either spouse (Reamy et al. 1982, p. 326). These negative effects are most likely to be found among couples who did not want to become pregnant and who, perhaps for religious, moral, or aesthetic reasons, feel that their sexual interaction must be limited to coitus.

Some time before the end of the first trimester, most women have chosen the physician or midwife whom they want to provide their prenatal care and assist in the birth of their child. Their care includes regular prenatal visits, routine tests, and monitoring of fetal growth. In addition, they may receive counseling about diet during pregnancy, exercise, weight gain, the options for birth, breastfeeding and other relevant topics. Identification of high-risk pregnancies by the twelfth week of gestation, followed by special treatment programs, has been shown to reduce the incidence of preterm delivery by more than half in one major teaching hospital (Arehart-Treichel 1982).

Richard E. Behrman, chair of the Institute of Medicine Committee of the National Academy of Sciences, reported that the entire cost of prenatal care for a woman is less than that of a single day of hospitalization in the intensive care nursery for a low-birth-weight infant. Behrman designated a 1.4 million population of women in the United States at highest risk for having low birth weight (6.8 percent of live births, proportionately more than in at least twelve other developed countries), to be found among "teenagers, unmarried women, the poor, black women and those with less than a high school education" (Miller 1985, p. 134).

The Second Trimester

The second trimester is marked by the beginning of the mother's awareness of fetal movement (quickening), usually somewhere between seventeen and twenty weeks. A human fetus is about 6 ¾ inches long at sixteen weeks and may reach more than a foot in length by the end of the second trimester, with a weight gain from a few ounces to as much as two pounds. The fetal heartbeat can now be heard with instruments, and its eyes are open. The mother-to-be looks pregnant and usually begins to wear maternity clothes. Some women begin to complain about feeling unattractive or clumsy, but most complaints in the second trimester are relatively minor.

By the second trimester, many pregnant women begin to gain weight. They will be less concerned about this gain if they understand that it results not only from the growing fetus, but also from uterine and breast enlargement, the placenta, amniotic fluid, and the significantly increased blood volume necessary to provide nutrients and oxygen to the growing fetus. Although some women and their doctors still worry about weight gain, most health care providers now feel that a weight gain of 25–30 pounds added gradually throughout the pregnancy is desirable. Many experts feel that if a woman eats a well-balanced nutritional diet regularly according to her own appetite, weight gain will not be a problem.

Recent research indicating that total maternal weight gain of less than fifteen pounds may be harmful to a developing fetus has lifted the burden of striving for minimal weight gain from most pregnant women. (Thirty years ago women were cautioned to keep their weight gain to no more than fifteen pounds, or about double the birth weight of an average baby.)

During the second trimester, the fatigue and malaise of the first trimester may have ended, and some women have increased energy. As a result, there is typically a marked gain in sexual desire over the low of the first trimester, although not back to prepregnancy levels (Reamy et al. 1982, p. 323). This may be due in part to increased blood circulation in the pelvic area. Pregnancy enhances normal pelvic **vasocongestion,** increasing warmth, lubrication, and sensitivity during sexual arousal.

The degree of sexual interest varies from woman to woman, just as at any other time, and is dependent on how the woman views the pregnancy and her relationship with her sexual partner.

Deep-seated attitudes about sex may be intensified during pregnancy. Women who feel that sex is dirty or sinful may now feel that they have added justification for rejecting their husbands; women who feel that sex is symbolic of love and unity may find security in it; women who feel that sexual interaction is a natural, delightful game may intensify their flirtatiousness.

The way a woman thinks of her body during pregnancy has a great effect on her sexual interest and on what she perceives her partner's interest to be. Is her body fat and ugly? Is it feminine, sensual, fulfilled? Is the woman glowing with good health, or is she sick?

The way people feel about their sexual selves is always dependent on their interpretations of potential partners' responses to them. A woman who believes (correctly or incorrectly) that her partner does not find her sexually attractive will respond by either repressing her interest in sexual interaction or finding a partner who does find her sexually attractive. Traditionally, "proper" pregnant women will do the former. If her partner seems more interested in the baby than in *her,* she may respond by taking a mother role rather than a lover role.

However the expectant mother and her partner feel about their sexual relationship during their pregnancy, communication is of prime importance. It is easy for either partner to mistake the message "I am not interested in sexual activity" for "I do not love you." It is equally important for the couple to communicate about how they will express their sexual feelings since the type of lovemaking that was comfortable before pregnancy may not be practical or comfortable as the pregnancy progresses. A couple with good communication skills can find mutually satisfying ways of maintaining a good sexual relationship during the middle months of pregnancy.

Most pregnant working women continue on their jobs until the end of the second trimester. A few continue throughout the pregnancy, although many women want time to prepare for the birth. Depending on the nature of their work, some women are obliged to quit working because of fatigue, which is accentuated by the added weight they are carrying. Some experts believe that continuing to work is an indication of good health during pregnancy. The president of a chain of maternity clothes shops has reported that sales rose 21 percent from 1979 to 1980. He attributed this to the growing number of pregnant working women who want to be fashionably dressed and who have more money to spend on clothes than they would if they were not working (*Marriage and Divorce Today*, July 28, 1980, p. 2).

The Third Trimester

The fetus is surrounded by amniotic fluid that protects it from infection, acts as a temperature regulator and a shock absorber, and serves as a medium for collecting fetal wastes. From the beginning of the third trimester, the fetus displaces an increasing amount of fluid in the **amniotic sac;** the fluid is either absorbed by the fetus or discharged through the placenta into the mother's system.

Early in the third trimester of pregnancy, the woman's pelvis begins to widen in order to accommodate the passage of the fetus through her pelvic girdle, causing her leg bones to rotate slightly outward in her hip joints. This results in the "duck waddle" walk characteristic of many pregnant women. This loosening of the pelvic joints, along with the change in her center of gravity, may also result in clumsiness or the feeling that her legs may not support her. Urination is more frequent in the third trimester of pregnancy because the bladder is crowded by the growing uterus. As the baby grows, the enlarging uterus fills more and more of the abdominal cavity, and the mother may suffer from heartburn, finding that she needs to eat smaller amounts more frequently instead of three full meals a day. She may also be bothered with backache as the baby descends into the pelvis and its increasing weight puts more and more pressure on her spine. She will need to experiment to find comfortable positions for sleeping that minimize back pressure.

At one time some doctors recommended that sexual intercourse cease during the third trimester of pregnancy in the belief that some damage might occur to the amniotic sac, if not to the fetus itself. Others feared that infection might result if the male's mouth, hands, or penis was not properly clean. Today, such precautions are usually advised only if there has been any vaginal bleeding, leaking of amniotic fluid, a history of premature births, or threatened premature labor.

Sexual activity often declines near the end of pregnancy. Many women report a sharp drop in sexual interest late in the third trimester, and most report that there is no physically comfortable position for coitus. There are, of course, many ways other than coitus for couples to achieve physical and emotional intimacy. This requires, however, open communication between partners and a willingness to experiment with new ways of meeting each other's changing needs for emotional closeness and sexual pleasure. Failure to make these adjustments can be a problem; the expectant mother misses the emotional support and physical affection that she needs, and her partner may have unrelieved sexual tensions unless she is willing to help meet his needs or he finds some outlet (such as masturbation) that does not involve her (Butler, Reisner, and Wagner 1979).

By the end of the third trimester, the fetus has grown gradually to its full size (twenty inches, seven and a half pounds, on average, although the first baby may be smaller). Its skin has smoothed out from its earlier wrinkled state and is covered with a creamy coating (**vernix caseosa**) for protection. Hair, fingernails, and toenails are obvious. The fetus settles into position for birth (normally head down), and it shifts lower in the abdomen, an indication that birth is approaching.

CHILDBIRTH

No two childbirths are alike. Not only is the experience different for different women, but each woman finds that each birth experience is unique. For one thing, labor and birth usually are longer for the first child. In addition, the size and position of the baby, the mother's muscle tone, her general physical and mental health, and the management of her labor all cause variations. Despite the dissimilarities, however, births follow a recognizable pattern.

During the last weeks of pregnancy, changes take place in a pregnant woman's body that may indicate to her that birth is approaching. Some women feel the baby's descent into the pelvis—"lightening" or "engagement"—as the baby gets into position for birth and the uterus readies itself for labor. They may notice the loss of the mucous plug ("bloody show") that has served as a barrier to infection in the opening of the uterus (the cervix). There may be increased pressure and backache as the baby shifts lower and exerts more pressure on the spine and more pull on the ligaments supporting the uterus. They may also feel more frequent contractions, tightenings of the uterine muscle that help ready the uterus for labor while making some of the changes that must occur before birth.

Labor

The end of a normal pregnancy is signaled by the beginning of labor. Labor is usually described as a process of three stages, although some term the immediate postpartum period as the fourth stage of labor. The *first stage* is marked by dilation (opening up) and effacement (thinning out) of the cervix, the lower portion of the uterus (see Figure 10.5). These changes must occur in order for the baby to be able to leave the uterus and begin moving down the vagina or birth canal, which occurs during the *second stage* of labor. The second stage ends with the birth of the baby. The *third stage* is the expulsion of the placenta.

The First Stage   The first stage of labor is usually described as being composed of three phases: latent, active, and transition.

During the *latent* phase, the mother's cervix usually begins to efface and dilate as a result of uterine contractions. Initially, the expectant mother may feel the contractions as cramps, abdominal tightening, backache, or even indigestion. But, unlike

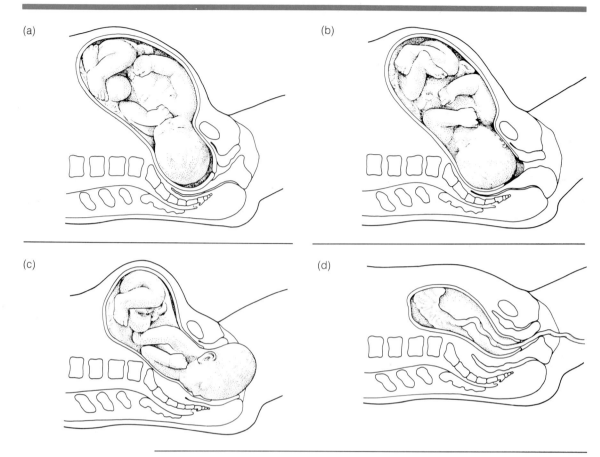

FIGURE 10 • 5

Birth Process (a) The most common fetal position when labor begins; (b) the early contractions of labor are accompanied by dilation of the cervix; (c) the baby crowns as its head appears in the mother's vulva; (d) the placenta remains to be delivered after the baby is born.

the other times she may have experienced these symptoms, during labor they come and go, usually at increasingly shorter intervals as time passes. In addition, these sensations gradually become stronger and last for longer periods of time, with shorter rests in between. Although she is "in labor," she may find it comfortable to continue her normal activities during this latent phase, only pausing to time her contractions in an effort to help her determine whether active labor has begun.

During the *active* phase of labor, the mother's contractions may become more regular. Certainly they are stronger and last longer. These contractions accomplish further dilation as the baby moves even deeper into the pelvis. The woman may now find it difficult to relax, and control of her responses begins to be less voluntary. If she has participated in childbirth preparation classes, she finds that the help of her labor partner can be invaluable in seeing that she is comfortable, as well as in helping her relax and utilize the breathing patterns that she has learned in her classes. She needs to remember to change positions frequently, and unless she's very tired, she may find that an upright position will encourage her labor to progress. Most women go to a hospital or alternative birth facility during this phase.

Transition is the last and most intense phase of the first stage of labor. As the cervix completes its dilation, the mother's contractions may last from 60 to 90 seconds each, and she may have as little as 30 to 60 seconds rest between them. A variety of other symptoms may occur during transition: nausea; increased sensitivity to heat, cold, lights, sounds, or touch; backaches or leg aches; trembling; and rectal pressure—among others. Because of the intensity of what she is feeling, she may want to give up and go home; she may become angry, discouraged, and fearful; and she may need all the support her labor partner can provide to help her cope with her contractions.

Although it is the most intense, this phase is also the shortest. For mothers having their first babies, labor averages between ten and sixteen hours, although there is tremendous individual variation. Transition for many mothers lasts only half an hour to two hours. During this phase, dilation of the cervix is completed—to ten centimeters, or about four inches. If it has not already done so, the amniotic sac will usually break or be ruptured by obstetrical attendants. Although this is not a painful procedure, since there are no nerve endings in the sac, the contractions that follow are usually felt more strongly, since the shock absorber provided by the fluid is gone.

It may be during the active or transition phase that the mother will consider medication or anesthesia to help her cope with her labor. Although many women find that they are able to cope with labor without medication, there are instances of tension and fatigue in which medication or anesthesia helps the labor move along more quickly, with the mother more relaxed and in greater control of her contractions. By and large, general anesthesia is not used today for normal vaginal births; most mothers prefer to be awake and aware during the birth of their babies.

Few physicians, midwives, or hospitals use medications routinely; it is often left to the mother to request medication should she feel it necessary. In making this choice, expectant parents should consider carefully both the benefits and the risks of any medication or anesthesia. Many medications given to the mother cross the placenta to the baby and have varying effects on the level of pain relief and ability to relax, the progress of the labor, and the well-being of the baby.

In the Hopkins Study, it was determined that the more drugs a woman is given during delivery, the worse she feels physically and emotionally immediately after the birth. In the ninth month, half of the women interviewed who eventually had normal deliveries hoped "to be awake and feeling everything," but only 50 percent of them actually were. Nearly as many (43 percent) expressed the desire to be "awake but numb." Only half of them were. About 30 percent were numb or sedated to the point that they were not aware of what was going on, which was not what any of them had said they wanted (Doering and Entwisle 1977).

With the current emphasis on improved communication, there is an increasing incidence of informed choice by expectant parents in consultation with their medical care givers. Thus, it is becoming increasingly possible for pregnant women to have, under normal circumstances, the kinds of births they hope for. Among the options open to them is, in many locales, the type of birth location. Most babies in the United States are born in hospitals; lesser numbers are born in freestanding or hospital-based birth centers; others are born at home. Even within a hospital setting, parents are often given the choice, assuming the birth is normal, of delivering in the traditional delivery room or in a birthing room. The birthing room is intended to be less like a hospital operating room and more like a home environment, while still providing immediate access to necessary medical technology. It also means that a woman can labor, birth, and recover in the same room without making one or more moves during the labor.

In many places, laboring couples can choose whom they would like to be present for the birth. In some cases siblings of the new baby attend the birth, and more frequently, the baby's grandparents or other relatives or friends may be asked to attend. In other cases the couple's childbirth educator or a *monitrice* (a trained labor partner) attends to offer added support for the couple.

The Second Stage   The second stage of labor, expulsion, begins when dilation is complete and the baby begins to leave the uterus and move down the vagina or birth canal. This calls for active participation by the mother and her partner, as the mother works with her contractions to push the baby down and out. Most women, especially those who have not had anesthesia, experience an urge to push, which results from the pressure of the baby's head toward the pelvic floor. For many women it feels satisfying to push, although for some it is painful; most find that it is the hardest work they have ever done. Expulsion usually takes about an hour for women having their first babies, although there is wide variation. Once the top of the baby's head is visible, the woman is prepared for the birth by her birth attendants.

If the baby's head and shoulders are so large that they threaten to tear tissues or muscles at the external opening of the vagina, a local anesthesia is used, and a small surgical incision (an **episiotomy**) is made to enlarge it. Then the baby can emerge without injury to the mother. After an episiotomy, a few pushes usually completes the delivery, and sutures can easily close the incision. Often, however, with controlled pushing by the woman and assistance from the doctor or midwife, episiotomy is unnecessary, especially if birth is in a squatting position.

In some cases, a vaginal birth is not possible, and a *cesarean delivery* through an incision in the walls of the abdomen and the uterus is necessary. Either the fetal head is too large to pass through the pelvis or the baby is in such a position that it will not pass through the pelvis. For example, the baby may be in *breech presentation* (that is, positioned head up). Sometimes an infection such as herpes (a virus that spreads easily and could infect the baby) is present in the genitalia.

> One-third of the newborns afflicted with equally dangerous Herpes I or Herpes II virus die from the illness, and another one-fourth suffer brain damage. The vast majority [who acquire it] acquire the disease at birth as they pass through an infected mother's birth canal. . . . An obstetrician alerted to the danger can deliver the baby by cesarean section. . . . But occasionally the episodes are not accompanied by obvious symptoms, and are probably the source for most cases of neonatal herpes, the scientists say. (*Science News*, December 24, 1983, p. 412)

Sometimes labor fails to progress as it should, and sometimes there are signs of fetal distress during labor, which indicate the need for the baby to be born as quickly as possible. In such cases, a cesarean birth is necessary to deliver the baby.

Cesarean delivery is considered major surgery, but, for the expectant couple, it is also the birth of their child. General or regional anesthesia is necessary, and except in emergencies, the parents often participate in the choice. With a regional anesthesia, the mother is numb from just below her breasts, but she remains awake. Although she does not view the surgery itself, she is able to see her baby as soon as it is born and often touch him or her even before the surgery is completed. Increasingly, fathers or other labor partners are choosing to be present for their children's cesarean births. Thus, regardless of the method of delivery, the birth becomes a shared family experience (Cain et al. 1984; Mutryn 1984, 1986).

After a cesarean birth, the mother usually requires as long a recovery period as she would for any other major surgery. Some women have more than one cesarean delivery, especially if the condition that necessitated the first cesarean is still present in a subsequent pregnancy. If the problem is not present again, the chances for a vaginal delivery in the future are good.

A minority of births are considered to require cesarean deliveries. The procedure is actually performed in approximately 16.5 percent of all births, with some teaching hospitals reporting an even higher rate—up to 40 percent (Mutryn 1984, p. 4). There is considerable controversy about whether the problems in such a high percentage of deliveries warrant this kind of intervention (Leveno, Cunningham, and Pritchard 1985; Young and Mahan 1980). On the other hand, obstetricians are reluctant to risk neurological damage to the baby from a difficult vaginal delivery, prolonged fetal distress, or a herpes-infected baby, or the malpractice suits that might result from them. In the Hopkins Study, nearly 18 percent of the mothers experienced cesarean deliveries. Only one of these cesareans was anticipated prior to the start of labor (Doering and Entwisle 1977).

The Third Stage   The *third stage* of labor occurs with the expulsion of the placenta After the delivery, the umbilical cord is cut. The placenta begins to separate from the uterine wall as the uterus continues to contract. Most women, excited by the birth of their babies and fatigued from the labor, pay little attention to this stage of labor, since the contractions will not feel nearly as intense as the earlier ones. As the placenta separates, the physician or midwife may simply ask the mother to bear down and push with a contraction to expel the placenta (the "afterbirth"). This process is usually uncomplicated and is completed in half an hour or less.

The *fourth stage* of labor is the onset of **involution** of the uterus. It is sometimes described as the immediate postpartum period when the mother is monitored carefully to make sure that her blood pressure is stable, her uterus is continuing to contract, and her bleeding is within normal limits.

Assuming that the baby was examined shortly after birth and was found to be in good health, parents who deliver in facilities that stress family-centered maternity care are able to spend the next couple of hours getting acquainted with their new family member. Contrary to earlier suppositions, newborn babies are often very alert and responsive in the first hour or two of life.

Unexpected Circumstances

In a small number of cases the newborn (**neonate**) needs expert medical attention supplied by hospitals and birthing clinics. For instance, a premature birth occurs for about 7 out of every 100 babies and is most likely to occur with a firstborn (Hurlock

1972, p. 87). Premature infants have more difficulty making postnatal adjustments in breathing, temperature regulation, and ability to suck. They are more vulnerable to infection because of their small sizes and relatively underdeveloped neurological systems.

Premature babies or other newborns with health problems are often taken to the hospital's intensive care nursery for special monitoring and treatment. This unexpected circumstance may be difficult for the new parents to cope with since it rarely meets their expectations about the birth and the immediate postpartum period. Intensive care nurseries now have open parent visiting and encourage as much participation in the baby's care as his or her condition warrants. This offers the new parents the chance to become acquainted with and begin bonding to their new babies in spite of the unexpected circumstances (Klaus and Kennell 1983a, pp. 93–139).

Blood incompatibility between the mother and the baby may require monitoring during pregnancy. When the mother's blood does not contain the **Rh factor** (a substance present in the blood of about 85 percent of the Caucasian population), she is classified as Rh-negative. If the father is Rh-positive, the baby will most likely be Rh-positive. The mother's blood will develop antibodies against the alien Rh-positive blood of the fetus and begin to destroy its red blood cells, and the baby will be born severely jaundiced. In the past, the newborn baby's blood had to be completely replaced to survive. Fortunately, an Rh-immune globulin has been developed to administer to the Rh-negative mother during the twenty-eighth to thirty-second weeks of each pregnancy or immediately after the birth of each baby; it suppresses the action of the antibodies.

Multiple gestations may receive special management. Because these babies are often born two, three, or more weeks premature, they may be smaller than average. Also, they may be positioned in such a way that cesarean delivery is necessary. Twins occur about once in every 85 to 90 deliveries. They may be **monozygotic** (one fertilized egg splits, giving each twin identical genetic material) or **dizygotic** (two eggs, each fertilized by different sperm cells). In the former case, the babies are *identical twins,* and in the latter, the babies are no more alike than any other two siblings and are called *fraternal twins.*

Triplets are born only once in 8,000 or 9,000 deliveries, and quadruplets only once in 500,000. Quintuplets or sextuplets are even rarer, although increased use of fertility drugs such as Clomid (which stimulates ovulation of more than one egg) has resulted in more multiple births recently (Menning 1977).

Multiple gestations are usually diagnosed sometime prior to delivery. Careful monitoring during prenatal care indicates a larger than average size of the mother's uterus for her length of gestation. Ultrasound examination can confirm the presence of more than one fetus. As the pregnancy progresses, additional ultrasound examinations can reveal if normal growth of both or all babies is occurring and, closer to the time of delivery, provide information on the exact positions of the babies.

Thus, most expectant parents have some warning that they will have more than one baby, allowing them time to plan for the unexpected increase in family size. They will have an opportunity to plan ways in which they can offer the physical and emotional support to each other that this sudden change will require and time to establish a good support system among their friends and families.

The maternal and infant mortality rates in the United States have dropped considerably in recent years, largely as a result of the availability of competent and

Monozygotic twins may be identical in every respect or one may be a mirror image of the other, depending on how the nucleus of their zygote split.

immediate medical care for births that are not routine, such as cesarean deliveries. Hospitals, advanced medical techniques, and lifesaving equipment are probably *essential* for very few childbirths. It is estimated that 90 percent of deliveries need little routine medical intervention in the normal birth process (Arms 1975).

Many of the hospital procedures necessary in emergencies are thought to interfere with normal birth. For instance, when the mother-to-be lies flat on her back during labor, she is working against gravity, as well as causing a decrease in maternal and fetal blood pressure that can be dangerous to the baby. Before the mid-nineteenth century in Western civilization—and still in many societies—women sat or squatted during labor to take advantage of the pull of gravity. A number of birthing facilities— for example, Michel Odent's birth center at Pithviers, France, and Michael Rosenthal's in Upland, California—currently use a variation of the squatting position. In the United States birthing chairs or beds that allow delivery in a more upright position are being used in many facilities. In addition, birthing women are being given more freedom to choose their own birthing positions and to change those positions as the labor progresses.

Queen Victoria of England is credited with the first use of a drug (chloroform) to ease the pain of birth. Since that time a variety of drugs have been given, sometimes routinely, to women before and during delivery, with a variety of problems resulting. Most research shows that drugs given before and during delivery affect the fetus and the delivery process itself. Some may lengthen labor; others lower the blood pressure and heart rate; certain drugs inhibit the mother's urge and ability to push during labor; and still other medications affect the baby's respiratory system and oxygen supply (Scanlon 1974). On the other hand, medication or anesthesia may provide welcome relief for the discomfort of labor—and, of course, is absolutely necessary for cesarean birth. Judicious use of medication may help a woman whose tension is interfering with the progress of her labor to relax so that labor will continue to progress normally.

In most parts of the United States medication and anesthesia are not used routinely for normal birth. Each labor is evaluated on an individual basis, taking into account the mother's feelings about the use of drugs and her ability to cope with labor using other methods.

Fetal monitoring has been of great importance in high-risk pregnancies, but its increasingly routine use in normal deliveries has been roundly criticized by some as a major interference in the birth process (Corea 1977). When the monitoring is done by attaching electronic devices to the mother's abdomen by straps, she may be required to lie still, on her back, for long periods of time. This can be uncomfortable and can cause circulation problems that may in turn decrease the oxygen supply to the fetus (Arms 1975).

Finally, forceps (tong-shaped instruments), which came to be needed as an aid in pulling the baby out in a slow or difficult delivery, are still used when medication either reduces the strength of the contraction, when there is fetal distress, or when the mother is too exhausted to push. Because of the risk of injury to the baby, the use of foreceps is not routine. They are no longer used so much to pull the baby out as to direct the baby's route and to guide the head and shoulders through the passage quickly. Some hospitals now use a suction cup device applied to the baby's head for the same purpose.

Changing Birth Practice

Recent critics of the "medical model" of childbirth (in which the mother is treated as a surgical patient) have encouraged a return to the natural birth process. European countries began the movement toward natural childbirth with medical intervention only when necessary. This change has perhaps been most noticeable in childbirthing clinics that use trained midwives for delivery with physicians on call if needed (Norwood 1978).

Although only about 2 percent of all births in the United States occurred in hospitals in 1920, 99 percent did by 1982. It appears that this rate has remained relatively stable since 1976 (*Los Angeles Times,* November 16, 1982, Part V, p. 15), despite the publicity received by those for and against home births and the increasing number of out-of-hospital birth centers. Such birth centers have been established, often to provide homelike alternatives with medical backup to home births. Alternative birth centers stress family-centered care, encouraging the expectant parents to have family and friends present if they wish. In some states, certified nurse-midwives staff birth centers and deliver babies, although other states require physician attendance at all institutional births. In some states home births can be legally attended by lay midwives; the practice is illegal in other locales. Although 95 percent of all births are uncomplicated, lay midwives sometimes have difficulty securing emergency medical care for their clients when complications arise. In recent years some have been subject to civil and criminal legal actions.

Other changes have influenced the increased interest in natural birth. There has in recent years been a growth in popularity of **prepared childbirth.**

In 1932 British physician Grantly Dick-Read began to question the widespread use of anesthesia to modify pain during childbirth (Dick-Read 1944). He attributed the extreme pain suffered by many women during the birth process to fear, which made them so tense that their pain was increased. He believed that ignorance often hindered the birth process, sometimes prolonging it and certainly magnifying the mother's discomfort. He pioneered a method of "natural childbirth" based on the philosophy that if a woman understands what is happening to her during childbirth, she will be less afraid and less tense and, consequently, will experience less pain. She will need little if any anesthesia and will be much more able to participate actively in the birth process.

Preparation for childbirth has gradually been accepted by parents-to-be and the medical profession. As recently as the mid-1960s, relatively few couples availed themselves of childbirth education classes, and physicians and hospitals were frequently reluctant to cooperate with those who did.

Since the early years of the childbirth education movement, other methodologies have evolved, based on the works of increasing numbers of educators, researchers, and practitioners. In addition to the Dick-Read method, expectant parents can now find classes based on the Lamaze (1970) method (psychoprophylaxsis), Bradley's (1962) husband-coached childbirth, and Kitzinger's (1972) psychosexual approach, to name only a few.

Regardless of the method, childbirth education, which is intended for the expectant mother and father (or other support persons) has become an important part of prenatal care. Classes taken in the weeks before the expected delivery date teach them what to expect during the birth process and how to cope with it (Lamaze 1970). Exercises, relaxation, breathing techniques and comfort measures are explained as ways of working with the laboring woman to minimize pain and allow her body to work efficiently. A number of other topics may also be discussed in childbirth education, including hospital and birth center policies and procedures, planning for birth based on available options, breastfeeding, parenting, problem labors, and sexuality.

▌ BONDING

A strong argument for natural childbirth over anesthetized delivery is that a great deal of evidence suggests that early contact between mother and infant is extremely important in affecting the way that a mother grows to feel about her child. Placing the newborn in an alert mother's arms or on her abdomen is thought to release feelings in her that strongly favor maternal attachment.

A famous study compared infants who had immediate contact with their mothers after birth with those who were treated in the pattern developed during the 1920s, when fear of infection led hospitals to isolate babies in aseptic nurseries, sometimes for several days. Marshall Klaus and John Kennell (1983a) demonstrated that babies who had immediate contact with their mothers—holding, vocalizing, rocking, kissing—cried less and smiled more. Other research has shown that newborns respond to sound and to movement. They are especially responsive to touch and to nursing at the mother's breast; the warmth of the mother's body and her rhythmic heartbeat and breathing are comfortably familiar (Spezzano and Waterman 1977, p. 110). The mother's alertness and readiness for such stimulation following delivery can be seriously impeded by anesthesia. Also, newborn infants may be drowsy if they have been exposed to anesthetics and thus may be less able to take part in this earliest of bonding experiences.

The mother who has been awake during the delivery, along with her husband or other labor partner, shares the moment of birth, witnesses her child's first breath, and hears his or her first cry. The parents are able to touch and hold their child and begin an enduring relationship as they start to know each other as a family.

This is not to imply that mothers who must have anesthesia cannot have adequate attachment to their babies. Bonding begins at birth, but it does not end there. The first weeks of life leave ample time for the closeness and attachment to form so that mothers whose initial contact is postponed by prematurity, cesarian sections, or otherwise difficult births should not be made anxious that their babies will suffer irreparably.

In the past, the traditional hospital routine after a normal delivery might have been the following: the umbilical cord was clamped and cut and the baby taken by a nurse to a far corner of the delivery room. The infant was checked carefully to be certain that air passages were clear (the old favorite technique was to hold the baby upside down by the feet and slap its back to elicit crying). Tests for vital signs— muscle tone, body color, heart rate, respiration, and reflexes—were administered. A rating scale (called the Apgar scale) was used to rate each of these five conditions as zero, one, or two (Apgar 1953). A total score lower than three was cause for great concern. A score of seven or more was considered to indicate a normal, healthy baby. Silver nitrate or an antibiotic was then dropped into the infant's eyes to counter infection (especially gonorrhea). An identification bracelet was snapped on the baby's ankle, and a matching one on the mother's wrist. A footprint may have been taken to ensure that no mistake could be made about the identity of the baby. The baby was shown to the mother (if she were awake); wrapped in a blanket; and taken to the nursery to be weighed and measured. There the father got his first look at the new arrival through a window.

In an attempt to humanize this method of hospital delivery, which prevailed for the past 50 years, birthing clinics and many hospitals have made significant progress toward family-centered maternity care. The infant may be given to the mother to hold even before the umbilical cord is cut. The father is present and is involved in welcoming the baby. After the cord is cut, a routine examination is made, and the necessary identification processes take place. Then mother, father, and baby are allowed to remain together. Necessary examinations, weighing, measuring, and the like are done at the mother's bedside. Mother and father are allowed to hold the baby as soon as these procedures are complete; breastfeeding is encouraged, and other family members may visit the new family. "Rooming-in" allows the mother and father to hold and care for the infant from the beginning.

A recent variation on this new treatment of the birth process focuses on the neonate and was pioneered by French physician Frederick Le Boyer (1975). His method attempts to make the transition from the womb less traumatic for the baby by the use of gentle handling, soft lights, lowered voices, immediate skin contact with the mother, and a warm bath.

Husband presence during a woman's labor has become increasingly usual since 1950. A study supported by the National Institute of Mental Health has reported that one-to-one support during labor leads to less pain for the mother, more positive feelings about the labor by both mother and father, and perhaps a reduction in cesarean delivery rates (Cogan and Hinz 1984).

Research by Klaus and Kennell (1976, 1983) has demonstrated the importance both to parents and to babies of the initial period of bonding, or attachment. Parents allowed to remain with their babies during this period can touch, hold, talk to, and establish eye contact with their new babies; mothers have an opportunity to begin to learn the art of breastfeeding if the couples chooses.

The bonding process is a continuous one. It is not limited to the first hours after birth, but many new parents feel that it is important to begin it early. Indeed, Klaus and Kennell (1983a) indicate that there can be long-range effects on the parenting behavior of both mothers and fathers when early interactions with their newborns have been rewarding.

▎ BREASTFEEDING

As interest in the natural birth process has increased in the United States, there has been a renewed interest in breastfeeding. Today's families are increasingly considering the positive aspects of breastfeeding for both parents and babies.

The benefits of breastfeeding for the baby are enormous, and there are advantages for its mother and father as well. Human milk is nutritionally ideal for a human baby. It is not high in fat. By keeping excessive fat cells from being laid down in the child's body, it may help prevent adult obesity. Both breastmilk and **colostrum**—the fluid produced by the breast before **lactation** (the production of milk) begins—contain antibodies that help protect the infant from a variety of diseases. Breastfed babies have fewer digestive upsets, fewer allergies, and fewer respiratory infections than those who are bottle fed (Nelson, Vaughn, and McKay 1969).

Breast milk is always available in adequate supply provided the mother understands the supply-and-demand principle of milk production and nurses her baby regularly while drinking plenty of fluids, eating a well-balanced diet, and getting adequate rest. Breastfeeding is convenient. There are no formulas to mix or heat at 2:00 A.M., no bottles to carry when going out, and no worry about sterilization or refrigeration. Economic considerations may be important for couples on limited budgets. Breast milk is free, and breastfeeding eliminates the need to purchase large supplies of bottles and other feeding paraphernalia.

Breast milk is the only nutrition that most babies need for the first four to six months, and because it contains a high percentage of water, supplemental bottles of water are usually completely unnecessary. By the time solid foods are added to the baby's diet, his or her digestive system is more likely to tolerate other foods, and physical development will allow the baby to adapt to spoon feeding.

For the breastfeeding mother, early and frequent nursing causes the uterus to contract and speeds involution, the return to its prepregnant size. Breastfeeding also suppresses ovulation and delays the resumption of the woman's menstrual periods. She should not, however, consider breastfeeding as a method of birth control since she will most likely ovulate once before having a period. Some studies indicate that sexual interest returns sooner in women who breastfeed, and some report that breastfeeding provides physically pleasurable sensations (Masters and Johnson 1966).

Important considerations about breastfeeding have to do with the development of maternal feelings and the process of mother-infant bonding. Maternal feelings are far from automatic, and some women report that it takes several months before they really begin to feel like mothers. The Hopkins Study reported that the average new mother developed maternal feelings in about six weeks, but half of the women who successfully breastfed did so after one week (Doering and Entwisle 1977). Two factors may contribute to these findings. The first has to do with the hormone *prolactin*, which is secreted by the mother as the baby nurses. Prolactin has been called the "mothering hormone" and has been related to breastfeeding mothers' feelings of relaxation, tranquility, and maternal fulfillment. The second factor relates to the fact that breastfeeding mothers automatically have protracted, intimate, skin-to-skin contact and cuddling with their babies. A breastfeeding mother cannot deny the reality of the baby, its dependence on her, and their complex interrelationship.

Significant as these advantages are, expectant parents may raise a number of important questions as they consider whether to breastfeed or bottle feed their babies. Couples may worry about the father's role. They express concern that if the baby is breastfed, the father will be unable to share in the workload and will have only the most limited contact with his new baby. It is important that parents consider the range of parenting activities other than feeding—holding, changing, bathing, calming, playing, carrying, talking to, dressing, singing—that are available to both mother and father (Kemp 1986).

There may be concern about the breasts themselves. Women with small breasts may fear that they will be unable to breastfeed. Women with larger breasts may worry that their breasts will sag. The size of a woman's breasts is largely a function of the amount of fat tissue they contain and does not determine how much milk she can produce. Breasts do enlarge for most women during pregnancy and again during breastfeeding. Use of a supportive nursing brassiere and nursing in positions that support the baby at the breast help to prevent sagging. Some women (or their husbands) consider breasts as sexual organs, and they may be uncomfortable with redefining the breasts as a source of food. For many couples, the current emphasis on the "natural approach" to pregnancy, birth, and parenting is helping them to accept this new definition.

With the increasing number of two-income families, the mother's return to work within a short period after the birth is becoming more common. Rather than choosing not to breastfeed at all, many women are choosing to give their babies the advantages of breastfeeding—if only for a short time. Still others find that they can return to work, supplement their babies' diets during work hours, and continue to breastfeed during the times they are at home—mornings, evenings, and weekends. Less common are arrangements that allow mothers to return home or to a baby-sitter's to nurse during lunch hours, or even to have the baby accompany mother on the job (Price and Bamford 1983).

Being tied down with a breastfed baby concerns many new parents, especially those who have been very active as a couple. It is important that they understand that babies are very portable, and going out is easier with a breastfed baby since it is not necessary to worry about taking formula and keeping it refrigerated or finding ways of heating it at feeding time. It is also important for parents to realize that once breastfeeding is well established after the first few weeks, it is possible to miss an occasional feeding and substitute a bottle without interfering with the breastfeeding routine.

A number of resources are available to breastfeeding parents. Breastfeeding classes may be available through childbirth education organizations or hospitals to encourage parents to learn more about breastfeeding before the births of their babies. Organizations such as La Leche League and nursing mothers councils offer information and support to mothers who want to breastfeed. If problems arise during the breastfeeding period, representatives of these organizations, along with lactation counselors and many childbirth educators, are available to provide individualized assistance in solving specific breastfeeding problems.

ADJUSTMENTS TO PARENTHOOD

Couples must make enormous adjustments after the birth of a first child. Although a growing number of parents are prepared for pregnancy and birth, few are totally prepared for parenthood. Many new parents have had little or no experience with infants, and most grossly underestimate the time and work involved and the change of routine that a baby necessitates. In addition, fathers may overestimate the mothering capabilities of their wives; at the same time women believe that men will be more help than they actually are (Doering and Entwisle 1977). Experts believe that inexperience as parents and romanticization of parenthood are major sources of stress in the emerging family (LaRossa 1977). Relatives who might be counted on for advice and support may live far away, may be unable to help for other reasons, or may not be those with whom the new parents are totally comfortable in this new situation. The new parents may be left pretty much alone with a copy of "Dr. Spock" to learn about baby care.

The birth of the first child has frequently been described as a crisis or a trauma for the new parents (LeMasters 1957; Hobbs and Cole 1976). Although many couples may not describe the impact of the first baby on their relationship as a crisis, the shift to parenthood rarely occurs without some marital conflict (Russell 1974). In a thoughtful analysis of the dynamics of the emerging family, McGoldrick (1980, p. 114) writes:

> Some couples find the level of responsibility required in having a child a great burden. They are able to handle the responsibility of living with another adult, realizing they are not responsible for the other's survival, or even for being emotionally available more than a certain amount of the time. There is a qualitatively different level of commitment to parenthood than to marriage. As everyone knows, marriage vows can be broken. Parenthood is forever.

On a cheerful note, a research program at the University of Texas reports that

> during feeding in the neonatal period, fathers have been found to be just as active participants in dyadic interactions as mothers; and for some affectionate-social stimulation behaviors, fathers were more active. . . . The fathers' involvement in triadic interactions with the mother and infant appeared to enhance the mothers' interest and affect directed toward the infant. . . . Fathers have been found to be just as sensitive and responsive as mothers to infant cues. Contrary to a number of traditional notions, the overall findings from this series of studies indicate that fathers are as competent as mothers in providing affection, stimulation, and the necessary care for newborn infants. (Sawin and Parke 1979, p. 509)

Parental Responsibility

In an early article on the transition to parenthood, sociologist Alice Rossi (1968) cited four basic reasons that becoming parents for the first time is often difficult. First is the crucial realization of the duration of the responsibility one assumes in becoming a parent. With the birth of each child comes a minimum eighteen-year contract of responsibility for the physical, mental, and social welfare of that child. Short of abandonment or putting the child up for adoption, there is no turning back, and facing this fact may be stressful. As one graduate student remarked a few weeks after her first son was born, "You have the baby in the hospital and you come home the next day and you go, 'Wow, this is my responsibility for a long, long time' " (Paula Ota, personal communication).

Role Change

The second stress of parenthood is that of role change. Rossi believes that women experience more difficulty in this area than men do because women usually become the primary parent to infants and small children. Additionally, the role change may be more dramatic since working women either substitute the role of mother for the role of worker or try to balance the two roles in what many view as an almost impossible combination. Legally and socially, an infant's needs take precedence over its mother's job; she may feel torn between her desire to be at home with her baby and the necessity or desire to resume working.

A recent study revealed that after the birth of their first child, women tended to reconceptualize their ideal families to include fewer children with longer intervals between children. Their husbands generally showed no change of view in either area, suggesting that there may be more maternal than paternal stress. Couples reported that there was more often disagreement on the number of children they would have after the first child's birth than before (Blehar 1980a).

Postpartum Depression

Many, if not all, women suffer from some degree of *postpartum depression,* or "baby blues," following the birth of a child. This can range from passing moods and anxieties to severe emotional disturbances (Eheart and Martel 1985). Although women who suffer from postpartum depression do not all follow a predictable pattern, they frequently share several characteristics. Almost without exception, the women involved were under psychological stress at delivery, and the added responsibilities of motherhood made them feel overwhelmed. Usually they felt helpless as they confronted an impossible array of unfamiliar and demanding situations.

Instead of reaching out for help (if it is available), a depressed mother may become withdrawn and feel drained of energy. She may feel guilty and upset with herself for not being a "good mother." She may try to hide her feelings and to deny that she is in trouble. She often cries a great deal, has trouble sleeping, and is joyless. Suicidal thoughts are not unusual, and these only intensify her anxieties and feelings of despair. These severe symptoms are temporary, sometimes requiring outside help and other times fading as the mother realizes that her child is thriving despite her self-defined "inadequacies." Sometimes, however, hospitalization is required. It has been estimated that such cases make up 10 percent of the female patients in mental hospitals (LaRossa 1977).

Fathers, too, suffer from baby blues. Kalter (1983), in studying the postpartum adjustment of first-time fathers, looked at the differences between expectations prior to the birth and realities after the birth. She found that, although men expected to devote less time to their worker/provider roles, 70 percent found that they ended up spending more time. She also found that a significant number of respondents volunteered comments that the financial worries had increased beyond their expectations.

From Dyad to Triad

The third area of transition to parenthood that Rossi identified as troublesome for the individual is the abruptness of the change from being part of a two-person unit to being part of a larger group (see also Broderick 1983). A great deal of help is available during pregnancy and birth itself, but little has been done to prepare the average couple for the impact of adding a baby to their family unit and for understanding what this will do to change their relationship with each other. In many ways it is as though the couple had applied for a job, were trained and aided in all the steps needed to be hired, and were then left without supervision on the first day of work. One parent may be more or less anxious than the other, more or less fatigued, more or less nurturant, more or less flexible; but both are usually novices in making the transition from a couple to a family.

Couples are usually unprepared for the changes that cause disruptions because they generally have focused on how a baby will enhance their lives. The notion that children improve a marriage has been around for a long time. "They will keep us young" or "They will cause us to settle down" are familiar and perhaps often true statements. Family-life experts acknowledge that a child serves as a link between the parents and that having a baby often has a stabilizing effect on the relationship. However, having a child is not a certain and immediate path to marital happiness; in fact, it is likely to increase dissatisfactions that the partners feel with each other.

The birth of a child changes the family's daily routine tremendously. The reason that parents fall asleep early may be that they have been awake since 5:00 A.M. If the baby has colic or is sick, they may also have been up two or three times during the night. Most parents report that a child's cry is impossible to sleep through. Children demand time plus physical and emotional energy that childless couples often cannot even imagine.

It is estimated that the amount of time a couple who are parents must spend on housework is at least double that of a childless couple. The time they spend in conversation is often cut in half. It may be that as a couple waits longer to have a child, their marriage becomes increasingly a companionship relationship with both partners having predictable schedules and patterns of responses. The birth of their first child may disrupt these comfortable patterns, causing marital crisis.

Before pregnancy there is a two-person system (a *dyad*). After acknowledgement of the pregnancy and more certainly after the child arrives, there is a three-person system (a *triad*). It is clear that the addition of even one member to a two-person system increases the number of possible interactions enormously in a geometric fashion (see Figure 10.6). The system must change to accommodate its new member.

FIGURE 10 · 6

Impact of First-Born Child on Marital Dyad

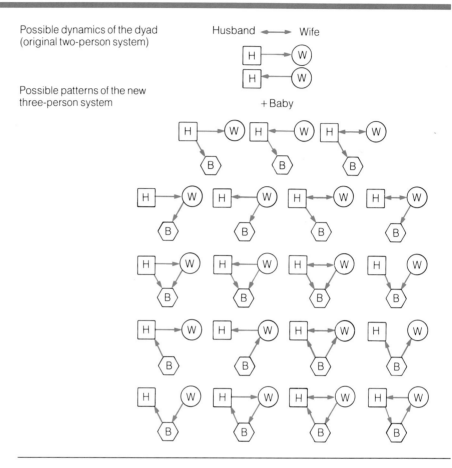

Possible dynamics of the dyad (original two-person system)

Husband ⟷ Wife

Possible patterns of the new three-person system

+ Baby

The parents must change to facilitate their added roles of mother and father without losing the roles of husband and wife.

A potentially unstable mother-father-baby triangle immediately replaces what may have been a stable dyad. As one parent draws closer to the baby, the other may feel left out and distant. Much has been written about the mother-child closeness that often pushes the father to the outside position. The necessity to work outside the home often increases the father's distance from both wife and child, but the child's dependence on the mother almost invariably increases the bond between mother and baby.

The dynamics of the triangle in a family system is a major interest of family therapist Murray Bowen. He sees "triangulation" in families in this way:

> In periods of calm, the triangle is made up of a comfortably close twosome and a less comfortable outsider. The twosome works to preserve the togetherness with one of the others, and there are numerous well-known moves to accomplish this.
>
> In periods of stress, the outside person is the most comfortable and in the most desired position. In stress, each works to get the outside position to es-

cape tension in the twosome. When it is not possible to shift forces in the triangle, one of the involved twosome triangles in a fourth person,* leaving the former third person aside for reinvolvement later.

When tensions are very high in families and available family triangles are exhausted, the family system triangles in people from outside the family, such as police and social agencies. (1978, p. 199)

Triangles frequently explain the dynamics behind feelings of jealousy that new mothers and fathers may have when they are the ones left out. Children learn at an early age to use the triangle by alternately shifting demonstrations of closeness from one parent to the other, thereby increasing feelings of jealousy or alienation that one parent (or both) may have.

New mothers in particular often feel that their husband's normal, healthy sexual interests are of secondary importance in the newly organized family. In the traditional sexually repressive family, steps may be taken even when the children are very young to conceal any evidence of sexual activity or interest. It is a short step for the husband to begin to blame his sexual rejection on the new competitor and an equally short one for the wife to see his sexual attraction to her as a demand that she devote time and energy to him that she should be giving to the much more dependent baby.

The new arrival also creates triangulation patterns involving grandparents since he or she has membership in both paternal and maternal families. In periods of stress for the new mother, a frequent triangle formed is grandmother-mother-baby. The new father may retriangulate with his own parents once more to overcome his feelings of distance from the wife-baby dyad.

Parenting Guidelines

Rossi's fourth troublesome factor in the transition to parenthood is that there are so few guidelines for raising children in today's world. Young parents often believe that their parents' and grandparents' methods are outmoded. They may not be pleased with the way they believe they were treated as children and may have sworn to avoid the mistakes they feel their parents made. Even if they approve of the way they were raised, they may believe that times are so different that the child-rearing techniques that worked successfully 25 years ago are not suitable for preparing children to live in the world as adults in the twenty-first century.

Research on families emphasizes the concern most parents have with being good parents in a "confusing and dangerous world and in the absence of clear role guidelines" (Blehar 1980b). The reading that they do seems to convince most parents of the powerful impact of the child's experiences in the first few years on his or her later development. This often increases their anxieties.

Fathers and mothers often are needlessly upset by normal infant behavior that they do not understand (such as the infant's irregular breathing or sneezing to clear the nasal passages). Being a parent for the first time means having to learn a great deal very quickly. Fortunately, babies are generally sturdy and resilient. If given reasonably good care and love, they cope surprisingly well with their inexperienced

---

*That is, one parent in a parents-child triangle introduces a fourth person to the system (for example, a grandparent) to form a new triangle with the baby.

CRYING

When and how much babies cry varies from society to society. Certain parenting practices seem to be the key to crying. In some societies, independence is not stressed as much as it is in the United States. Babies are carried in their mothers' arms or on their backs during most of the day, and they have constant attention to their needs. In the United States, as well as in most industrialized societies, children are left alone in their cribs or their play pens much of the time. They are put to bed in a darkened room with the door shut rather than having the company of parents or siblings in bed. This is evidently designed to teach children to be self-reliant at an early age. Crying is greater under these circumstances than in nonindustrial societies, where babies are held more and do not sleep alone.

New parents have often consulted us about what to do when a baby cries. Sometimes they can find no cause for crying. Can you "spoil" babies, they want to know, if you pick them up at such times? Some parents may remember reinforcement theory from their basic psychology courses and fear that their baby will learn quickly that crying can bring someone running.

Our advice, based on research with which we are familiar, years of counseling new parents, and our own fumbling parenting years (before we knew very much about how to be parents), is that in the beginning—for the first few months, in fact—babies cry as a natural response to some distress. Crying usually peaks at about six weeks in a normal, healthy baby. They should not be ignored, and spending time comforting will not spoil them. In fact, holding infants and responding to their needs right away in the first few months cuts down significantly on the amount of crying later on.

From age seven through twelve months, responding by talking and with visual distractors but not picking the child up also seems to diminish future crying. Crying to manipulate as a result of having learned that attention follows crying is not usually seen until near the end of the first year. By this time, most parents can identify their child's various types of crying and therefore can be selective in responding. Babies whose parents or sitters do not respond selectively learn quickly to cry for whatever they want. Some go on to become spoiled and may graduate from crying to crying tantrums to gain their objectives.

parents in the first months of life. Being a baby for the first time means having to learn a great deal very quickly, too, but no baby has ever had another mother or father to compare with his or her new parents!

There is no question, however, that parents (particularly first-timers) need help with learning to parent. Pediatrician T. Berry Brazelton (1980) has written:

> In other cultures that I have studied in Europe, Asia, and Africa, including [those of] many economically underdeveloped countries, young parents are cushioned from the beginning by a caring, extended-family system that not only nurtures them but also provides relatively clear guidelines for bringing up their children.
>
> In my pediatric practice, behind every question a first-time mother asks me about how to bathe a baby or how to know if he "really" is upset, are ten or twenty more that she doesn't ask me. What she needs—and both she and I know it—is someone who has had the experience, who can answer each question as it arises.

With all the adjustments that must be made when a child is born, there seems to be a good reason to ask, "Why have them?" We have asked uncounted numbers of parents whether they would plan to have children if they could roll the clock back and begin their marriages again. A few parents said that they always felt negative about being parents, an admission that points up the fact that not everyone is suited for parenthood. Some replied that there were days when nothing went right and when their children's behavior would have tried the patience of a saint; on such occasions the answer would be a resounding "no." Most parents, however, reported that, even with the problems of parenthood, once their children became part of their lives, they could not even imagine being childless.

Since most couples do have at least one child, perhaps the emphasis should be on how to minimize the negative aspects of adjustment. Few couples are sufficiently objective to be able to predict their reactions to all of the crucial aspects of adjusting to parenthood; guidelines are needed to handle the emotional effects they will feel. Here are three we recommend:

1. Couples who have not yet had a child but are considering starting a family need to explore honestly how they would restructure household duties, finances, and work schedules once the child arrives. Realism as well as honesty is important because too many couples have expectations for themselves or their partners that border on the unachievable ideals of "superparents."
2. Partners need to explore each other's attitudes toward various aspects of child rearing. One way to do this is to look back to their own childhoods and analyze how they were parented in their families of origin. Family therapists state that the agreement of parents on their philosophies of child rearing is one of the most crucial factors affecting the later marital adjustments.
3. Couples should understand clearly the distinction between their roles as parents and their roles as marital partners. Being a parent has a way of becoming all-consuming, and life can easily come to revolve almost entirely around children's needs, schedules, and demands. Couples must find ways of meeting these demands without abdicating their roles as husbands and wives. In virtually every survey of what people want from marriage, companionship ranks at the top of the list. It is important that the birth of a child not create emotional distancing in the marriage that undermines companionship.

Eventually, nearly every marriage that endures will be again the dyad that it was in the beginning: just the couple. Parents must not lose sight of the fact that most married couples have far longer to live together without children in the home than with children in the home. We are reminded of a young couple with three children who told us of their infrequent weekends spent away from their children in order to reestablish their bonds as husband and wife:

> As rarely as we go away, the children still seem to resent it and always make a fuss to go along. Finally, one day in near desperation over their whining, we hit upon an explanation that seemed to work. We told them that in only a few years they would be grown and would be leaving us. So we needed these weekends away to begin to practice being alone.

SUMMARY

1. Life as a couple will change as partners take on the roles of parents. Nearly every survey on the subject reveals that the birth of the first child has significant effects on the couple's marriage.

2. Pregnancy, whether it is greeted with delight or with apprehension, requires major adjustments. Financial plans are necessary since pregnancy, childbirth, and the baby's first year may cost $5,000 or more and the cost of rearing the child to age eighteen may reach $100,000.

3. Pregnancy and childbirth have traditionally been viewed as a woman's experience, although in certain societies men ritualistically participate. The traditional view is undergoing substantial change in the United States. It has been shown that a man who becomes highly involved in his wife's pregnancy and who takes part in the actual birth is a better father than one who leaves it all up to his wife.

4. Pregnancy lasts for nine calendar months or approximately 280 days. Clinically, the gestation is divided into three periods called trimesters. During the first trimester, the fertilized egg undergoes cell division and implants in the uterine wall. The embryo takes on a human appearance and thereafter is referred to as a fetus. It is during the first trimester that birth defects are especially likely to be caused by the mother's exposure to radiation, viruses, diseases, and harmful drugs or other toxins.

5. The second trimester is marked by the beginning of the mother's awareness of fetal movement. Most women feel healthy and may continue a normal schedule of activities. Weight gain is noticeable, they clearly appear pregnant, and, in most cases, they begin to wear maternity clothes.

6. In the third trimester the fetus completes its growth. The mother may experience a variety of symptoms related to the increasing size of the uterus. Near the end of this period, the baby usually settles into a head-down position as birth approaches.

7. Although no two childbirths are exactly alike, there are enough similarities to form a recognizable pattern. Four stages of labor can be identified: (1) dilation of the cervix, (2) expulsion of the baby, (3) expulsion of the placenta, and (4) the onset of involution. Labor usually lasts from ten to sixteen hours for the firstborn and less than half that time for subsequent births, although there is a wide range of variation.

8. The first stage of labor ends with transition, during which the cervix reaches complete dilation. As the second stage begins, the baby enters the birth canal, and the mother pushes the baby out. The second stage ends as the baby is born.

9. The third stage of labor involves separation of the placenta from the wall of the uterus and the placenta's expulsion. In the last stage, or involution, the uterus begins its return to its nonpregnant size—about that of a fist.

10. Most childbirths are fairly routine. Drugs, cesarean delivery, and other obstetrical interventions may be used under unusual circumstances. Multiple or premature births, unusual positioning of the fetus, maternal health problems, and fetal distress may be cause for medical intervention in this otherwise natural process.

11. Early contact between parents and infant is enhanced by alertness on the part of the mother and infant following birth. With the increase in requests for family-centered maternity care, hospitals and medical staffs are responding by emphasizing prepared childbirth, less medically oriented delivery processes, and "rooming-in."

12. Breastfeeding is increasing as an accompaniment to the growing interest in the natural birth process. The nutritional superiority of breast milk and the enhanced physical contact of mother and child are two advantages that encourage mothers to breastfeed their babies.

13. Although before it occurs few couples define the birth of their first child as an impending crisis, new parents find that their lives change rather dramatically. Four basic reasons have been cited for difficulties they encounter: (1) realization of the duration of the responsibility undertaken; (2) role change from husband to father/husband and from wife to mother/wife; (3) the abruptness of the change from a dyad to a three-person group; and (4) the lack of guidelines for raising children for tomorrow's world.

14. Triangulation is a frequent problem for new families. Family coalitions that leave one person out cannot happen in dyads; the feeling of being an outsider may be new and painful.

15. Some couples have trouble making space for the baby in their lives. Others may use the child to fill a void between them. All parents face the task of finding a middle ground that includes good parenting but also allows them to maintain a strong marriage relationship.

16. Eventually every enduring marriage will be a two-person unit again, just as it began. Because most married couples spend far fewer of their years with children in the home than without, the couple bond must remain strong.

GLOSSARY

Amniotic sac The protective fluid-filled membrane that surrounds a fetus during pregnancy. (p. 306)

Bulbourethal glands (Cowper's glands) A pair of small glands, situated adjacent to the male urethra, which secrete preejaculatory fluid in response to sexual excitement. (p. 294)

Cesarean delivery (cesarean birth) The delivery of a baby through an abdominal incision, a procedure restricted generally to cases in which vaginal delivery is medically impossible or undesirable. (p. 298)

Colostrum The fluid secreted by a woman's breasts during pregnancy or after delivery before milk develops. Colostrum is high in protein and contains antibodies that provide an infant with immunities to certain infections during the nursing period. (p. 317)

Couvade The practice in some societies in which, with the onset of labor, the expectant father takes to his bed and behaves as though he is in labor. (p. 298)

Dizygotic Produced from two fertilized egg cells; used to describe fraternal twins. (p. 312)

Embryo The developing human organism during the period from the second to the eighth week of pregnancy. (p. 300)

Episiotomy A small surgical incision sometimes made at the time of birth to enlarge the vaginal opening and facilitate the birth of the baby. (p. 310)

Fetus The developing human organism from the eighth week of pregnancy to birth. (p. 300)

Gestation The state, period, or process of development of a fertilized ovum to an embryo, a fetus, and a child leaving its mother's uterus. (p. 299)

Involution The return of the uterus to its prepregnant size and shape following birth. (p. 311)

Lactation Milk production. (p. 317)

Monozygotic Produced from one fertilized egg cell; used to describe identical twins. (p. 312)

Neonate A term used to describe the newborn baby during approximately the first month of life. (p. 311)

Oogonia Female germ cells at the stage of division. (p. 295)

Ovum Female reproductive cell. (p. 294)

Prepared childbirth Prepared childbirth includes the mother and the father (or other birth partner) receiving instruction, including information about the birth process, techniques for coping with it (such as special breathing and relaxation techniques), and options for birth location. (p. 314)

Rh factor Any of several substances in the blood that can cause reactions in a second or later fetus if the mother is Rh-negative and the father is Rh-positive (due to the mother's having developed antibodies to the Rh factor present in the blood of the first fetus). (p. 312)

Seminal vesicles Saclike structures on either side of the prostate (the gland surrounding the male urethra) that produce prostaglandins and part of the seminal fluid. (p. 294)

Sperm Male reproductive cell. (p. 294)

Umbilical cord The tube, connecting a fetus to its placenta, through which nutrients pass and waste materials are removed. (p. 300)

Vasocongestion The engorgement of tissue with blood. In response to sexual stimulation, vasocongestion of the genitalia produces erection of the penis and the clitoris and lubrication of the vagina. (p. 305)

Vernix caseosa The creamlike coating on the fetus that has served as protective shield during prenatal development; literally, "cheesy varnish." (p. 307)

Zygote The cell formed when a sperm fertilizes an ovum. (p. 296)

11

There are only two lasting bequests we can hope to give our children.
One of these is roots; the other, wings.

arenthood is usually a complicated undertaking. It transforms one generation automatically into the next as adult children become parents and their own parents become grandparents. The considerable research attention that the transition to parenthood has received has shown that most parents agree with family-life professionals that children do modify parents' lives with their needs for time, energy, and other parental resources. Not only do children change their parents, but there is also ample evidence that parents are major determiners of how their children grow up to be adults. The lack of training—other than "on-the-job" training—for parenthood leaves many parents ill prepared to meet the challenges of child care. However, the parenting process is of sufficient interest to parents and to nonparents alike that nearly everyone has developed a personal philosophy about "right" and "wrong" ways to bring up children. Every human society has some ways of assisting or even replacing parents if the physical or moral welfare of children is seriously threatened. This chapter is designed to help to evaluate philosophies, methods, and outcomes of parenting in the light of current knowledge in the fields of child development, psychology, and sociology.

PARENTING: ON BEING MOTHERS AND FATHERS

Hodding Carter

*A*lthough there is no agreement among Americans on one best way to be parents, it is agreed that parents have a vital socializing influence on their children and that children play an active role in how their parents behave toward them. The many variations of parenting seem to have in common a strong conviction that parents must assume the basic responsibilities for child rearing, including ensuring their children's chances for survival, good health, an adequate education, conformity to the community's standards, social adjustment, and eventual self-sufficiency. Community members are on the alert for evidence of child neglect or child abuse, and school and religious groups encourage parents to meet their obligations. As a result, most parents soon learn what generally is expected of them (even though some may not always comply).

Child-rearing changes parents as persons, beginning with the moment the mother-to-be and the father-to-be become aware that they have created a new life. Each of them experiences the beginnings of attachment to (or sometimes rejection of) another human in a way that may be more intense than any previous emotion. There is an immediate shift in role relationships. A change in the way they think about society and the way their child will or does interact within it and a dramatic new growth in *feeling* capabilities begin (Newman and Newman 1984, p. 2).

IDEALIZATION

The mental picture of a family that many people have is of a father and mother, married to each other for a year or more, who have given birth to a wanted child who is a product of their own conception. However, the parent-child relationship can begin with single parents of either sex; it can begin with parents in their late forties; it can begin with an unwanted child; it can begin with an adopted child; it can begin with a homosexual couple. There is no end to the variations that can occur.

The mental pictures that people in a parenting system have of one another begin to take shape long before the first child is born or adopted. By the time a pregnancy or adoption has occurred or even when it is seriously contemplated, a process called *idealization* may have begun, which includes not only some thoughts about the physical appearance of the coming child, but also assumptions about his or her intelligence, health, affectional behavior, and even performance later in life. Idealization does not stop at birth or adoption. As long as they live, parents may continue to have mental images of their children that have varying degrees of accuracy. As the children grow older, they likewise form idealized images of their parents. By the time a child learns to talk, he or she has definite mental pictures of mother and father with special qualities that no others have (Feldman and Ingham 1975).

FAMILY ROLES

Besides idealizations about what a family should be, there are also usually ideas and feelings about the "rightness" and "wrongness" of actions for each specific person in the family. Although some of these ideas are unique to one specific individual ("David is always the first to clean his plate"; "Carrie is the family diplomat"), others refer to rules that are believed to be proper or improper for all families ("Mothers and fathers always put their children's welfare ahead of their own"; "Children shouldn't be allowed in their parents' beds at night after they are four years old"). Such rules characterize family roles—what persons in a family are expected to do or *ought* to do. The sources of these rules are varied and complex—observing other families, reading about how others live or believe life should be, watching television and movies, and so forth. For parents, perhaps the most important source of ideas about parent-child roles is their knowledge of how their own **families of orientation** functioned (Framo 1981). If the childhood home is remembered fondly, it may be emulated. If not, most parents probably hope to be better parents than their own were. Children, meanwhile, are learning from their parents how or how not to be parents themselves someday.

From these various sources, parents and children usually develop an idea of what a good outcome for their family would be if each member fulfilled his or her roles properly. The definition of "good outcomes" may differ considerably among family members, as may ideas about how to achieve them. To complicate family life further, family members' definitions are not always verbalized (sometimes they are not even consciously formulated) and, like other elements in the parenting system, are subject to change.

A mother may consider that a good outcome of parenting for her son would be his successful and happy marriage and subsequent fatherhood, whereas the son may define a good outcome as having his parents retire and turn over the family business to him. At another time a mother may consider as a good outcome for her son his becoming a priest, whereas the son may think of a good outcome as being "liberated" from his family responsibilities altogether.

Not only may ideas and feelings about the "correctness" of roles of family members differ at any given moment, but these ideas are also in a state of ongoing change for each person. Although this fact invariably creates some degree of disorganization and stress ("Connie, from now on you ought to earn your own spending money"; "Don't come in my room without knocking!"), it also is the way that such systems grow and adapt to ongoing changes in individual members.

In a family system, parent and child roles are *reciprocal*. In other words, a person cannot assume a parent's role unless another person assumes or accepts a child's role. Similarly, to define oneself as a child, one needs a parent. Systems theory has provided us with a special way of understanding these interrelationships. The theoretical insights help us describe the effects of each member's roles on every other member and the energy and life of the system as a whole. If even one member is absent or behaving differently, the entire system will be altered (Broderick and Smith 1979).

If and when family members give up their parent and child roles and relationships, the parenting system comes to an end. Every state has laws defining the age at which children legally become adults for various specific activities, but even within states the ages vary. A child may legally become an adult at the age of 18 for purposes of registering to vote or of being subject to a military draft, for example, but may not legally purchase tobacco or alcoholic beverages in some states until he or she is 21. The age at which child roles (and thus parent roles) end often has little to do with legal adulthood, however. Sometimes young adults who have given up the child role have considerable difficulty in convincing their parents to quit acting like parents. Parents, too, often have their share of difficulty in trying to persuade their grown children to give up childlike dependencies. A few parents and their grown children never give up their reciprocal roles even when the "children" are themselves parents. When family members disagree about whether parenting has ended or not, there is almost always stress, disorganization, and pain (Gottlieb and Chafetz 1977).

Children are living in their parents' households longer than ever. In 1984, over half (52 percent) of men 20 to 24 years old were living with their parents, compared with 43 percent in 1970; as were 16 percent of men 25 to 29, compared with 11 percent in 1970 (see Figure 11.1). Although women tend to leave home earlier, 32 percent of those aged 20 to 24 and 8 percent of those aged 25 to 29 were still living at home in 1984, compared with 27 percent and 5 percent in 1970 (U.S. Bureau of the Census 1985h, p. 18).

A parent's demands that a child be an independent, self-sufficient adult (or a *former child*) may seem to a late adolescent to be inconsistent with other parental demands that seem appropriate to a dependent child role.* For instance, parents often want a child to live on his or her own while at college but still want to impose limitations on with whom the child lives and other aspects of his or her life. The child's argument is familiar: "If I am mature enough to move from home to college to live, I am mature enough to live where I please and with whom I please!" On the other hand, parents may reply, "As long as we pay the bills, we make the rules!" Conflict over appropriate parent-child roles in a family system is very familiar in adolescence and may indeed be a necessary step in a child's redefinition of himself or herself as an adult (Erikson 1968).

Changing Parent-Child Roles

One of the chief problems in defining parent-child relationships is that they are constantly changing. Although it is appealing to believe that persons in a social system of any sort are reliable and therefore predictable, such stability is rarely found. Paradoxically, in fact, stability in a family system may be less adaptive to a changing world and to changes in family members than a system characterized by "creative flexibility."

Change is inevitable in a family, if for no other reasons than the growth and development of the children and the physiological aging of the parents. Change is a necessary condition of any kind of growth, in fact. In addition, parents and children are always adapting to changes in other institutions—schools, churches, and government, to name but a few—in order to survive in a constantly changing world. There is a growing belief among family-life observers that understanding how families adapt to both internal and external change is an important source of knowledge about family strength and solidarity. Patterns of adjusting to change develop over time, and each family has its unique coping mechanisms. In a thoughtful appraisal of parents, children, and change, McCubbin et al. (1980, p. 865) concluded:

> Because the family is a system, coping behavior involves the management of various dimensions of family life simultaneously: (1) maintaining satisfactory internal conditions for communication and family organization, (2) promoting

---

Former child is a term used by James Framo (1981) to describe an adult's relationship to his or her "former parent."

CHAPTER 11

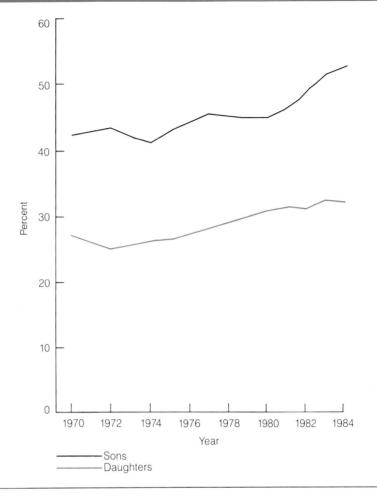

Source: U.S. Bureau of the Census, *Current Population Reports,*
Series P-23, No. 145 (September 1985), p. 19.

member independence and self-esteem, (3) maintenance of family bonds of co-
herence and unity, (4) maintenance and development of social supports in transactions with the community, and (5) maintenance of some efforts to control the
impact of the stressor and the amount of change in the family unit. Coping then
becomes a process of achieving a balance in the family system which facilitates
organization and unity and promotes individual growth and development.

As noted in Chapter 10, when the first child is born, even the happiest and
most well adjusted new parents make drastic changes in their own behaviors and in
their expectations of their partners. Budgets, leisure activities, household duties, even
sleeping hours and sexual behaviors are reorganized and redefined. Unless communication between partners is exceptional, each will be forced to engage in spontaneous
decisions and behaviors that the other does not expect. New babies often create stress,
although they also can be fulfilling and can strengthen the bond between the parents

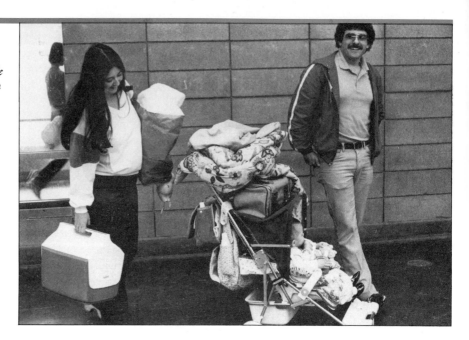

New parents find that their ability to act spontaneously as a couple changes drastically when a baby (with paraphernalia) must be accommodated. A day's outing with a baby requires planning, and it may almost seem like more effort than the activity is worth. Keeping a sense of humor definitely helps.

(Sollie and Miller 1980). Whatever the direction—toward stress or toward fulfillment or both—change is the rule.

Psychologists Lois Hoffman and Jean Manis found some of the role changes that first-time parents experienced included a sense of full entry into an expected and enacted adult role; a sense of having a new status in the community, especially among relatives and friends; a reassessment of the spousal division of labor; a transformation from identity as "a couple" to identity as "a family" (cited in Newman and Newman 1984, p. 14). As sociologist Edward McDonagh (1950, personal communication) once phrased it, "A married couple without children is more like an unmarried courting couple than either is like a married couple with children."

One study found that the poorer the marital adjustment, the more negative was the perception of both husband and wife of the changes in their relationship that accompanied the birth of a child. Whether the pregnancy was planned was significantly associated (positively) with the parents' marital adjustment and also with the parents' educational level. Both husbands and wives reported negative feelings about having less time to spend with their partners and their sexual responsiveness to them (Harriman 1986, p. 237). At the same time, the birth of the first child is positively associated with the probability that the marriage will last for another year (Waite, Haggstrom, and Kanouse 1985, p. 850).

About the time that new parents have reorganized their behaviors and expectations in order to deal comfortably with the 2:00 A.M. feeding of the infant, the baby begins to sleep through the night. By the time all the breakable objects have been put away in cupboards, the child has learned to open the cupboards. Just when the family has adjusted to allowing the necessary space and facilities for bottle feeding, the child begins to drink from a cup. If anything is constant in the parenting process, surely it is change!

Roles and Family-Size   The birth or **adoption of** any additional children also calls for reorganization of the parenting system. Relationships between brothers and sisters must be defined and redefined as the children grow up together. An endless series of decisions must be made—including who will make the decisions. Will Cindy and Michael share a bedroom? If so, for how long? Should they be consulted, or should one or both of the parents make the decision? The addition of each child changes the family structure. Not only does each sibling change the parents' relationship with each other, but the children's relationships with each other also undergo a change. A boy added to a family with girl siblings or a girl introduced into a home in which her brother has had all the attention produces a very different mix of emotions and behaviors from other possible combinations. Children who are widely spaced form family patterns that differ from those of siblings who are close together in age.

Studies of family size indicate that parenting roles take on different dimensions as the size of the family increases (Kunz and Peterson 1975). Particularly in middle-class families, parents tend to become more authoritarian in their attempts to modify or direct their children's behaviors according to predetermined standards of conduct. In one study, boys in large families reported greater parental control as family size increased than girls did (Zussman 1978). It is not clear why sons reported more authoritarian control than daughters. Perhaps it was simply that boys viewed control more negatively than did girls.

Psychologists Philip Newman and Barbara Newman (1984, p. 16) comment that "parents worry more about girls than [they do about] boys. This observation is of striking significance when we think about the survival mission of parenting. While we tend to think of the importance of male children for carrying on the name of the family, it is the female children [who may] eventually bear offspring." Even though the sons perceived more authoritarian control than daughters, it may be the anxiety of parents about protecting their daughters that produced Montemayor's (1982) findings of more frequent parent-daughter conflict than parent-son conflict. Further, conflicts between mother and daughters were found to be not only most frequent, but also most intense (Montemayor 1982; cited in Newman and Newman 1984, p. 17).

Birth Order   Although child psychologists do not agree on the effects of birth order on children's personalities, there is no doubt that parents' interaction with their children changes as each successive child appears. Part of this is due simply to the aging of the parents. Christine may learn to roller-skate, for example, by having her parents hold her hands as they skate along on either side of her; her brother Stephen, who is six years younger, may never even see his parents roller-skate.

Another aspect of the changed parent-child interaction can be traced to the impact of a new child on the family's financial status. Middle children have the least probability of being sent to college, for example, when family size is held constant (Bayer 1966, p. 484; see also Finlay 1981, p. 1000). Every coat that Debbie ever wore was new when she first wore it; her sister Alison—two years younger—*never* had a new coat until she went away to college.

Psychologist Walter Toman (1961), after studying thousands of persons, concluded that firstborns are most achievement motivated because of parental expectations; younger children are more likely to be interested in music and art because their parents are more relaxed (see also Forer 1976). Family specialists Brent Miller and

Diana Gerard (1979, p. 295), on the other hand, summarized studies whose findings on the relationship of creativity to birth order were inconsistent—except that younger children distant from their siblings in age tend to be less creative.

Child Development and Parental Roles and Responses

Parents, as well as children, grow older, more mature, and different in their needs, wants, and expectations. Parents also change in response to their children's developmental stages. Some parents seem to enjoy babies more than older children. Others relate better to children who are old enough to be companions and find the infant stage burdensome. Parents may have different kinds of parenting styles and different ideals for the outcome of their parenting roles at different periods of the life cycle. An anxious first-time parent may relax as he or she becomes more experienced, for example. Adolescent behavior may increase parents' stress as they question their own and their children's values and behaviors.

One virtually inevitable outcome of the parent-child interaction is that children develop their own styles and philosophies for relating to other family members. Some of these styles are intentionally taught to a child by parents ("Always say 'please' when you ask a person for a favor and 'thank you' for any favor given to you"), but many are learned by children from models set by parents (and others) without specific instructions. Not only may emulating parental behavior gain the child favor with the parent who is modeled, but children also seem to be gratified by being similar to parents who provide them with security and ways to gain a sense of mastery over their environment.

There is an old saying that children learn more from what their parents *do* than from what they *say*. Erikson has put it more bluntly: "Parents get the kinds of children that they deserve" (Erikson 1968). Besides being readily available for imitation, parents hold the keys to rewards and punishments and are therefore seen as worthy of being imitated. Furthermore, because parents usually offer security and love, children want to be like them as a way of being as close to them as possible.

Developmental Levels It goes without saying that a parent cannot teach a child something that the child is not capable of learning. Successful parenting, therefore, involves parents' reasonable assessments of the **developmental levels** of their children. Newborn children are necessarily dependent on the activities of others for their satisfactions, pleasures, and comforts—even for their very survival. As a kind of social relationship, dependency means that someone must care enough about the dependent children to supply the materials, energy, and behaviors for their survival needs. Although dependency does not need to be taught, it obviously and definitely requires a very specific kind of social relationship that parents (or other caretakers) must create if children are to survive infancy. Studies have indicated that an atmosphere of interpersonal warmth (including reasoning and explanation) and acceptance of the child sets the stage for the child to learn to trust and to want to identify with his or her parents (Erikson 1968).

As infants develop, they establish memories of events: a simple memory might be that hunger is reduced by the feeding process—the act of nursing from a breast or bottle is followed by a "good" feeling (or the absence of a "bad" feeling). Perhaps incidentally, the infant is exposed repeatedly to situations in which the breast or bottle appears when he or she cries. After a series of such occurrences, the child may remember that crying is followed by feeding, which is, in turn, followed by gratification. Cognitive and motor developments are now adequate for the appearance of a second level of social relationships. The child progresses from total dependency to a point at which he or she can influence certain facets of the environment.

In an influential social relationship one person deliberately engages in behavior intended to affect the behavior of another person in a particular way. This new style of social relationship gives a child an alternative to dependency for survival and gratification. At this point, parent-child communication can be said to exist. The child has learned to express an idea ("I am hungry") through a motor activity (crying) that produces the same idea ("The child is hungry") in the mind of the parent. As the parent responds to the child's "statement" with rewarding behavior, the child learns the effectiveness of crying behavior in influencing the parent's behavior.

The importance of the parent role during a child's development of influencing capabilities cannot be overstated. The parent's responses directly affect the child's development of communication, secure attachment, and trust. A parent who responds immediately to a child's needs teaches the child to trust that his or her needs will be met. Parents who fail to respond communicate to the child that his or her needs are not important or that the parents' needs take precedence. If no caring adult ever consistently responds to a particular infant's activity, the child's motor activity becomes random, and cognitive development is impeded. Continued absence of adequate parenting beyond the fifteenth week of infancy may lead to a condition called *marasmus,* in which the infant is not only retarded in cognitive and motor development, but also falls behind in growth, weight, and physical health and has a much greater probability of dying during the first year of life than has the average infant (Spitz 1975).

Self-Sufficiency   As children's motor and cognitive capabilities continue to increase, the probability of being able to relate to others as self-sufficient persons also increases. As an illustration, children learn to grasp and pull a blanket over themselves and develop the cognitive capabilities (1) to recognize that they feel chilly, (2) to remember that the stress of being cold is absent or reduced by being covered with a blanket, and (3) to *know* that they have the motor skills to pull on the blanket. With this increased capability, children now have at least *three* options for reducing certain stresses or gratifying certain wishes: (1) "Let my parents decide what I need and provide it" (dependency); (2) "Tell my parents what I need and ask for it" (influencing); or (3) "Do or get what I need myself" (self-sufficiency).

The impact of parental behavior on a child's self-sufficiency may seem less dramatic than how they respond to their child's attempts to influence them, for the child is not likely to die if self-sufficient development is frustrated. Nevertheless, parents' actions are important at this step for enhancing the child's self-esteem and self-confidence. A child who is too rigidly controlled by autocratic parents has at least two "regressive" options: (1) he or she may resort to attempts at influencing the parents' behaviors, from which a child may learn either assertiveness or seductiveness, according to the rewards received from each; or (2) the child may regress to the less mature option of dependency. (Influential behavior is considered more mature because, unlike dependency, it demands both cognitive and motor capabilities.)

SUGGESTIONS FOR EFFECTIVE DISCIPLINE

Child psychology provides many practical guidelines for parents who want their discipline to be both effective and humane. Underlying all of the guidelines, however, is the basic notion that all parents should become informed about child development so that they know what to expect of children at certain ages. Most children most of the time want to be good and to please their parents. Much of the behavior that parents see as problematic may result from the child's lack of experience and poor judgment.

1. Parents should make clear rules that are consistently enforced. The reasoning behind rules can be explained to children as soon as they can understand. Having fewer rules consistently enforced works better than having many rules frequently broken.

2. When a child appears to be misbehaving, parents should find out what really happened before jumping to conclusions.

3. Never punish a child for feelings, only for actions. A child has a right to his or her feelings, but how they are expressed may need guidance. "I feel like hitting you" can be met with "Why are you so angry?" "I am going to hit you" can lead to a discussion of the consequences of such behavior and an exploration of better ways to handle anger. If, however, a child does hit a parent, the action calls for discipline (unless the parent wishes to encourage hitting).

4. The timing of intervention following misbehavior can be critical. The longer the interval between the act and the intervention, particularly with young children, the less effective the parent will be in changing the child's behavior. However, older children sometimes find the waiting period while parents decide on a punishment worse than the punishment itself.

5. The simplest way to eliminate negative behavior is to be certain that there are no rewards attached to it. It is rare that any behavior continues unless it is somehow reinforced. Of course, parents are not always able to eliminate rewards (such as attention from friends or the perverse pleasure some children gain from riling their parents). In such cases, rewarding behavior parents want to encourage can work nearly as well.

6. Parents should refrain from intervening if they feel out of control. Allow a cooling-off period that is long enough to restore calm but not so long as to render the intervention unsuccessful. "Time-out" (by sending a child from the room, for example) can help both parents and children calm down.

When children reach the self-sufficient stage, parents face decisions about guidance and discipline. Child psychologists have been interested in the mix between the support parents give a child in his or her struggle for self-sufficiency and the control that they attempt to exert to keep children compliant. The ratio of parental support to control has been shown to affect a child's later self-esteem and social competence (Thomas et al. 1974). The more affirmative that parents are, the better the child's evaluation of his or her self-worth.

Parental support is that quality in the relationship between parents and their children that creates a warm, positive environment in which the children are not afraid to show individuality. There is a mutual give-and-take that encourages a child to try new skills and gives positive feedback that builds self-esteem. Such support is believed to be essential to the development of **ego strength**. Essentially, ego strength is the capacity to choose between alternatives for dealing with the environment and to accept the responsibility for having chosen the alternative that one did (Erikson 1963, pp. 248–249). Although for some persons this capability does not develop fully until adulthood (and for a few it never becomes adequate), a few children develop it by the time they are in elementary school—usually with the aid of their parents.

The parents' roles in responding to their child's efforts toward developing ego strength requires the practice of an art, although it often appears to be intuitive. Parents must be extremely sensitive to their child's self-definition—sensitive enough to affirm or validate the child's accomplishment of his or her own goals or objectives. The criteria by which "accomplishments" are judged must be realistic enough that the child will achieve a fair measure of personal successes, but also challenging enough that he or she does not develop an inflated or unrealistic definition of his or her capabilities that may be shattered eventually by criticism from others.

Parental control can be coercive, with the parents demanding compliance and punishing any infraction. The affective climate of the home can easily become one in which the children feel dominated or exploited. Even when punishment produces compliance, it may also create hostility toward the punishing parents. A pattern of constant criticism and frequent punishment is termed **serial invalidation,** which leads to low self-esteem, lack of self-confidence, anger toward parents (and usually toward other authority figures), and erratic behavior patterns of children (Sze 1975).

The parent who encourages a child's self-sufficient behavior must also give judicious reassurance, approval of successes, and guidance about hazardous or potentially hazardous activities. An important part of the parental role is also self-restraint. A child's capability of carrying out a task cannot possibly be confirmed if he or she is not allowed to complete the task. Self-confidence and self-esteem grow through parental affirmation of their child's behaviors. In the absence of such positive feedback, a child may be unable to distinguish between socially approved and socially disapproved behaviors.

PARENTING STYLES

Parenthood is one of the few jobs in life for which there is little preparation other than on-the-job training. This lack of preparation is puzzling in view of the great concern evidenced generally about the welfare of children in the United States. It is almost as though couples believe that the big hurdles are pregnancy and childbirth and that the actual parenting will take care of itself. Many couples take classes in childbirth preparation, but relatively few take instruction in parenting. Of course, many read books such as Dr. Spock's *Baby and Child Care,* which was first published in 1945—just in time for the baby boom that began that year—and has been revised frequently since then (Spock 1976). Still, compared with nearly every other important task in life—many of which require licenses or degrees—parenting seems to suffer.

A poll of parents asked, "How much effect can parents have in determining how children will turn out?" Men and women did not give significantly different answers, but there were differences according to education and race. Of those who had a grade-school education, only 48 percent believed that parents have a strong influence, compared with 66 percent of those who were college educated. Blacks were less likely (39 percent) than whites (59 percent) to believe in parental influence (Roper Organization 1974, p. 77). The poll did not control for economic factors; nor is it

Children thrive under a variety of parenting styles. What appears to be most important are love and consistent rules.

clear whether college-educated blacks were more like all other blacks or more similar to college-educated whites. It appears from the responses that at least those who were well educated believed that there are cause-and-effect relationships between what they do and how their children grow up. College-educated parents may have had more training for parenthood and more resources to use in active parenting.

Countless studies have reported that parenting can be learned and that parents do indeed have an impact on their children's lives, whether they learn to parent well or leave parenting to chance (Willis, Crowder, and Willis 1975; White, Watts, and Barnett 1973). Parent-training programs developed to teach more effective parenting procedures have had quite positive results. In a recent review of two types of training for more effective parenting, both **behavior modification** and **parent effectiveness training** were shown to be useful for reducing parent-child problems and increasing parents' knowledge of how to work with their children (Pinsker and Geoffroy 1981). In behavior modification instruction, parents are taught systematic methods for modifying children's behaviors that they judge to be inappropriate. As a result of putting their training into action, deviant child behaviors have been reduced, and parents' perceptions of the problems have been altered. Parent effectiveness training, which focuses on communication patterns between parents and children, has been found to increase family cohesion and decrease family conflict.

Studies of various parenting styles and the results of each have provided information about basic approaches that are frequently followed. For nearly twenty years a study has been continued that began with observations of children of preschool age. Their behaviors were observed both at home with their parents and in nursery school classes. Follow-up studies were made when the children were between eight and nine years old, and the research is still in progress (Yahraes and Baumrind 1980). Three main parenting types were found, each of which had a different effect on the children:

1. *Authoritarian:* these parents valued **obedience** and believed in restricting the child's freedom. They did not encourage verbal give-and-take and expected the child to do as told. The highest value for these parents was found to be unquestioning obedience.
2. *Authoritative:* such parents directed their children firmly and rationally. They focused on issues and set standards, but they also listened to their children's views and encouraged children to express their opinions. The children were allowed a certain amount of independence and could make many of their own decisions.
3. *Permissive:* this kind of parent gave the children little restraint and had little parenting philosophy other than giving children all the freedom they could handle, believing that they would naturally fulfill their potentials.

The second style, *authoritative*, was shown to produce the most responsible, self-reliant children. Parents of this type were responsive to their children, flexible in their roles, and apparently confident in their child-rearing practices. In the follow-up studies these children were judged the most competent by their peers, significant adults, and the research observers (Baumrind 1975).

Authoritarian parents produced children who were obedient at home and often dependent and passive in other authority situations. They often displayed withdrawn behavior and were frequently distrustful and discontented.

Children from homes that were judged permissive often lacked self-control or self-reliance. Children raised under such influences tended to be afraid of new experiences, probably because they were unsure of what would be acceptable behavior in more authoritarian climates.

Parenting and Social Class

Members of different social classes view parenting differently. The authoritarian pattern has been described as more popular with blue-collar families; the authoritative style is more frequently favored by middle-class parents. Another study of 400 families found that insisting on obedience, teaching children to control their impulses, and using physical punishment were most often characteristic of working-class parenting. Parents in the middle classes were more likely to be authoritative, prizing the child's individuality, explaining rules to the child, and emphasizing verbal discipline (Kohn 1959).

Perhaps the most comprehensive report of the impact of social class on personality development was made by sociologist Margaret Lundberg (1974). After summarizing research on social class differences in what children learn from their parents about styles of thinking, feeling, and interacting, she examined these differences as they might relate to theories of human development and personality: "The mounting evidence of a systematic, positive relationship between the child's personality development and his social class position cannot be ignored. . . . The overall conclusion from the behavioral science literature is that the chances of achieving full personality development increase with each step [of] increase in social class position" (p. xiii). "Social class position affects personality development by providing differential learning experiences, which for any given class consist of its distinctive value system and interaction patterns" (p. 13).

Sociologist Alan Kerckhoff (1972) explored the social class differences in child rearing by investigating those differences from the perspectives of social context—families, neighborhoods, and schools—and parental expectations. He noted that socialization outcomes influence both the child's choice patterns and his or her opportunities.

> Middle-class parents generally rear their children in such a way that they develop greater self-control, a stronger achievement orientation, greater sensitivity to others, and a more complex linguistic and cognitive structure than lower-class children show. Such characteristics are well suited to the expectations of the school, and middle-class children thus tend to be more successful in school from the beginning. This initial advantage tends to snowball, so that an increasing gap occurs between those who are initially more and less successful. . . . Those who are less successful in school thus tend to leave the system earlier. . . . they are not well prepared for many adult occupational positions . . . they marry and have children at a relatively early age. . . . Thus, those who start life at higher status levels seem to be destined to remain there, and those who start life at lower levels seem unlikely to rise in the system.
>
> Yet we know that mobility does occur. (p. 121)

In a study of a working-class neighborhood, black, Mexican-American, and Anglo parents were compared (Bartz and Levine 1978). Black parents were found to exhibit high levels of support, control, and open communication. Although they were strict, they also involved their children in decision making. Mexican-American parents were the most protective and were very consistent in rewarding and punishing their children. Anglo parents were less protective than Mexican-American parents, were more likely to use guilt to control their children than were black parents, and were less likely to expect their children to obey at an early age than were black parents. Actually, most children thrived (or at least were not seriously damaged) under all three parental styles (as they do under a variety of others).

Perhaps more important than style is consistency and an atmosphere of caring. Lack of involvement with children or harsh, exploitative, and inconsistent parental behavior have been shown to be the most destructive parental qualities (Rosenberg 1965). In their research on the delinquent behavior of adolescents, the Gluecks (1968) studied several hundred delinquent boys. They reported that the families from which these boys came were generally unsupportive and unaffectionate, and that punishment was more likely to be harsh and physical than in families of nondelinquent boys.

Models of Parenting

Some other models of parenting have been described (LeMasters 1974). One is the *martyr* model. Parents with this style make sacrifices for their children and often seem to feel they must compensate for what was lacking in their own childhoods by seeing that their children want for very little. Such parents often are overprotective, regarding it as their duty to provide a "safe" world for the child. Often parents of the martyr type exhibit guilt over not doing enough for their children, as well as guilt when they take some time for themselves. For example, a mother who has not been employed outside the home while her children are small may suffer tremendous guilt when she decides to go back to school or to take a job for her own sake. Children often resent parents who overprotect. At the same time they are likely to feel angry when the parents' total availability for them is lessened. Some children rebel and break out of the overprotective environment (often a healthy move), whereas others are handicapped by having had too much done for them.

The second model described by LeMasters is the *buddy* or *pal* type. Parents often attempt to blur the boundaries between the generations by attempting either to become a part of the child's world or to make the child grow up too quickly to become an "instant adult." Research suggests that early marriages and young parenthood may have helped this model to develop. Many young parents and their children appear to be growing up together. When the children reach adolescence, their parents are still young and may have trouble visualizing themselves as parents of teenagers. A "buddy-pop" might tell his fifteen-year-old son, "Look, I'm only eighteen years older than you are, so I don't know a whole lot more about life than you do." Children whose parents adopt this model are often confused and may not know where to turn for the kind of parental expertise they need when they have problems.

A third model is the *police* or *drill sergeant* type. These are autocratic parents, versions of the controlling parents described earlier. They often appear more interested in the rules than in the child. Parents of this type fall on hard times when their children reach adolescence because teenagers are often ingenious in finding ways to avoid their parents and to get around the rules. Only when warmth and love are plentiful and obvious are such parents likely to succeed beyond the first few years of parenting. Sometimes a "benevolent dictatorship" can be developed, in which parents are very strict and controlling but their children tolerate them because they also feel loved and believe that their parents have their best interests in mind.

Another model is the *teacher-counselor* type of parenting. Here, the children's needs always come first, but within the tolerance limits of the family system. Parents set themselves up as experts. They participate in trying new techniques, read the latest books on child psychology, and are involved in most aspects of their children's lives. Such parents often report feeling anxious about making mistakes in their parenting and feeling guilty when they inevitably do.

The final model discussed by LeMasters is the *athletic coach* type of parent. This type often seems to have success since such parents evidently exhibit a good balance of cooperation, assertiveness, and concern for each member of the "team." This model involves being fit, knowing the rules, mastering skills, and developing self-discipline. Perhaps most important is the realization that the coach cannot play the game for the players—parents cannot live their children's lives—but are there for guidance, instruction, and emergency advice. The drawbacks are that there are fewer schools or training programs for parents than for coaches, and life is not as simple as a football game. Furthermore, coaches can select their players, and players can choose not to join a team. The coach gets a new team every year or so, but parents have the same players for twenty or more years.

Parental Attitudes

An interesting patterning of parental styles and values is taken from a widely used test called the *Parental Attitude Research Instrument,* which measures parents' implicit and explicit attitudes about parenting (Sims and Paolucci 1975). Points of view that were examined included:

1. *Parents know best.* Those who believe that this is true tend to expect their children to accept their opinions unquestioningly.
2. *Children's opinions should receive equal treatment with those of parents.* Parents with this viewpoint strive for an egalitarian relationship with their children.
3. *Children should have unquestioned loyalty.* Those with this perspective feel that children should never oppose their parents, nor should they ever doubt that the parents' word is to be respected.
4. *Deception is a legitimate part of parenting.* Sometimes parents believe that they must keep the truth from children since children do not always understand. (This is part of the notion that parents always know best and that children should trust them.)
5. *Children are demanding and bring occasional dissatisfaction.* This attitude implies that children are often a burden and that there is an annoying aspect to child rearing.

Still another look at parental models suggests that there are four major roles that parents play in shaping and molding their children: (1) the "potter," who shapes raw material into a finished product; (2) the "gardener," who provides the climate and nutrition for the child to grow; (3) the "maestro," who conducts the symphony of a child's life but lets the child develop into a fine performer; and (4) the "consultant," who is less authoritarian and serves as a guide and a mentor to the child (Wood, Bishop, and Cohen 1978).

Although there are probably almost as many models for parenting as there are parents doing the job, parents clearly socialize their children by the behaviors that they themselves exhibit. Their own upbringing and their notions of right, wrong, good, bad, proper, and improper all mold their unique styles.

DISCIPLINE, COOPERATION, AND COMMUNICATION

Most parents use some form of discipline. Children who come from families with no control at all often fare poorly. Evidence from most studies of discipline indicates that it is neither how much discipline is used nor what kind of discipline (short of real abuse) that makes a difference in the outcome for the child. Rather, it is the total pattern of parental control and the emotional climate of the home that really count.

A home in which there is positive support, love, and security is more effective for shaping children's characters than any one style of discipline. Rewarding behavior that parents favor and ignoring most other actions is probably the most effective technique. This is not to say, however, that occasional punishment is not needed for those willful acts of disobedience that happen from time to time. To let such acts go unpunished would be a form of reward for the behavior. If a child gets by with an act for which he or she expected punishment, this nearly always strengthens that response.

Discipline does not need to be harsh to be effective. From a review of the research on punishment (Baumrind 1977), the following facts emerge:

1. Punishment is most effective when it is closely associated in time with the undesired behavior.
2. Punishment should be accompanied by an explanation of why the behavior was wrong, and alternate behavior should be offered so that the child can be redirected.
3. The punishment should "fit the crime" as much as possible so that the child makes an association between the act and the punishment.

Children generally accept discipline when it is rational and shows their parents' concerns for their welfare. Children who come from homes that are predominantly supportive and generally positive require less frequent punishment because they voluntarily conform more often to their parents' wishes. They also require less severe punishment because they are more sensitive to their parents' displeasure and respond to milder sanctions (Rollins and Thomas 1979).

Child Maltreatment

Unfortunately, not all parents are wise disciplinarians. Fatigue and stress often cause parents to behave in ways that may harm their children. Many parents defend physical punishment—usually because that is how their own parents dealt with them. The idea seems to be, "I didn't turn out so bad, so what was good enough for me will be good enough for my children." The problem however, is that physical punishment is usually delivered in anger and exasperation. When parents' emotions run high, they can easily lose control.

Every year over a million American children are seriously hurt by their parents. Children are beaten, burned, thrown to the floor or against a wall, put outdoors in extremely cold or hot weather, tied up, locked in closets, and denied food or water. Child abuse seems to peak at about age three; the leading cause of death for children under the age of three is parental violence (California Commission on Crime Control and Violence Prevention 1981).

The research on child abuse indicates that the causes of child abuse are many. Parents who are immature and troubled are often easily stressed by normal childhood behavior. Inexperienced parents may have unrealistic notions about how children should behave in general and about what is appropriate behavior for the age of the child. Often one child in a family becomes the target of parental displeasure. These children may be at high risk because they are difficult, handicapped, unwanted, or sometimes just because they look like a relative or ex-spouse whom the parent does not like. Some people seem predisposed to react to any stress with violence, and when the stress is caused by a child, the stage is set for abuse.

Sexual abuse of children by one of the parents or stepparents also frequently occurs in the home. Most such cases are probably never reported, and statistics, for that reason, are likely to be low. One reason that such acts are not reported is children are often not believed when they report such abuse. Many children who are sexually molested are preschool age and are often too young to know exactly what is happening to them. If they are aware of the significance of what is happening, children sometimes are afraid of retaliation or punishment if they tell. Others may feel guilty.

Child neglect is another form of maltreatment of children. While child abuse is an overt act of violence to a child, neglect is failure to take care of a child's physical and emotional needs. Neglect is often more difficult to ascertain than abuse, unless of course, the neglect can be seen by outsiders, as when children are hungry, not properly dressed, left unattended under risky circumstances, or not given proper medical care.

Thousands of cases of child abuse and neglect probably go undetected each year. Often injuries are judged to be accidental and therefore go unreported. Neglect and sexual abuse are even more difficult to prove. All states require that if there is even a suspicion of maltreatment, however, the case must be reported to Child Protective Services. Child maltreatment is a crime, and guilty parents may face prison terms, be required to undergo psychological treatment, and lose custody of their children.

There is help for abusive parents. Parents Anonymous is an organization with chapters in nearly every major city; their telephone numbers are listed in the directory. Groups meet on a regular basis; members share phone numbers so that they are available to each other for immediate support and to help each other to deal with stress more constructively. Other cities have hotlines, which parents can call if they feel overwhelmed and fear they may abuse their children. Treatment programs by qualified mental health professionals can be located through local mental health clinics.

Cooperation

Family therapists believe that competent families, no matter what their values, rituals, or other cultural uniquenesses, have a number of similarities that distinguish them from families that function less well or that may even be in crisis regularly. Two similarities stand out as especially significant patterns of competent families: (1) the parents work cooperatively as a team, and (2) there are good communication patterns in the family.

Parental coalition is the concept that describes parents who stand unified and do not allow children to play one against the other. When the relationship between a mother and father is fragile, children may learn to use the rift between their parents as a means to achieve their own ends. Often couples with children are unable to form a parental coalition because of emotional conflicts between them. They may be unconsciously caught up in a fight for family power, for example, and children who sense the struggle may side with one parent or the other—perhaps with the one who offers the most. Compatibility of the parents' philosophies about child raising is one of the most crucial factors in parental coalition formation. Learning where they agree and working out compromises when they disagree helps them avoid many of the conflicts that lead to disharmony in families.

Communication

Good communication patterns in families have been the objects of a great deal of family research. Family-life experts stress that effective family functioning necessitates clear communication channels between family members. A pioneer in the study of communication in the family, Don Jackson (1967, p. 174), remarked:

> The family is an interacting communications network in which every member from the day-old baby to the 70-year-old grandfather influences the nature of the entire system and in turn is influenced by it.

Jackson stressed that in communication what is said is only a part of such influence. Just as important are how it is said and what the intention behind the communication is. Clear communication takes into consideration the levels of communication—from the first level, which is content, to the deeper levels involving tone of voice, body movements, inflections, emphasis, speed of the communication, and other nonverbal behaviors that give clues to various levels of meaning in the interchange.

Another of those who has emphasized clear communication as a necessary ingredient in functional, healthy families is Virginia Satir (1967, p. 97), who wrote:

> There are four wrong ways people communicate. You can blame, you can placate, you can be irrelevant or you can be "reasonable." There's something incomplete about each way. The blamer leaves out what he feels about the other person, the placater leaves out what he feels about himself, the reasonable one leaves out what he feels about the subject being discussed and the irrelevant one leaves out everything.

Satir believed that each family develops its own rules of communication. In some, only positive comments are allowed and only good feelings may be expressed. An angry child is banished to his or her room or made to feel guilty about such feelings. No space is allowed for real feelings, and the family ceases to be a place where members can have their emotional needs met.

Successful families, on the other hand, foster an environment for growth in all dimensions of their members. Clear, open communication frees both children and parents to understand each other, support each other, and encourage each other to grow.

FATHER-MOTHER DIFFERENCES

Studies of parent-child relations have typically been concerned with the influences of the mother on the child. Most of the early research placed a heavy emphasis on the mother-child interaction—almost as though fathers were hardly in the picture. In fact, the word *parenting* is of rather recent origin, having replaced *mothering*, which was used almost exclusively until recently.

Current research recognizes that fathers play roles as significant in parenting as do mothers. As fathers spend more and more time with their children, their influence shows an increasing impact. Both parents can be blamed or praised for the way their children develop. Fathers have been declared "just as nurturant as mothers" and, given the opportunity, are as competent and enthusiastic about taking care of children as mothers are (Sawin and Parke 1979; Parke and Sawin 1976, p. 368).

Parental Satisfaction

A study reported in 1978 found that only about 5 percent of parents failed to derive great satisfaction from their parenting when their children were in preschool or elementary school. Mothers consistently found parenthood their greatest source of satisfaction among their life's activities, but fathers' sources of satisfaction varied with the ages of their children. At certain ages of their children, fathers rated their marriage relationship as more important than their parenting relationship, although they more frequently ranked the amount of satisfaction from parenting as greater than that from their occupations (Hoffman and Manis 1978; cited in Newman and Newman 1984, pp. 14–15).

In traditional homes the father's role was seen as an important supporter for the mother, who usually assumed the role of primary caretaker. The father was seen as the disciplinarian and the chief wage earner and financial support for the family. There still is a tendency in many families to assume that providing financial support is equivalent to being a good father (Biller and Meredith 1974). Recently this notion has been seriously questioned with the realization that earning a living has in fact frequently interfered with the father role. However, when there is great time pressure, as there often is in the strain from the many roles of parents, institutionalized definitions provide an immediate pattern of response to unexpected events. If a button pops off father's last clean shirt at the same time the car battery goes dead, father may almost automatically hand the shirt to mother while he reaches for the telephone to call the auto club—otherwise the children would be late for school. The traditional solution does not require time to think through novel solutions or to experiment with trial and error to discover the most equitable outcome. It solves an immediate problem, which at the moment seems more important than debating the appropriateness of gender roles.

Housework

Over ten years ago a research project widely cited in feminist literature explored men's family roles, including their participation in housework and child care. At that time it was found that men were involved in "family work" only between one and one and a half hours a day, with child care occupying only a short period of each day (Pleck 1975b). Men's work roles were to some extent blamed for their minimal involvement; but, more than anything, the author cited "parental differentiation" as the cause. Women who did not work outside the home took the major child-rearing responsibilities, and men took the major financial responsibilities.

A special study of the U.S. Census Bureau, published in December 1983 and September 1985, showed dramatic changes. The civilian labor force participation rate for women rose from 43 percent in 1970 to 53 percent in 1983; that of males declined from 80 percent to 77 percent. The largest increase in participation was for women with husbands present who had children under the age of six years at home; the fraction of such women employed rose from 30 percent in 1970 to 49 percent in 1982. Married women with school-age children (six to seventeen years old) increased their participation rate from 49 percent to 63 percent during the same period (U.S. Bureau of the Census 1983e, p. 24; 1985h, pp. 24–25). A recent

Fathers generally enjoy "rough and tumble" play with their children—especially sons—and children seem to enjoy this as well as the quieter play they have with their mothers.

national time-use study of employed wives found that they spent only twelve more minutes per day in combined paid work and family work than their husbands did (Lewis 1984, p. 70). This conflicts with older research showing that women work longer hours. It is probable that women work fewer hours in paid employment than men do but make up the difference (plus 12 minutes) by working more at home than men do.

As increasing numbers of women are employed, many men are taking more active parenting roles. The number of "househusbands" increased from about 54,000 in 1973 to 93,000 in 1983 (U.S. Bureau of the Census 1985h p. 24). (For a comprehensive resource guide presenting information on single fathers, gay fathers, adoptive fathers, working fathers, stepfathers, and others, see Bank Street College of Education 1983, cited in Klinman and Kohl 1984.)

Play

An earlier study indicated that as children grow older, they showed more desire to play with their fathers than when they were younger and that fathers also showed more interest in their older children—particularly their sons (Lamb 1977). Fathers generally played more vigorously with children than mothers did, and children responded positively to this style of activity. It has been concluded that it may not be fathers per se that children prefer but the "physically stimulating, rough-and-tumble nonintellectual nature of paternal play" (Clark-Stewart 1978, p. 475). Children whose fathers spent a substantial amount of time with them adapted more readily to new situations and were better able to withstand stress (Lamb 1977). Active stimulation by their fathers seems to be one key to children's greater adaptability. Another is that the presence of two active parents caring for a child increases the child's diversity of responses.

Responsiveness

A study at the National Institute of Child Health and Human Development found that a father's responsiveness to his child is significantly related to the infant's ability to manipulate toys successfully (*Science News,* September 6, 1984, p. 153). Sociologist Joan Aldous (1975, pp. 719–720) reported that, in a highly selected sample of families, fathers' directive behavior toward their daughters was positively associated with the daughters' ability to give original responses to assigned tasks, even though the same behaviors on the part of mothers had no such effect on children of either sex. Mothers tended to give help to their daughters faced with such tasks, but not to their sons, when they requested it.

In a comprehensive cross-cultural analysis of men and children, males were observed in their relationships with children in the United States, Ireland, Spain, Japan, and Mexico (Mackey and Day 1979). These were not necessarily father-children observations since the observers made no attempts to determine kinship. However, the findings may well serve as an indication of "fathering-type" behaviors. Some of the major findings were that men in all five nations associated and interacted with children in very much the same manner. In general, the younger the child, the more likely the man was to touch the child. Men made no distinction between girls and boys, and in no instances did men interact less with children than did women who might also be present.

Some studies have suggested that fathers and mothers influence the development of their children differently. It has been reported that fathers respond to their sons more and that they tend to spend more time with them each day than they do with daughters. The research is often contradictory, however, since most studies have not taken into consideration the total amount of time that fathers spend with their children. For instance, fathers who stay at home to take care of their children or who have primary care of them in single-parent households interact with their children much as mothers do (Parke and O'Leary 1975). When fathers spend more time caring for their children, they are believed to establish a nurturant relationship with them rather than the "pals" interaction that is often typical of many father-son relationships (Pogrebin 1980).

Other studies have reported on the fathers' socioeconomic status and their parenting practices (Kohn 1977). Fathers are thought to be instrumental in forming their children's lives by translating their socioeconomic values into behaviors toward their children. Higher-status fathers were reported to reward their children for thinking through problems and for being inquisitive about alternative approaches, and to tend to examine the children's motives and feelings more when they misbehaved. Lower-status fathers, on the other hand, tended to reward their children for unquestioning conformity. Deviation from the rules was more emotionally threatening for these fathers. Since children whose fathers were in the lower socioeconomic category were expected to conform to their fathers' values, they were also found to have identified their gender roles earlier in life and more narrowly than did children from higher-status homes (Lynn 1974). Leisure activities were more likely to be sex-segregated in homes at lower socioeconomic levels than in upper-class ones, and being a "tomboy" or a "sissy" was a more serious violation of the rules.

Until rather recently most of the studies of children and adults either focused on mothers and children exclusively or gathered information about the father's role from the report of the mother. Since the father's role is defined in part by his relationship with his wife and how she sees his behavior as a father, her report of his relationship to his children was thought to be subject to bias. In his study of the role of fathers, educator Michael Lamb (1977) not only confirmed this suspicion but also found that the child's perception of his or her father is influenced significantly by the mother's attitude toward the father. A mother who warns the child, "Daddy will be tired and cross when he comes home, so stay out of his way," or "Wait until your father comes home and he will spank you," puts the father at a real disadvantage in relating well to his children. On the other hand, even when the father is absent from the home for extended periods of time (for example, for business or military duty), his picture on the wall and the anticipation of his letters, eagerly shared, can convey to children that their father is a very special person.

Fathers are not totally at the mercy of their wives' interpretations of them, however. Fathers' direct relationships with their children are more important and permit children to make their own judgments. It is true, however, that both mothers' and fathers' parenting behaviors are affected by the opinions of one another each conveys to children.

There is significant research showing that one parent's behavior is changed by the presence of the other during parent-child interaction (Clarke-Stewart 1978, p. 475). For example, fathers talk to and touch children more when the mothers are also present. Mothers tend to respond to and play with girls less when the father is present. With boys, mothers smile and touch more when the father is also present than when they are alone with the boys (Parke and O'Leary 1975). It might be concluded that fathers can enhance the mothers' interactions with their sons by being present during their times together. It is as though the father's presence encourages the mother to spend more time stimulating her son.

A study of touching in the family has shown that parents tend to reach out and touch children more often than children reach out to touch their parents; that fathers were more likely to touch mothers than vice versa; mothers were more likely than fathers to touch children; and that mothers received more body contact than any other single family member, getting as many touches as the older child in a two-child family (Grusky, Bonacich, and Peyrot 1984, pp. 720–721).

Since the evidence indicates that parents respond differently when they are alone with a child from the way they do when the other parent is present, understanding the true picture of *family* life requires that all members be seen in relationship to each other with other members also present. In their review of parent-child research of the 1970s, James Walters and Lynda Walters (1980) recommended that family studies focus on mother-father-child relationships and on mother-father-child-sibling relationships rather than (as has been done in the past) on mother-child relationships or, more recently, father-child relationships. This is in keeping with the belief that families are systems in which each member affects every other member.

INFLUENCES OF CHILDREN ON THEIR PARENTS

Almost without exception, the literature on parent-child relationships has emphasized parents' influences on children. Until about ten years ago the powerful influences that children have on their parents were largely neglected. During the past decade a shift toward studying these influences has begun, although there is still relatively little research on the effects of children on their parents compared with those of parents' impact on children (Walters and Walters 1980).

The notion that children affect a marriage has been around for a long time. Family sociologists have reported that children tend to detract from rather than to contribute to marital satisfaction. Wives especially report that children have negative impacts on the quality of marriage (Hicks and Platt 1970). On the other hand, in a study of couples with low levels of marital satisfaction, many reported that their children were among their only sources of mutual satisfaction (Luckey and Bain 1970).

Most of the current evidence about the impact of children on their parents' marriages seems to support the notion that parents manage to weather the child-rearing period if the marriage is intact and reasonably satisfying to both partners, although the drain on their time, energy, and economic resources may decrease their marital satisfaction. Children do not make marriages better, but they do not ruin them either (Rollins and Galligan 1978).

We have often remarked to our classes in response to student complaints that some of their assigned reading was confusing that "confusion is the first step in learning. A person who already has a full understanding of a new experience is not going to learn anything from it." From that point of view, it can be observed that parenting certainly presents ample opportunities for learning (see Newman and Newman 1984, p. 28).

One of the advantages of parenthood is that it stimulates growth through new experiences. In one analysis of parenthood, the authors comment:

> Parents learn, through parenting, something about what kinds of persons they are. Many of their reactions and feelings in this new situation tell them something about themselves and their attitudes and values to life as well as about their capacities in the specific role of parent. They see themselves exposed to experiences such as the handling of stresses and discomforts that may be new to them, and what they see may require a reappraisal of themselves as people. (Rapoport, Rapoport, and Strelitz 1980, pp. 27–28)

One of the most complicated issues concerning children's impact on their parents has to do with how parents reconcile their personal needs with those of their children.

> Parents are not only vehicles for the care of their children. They were persons before the child arrived; are persons while they are parents; and will be after the children leave. They were once told to listen to their parents. They are now told to listen to their children. They must, in addition, listen to themselves. (Group for the Advancement of Psychiatry 1973, pp. 131–132)

Parents' and children's needs do not always mesh. In the past, when children were often treated as ones who should be seen but not heard, parents' social needs came first. More recently, there has been a child-centered approach, with children's social needs coming first. The search for some balance seems necessary if family life is to meet the demands of individual family members and those of the outside community. Since the social needs of parents and children sometimes do not coincide, arrangements need to be made so that neither children nor parents suffer unduly.

"For the parent, no matter how devoted to the joys of parenthood, it is desirable—for the child's sake as well as the parent's—to avoid martyrdom. Arriving at compromises, exchanges, and settlements for families to achieve a tolerable degree of harmony is a major part of the work of parenting (Rapoport, Rapoport, Strelitz 1980, p. 21).

Many of the discomforts and anxieties of today's parents and much of the unhappiness they reported as a result of trying to raise children satisfactorily seem to be directly related to how much the parental role totally eclipses the parents' individualities and their relationship as husband and wife. Too many couples seeking help for their troubled family relationships tell us that they "have nothing in common anymore except the children" or that they feel guilty if they take time for themselves, either individually or as a couple.

There is little question that parenthood and marriage compete for the same resources of time, energy, and money. One of the most frequent complaints of young parents is that they feel conflict between the demands of their family responsibilities and the desire to spend time maintaining their bond as a couple (Walters and Walters 1980).

Klaus Riegel (1976, cited in Newman and Newman 1984, p. 34) defined one characteristic of adult cognition as the capability of entertaining two or more conflicting ideas in one's mind at the same time. Newman and Newman (1984, p. 34) point out that parenting enhances the development of this capacity. They believe that as a result of such **dissonance reduction**, parents feel closer to one another. When parents manage to find a balance between their own social needs and those of their children, not only do they become better parents, but they also report a greater satisfaction with their lives and their marriages (Group for the Advancement of Psychiatry 1973).

In a major cross-cultural study of parents' reactions to their children, it was found that parents ranked the emotional cost of having children as the most stressful disadvantage and ranked the psychological factors of happiness, love, and companionship that children bring as the main advantages of having children (Arnold et al. 1975). Sons were preferred—usually to ensure that the family name would be passed down to another generation. Also, some families believed that sons would bring more of the joys of parenting and might be of some economic help as well. In general, however, in the six societies studied, psychological reasons were the main motives for having children and also brought the greatest problems to parents.

Two particular events in parenting have been singled out as especially likely to upset the marital balance (Lasswell 1984). The birth of the first child produces the most impact because the child forces the couple to add new and unaccustomed roles. Moreover, the first child is a novelty and will remain so as he or she reaches each new stage. In effect, the first child blazes a trail for those siblings yet to come and trains his or her parents. Each major transition period for the firstborn may be a source of stress for the parents. This is especially the case when the oldest child reaches adolescence and the lack of role clarity experienced by the child and parents frequently causes great stress.

The youngest child has also been shown to serve as a definer of parents' lives. In contrast to firstborns, however, the youngest child's entry into school and ultimate departure from home more often than not have a positive effect on the parents' lives. Sometimes the last child's departure leaves an empty nest, which has been said to be difficult for some parents. It is the end of a long phase of parenting—usually twenty or more years—and many men and women who are already battling feelings about the waning of their youth find it even more disturbing to have the onset of middle age reinforced by the end of their child-rearing years.

Children with Handicaps

Parenthood at its best is rarely uncomplicated, but when a child is handicapped in some serious way, the effect on the parents' lives is often drastic. Whether the handicap is physical or mental, it is often very difficult for the parents to accept. Some parents become overly involved, devoting their entire lives to the child; others run the danger of rejecting the child as a result of their disappointment or feelings of guilt (Ferbolt and Solnit 1978). The parents may interpret the birth of such a child as the result of a flaw in their heredities. Sometimes the mother blames herself, believing that she may have been careless during pregnancy, that she failed to provide an adequate intrauterine environment, or that she is somehow being punished for some act or thought.

Although some parents may reject a handicapped child, overprotectiveness is a far more common reaction (Bell 1964). This was found to be so for children who suffered from blindness, congenital heart defects, Down's syndrome, and cerebral palsy. Excessive vigilance and restriction of both the child's and the parents' activities are often seen. It has been suggested that since our society places such emphasis on a child's development of independence, raising a handicapped child may cause greater stress for parents in the United States than in some other societies (Jordan 1962). Support groups such as Parents Helping Parents can provide help, advice, and encouragement (telephone: 408-288-5010).

Besides the obvious emotional factors involved in having a handicapped child, a considerable additional financial burden is often placed on parents. Family activities may be curtailed and other children in the family may feel slighted as a result of the parents' involvement with the handicapped child. The younger the handicapped child, the more the parents seem to be involved and the more the siblings are influenced (Farber 1959).

One-Parent Families

Children who are brought up in one-parent homes often are those whose parents have been separated or who are divorced. Most commonly the mother has custody in such cases. However, there are many children who have only one parent present because of a death or because they were born out of wedlock. A discussion of single-parent homes does not include those in which a parent is away for long periods of time as a result of job requirements; however, the problems may be very nearly the same except that the absent parent's financial contribution is very valuable. Children whose parents are divorced also may have financial help from the noncustodial parent. In Chapter 13 we will discuss the homes of divorced parents and their children. However, to cover the full range of parenting behavior, we must deal with those children who are brought up by only one parent (usually the mother, but sometimes— more often than ever before—by the father).

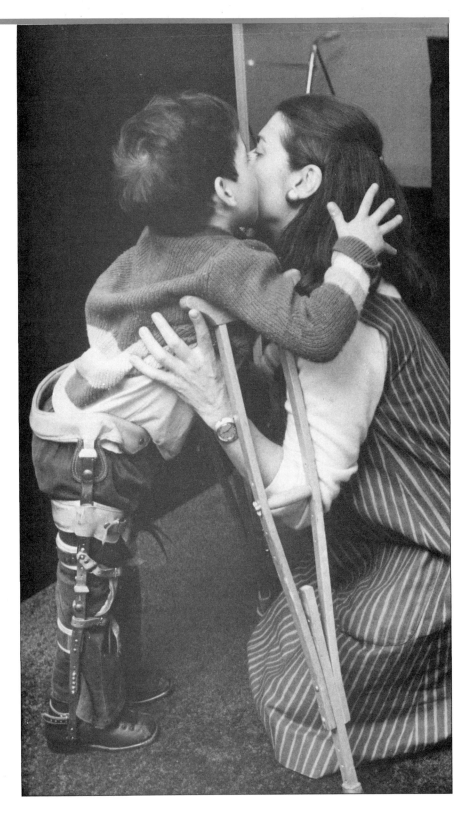

Parents of children who are handicapped have special responsibilities and concerns. Support groups can provide help, advice, and encouragement.

In the United States today there is a definite increase in the number of unmarried mothers who are choosing to keep their children. Over the last two decades, the Bureau of the Census has documented the number of families maintained by women with no husband present. During the 1970s this type of family had a higher rate of growth than any other type. There were about 33.2 million households in the United States that had children of their own under the age of eighteen years present in 1984; 8.5 million of them were single-parent households, two and a quarter times as many as there were in 1970 (U.S. Bureau of the Census 1985a, p. 4). The racial distribution of single-parent households is remarkable. Whereas 81 percent of white households with children present were headed by married couples and 72 percent of Spanish-origin* households were, only 41 percent—less than half—of black households with children had two parents present (U.S. Bureau of the Census 1985b, p. 4). (See Figure 11.2.)

In 1983, the type of family most likely to include a child was one that was maintained by a woman with no husband present (60 percent of households headed by women had children), followed by married-couple families (49 percent had children), and families maintained by a man with no wife present (37 percent had children) (U.S. Bureau of the Census 1984f, p. 6).

Single parents have tended to be less well educated. More than half the female heads of households in 1970 had not completed four years of high school (U.S. Bureau of the Census 1980c, p. 7). Paradoxically, as the population of single-parent house-holders had become more youthful, this percentage has decreased. In 1983, nearly 70 percent of women who were single parents were at least high school graduates, and over 25 percent had attended college (U.S. Bureau of the Census 1984b, p. 8).

It has been found that single-parent households have lower average incomes than do two-parent homes; in 1983 the median income of woman-headed households ($11,790) was only 43 percent of the median income of two-parent households ($27,290) (U.S. Bureau of the Census 1984i, p. 2). The contrast was even greater for married-couple families with wives in the labor force ($28,570). If both husband and wife worked year-round, full-time, the family income in 1983 was $39,390 (U.S. Bureau of the Census 1986b, p. 1). In the last case, the median income of a female householder with no husband present would have been approximately 30 percent of such a household. To aggravate the situation further, families with female house-holders, no husband present, had 29 percent more children under the age of eighteen years present in the home than did married-couple families (U.S. Bureau of the Census 1984f, p. 11). Financial problems often are of greater concern than the fact that there is only one parent.

Besides their financial difficulties, single parents, who usually have full responsibility for their children, are generally overworked; fatigued; and lacking in the emotional, social, and material support provided by a spouse. Children brought up in homes with only one parent are more likely than children with two parents present to have behavioral problems (Rutter 1975). However, the fact of having only one parent is not necessarily the primary cause of behavior problems. Rather, the many difficulties associated with having only one parent—lower income, parental stress, and social privation—may be the major factors.

---

*The Bureau of the Census notes that "persons of Spanish origin may be of any race."

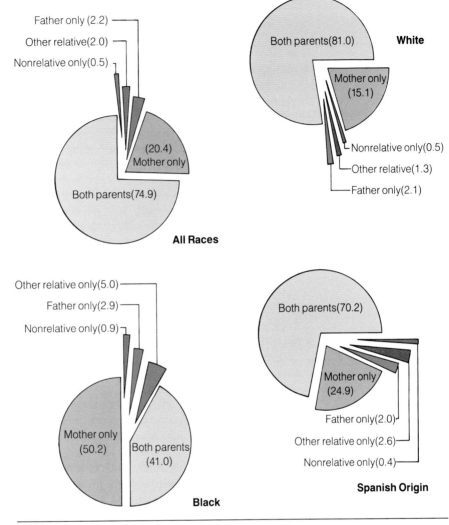

FIGURE 11 · 2
Living Arrangements
of Children under 18,
by Race and Spanish
Origin, in Percent,
March 1984

Father only (2.2)
Other relative(2.0)
Nonrelative only(0.5)

(20.4)
Mother only

Both parents(74.9)

All Races

Both parents(81.0)   **White**

Mother only
(15.1)

Nonrelative only(0.5)
Other relative(1.3)
Father only(2.1)

Other relative only(5.0)
Father only(2.9)
Nonrelative only(0.9)

Mother only
(50.2)

Both parents
(41.0)

Black

Both parents(70.2)

Mother only
(24.9)

Father only(2.0)
Other relative only(2.6)
Nonrelative only(0.4)

Spanish Origin

Source: U.S. Bureau of the Census, Current Population Reports,
Series P-23, No. 145 (September 1985), p. 18.

Some single men and women adopt children. This is usually very difficult to
accomplish unless the child is a relative or is difficult to place. In California, in 1974,
the first single parent to adopt was apparently approved only because the child had
handicaps and had been rejected by several couples. The adoptive parent was a male
who presumably wanted to be a father but did not want to marry. Some single women
who have not married also have adopted children. The new role of women and their
increasing financial independence has enabled many who wish to do so to adopt
children and continue to work, much like married men or women who have children
and then divorce before the children are very old.

Single parents still report that they lack much of the social support given to two-parent families and that their children often are targeted as "different." They report occasional embarrassment in explaining that there is no father (or mother) present (Chester 1977).

Teenage Parents

As we saw in Chapter 9, premarital childbearing, especially by teenagers, has been a growing national concern in recent years. There are serious economic disadvantages for the mother and child. There are similar disadvantages for couples who marry as a result of the discovery of a premarital pregnancy (Freedman and Thornton 1979). In general, the older an American woman is when she marries, the more likely her first child is to be conceived in wedlock (see Figure 11.3). As of June 1982, only 25 percent of the births to white women aged 15 to 17 were conceived after marriage; 93 percent of the births to white women aged 25 to 29 years were. For black women the comparable figures were 1 percent and 64 percent (U.S. Bureau of the Census 1984e, p. 9).

Earlier studies have shown that the partners of teenage women who are married are, on the average, two years older than the mothers. If the young parents are still in school when their babies arrive, their educations usually must be interrupted. Studies show that men who marry in their teens are more likely than those who marry later to have unskilled, low-paying jobs. Even so, the father has a legally enforceable obligation to support his child for the next eighteen years (Nye 1976).

Having a baby in the teenage years tends to be related to having additional children in rapid succession. One-sixth of all mothers under eighteen who give birth to a child are, in fact, giving birth to a second or a third child (Nye 1976). This is especially likely to be the case if they are married. Several studies during the 1970s have indicated that teenage parenthood may be less disruptive if the parents do not marry, especially if the mother's family helps her and if she returns to school (Furstenberg 1978).

Marrying and not returning to school usually result in a lack of the education that these young people need to secure the kinds of jobs that will enable them to support themselves and their child(ren). Unless the father is considerably older than the mother, the couple may be doomed to years of low income. A large nationwide survey found that of those who became mothers between ages thirteen and fifteen, only 11 percent ever graduated from high school. Of women who became mothers before age sixteen, 31 percent were living below the poverty level when interviewed (Bacon 1974).

Some scholars see single parenting by teenage mothers as having an increasing effect on the equality of women to men in employment opportunities. Margaret Mooney Marini (1984) concluded that "to the extent that early childbirth continues to interfere with the educational attainment of women, it will preclude women from attaining educational parity with men."

The divorce rate for couples who have a child in their teen years is about two and a half times as great as that of those who wait until they are 22 or older (Bacon 1974). Those couples who wait two years or more after marrying before having a child are less likely to divorce. Research findings imply that marriage and parenthood

FIGURE 11 · 3
First Births of
Women by Age of
Mothers (15–29),
1977–1982

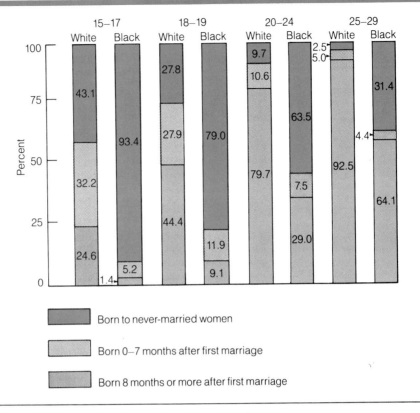

Percent

	15–17		18–19		20–24		25–29	
	White	Black	White	Black	White	Black	White	Black

Born to never-married women

Born 0–7 months after first marriage

Born 8 months or more after first marriage

Source: U.S. Bureau of the Census, *Current Population Reports,*
Series P-20, No. 387, pp. 8–9.

are likely to be more satisfying if couples do not hurry their "life schedules" (Nye 1976). The following suggestions are given for a "life schedule" in which a person is more likely to develop a satisfying marriage and good experiences as a parent (Nye 1976):

1. Complete an education.
2. Gain some work experience.
3. Find a person with whom you would really like to share your life and take time to become well acquainted.
4. Delay parenthood until the marriage has been tested for a couple of years.

SUMMARY

1. The notions that people have about parenting begin to take shape long before the first child is born or adopted. The "idealization" process that occurs includes how the baby will look, how intelligent the child will be, and myriads of other expectations.

2. There are also parental notions of "rightness" and "wrongness" of a child's behavior as well as of what parents "should" do. Many of these ideas are based on the parents' own childhood experiences—if good ones, to be emulated; if poor ones, to be corrected.

3. Parents go through cycles of "parenting" in which they play a variety of roles much as children go through developmental stages. Eventually, parenthood must end, although some parents find it difficult to give up that role, just as many adults find it difficult to quit being children.

4. One of the chief problems in defining parent-child relationships is that the life cycle mandates change. About the time that parents have adjusted to the new baby, for example, the baby changes. Then another child is born; then the children grow up and leave home. Parents, too, change over the life cycle, both as individuals and in reaction to their children's developmental needs. Family size also mandates not only the length of the parenting years but the time and energy that can be given to each child's needs.

5. Children learn from their parents both by direct teaching and by imitation. Children go through developmental stages from dependency to influencing to self-sufficiency. Parents have the opportunity to contribute significantly at each level by creating a warm, supportive environment in which children can develop as individuals.

6. Parents do affect their children's lives, whether positively or negatively. Good parenting can be learned, and parent-training programs are proving to be highly effective.

7. Various parenting styles and the results of each have been the subject of numerous studies. Three styles that have been distinguished are authoritarian, authoritative, and permissive. Members of different social classes often differ with respect to which of these patterns is preferred. The authoritarian style was found to be more popular with blue-collar families. Middle-class families were more likely to be authoritative. Other types of parenting styles have been described as martyr, buddy, drill sergeant, teacher, and coach.

8. Most children do well with any of the types of parenting styles as long as parents are consistent, caring, and involved. Delinquent children most often come from homes where these factors are absent.

9. Punishment is often necessary but should be used judiciously. It is most effective when closely associated in time with the undesired behavior; when it is accompanied by an explanation and a suggestion of alternate behavior; and when it "fits the crime."

10. Family therapists believe that competent families have some things in common. Chief among these are that parents work cooperatively as a team and that there are good communication patterns in the family.

11. Early research on parenthood focused on mother-child interaction, but recently, as fathers have come to be studied, it has been determined that they can be just as nurturant as mothers if given the opportunity. Typically, however, fathers have been defined socially and legally as support resources for mothers (who have had the primary responsibility for child care) and as wage earners for the family.

12. Fathers respond differently to children from the way mothers do and tend to treat their sons differently from their daughters unless they are in a primary care position (in which case they tend to interact with their children much as mothers do). Fathers tend to play with their children differently from mothers and to play differently with sons than with daughters.

13. The role of father as culturally defined in the United States is affected by socioeconomic status. Since men are so often absent from the home during the child's waking hours, many mothers "interpret" the father role to the child. Parents tend to behave differently when they are in each other's presence. For this reason, it has

been suggested that future parent-child studies should include all members of the family in interaction together as a system.

14. Children affect parents just as much as parents affect children. Research has shown that marriages are generally less satisfying after the birth of children, although parents also report that children bring satisfactions. Many of the reported dissatisfactions with parenthood appear to result from the pressure parents feel to subordinate their own needs to those of their children. Satisfaction seems to increase during the middle years of child-rearing but to decrease again during adolescence.

15. Children with handicaps present special problems for parents. The twin dangers are that parents may reject the handicapped child or that they may go to the other extreme and become overly involved to the detriment of their other children, their marriage, and their own needs.

16. One-parent families are a growing phenomenon in the United States. Traditionally single-parent families resulted from divorce or death, but the number of unmarried mothers has grown rapidly in recent years. There are a few single fathers, virtually all of whom are divorced or widowed.

17. Teenage parents have a particularly difficult time because they so often quit school and settle for low-paying jobs. The divorce rate is high for such young couples. Recent research has indicated that a teenage pregnancy is less of a problem in the long run if the couple do not marry, if they continue school, and if their parents help out.

GLOSSARY

Behavior modification The systematic attempt to change a subject's behavior patterns by responding to desired behaviors with rewards to the subject and by ignoring undesired behaviors (or by responding to them with punishment). (p. 342)

Developmental level The stage of the maturational process at which a child is currently functioning. (p. 338)

Dissonance reduction Taking steps to reduce tension that has resulted from contradictions between one's beliefs, emotions, and actions. (p. 355)

Ego strength The ability that an individual has to adjust to life, or the kind of character strength that he or she possesses; the ability to make decisions and the characteristic of taking personal responsibility for the decisions one has made. (p. 340)

Family of orientation The family in which one grows up. (p. 333)

Parent effectiveness training A program of instruction, developed by Thomas Gordon, in which parents receive guidelines for increased intimacy with children and for less authoritarian parenting. (p. 342)

Serial invalidation Consistent definition of a person's behaviors as inept, inappropriate, or incorrect by significant others. (p. 341)

There is in marriage an energy and impulse of joy that lasts as long as life and
that survives all sorts of suffering and distress and weariness. The triumph of marriage
over all its antagonists is almost inexplicable.

Every American family is subject to a host of outside influences. Some families passively accept what happens to them, and others react by attempting to change things when they can—sometimes constructively, sometimes not. One of the chief sources of outside pressures on families is the work life of the parents. Dual-income families have become the norm rather than the exception as a rising number of married women have entered the labor force. Child-care problems and overloading of time, energy, and coping strengths are still unresolved problems of this new lifestyle. Other sources of outside influences that affect the quality of marriage and family life are kin and friends. All hold the potential for being supportive and rewarding or for creating potentially destructive stresses and strains.

OUTSIDE INFLUENCES ON RELATIONSHIPS

James Douglas

*I*t is very important that marriage and the family be viewed in a broad context—not simply as parents and children with their own resources living in a relatively closed system, but rather as individuals who go outside the home daily to interact with members of the community at work, at school, in the neighborhood, at church, and at social functions. Kin and friends have an influence on the family unit as do the economy, politics, the weather, television, newspapers, and the educational system, to name but a few external phenomena.

Some outside influences are clearly under the control of the individual family members. They can choose whether to be receptive, indifferent, or hostile to them. They can turn off violent programs on television, choose certain friends over others, form a carpool, or turn down the furnace to confront the energy crisis. Some outside influences are not as much a matter of choice, however. An individual cannot always change jobs easily if the old one becomes stressful, for instance. It may not be possible to move just because the neighborhood is changing or the air is polluted. One may have to put up with troublesome behavior from kin because they also offer some things that are valued. To change many of the outside influences on families often necessitates paying such a price that people choose to put up with them instead. Social exchange theory speaks of the **cost-reward ratio** and explains that although we may pay dearly in some respects for what we receive, as long as the rewards outweigh the costs, we will usually continue to pay the price.

Finally, some outside influences seem totally out of control. The most obvious are what are called "acts of God." These may be natural disasters—floods, fires, earthquakes—that can leave a family in a state of shock and near ruin. The eruptions of the volcano Mount St. Helens reportedly caused unusual amounts of stress, anxiety, anger, and depression in the communities near the volcano. Physical abuse, suicide attempts, and calls to the community crisis line doubled, according to Washington State mental health authorities. Research on the effect of natural disasters on families has shown that to some extent the way the family defines the event is the most powerful determinant of how family members meet a stressful occurrence (McCubbin and Olson 1980).

Having the family home burn to the ground, with the loss of all their possessions, may be seen as the end by some families, but others—especially if they are well insured—may see it as a chance to rebuild. Not only the attitudes of family members, then, but also their resources account for the impact of a blow over which they seemingly have no control. Poor people and the elderly (who may also have low incomes) may be more severely affected by such traumas and are, in fact, more likely to be the victims. They are more likely to live in older, less adequate dwellings that are subject to fires or to flood or wind damage. Generally, however, natural disasters are not selective. The fatigue, anxiety, and worry that they cause provide fertile soil in which marital and family problems can grow.

Less dramatic, but not within an individual family's control, is the state of the economy—depression; spiraling inflation; the rising cost of housing, food, and medical care—all these influence the family unit. In times of economic recession, for instance, mental health experts report increases in marital problems, drinking, child abuse, and suicide attempts (McCubbin and Olson 1980). Although the economy is not directly responsible for these behaviors, financial stress may cause those persons already predisposed to such actions to carry them out. It is as though the economic frustrations push people over the brink (Moen 1979).

Inflation, a feature of an economy over which individuals have virtually no control, has profound implications for some decisions a family makes. Changes may have to be made in standards of living. What was once taken for granted may be deemed a luxury in a few years. Women have gone to work in growing numbers to increase family incomes in order to stave off the effects of rising prices. Perhaps most adolescents also will have to work in the future to provide family resources or at least to help defray the cost of their own needs.

High mortgage rates, which keep families from buying homes at all or strap them financially if they do buy, have created enough financial pressure that mental health workers are reporting increases in family discord and breakup. In communities where rentals are scarce (New York City reportedly has less than a 1 percent vacancy rate), it is reported that as families grow but cannot afford to move, crowding is becoming a serious source of stress.

STRESS IN FAMILIES

In a now classic piece of research conducted after World War II on separations and reunions caused by war, sociologist Reuben Hill (1949) outlined a set of variables and their relationships that has served as the foundation for research on family stress ever since. It is called the *ABCX* framework: *A* represents the event itself and the resulting hardships, *B* the family's resources for meeting the problems, *C* the definition the family gives to the situation, and *X* the crisis that results. The process underlying the *ABCX* pattern leading to the family's eventual adjustment involves an initial period of disorganization followed by a period of recovery and, finally, a new level of organization.

Family-stress research has focused on the impact on marriage and family life of stressor events and has noted that families can be very vulnerable and may even disintegrate unless they can muster resources to help them to cope (Burr 1973). Three important areas must be considered in understanding the impact of outside influences on marriages and families: (1) resources of members; (2) the family's definition of the situation; and (3) the degree of stress present in the family at the time.

The degree of stress experienced by a family is inversely related to the *resources* of its members for dealing with an incident or activity. Their resources include their coping skills, their personality strengths, their talents, their health, and their finances. Most families get through stressful times because they have learned to respond to any given situation in whatever ways the situation demands. They are usually versatile and flexible and are constantly adding to their repertoire of coping behaviors. In fact, some stress from external sources often has a positive effect on families. Family psychiatrist Jerry M. Lewis (1979, pp. 142–143) remarks:

> There is something about being exposed to some stress that jolts the family into re-evaluating its skills and characteristic ways of dealing with life. Assets that are hidden or little used may be discovered. The sharing can lead to deeper appreciation

of each individual's humanness. Family stereotypes may be shattered and myths dissolved. Coping successfully with stress can lead to increased family confidence in the ability to deal with future difficulties.

Family-stress literature indicates that families cope with outside influences both by mobilizing these inner resources and by utilizing resources available from the outside (Pratt 1976). The social structure in which family units are enmeshed has a powerful impact on them both by creating stress and by offering assistance to deal with it. Outside help from the community, friends, and kin comes not only through direct gifts of services and goods but indirectly as well through information, mediation, feedback, and validation of the family members' efforts to help themselves.

The family's *definition of the situation* is a second important variable in determining how they will respond to stress. Some families even choose a lifestyle that they know will be stressful rather than one that is lower in stress. Families who chose to move to Alaska to work on oil pipeline projects, for example, endured long separations while fathers were working and often traumatic reunions when they returned. Mental health workers in Alaska reported high incidences of family disruption as a result (Leon Webber 1980, personal communication). Nonetheless, these families chose to stay in Alaska to work and to make their homes.

Military families have also been shown to be vulnerable to strains that other, more conventional families may not experience. They endure frequent moves; separations in times of duty; and threats of injury or loss, especially during wartime. Loneliness, sexual tension, and dealing with children are major problems aggravated by military life. Although retention of military personnel is an acknowledged problem, attributable in part to family difficulties, many career military personnel have chosen this lifestyle despite its hardships. Studies have indicated that although military wives rate their marital satisfaction lower than their husbands rate theirs, over half of the wives would be willing to have the men reenlist at the end of their terms (Grace and Steiner 1978). A similar finding was made with army officers, over 60 percent of whom reported that their decisions to reenlist were influenced positively by their wives (Lund 1978). It is clear that either the advantages of some extremely stressful lifestyles outweigh the stresses for many families or else these families do not perceive the disadvantages in the same way as do those who cannot cope.

Choice itself seems to explain a good deal of why some families are better able than others to cope with the stress imposed by their lifestyles. When families view their lifestyles as the best among the various alternatives for themselves, they tend to minimize the negative aspects and to view their situations more positively (Bebbington 1973).

The third important factor in how outside influences affect marriages and families relates to how many *other simultaneous sources of stress* exist in addition to what the family may currently be suffering. For instance, a parent's loss of a job because of an economic recession will place great stress on the family unit. Most families can survive for a short period of time if they have other resources (savings, the other spouse's earnings, unemployment benefits) to call on. However, if they also have the coexistent strain of a child being hurt in an accident, for instance, or the serious illness or death of an elderly parent to compound their problems, the overload may prove too much.

Under conditions of stress that are sufficiently severe or prolonged, even families who cope well under most circumstances can become very disturbed. It does not

Military families experience separations not common to most families. At right, a prisoner of war returns after months away from his family to greet his daughter and to pick up the pieces of his life.

always take major stresses to push a family over the brink; often it is simply a series of incidents, each of which the family might be able to handle well, but which, when put together, add up to too much stress. Even minor stressful events can cumulatively reach unmanageable proportions. It may seem like a constant run of bad luck, one thing right after another—any one or two of which could be managed but which, taken together, cause such tension that the family unit begins to suffer.

WORK

Work is one of the most pervasive influences on the average family. Sigmund Freud is reputed to have said that the two most important things we can do as adults are to work and to love. In Chapter 3 we looked extensively at love; an exploration of the effects of work is important for understanding the impact of outside influences on marriage and family life. Most adults work half or more of their waking hours each weekday. Jobs and those with whom we work are sources of some of the major satisfactions in life as well as of some major stresses.

Work and Stress

In research on stress that uses a scale of items that cause stress in life, work-related events were found to account for one-quarter of the stressors in the average adult's life (Dudley and Welke 1977). Some of the events are pleasant and desirable ones, but they may produce stress nonetheless. Each event on the scale is given a stress value, and research has indicated that when one accumulates 150 points within a two-year period, there is a strong possibility of an illness or accident resulting. Table 12.1 shows some of the work-related items and their values from the longer list of items.

TABLE 12 · 1	Life Event	Mean Value
Work-Related Stress	Fired at work	47
	Retirement	45
	Business readjustment (e.g., merger, reorganization, bankruptcy)	39
	Change in financial state (a lot worse off or a lot better off than usual)	38
	Change to different line of work	36
	Change in responsibilities at work (promotion, demotion, or lateral transfer)	29
	Spouse begins or stops work	26
	Trouble with boss	23
	Change in work hours or conditions	20

Source: Table from *How to Survive Being Alive* by Donald Dudley and Elton Welke. Copyright © 1977 by Donald Dudley and Elton Welke. Reprinted by permission of Doubleday and Company, Inc.

Theoretically, if one were promoted (29 points) to a different line of work (36 points) with a nice pay raise (38 points), but with many more hours per week required (20 points), one would have 123 points—almost enough stress for trouble to be just around the corner. If, in addition, one or two other stressful events accompanied the foregoing—such as a move to a new location (20 points) and a traffic ticket (11 points)—a dangerous level of stress would be reached. Not only is there the increased possibility of health problems and accidents, but the tensions also may lead to more arguments with a spouse (35 points), sex difficulties (39 points), and possible separation (65 points). (The numbers in the parentheses are mean values, according to Dudley and Welke.) When such a high score is reached, a downward spiral often begins, with the work-related stress spilling over into the marriage and family life.

Couples who seek marital and family therapy often are experiencing a great deal of stress at work or school in addition to having serious problems getting along with each other. It is easy to understand and to blame job stress when what is happening is obviously bad—such as being fired or demoted. However, couples may not realize that marriage-threatening stresses also result from good things happening at work. A sudden increase in income, status, or responsibility in one partner's job may place a tremendous strain on a marriage relationship, even though the couple would not want to change their good fortune.

We also know that relationships at home can affect work performance; similarly, however, we do not usually recognize happy occurrences as stressful—even though indeed they may be. For instance, if one gets married (50 points), buys a condominium with a good-sized mortgage (31 points), moves into it (20 points), and begins a new job (36 points), with one's mate also beginning a new job (26 points), the stress level is very high. Troubles with the boss might well begin (23 points), and consequently one might even receive a lateral transfer to another department (29 points) or be fired (47 points).

Since in more and more marriages both partners work outside the home, the chances for job-related stress to affect a marriage are very great. Only slightly over 5 percent of the families in the United States fit the stereotypical model of a family in which the father is the sole wage earner for all the years the children are at home, while the mother remains at home, caring for it and for the children. In part this figure is so low because of the large numbers of single-parent households and of couples who have no children. Almost all fathers work outside the home, and 75–90 percent of married women who have no children work outside the home during their years of fecundity; younger wives (21–29 years) are twice as likely to be working as older wives (30–44 years) (U.S. Bureau of the Census 1984h, pp. 6–7). Currently more than half (55 percent) of all married women with minor children are in the labor force (U.S. Bureau of the Census 1984g, p. 26). Nearly half of those work part-time—usually those with small children. The average male in the labor force spends about 3 percent of the time between the ages of 21 and 64 out of work because of unemployment, illness, or family reasons; the average female spends about 31 percent during those years, overwhelmingly for "family reasons" (U.S. Bureau of the Census 1984h, pp. 6–7) (see Figure 12.1).

Dual-Worker Couples

The increase in the number of two-paycheck marriages is one of the most important changes that has taken place in recent years in the American family. At the turn of this century, only 18 percent of the labor force consisted of women, and 85 percent of those women who did work outside the home were single (Kimmel 1976). For over 150 years middle-class women were taught that their roles were concerned with the internal maintenance of the family and that their husbands' roles were concerned with the family's interface with the world outside the home.

Although sociologists and economists have termed the surge of women into the workplace one of the most outstanding phenomena of this century, it is not as though women had not previously contributed to the economy of the family. Women worked alongside men when the United States was predominantly an agricultural nation. From the earliest days of the industrial revolution, large numbers of women worked outside the home. Most who were single contributed to their parental home, in which they maintained their residence.

Changes in the Work Force   The change in the last three decades in the number of married women working outside the home for wages has been phenomenal. As late as 1900, only 5 percent of all married women in the United States were employed, and as recently as 1940, the proportion was no higher than 15 percent. Then during the four years of World War II, the government urged single and married women to fill the jobs vacated by men who had joined the armed services, pushing the total to 35 percent.

Following the war, many women dropped out of the labor force to become homemakers, although the decline in employed women was small and temporary. There were steady increases in the number of women in the labor force throughout the 1950s even though the postwar years glorified motherhood and domestic life. "For the first time in the history of any known society, motherhood became a full-

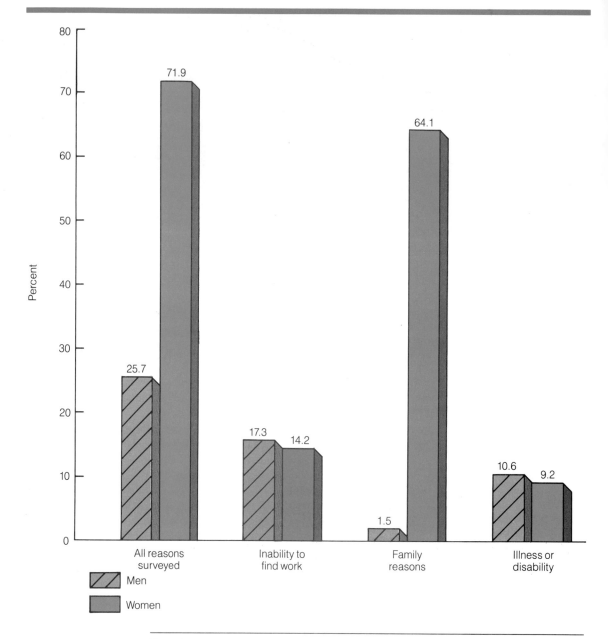

FIGURE 12 • 1

Percent of Persons Aged 21–64 Who Ever Worked and Who
Had One or More Work Interruptions Lasting 6 Months or
More, 1979

Source: U.S. Bureau of the Census, *Current Population Reports,* Series
P-23, No. 145 (September 1985), p. 28.

time occupation for women," wrote sociologist Alice Rossi (1964). In spite of the emphasis on traditional roles, by 1970 millions of women, spurred by economic needs, personal desire, and the effect of the women's rights movement on traditional roles and values, had poured into the labor market. Of the nearly 28 million employed wives in the United States, well over half (55 percent) have children under the age of eighteen at home, and almost a quarter (23 percent) have at least one child under the age of six (U.S. Bureau of the Census 1984g, p. 26).

Wages and Income Working only part-time enables many mothers to manage their heavy responsibilities. Part-time work schedules are easier to accommodate to school hours and to marketing, meal preparation, and other homemaking duties. Part-timers earn a much lower wage as a result, however—not only because they are employed for fewer hours but also because part-time jobs are usually at the low end of the pay scale and are not ones in which advancement is likely. Jobs that are available as part-time work often are ones that can be filled easily if the employee has to quit and consequently may not engender the kind of involvement that full-time jobs do. Research on job satisfaction indicates that it is positively related to hours worked and to fair pay. A study of employed married women showed that they are much more satisfied with their work when they have hours, salaries, and responsibilities equivalent to those of similarly employed men (Van Sell, Brief, and Addag 1979, pp. 38–42).

The dual responsibilities of most working women as both homemakers and wage earners often means that they work part-time or seasonally or as needed in a financial pinch. As a result, their pay stays at a level below that of men who are consistently in the full-time labor force. Another factor in the lower incomes of women is that most full-time pay schedules recognize seniority, or length of time employed by the company or agency; since women are ten times as likely to be employed intermittently (U.S. Bureau of the Census 1984h, pp. 6–7) or for fewer years at the same job, their pay is proportionately lower.

One in three employed women, however, earns at least as much as her husband (U.S. Bureau of the Census 1978b, p. 33); one in six earns more (U.S. Bureau of the Census 1984g, p. 1). Women who earn more tend to be married to men located disproportionately at the lower end of the income scale (or occasionally, at the upper end in the case of two professionals, for example). The majority of the six million households in which the wife outearns her husband involve men who have had difficulties finding work. More than half are cases where the husband has lost his job or only works part-time. In 1983, 12 percent of all households had women as the primary wage earner; that figure rose to 19.5 percent among blacks, but dropped to 10 percent for Hispanics. Black women have made significant wage gains since 1956. After-inflation pay for black women has increased 57 percent, nearly erasing the disparity with the wages of white women (Smith and Ward 1984). A few households involve a "female superstar," who is generally both highly educated and in a high-income professional job. There may be an increase in the numbers of high achieving women in the future because women are staying in school longer and are aiming for professions that pay the most. Women received about half of the master's degrees in 1981, over 30 percent of the doctorates (up from 13 percent in 1970), and 25 percent of the medical degrees (Tumulty 1984).

In 1983 the average man in the United States who worked year round, full time earned $22,508, but the average female year-round full-time worker earned

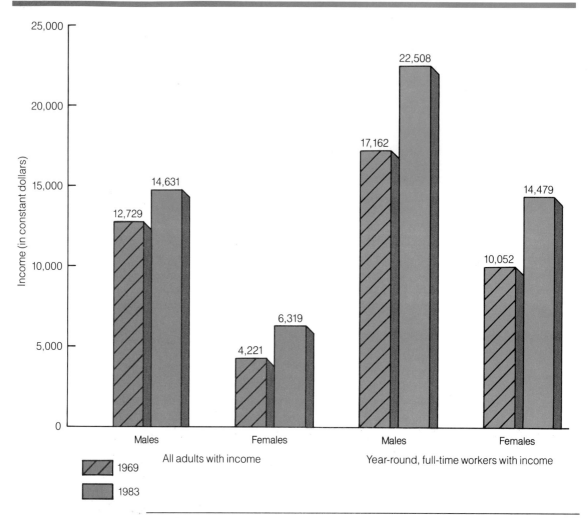

FIGURE 12 • 2

Median Income for Males and Females 14 Years and Over
with Income, by Work Experience, 1969 and 1983

Sources: 1969—U.S. Bureau of the Census, *Current Population Reports,*
Series P-20, No. 363 (June 1981), p. 40; 1983—U.S. Bureau of the
Census, *Current Population Reports,* Series P-60, No. 146 (April 1985),
p. 119–120.

$14,479. Between 1969 and 1983, the real median income for all males fifteen years
old and over increased by 15 percent, while there was a 50 percent increase for women
(U.S. Bureau of the Census 1985k, pp. 119–120) (see Figure 12.2).

Female-headed households were much more likely than married-couple families
to have low incomes. About 24 percent of families with female householders had
incomes of less than $5,000 in 1979, compared with about 4 percent of married-
couple households; at the other extreme, about 40 percent of married-couple families
had incomes above $25,000 in 1979, but only about 9 percent of families with female
householders had incomes in this range. In married-couple families, nearly all the

husbands and 88 percent of the wives received at least some income in 1979 (about 30 percent of the wives had no earnings but received income from jointly owned assets or other sources): 89 percent of white wives, 83 percent of black wives, and 78 percent of wives of Spanish origin. The black wives had the highest mean income in 1979—$6,260, compared with $5,551 for white wives and $5,151 for wives of Spanish origin (U.S. Bureau of the Census 1981a, p. 39).

Recent studies on the male-female wage gap predict that even though entry-level salaries for males and females in the same occupation are nearly equal because women's market skills have improved vastly, the chances of the overall gap closing in the foreseeable future are minimal (Smith and Ward 1984). This is due to several factors that are likely to change very slowly, if at all. An important reason is that women are concentrated in occupations—service and clerical—that pay less than traditional male jobs. It is possible that more women than men in their twenties are hesitant to commit themselves to a year-round, lifetime career or job for many reasons. There is a lingering attitude on both the part of women and their employers that women are not cut out for certain jobs. Not only does this attitude channel women into lower-paying work, but it also serves to keep them from top management positions.

Another significant factor in the widening wage gap between men and women after entering the work force, even in comparable jobs, is that women often drop out at critical points in their careers to have a family (see Figure 12.3). Women still have the primary responsibility for child rearing; even if they continue to work, they often forgo overtime and promotions that would conflict with home responsibilities. The ages of 25 to 35 have been shown repeatedly to be the period when working consistently and hard is vital to advancement and job security. These are precisely the years when women are likely to have children and begin to slide away from men in earning power. Consequently, a woman's income is more likely to be seen as secondary to her husband's.

Recent high unemployment figures in the United States (over 10.7 million people were unemployed in 1983) have been blamed for marital and family problems that typically surface with reduced financial resources. Not only are there obvious stresses surrounding economic survival when men and women are unable to find jobs, but there are problems involving self-worth and role changes as well. Many men have been put out of work by a decline in male-dominated jobs in construction and manufacturing. Their wives, on the other hand, who more typically are employed in clerical and service jobs often have found themselves the chief breadwinners. Their wages are lower than those earned in the higher-paying jobs husbands once held, but nonetheless, the wives' paychecks support the family. As a result, adjustments in child care and domestic duties as well as changes in decision making often become causes of conflict in these changed circumstances. As joblessness persists, many men's traditional position and power within the family become diminished. The more traditional the marital roles were before the husband's unemployment, the more stress seems to take its toll on the marriage (Larson 1984).

Work, Marriage, and Family Life   Many women are postponing childbearing either because they want to keep jobs they enjoy or because they need the income. Once they have children, many women quit their jobs to stay at home for a few years before returning to full-time or part-time outside employment. The length of time women stay at home depends on the number and spacing of their children, the family's financial

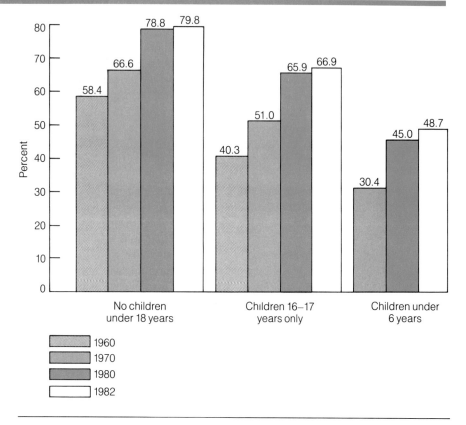

FIGURE 12 • 3

Labor Force Participation Rates for Married Women Aged 16–44 with Husband Present, by Presence and Age of Children, 1960*, 1970, 1980, and 1982

Percent

80 — 78.8   79.8
70 — 66.6   65.9   66.9
60 — 58.4
50 —   51.0   48.7
                                                 45.0
40 —   40.3
30 —   30.4
20 —
10 —
0 —

No children under 18 years   Children 16–17 years only   Children under 6 years

1960
1970
1980
1982

Sources: 1960, 1970, and 1980—U.S. Bureau of the Census, *Current Population Reports,* Series P-20, No. 363 (June 1981), p. 30; 1982—U.S. Bureau of the Census, *Current Population Reports,* Series P-23, No. 130 (December 1983), p. 25.
*Data for 1960 relate to persons aged 14–44.

condition, and whether or not they are in careers they enjoy or that they cannot leave except for a brief maternity furlough. (Figures 12.3 and 12.4 show the participation of women in the labor force by age and number of children.)

If women with young children return to outside employment, the most common pattern has been one in which their family responsibilities are still paramount and the job is in an important second place. Recent studies have suggested that women who have outside employment still assume major responsibilities for home and children (Haverstein 1980). Many women may thus have two full-time jobs—one at home and one outside—or one full-time homemaking job and one part-time outside one. This appears to be shifting in the direction of more equal husband-wife participation. One sociological study found that most working women believed that their husbands' careers were more important to the family than their own and that they would give up their jobs if they conflicted with family needs (Mason and Bumpass 1975).

An English study showed that the average wife and mother who also works outside the home in that country puts in a total of six more hours a week on both activities combined than her husband does on his job (Rapoport and Rapoport 1978).

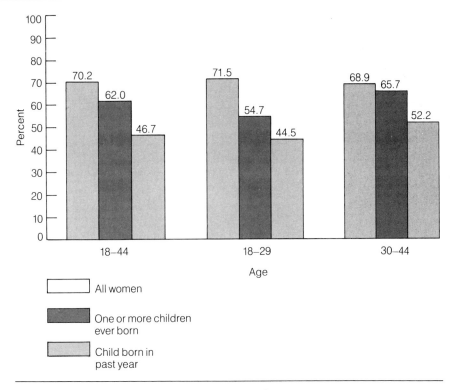

FIGURE 12 • 4
Percent of Women in
the Labor Force, by
Age and Children Ever
Born, June 1984

All women

One or more children
ever born

Child born in
past year

Source: U.S. Bureau of the Census, *Current Population Reports,*
Series P-20, No. 401 (November 1985), p. 5.

A poll in 1984 of over 2,000 men and women revealed that although most believe that child care and domestic duties should be shared when both partners are employed, 20 percent of the women still believe it is chiefly "women's work." None believed it to be "husband's work." When respondents were asked to rate the importance of family and work, women chose work only 8 percent of the time whereas more than half of the men ranked family second to work ("The Times Poll," *Los Angeles Times*, September 10, 1984, p. 1).

Men who have traditionally borne the burden of family support often work at two jobs, too, or may put in a great deal of overtime to fulfill their responsibilities as providers. Nearly half of the men in the labor force do skilled or unskilled manual work requiring considerable physical effort. Thus work may take not only much of their time but also most of their energy (Wallum 1977).

Marital Satisfaction   Many studies have focused on the level of marital satisfaction that exists when both partners are employed outside the home (Booth 1979). The findings are that any outside influences that produce major strains usually have a negative impact on husband-wife relations. Employment is no exception. One of the earliest studies of the effect of the wife's employment on marital happiness determined that the marital relationship suffered by comparison with couples with nonworking wives only when the couple had preschool children. Once the children were of school age, however, those couples in which the woman was working by choice and liked her work reported better marriages than did either those couples in which the wife disliked going to work or in which the wife was not employed outside the home (Orden and Bradburn 1969). The woman's choice of employment and the pressures of child care for very young children were the two factors that made the difference in stress and, therefore, in marital satisfaction. Other more recent studies have pinned the source of any marital upheaval caused by both partners being employed more specifically on major overload and on stresses involved in working out a lifestyle based on nontraditional roles (Nadelson and Eisenberg 1977).

Six national samples of employed and unemployed wives were made between 1971 and 1976 to study marital happiness and other overall life satisfactions of these women and their mates. The general conclusions were that "both work outside the home and full-time housewifery have benefits and costs attached to them; the net result is that there was no consistent or significant difference in patterns of life satisfaction between the two groups" (Wright 1978). In other words, these studies reported that women who work outside the home had neither greater satisfactions nor greater dissatisfactions in their lives generally or in their marriages than did women who worked full-time as homemakers. These studies, however, did not divide the women into categories separating out those with preschool children—a factor that has been shown to make a difference. Nor did they ask the women whether they chose their occupations willingly and liked what they were doing—whether the job was homemaking or something else. Most important, perhaps, no consideration was given to the women's income or educational levels.

Studies have shown that women from lower socioeconomic levels who are homemakers report less stress and more marital satisfaction than do women from the same background who are working outside the home (Reiss 1980). It has been hypothesized that husbands may be less helpful and supportive at this lower socioeconomic level so that women not only have outside work but also nearly all the responsibility at home. A low income (below the national average) earned entirely by the husband seems to enable the wife to be more satisfied with her marriage than if he earns only a portion of it and she must also work just to meet minimum standards.

Studies indicate that working women are generally satisfied with their lives and their jobs. More men than ever before support the notion of their wives' working, and many prefer it, especially younger men. Many younger men have grown up with new ideas of women in the labor force because some of them have mothers who were employed. Most have grown to expect that wives will work before they have children, and many expect—or even demand—help in supporting a family (Aldous 1982).

Some studies have been done to determine the effects of his wife's employment or lack of employment on the husband's satisfaction with marriage. One study revealed that men whose wives are employed experience no more marital discord and are under no more stress (although perhaps different kinds of stress) than men whose wives are homemakers. Many, in fact, reported that the extra income relieved a great deal of stress (Booth 1977). One study in particular made the interesting discovery that there was likely to be more stress in dual-worker families if the wife had worked less than one year at the time of the interview. There was also more stress if she was a housewife at the time but had previously been employed (Burke and Weir 1976). Perhaps the transition from one role to the other for her and the adjustments her husband had to make were the real stressors.

SALLY FORTH

It has often been hypothesized that there will be a strain on a husband and resulting marital dissatisfaction if his wife has a better job or earns more money than he does. He may be proud of her and pleased with the money, but questions have been raised about his feelings of envy or loss of self-esteem. Research so far has produced mixed results on whether marriages are any worse off or whether husbands are particularly unhappy about being married to women who make more money or who have more prestigious jobs (Richardson 1979). Unfortunately, few data were collected about the socioeconomic backgrounds of the couples, although it has been determined that of the six million or so women who earn more than their husbands, most are at either the upper or the lower end of the salary scale. Little mention is made of their occupations, ages, or educational levels, all important factors to consider. No doubt some men do resent wives who are more successful, and others may suffer loss of self-esteem.

A study published recently by Michigan's Institute for Social Research reports that although men may initially have problems adjusting to a loss of status as chief breadwinner, once they do accept the fact that their wives are major contributors most do not continue to be upset (Kessler and McRae 1984). In fact, the Michigan study found that about 12 percent of men whose wives earn more than they do report *no* problems dealing with the situation. If, however, a woman is earning a good deal more than her husband, he may not adjust so easily. If the wife's success is in a female-dominated field, it is less a problem for the husband's self-esteem than if she works in a male-dominated occupation (Lasswell and Lobsenz 1983). Some women feel envious and resentful of their husbands' successes as well (Macke, Bohrnstedt, and Bernstein 1979). We often hear a woman refer to herself as "just a housewife" or say that her economic contribution as a homemaker is scanty compared with that of her husband.

The one distinguishing feature of the marital relationship of dual-worker couples that has been found consistently is that women who are also earners typically have more say in family decisions. They assert themselves more readily, and their "bargaining power" increases (Moore and Sawhill 1976). This phenomenon has been explained by the obvious fact that when women earn enough money to support themselves (even if not at the level to which they are accustomed), they no longer believe they must give way to husbands who provide the family resources. This view may be too simplistic, however. It is more likely that employed married women take a more active part in the decision-making process not just because they are earning money. Instead, their new financial status may be a reflection of their upgraded feelings of competence and self-worth and of their increased awareness of how other couples balance the power between them (McDonald 1977). Changes in the way a husband and wife relate to each other as a result of the wife's employment can create stress if the couple fails to reach a balance that allows them to view themselves as a cooperating team rather than as adversaries in a power struggle.

The key to whether dual paychecks result in more or less marital satisfaction seems to lie in whether the couple is capable of working as a team. Qualities such as open communication, mutual respect, sensitivity to each other's feelings, and the ability to be fair and supportive are qualities of a functioning team that appear to compensate for the overload and other stresses inherent in such a lifestyle.

Work Overload

A major source of strain on modern dual-worker families is that of having far too much to do in much too little time. Fatigue, irritability, and "burnout" are commonly reported accompaniments of the increased volume of responsibilities and activities dual-worker families face. Particularly where both partners are working eight-hour-plus days outside their home and where there are children, there are nearly always strains to get everything accomplished. In their study on working couples, Rapoport and Rapoport (1976) suggested four conditions that affect the issues of overload: the degrees of (1) familism, (2) anxiety about household standards, (3) sharing of chores, and (4) interpersonal stress.

1. *The emphasis placed on the degree of family life desired:* parents not only have internalized standards about what a family is and how involved good parents must be with their children, but many also are subject to outside pressures from relatives and the community to conform to a socially approved family structure. Insinuations that they are not good parents if they do not get involved in the PTA or serve as Cub Scout den parents or Little League scorekeepers can cause guilt and even more stress for the parents.

2. *The standards the couple hold for housekeeping and other domestic living:* the fact that both parents are employed outside the home does not relieve them of the responsibilities for the daily tasks necessary to run the household. These duties are generally handled as "overtime," and much of the literature emphasizes that women pick up the lion's share of them (Hopkins and White 1978). Less than 10 percent of the families have paid household help. Instead, most parents report that they get up extra early in the morning, stay up late at night, and spend time on weekends to finish the house and yard work. Most complain that they really never finish and that they are not satisfied with the standards they keep. Most have learned to compromise their standards—to live with some untidiness and with quick meals—whereas others use some of their extra income for time- and effort-saving appliances, permanent press clothing, or eating out. Outside social pressures (real or

imagined) often cause couples to feel guilty about these compromises even though they find them necessary.

3. *The degree to which tasks are evenly divided and accepted by family members:* although the average working wife is seen as helping her husband support the family, most people still consider it the man's responsibility. Conversely, men help with what both partners usually view as the wife's job of homemaking and child care. The involvement of children in home duties varies with their ages and the parents' attitudes about their help.

Some experts have suggested that when mothers feel guilty about working outside the home, they are likely to ask for less help from the children. Such guilt seems to occur most frequently when women do not believe that they have to work for financial reasons but that they have chosen to be employed for personal reasons. Women who seek outside employment to help out financially seem more likely to insist that children carry their fair share of the workload, especially if the mother feels her employment is not a matter of choice but one of necessity (Rapoport and Rapoport 1976). An interesting finding was reported in 1983 from a study of employed mothers between the ages of 30 and 44. As the husband's income increased, the wife's home responsibilities increased. As the wife's income increased in relation to that of her husband, her share of home responsibilities declined (Maret and Finlay 1983).

In an article on dual-worker families, *Ms.* magazine editor Letty Pogrebin (1978, p. 52) said: "Housework is not trivial on any level. It even has an impact on future generations, for how the work is divided tells children how valuable males and females are and what their time is worth." It is Pogrebin's opinion that both boys and girls learn from their parents how to value housework as well as outside employment. In the United States, she believes, housekeeping is low on most status rankings. Pogrebin goes on to list two opinions about division of household responsibilities in dual-worker families: (1) tasks should not be apportioned with respect to who earns more or less, since each partner's *time* is equal; (2) no task should be seen as inappropriate for one partner or the other by virtue of sex. Work should more fairly be divided in terms of who is capable and who currently has the time and energy.

Some couples report that they are their own worst enemies in accepting new standards because of their internalized values about masculinity and femininity—that men and women "should" do only certain tasks. Departure from these values can produce embarrassment or guilt. Others' expectations that couples behave in traditional ways also are cited as sources of strain. Social pressures often are equal to or greater than those that couples put on themselves. Some dual-worker couples, for example, report that they rarely entertain, not because they are too tired or do not have the time, but because their housekeeping standards have slipped so that they are embarrassed to have more traditional family and friends visit.

4. *The degree to which the couple can minimize the physical, social, and psychological strains:* couples use a variety of techniques to manage work-related stress reduction. One frequently mentioned strategy is to compartmentalize work and family roles as much as possible. Most employers expect or even demand that employees give full attention to their work without interference from spouse or children (frequent telephone calls or visits, for instance, are usually discouraged). A bigger problem seems to arise in leaving work behind at the end of the day so that it does not interfere with family time. Many dual-worker couples believe this is important since their time with the family is so limited that they want it to be quality time.

Another way that dual-worker couples manage to minimize some strains inherent in their lifestyles is to change the nature of their social lives. They are likely, for instance, to have friends who are also dual-worker couples. They avoid persons as friends who do not approve of their way of life or who make friendship demands on them that are impossible or uncomfortable to meet. Dual-worker parents often prefer to spend leisure time with their children or alone with each other. They are also less likely to go to functions as a couple than are those in which the wife is not employed outside the home. Many of the functions they attend are related to their jobs (business entertaining, a baby shower for a coworker, or a retirement dinner); since both partners work, there are double the number of functions for each if they go together.

Many of the strains of dual-worker overload may be explained by the fact that only recently have many middle-class families begun to follow this pattern. In the past they would have been subject to significant social disapproval, as has often been the case for those who change traditions. With little in the way of social support, dual-worker families have had to battle the overload inherent in having both parents working outside the home in addition to the stress caused by criticism of their lifestyle from outsiders.

Dual-Career Marriages

A small but important segment of dual-worker couples are those who have careers. A *career* is defined as a self-selected identification with a lifelong occupation. Most careers involve years of schooling and training. Demands on time and energy are great and often are self-determined rather than set by an employer, and the work week may be as much as 60 or 70 hours. Usually, because of the self-dedication, the nature of the job, and the hours spent, the pay is good and job satisfaction is high.

It is estimated that only 15 to 18 percent of the total work force is engaged in professional careers. Few of these are married women (Shertzer 1981). Somewhat over three million married women in the United States (approximately 1 percent of women who are employed) pursue a profession distinguished by specific training for that occupation and a high level of career development, such as medicine, law, or engineering (Thomas, Albrecht, and White 1984). The number of women in careers is growing, however. Women now make up over 30 percent of all workers in executive, administrative, and managerial positions, up from 19 percent in 1970. The percentage of physicians and lawyers who are women has increased dramatically since 1960. Although the increase of married women in professions still remains below what might be expected in light of those who receive advanced education, the two-career marriage will be a major social change of the twenty-first century (Rytina and Bianchi 1984).

Studies have indicated that dual-career partners are usually competitive individuals who need recognition and are achievement motivated. In addition, they are ambitious and have high energy levels (Rice 1979). Such couples report almost all

Research indicates that married women in demanding careers are almost all satisfied with their lives and credit their husbands' emotional support as a major factor in how they are able to balance career and family.

the stresses that dual-worker couples do (although more money may be available to buy services that can ease some of the strains), but they typically have additional stresses as well to compete with the positive aspects of having a career. A source of much of the reported strain in dual-career marriages stems from the fact that until very recently couples have had no models to follow. Having both partners engaged in demanding careers is a new way to live, and only a minority of husbands and wives attempt such a lifestyle. Each couple is forced to be creative in arriving at individual solutions to the challenges of work and family life.

A problem often mentioned by both husband and wife in a dual-career marriage is that of one or both being overinvolved in the job. Not uncommonly, an all-consuming involvement in the career takes over, making family obligations difficult to fit in. Children usually get first call on whatever time is left, so it is the spouses who are likely to feel the most neglect. It is not surprising, then, that marital strain is often reported. Tension may occur if either partner's involvement makes the other resentful—particularly if both partners are overinvolved in careers (Ridley 1973).

Workaholics   The **workaholic** has become a familiar figure among career-oriented people. Such a person's work life takes over almost to the point of obsession, with the result that family life and, often, physical and emotional health suffer. Workaholics have what psychoanalyst Karen Horney (1950, p. 64) has called the "tyranny of the should." It is difficult for them to enjoy even weekends and holidays because they think they "should" be working. Often the employer encourages this attitude and may even demand such dedication as evidence that a promotion or a raise is warranted. As a result, such intense job involvement usually does lead to high achievement and a successful career.

Rewards keep the workaholic pressing on. A recent survey by a major business magazine identified a category of "megacompulsives" who work from 70 to 105 hours per week (*Venture*, January 1985, p. 24). Only 5 percent of those who worked over 80 hours were currently married. A large number reported no vacations in the previous three years, and several had not taken an official vacation for over twenty years. Many reported no time for any activity except work.

Marital Adjustment   Dedication to work and the resulting rewards may contribute positively to marital adjustment, of course, besides being a source of strain. Success usually brings financial gain, more material advantages, and a generally higher standard of living accompanied by a solid sense of security and of achievement.

Dual-career couples usually expect and understand each other's need for dedication, although the extreme cases still cause marital dissatisfaction. Women report more difficulty as a result of their high job involvement than men do (Holmstrom 1972). Part of their problem, no doubt, is that neither they nor their husbands can totally rid themselves of notions of sex roles that usually place a heavier domestic responsibility on wives. Although many women accuse men of resisting full equality for women, women often feel that they "should" assume more homemaking and child-related duties. Not only do the partners themselves often become trapped in traditional role expectations, but they frequently complain that friends, relatives, and sometimes their own children expect that they behave in traditional ways (Heckman, Bryson, and Bryson 1977).

The new freedom to be away from home, to meet new people, and to travel, as well as not being available when husbands want time with them, can create dissension between husbands and career-oriented wives. Most of the research on dual-career marriages reveals that even when husbands are supportive of their wives' careers, they tend to accord them less importance than their own (and often so do the wives) (Safilios-Rothschild 1970). Clearly, even among dual-career couples the old traditional sex roles still have a foothold. Several studies of such couples have revealed that the women, on the one hand, compromise more in their career ambitions than the men do in order to relieve stress in the marriage, and, on the other, work harder at their careers than do other women who hold similar positions (Poloma, Pendleton, and Garland 1971; Martin, Berry, and Jacobsen 1975).

Parenting   Both the presence of children and the stage of the family life cycle affect expectations and overload issues. In a large-scale study of dual-career couples, it was determined that sacrifices for the sake of work are likely to be made in the early years of a career (Hall and Hall 1979, pp. 51–53). After partners become better established and have more career security, they can afford to devote a greater proportion of their time to family interests than they could at earlier periods. Family demands may also decrease as children grow older.

Younger dual-career parents, in particular, report the most stress, whereas older professional couples and those without children have a far easier time of it (Gove and Greerken 1977). There is no evidence that children are affected by the dual-career pattern in more negative ways than in other two-paycheck families; but there is evidence that dual-career parents do experience extra strain from attempting to fulfill their responsibilities to their children in as close a manner as possible to more traditional parents (St. John and Parsons 1978). Because the demands of both parents' careers are equally high, they are not able, as many other parents are, to have at least one of them (usually the mother) give priority to family over a job. Long hours are usually demanded of those in careers, particularly at the beginning and middle stages when those who are also parents find the family responsibilities the most taxing. A recent poll of 200 top managers at Fortune 500 firms found that their average work week was 65 hours and that almost all took work home for evenings and weekends (*Working Woman*, August 1984, p. 30).

Fathers in dual-career families spend more of their discretionary time in child rearing than fathers from traditional households do. There appears to be a gender difference in what activities mothers and fathers undertake, however. Fathers are more likely to play with children, read to them, supervise bed times, homework, and outside activities than they are to wash and iron their clothes, clean their rooms, cook their food, or change diapers (Pleck 1981). Recent research indicates that even dual-career marriages are not truly egalitarian. What happens in most dual-career families is that women hire household and child-care help to do what they can no longer do (Hunt and Hunt 1982).

Because having children complicates a dual-career lifestyle tremendously, large numbers of women who wish to pursue careers either plan to remain childless or postpone children until after their careers are well launched. Research often is pessimistic about the chances for mothers to have career lives like those of their husbands. An understanding and helping husband alleviates some of their pressures, but for most career-oriented women having children means that either their job or their children will sometimes suffer unless there is reliable and top-quality hired help in the home (Poloma et al. 1982).

Job Relocation   A strain found particularly often in dual-career marriages arises from pressures for geographic relocation. Transfers within a company or lucrative job offers outside the company that require moving to another location are real threats to a dual-career marriage. Whereas the average working wife may take it for granted that she will move with her husband, a woman with a career knows that relocating to accompany her husband may mean starting all over at a lower position.

Many dual-career couples agree always to live in a large city where both can engage in their careers with ample opportunity for mobility within that city. Others agree that a move will be made only if both partners are able to relocate in jobs equal to those they currently hold. This is often impossible, however, because of the types of work involved. There may be few openings, or every move may hold the inevitable risk of losing seniority, benefits, and the network of contacts built up over the years. Other couples take turns accepting relocation for job upgrading. A few live apart in what have been called "dual-residence" marriages, with one partner commuting on weekends or, in rare cases (usually when there are no children to care for), both partners taking turns commuting. This obviously is expensive, and typically these are upwardly mobile couples with high incomes. According to one report, some such couples spent $10,000 each year on commuter travel (*Business Week*, April 3, 1978, p. 68).

Most dual-career couples resist the idea of living apart, especially when children are involved. Those couples who choose this path usually have an extremely high commitment to their respective jobs. Most emphasize that the arrangement is a temporary one, and it usually is. As one counselor analyzed commuter marriages, "A commuting relationship either brings out the best in a marriage or it's the last nail in the coffin" (Cecre 1982). In other words, a prolonged separation can test strong bonds, or it can make a couple realize that they are using the distance as an excuse to end the marriage.

Business and industry are beginning to try to help relocate the spouses of highly desired career personnel (*Business Week*, April 3, 1978, p. 68). In many instances, however, couples either pass up the opportunity, if both cannot successfully relocate, or else one sacrifices to aid the other. Women, more often than men, still seem to be the ones who sacrifice, either by moving or by not accepting positions that require them to relocate (Duncan and Perrucci 1976).

A nonprofit organization to promote the participation of women in the work place interviewed 160 of the nation's largest companies to gauge how they deal with transfers for employees in dual-career marriages. The survey found that following concerns about housing and other economic costs of moving, the spouse's career was the second most prevalent reason for resisting relocation (*Los Angeles Times*, February 17, 1984, Part V, p. 30).

Two careers seem to be less stressful if both partners are in similar fields, although there is also an increased possibility of competition between them. Being in similar occupations seems to give husband and wife an understanding of the pressures and duties the jobs entail. Listening and being sympathetic is easier when the nature of the mate's job is at least familiar. Since mutual support seems to be the key to making most dual-career marriages work, having an understanding of a partner's work life goes a long way toward empathy.

Whether dual-career spouses are mutually supportive or competitive may be as much influenced by their personalities as by the nature of their jobs. Some spouses are caught in a power struggle with each other from the beginning and make almost any situation a win-or-lose contest. Such couples often use money as a yardstick to measure who is winning. As we have already noted, research has repeatedly suggested that some husbands feel competitive distress if their wife's salary is comparable or higher, especially if they are in the same field (Fendrich 1984).

Although the stresses are even greater in some respects on those with dual careers than on dual-worker couples, the rewards seem to be greater as well (Heckman, Bryson, and Bryson 1977). Studies have shown that the relationship draws strength from the fact that each partner is economically self-sufficient. An important point is that both are more likely to be in the marriage by choice rather than from necessity since each is capable of earning a good living independently. There is usually more money to ease financial demands and to spend for items and services the couple value. However, the biggest reward seems to be in the freedom each has to pursue what he or she most wants to do occupationally (Pleck 1977, p. 231). A man is freer to change from a less desirable position to one he really wants when his wife also provides an income. He is free from total responsibility for financial support and consequently is

Husband-wife astronauts William and Anna Fisher illustrate a dual-career marriage in which each must understand the other's need for dedication and time devoted to a demanding career.

able to get out of a job that feels like a trap. A woman in this situation, too, has the freedom to develop her potential and to choose her occupation rather than to accept a role that society has assigned to her.

> It means the couple must plan and negotiate, argue and compromise, deal with a host of unexpected feelings and reactions. But those couples who are already finding it a good way to live report that the gains are worth the troubles. When you have real and free choices, you can no longer blame each other for unhappiness or frustrations. (Lasswell and Lobsenz 1976, p. 231)

Child Care

Tensions over child care are among the most severe that working parents face. They must work, or prefer to, but also want to be certain that their children have good care. Leaving and returning to a happy child each working day relieves much of the stress that dual-worker couples already feel. Child experts have determined that *where* the child receives care is less important for his or her development than is the quality of the care received (Rowe 1978).

Effects of Child Care   Studies have reported that having both parents employed outside the home is usually stressful to the children only if the parents are suffering from stress about it. In an important study of the effect of the mother's outside employment on her children, sociologist Lois Hoffman (1974) concludes that "the working mother who obtains satisfaction from her work, who has adequate arrangements so that her dual role does not involve undue strain, and who does not feel so guilty that she overcompensates is likely to do quite well and, under certain conditions, better than the nonworking mother." Hoffman's conditions add up to a tall order for working mothers, and few studies have located enough parents who meet all of these specifications to reach any definite conclusions about the effects of dual-worker parenting. It appears that there are too many other variables involved, beyond the fact of the mother's employment, that affect the adjustment of children. Anything that affects the stress level of the parents is likely to disturb their children. For instance, if the parents disagree about the mother's employment, the stress level of either or both of the parents may affect their children much more than does the simple fact of whether she is employed.

What is certain for many is that it is increasingly necessary for both parents to contribute to the family income and that trying to manage child care is one of the most difficult problems couples face.

Family experts have debated the effects on children when both parents are employed outside the home. The studies range from those that lay considerable blame for children's problems on working mothers to those that emphasize positive results to children when both parents are employed.

The rapidly rising divorce rates of the 1950s and early 1960s were widely defined as a worse form of family disruption than the earlier more common patterns of parental death or desertion. Millions of newly single parents were seeking employment, and newly formed models of family life appeared to be threatening traditional models. Mothers who were employed were not well accepted; many employers fired female employees if they married—school boards in particular were noted for requiring female teachers to resign if they married. Many studies reflected this bias by highlighting any negative effects of nontraditional family patterns. Selma Fraiberg (1977)—one of the most influential child psychiatrists of those years—spoke for the conservative side of the maternal employment battle, contending that few mothers really needed to work and that their selfish pursuit of material goods did irreparable harm to their children.

The research of the 1970s swung to a bias in the opposite direction from that of the earlier decades, emphasizing positive results of the employment of mothers. Nearly all studies focused on the potential effects of a mother's absence from her home, and many seemed attuned to absolving the mother of guilt over having "abandoned" her children (Hoffman and Nye 1974).

More recent studies have found little evidence that parental employment itself is the crucial factor in how children develop. The National Academy of Sciences (1982) published extensive findings that concluded that parental employment in and of itself is not necessarily good *or* bad for children. Some are better off, some worse off, and some not influenced much one way or the other.

It is comforting to employed mothers to know that research has not proved that there are developmental differences between children of employed or nonemployed mothers. Activists argue that it is wasting money on research to find answers to the question of what effect mothers' employment has on their children. What is needed instead is research on what inadequate care does to children. Parents need support in the form of flexible work hours, job sharing, day-care centers, and subsidized child-care programs for employees' children that are provided by business and industry as fringe benefits.

Labor force projections for 1990 predict that there will be nearly double the number of working mothers with children under the age of six (Smith 1979). These mothers will be working for the same reasons that fathers do. The character of the American family is changing, and the need is for support for the creativity with which families are coping rather than criticism for their efforts. Even so, there is at least as great a need for valid information about the effects of various forms of support as there is for support itself. A small minority of citizens—mostly scholars—argue that 0.5 percent of all social-action expenditures should be allocated to research to learn what actions produce what effects in family processes as well as in business and industry. They believe that policies should be based on facts rather than on opinions, customs, or wishes.

Job Sharing and Split Shifts   Unavailability of high-quality care is one of the main reasons that, if they can manage financially, many women do not return to outside employment until their children are in school (Gove and Greerken 1977). Both parents appear to feel responsibility for parenting their children, but if satisfactory child care is not available, it is rarely the man who stays at home.

Many experts believe that the unresolved problem of child care may be the biggest deterrent to equality in employment in the United States. Other countries have tried innovative methods that permit both parents to work while still caring for their children. For instance, in many families in Sweden both mother and father hold part-time jobs and share home responsibilities. **Job sharing** is being tried in some other countries, as are flexible schedules that enable the parents to pick the hours they would like to work. A father, for instance, might choose 9:00 A.M. to 5:00 P.M. so that he can get the children off to school, but the mother might choose 7:00 A.M. to 3:00 P.M. in order to be at home when the children return from school. Parents in this country sometimes work different shifts to gain flexibility in child care. However, split shifts create their own stresses on a marriage.

In the United States, flexible scheduling is easier in some jobs—such as those in which the worker is self-employed or is not confined to an office or factory. Usually, however, the hours are set by employers, not employees, although some companies are cooperating in "flextime" for some of their valuable employees who might otherwise look for some other job that allowed them needed family time. Some companies have tried a ten-hour, four-day work week, which can help if husbands and wives choose to take off different fifth days. For most couples who are finding an inflexible work schedule difficult to reconcile with family responsibilities, however, employers are not doing enough to help them work out solutions.

Job sharing is a small but growing phenomenon in certain professions in the United States. Usually two women share one position, each working half-time; very few men share one position. There are a few job-sharing couples—usually professionals who can live on one salary (two halves), but who both want to work and to share household and child-care duties. Faculty positions at colleges and universities are occasionally filled by a husband-wife team, for instance.

Most employers still resist the idea of job sharing because they have a negative attitude about the "half-time effort" they believe will result. Actually, research has shown that job-sharing couples typically put in more than half-time each, so that their combined efforts result in increased productivity for the employer (Arkin and Dobrofsky 1978). Job sharing in another form, of course, has often been expected by employers. Many men have jobs that require the active participation of their wives even though there is no direct wage for that contribution. This has been termed the "two-person career," in which the nature of the work demands a backup person. The clergy is one such occupation, as is a political career or any job that requires entertaining for business as a part of the wife's responsibilities.

Some couples have attempted their own time management by working split shifts—one on the day shift and one on the night or swing shift. For child care, there are very real advantages to this pattern, of course, since the children have 24-hour coverage and each parent has time alone with the children and for himself or herself. However, the partners' time together as a couple is necessarily extremely limited. In a study of such couples, the uniform complaint was of no time to talk, to do things together, or for sex. One couple reported that they saw each other only about 45 minutes each day. The husband worked as a plant foreman from 5:00 P.M. to 1:00 A.M., and the wife was a nurse on the 7:00 A.M. to 3:00 P.M. shift. She got home at 3:30 P.M. after picking up the children from school, and he left at 4:15 to commute to work. Their sex life was restricted to weekends, although they reported that each took an occasional day of sick leave or vacation so they could have extra time together (Cole 1980).

Costs and Types of Child Care   There are eight million working women in the United States whose children are too young to be in school. Most working parents with children must arrange for paid, full-time child care—in their own homes, in the home of a sitter or of a relative, or in a day-care center. Each plan has its merits and its drawbacks. If a child is ill, he or she cannot be taken where other children are—and young children have frequent fevers, colds, and earaches. On the other hand, a sitter can become ill, too, often at the last minute when a replacement may be impossible to find.

The financial costs of the various forms of child care are about the same—day-care centers and schools vary in price a great deal, generally running from $65 to $150 a week depending on the hours the child stays, the age of the child (infants cost the most), and how many children the parent leaves. Some centers are publicly supported and charge according to ability to pay. Home care costs from $3.00 to $5.00 an hour on the average (thus a 40-hour week would range from $120 to $200). There may also be unemployment and worker's compensation payments on the sitter's wages, making home care the most costly option. Still, where there are two or more children, this choice may be cost-effective. Charges vary from region to region, with large cities and the East and West coasts being the most expensive.

Over 25 percent of all children of working parents are cared for by a relative, often an older sibling, while their parents work. Another one-quarter take care of themselves until one of their parents returns from work (primarily older children, although some younger school-age children also fend for themselves) and are sometimes called "latchkey" children. The remaining 50 percent are cared for in some other type of child-care arrangement, most commonly by one parent or the other (as in split-shift families), with limited help from a sitter or older sibling, or by using part-time day care.

Most working parents use a home environment (either their own or the sitter's) for child care; a smaller percentage use day care as their principal means of help (Rodes 1976). The school-type settings (day care, nursery school, before- and after-school programs) that are popular in much of the rest of the world but used by far fewer working parents in the United States for child care have come under heavy criticism recently. Some critics of day care argue that parents obviously do not like such arrangements; otherwise, they would be more popular.

The chief drawbacks to the use of day-care centers are not that parents would not like to use such facilities but that the easiest in which to enroll children may be of questionable quality whereas the good ones have waiting lists. Recent scandals involving abuse in day-care centers have frightened parents. There is a lack of uniformity in state licensing standards. Pay is often poor for persons who work in day-care facilities. The shortage of care for infants is particularly noticeable even though the fastest growing number of working mothers are those with children under two years. The truth of the matter is that parents often feel that to find good child care, they must resort to arrangements other than care centers.

Recently, employer and community information and referral services have begun to increase in number to aid parents to find openings in approved facilities. Some companies are providing on-site centers for employees, but the practice is not widespread, largely due to the cost of maintaining quality programs and the reluctance of boards of directors to assume what might be enormous liabilities for the malpractice or incompetence of personnel.

FRIENDS

Friends, neighbors, and coworkers are a major outside influence on marriages and families. Friends can be positive in that they offer support and share experiences. They also can cause stress in that they usually demand a certain amount of time and energy.

Balancing Friends and Family

Research indicates that problems are likely to occur in several areas. The first centers around friends who relate only to one of the partners. These may be either old friends from before the marriage or new friendships maintained outside the marital relationship. Such friendships are especially likely to pose a problem when they involve opposite-sex friends. Most couples seem to have difficulty accepting that a husband can have a close woman friend or a wife have a close man friend without at least some jealousy or anxiety. Dual-career couples seem to adapt to the idea of male-female friendships more easily than most couples since they are used to the idea of work colleagues of both sexes. There may still be problems, however, if the spouse feels excluded or threatened by the closeness between his or her mate and a third person (Clanton and Smith 1977).

Jealousy   Jealousy is one of the most difficult emotions to cope with and is nearly always directed at an outsider who is believed to be intruding. Studies of jealousy have shown that the emotion goes hand in hand with a feeling that one's partner might easily find someone else better for him or her and with a feeling of such dependence on the relationship that the threat becomes almost an obsession (Bringle and Evenback 1979). Some family sociologists believe that marital jealousy is declining as the notion of marriage as a possessive "ownership" of the mate changes. As women become less dependent and as the balance of power between mates equalizes, it is argued, human beings will have less reason to experience jealousy (Bernard 1971a). However, jealousy often can be an almost irrational emotion rooted in long-standing feelings of personal insecurity. If this is true, then the problem is much too complex to be solved merely through male-female equality.

Couple Friends   Outsiders can contribute support, or sometimes they can add to marital stress when a couple makes new friends together. It is typical for women to be more sociable and to initiate contacts, usually with other women. They then attempt to integrate the men so that they can be "couple friends." This is especially the case with employed women who seem to seek other women as friends who offer support for their working lifestyle. (The opposite is rarer in contemporary society—that is, husbands pressing to make couple friends with their personal male friends and their spouses.) Establishing friendships with couples similar to themselves not only helps to validate their lifestyle but provides a supportive structure (Rapoport and Rapoport 1976).

Making couple friends can be complex. Not only are the men expected to like each other, but each woman is expected to accept the other's husband and each husband to like the other's wife—but not too much. The complexity of such relationships often leads to stress when one or more of those involved proves unable to participate or to be accepted. If there are children, they, too, can be a source of conflict if socializing involves families. Sometimes children do not get along, and often there is a problem between one set of parents and the children of the others.

On occasion a couple becomes intensely involved with another couple. The four persons may spend so much time together that they lower their horizons of experience and even stifle their growth as individuals. Such closeness has the potential to overwhelm a marriage. If something goes wrong between any two of the parties, it can create serious problems for the others. In one case, two closely linked couples, who spent most of their leisure time together, who usually took their vacations together, and whose children were also best friends, ran into serious difficulty when one of the men became sexually aggressive with the other woman. "My feelings for him cooled at once," she reported. "I couldn't tell his wife why and risk hurting her, and if I told my husband, he would have done something so she would know anyway. Besides, he and my husband really like each other and have some business ventures together." In this case, the wife was burdened with a secret but felt that the friendship between the families must continue. She simply stayed as clear as possible from ever being alone with the other man.

With couples increasingly busy trying to combine work and family life, spending time that is already in short supply with friends often takes time away from children or from a spouse. How much time to spend with friends too frequently becomes an issue. Even time spent on the telephone with friends often displaces opportunities for family interaction.

Supportive Friendships

The support that friendships offer and the positive roles that friends play in a family's life have been well documented. It seems especially important for couples to have friends who are experiencing with them the same stage of the family life cycle and the same demands and joys. For example, newlyweds whose friendships may have been primarily with those who are single seem especially in need of making new couple friends who are also undergoing the change to married life (Titus 1980).

Young parents often band together in friendship networks to help with child care, transportation, and leisure activities where children are welcome and for general closeness and support. As children grow older, parents often meet and become friends because their children like each other and bring their parents together. Children's activities such as Scouts, Little League, soccer teams, or dance classes give parents opportunities to get acquainted and to share a time of life in common. Sociologist Lillian Rubin (1985, pp. 135–150) reports that by the end of the anxious years of child rearing, friendships as individuals rather than as couples come into their own again. These individual friendships fill the gaps that a mate, no matter how loving, cannot fill. They support one's individual identity, whereas other friends maintained by the couple buttress the twosome and help to bind the partners to their marriage.

In a review of friendships over the life span, it was noted that friendships come and go as needs of couples change. Most friendships endure as long as the need exists or perhaps until there is a geographic move that puts emotional as well as physical distance between the friends. A few friendships endure the passage of time, but most friendships reflect a connectedness primarily of those of similar ages, stages, tasks, and economic and social aspirations (Brown 1981).

It seems clear from the research on friendship that friends serve a purpose for families that is both supportive and supplemental to the backup that was once given by the extended family.

Other Demands

One stress that couples report involves those outsiders who make demands on the couple that interfere with their marriage and family life. This is of particular importance to dual-worker families who often already feel overburdened. These demands may come from neighbors, from the community, or from adults involved with children of the couple. It is easy to find most of a family's extra time spoken for by those whose requests, taken individually, seem reasonable and are not easy to turn down. Collectively, however, when added to an existing overload, these demands produce stress by devouring all of a couple's leisure time. Often the time to collect for a charity or to be a club officer is taken at the expense of the couple's time to be alone with each other. Some studies have indicated that, as a result, dual-worker couples may spend less than an hour a week in conversation and intimate contact with each other. Often what time together they do have deteriorates into problem-solving sessions rather than time for intimacy. Some couples complain that communication is all but nonexistent except for routine matters and discussion of problems. Sex may be infrequent because there is so little time as a result of outside demands. Some couples, of course, let outside demands detract from their time together as a device to avoid being together. Patterns of overactivity may be a sign of trouble in the marriage if the partners desire to spend as little time as possible with each other. However, most couples, even those with conflicts between them, seem serious in their desire to find more time to spend with each other.

KIN AND IN-LAWS

> When you fall in love or marry, you think you are involved with just the other person. But you are not. You are involved with your partner's family—with their traditions, attitudes and ways of living. Similarly, he or she is involved with your family. And each of you also brings to the relationship all of the feelings, acknowledged or repressed, you have about your own parents. (Alexander Taylor, personal communication)

This statement by a marital therapist concerns the most widely discussed "outsiders" in any couple's relationship—in-laws. One partner's in-laws are, of course, the other's kin. They can be wonderful and highly supportive; they can be distant and rarely (if ever) in contact; or they can be critical and interfering. Whatever behavior they choose and however the husband and wife choose to react to them, in laws have an impact, directly or indirectly. Each of us is a product of his or her past, and there is no more important influence on us than our families of origin. If we have not been positively molded in their pattern, we may have chosen to be negatively influenced by being as different as possible. Either way, what we are is measured by some yardstick drawn from our roots in that family.

The Family Unit

The family unit in the United States has been described as an **"isolated nuclear" unit** (living apart from and in infrequent contact with kin) (Parsons 1951). Many family sociologists have taken exception to the "isolated" notion by demonstrating that most families and their kin have frequent contact (Sussman 1965). This is particularly the case with parents and their grown children who often live remarkably close to one another and maintain frequent contact. In the United States a large percentage of older persons lives either with a grown child or within a few minutes' distance. In one study, about half the parents living apart from their children reported having seen one or more of them within the 24 hours previous to the interview, and 78 percent had visited within the previous week (Shanas 1973). A recent poll of married women under the age of 35 reports that 70 percent live within 100 miles of their in-laws and approximately 50 percent live in the same city (*Redbook*, June 1980, p. 62).

Even when there is a geographical separation between adults and their parents and siblings, surveys show that there is frequent contact by mail and telephone and occasional visits from parents to grown children, from adults to their parents, and between grown siblings. As longevity increases, there is a greater likelihood of several generations being alive and in contact. Married couples may have parents and their grandparents, children, and perhaps grandchildren to consider as family. These statistics would fit many families:

- Age 90: great-grandparents (married at age 22 in 1919)
- Age 66: grandparents (born 2 years later in 1921)
- Age 44: middle-aged offspring (born 22 years later in 1943)
- Age 22: grown grandchildren (born 22 years later in 1965)
- Age 6 months: great-grandchildren (born 22 years later in 1987)

This affords some idea of the size of the **extended family** kin network that one might have and that one's partner would inherit with marriage. There will be siblings, parents, grandparents, uncles, cousins, and their in-laws. In a study completed several years ago, sociologist Bert Adams (1968) asked respondents how many blood relatives (not their in-laws) they would recognize if they saw them on the street. The average was 30 for women and 26 for men. Adding in-laws could double that number.

In-Law Influence

In-laws have not enjoyed a good reputation in the folklore of the family. There does seem to be evidence of a fair amount of troublesome interference. Marital therapists list in-law problems among the most common marital complaints. Even when they are not the primary problem, they are mentioned by a sizable percentage of those couples who seek marriage counseling as incidental to their troubles. Even "Dear Abby" says that in-law problems rank second only to romantic troubles among her readers.

Mothers-in-law have been especially singled out as the source of trouble, probably because women are more likely than men to be involved with each other in a direct, emotional way, as a result of women's more social role. They are usually charged with the responsibilities of maintaining ties to parents and to siblings. Wives generally keep the social calendar and handle family correspondence. Family sociologists have noted that women usually maintain closer ties to their own families of origin than they do to the husband's parents and brothers and sisters (Adams 1970). Interestingly, though, the source of contact—no matter whose side of the family it is on—is more often from woman to woman. Consequently, the wife will have the most frequent contact with her own mother and sisters, followed by her mother-in-law and sisters-in-law. This situation may account for the fact that twice as many women as men complain of in-law interference (*Redbook*, June 1980, p. 62).

The influence of kin and in-laws is felt in several ways. The first of these is direct interference, which may take the form of criticism or of attempts to influence the couple. This behavior is not difficult to recognize; when an in-law makes critical remarks to or about the member related by marriage, it is at least out in the open. However, other direct interference may be less obvious—for instance, behavior that is too helpful. This more subtle type of interference couched in helping behavior is generally harder to combat. For example, the father who gives his daughter money because he does not feel her husband earns enough can be a source of great frustration and anger to his son-in-law. The mother-in-law who takes over in the kitchen or cleans house for her employed daughter-in-law in order to "help" may easily convey to her the criticism that she is not a good homemaker. Overruling parents' discipline or regulations when grandchildren visit is a frequent source of trouble.

Sometimes in-laws criticize in the guise of "helpful" suggestions—for example, the mother-in-law who says to her daughter-in-law, "Bill looks so thin and tired. Have you thought of trying to get him to go on a little vacation by himself?" or the father-in-law who remarks to his son-in-law, "Sue has had that car since we bought it for her in college. I'm worried it will die on her one of these days. It seems like a good time to replace it." As irritating as such comments may be, they are hard to combat because the in-laws will claim to be misunderstood—they are only trying to be helpful.

Caring for Elderly Relatives

An increasing source of in-law and kin stress involves caring for elderly relatives. It is as directly felt as other pressures but does not involve an intentional effort to stir up trouble. For instance, this is often the case with responsibilities toward aging parents and grandparents, which is of growing concern as the life cycle is extended. In the United States in 1900 there were only three million people over the age of 65. Today there are more than 25 million, and it is estimated that by the year 2000 there will be over 30 million (Ward 1978). There is considerable evidence that kin—primarily grown children—are the primary source of support for the elderly. In a study of over 2,000 adults to determine their major areas of stress in life, it was found that, after their own mental and physical health, "parent caring" was what worried them most.

Women traditionally seem to bear the principal burden of the physical care of older family members, but men are the primary source of the financial support, whether of their own parents or of their in-laws. This may be changing as women earn a greater percentage of the family income and may have less time to care for elderly relatives. When the care is for in-laws, there may be conflict between the care given and his or her spouse. A daughter-in-law may resent having to run errands for her in-laws or having to drive them to the market or to the doctor because her husband is too busy. She may also resent his siblings, if she perceives they are not doing as much for their own parents as she is doing.

When the issue is money used for the parent's support, the child-in-law may resent the expense. When their own family expenses are high, having to send money to parents may be a hardship. As one woman told us, "Just when we got our children through college and saw a chance at last to do some long-postponed travel, we now have to send money to my mother. And my father-in-law has to be put in a nursing home. We love them, of course, but it hardly seems fair that we end child responsibilities only to take on those of our parents."

Some adults find they have angry feelings at their aging parents' dependence, feelings left over from the anger they felt when they themselves were the dependents: "Why should I be good to them when they were so rotten to me?" If the aid goes to in-laws, the angry feelings may be directed at the spouse: "Why should I send money to your parents when you aren't giving me what I want?"

Extended Family Support

Of course, kin and in-laws, besides being sources of stress to couples, can also be of great help. Studies have shown that support goes both ways—from parents to adult children and from adult children to parents. In a recent report on black families in

Kin and in-laws often are valued family members who give support in a variety of ways.

the United States that covered a period of eight years in the lives of the families studied, the mutual aid between generations was clear (Martin and Martin 1978). Those interviewed were usually a part of a multigenerational, interdependent kinship system with a definite sense of obligation to relatives and generally guided by a dominant family figure.

Similar research has shown that the extended family plays an important mutual-aid role in Mexican-American, Chinese-American, and Japanese-American families as well. Sociologist Bert Adams (1968) concluded that "minority status tends to result in residential compounding, and in strong kin ties for the sake of mutual aid and survival in a hostile environment." A recent look at family circles and "cousins' clubs" of New York City Jews of Eastern European background shows an innovative way that these family members have developed to stay in touch in a large urban setting. Clubs composed of cousins enable even distantly related members of the same generation to stay in touch and to be supportive of each other. Older generations of cousins give a helping hand to younger ones as they make their way in establishing their occupations and families (Mitchell 1978).

Indirect Influence from Kin

A major influence of kin and in-laws may actually have little if anything to do with these family members directly. Instead, the influence comes indirectly from the ways in which families of origin still affect their grown children. The influence comes from the old (and often unacknowledged) feelings each partner has about his or her own parents. Basically, these unresolved feelings are of two types—both sides of the same emotional coin—unresolved dependence on parents, on the one hand, and unresolved hostility toward them, on the other. Younger couples are more likely to have one or both of these unfinished ties to their parents, although age alone does not necessarily resolve the feelings that seem to keep some men and women forever children when they are in the presence of their parents.

Dependence may send one spouse running home to parents every time there is a disagreement—if not literally, then at least figuratively. There may be interminable long-distance telephone calls or relayed advice from absent parents about what the couple should do to solve their conflicts. Men as well as women may remain so attached to their parents that their mates feel in competition with the parents for attention and affection.

Unresolved hostility toward one's own parents also may cause difficulty. It may be projected onto in-laws who themselves are innocent of any wrongdoing but who nonetheless become targets of the angry feelings. Sometimes these hostile feelings are actually ones toward the mate that cannot be expressed directly. For instance, a man might say he hates his father-in-law if his wife is always comparing the business acumen of the two men, or a woman might say she dislikes her mother-in-law if her husband thinks his mother is perfect. The in-law may not even know the comparison is occurring.

Often the comparison of the two families is the focus of indirect in-law interference. Without their being aware of it, parents-in-law may be cast by their married children into competing roles. Gifts, financial aid, and even affection may be the source of conflict, whether they flow from parents to children or from children to parents. Thus the arguments may be more *about* the parents than directly *with* them. Sometimes in-laws give costly gifts as a way of showing love and do not realize that they may be conveying to their children or grandchildren a message they do not intend. For example, a daughter-in-law may resent her in-laws' aid or gifts in the belief that the in-laws are competing with her own parents who either cannot or will not do as much for her. Or a son-in-law may believe his wife gives too much of her time, energy, or financial support to her parents because she does not give as much to his. In each case the in-laws may have no knowledge of their role in the conflict. The couples, however, use the in-laws as a focus for disagreements with each other.

In spite of stresses and strains produced by in-laws, a 1980 magazine survey of 300 young married women (18 to 34 years of age) representing a random, nationwide sample of almost nineteen million such women, revealed that in-law relationships are generally quite good. One reason seems to be that both in-laws and their married children are leading busier lives, particularly the women, who are more often employed or busy with volunteer work. This keeps them from being too intensely involved in each other's lives. The arrival of children reportedly strengthened the in-law bonds as both grandparents and new parents were reminded of the continuity of the generations. Another reason given for improved in-law relationships was that there has been a general increase in our society in tolerance for one another's differences, a tolerance that seems to be extending to in-laws (*Redbook*, June 1980, p. 62).

RELIGION AND CHURCH

With few, if any, exceptions organized religions are big supporters of marriage and the family. We have already noted that a majority of weddings are in places of religious worship or have some kind of religious focus to the ceremony. In addition, family life-cycle events such as christenings, rituals of passage into religious responsibility (confirmation, bar mitzvahs, bat mitzvahs), and, finally, the end of life ceremony—the funeral—are frequently connected to religion and to places of worship.

Religious Commitment and Marital Success

Research has consistently shown a strong positive correlation between religious commitment and marriage success and happiness, revealing a belief that religious involvement is a major cause of marital and family solidarity (Stinnett 1983). It is not clear whether the positive correlation between religion and marital and family stability is really a matter of cause and effect or whether other factors present in the personalities and backgrounds of religious people work to keep their marriages together. It has been suggested, for example, that those who are religious are more conventional and, as such, are more likely to follow a "conventionalized" pattern of marriage for life. To investigate this point, the variable of conventionality was controlled for in one study, and it was reported that there was still evidence that marital satisfaction and religious participation were positively correlated (Hunt and King 1978).

As a support for marriages and families, religion serves as a set of guiding principles teaching the importance of love and personal sacrifice for the good of those who are loved. Religion also stresses duty and responsibility as good qualities to embrace not only as personal attributes but as enhancers of good relationships.

The Church as a Resource

Churches often serve members as a supportive resource in time of trouble. Help comes in a variety of forms from companionship and advice in time of need to programs for education for marriage and parenting. Religiously inclined couples in distress frequently turn to a clergy person for counseling. Since 62 to 65 percent of American adults belong to a religious organization, this is a significant resource for families (Roof and Hage 1980).

Religion as a Source of Stress

Religion is sometimes a stress in marriage and family life as well as a supportive factor. When partners' belief systems are at odds or when participation becomes a time and energy drain, it is often the case that religion is blamed. In addition, some people view certain teachings of religion as oppressive and restrictive. For example, historically, the religious emphasis on duty and commitment to the responsibilities of marriage and parenting led to prohibitions on divorce and, in some religions, to sanctions against family planning. These sanctions continue to be a part of some modern religions. The personal relationship between husband and wife was not considered as important as was their responsibility to stay married and bear and bring

MARRIAGE ENCOUNTER

Marriage encounter is a popular program sponsored by religious denominations to provide support and enrichment for intact marriages. It was begun in 1967 by a Spanish Jesuit priest, Father Calvo, and since that time it has been adopted by other denominations to meet the needs of their members. It is estimated that as many as a million couples have participated in weekend encounter workshops both for married couples and for those engaged to be married.

Basically, marriage encounter teaches couples how to share their feelings on a deeper level and to explore the meaning of their lives and of their marriages. There is virtually no group interaction; instead, the emphasis is on a dialogue between partners. Exercises and assignments encourage couples at the workshop and in follow-up programs that may be done at home.

Does marriage encounter work? There have been a handful of studies on the effects, both positive and negative.

PRO. Couples do show improvement in dialogue technique and empathy at the end of the weekend compared to the Friday night before and continue to show the gains six weeks later (Newhaus 1977; Huber 1977).

Teaching couples how to share feelings, including hurt and the fear of being hurt, can lead to increased competence in the tasks of marriage that require such sensitivity. Empathic ability and marital adjustment are positively correlated (L'Abate 1977).

CON. Some couples have become so caught up in a kind of religious experience about the process of dialogue that they become dependent on it to the exclusion of other methods of interaction. There are even some who have become so enamored of the technique that they have alienated relatives and friends, causing themselves new problems (Doherty, McCabe, and Ryder 1978).

Marriage encounter sometimes draws couples whose marriages are in serious trouble because there is no screening for problems of those couples who take part. The program is not designed as therapy; therefore, the encounter actually may worsen the problems of couples who need professional help (De Young 1979).

Based on these limited studies, it appears that marriage encounter can be a valuable experience for couples who have good marriages that they want to make better but not for couples who have serious problems. And dialogue is a valuable tool for gaining empathy but should not become a religion in itself.

up their children. Today the husband-wife relationship is usually viewed by religious leaders as the basis for a healthy family; still, religions, for the most part, place a higher value on marriage and the family for their own sake than do more secular marriage and family theorists (Barnhouse 1981).

Secularization is a term used to describe a process of a decline in religiosity and an increase in reliance on other sources of information. Many experts in the sociology of religion point to this trend—which seems to have increased in the twentieth century—as an irreversible process (Wilson 1982). Still others believe that religion is as powerful a force as ever and may even be increasing in influence (Bahr and Chadwick 1985). They point to the increase in the number of religious books, religious television programs, church weddings, and the rates of church attendance. Wherever the truth lies, it is clear that religion and the family are intertwined and that the church remains an outside force on marriages.

SUMMARY

1. Marriages and families are not closed systems but instead interact daily with kin, neighbors, and community members. They are also affected by the economy, the weather, the media, and a host of other influences.

2. Stress from outside sources can be as powerful an influence on marriage and family life as are internal stresses. Some stresses can be partially controlled, but many—such as "acts of God"—are not within the family's control.

3. Three important areas to consider in understanding the impact of outside influences on family life are (1) the resources of family members, (2) the family's definition of the stressful situation, and (3) how many other sources of stress the family is simultaneously facing.

4. One of the significant changes in married life in the past two decades is the rapid increase in the number of middle-class women in the labor force. Dual-income marriages have become the norm rather than the exception.

5. Marital satisfaction of dual-worker couples compared with that of traditional couples depends on many factors other than the single variable of whether the wife works. The key seems to lie in whether the couple is capable of working as a team to compensate for the strains of child care, overload, and social pressures.

6. Overload is another major source of stress for working couples. Many attempt to keep up the household standards that were possible when the wife was a full-time homemaker. Often these pressures come as much from outsiders as from the couples' own expectations for themselves. Until recently, the middle-class working wife was generally denied social approval.

7. Dual-career marriages are a relatively new, small, but significant outgrowth of the past two and a half decades—a result of the women's movement, of family planning, and of more women being as well educated as men. Dual-career marriages have many of the same stresses as do dual-worker marriages, as well as others resulting from the dedication and motivation a career demands. There are high rewards for dual careers, however, the chief of which seem to be the opportunity for women to be as free to pursue a rewarding career as men are and the relief men receive from the total burden of family support.

8. Child care is a major source of stress for most two-paycheck families. Mothers still bear the major responsibilities for children, although fathers are becoming more involved. The United States lags behind much of the world in offering support to dual-worker families by providing adequate child-care facilities.

9. Friends, neighbors, and other community members can also exert influence on marriage and family life—both supportive and stressful. Problems arise, for example, in making "couple friends," maintaining friendships that do not include the partner, avoiding jealousy, and dealing with the time and energy demands of friendships.

10. In-laws and other family members have come in for their share of attention as influences on marriages and families. Usually, the implication has been that they are often more trouble than help. However, recent surveys have reported that families interact helpfully much more than has been realized by family-life experts in the past. As the life cycle lengthens, grandparents and great-grandparents are becoming more numerous, with the implication that multigenerational contacts will likely become more prevalent. As more women enter the labor force, some experts predict that "mother-in-law problems" may diminish since women will have less time to be so intensely involved in each others' lives.

11. Religion plays an important role in marriage and family life. Organized religion is a major supporter of stability and commitment, love, and nurturance. Research shows a positive correlation between religious involvement and marital stability.

GLOSSARY

Cost-reward ratio   The balance between what one gains from any given transaction and what the transaction costs—including the costs of time, energy, emotion, or anxiety. (p. 366)

Extended family   Kinship involving at least three generations living together in the same household or, in a modified form, living in such close physical proximity that they are in frequent intimate contact. More recently the term has come to denote those relatives who are personally known and with whom one has some regular interaction. (p. 395)

Isolated nuclear unit   A term used to describe a family unit that resides apart from extended kin and that is not in frequent face-to-face contact with them. (p. 394)

Job sharing   Usually, the division of a job between two people, each of whom works half-time. (p. 389)

Secularization   A process by which the domination of religion on society is weakened and replaced by values gleaned from other sources, such as science, education, and personal experience. (p. 400)

Workaholic   An individual whose work consumes his or her life to the point of seriously interfering with relationships and personal, mental, and physical well-being. (p. 383)

13

Jane Cox Vonnegut and I, childhood sweethearts in Indianapolis,
separated in 1970 after a marriage which by conventional measurement was said
to have lasted twenty-five years. We are still good friends, as they say.
Like so many couples who are no longer couples these days, we have been through
some terrible, unavoidable accident that we are ill-equipped to understand. Like our six
children, we only just arrived on this planet and we were doing the best we could. We
never saw what hit us. It wasn't another woman. It wasn't another man.
We woke up in ambulances headed for different hospitals, so to speak, and would never
get together again. We were alive, yes, but the marriage was dead.

iving together intimately for a lifetime is difficult for many couples and apparently impossible for the growing number who eventually divorce. Most marital and family therapists are equally adept at working with couples to resolve their marital problems and at providing divorce therapy to help couples end their troubled relationships as peacefully as possible. Although divorce may be the best solution for some couples, it is rarely an easy path to take, particularly when there are children involved. The number of divorces in the United States has risen to a historically high level. The period leading up to a divorce is traumatic for couples and children alike. Postdivorce adjustment is likely to be equally difficult for some divorced individuals, although those with the most resources—youth, money, friends, self-confidence—have an easier time.

DIVORCE: CAUSES AND CONSEQUENCES

Kurt Vonnegut,
Palm Sunday

*F*rom the beginning, virtually all couples want their marriages to succeed. However, marriages often run into trouble, and not all couples manage to salvage their hopes and dreams. "Marriage has been called the most difficult—if not impossible—social enterprise. Considering how poorly most people are prepared for it, and how immense their expectations of it are, the description more often than not unfortunately proves correct" (Lasswell and Lobsenz 1976, p. ix).

Divorce is a solution to unresolvable problems for a growing number of disillusioned couples. Divorce has become familiar to all Americans who may experience it directly themselves or in their family or indirectly through their friends and acquaintances.

Most thoughtful persons realize that not every marriage should endure. Some marriages are troubled from the beginning; others have reached a state where the relationship is destructive to both partners. Because all societies recognize that a certain number of marriages will not succeed, virtually all societies provide ways of ending them.

Divorce rates in many countries are higher than those in the United States; often this reflects the ease and social acceptability of ending marriage contracts in those countries. For instance, some Islamic societies permit a husband to divorce his wife by repeating "I divorce thee" three times. In societies in which divorce is difficult to obtain, there are fewer legal divorces but often a higher rate of separation and desertion: the husband or wife simply leaves. Desertion for a specified number of months or years is grounds for divorce in many countries; where it is not, however, the parties may remain legally married for the rest of their lives, even if they never see each other again. Many marry again illegally. Bigamous marriages can easily remain undetected if the couple moves a sufficient distance away from friends, families, and original spouses. It is impossible to know how many such marriages exist.

▌ DIVORCE IN THE UNITED STATES

For generations the United States made divorce difficult to obtain. In the northern colonies of pre–Revolutionary America, it was not unusual for a divorce to require an act of the legislature, if it was granted at all; as a result, there were very few. The southern colonies had no provision for divorce; couples could only separate from "bed and board."

All states now sanction divorce, but until 1966 New York granted divorces only in cases of proved adultery. Many other states had very few acceptable grounds. Beginning in 1970, states began to liberalize divorce laws by granting dissolutions on the basis of testimony that the two partners could not resolve their differences. The effects were predictable. From the trends in the United States, it is readily apparent that as laws have been liberalized, the divorce rate has steadily climbed. Wars and depressions temporarily affected the rates—wars were followed by sharp increases, and depressions lowered the rate—but the overall trend was upward over the years until 1982, when the number of divorces fell for the first time in two decades (see Table 13.1).

	Year	Number of Divorces
TABLE 13 · 1 Number of Divorces in the United States	1920	171,000
	1930	196,000
	1940	264,000
	1950	385,000
	1960	393,000
	1970	715,000
	1980	1,189,000
	1983	1,179,000
	1986	1,188,000

Source: National Center for Health Statistics, *Monthly Vital Statistics Report* 32, No. 13 (1984); *Monthly Vital Statistics Report* 35, No. 2 (1986).

The upsurge in numbers of divorces was, in part, due to the increase in population during the years that divorce statistics have been kept. The more people there are, of course, the more will marry. More marriages provide more potential for divorces.

No one is quite sure why the divorce rate fell, but one popular theory is that the economic recession in 1981 caused couples to think twice about going off on their own because they simply could not afford it. Jean van der Tak of the Population Reference Bureau, an independent Washington, D.C., research group, said: "Divorces cost money. Divorce often is a reflection of the economic times. I believe the recession was the prime cause of the decline" (*Los Angeles Times,* January 4, 1986, Part I, p. 31).

Social Factors Contributing to Divorce

Divorce statistics can be quite misleading if one counts only the increase in numbers over the years. A more meaningful figure is the number of divorces per 1,000 population. In 1920, for instance, the number of divorces per 1,000 population was 1.6; in 1970 the rate was 3.5 per 1,000; in 1976 it was 5.0 per 1,000; in 1981 it was 5.3 per 1,000; it is estimated that the figure will stay around 5.0 to 5.5 per 1,000 (National Center for Health Statistics 1980). Recent decreases may have been due not only to the economic recession but to demographic factors such as the trend toward later ages at marriage—which usually give marriages a better chance of success. Another factor contributing to the decrease may well be the larger number of unmarried couples reported living together. Should they break up, there is no divorce to add to the statistics.

Some experts have suggested that since divorces have increased so dramatically, more people are seeing the trauma of divorce. As a result, attitudes have changed that divorce always brings relief from problems and brings chances for a more satisfying life. The pain of friends and relatives who struggle with loneliness, single parenthood, financial crises, and emotional stress following divorce gives couples reasons to work on marital problems rather than to escape them through divorce.

The dramatic rise in the number of divorces in the United States came between 1963 and 1976, a period of other radical social changes. It was generally a time of affluence, of improved availability of birth control, and of the women's movement.

Some who watch divorce trends believe that the divorce rate may continue to level off in the immediate future and that the prediction that half of the couples marrying today will eventually divorce is unfounded. All of this remains to be seen; what we do know is that the courts dissolve 1.2 million marriages each year.

Even the method of calculating divorce trends by the number per 1,000 population can be misleading unless one looks at other factors affecting divorce statistics. For one thing, general divorce statistics include all divorces whether they are dissolutions of first marriages or sixth. First or second marriages, however, have a much lower likelihood of divorce than do third, fourth, and subsequent marriages (Cherlin 1978). Another factor that causes variation in the meaning of this divorce statistic is change in the relative size of age categories. An increase in the population under the age of fifteen, for example, would add to the population base but would not add a number of divorces proportionate to the number in the total population. The *divorce ratio* is defined by the U.S. Bureau of the Census (1985h, p. 19) as "the number of currently divorced persons per 1,000 currently married persons living with their spouses." It is subject to several criticisms, but it serves as an arbitrary standard by which to estimate trends.

Population   Certain population categories have higher divorce rates than do others. For instance, there are more divorced persons in urban areas than in rural ones. Western states have three to four times more divorces than do the states in the Northeast, which have the lowest rates. The North Central states are the next lowest, and the South ranks second to the West. Obviously geographical area does not make a difference per se; however, the attractive climates of the West and South are probably factors in their recent rapid growth, and family sociologists note that rapidly growing areas have less stable social environments and that couples who migrate may have less stable marriages with fewer support groups to aid them (Reiss 1980).

Age   Age at marriage is related to the likelihood of divorce, particularly if the partners are both teenagers when they marry. Teenage couples who marry have nearly twice the probability of being divorced than do those who marry later. It has been suggested that age itself is not the only reason for their high divorce rate, although inexperience and immaturity can be real detriments to marital adjustment (Bumpass and Sweet 1972). Teenagers who marry usually interrupt or discontinue their educations when they marry; thus they must often settle for unskilled jobs that pay less, a situation that puts stress on their marriage. They are more likely than older couples to have married despite parental opposition. Often very young couples marry because of pregnancy, and that frequently involves hostility of one or both sets of parents toward one or both of the couple, and perhaps guilt, blame, and anger between them. In a five-year study of teenage mothers, it was reported that over 50 percent of those who married when they became pregnant were divorced within four years (Furstenberg 1976a). No matter what the age of a couple when they marry, if they have these limitations, they may be in trouble from the beginning.

Education   College-educated couples usually have a much lower divorce rate than those with less education, but they also tend to marry several years later than the average person. More education affords them a higher standard of living; they are less likely to marry because of pregnancy or against parental opposition.

The only exception to the generally lower divorce rate for well-educated persons is that of women with seventeen or more years of education; they have a slightly higher average divorce rate than women with only four years of college. The reason may be that well-educated women are more likely to have professional careers and to be financially independent. Both factors have been blamed for marriage breakups, for (1) a self-supporting woman usually has attractive alternatives to remaining in an unhappy marriage, and (2) the complexity of the lives of two-career couples may be distressing to some (U.S. Bureau of Census 1977b, Table H). Men who are married to such women may feel freer to divorce if their marriages are unhappy since they are less likely to feel wholly responsible for their wives' financial support.

Religious Beliefs   Interfaith marriages (which have increased since 1900) have been thought to have a higher failure rate than do marriages in which couples share religious beliefs. However, once again other factors intrude to make the findings more complex than they first appear. The ages of an interfaith couple at marriage make a significant difference in the probability of survival of their marriage, for instance. Age at marriage, as we have seen, is related to educational level and to social and economic status, and these are highly correlated with the likelihood of success or failure of a marriage. An example of how these factors operate can be seen in divorce rates for Catholics who marry Catholics and for those who marry non-Catholics, considering the age variation (see Table 13.2). The rate of divorce is considerably higher for younger couples whether they are of the same faith or not, although Catholics who marry non-Catholics have a greater risk generally. Research has indicated similar findings for other religious groups (Burchinal and Chancellor 1962).

Intergenerational Patterns   Early research found that divorce was more likely for couples whose parents had been divorced. One study reported that when neither set of parents was divorced, there was only a 15 percent chance a couple would divorce. This figure rose to 24 percent if one set of parents was divorced and to 38 percent if both sets of parents were divorced (Landis 1956). There appeared to be a logical explanation for this intergenerational effect. If one's parents had divorced, any strong family opposition to divorce had already been tested. The couple had a model from their own parents of how to solve difficulties through divorce. However, once again matters are more complex than they may seem from the findings. Educational, social, and economic variables were not controlled. More recent research has shown that although there may be some truth to the foregoing arguments, divorce may be "contagious" in some families more because the parents and their married children share other factors that increase the likelihood of divorce, such as being of a lower social class, having less education, and marrying at an early age (Mueller and Pope 1977).

The Marital Life Cycle

For those couples who have troubled marriages, the first few years hold the greatest risk of divorce. The divorce rate peaks somewhere around the third year. Although divorce can occur at any time during a marriage, and the median duration of marriages ending in divorce is seven years (half the divorcing couples had been married

TABLE 13 • 2
Divorce Rates for
Endogamous and
Exogamous Catholics

Religious Combination	Age at Marriage	Divorce Rate	Average
Catholic-Catholic	Below 20	11.7 ⎤	
Catholic-Catholic	Over 20	0.6 ⎦	6.1
Catholic-other	Below 20	39.7 ⎤	
Catholic-other	Over 20	9.0 ⎦	24.3

Source: I. Reiss, *Family Systems in America,* 3rd ed. (New York: Holt, Rinehart and Winston, 1980).

less than seven years and half longer), at no time does the divorce rate again reach that of the first three years. Because the divorce itself rarely occurs until several months after the couple part, it is the first year or two of marriage that carries the most peril. One of the later peaks is at seven to ten years after marriage, another at eighteen to twenty years after marriage. Both of these coincide with "life-cycle crisis" periods that may cause discontent with many facets of life, including the marriage (Gould 1978).

Since the average person marries in his or her early twenties, seven to ten years later that person will be somewhere between 28 and 32 years old. Almost half of divorcing spouses are between 25 and 34 years of age (National Center for Health Statistics 1984a). Studies have determined that many people experience dissatisfaction with themselves, their work, and their marriages at this time. Some decide to change jobs; others decide to change spouses or to try being single. This phase has been dubbed the "seven-year itch" by those trying to explain the upheaval in the marital relationship. It may, however, be better named the "thirty-year blahs" to indicate a general dispirited attitude.

After eighteen to twenty years of marriage, the average spouses are 40 to 45 years old (give or take a year or two). Their children may be away at college or working, and the two partners may decide that although they are not yet old, they are not getting any younger either. In taking stock of life, they may decide that they do not want to live the rest of their years without realizing more of their hopes and dreams. They may blame each other for their failure to succeed or may believe that having a different partner or being single will help them to find what is missing. Therefore, a number of persons end long-standing marriages in their early forties, although nowhere near the number who end marriages of three or four years' duration when they are still in their twenties.*

Each year, millions of couples contemplate divorce. Over one million of them actually do. Often, when one partner is reluctant to dissolve the marriage, the other initiates the final action. Sometimes the conclusion is reached jointly after a long period of unhappiness and tension. The couple may have separated and then reconciled. They may have sought professional help for their problems. They may have had

*The U.S. Bureau of the Census (1977b, p. 12) made an effort to find evidence of an increase in divorce rates as the youngest child approaches maturity, but found none.

loud arguments, or they may have carried on a "cold war." Finally, somehow, one or both make the decision and contact lawyers.

CAUSES OF MARITAL DIFFICULTIES AND DIVORCE

What are some of the most frequent complaints that spouses claim ultimately lead to divorce? Marriage experts have long been puzzled why two people who love each other when they marry can turn so distant, so angry, so hurtful to each other that they want to end their relationship. What are the "irreconcilable differences" that lead to marital **dissolution**? The reasons couples give for wanting to separate or divorce—adultery, poor communication, lack of similar values—never quite describe the complexity of the turmoil of a marriage. The problems are never so simple and clear-cut. They rarely are entirely the fault of only one spouse, with the other totally innocent, as traditional grounds for divorce have so often implied. By the time two people decide to part, their conflicts are bound to have grown and to have spilled over into nearly all facets of their relationship.

Some troubled couples seek professional counseling for their marriages and succeed in getting them back on track. For some, however, counseling comes too late or does not solve their problems. Other couples manage to work things out for themselves. The reasons some couples succeed in staying together and others do not depends on a number of factors. There are a number of marital climates that hold the greatest risks for divorce and that indicate the need for professional help.

Studies have indicated repeatedly that most divorcing persons report that their marriages broke up for multiple reasons. For example, in a recent study, sexual incompatibility was the leading cause, followed closely by lack of communication and lack of time spent together (Burns 1984). These three are without doubt closely intertwined; to tell whether sex was not good because the couple did not communicate well and spent a great deal of time apart, or vice versa, would be difficult.

Marital Danger Signals

A problem that may be less obvious and certainly less dramatic than some other marital danger signals, but that is perhaps the most common, occurs when conflict has gone on so long that it has hardened into rigid confrontation, and the two partners seem unable to budge from their inflexible positions. Their viewpoints may be as unrealistic as they are resistant to change. Each may assume that only he or she sees the truth and that the other is an enemy. The struggle for power between the two may make it impossible to compromise or to cooperate. When, in addition, there is a definite imbalance of power between them—that is, one partner has the most resources—and the more powerful partner takes advantage of this position to "win" by intimidation, the relationship is usually in danger, if not already lost. Resources in power struggles may be sexual, financial, social, or psychological—whatever gives one partner an edge in controlling the other.

Sometimes one or both partners in a marriage have a need to hang on to a past hurt and to use this in an ongoing battle. They may not want to forgive the past but

DIVORCE AMONG THE ELDERLY

Approximately 6,000 divorces every year involve couples who are over 65. Sometimes these are couples who have had a long history of unhappiness. Often, however, they have had reasonably successful marriages through all of the previous transition points of their married life, but they run into trouble in the later years.

Older couples in troubled marriages are less likely to seek marriage counseling than younger couples are, probably because older people often are wary of mental health services. In their formative years such services were not available except for those who were mentally ill, and many still believe that only seriously disturbed people seek counseling. However, we see one or two elderly couples in our practice every year.

One of the most prevalent reasons behind divorce among older couples who have previously had reasonably successful marriages is that they have diametrically opposed ways of adjusting to their aging. Typical of such couples was 77-year-old John and 67-year-old Martha, who had been married for 46 years. John wanted a divorce "to have peace and quiet" in his last years, he told us. It seemed that Martha was on him continually because he was never home. She said she was lonely and disappointed at how their retirement years were going.

Upon investigation, their story unfolded. John had always been an active, hardworking man with many irons in the fire. True, he had sold his businesses in the preceding year, promising Martha that they would travel, play golf, and generally spend their days together. But John couldn't stand retirement and had just bought another business without telling Martha. She thought he was staying away so many hours a day because he did not want to be with her. The more she fussed, the more this was true—John did not want to hear her complaints. John wanted to stay active; Martha wanted to retire. They had developed a classic impasse.

Happily, this marriage was saved after much negotiation and compromise. John kept his business but agreed to give considerable time to being a companion to Martha. Her part of the bargain was to make their time together positive instead of complaining that she didn't have more of his time. Neither had it exactly as he or she would have liked, but both agreed that the compromise was far better than a divorce.

Other cases have not worked out so well. One reason that older couples divorce is that sometimes personalities change as people grow older. Character flaws and idiosyncracies may become exaggerated. What may have been tolerable when the couple spent significant time apart from each other during the workday may be impossible to live with after retirement, especially if the traits have grown more unpleasant.

Impending retirement often precipitates an identity crisis in one or the other partner. He or she may opt for one last fling at life before giving in to old age. A man, in particular, sometimes leaves a longtime marriage to find a younger woman. Perhaps he believes that her youth and energy will rub off on him. Women do not trade husbands at this age as much as men change wives because women's pool of available choices is far more limited due to the shortage of men in a suitable age bracket.

Women sometimes leave a long-term marriage to escape caring for a man who is chronically ill, senile, or otherwise seriously impaired (from a stroke, for example). Since husbands are, on the average, older than their wives and die younger, many women are faced with years of caring for an invalid spouse. It may strike some as unthinkable to leave a partner because of illness, and most spouses do not, of course. However, when over the years the marriage has become only tolerable at best, a long-suffering wife may decide that when love is gone, she cannot stretch her sense of responsibility any further.

The 6,000 divorces per year among couples over age 65 is but a small fraction of the more than one million total divorces granted each year. However, many find it surprising that even this small number of couples, some married more than 40 years, would think of divorcing. (Of course, not all of these are first marriages.) Apparently, longevity in a marriage does not always equal satisfaction.

instead continue to punish each other and to seek revenge. They may be completely blind to any part they have played in causing the painful episodes. The past is alive for them, as though past events had just occurred. Often such couples are afraid of intimacy or commitment and therefore actually sabotage any attempt, either their partner's or their own, to settle any differences.

Fear of intimacy may be of long duration, even predating the present relationship. Usually in such cases couples consistently have what is called the *conversation of divorce*. Accusations, insults, and threats all become increasingly ugly and wind up with talk of ending the relationship rather than with suggestions for solving the problems. Sometimes a partner becomes desperate enough to make a dramatic gesture such as moving out or seeing an attorney. Others may be driven to the point of threatening or even attempting suicide. Should any of these happen, there is no question that professional help is needed, although the partner who needs it the most may not be willing to seek it. In such cases the other spouse is encouraged to go alone. It is valuable to know how to react to such behavior so that it does not become more serious or how to cope with it should it continue.

Couples can find themselves in a particularly difficult situation when the conflict they are experiencing is deeply rooted in or inextricably linked to neurotic personality patterns of one or both partners. These can include character disorders such as compulsive gambling, constant lying, or lack of impulse control leading to suicidal tendencies, severe depression, or acute nervousness, and deep feelings of insecurity or inadequacy. These are problems that usually were present before the marriage occurred, but that did not give strong enough warning signals to discourage the marriage.

Often individuals who marry those with character disorders or with severe psychological problems either have serious but complementary disorders of their own or believe that they will effect miraculous changes in their disturbed partners. The psychological problems of one or both partners subsequently may either cause, or at least get in the way of solving, their controversies (Lasswell and Lobsenz 1976, pp. 235–239).

In contrast to those couples locked in an ongoing battle, there are as many more who speak of the lifeless quality of their marriage. They say they have nothing in common—a state often called *marital divergence*—because largely they have each been traveling separate roads. Such couples often say they no longer love each other. They know that something important is missing, and they often want the chance to find it with another partner. Some already have done so.

Extramarital Affairs

An affair often comes about when the marriage has grown cold. Most experts agree that the third person in a cold marriage is not usually the principal cause of the eventual divorce. Usually the third person is used only for comfort or to call attention to the problems that already exist. Marital therapist Carl Whitaker (personal communication) has said: "The third person is an amateur therapist. He or she teams up with one of the partners against the spouse. The spouse now becomes a bad parent and the lover a good spouse, but you really can't get rid of your problems with this kind of triangulation."

Most marriages in which affairs occur do not dissolve. If that were the case, the divorce rate would be even higher than it is. Even in ongoing affairs, the third person usually loses out to the spouse. It is true that some divorcing persons have someone waiting in the wings. The question for marital and divorce experts has always been whether there are some people who cannot leave one relationship, no matter how bad, until they have someone else with whom to be. It is as though the other person is a crutch to enable a man or woman to leave what is considered an unsatisfactory marriage.

Family Violence

Physical abuse, which results from lack of control over impulses, is a most damaging problem. Family violence has been a target of much research recently, after having been virtually ignored by the public and by professionals for years. Family violence—including wife abuse, husband abuse, **child abuse,** sibling abuse, parent abuse, and sexual abuse—has probably always been with us. It has played a part in many divorces.

The growth in both research and public interest in family violence has largely come about since 1970. The picture today is one of changed cultural norms. Since family violence is not considered acceptable behavior in the United States today—even though it has been in other places and at other times—what should be done about physical abuse has become a topic of major concern.

It is known that one-quarter of all the murders in the United States begin with domestic quarrels. Love triangles account for another 7 percent. In California, for instance, it is estimated that well over half the women murdered have been killed by a husband or lover (Meyers 1978). Wives kill husbands and lovers, too. According to FBI statistics, in cases of homicide involving one spouse murdered by the other, there is no difference between the percentage of wives and that of husbands who are offenders (National Center for Health Statistics 1976).

Wives are more likely to murder husbands for reasons of self-defense. Husbands are most frequently motivated by anger or jealousy. Many men report later that they were in a rage and did not intend the result of their violence to be homicide. More women report later that their intent was to kill to protect themselves.

Spousal homicides are said to occur across all socioeconomic, racial, and ethnic lines. However, a study of homicides in Chicago in 1981 revealed that not one person with a Hispanic surname arrested for homicide (about one-fifth of all suspects) had killed a spouse or lover. Among black couples, approximately two black men were killed by a black woman for every black woman killed by a black man. White intimates showed the opposite pattern: two white women were killed by a white man for every one white man killed by a white woman (Zimring 1983).

Fortunately, most spouses use the threat of violence to end a marriage by divorce rather than by death. In fact, it has been suggested that the relative ease and acceptance of divorce may actually be keeping the number of spousal murders from increasing as rapidly as have homicides involving strangers or casual acquaintances.

Battering of spouses, however, continues at an alarming rate and has become the focus of much research on social problems.

Spouse Abuse   An estimated 6 million women are victims of some form of abuse annually. Studies of couples now living together indicate that 3.5 million wives and over 280,000 husbands experience severe beatings from their spouses (Steinmetz

The intervention of a professional counselor in family violence cases provides advice and direct help for family members who must protect themselves or be protected.

1977a). If we were to add to this the violence between partners who are separated but were formerly married or that between unmarried persons who are living together, the total would be much higher. Even more devastating is the statistical evidence that in physically abusive couples these attacks happen several times a year. Financial analyst Sylvia Porter reports that abuse-related absenteeism on the job results in an estimated economic loss of $3 to $5 billion annually. Medical expenses add another $100 million or more to that bill (*San Fernando Valley News*, November 1, 1979, p. 12).

Hard times add to the incidence of spousal abuse. Statistics in Ohio for 1982 showed that the unusually high 21 percent unemployment rate in Youngstown was accompanied by a staggering 404 percent increase in domestic violence over 1979 (*Time*, September 5, 1983, p. 24).

Child Abuse   Child abuse is even more prevalent than spouse battering as a form of family violence and is often an issue in a troubled marriage, although it seems to be more common in single-parent families. Very young children often suffer such abuse. Although accurate statistics on the incidence of child abuse are extremely difficult to obtain, estimates range between 1.5 and 2 million cases each year. Approximately 8 percent of children are kicked, bitten, or punched, and 3 percent have been threatened with a gun or a knife (Gelles and Straus 1979, p. 12). In 1974 Congress passed the Child Abuse Prevention and Treatment Act; as a result, all 50 states now require that persons knowing of abuse report it. In 1984, the act was amended to include withholding medical treatment from children in life-threatening conditions as a criminal act.

The psychological damage to children who are victims of abuse is of almost as much concern as is their physical danger. Likely outcomes to the children have been shown to be negative self-images, difficulty in relating to others, failure to trust others, and poor ability to handle their own aggressive impulses. The last is of special importance, since adults who abuse children very commonly were themselves abused as children (Kinard 1979). Thus abused children are likely to repeat the pattern when they become parents. Often in families in which there is spousal abuse, child abuse also occurs. Research reports that of women seeking protective shelter who take their children with them, nearly half of their children have been physically abused, seriously neglected, or both. This is 1,500 percent higher than national averages for parents in the general population (Stacey and Shupe 1983).

Sibling Abuse Violence between siblings has been slow to be recognized as the severe problem that it is. Many parents accept as normal acts between siblings that would be considered cause for intervention if they took place between husband and wife or between parent and child. Actually, violence between siblings occurs more often than violence between parent and child or between husband and wife. Fifty-three of every 100 children seriously beat up a sibling each year (Straus, Gelles, and Steinmetz 1978). Although brothers hit, push, and throw things at each other more than sisters do, the greatest amount of physical violence occurs between brother-sister pairs (Steinmetz 1977b).

Parental Abuse Abuse of parents has only recently begun to be recognized as a problem. Although there are often instances of adolescent children physically abusing parents—usually mothers—and occasionally murdering one or both parents, the most typical parent abuse is of elderly, dependent parents. This is a growing problem, in part because of the increasing numbers of old people in our society who, forced to retire from jobs, often become dependent on their grown children.

In her study of battered parents, sociologist Suzanne Steinmetz (1978, pp. 54–55) remarked: "It may well be that the 1980s will herald the 'public' awareness of the battered aged—elderly parents who reside with, are dependent on, and battered by their adult, caretaking children." The problem is also a recognized one in England, where one study reporting on violence to the elderly concluded "Individuals exposed to a high degree of physical punishment as children are more likely to resort to family violence as adults" (Freeman 1979). Children reared in an environment of violence tend to batter their children and spouses and in turn may find themselves exposed to violence later in life from their own children—who, of course, have been brought up by violent parents.

Sexual Abuse Sexual abuse is usually separated in most persons' minds from the physical violence that goes on in families. However, even when physical damage is not a major concern, the psychological damage of such abuse can be very great and the fear can be overwhelming. Sexual abuse is usually linked to the abuse of children by adults—often parents, stepparents, or other relatives. Such acts are considered criminal offenses, and the adult, if convicted, faces the possibility of imprisonment. In reality, however, of those acts ever brought to light, most result in probation with the stipulation that the offender seek counseling. In addition, contact with the victim is forbidden for a specified period of time—sometimes indefinitely. Needless to say, when a parent or stepparent sexually abuses a child, the marriage is usually in serious jeopardy.

Another kind of sexual abuse has gained attention recently. Research on marital violence has found evidence that many men have forced or threatened to force their wives to have sexual intercourse—**marital rape**—on at least one occasion. Some of these cases have been brought to trial, and several states have adopted legislation protecting women from coitus by force or threats of force. Unfortunately, the parameters of rape have become increasingly difficult to determine, especially when no clear objection to coitus was stated by the woman at the time of the incident, but she reported that she believed that force might be used, money might be withheld, or other retribution might be forthcoming if she did not submit on an occasion when she was not interested in coitus. If there are irreconcilable differences about the desired frequency of coitus, sex therapy (or marital dissolution) are more acceptable.

Prevention and Treatment   Effective prevention programs are being developed to aid families who are identified as high risks for violence. The mass media—radio, television, and newspapers—are offering programs of education about family life and its stresses that lead to sexual abuse. Programs for aid to the abused and to abusers have been increased significantly. Crisis lines and protective agencies are available in most communities so that people can look for help at all hours. Meanwhile, victimized family members are advised not to remain in the home with any person who has an impulse control problem of this nature.

When treatment is either refused or is unsuccessful, divorce is seen as the only ready answer in many abuse cases. It is believed that violence is the underlying cause of thousands of divorces each year. Some states still list "physical cruelty" as a basis for divorce, but in most states, in which the usual reason given for marital dissolution is "irreconcilable differences," it is difficult to determine exactly how many divorce cases involve physical abuse.

Substance Abuse

A serious problem that affects millions of homes each year and is at the root of countless divorces is substance abuse, including alcohol and other drugs. It is commonly recognized that alcohol is often involved in family violence. Some studies have reported that approximately 80 percent of all such cases involve drinking before, during, or after the critical incident (Flanzer 1977–1978).

In the past, most of the literature on "problem drinking" focused on the husband and viewed his wife and children as the victims. More males than females abuse alcohol; however, many women also are problem drinkers. It has been estimated that at least 20 percent of the five million alcoholics in the United States are women (Beckman 1975).

A family with a drinking problem is always a family in trouble, although outsiders may be unaware of it unless the drinker creates a disturbance that arouses the attention of neighbors, employers, friends, or the police. In most homes with a problem drinker, both the drinker and the spouse are likely to "cover up" and to distort the facts to excuse the drinking behavior. Specialists in the treatment of alcohol abuse believe that covering up is a serious mistake that can lead to even more serious problems such as physical abuse, financial difficulties, and eventual breakup of the marriage.

According to the National Council on Alcoholism, half of the nation's divorces include alcohol abuse as a major factor (Roth 1981). Although alcohol abuse was less frequently mentioned than some other marital complaints, it was often a facilitator of the most common ones—constant arguments, sexual dissatisfaction, communication problems, and financial disagreements.

Not every problem drinker is necessarily classified as an alcoholic. Alcoholics not only drink excessively but also are unable to control their drinking and, in many cases, do not recognize that it is out of control. Obviously, they harm both themselves and those whom they love. Problem drinkers, too, drink so excessively or in such a pattern that their relationships necessarily suffer. Whether or not there are marital problems, any drinking behavior that creates discord is a serious problem even if the drinker is not labeled an alcoholic.

The best-known treatment plan for alcoholics is that of Alcoholics Anonymous (AA). Another organization, Al-Anon Family Groups, works with families of alcoholics. The AA plan has been highly successful and has served as a model for many self-help programs for problem drinkers. Other treatments that have been successful may use drugs to alter the effects of alcohol or behavior modification to retrain the drinker to avoid alcohol. The best treatment depends on the personality of the drinker and on his or her motivation for drinking. The most widely successful treatments combine elimination of all alcohol use with helping the alcoholic handle his or her life stresses and anxieties in other ways.

Since many of a problem drinker's difficulties may involve his or her family, family treatment is important. This treatment approach recognizes that the family is a system in which each member influences every other member. The goal is to change the system in which the problem drinker lives while helping him or her and the others involved to understand the illness. Family members must be encouraged to deal with their problems of living together in such a way that alcohol is not automatically blamed for every problem they have. "If only you didn't drink, everything would be fine" is not true for most of these families. However, many therapists believe that not until alcohol is eliminated can they begin to focus on the problems (Zimberg, Wallace, and Blume 1978). Others believe that until the causes for alcohol abuse are dealt with, it must be viewed as a symptom of other problems, which will not be solved simply by eliminating alcohol.

Statistics on how substance abuse other than that involving alcohol contribute to divorce are hard to come by because of the illegal nature of drugs. Marital therapists report that they are seeing an increasing number of young couples who mention drugs as a factor in their marital troubles. However, couples usually cover up the extent of drug usage even when directly questioned by the therapist. Denial is one of the most frequent characteristics that a drug user displays, and the damage such usage is causing the marriage is often minimized both by the user and by his or her spouse.

The executive director of the Commission on Organized Crime recently reported that the number of Americans who are chronic cocaine users (4.2 million) rose nearly four times from 1977 to 1982 (*Los Angeles Herald Examiner*, November 27, 1984, p. A-8). These are not just the criminal users or very wealthy sophisticates. Instead, cocaine usage is common among the young middle class and frequently becomes an issue in marriage problems.

Many companies are asking employees to supply urine samples because illegal drugs have become so pervasive in the work place. Countless others who do not use drugs on the job use them at home or elsewhere. The costs of drug abuse on the job are staggering; the costs of drug abuse at home are as enormous.

In California, as in some other states licensing marriage and family therapists, it has now become mandatory for those in the profession to be trained in substance abuse. This law recognizes the frequency with which drug abuse and dependence are a part of married life.

PROFESSIONAL HELP

Couples in serious marital trouble often choose professional help, hoping to head off a divorce or, at least, to minimize the problems in getting one. Once a decision has been made to seek help with marital or family problems, it is often difficult to know how to find the most effective guidance. Counselors and therapists provide help by means of various methods that are available to them. Such counselors come from a variety of training backgrounds. The intervention of a professional person in problems as intimate and crucial to one's life as are most family difficulties is cause for careful consideration. Persons contemplating therapy may be filled with anxiety. However, there are guidelines that can be followed for seeking the best help possible. These involve knowing where to turn for a referral to a qualified therapist and what questions to ask of the person one is considering.

Referrals are made in two general ways—informal and formal. Informal referrals are generally by word of mouth, either by having heard others speak highly of a therapist or by asking family, friends, or others for suggestions. Sometimes persons will suggest a therapist they have seen personally; sometimes they know someone else who has gone to a particular therapist. A therapist's good reputation with past clients is usually an indication of competence, although it is not always enough to ensure that he or she will suit you personally.

In addition to recommendations of friends and family, we suggest that the informal referral be combined with a more formal one made by reputable professional organizations representing family therapists. Some organizations that give referrals to highly trained therapists who work with individuals, couples, and families include:

- **American Association for Marriage and Family Therapy**
  1717 K Street, N.W., Suite 407
  Washington, DC 20006
- **National Council on Family Relations**
  Fairview Community School Center
  1910 West Country Road B, Suite 147
  Roseville, MN 55113
- **Family Service Association of America**
  44 East Twenty-third Street
  New York, NY 10010
- **American Family Therapists Association**
  1815 H Street, N.W., Suite 1000
  Washington, DC 20006
- **National Association of Social Workers**
  7981 Eastern Avenue
  Silver Spring, MD 20910

- **American Psychological Association**
  1200 Seventeenth Street, N.W.
  Washington, DC 20006
- **American Psychiatric Association**
  1700 Eighteenth Street, N.W.
  Washington, DC 20009

One can also ask a clergy person; a physician; or the psychology, psychiatry, social work, sociology, or family-life departments of a nearby college or university for referrals. State and local agencies also sometimes provide low-cost care in mental health clinics.

Once a prospective therapist is found, a telephone inquiry about methods, fees, and other pertinent matters can be made. It is especially important to determine that the focus of the therapy will be on the relationship and the interaction between the partners and other family members rather than on one particular member of the system. This does not mean that partners or other family members may not have individual sessions when the therapist believes that these will be beneficial. It is important, however, that the therapist believe that the actions and reactions of any individual are at least in part determined by the persons with whom he or she is interacting. This is especially so in a marriage or in a family, where change in the behavior of one member can easily cause change in that of other members. Counseling both partners together or all family members as a unit has been shown to be considerably more effective than working with only one member of the unit. The reasoning behind systems therapy is that—at least a majority of the time—the cause of problems between two or more people lies in their relationship rather than in the actions of any one of them alone.

Marital therapy can help; many couples credit it with saving their marriages. For those couples who want to work out their problems and who still love and respect each other, the rate of success is high. Many couples end their marriages only to regret it later. One investigation of postdivorce adjustment reported that two years after their divorces fully 25 percent of the women and 20 percent of the men expressed strong feelings of regret that they had not worked out the problems rather than divorcing (Hetherington, Cox, and Cox 1976). Meyer Elkin (personal communication), a long-time court of conciliation director, commented: "Every year we bury thousands of marriages that are still very much alive."

Successful marital therapy depends on several factors: how willing both partners are to cooperate for the necessary length of time, how determined they are to make their marriage work, at what point in the marriage they bring their difficulties to a counselor, and what level of maturity and state of emotional health each partner has.

Counseling does not always head off divorce. Experts estimate that about two-thirds of all clients report being helped by counseling even though the decision made is to divorce (Lasswell and Lobsenz, 1976). At best, successful counseling improves communication, may result in a happier sex life, and may give a more positive view of marriage. It also makes for "better divorces," if that is a couple's chosen path, by helping to work out personal problems and decisions that make parting less traumatic.

Most experts agree that not every marriage is destined to survive. In such cases, counseling can help to alleviate pain and bitterness. Couples may use it as a kind of predivorce counseling that enables them to weigh the issues and to make a rational decision to end their marriage. It can make a couple aware of the effort required to make a marriage work so that a future marriage may have a better chance to succeed.

STAGES IN THE DIVORCE PROCESS

For those who do not regret their divorces, one can only conclude that an adjustment has been made following the divorce that is judged to be an improvement over the troubled marital relationship. However, there is no smooth road from the time of decision to the time of feeling good about the action.

Most experts believe that resolution of a broken relationship takes a minimum of one to two years following a legal divorce decree. In a study that surveyed couples after a two-year interval, it was determined that there was great difficulty in letting go of the ties the couple had to each other. In the two months immediately following the divorce, 70 percent of the wives and 60 percent of the husbands said that should a personal crisis arise, the first person they would call would be the ex-spouse (Hetherington, Cox, and Cox 1976). The higher percentage for women may reflect the dependence they feel if they have child custody. It also may imply that women are somewhat more distressed by a divorce than men are, as other research has also indicated. However, a recent study has reported that men have a much higher need of psychiatric help following a divorce than do women (Bloom, Asher, and White 1978). It is probably safe to say that divorce is not easy for either of the partners.

Men seem to have a tendency to keep their feelings to themselves and to be less likely to discuss problems with relatives and friends than women are. Interviews with divorced men have shown that they often deny they are having difficulty in adjusting and, in general, seem to have a poorer grasp of why the divorce actually occurred than do women (Kressel 1980).

Other research on adjustment to divorce has indicated that the two-year figure is somewhat arbitrary and often misleading. Instead, it is suggested that many factors mitigate adjustment and that even though relationships may smooth out for months or even years at a time, turmoil frequently erupts over events such as children's problems, graduations, or weddings, for example.

Psychologist Constance Ahrons's (1985) five-year study of divorced persons indicated, in addition, that there is definitely a "his" and a "her" divorce; each sex may view divorce very differently and, therefore, adjust in different ways. Stages in the divorce process have been proposed by nearly a dozen family sociologists (Price-Bonham and Balswick 1980, p. 963). Although every divorce is unique, most couples seem to follow certain general patterns. A look at these stages may help to shed light on the coping process couples use to get through the traumatic months following a divorce. Very few escape the depression, the sense of personal failure, and the diminished ability to function that follow the breakup of the long-standing emotional bonds of a marriage.

The most traumatic effects of divorce usually occur when only one partner wants to end the marriage and initiates the divorce. It is never easy to be rejected; when, in addition, one's whole life is upset against one's wishes, the results can be devastating. The responses to such a loss are very similar to those noted in persons who have been victims of natural disasters, have lost a loved one by death, or are facing the prospect of their own deaths. They go through a period of denying reality.

This is followed by a period of despair and confusion. The repression of their feelings may cause them to develop psychosomatic disorders or other types of problems that lead them to seek professional help. Typically, anger follows, along with a feeling of betrayal. Finally, realistic planning and adjustment to the situation gradually begin to take over (Falek and Britton 1974).

In viewing the stages of the divorce process that have been proposed in the literature, it may be helpful to put them into two broad categories: adjustments to the end of the marriage and adjustments to a new lifestyle.

ADJUSTMENTS TO THE END OF A MARRIAGE

Nearly all those who have carefully studied the divorce process concur that the period during which the partners actually separate is one of the highest points of stress—far greater than the time of the legal divorce. In a study comparing recently separated men and women with those who were married and those who were already divorced, the separated showed the highest levels of stress and depression (Pearlin and Johnson 1977).

In a comprehensive look at the divorce process, social scientist Paul Bohannan (1970a) used six overlapping phases to explain the complexity of divorce. The first five are useful for examining the early adjustments that divorcing persons must make. The sixth (the psychic divorce stage, in which individual autonomy is regained) deals more with the development of a new lifestyle.

The Emotional Divorce

The first of Bohannan's "six stations of divorce" is the *emotional divorce,* which centers around a deteriorating marriage. Research on this phase has been aimed at determining the causes of marital strife that ultimately lead to divorce. Specific problems—finances, alcoholism, extramarital affairs, and poor communication—are often blamed. However, most experts agree that these problems are not the real causes of divorce but only the visible symptoms of an unlivable situation that gradually worsens over time. Divorce expert Sheila Kessler (1975) has divided this stage into three phases—disillusionment, erosion, and detachment—that may reflect the real causes more accurately.

Couples first concentrate on each other's weak points and blame each other for unhappiness that may actually lie within themselves. They may be trying to judge their relationship through unrealistic or even offensive comparisons. Eventually, disillusionment leads to an erosion of their affection for each other either as a result of low priority for the other's emotional needs, constant bickering, or of cold silence. Most people assume that the greatest marital stress occurs at the time of crisis. Marriage therapists, however, know that although a crisis often brings stress to its breaking point, the stress itself is due more to the gradual erosion of the marriage than to any one special event. At some point, detachment occurs when both believe that the continuation of the marriage is untenable.

The Legal Divorce

By the time that one or both of the partners decide to move to the second stage described by Bohannon—the *legal divorce*—marriage may have ended emotionally months earlier.

The legal divorce begins with the decision of who will file and on what grounds. In the past this was a far more difficult step than it is today. Until recently, it was necessary for one spouse to prove that the other had "damaged" him or her in some way, such as by adultery, mental cruelty, or impotence. Today almost all states have some form of "no-fault" divorce that allows partners simply to agree that they have "irreconcilable differences" or an "irretrievable breakdown." Some states have other grounds as well (such as insanity or long-term separation), although these are only infrequently used. If two spouses disagree about whether there is or is not an irreconcilable difference, their persistent disagreement makes it so.

Lawyers   Most persons turn to a lawyer at this juncture. Lawyers perform a number of important functions during the entire time of the divorce, but in this phase they are particularly valuable as sources of information about laws and rights. If two people can agree on grounds, support, custody, and visitation, a lawyer may serve only to review their decisions for clarity and legality and to make sure that proper legal procedures are followed and that various forms are completed and filed. A couple in some states, if they have limited assets and there are no issues involving children, can secure a marital dissolution simply by filing a request for one.

Divorce Mediation   A comparatively new field of help for divorcing couples has grown increasingly popular in the last decade. Divorce mediation is a process in which the couple together work out the issues involved in their divorce agreement—division of assets and debts, custody and visitation, child and spousal support—with the help of a third party, either someone trained as a counselor but knowledgeable about law or a matrimonial lawyer who is knowledgeable about counseling. Sometimes a team— one a lawyer and one a divorce counselor—work together to help couples at a very vulnerable time in their lives to make good legal and emotional decisions.

Divorce mediation causes the separating spouses to focus their efforts on reaching a mutual solution to the many issues that must be decided in a divorce. Through mediation, they have the opportunity to explore options and to work on joint strategies to end their marriage but to continue parenting if they have children.

Of course, mediation does not work for every couple because one or both may have an uncooperative attitude or be too angry and hurt even to face each other in the same room, let alone work together on emotional issues. There is not yet a great deal of research to document the value of mediation over the usual process of using attorneys to settle the issues that the ex-partners cannot decide. However, a few studies have indicated that couples who choose mediation over the adversarial system seem more pleased with the results and are less likely in the future to return to court to change the decisions they have made (Pearson and Thoennes 1982, p. 3; Bahr 1981).

In approximately 10 percent of divorce cases, parents cannot settle custody and visitation issues and wind up in court to fight it out (Drapkin and Bienenfeld 1985, p. 63). Children feel tremendous pressure and divided loyalty when they are the pawns in their parents' battle. Other research shows that of those couples who choose me-

Legal advice is considered essential for most divorcing couples, particularly when property, custody, and support issues are involved.

diation, there is disagreement between the parents about the best interests of their children in half of the cases (Little 1983).

On occasion children are included in custody and visitation mediation. Children are afforded the opportunity to express their concerns and tend to leave the sessions feeling less anxious and with a better understanding of both their own and their parents' feelings and expectations.

Annulment   Under special circumstances an annulment may be granted to a couple to end their relationship. Annulment is not, strictly speaking, a legal divorce. It is a legal process used in only about 3 percent of the cases of legal breakup; however, it is interesting because of the conditions under which it is allowed. An annulment actually decrees that a marriage never really existed because for some reason it was not legally contracted. The grounds for annulment are quite uniform in the United States and are similar to the grounds for declaring any legal contract invalid.

Some of the reasons for the judgment that a marriage was not legally contracted involve the "competency" of either or both of the parties to enter into the agreement in the first place. For instance, they may have been below the legal age to marry. Approximately 25 percent are granted for this reason. One or both of the partners may have still been married to another person. This happens fairly often, as when a person remarries before a final divorce decree is granted from a previous spouse. However, it does not often become an issue since none of the persons involved usually has anything to gain by filing charges of bigamy.

The marriage contract may be void if it is determined that the parties are blood kin to some degree that is against the law for marriage. A few cases of incompetency to marry have been recorded in which one party was drugged or drunk or judged to be temporarily insane and therefore unable to consent to the legal agreement to marry. This happens only rarely because most states require a waiting period from the time the license is taken out to the time of the ceremony, and it is not likely that such an incompetent condition would go undetected for several days. However, there are states in which a couple could meet and marry within one day—even within a few hours.

A second major determination of whether an annulment can be granted is the proof that one party has "defrauded" (misrepresented or concealed important information from) the other. It is surprising that more annulments are not granted, considering the range of information that is considered important when withheld: pregnancy of the bride without the groom's knowledge, or a claim that she is pregnant when she is not; concealment of impotence or knowledge of one's sterility; concealment of a venereal disease; misrepresentation of one's intentions to have children; concealment of prison records or other illegal acts that may affect the spouse; concealment of debts or deliberate misrepresentation of income or assets; or misrepresentation of one's intentions to consummate the marriage (to have sexual intercourse). In addition, the use of force, threat, or other coercive measures to make one person marry the other constitutes grounds for annulment.

Should an annulment be granted, it takes effect immediately since the marriage is judged never to have existed. This makes annulment attractive to those for whom a divorce is an impediment to remarriage—for example, adherents of religions that do not recognize divorce. It should be noted, however, that legal annulment and religious annulment are two separate processes. For instance, one may have a church annulment following a legal divorce.

Some couples who have been married for years and who have children are granted annulments. However, there are some serious questions about the consequences. Their children are technically illegitimate since it has been decreed that a marriage never existed, and in some states this may affect inheritance and child support. Community property rights and spousal support may also be affected. However, some persons choose this route despite the problems.

The Economic Divorce

The *economic divorce* is the third of Bohannan's phases. This is a crucial period filled with negotiations about child support, alimony, and property settlements. A thoughtful analysis of this phase has proposed that how well or poorly the negotiations proceed is a function of four primary factors: the emotional state of the divorcing partners, their ability as negotiators, the assets to be divided, and the power base from which each is operating (Kressel and Deutsch 1977). Emotions often get in the way of rational settlements, as powerful feelings of anger, guilt, and vengefulness interfere with sensible negotiations. With couples who are divorcing, finances and children seem to be the topics that arouse the most passions.

In no-fault decisions, child custody and child support are decided separately from financial issues of the divorce such as property division and spousal support. In reality they often become confused with each other since money paid to children is often viewed by the noncustodial parent as payment to the parent with custody. Thus children, alimony, and child support often become intermingled as emotional issues in the minds of divorcing parents. If there are no children, then obviously property and spousal support have clearer boundaries. Since large numbers of divorced couples also are parents, however, confusion often arises.

As mentioned previously, in many family court systems, trained mediators can guide the divorcing parties to an equitable and effective solution to their differences. The couple can avoid costly proceedings and may have a better chance to part on amicable terms than if they go through a prolonged legal fight during which, too often, the ex-spouses abandon all communication except through their respective attorneys. "We try to help people close the book gently," says Meyer Elkin (personal communication), a pioneer court of conciliation director.

Property Agreements   In many states, property distribution is done on an equal basis; hence, any advantage held by one who is a better negotiator is minimized. Some states have legislation mandating *community property,* which means that all assets and debts accumulated since the wedding date are divided equally unless the partners had a prior legal agreement to some other distribution. In other states, fault (grounds for divorce) may decrease the share that the "guilty" partner (the one deemed at fault) is awarded. Usually, a parent who retains child custody is given some advantage in terms of maintaining a home for the children. The house, the furniture, and often a car are awarded when possible to the custodial parent. In community-property states, however, homes frequently must be sold to balance out the debts and assets equitably.

Recent court cases have tested the definition of marital property. Typically property is defined as furniture, real estate, cars, and other tangible assets as well as future benefits such as pensions and intangibles such as professional "goodwill" that have recognized value (for example, a physician's reputation in the community that more or less ensures continued or increasing income). Since 1983, courts in several states have begun to look at professional degrees earned during marriage to determine whether they may be considered community property. In Wisconsin a statute now provides for compensation for spouses who have contributed to their mate's education. Frequently, one spouse works to support the other's education, sacrificing equal advancement for himself or herself. Often this is a woman who ten years later is still at the same job while her husband has enhanced earning capacity due to his degree. At least one court has ruled that such a woman is entitled to recover the actual amount she paid for her husband's educational costs (tuition and books, for example) upon dissolution, but not the increased income that she believes he is likely to receive after the divorce as a result of his education.

Spousal Support   Spousal support is money paid regularly to one spouse by the other in addition to any child support that may be due. **Alimony,** as distinguished from spousal support, is a kind of restitution for "damages" or for "loss of marketable assets." Alimony is almost always a fixed amount, which the court may order to be paid in monthly installments or as a lump sum, due whether the partner remarries or not. Spousal support, in contrast, is usually a fixed stipend to be paid monthly until the partner remarries; dies; or, sometimes, has time to become self-supporting. Spousal support is intended to permit the spouse who may be left with the fewest resources to live in a manner that is not drastically different from that of the married years. Usually, however, both partners have to lower their standards of living substantially since rarely is there enough combined income for them to maintain two households at the same level at which it was possible to maintain a joint one.

In recent years, alimony has been ordered less often by courts, especially when there is no evidence that the marriage has "taken the best years" of the spouse's life.

It is rare for alimony to be awarded in addition to support. Usually the husband is ordered to pay his ex-wife either alimony or spousal support either because she has been a homemaker or because, if she has had outside employment, it has been less continuous than his and she has therefore earned less. If she earns as much as the husband does, usually no award is made to her. A growing number of courts are requiring a woman to pay support to her ex-husband should her income be greater than his and should he need such assistance.

Spousal support is based on both partners' abilities to earn, their standard of living during the marriage, the number of years they have been married, and the growth of their assets since they were married. It is considered that both have contributed to their financial prosperity by fulfilling whatever contract they made when they were married. Among high-income couples support can be a very complicated issue, with significant tax implications. The one who pays spousal support or alimony can deduct payments from his or her income tax totals, although child support is not deductible.

Couples who have not prospered or who are too newly married to have accumulated assets are more likely to avoid arguments about spousal support. Some courts view the age of a woman who has not had outside employment for years as a factor in her ability to support herself. If she is young, she should be able to work; but if she is older, her "marketability" may be doubtful. Her health and her job skills are also taken into consideration. Some studies have shown that women who receive support from ex-husbands report less satisfactory postdivorce adjustment (Raschke 1977). Continuing to depend on an ex-husband financially may be detrimental to a divorced woman's feelings of self-worth. However, it may be that more traditionally oriented women (who would be most likely to receive support since they would not have been employed) report a lower level of postdivorce adjustment (because their status has changed more drastically) than do women who have held outside employment. Those who are in the labor force are the ones who report better adjustment (Raschke 1977).

Spousal support usually is ordered for a specified period—until the supported partner remarries or until his or her income reaches a specified amount. Support may be jeopardized in some states if the supported partner lives with someone on a more or less permanent basis and it can be shown that the other person is also contributing to his or her support. Usually, this becomes an issue when a man who is paying his ex-wife support learns that she is living with another man who is supporting her or contributing significantly to her support.

The Coparental Divorce

The fourth of Bohannan's phases of divorce has been termed the *coparental divorce*. This phase deals with issues of custody, visitation, and child support.

Child Custody   Historians note that prior to this century, fathers were more likely to have custody than were mothers, due, in part, to the high maternal death rate and also to the belief that children were the property of their fathers (Polikoff 1982). By the late nineteenth century, the notion that the child belonged to the father slowly changed to a belief that mothers were essential to child rearing, especially from birth to school age. No doubt, this notion was strengthened by society's industrialization, which sent fathers to work outside of the home for long hours (Trattner 1979). Ultimately, the bias toward the mother's custody (in legal language, "the doctrine of tender years") was so entrenched that fathers rarely asked for or received custody. Knowing that mothering would be their major role in life caused most women to accept that they were the better "nurturers" and to have strong sentiments that they must have custody if they were to define themselves as good mothers and good women. It did not matter much that many times the father was the better parent or that the children preferred to be with him. The reasoning was that unless the father was happily remarried, he could not make as good a home for the children as their mother could since he would be away all day at his work. Therefore, if a father gained custody of his children, the assumption was that the mother was out of the picture (dead, a runaway, or institutionalized) or that she was otherwise unfit for motherhood.

Historically, being "unfit" often was related to a mother's past or current sex life. If it could be proved that she was living with a man (or, in the case of a lesbian, involved in a sexual relationship with a woman) or was entertaining partners sexually while the children were in the home, her ability to be a good parent was considered to be impaired. Currently, however, "living together" is becoming more acceptable in the eyes of the courts, and some judges even take the view that another responsible adult in the home is an advantage for the children.

An important traditional reason for awarding mothers custody involved the nature of the divorce itself. Only recently have divorce laws been changed in most states to eliminate the notion of guilt or innocence over the breakup of a marriage. Under the old system, one party sued the other by bringing charges that were grounds for divorce. If those charges were proved and if the divorce was granted, the one who sued was the "innocent party" and often was awarded the children as well as a larger part of the property. It was not that women were usually "innocent" but that since women were expected to get the children anyway, they were the ones most often delegated to sue. In addition, many people believed that it was more "chivalrous" for a man to allow himself to be found "guilty" in a public trial than to "besmirch the character" of a woman by accusing her of wrongdoing, especially when she was to have custody of their children.

The belief that divorced mothers could stay at home to care for children whereas fathers must go to work and would be unavailable for their care was another reason for awarding custody to mothers. In most cases, however, divorced women today must work outside the home, causing their lives to be as fragmented as a custodial father's would be. In 1983, 51 percent of divorced women were employed outside the home on a year-round, full-time basis (U.S. Bureau of the Census 1985j, p. 147).

Not until the last few years has this strong bias toward mothers been challenged. As a result, the number of fathers granted custody has been on the increase. The number of fathers with sole responsibility for their children has almost tripled since 1970; it is currently estimated that they number around 600,000 (U.S. Bureau of the Census 1984f, p. 7).

Until relatively recently, the decision concerning custody was usually made by the divorcing parents and was based on such factors as time available for the child or children, each parent's desire to have custody, the perceived need to keep siblings together, each parent's suitability for custody, and even the preferences of the children. However, fathers have increasingly been challenging the policy that, even though they might fill the requirements better, the children's mother (except in rare cases) should be awarded custody.

Joint Custody   Shared custody has grown more popular in recent years. Shared custody may take the form of *joint custody,* in which both parents retain legal custody just as they had while married to each other. Joint custody is not necessarily shared physical custody, in which the children live an equal amount of time with each parent. It does mean that each parent has access to the children and has an equal voice in making major decisions pertaining to education, health care, religious training, and other kinds of parental decisions that were made when the parents were married.

In most custody arrangements, all of the children initially live with one parent—usually the mother—for the school week and visit with the other parent on some weekends and some vacation periods. As time elaspes one or more children may reverse the original plan. This is particularly the case with boys, who more frequently than girls move to live with their fathers. Mothers and sons in particular seem to have problems after the divorce, and mothers often ask for help from the boy's father (Hetherington, Cox, and Cox 1976). Occasionally, when someone remarries, the new spouse does not get along well with the children, and a move is made to have them live with their other parent.

Not all divorced parents are pleased with the greater ease with which joint legal custody is being awarded. Many critics of joint custody point out that now fathers receive equal legal rights to determine how their children will be reared while the children actually live with their mothers, who have all of the actual responsibility.

One of the most important effects of either joint legal custody or shared custody is that they necessitate cooperation between the parents if they are to work. Both plans eliminate custody battles (devastating to children and parents alike) in which children's loyalties are constantly at stake. Parents who have made joint legal and shared custody work report that the process of negotiating the arrangements was a positive factor in achieving an amicable divorce. For instance, the father who has more contact with his children and makes more decisions about them is more likely to be willing to help pay for their support. Many fathers who fail to pay child support say that they withhold the payments because the mothers are not allowing them to see their children on a regular basis.

A growing number of parents are sharing physical as well as legal custody, using a variety of innovative plans. The children, for example, may live for half of the year, half of each month, or every other week with each parent. In such cases, the parents usually live in the same school district, and each maintains a room, clothes, and toys for each child. Parents usually like the shared responsibility and the opportunity for more personal freedom. Child therapists believe that the close contact with both mother and father is especially valuable (Cox and Cease 1978). Studies show that parents who have shared child raising during marriage are the most likely to choose shared physical custody when they divorce (Takas 1986).

Since being a single parent after divorce is often difficult, a trend toward shared custody seems to hold promise. Although many questions about shared custody remain to be answered—such as how two parents who got along so poorly that they divorced can now cooperate in a joint custody arrangement—there are distinct advantages. It is estimated that approximately 35 percent of divorced parents in the United States have some form of shared physical custody (considering the number

More and more divorced parents are choosing to share custody of their children. While many questions about the logistics of such plans remain to be answered, child therapists believe the idea shows promise since close contact with both mother and father is almost always a positive experience.

of teenagers living with their fathers). This fact has emerged as a topic of major interest to the legal profession and to divorce therapists (Abarbanel 1979).

Some parents and children report drawbacks to shared physical custody. From the standpoint of the children, there is something called the "suitcase phenomenon." Children sometimes resent, or simply get tired of, packing and unpacking to move from Mom's house to Dad's house. Some parents who can afford to do so have clothing, toys, and other supplies at each home so that children minimize the feeling of visiting each site with their possessions in hand.

More than the transient feeling, however, bothers older children, who seem to dislike making friends at both places and then separating from them on a regular basis as they alternate where they live. If parents reside in close proximity to each other, it helps to alleviate this problem.

Parents, too, have some complaints about sharing physical custody. A frequent problem is the competition that can develop over who provides the "best" home. Children often compare discipline, attention, and the standard of living provided by each parent. Parents may feel the pressure to keep up with each other. Mothers frequently feel at a material disadvantage since very few ex-wives have the income their ex-husbands do. The effect of the average divorce is to decrease the standard of living of women by 73 percent and to increase that of men by 42 percent, according to a recent extensive review of divorce in the United States (Weitzman 1986). This discrepancy in income is compounded by the fact that when mothers and fathers share care of their children an equal amount of time, often neither pays the other child support. For many women, child support makes the difference between a comfortable existence and a real financial struggle. Just because the children spend considerable time with the other parent decreases actual expenses very little. Costs of housing, utilities, and other fixed expenses must be paid whether the children are there or not. Only food and clothing costs may decrease.

Custodial Fathers   The reasons that fathers rather than mothers sometimes gain custody fall into four broad (and overlapping) categories: in 60 percent of the cases, the mother did not want custody; 35 percent of the fathers reported that the children chose this arrangement; 30 percent of the fathers believed the mother was not a competent parent (many of these cases were fought in court); 20 percent of the fathers wanted the children and the home so that they could hold onto a sense of family

(Greif 1985b). In addition, divorce advocacy books for men seem to argue that men have been taken advantage of in the custody process long enough and that they should fight for custody just to end such discrimination (Kerpelman 1985).

A growing number of fathers have organized to protest the traditional custodial process. They resent giving up the legal right to be fathers to their own children. Presently there are more than 80 groups of divorced fathers in the United States—including Fathers for Equal Justice, United Fathers' Coalition for Fair Divorce and Alimony Laws, and Male Parents for Equal Rights—attempting to change a father's chances to share in custody of his children after a divorce. These groups estimate that in 1985 over 600,000 separated or divorced men were raising approximately one million children.

Some women's advocates have suggested that some men seek physical custody not because they really want it but because they want to gain leverage in financial bargaining. In her book based on hundreds of interviews with parents, children, and divorce and family counselors, Phyllis Chesler (1986) found that in custody battles in which the mothers had been primary caretakers prior to the divorce, fathers still often asked for and received custody. Often the decision was that the father was better able financially to provide an adequate home.

Research on custodial fathers has been meager until recently, but new studies show that such fathers adjust as well as mothers. They provide somewhat different but equally good care for their children. Once fathers obtain custody, they use grandparents, baby-sitters, day-care centers, and schools to help with child care while they work—just as custodial mothers do. Custodial fathers report personal growth and increased sensitivity to others as a result of assuming greater responsibility for their children's needs (Rosenthal and Keshet 1978).

Much of the research on custodial fathers who are single comes from a study in England that indicated that although almost all single parents have similar problems regardless of their gender, men and women do differ on some issues (Hipgrave 1981). Fathers received more help from family and friends than mothers did, even though they were less likely to ask for it directly. Single fathers are more consistent, stricter disciplinarians and, consequently, report fewer discipline problems than do "solo mothers." The men reported anxiety about raising daughters, especially in giving them good emotional support. Women worried more about discipline problems, especially with sons. These findings have been replicated in many respects by studies in the United States (Santrock and Warshak 1979).

A recent study of over 1,000 fathers raising children alone found that single fathers experienced the most difficulty—just as single mothers do—in juggling work and a social life with their parenting. Least difficult for the fathers were maintaining strong bonds with their children and housekeeping even when they had done little of the latter while married (Greif 1985a).

Another recent study of the effect of children on father custody compared with that of mother custody has shown that children can fare well no matter which parent has custody. However, boys seem to do better with their fathers and girls with their mothers, all other things being equal (Santrock and Warshak 1979). This observation may be the effect of sex similarity resulting in a greater understanding between same-sex persons or, conversely, of male-female antagonism—whatever the reason, there does seem to be ample evidence that the courts should perhaps reconsider the usual judgment that brothers and sisters should not be separated in custody decisions.

Visitation   Most divorced fathers are "part-time" and see their children only as arranged by the court's visitation orders. This may be, for example, every other weekend, alternate holidays, and one month in the summer. Sometimes the court inserts the words "reasonable visitation" into the order, but too often bickering ex-spouses have difficulty deciding what "reasonable" is. Thus visitation is usually spelled out, taking into consideration both parents' wishes and the best interests of the children.

Many fathers report difficulty in making their visits with the children normal and easy. There is a temptation for the father to try to make every minute count in order to reestablish himself with his children as a "good guy." Fathers may try to do only things that are fun to make up for all of the pain of the divorce and to ensure that times together with their children are good. Visitation may be spent as a vacation would be—no set bedtimes, eating out, no homework—especially in the first months after the divorce. Custodial mothers complain that the children come home confused and resenting the discipline and responsibilities demanded of them. As one mother (personal communication) put it, "Daddy looks awfully good, taking them to the movies and to the ball game. Then they come home to a regular routine, plus taking out the garbage and picking up the dog's mess, and they scream that they want to live with their dad." In California and Florida, this has been termed the "Disneyland-Dad syndrome" since every weekend the amusement parks hold many such fathers and children.

Over half of divorced fathers remarry within three years of their divorce. The new wife may have children of her own, to whom he becomes a live-in stepparent. He may begin to see his own children less often as he involves himself with his new family. Visits may be difficult because of crowding or of poor relationships of either the father or his children with stepsiblings or of the children with the stepmother. The children's mother may also have remarried, so that there is now an "in-house" stepfather to fill many of their needs. The result is often an emotional distancing with the noncustodial parent. Sometimes there is a geographical move away as well, often because employment demands mobility among many men and women in our society. Visitation rights are not lost by moving, but if the distance is great, they may be very difficult or inordinately expensive to exercise frequently.

Recent studies have indicated that the patterns and levels of contact between children and their noncustodial parents vary widely among divorced families. Some fathers see their children several times a week and have telephone contact at other times. Boys see their fathers more frequently than girls do and for longer periods. Some children spend enough time with their fathers to be a part of their lives and their households, which become like their second homes. When children are seen as part of two households, whether or not the parents share legal and physical custody, they are said to belong to *binuclear families* (Ahrons 1979). They are given responsibilities and are not treated as guests. This is in contrast to other children who see the noncustodial parent rarely and with little, if any, predictability.

A rather surprising finding of most research is that the frequency of visits is not the major factor in the quality of father-child relationships. The nature of the time spent together is what gives the child a secure feeling of a primary bond with the father. The studies conclude that relationships between noncustodial fathers and their children have a good chance to be maintained even when busy schedules, mothers' preferences, business demands, and geographical distances interfere with frequency (Hess and Camara 1979).

Noncustodial mothers have visitation patterns that are very similar to those of noncustodial fathers. In a recent study of custodial fathers, it was reported that mothers were a little more likely to visit when the father was raising only girls than when there were only boys. Approximately 25 percent of the noncustodial mothers visited weekly, but nearly ten percent never visited (Greif 1984).

Child Support   In most states, child support is ordered until a child is eighteen. It is usually figured on the basis of both parents' incomes, the number of children involved, and their former standard of living. Most courts will not permit an award to give a noncustodial spouse more of the necessities of living than the dependent children. In many states, this is translated to mean that the noncustodial parent shall contribute up to 40 percent of his or her net income to the children's support (depending on the income of the custodial parent).

However, awarding child support does not mean that it is always paid. Of the four million divorced women with children under the age of 21 who were awarded child support by courts, only about 47 percent received the full payment due to them in 1981; another 25 percent received partial payment. The average payment received was about $115 per child per month (U.S. Bureau of the Census 1985f, p. 1).

Fathers who do not have custody complain that they can go to jail for nonpayment of support but that nothing happens to ex-wives who make visitation difficult or even impossible. They are accurate in saying that they could be imprisoned, although most courts believe that such action only compounds the problem. Extreme measures are used only when a father who has the money to pay willfully disobeys orders to support his children. Again, there is a kernel of truth in the argument for a law to enforce payment of child support. The financial situation for millions of mothers with custody of their children is perilous. A great part of the problem is that today it is difficult to make ends meet even with two incomes for one family. When divorce occurs and the total income must now support two households, there is often just not enough money to go around. Most women report a sharp drop in their level of living following a divorce. Fully one-third live below the poverty level.

It may be difficult for fathers to pay child support regularly, especially if they remarry and begin a new family. Since money is at a premium under such conditions, many begin to lag behind. Nonsupporting fathers are sometimes arrested at work and may even be jailed, as mentioned earlier, although this social cost is high (Chambers 1979). Not only is it usually impossible for a father who is in jail to continue to earn money, but also the stigmatization and the alienation are great.

A federal child-support enforcement program became effective in 1975. It requires that absent parents (usually fathers) be located and required to help support their dependent children if they have failed to do so. Social Security numbers and Internal Revenue Service records can be used to track down these delinquent parents. There is a minimal cost to the custodial parent unless she or he is on welfare; then it is free since locating a paying parent can potentially cut the cost of Aid to Dependent Children payments. Under current laws, states must require payroll deductions for delinquent child-support payments. Support payments are withheld from the parent's paycheck by his or her employer and paid directly to a support collection agency. Federal Income Tax refunds can also be intercepted to collect support payments.

As noted previously, many noncustodial parents confuse the concept of child support with that of spousal support and refuse to pay for their children's support because they resent the divorced spouse's having access to the money. Finances are often used as a weapon to continue the battles that led to the end of the marriage. Children are the innocent victims. "I will quit my job and move out of the state before I will give her one dime," said one bitter husband whose wife left him for another man (personal communication). A woman whose husband was awarded custody in a contested suit was so angered when she was ordered to pay child support to him that she kidnapped their children and fled the country.

The Public Divorce

The fifth stage of divorce described by Bohannan deals with *friends and community,* which affect every divorced person. We have often heard the remark that when we marry, we choose not only a mate but also his or her family and friends as well. An insightful analysis of the changes in relationships with kin and friends is provided by family sociologist Robert Weiss (1975). He stresses that it is not unusual for the decision to divorce to be postponed because the thought of telling family and friends just cannot be faced. Relatives, close mutual friends, and sometimes work colleagues are frequently supportive, of course, but can also be judgmental. Telling one's parents seems to be the hardest, perhaps because it is difficult to face disappointing or upsetting them.

Relatives   In our clinical experience we have known couples who, living apart prior to a divorce, make a great show of still being together for the sake of their kin. They call family members regularly, never mentioning the split. If relatives are planning a visit, they temporarily reconcile in order to keep the secret a bit longer. Although their greatest fears of condemnation by family members may come true, most kin rally around after asking questions about what went wrong and offering advice for how to reconcile. Their reactions depend on how they evaluate the reasons for the divorce. If violence, alcoholism, gambling, or another lover has been in the picture, sympathy usually goes to the spouse who is seen as the victim. Parents may be critical of their own sons or daughters who have misbehaved and may side with their in-laws, at least at first.

A study of 78 grandmothers (aged 52 to 91) with a divorced child analyzed the changes in their relationship with their son or daughter, their former in-law, and their grandchildren. Twenty percent of the grandmothers reported negative changes in all three areas; in view of the large numbers of grandmothers this may represent, it is not an insignificant effect of divorce. However, the study also suggests that grandmothers are much more often an important source of support and that they experience little, if any, negative changes toward their children and grandchildren (Ahrons and Bowman 1984). It appears that the old adage "blood is thicker than water" usually proves true in the long run, and blood relatives eventually pull together.

Sometimes a divorced man or woman moves back to the parental home. This is far more common among relatively young divorced persons, and more frequently it is the woman who has small children who seeks such refuge. Although this may be her only good choice, moving back with her parents often is distressing. Parents—especially white, middle-class parents—may treat grown children as if they were adolescents when they return. It is as though their "parent buttons" are pushed again by the dependency of the returned child. Although such an arrangement may be practical for a short time, it is usually temporary for that reason.

A custodial parent usually maintains some relationship with his or her in-laws. Since grandparents are blood relatives to their grandchildren, they are usually concerned about losing touch with them. If the divorce has been a bitter one or if the children live some distance from their grandparents, contact may be confined to times when the children are visiting their noncustodial parent.

Some states are beginning to make laws to protect the rights of grandparents to visit their grandchildren. In 1983, Texas passed over a dozen new laws in an attempt to create more fairness in issues of divorce, custody, and visitation. One such bill was the Grandparents' Visitation Act, which protects visitation rights even if their own child (the parent of their grandchildren) should die.

Women usually have established stronger bonds with their in-laws than men have. This is probably because women traditionally plan family functions, keep up correspondence, buy gifts for special occasions, and see that children keep in touch with their grandparents. However, some men who are not close to their own families of origin may "adopt" their in-laws. If they are involved in a family business with in-laws, changes in relationships can be upsetting. Divorce may mean more than losing a family—it may also mean losing a job.

Friends   A divorcing person often has trouble continuing relationships with friends. He or she may feel let down or rejected at the very time when support is needed. Often friends have been primarily attached to one partner; after the divorce, they quickly lose touch with the other. They may take sides, blaming one spouse for the divorce. In the days before no-fault divorce, friends were often called on to testify for a person suing for divorce. Such testimony was a clear case of taking sides that understandably alienated the spouse, usually irrevocably.

Sometimes couples' friendships are based on their marital status—as in couples' bridge clubs or square-dance groups—so that a divorce terminates relationships with other couples for both of the divorced persons. When one's friends divorce, anxiety about the state of one's own marriage may be aroused. Some married couples try to avoid friends who are divorced, as though divorce might somehow be contagious. Newly single women in particular report feeling unwelcome at gatherings of their married friends. They may be anxious about being seen as threats to the other women, who may not trust them or may mistrust their own husbands around them.

Friends can, however, be very helpful and supportive in the months following a divorce. Eventually, ex-spouses usually begin to make new friends who know nothing of their past troubles or who themselves are divorced and trying to make a fresh start. Until this happens, there can be a time of loneliness ameliorated only by those friends who rally to one's support.

ADJUSTMENTS TO NEW LIFESTYLES

As difficult as it is to get through the emotional turmoil of ending a marriage and to live through months of legal negotiations and radical changes, many divorced persons report that starting over is in many ways an even bigger problem. Bohannan calls this stage the *psychic divorce*. It can be a rewarding period, in which growth begins to take the place of destructive forces and autonomy replaces dependency, or it can exact a greater and in many cases a longer-lasting toll than virtually any other life stress.

The Psychic Divorce

Adjustments to the divorced status usually involve problems of finances, companionship, children, and self-concepts. Those who have the most difficulty developing a new lifestyle are likely to be those with the fewest resources (and therefore, the fewest alternatives), whether in money, friends, family, sexual gratification, and/or in inner resources of self-confidence.

The stage in personal and family life cycles during which a divorce occurs has a great impact on how the ex-spouses adjust. Young, childless couples who divorce generally blend back into the young singles' world with relative ease. Usually both are employed, and they have no responsibilities other than themselves. Their individual adjustments still involve starting over, but most young persons have hope that they will find new love and success in a remarriage. Adjustment is closely tied to how successful they were at single life previously and to the kind of supportive network they have during and immediately following the divorce.

Couples who have been married longer and particularly those with children have many more problems to face in their postdivorce adjustment. A parent with sole custody of his or her child(ren) often has little time, energy, or money to go out; yet having visitors in the home may prove troublesome for the same reasons. In addition, some children can be very difficult when they are asked to make room in their lives for their parents' friends.

Many custodial parents report that their sense of alienation and isolation can become acute. There is the need for internal reorganization of feeling and thinking as well as for adjustment to the external changes due to the divorce. It usually takes a minimum of one to two years to recover; even longer may be needed should the external changes involve poverty or problems between the former spouses. Unlike younger, childless couples who may never see each other again should they choose, parents usually continue their contact even though they might wish not to.

Older divorced men and women also have their special adjustment problems. Older divorcees may have a more difficult time adjusting because fewer older people do divorce. Consequently, they may feel out of step with their contemporaries and have a more difficult time reentering an ordinary social world.

Older men, of course, are often at a premium since there are so few of them compared with the number of older women. They have a good chance to remarry, and most do so. Older women, particularly those who have made the focus of life around home and husband, have an unusually difficult time. Usually, they do not initiate a divorce no matter how troubled the marriage because they are dependent. When men or women who have been married for over 25 years decide to divorce, they often find that cutting the ties of responsibility for each other and disrupting the family bonds with children and grandchildren are more problematic than they had anticipated. It is not unusual for one divorced partner, even though remarried, to be available for aid to the former spouse in time of need. It is almost as if they now were married to two partners in some respects.

Problems of Women

Often women are at a distinct disadvantage after a divorce because they may be expected to make the most drastic changes with the fewest options open to them. A woman who has few marketable skills except those needed for homemaking may now have to earn a living working in industry or in an office or a store. This is particularly difficult for mothers of young children who married at an early age and have little or no work history.

Immediately upon separation, divorced women who have worked little, if at all, outside the home must face child-care problems and a transition from the financially dependent status of wife to that of head of a household with responsibility for making many unfamiliar decisions. Many such women moved at an early age from dependency on their parents to dependency on their husbands. They did not have time to experience the self-sufficiency that comes with living alone and supporting themselves for a few years or, in some cases, even a few weeks. It is not uncommon to find that a woman who has been married for several years does not know how to file a tax return, for instance, or when or how to buy new tires for the car.

Middle-aged or older women who have spent their lives as homemakers and mothers have an additional set of problems. They not only may have no way to earn a living except, as one woman put it to us, "as a maid in someone's home," but they often suffer from lack of confidence and from the fear that their social value has vanished with their youth. Again, the grain of truth is that many employers and personnel officers (both male and female) give preference to applicants with youthful appearances. Corporate pressures for early retirement may intensify the emphasis on a youthful work force, although it is usually explained by the willingness of younger people to work for lower pay. In recent years, however, many large corporations have been forced by both union pressures and court decisions to give up age discrimination. Still, older women may feel too old to be trained for a job and unsure, if they find one, that they can compete with younger women.

Problems of Men

Many men have severe problems in starting over after divorce, although they may have more alternatives than their ex-wives. The hardest part for many men may be moving away from a home and children they have valued highly; men who have never lived alone may feel lonely as well as relatively helpless about domestic tasks that have always been done for them—first by their mothers, then by their wives. Psychiatrist Robert Robertiello (1979) says: "Divorce is one of the most highly traumatic things a man can go through. Men whose wives have left them are shattered, and they really do withdraw." Learning to be alone after many years in a family may be the most difficult adjustment a man has to make. Often he is struggling financially to pay child support; if he did not want the divorce in the first place, he may be bitter as well. Many men fill their lonely hours by work or television, or haunt singles' bars in an attempt to begin to feel attractive and to fill time.

In general, however, men fare better financially, if not always emotionally, following divorce. It has been shown that in all income groups the postdivorce income of men is substantially higher than that of their former wives. In addition, men are far less likely to have dependent children living with them and their income is treated as "his" rather than "theirs" (Weitzman and Dixon 1980).

Social Life

Beginning to date is not an easy task for either a man or a woman who has not done so for years. The average newly divorced man is 32 years old and the average woman almost 28. They have been closely related in the processes of courting, being married, perhaps raising children, and divorcing for an average of nearly seven years. The longer they have been involved with each other, the more things will seem to have grown different in the singles' world—and, of course, the more the man or woman has changed from the young, relatively immature person he or she was in previous dating experiences.

Seventy-five percent of divorced persons begin dating within the first year after divorce; by the end of the second year, all but 10 percent have done so (Hunt 1966). Those who find dating the easiest, again, are the ones who have the most resources—youth, good looks, money, self-confidence, and know-how.

A major difference in the "world of the formerly married" that is often a surprise to a man or woman is how early in a new dating acquaintance the topic of sex is raised. The assumption seems to be that both individuals are sexually experienced, both have sexual needs, and the games of teenage flirtations are a waste of time.

In one survey, six out of ten women reported that most or all of the men they had dated made serious sexual approaches on the first or second dates. Nearly three-quarters of the men and nearly two-thirds of the women had sex on this more or less casual basis. Of those who had been divorced for a year or more, only one man in twenty and one woman in fourteen had not had sexual intercourse. Nearly all reported that the effects were generally beneficial in terms of restoring their self-worth and enabling them to believe in love again. The Hunts (1977) comment: "Good, bad, or indifferent, the early dates of the formerly married are a virtual laboratory, an environment in which to observe behavior, perform tests, and make a number of discoveries about others and themselves."

Some men and women receive professional help during these months of transition to a new life. Many divorced persons attend seminars or join self-help groups to meet others who are involved in similar struggles. Divorcing partners report that groups can serve as vehicles to help them get over hurt feelings and anger as well as expand their activities and establish new friendships.

There are many organizations for those who are divorced. Perhaps the largest is Parents without Partners (8807 Colesville Road, Silver Spring, MD 20910), which has over 1,000 chapters and organizes social and educational events for parents and their children. Churches, universities, and men's and women's organizations are all beginning to offer special interest groups for divorced persons. Newspapers routinely carry notices of meetings and events for singles (often specifying age groups that might be most welcome). These events range from social activities or trips to lectures or discussions about problems of adjustment. Studies of postdivorce adjustment report that the more divorced persons participate in social activities, the better is their adjustment (Spanier and Casto 1979). Of course, the argument could be made that those who have the best adjustment are the most likely to feel like going out. This is

Not all divorced persons find (or want to search for) desirable and accepting partners among their personal contacts. Advertisements are a way of searching anonymously.

Single BF 29, healthy, attractive, active, aware, smoke/drink/drug-free, vegetarian, therapy veteran, seeks fit man 30–40 for friend, lover, lifetime companion. I value: honesty, gentleness, tolerance, forgiveness, nurturance, stability, courage. If you care deeply for something other than yourself and work to improve the quality of life, please write Box #————.

My 30th is approaching soon. Help me celebrate. WM, 29, very nice, from Midwest, tall, slim, good-looking, low key and patient. Would like to meet intelligent, dark-haired, attractive white or Asian female 25–31.

no doubt the case, but dating and companionship do tend to relieve the pain of rejection and to reassure the person that he or she is socially acceptable and perhaps likable or even lovable once again.

Divorced persons have a tendency to use each other for support, and groups for postdivorce adjustment can help them come together. Experienced divorce counselor Esther Fisher, editor of the *Journal of Divorce,* believes that group support is one of the most valuable paths to adjustment following a divorce. As she states (1974, p. 119), "Post-divorce adjustment includes a variety of goals; namely, a reduction in feelings of bitterness and hostility; more understanding and acceptance of self, children, and ex-spouse, and of society generally; a return to work and social activity; and better management of personal affairs and the ability to handle the new problems that follow divorce."

Adjustments of Children

Currently over one million children each year must face the divorces of their parents. It is predicted that by 1990, one-third of all children under eighteen years of age will have lived with a divorced or otherwise single parent at some time. Some of the children will have been through the experience more than once (Glick 1979).

It is difficult to determine exactly how much psychological damage children suffer as a result of possible predivorce traumas and how much can be attributed to the actual separation and postdivorce adjustment. However, most experts argue that adjustments following their parents' divorce are difficult for all children. The range of reactions is wide, however, and the time needed to recover is variable. Some adjust well in a relatively short period of time, but others never quite recover. Parents who belong to Parents without Partners have estimated that their children take from one to three years on the average to adjust. Approximately 9 percent reported that even

The range of reactions
that children experience
as a result of divorce is
varied. Some adjust
well, but others have
stress from which they
are slow to recover if
they ever do.

after many years, a child had not recovered (Parks 1977). Those children who have personality and behavior problems even before their parents divorce usually suffer the most serious adjustment difficulties. Often they must receive professional help for such problems as antisocial behavior, serious school problems, and personality maladjustments. The most common reaction is depression. One study concluded that "divorce may now be the single largest cause of childhood depression" (McDermott et al. 1978).

The first year following a divorce is typically filled with great stress and disorganization for the children, which may prompt negative behavior—nagging, whining, dependency, demanding behavior, rebelliousness—that causes the custodial parent to become cross and restrictive (Hetherington, Cox, and Cox 1978).

The most distressed children are those who are caught in the crossfire of their parents' battles and whose parents themselves are having the most difficulty adjusting.

Another important variable in a child's adjustment has to do with the financial condition in which the custodial home is left. Most intact families have a difficult enough time making financial ends meet in this time of escalating costs of living. When a family divides, there is often economic hardship. Income is a key factor in the adjustment of divorced couples and of their children.

A recent longitudinal study begun in 1976 and continued in 1981 studied a large sample of children whose parents were separated or divorced by 1976. The conclusions were that divorce often tends to undermine the relationship a child had previously with each parent. These weakened relationships may be among the most important factors in adjustment problems children have after divorce (Peterson and Zill 1986).

An ongoing study of children and divorce has been conducted by psychologists Judith Wallerstein and Joan Kelly (1974, 1975, 1976) in California. The age of children at the time of a divorce became an important clue to how the children went about adjusting. Preschool children typically react with denial and may ask, "When is daddy coming home?" They often talk and act as though nothing has changed, although on deeper investigation it is shown that they may harbor fantasies that the separation has occurred because they have been bad. Many children of this age believe that they have somehow caused the problems between their parents.

Somewhat older children (seven or eight years old) are less able to use denial than are younger ones. Their reaction is often one of sadness and withdrawal. Parents report the most difficulty in getting children of this age to talk about how they feel. Tears are common, but the children are unable to verbalize their emotions.

Children of nine and ten are often very angry and may blame one or the other parent (sometimes both) for the distress they feel. They may resent having to help more and become unpleasant about financial hardships. They often report feeling ashamed of what their parents have done.

Older children, particularly adolescents, realize the impact and finality of the divorce and may need to make sense out of why the marriage ended. They may take sides and withdraw emotionally from one or the other parent. They, more than younger children, will base their reactions on how the parents respond to their questions and on how the parents resolve conflicts.

In a 1984 follow-up Wallerstein and Kelly reported that children of divorce often looked back on their childhoods with lingering sorrow and were extra cautious before marriage and childbearing. Their feelings of anger at their parents abated with the passage of time and the growth in their own maturity. However, a few continued to have problems with trust related directly to their parents' divorce (*Los Angeles Times,* Part V, February 17, 1984, p. 32).

Although most children recuperate from the effects of divorce within a year or two, research has shown two basic differences found in later life between those who experienced a parental divorce prior to age sixteen and those who lived in intact families. First, those from divorced homes have a greater tendency as adults to identify childhood or adolescence (or both) as the unhappiest period of their lives. The exception to this is among those who have also been divorced themselves, in which case their own divorce may take precedence. The experience the child had when his or her parents divorced becomes a kind of yardstick by which to measure future misery.

The second major difference in adults whose parents divorced is that they are more likely than children from intact homes to experience later events as ones that produce high anxiety. This is especially true for males (Kulka and Weingarter 1979). Interestingly, this finding is similar to other research suggesting that girls adjust to their parents' divorces sooner than boys do. Until 1976 children whose parents had divorced were also more likely to have sought professional help for their anxieties and personal problems than were those from intact homes (Kalter 1977). In 1976 the trend was for more people in general to seek professional help for their problems; this ended the disproportion in the number of clients whose parents had been divorced.

When adults who experienced parental divorce as children are compared with those who did not, the differences in reports of childhood happiness and current anxiety levels are statistically significant. However, recent research has shown that experiencing a parental divorce, though traumatic in the short run, is in the long run, as Wallerstein suggests, one that most adults outgrow. Many come to believe that their parents made the right choice in parting. The parental divorce tends to remain as a subtle influence helping to shape the child's views of adult life roles.

What is significant in understanding both the short- and long-term impact of divorce on children is that for children the threat of divorce and the problems following divorce are determined by how the parents adjust. Since most parents have readjusted (and a sizable number have successfully remarried) within one to three years following divorce, it is not surprising that most children also have made a good recovery within a similar period of time.

Most studies of readjustment involve the reactions of the mothers since the overwhelming majority of children of divorced parents have been placed in the custody of their mothers. Some studies have shown that children and adolescents who live with mothers who have remarried have self-concepts that are much better than those of children whose mothers have not remarried (Parish and Copeland 1979). The mothers' readjustment seems to be the most important key to the children's readjustment. In fact, a study of schoolchildren showed that emotional problems evidenced by children depend on the amount of conflict experienced in the home, regardless of whether the parents are divorced, still married to each other, or remarried (Raschke and Raschke 1979). A stable single-parent home is more conducive to a conflict-free childhood than is a two-parent home filled with turmoil. The fact that most children show a good adjustment when their mothers remarry is thought to be a direct result of her good adjustment.

Although most divorced parents eventually remarry, children may live in single-parent households for a number of years. At any given time, it is estimated that over one-third of all children will spend some time in a single-parent family before age sixteen because of marital disruption (Bumpass and Rindfuss 1978, p. 1). A 1985 census report indicated that in March 1984 over five million minors were living with a divorced parent who had not remarried (U.S. Bureau of the Census 1985a, p. 145). Most such families face major difficulties—finances, fatigue, unfamiliar tasks usually performed by the other parent, added child responsibilities, sibling quarrels brought on by stress and uncertainty—but with effort, these families do survive and most of them thrive.

Most single-parent families are headed by women—89 percent in 1984 (U.S. Bureau of the Census 1985a, p. 5)—although there are some recent indications that this may change as a result of joint custody trends. The father was the lone parent in about 3 percent of the family groups with children under eighteen in 1984, triple the figure of 1970 (U.S. Bureau of the Census 1985a, p. 5). Many fathers who are single parents report that their jobs suffer because employers do not expect men to have demands made on their time by children.

Divorce has become such a commonly shared experience for children that in some communities they have banded together in support groups. In a Lexington, Massachusetts, high school the Divorced Kids Group was formed several years ago to help create a more accurate picture of how divorce affects children's lives (*Marriage and Divorce Today* 6, No. 46 [June 22, 1981], p. 2).

SUMMARY

1. Virtually all societies recognize that some marriages are better ended and therefore provide ways to end them. In the United States, until relatively recently, divorce was difficult to obtain.
2. As a result of liberalized divorce laws, a lessening of social stigma attached to divorce, the ability of more women to make their way financially, and other social variables, the divorce rate in the United States increased until 1982. Not all marriages are equally vulnerable to divorce. Age, geographic location, education, income, religion, and marital status of a couple's parents are all factors affecting divorce.
3. Professionals and organizations for divorced persons can assist individuals who are making the adjustment to single life again. There is a tendency for divorced persons to group together to support each other through the adjustment process.
4. Adjustment to divorce follows a series of stages for most individuals as they face the inevitable changes necessary when a marriage has ended. Many divorce experts believe that the process of deciding to divorce and the actual physical separation create the greatest stress in the divorce process. This stage is termed the *emotional divorce*.
5. A *legal divorce* involves attorneys, courts, and arguments over support and custody issues. The legal issues are heavily dependent on the emotional state of the divorcing partners, which affects their ability to negotiate, and on the assets and liabilities to be divided. No-fault divorce legislation has helped reduce the likelihood of one ex-partner taking advantage of the other although there are still loopholes in the law that allow for serious problems to arise.
6. The *economic divorce* involves issues of division of property and other assets and liabilities, as well as possible provision of spousal and child support.
7. Parental issues are difficult to decide. For most of the twentieth century, when divorces have occurred, women have received custody of children and men have paid child support. The picture is beginning to change gradually as more men are receiving custody of one or more children or are sharing custody with their ex-wives.
8. Annulment is a legal process sometimes used to end a marriage when it can be proved that there was some defect in the union. There is also religious annulment, which is granted for reasons comparable to those for a legal annulment and which may be useful to those whose religions prohibit remarriage after divorce. An annulment decrees that the marriage never existed.
9. Family, friends, and the community can be important sources of either stress or support for a divorcing couple. Reactions depend on how these outsiders evaluate the reasons for the divorce. They are usually supportive to the partner who has

been "wronged," although in the long run kin tend to side with their own blood relatives.

10. Adjusting to the status of "divorced person" can be nearly as difficult as the separation process. Adjustments are easier for those who have the most resources: youth, money, friends, know-how, and self-confidence.

11. Both men and women report problems in beginning a new lifestyle. Women, however, are usually asked to take on the responsibility of child custody. Since most divorced women must work outside the home, those who have not previously done so may find the transition to be dramatic and demanding.

12. By the end of the second year after divorce, nearly all men and women have started to date again. They often have to relearn how to behave in the courtship process. They have different dating norms, particularly with respect to early sexual involvement.

13. Adjustments to their parents' divorces are difficult for all children, although most research indicates that in the long run all but a small number adjust well. Those who have personality and behavior problems before the divorce seem to have the most serious adjustment problems. The key to the children's adjustment appears to lie in that of the parents, as well as in the financial state in which the children must live.

GLOSSARY

Alimony Court-awarded payment to a spouse upon separation or divorce. Alimony, which should not be confused with support payments, is paid for restitution of losses or for remedy of wrongs done. (p. 426)

Child abuse Violence against or extreme neglect of a child; sexual interaction of an adult with a child. (p. 414)

Dissolution The formal, legal termination of a valid marriage by any means other than the death of one or both spouses. (p. 411)

Marital rape Coitus between married persons that is accomplished by force or the threat of force by the male partner, or coitus to which a wife submits because of her concern about what her husband might (or might not) do if she refuses. (p. 417)

14

After a divorce, and to an even greater extent after a remarriage, many individuals
experience the insecurity of sharing children and sharing parents.
Compassion and understanding can lessen the hurt, and aid the healing process.
Individual growth can then occur, bringing with it an interpersonal warmth and a
deep understanding of other human beings.

As the number of divorces has grown in the past two decades, so has the number of remarriages and resulting stepfamilies. Couples who divorce clearly are not permanently disillusioned with marriage—only with the person to whom they were married. Most divorced persons remarry, and rather quickly at that. Second marriages fare quite well and give strong evidence for the belief not only that divorce may be the best solution for some troubled marriages but also that many couples who divorce do learn how to succeed better the second time around.

Of the approximately 40 percent who divorce a second time, their chief complaints vary considerably from those that caused them to divorce the first time. Conflict in remarriages usually centers around finances, in-laws, ex-spouses, and children. Stepfamilies—sometimes called "blended" or "reconstituted" families—offer great challenges for both the parents and the children. With over sixteen million children living in stepfamilies, the blended family is no longer an oddity. In some communities, children who live with both natural parents seem to be hardly more numerous than those who have a stepparent.

REMARRIAGE AND STEPPARENTING

Emily E. Visher and John Visher, *Step-Families: A Guide to Working with Stepparents and Stepchildren*

*E*ventually, the desire to marry again arises in nearly all divorced persons. Even those who loudly proclaim "never again" at the time of their divorce find that, as time heals most of their wounds, they begin to feel the desire for companionship and for someone with whom to share life. Furthermore, the social expectation that one ought to have a successful marriage usually leads people to try again. Four out of every five divorced persons eventually remarry; most within three years of their divorces. Currently, over 30 percent of the total marriages in the United States are remarriages (Price-Bonham and Balswick 1980).

REMARRIAGE

Divorced men are more likely than divorced women to remarry, although the difference is not great (three of four women and five of six men) (U.S. Bureau of the Census 1981b, pp. 1–6). Of those women who are divorced before age 30, 91 percent remarry within nine years of their divorce, most of them within three years (National Center for Health Statistics 1979b). The reason is probably that older women's chances of remarriage are diminished because there are many fewer men in their age range (see Table 14.1). Men are usually older than their wives, but die several years younger than women on the average. There is also some evidence that a woman with several children at home is less likely to remarry. By the time her children are grown, she may be in the pool of older women and have a limited choice of partners. A recent national survey of divorced women between the ages of 15 and 44 found that whether a woman remarries is determined primarily by her age at divorce, her educational level, and her race. The younger she was when divorced, of course, the greater the likelihood she would remarry. College-educated women were less likely to remarry, as were black women (National Center for Health Statistics 1980).

The number of black males equaled the number of black females at age 18 on July 1, 1984. Black women outnumbered black men in every subsequent age category. This was not true for the white population until age 27 (U.S. Bureau of the Census 1985i). This fact, coupled with the additional facts that black males are much more likely to marry white females than white males are to marry black females (see Chapter 6) and that women marry men somewhat older than themselves helps to explain the low remarriage rate for black women. The low remarriage rate for college-educated women is probably due in part to the greater likelihood that they are financially self-sufficient, partly because of the later age at first marriage of college-educated women and partly because of the tendency of never-married women to stay in school longer.

From Divorce to Remarriage

The average interval after which divorced persons remarry has changed from approximately four years from the time of divorce in the 1950s to the current average of three years (National Center for Health Statistics 1980). It is interesting to speculate about the reason for this. One factor may be simply that there are more divorced persons from whom to choose than there were previously. Since those who are di-

TABLE 14 · 1

Males per 100
Females: 1970, 1979,
and 1984

Age	1970	1979	1984		
			Total	White	Black
All ages	95.9	95.0	94.9	95.5	90.4
0 to 9 years	104.0	104.5	104.7	105.4	102.2
10 to 19 years	103.5	103.7	104.4	104.8	101.8
20 to 24 years	101.2	101.4	102.0	102.9	95.2
25 to 34 years	98.0	98.8	99.5	101.3	89.2
35 to 44 years	95.7	95.4	97.1	99.0	83.8
45 to 64 years	91.7	92.1	91.4	92.7	81.9
45 to 54 years	93.3	94.3	94.4	96.2	82.1
55 to 64 years	89.7	89.8	88.4	89.4	81.7
65 to 74 years	77.7	77.0	77.6	78.0	72.0
75 to 84 years	65.9	60.4	59.3	58.8	61.5
85 years and over	53.2	44.7	40.6	39.8	47.4

Sources: U.S. Bureau of the Census, *Current Population Reports*,
Series P-23, No. 111 (June 1981), p. 3; Series P-25, No. 965 (March
1985), pp. 9–10.

vorced tend overwhelmingly to marry other divorced persons (just as never-married people tend to choose other never-marrieds and those who are widowed usually select others with the same histories), the increased availability of potential partners may also increase the speed with which they can be located. Perhaps another reason for the shorter time span from divorce to remarriage is the change in attitudes about the morality of divorce and subsequent remarriage. Rather than viewing either divorce or remarriage of divorced persons with the alarm that was common even one or two generations ago, most people view divorce as preferable to years of unhappy marriage, and remarriage as more desirable than celibacy and loneliness.

As life expectancy has lengthened from about 45 years at the beginning of this century to well over 70 years currently, the period of adulthood has almost doubled. The average length of married life has increased accordingly. With the increase in the number of years that couples *can* be married and with the consequent decline in the proportion of child-rearing years to years with no children in the home, a reconsideration of the morality of divorce is appropriate. Although there is a sadness at the pain and personal losses that occur in divorce, most people are no longer outraged by it. Most believe it would be cruel to force couples to stay married for 40 or 50 years because of an error in judgment or unexpected situational or personality changes. The fact that over 30 percent of all marriages are remarriages has done much to reduce the stigma once associated with divorce and remarriage. Divorce is seen not as a sign of disenchantment with marriage itself but as a temporary state until a more satisfactory mate can be found (Goode 1956). It does not take as long as it did in the past to recover from a divorce and to turn to the possibility of making a new life.

Some divorced persons (over 15 percent) marry as soon as the divorce is final, often only a few months after they were first separated from the ex-mates (U.S. Bureau of the Census 1976, p. 15). This has led to speculation that many marriages end so that one or both parties may be free to marry a person already selected. However, there are indications that other factors may account for this statistic, at least in part, since some couples remarry quickly to persons they did not know before the divorce. Marital therapists have found some divorced persons have a strong need to convince themselves and others that they are capable of a successful marriage. Often they blame their ex-spouses for the breakup and need to show them as soon as possible that other partners find them desirable.

Choosing a New Partner

Most divorced persons move cautiously, however, as they sort through their doubts about whether they are likely to pick carbon copies of their mischosen ex-mates or whether their own faults might contribute in a similar fashion to still another troubled marriage. In their study of hundreds of separated and divorced men and women, Hunt and Hunt (1977, p. 223) reported that prior to a remarriage most formerly married persons

> have one or more relationships of some emotional intensity or importance. They are not all major love affairs: most, in fact, are trial runs or experiments: skyrocket infatuations that flare and burn out in a few weeks; dating relationships that gradually grow close and loving, then, unaccountably, waste away; friendships—with sexual intimacy—that are comforting and pleasing but never more than that. For most of the formerly married, such trials are an essential part of the process of self-discovery and development; the typical man or woman has three imperfect or abortive love relationships before entering one that is deep enough and "right" enough to seem like a realistic basis for remarriage.

Psychologists and marital therapists have long been concerned with the question of whether divorced persons tend to choose new partners who are similar to their ex-mates. No doubt some do, although others go to the other extreme, picking someone diametrically opposite to the former spouse. In either of these situations, however, the new partner will possess qualities unique to him or her. As a result, the quality of interaction of the couple will be different from that of the former marriage. For instance, even if the new spouse has a bad temper, just as the ex-mate did, he or she also may have redeeming qualities that were missing in the former mate. In a survey of remarried couples, not one reported having married a carbon copy of an ex-spouse. In fact, many reported ending love affairs because they recognized troublesome traits similar to those of their divorced partners (Westoff 1977).

Not only counselors but also most divorced men and women wonder whether they are likely to commit the same mistakes in a future marriage or whether they have learned something from the divorce experience that will make the next marriage better. Obviously, a divorce cannot create whole new persons; basic personality traits remain essentially the same. Even so, new partners are unlikely to react to those traits precisely as the ex-spouse did. Since each partner is affected by the actions and reactions of the other, the new relationship will be different (Weiss 1975).

The following wedding ceremony was written by a couple, each of whom was remarrying, and reflects their experiences of divorce and an increased awareness of the new vows they were taking:

We are both entering intimacy with each other, but one which must inevitably bear the burdens of a first sundered intimate relationship with other partners. We bear scars and wounds unknown to other brides and grooms: fears, doubts, and weaknesses of which only we are aware. But in these is our mutual strength to be found. Our love has gradually healed the wounds, calmed our fears, and established trust like a strong rock at the center of our mutual lives. (personal communication)

Using Bohannan's six stages of divorce (See Chapter 13), family-life expert Ann Goetting (1982) has described six stations of the complex process of remarriage: (1) *emotional remarriage*, which is the reestablishment with a new partner of the bonds of trust and commitment following the hurt and disillusionment from the previous bond; (2) *psychic remarriage*, which involves becoming part of a couple again and means a change of lifestyle and a shift of attitudes away from independence; (3) *community remarriage*, which usually involves a change in friends and activities from those of the single world to those of the new social status of remarried; (4) *parental remarriage*, which is unique to those with children but nonetheless very common since a growing number of divorced persons are parents who come as a package with their children to the new marriage; (5) *economic remarriage*, which seems to be a particularly difficult stage in which resource distribution may challenge the remarried couple; and (6) *legal remarriage*, which is partly dictated by state legal codes but interpreted by each couple as they deal with new wills, insurance beneficiaries, property, and responsibilities to children.

Remarriage Satisfaction

Almost all studies of remarriages have concentrated on partners who have *both* been previously married. Many researchers have gone right to the point and have asked couples how the new marriage compares with the old. It is not surprising that an overwhelming number report that the present marriage is much better since the former marriage was obviously not good and the remarriage is not bad enough to have left. But three-fifths report that the present marriage is better than those of other couples they know, and 67 percent report the current marriage to be even better than they had expected (Albrecht 1979).

The figures on the marital happiness of remarried persons may be inflated because of the tendency of couples to report positively on themselves and the tendency of couples who are having serious problems not to report at all. However, other national surveys have also indicated that second marriages are as satisfying and nearly as successful as first marriages and have a very good chance to last (Glenn and Weaver 1977). In fact, there is a greater probability (56 percent) that a second marriage will end by the death of one spouse than that it will end in divorce (Glick and Norton 1971). In other words, of the one-third whose first marriages end in divorce, about 44 percent will be divorced a second time, but 56 percent of them will be successful the second time around. Clearly, some do learn something about picking a mate and making a marriage work. The fact that the average remarried couple is older undoubtedly contributes to this effect. Because most first divorces and subsequent remarriages occur when the partners are still in their twenties or early thirties, there is a good chance that many second marriages will last to celebrate a golden wedding anniversary.

Remarriages usually involve people who are fairly close in age. If both parties have been previously married, their age difference is, on the average, four years. If a bride has never been married before but her new husband has, he will be, on the average, six years older than she. If a man has never been married but his bride has, the average difference between their ages is only a few months. Contrary to popular myth, very few divorced men marry women who are a great deal younger than they are. Only one divorced man in 25 marries a woman twenty years or more younger than he is. It is even rarer for a divorced woman to marry a man significantly younger than she (Weiss 1975, pp. 305–309).

The average age for a second marriage for men is approximately 34 years and for women nearly 31 (Glick and Norton 1977). As we have previously noted, the obvious fact that couples are older on the average at the time of remarriage than are couples marrying for the first time is one factor in favor of these marriages. Immaturity plays a large role in marital dissatisfaction and discord. We have already seen that those who marry young have a higher divorce rate.

Population specialists Arthur Norton and Paul Glick (1976) estimated that one of three first marriages of younger persons (aged 25 to 29) will end in divorce (34 percent) and that for the same age group 38 percent of second marriages will. Since other research reports indicate that those who decide to end a second marriage do so because they have less tolerance for a poor marriage and, therefore, will end it sooner than they did their first one (by an average of two years), it is even more likely that when second marriages succeed those couples have profited from the mistakes made in their first marriages (Hunt and Hunt 1977).

A recent study of 1,673 married persons has indicated that there is a difference in satisfaction and stability between remarriages in which both partners are divorced and remarried and remarriages of a divorced person to a previously unmarried individual (White and Booth 1985). The latter were not significantly more likely to end in divorce than when the marriage was the first for both partners. On the other hand, double remarriages are at higher risk for divorce. The findings are that when both partners have previously been married, there are more likely to be stepchildren present. This involves ex-spouses as coparents, which complicates matters.

Multiple Remarriages

Most studies of remarriage have used samples of persons who have been divorced only once. However, the adjustments faced by those who may have more than one remarriage are receiving increasing attention as their numbers grow. The proportion of second, third, fourth, and fifth marriages ending in divorce raises the divorce rates significantly.

Those who have multiple divorces and remarriages often remarry before they finish analyzing their own roles in their divorces. Some persons seem to have a **repetition compulsion** in mate selection, repeatedly making the same kind of choice that has failed in the past or overcorrecting by choosing in an opposite—but not necessarily better—direction.

The United States Bureau of the Census refers to those who have been divorced more than once as **redivorced.** Redivorced persons make up a relatively small proportion of the population; however, in 1975, there were over a million such persons.

From 1967 to 1980, the number of men married three or more times increased by 103 percent (15 percent of marrying males). Women's rates increased nearly as much; 13 percent of marrying females have been married three or more times (*Marriage and Divorce Today* 10, No. 33 [March 18, 1985], p. 1).

It is not altogether clear why a first divorce makes for a relatively successful basis for remarriage, yet redivorces do not have the same effect. We can hypothesize that most first divorces are granted to those who married too early to have chosen wisely. A second marriage allows them a more mature choice and thus is more likely to be successful. Perhaps those who redivorce choose their partners poorly, have personal problems that keep them from relating well, do not understand what it takes to make a successful marriage, or have unrealistic ideals or expectations about married life. Remarriages (especially those involving children) necessitate different adjustments on the part of the partners from the adjustments faced in most first marriages. No doubt, many remarriages are disrupted over such issues as stepchildren, ex-mates, and support payments, to name but a few.

Couples who report significant difficulties in a remarriage following divorce usually cite quite different problems from those they list for their first marriages. Infidelity, loss of love, physical abuse, alcohol, and communication difficulties—all major factors in troubled first marriages—are much less often mentioned as problems in remarriages. Instead, financial problems are most often stated to be the single biggest trouble area in remarriage. Others are problems with in-laws, conflicts over children, and involvement with former marriage partners (Albrecht 1980).

A popular explanation for the higher rate of redivorce for persons in remarriages than for those in first marriages is that remarriages have no clearly defined patterns of behavior. Social and emotional issues arise that have no socially standard answers due to the complicated intertwining of past and current relationships. Sociologist Andrew Cherlin (1978) explains that because of the "incomplete institutionalization of remarriage," such couples must make up their own rules and devise their own solutions. This increases the potential for conflict and for unresolved differences.

A more recent explanation for the higher divorce rate for the remarried is based on a growing body of research. While acknowledging that remarried life is more difficult, less predictable, and different in many respects, it is postulated that those who marry only once and never divorce may have certain value differences from those who remarry (Halliday 1980). It is possible that those who never divorce include a higher number of persons with "staying power" due to their religious, social, or personal opposition to divorce. Others have suggested that those who have divorced once may be more willing to leave a subsequent unhappy marriage because they have dealt with such an experience before and know that they got over the trauma. Remarriages that break up do so more quickly than first marriages, lending support to this latter notion (Furstenberg and Spanier 1984).

At any rate, remarriages after divorce seem to have somewhat different sets of problems from those that first marriages encounter. Many of the differences are determined by whether the remarried couples have children by former marriages. Some studies have implied that having children from a previous marriage heightens the risk of divorce in the remarriage (Becker, Lanes, and Michael 1977). However, research shows that although children from previous marriages are often the focus of problems in remarriages, the probability of divorce is only slightly higher than for remarriages where there are no children involved (McCarthy 1978).

In the following sections, we will look at the problems and issues involved in remarriages—financial concerns, stepparenting, in-laws, ex-spouses, and friends.

FINANCIAL CONCERNS

Financial strains are felt by nearly all American families today, but in remarriage these usually involve the added burden of helping to support two households. The husband may make child-support payments to his own children who live with their natural mother, or he may have one or more children living with him. He may also pay spousal support to his ex-wife if she has not remarried. His new wife may have children he is supporting or helping to support. Her ex-husband may not keep up support payments once she has remarried, or he may be able to afford very little as a result of his own remarriage.

Child Support

In a survey of **stepfamilies,** it was discovered that 69 percent of stepfathers fully supported their stepchildren, receiving no money for child support from the natural fathers or from their mothers' employment (Duberman 1975). For women who actually received child support from the children's fathers, the average amount received was $2,340 in 1983. Over 42 percent of the mothers never were awarded support for their children at all, and of those who were supposed to receive support, half received the full amount due and one-fourth received nothing at all (U.S. Bureau of the Census 1985h, p. 1). A remarried couple may have additional children together and, because they are older on the average, are more likely to have elderly parents who have become dependent. All in all, a family formed by remarriage frequently feels a financial pinch.

Financial problems may not always have to do with hardship. For instance, the stepfather may resent that he is solely responsible for children of a man who contributes little or nothing to their support. Or he may feel guilty that his own children cannot have more support from him because of his responsibilities in his new marriage. A wife in a remarriage may understandably grow resentful if she is working to earn money that is sent on to an ex-wife who chooses to stay at home with her children. Although she may not object to working, she may object to doing without the things she could buy with that money. If the ex-wife or her new husband can provide luxuries for the children, the new wife may resent *any* gifts to them if she perceives that her own children are less well off. As one remarried mother said to us, "He took *his* children to *Disneyland* on his visitation day, but he complains about the cost every time we take mine to the movies." No wonder studies consistently show that higher incomes are extremely favorable to the success of remarriages!

Income and Financial Arrangements

An interesting aspect of the financial condition of remarried couples is that men who remarry have higher incomes on the average than do men in first marriages. Of course this is due in part to their being, on the average, somewhat older. They may have many more expenses as well, but they also have more money coming in. Women, on the other hand, tend to have lower family incomes in remarriages than in their first marriages. This has been explained by the fact that divorced women with children may feel an urgency to remarry that puts them at a disadvantage, so that they often "marry down" financially. There is clear evidence that women who are poorly educated, disenchanted with work, or unemployed during the year following divorce are the quickest to remarry. Women who were able to support themselves were much less likely to marry soon after a divorce (Mott and Moore 1983).

Women in remarriages also report being less happy than women in first marriages do, but men in remarriages report being happier than men in first marriages say they are. Men in remarriages report being significantly more satisfied than their wives do (White 1979). Perhaps finances are the key, or perhaps women who have settled for a lower standard of living than they would have had by staying in the first marriage consider this a cause for discontent.

Equally important to the inadequacy of income in creating discord in remarried couples is the *emotional* aspect of family finances. Transmission and discussion of money continues to tie ex-spouses together, especially when there are children. When there have been financial conflicts in the recent divorce, men and women become wary and often hesitant to pool their resources again in a remarriage. In her study of remarriage, divorce specialist Lilian Messinger (1976) reports:

> Many remarried men were reluctant to speak freely about their financial assets and remarried women were often secretive about monies they had brought into the marriage. . . . Some women confided that they felt it necessary to keep some money aside in the eventuality of yet another divorce . . . some men appeared reluctant to revise their wills, insurance, and property assets.

Some couples who remarry draw up prenupital agreements to state how money and property will be handled in the marriage. Each can agree to keep separate any property or money they bring with them to the marriage. Unless the agreement violates existing state laws, they can agree on how to hold title to any property and earnings acquired while they are married. This can ensure that property and earnings will be kept unentangled if a divorce occurs—a comforting safeguard, especially when a partner has children by a previous marriage. However, because such precautions may make it seem that one or both partners are not fully committed to the marriage, some couples are hesitant to draw up such agreements.

BLENDED FAMILIES

Couples in a remarriage almost invariably report that integrating children into the new home is of major concern and is a source of frequent conflict. It is also the consensus of those who study remarriage that stepparent-stepchildren relationships are crucial to the success of the new marriage and vice versa. It is reported that over sixteen million minor children now live in stepfamilies, with an increase of nearly a million every year. Approximately 60 percent of all divorces involve children (Glick 1980).

Of course, not all stepfamilies are the result of divorce. Each year in the United States approximately 400,000 children experience the death of a parent. Also, roughly

THE BLENDED FAMILY

Television has not portrayed the blended family in a realistic way in the few shows that have dealt with this issue. Well-known sitcoms such as the *Brady Bunch* and *Eight Is Enough* make it look easy compared to real-life experiences. Parents and children who believe the TV versions often are frustrated and disenchanted.

In our work we frequently see two families attempting to merge under one roof, with differing measures of success. The qualities that stand out in those who have high- versus low-quality blending seem to be versatility, creativity, and fairness. Such families allow for individuality, and they are not afraid to create new ways of doing things.

Some examples of versatility, creativity, and fairness that families have exhibited and that have worked follow:

- Mary and Brad combined three of her children and five of his. Some of the children got along famously while others quarreled constantly. Their solution: they bought two apartments across the hall from each other and divided the children into living quarters according to their abilities to live peacefully. The children loved it, and it became a reward, especially for the friendly ones, to have a retreat away from their bickering siblings.
- When Joe and Sue married, they brought together five children ranging in age from two to seventeen. The younger children were Sue's, and the three older ones were Joe's. They needed a solution to discipline and each parent agreed to be the disciplinarian for his or her own children, although either Joe or Sue could recommend to the other a course of action. If they could not agree, the natural parent would prevail. They carried this off so well that when the children were asked who disciplined them, they said, "Both do."
- It became apparent to Linda and Mark after the first year of combining their children that not only they but also their children were missing the closeness they had achieved as single-parent family units prior to remarriage. As a solution, they each planned to spend time with their own children—movies, picnics, weekend trips—as they previously had done on a regular basis. "It was amazing," they told us, "how reassuring those times made us feel. We came home recharged to work as a total family."

More and more, divorce and remarriage involve couples with children. Joint custody is growing in acceptance, thus creating more homes in which his, her, and their children must come together to become families. There is no model that works in all families; even a successful plan may not work from one stage to the next as the children grow older. With few guidelines or role models—television is certainly no help—blended families have been left to fend for themselves. Sometimes they are not successful; however, for those who are, their creativity is to be applauded. Family experts are doing a great deal of research on the ways that blended families cope creatively. Perhaps one day soon there will be valuable data to help this growing segment of the population in the United States.

625,000 babies are born annually to unwed mothers. Although only a small proportion of mothers are under age eighteen, 85 percent of all births to women between the ages of fifteen and nineteen are out-of-wedlock, and 98 percent of births to women under fifteen are out-of-wedlock. Many of these young mothers eventually marry and establish stepfamilies. Many widowed parents remarry, of course, and most unwed mothers eventually do. But the estimate is that well over a million stepchildren each year owe their new status to divorce (National Center for Health Statistics 1985, p. 2).

Children from former marriages almost always become part of a "remarriage package." Whether the children live with the newlyweds or not, a new family form is established that necessitates a prolonged period of adjustment.

Adjusting to Blended Families

The bulk of the stepparent homes (often called **"blended"** or **"reconstituted"** families) involve a stepfather whose new wife has custody of her children (nearly nine times more common than the case in which the husband has custody and the stepmother moves in). The children become a part of a "remarriage package," usually through no choice of their own. Usually the mother and her children have been in an established single-parent home for months or even years prior to the remarriage. (The term *single-parent home* is used when only one parent has custody even though the children's other parent may be quite actively involved with them. It has been suggested that the term *single-custody home* may be more appropriate.) Whether a stepfather moves in with them, they move in with him, or they find a new place to live, major adjustments must be made. The longer a single-parent home has existed, the more difficult it will be for a stepfather to become a part of it. Research indicates that on the average it takes from one and a half years to two years for the adjustment to take place. The process goes more smoothly if the children are young (Stern 1978). Marriage therapist David Mills (1984) has suggested that it takes as long for children to adjust as the period they lived prior to the remarriage. If a child is three, it may take three years; if a child is eight, eight years. Although this formula may seem to make adjusting take longer than other studies suggest, it is support for the fact that older children usually adjust more slowly than younger ones do.

Adolescents in a remarried home prolong the adjustment time for the new family. Several studies have determined that teenage children reported significantly more conflict with both parents and were significantly less likely to be supportive of a stepfamily situation (Visher and Visher 1979).

Stepfathers

Stepfathers who have no children of their own may be very inexperienced at parenting. The founders of the Stepfamily Foundation of California comment: "While the mother has been filling many roles, the divorced man has had little family life. The mother may be feeling overwhelmed by all her parental responsibilities, particularly those of discipline, and imagine that the new husband will help her with all of her problems—financial, personal, and parental (Visher and Visher 1979, p. 91). It is very hard for any husband to live up to such a role, especially if he is coming into an ongoing system. Understanding the behaviors of children may be difficult for a man who has lived only with adults previously. Perhaps the most troublesome area involves their discipline. Studies of stepfamilies have reported that the touchiest point in all such families is how discipline is handled (Bohannan and Erickson 1978).

In a study of discipline in homes with a stepfather present, it was reported that unless a new husband has been accepted into the family before he tries to become a disciplinarian, there will be serious problems: "The stepfather who moves slowly and attempts to make a friend of the child before moving to control him has a better chance of having his discipline integrated into the sentimental order of the family" (Stern 1978).

It is easy for a stepfather who disciplines too soon and too harshly, or just differently from the mother, to cause a rift between himself and the children and often also between himself and his wife. Of course, this is also true for stepmothers who move too quickly to become disciplinarians to stepchildren. Children in such cases often play a "divide and conquer" game that leaves the stepfather or stepmother an outsider. One study has reported that the most glaring problem of the reconstituted family is "freezing out" the stepparent (Goldstein 1974).

Although a stepfather who has no children of his own may be at a real disadvantage because of inexperience, he still may have an easier time of it than does a man who is separated from children of his own. The latter must deal with his feelings of being a "live-in father" to his wife's children but only a "visiting father" to his own. His role may be poorly defined with both sets of children. When his own children come to visit, does he take them to the park or the ball game separately, or does he make them a part of his new family? If he succumbs to the temptation to devote all his time to his own children, since he sees them infrequently, how will this affect his stepchildren and his wife?

A new stepfather may find that it is less stressful for him to see his own children often and for long periods of time than when he was living alone because he, as a remarried person with stepchildren, now can provide a family setting for his children's visits. On the other hand, the problems of having his children visit may be so great that the stepfather sees them less frequeqntly. His wife may resent the additional time he spends with his children. The stepsiblings may have a hard time understanding their status and may resent the "intruders." In that case, his guilt may mount.

Fathers who become stepfathers often have high expectations for themselves and also often report trying harder to live up to their responsibilities than they did in their first marriages. Since there are no established guidelines, they try one set of behaviors after another, looking for a formula that will work. As a result, stepfathers view themselves as less successful parents than do fathers living with their own children (Bohannan and Erickson 1978).

Stepmothers

Stepfathers seem to fare better than stepmothers. Most stepmothers do not have their stepchildren living with them, but even the children's visits may be difficult. A stepmother may notice competition between her husband's children and hers. When hers are away visiting their father, she may have to take care of his or help entertain them.

Stepmothers seem to get along better with stepchildren who are not teenagers, and younger stepmothers (under 40) seem to have better relationships with step-children than do those over 40 (Duberman 1975). Generally, however, stepmothers report that they find their roles stressful. Perhaps the reason is that stepmothers are traditionally more directly involved with the daily care of children than are stepfathers. They often report that their involvement with and attempts to care for their stepchildren are interpreted negatively by the children, as though they were asking them to be disloyal to their "own" mothers (Goldstein 1974). Virtually all children have been exposed to the long-standing myth that natural mothers instinc-tively care more and better for their own flesh and blood than anyone else does or ever can. It has been suggested that stepmothers step into the role with two strikes against them because of the images of wicked stepmothers in children's fairy tales (Simon 1964).

One stepmother wrote of an experience she had when she was driving her young stepdaughter and a little friend home from a birthday party: "Suddenly the friend asked, in a crystal English voice, 'Is that your stepmother?' The answer came, slightly shaky: 'Yes.' There was a pause. 'Oh. I always thought a stepmother was something like a witch' " (Maddox 1975, p. 16).

Most stepmothers are involved with their stepchildren only through visitation, although the myth of the "wicked stepmother" is generally based on having her husband's children living in the same house with her. Even though their contact with stepchildren is usually relatively infrequent, stepmothers often take the bulk of the child-care responsibilities during those visits.

Perhaps in an effort not to be stereotyped, many stepmothers make noble efforts to love the husband's children and to be good to them. In her work with stepmothers, family therapist I. Sardanis-Zimmerman (1977) has found that most stepmothers begin with a "honeymoon" stage not only with the husband but also with his children. They often deny problems that exist—as well as their own feelings—because they do not want to put their husbands in a position of divided loyalty. Many women report feeling trapped because they are afraid to complain and are even more afraid to act on their negative feelings.

A stepmother's own children often notice how differently she treats them when the stepsiblings arrive for a visit (or when her own come for a visit, if she is the noncustodial parent). She may be nicer to all of them, or she may hold the line with her own while treating the stepchildren as guests. Many stepmothers are aware that they make this distinction but report that their own children know they are loved, but their stepchildren must be convinced that they are. The belief that a woman must immediately love her stepchildren and that they must return her love has been labeled "the myth of instant love" (Schulman 1972). Stepmothers report feeling that they have somehow failed when these expectations do not materialize. On the other hand, they may blame the stepchildren, consoling themselves that their own efforts have gone unrewarded. Commenting on the problems of love in a stepfamily, authors Ruth Roosevelt and Jeanette Lofas (1976, p. 69) say:

> Feeling obliged to love a stepchild and getting withdrawal sprinkled with hostility, a stepmother may tend to resolve the discrepancy by constructing an emotional brief of . . . her stepchild's faults and inadequacies. Who, her thinking goes, could ever be expected to love this child? . . . The stepchild finds his original negative assumption confirmed ("I always knew she was mean").

There are fathers who have sole custody of their children, usually because of the mother's death, abandonment, or incapacitation. Sometimes custody is transferred at the mother's request because she is unable to cope with the problems her children present. In father-custody homes, the stepmother plays a very important role and may be the most active caretaker of the children. Three models for stepmothers have been proposed by psychologist M. Draughon (1975) in her work with families in which the father has custody: friend, primary mother, and other mother.

1. *Friend:* this role seems to work best with those children whose natural mothers see them regularly and are active though noncustodial. The stepmother is the other responsible adult in the household but does not try to fill the role of mother to her stepchildren. In such an arrangement, the children usually call her by her first name, and the friendship can range from very close to casual. Stepmothers in this role generally take a light hand with discipline. This pattern seems to work well with older children, who often resent a stepmother entering the family—especially if she attempts to be a disciplinarian. This role can be difficult for a woman whose own children also live in the same home. Being a mother to one set of children and an adult friend to the others can be confusing to all family members.

2. *Primary mother:* this role is most successful when the natural mother is permanently out of the picture or when there is a mother-child estrangement. Very young children often feel comforted after the loss of their own mothers by having a complete family again. They usually call the stepmother "mother." Without a biological mother in the picture, the question of divided loyalty occurs less often. There may be difficult moments when the child confronts the stepmother with, "You're not my real mother. You can't tell me what to do." However, since the children are not members of two households and have no "real mother" to turn to, such outbursts seldom last long.

3. *Other mother:* this may be the most prevalent stepmother role and is possibly the most confusing and troublesome. This model is ambiguous, and the children often feel a conflict of loyalty. They may threaten to return to live with their "real" mothers whenever the stepmothers cross them. They may appeal to their fathers, who do not want the children complaining to their mothers about their new wives. If a father tries to intervene, his present wife may feel that her feelings are less important to him than his children's or even his ex-wife's. Studies of stepfamilies reveal that children often come between the spouses in the "other mother" or "other father" situation. The couple must form a cohesive unit to withstand such pressure. If their alliance is strong, the chances for success of the stepfamily greatly increase (Lewis et al. 1976).

Stepmothers who have no children of their own have the same problems of inexperience that childless men have in becoming stepfathers. The most stressful stepparent homes we have seen involve a father who has custody of his children and a woman who has never had children. It is difficult for a woman to become an "instant mother" and a new wife at the same time. Childless women often have careers that they resolve to give up to become homemakers and mothers. Making so many changes at once in their lifestyles can place a great strain on them.

New stepmothers who continue to work outside their new homes may be overburdened and may fail to meet their own and their husbands' expectations for their roles as stepmothers. They are often upset by the amount of contact that their husbands and their ex-wives have to discuss matters of visitation and financial arrangements, especially if the contact seems friendly. Some new stepmothers are upset if they are asked to participate in these discussions; others are upset because they are not.

One stepmother told us that she had no idea what she was getting into when she married a man who had custody of his children and whose ex-wife was always in the background:

> I feel more like an employee hired to take care of his children than like a new wife should feel. Everything centers around their welfare, their activities, what they want to eat, where they need to go. But I not only don't get paid, I get criticized by the children and also by my husband for not doing a better job. At the same time, their mother is always ready to pounce on us to regain custody. That doesn't help me to feel secure.

Having a child by her new husband to add to their family usually seems to help all family members adjust. Not only is the stepmother now a mother, but the stepchildren's father is her baby's father as well. The existing children and the new baby are blood relatives. The baby often acts as a link between the stepmother and the stepchildren (Duberman 1975). The birth of the new baby may end the fantasies some stepchildren have of breaking up the new marriage so that their parents can reunite. Of course, there may be jealousy and anxiety about being displaced by the new baby, but these feelings are also common among children who are living with both natural parents.

Binuclear Families

A new form of stepfamily, the **binuclear family,** has emerged in recent years with the growth of the joint custody phenomenon. A child actually has two homes and two families of which he or she is a member. Both parents share physical care of their children on a regular and somewhat equal basis. For example, children may alternate parental households week by week; another frequent arrangement is summers and holidays with one parent and the school year with the other (Ahrons 1985).

Binuclear families in which the children are a part of two homes and two family groups are increasing in numbers. However, since custodial fathers—even joint custodial fathers—are still in the minority, little research has been completed to answer such questions as whether they are similar to custodial mothers in their relationships with their children, whether they were more involved before their divorces than were noncustodial **fathers**, and whether they select wives who are different from those that noncustodial fathers choose.

The term *binuclear family* usually implies that each parent has remarried and provides space for children to live when it is their turn to reside with each parent. There are no "guest children" on weekends and holidays. Sometimes both parents in a remarriage have their children in this shared fashion. The issues can be complex, but there also is a positive side. Both parents not only have their own children living with them, but each also has an experienced partner to help out. Each has a better basis for understanding what is happening to the other.

Stepsiblings

Stepsiblings often have an easier time getting along with each other than with their stepparents. Young children in particular may develop strong bonds, although, as in natural families, there is bound to be rivalry, conflict, and some instances of real dislike for each other. The better the stepsibling relationships generally, the better the reconstituted family adjustment (Duberman 1975).

A problem that is being addressed currently in the literature on stepsiblings has to do with sexual activities between unrelated children who are now sharing a home (Duberman 1975). Sexual activity between siblings (even sibling incest) is not uncommon, but sexual activity between stepsiblings is thought to be more common. The process of growing up together from birth seems to dampen sexual interest between natural siblings or to lead to its repression or sublimation. Sometimes it appears as hostility. However, teenagers in particular who suddenly are thrown together in the intimate atmosphere of a home by a parent's remarriage often report being sexually aroused by close contact with an attractive stepsibling. Although incest may have been defined as taboo or unattractive, this new relationship is often undefined. Even parents may be uncertain about the "proper" rules for tickling, wrestling, kissing, and nudity, especially if these rules have been casual for the natural siblings (clinical files).

When the sexual urgency of adolescence is growing and the consciousness of sexual activity is heightened by knowing that their newly wed parents are sexually active, the enticement of a stepsibling may be a temptation some teenagers cannot resist. No one knows exactly how many sexual relationships exist between stepsiblings, but the growth in numbers of stepfamily homes, combined with increasingly permissive norms for adolescent sexual behavior, seems likely to make for increases each year.

It may appear from the myths and very real problems of stepfamilies that the picture is rather bleak. Much recent research, however, has given a more positive outlook and has suggested that the major reason that stepfamilies were initially given low marks was because they were being compared to traditional nuclear families. The very word *stepfamily* connotes something less than a "real" family, and it has been popularly assumed that living in a remarried household would be less than satisfactory for everyone concerned. The unfair comparisons with biological families have not taken into consideration the incredible creativity and resiliency of the millions of parents and children who have very successful blended families. Considering that

The complexities surrounding remarriages and blended families are illustrated here as a father's 21-year-old daughter helps him care for his children from his second marriage—her half-siblings.

members of stepfamilies may come together from very different backgrounds and form a structure quite distinct from biological families, it is a disservice to judge them by the same standards (Mills 1984).

Most studies suggest that stepchildren do not have significantly more problems or negative attitudes toward themselves and others than children from traditional nuclear families have. Neither do stepchildren differ much from other children in terms of school grades, personality characteristics, social behavior, or marriage attitudes (Ganong and Coleman 1984). Although children from stepfamilies acknowledge that there are problems, most rate their new family rather positively, considering the difficulty of the task of blending many diverse elements (Knaub and Hanna 1984).

IN-LAWS

After problems with finances and children, couples in a remarriage rank outside family (kin) as the third major problem they face (Bernard 1971b). Where there are children, grandparents may have played an active role following the parents' divorce. They may not wish to give up this new closeness and may oppose the remarriage. They may not be able to accept their stepgrandchildren, or they may favor their own grandchildren to the point of causing conflict. They may interfere with already touchy discipline controversies in the new home.

Typical of the sensitive situations that can develop is one that occurred in the home of a divorced man who gained custody of his two children. His retired parents moved in with him to help with family responsibilities. They were very fond of the children and, in the three-year period before he remarried, had established themselves as prime parent substitutes for the busy father. After the newly married couple returned from their honeymoon, the grandparents moved to a house a few blocks away but dropped in daily to be certain that the children were being cared for properly. The children's father was grateful for all his parents had done for him and felt very close to them. His new wife, however, was resentful of their mistrust of her parenting abilities. The children adjusted poorly because their grandparents had sympathetic ears for even the most minor complaints. It took family therapy for all three generations to unravel their tangle of problems with each other.

Ex-in-laws sometimes are the source of problems in a remarriage, although they may not actually *cause* the problems. Most often the problems lie in the reaction of a new spouse to his or her mate's ex-in-laws. Just as some stepparents feel resentful or jealous over the constant reminders of a former family that stepchildren generate, so ex-in-laws in the picture may also be seen as threatening by the new spouse.

Divorced men are more likely than divorced women to end relationships with their in-laws, partly because they usually do not have custody of their children—who serve as the link to the in-law grandparents. Most such men mention no hostility toward former parents-in-law (only 18 percent do), but they report that there does not seem to be any reason to keep in touch or that it is geographically difficult (Spicer and Hampe 1975).

Women who are divorced, on the other hand, interact more with family members of their ex-husbands. Children are an important reason that custodial mothers maintain contact with their children's paternal kin. Many mothers report feeling some obligation to allow the grandparents and grandchildren to have access to each other. However, divorced women report that the chief reason they maintain contact is for affection, whether they have children or not.

Women have been shown to be the chief source of kin contact both with their own families and with those of their husbands. When such contact has been positive, that commitment seems to work to minimize disruption with the in-laws after a divorce. In fact, over 40 percent of the women in the Spicer and Hampe study (1975, p. 115) reported seeing their ex-in-laws as much or more than they did prior to the divorce. Only 17 percent of the men saw as much or more of their ex-wives' families.

EX-SPOUSES

One common stress in remarriage comes from the necessity for frequent contact with ex-spouses. As one ex-wife and writer on remarriage has said:

> The majority of ex-husbands and ex-wives seem not to like each other, even when it's all over and when they could presumably be friends again. There is something about being an ex- that, very often, causes any interaction to become extremely difficult and exacerbates any problems that may arise.
>
> When one remarries, one is never alone with a new mate. One lives with vibrations of other people who were part of one's old life and the new partner's former life. There are constant reminders of the past spent with others—portraits, photographs, monograms, laundry marks, furniture, tastes, habits—living ghosts that go along with every remarriage. (Westoff 1977, pp. 43, 46)

Child Custody Issues

Most of the problems that arise with ex-spouses have to do with children—visitation, custody, child support. These are all issues that the divorcing couple considered to have been settled in divorce court. It is not at all unusual for divorced parents to go back to court again and again for postdivorce litigation over such issues. Although there may, of course, be legitimate cause to file for change of custody, to seek increased or decreased support payments, or to ask for a ruling on disputed visitation rights and responsibilities, marital therapists believe that there are usually underlying dynamics between the divorced spouses that cause them to keep upsetting each other. In a study of 300 such cases, certain psychodynamics underlying conflicts between divorced spouses were found to exist in varying degrees and combinations (Elkin 1976).

1. Divorce frequently does not end feelings of anger, hurt, rejection, and vengefulness. Some persons are "hostility junkies," who hang on to the divorced spouse by displacing this anger onto matters concerning their mutual children. As long as the bitterness can be focused on the ex-mate, no self-analysis need take place.
2. If one partner remarries, the single ex-spouse may feel jealous, especially if he or she had not wanted the divorce in the first place. The battles may actually represent a conscious or unconscious wish to get revenge by causing trouble so that the new marriage has less chance of success. The need to hold on to the ex-mate may be so strong that there is no acceptance of the reality that the marriage is over.
3. Occasionally, the new spouse is resentful of ongoing needs of the divorced parents to communicate about the children. He or she may cause trouble between the parents or between the children and the noncustodial parent. Children who refuse to visit their noncustodial parents are often acting out the custodial parent's problems. Often these stem from the knowledge that the contact necessary to arrange a visit will anger the stepparent.

On occasion, the battle between divorced parents results in **child snatching**, which occurs when the noncustodial parent does not return the children from a visitation or when he or she picks them up at school, for instance, and then leaves for parts unknown. It is reported that there may be as many as 150,000 child stealings every year in the United States—one child stolen by a parent for every 22 divorces nationwide (*Family Therapy News*, July-August 1984, p. 11).

Family sociologist Richard Gelles (1984) believes that the incidence of child snatching is dramatically higher than actually reported. He conducted interviews with a representative cross section of over 3,700 divorced adults with children and found that 1.5 percent reported personal involvement in an incident of child snatching in the previous twelve months. Projecting this rate to the 83.5 million households in the United States in 1982, he estimated that the incidence of child snatching each year is probably between 459,000 and 751,000.

The rivalry between divorced parents that precipitates such action is so intense and so bitter that an attorney often must be appointed to represent the best interests of the children against their battling parents. Until recently there has been no interstate mechanism to help locate stolen children. When they have been found, there has been a good chance that the case would be heard in the state in which the children have been relocated, often making it difficult for the parent who originally had custody to appear in court.

In 1975 the Federal Parent Location Service was created to help locate absent parents who had failed to meet their child-support obligations. In 1982 this service was expanded to include locating children who had been kidnapped. However, implementation has been slow, and a national computerized system to locate children is not yet a reality (*Marriage and Divorce Today,* June 14, 1982, pp. 7, 45).

Private agencies, such as ADAM, are actively assisting distraught parents whose children have been abducted. ADAM is the popular name for the Adam Walsh Child Resource Center in Florida, founded by John Walsh after his six-year-old son Adam was abducted and murdered in 1981. In 1984, with a grant from the Justice Department, a Washington, D.C., private center modeled on ADAM opened to educate parents and law enforcement agencies on locating missing children (*Family Therapy News,* July-August 1984, p. 11).

Defining Roles

Not all problems with ex-spouses directly concern children. Other difficulties stem from the trouble some couples have in separating spousal and parental roles. These roles may have overlapped greatly when they were married. Studies have shown that in addition to continuing to relate to each other as parents, most divorced persons also keep in touch on non-child-related subjects. The most frequent topics they reportedly discuss, other than their own common problems, were news of their respective families and of their mutual friends. Most of the contact came when a noncustodial parent picked up or delivered the children or during telephone conversations. However, these friendly "news reports" were cited as the cause of trouble in their remarriages by a large number of couples (Ahrons 1978).

Relations between Current and Ex-Spouses

Research indicates that relationships between former spouses usually are not well defined and that couples seldom know how to respond appropriately to each other once they are divorced. Even less well defined is how the current wife should behave toward the former wife and how the current and ex-husbands should relate, if at all. The "divorce chain," as Bohannan (1970b) calls it, gets even more complex when the ex-spouses of the remarried couple have also remarried. They form a new kind of extended kinship system; an etiquette for proper social relationships is often nonexistent.

Those who have not previously been married but whose mate has an ex-spouse often may have difficulty understanding the bond—negative or positive—that the ex-partners feel toward each other. As one woman told us, "My husband hates his ex-wife so much that it is almost as though she is still a member of our family. I don't understand why he can't let go and keep her out of our daily lives." Indeed, many divorced persons bear hostilities that are kept fresh by frequent rehashing of old hurts.

However, we just as often see couples where the previously unmarried spouse feels jealousy toward his or her partner's former mate because the two continue to be very friendly.

To gain insight into the types of relationships that remarried persons maintain with their partners' ex-mates, couples who have been remarried just under a year were interviewed (Goetting 1980). For 86 percent of the men and 87 percent of the women in the sample, this was a second marriage; for 11 percent of the men and 13 percent of the women, it was their third marriage; and for 3 percent of the men but none of the women, it was a fourth marriage. Men and women showed general agreement that they and their current spouses should be courteous (should say "hello" in public places, for example) to each other's ex-spouses. They also agreed that they should inform them of any serious illness or accidents either to the ex-spouses or to the children.

The agreement of recently remarried persons to exchange information on sickness and injuries is in keeping with other research findings that crisis situations increase communication and social solidarity, whether the crisis is a neighborhood emergency or a health-related problem in the family (Dovidio and Morris 1975). There seemed to be little agreement on other relationship issues by current wives about ex-wives, current husbands about ex-husbands, wives about current husbands, or husbands about what current wives should do concerning ex-mates. On each issue, however, there was distinctly more social distance preferred by wives toward ex-wives than by husbands toward ex-husbands.

Ann Goetting (1982), who has done extensive research on divorce, suggests that an explanation of the distance desired by ex-spouses lies in social exchange theory. Exchange theory would predict that the more unpleasant a past marriage and divorce had been, the more contact with anyone connected with it would be avoided.

Several studies have indicated that women have the most stressful time adjusting to divorce and stand to lose the most both in status and financially (Raschke 1976). This may account for the greater social distance women prefer to keep from their husbands' ex-wives. Perhaps one could generalize to say that if the past marriage was "punishing," both women and men might vote to keep more distance from ex-spouses. At any rate, there are great individual differences in what is considered appropriate behavior for remarried persons and their ex-spouses. Some socialize comfortably; others do not even speak. Most ex-spouses relate in patterns between these two extremes.

▌ FRIENDS

Integrating old friends from the past into a remarriage is often a source of difficulty since these persons may very well have been friends of the ex-spouse as well. Many of them may still continue to see both divorced partners, and this situation can be a source of discomfort to new spouses. A recently married woman spoke of her husband's friends left over from his past marriage:

> I hate it when I know that people are also friends of my husband's ex-wife. Sometimes they let something slip into the conversation about her. Or they forget and start to reminisce about old times. One man even called me by her name

once. I feel like a real outsider usually and I sometimes wonder if they are comparing me to her. I'm afraid I might say the wrong thing and they'll let it slip around her just as they get careless around me. (clinical files)

An especially difficult situation seems to arise when a remarriage takes one partner to the other's home town or neighborhood. Remarrying women often move from their previous residences to join their new husbands and face the decision of whether to make friends with people who were friendly with both him and his ex-wife. When a woman brings her children into the remarriage, they often attend the same schools as do their stepsiblings, who may live with their own mother in the same town or neighborhood.

Men who have been living in apartments often move into the new wife's home, where she has been living with her children. The new husband, too, must make his way with neighbors and tradespeople who may be uncomfortable with this new man in the house. The very fact that the couple seem so happy and satisfied with their new relationship may create anxieties in those friends whose marriages are not doing so well. Many remarried couples report that they moved to a neighborhood or city new to both of them or changed churches to avoid contact with mutual friends from their previous marriages. They find it easier to make new friends than to face the problems created by maintaining old friendships.

Many remarried couples join discussion groups or attend workshops that focus on the special problems of remarriage. These partners may make new friends and develop a support group of understanding peers who can offer advice on, and serve as models for coping with, difficulties that may arise in remarriage.

REMARRIAGE AFTER WIDOWHOOD

Although most remarriages follow divorce, thousands of widowed persons also remarry each year. Only as recently as 1973–1974 did marriages ending in divorce begin to equal those disrupted by death (Glick 1980). It is true that most persons whose spouses die are older—and they are predominantly women. Consequently, the stereotypical widowed person is an older woman whose husband has died, leaving her to melt into the "never-to-marry-again" population.

A widow who is over 55 years of age when her husband dies has less than half the probability of remarrying that a widower her same age has (Cleveland and Gianturco 1976). A woman may wish to remarry but may find no available men since not only do women far outlive men, on the average, but widowers also often remarry somewhat younger women. Twenty percent of widowers over age 65 who remarry choose women ten or more years younger than they are. Fewer than 3 percent of widows marry men that much younger than they are (Treas and Van Hilst 1976). So many more women become widows compared with men who become widowers that there is only the word *widowed* to describe the state following the death of a spouse. Although we speak of "widow" and "widower," there is no such word as "widowered."

The median age at widowhood is in the early fifties. Since this is a median, it means that half of the men and women who lose their spouses by death are younger. Many of them have minor children (approximately 400,000 minor children a year experience the death of a parent). Men and women with minor children commonly

Marriages between two older persons have a high rate of success. Such couples are usually in better health and have a higher probability to live happy lives than those who remain single.

remarry, often to another widowed person. Since there are many fewer of them than of persons who remarry following a divorce, few research studies have been done to determine how similar they are to couples who remarry after a divorce. The small number of studies, however, has been offset by the high quality of those that have been done. Some of the best research has concerned itself with older women who remain widows—those three currently unmarried women to every currently unmarried man over the age of 65. Fewer than one-fifth of such women even declare a wish to remarry (Lopata 1973).

Adjusting to a Partner's Death

Younger widows and widowers received attention in a study emerging from the Harvard Laboratory of Community Psychiatry (Glick, Weiss, and Parkes 1974). The subjects were men and women under the age of 45. There were interesting differences between the adjustment patterns of women and men whose spouses had died. The two sexes organized their lives differently following loss of a mate. Widowers tended to view the death of a wife as a loss of part of themselves. They had difficulty mobilizing themselves to work, were very lonely, and felt sexually anxious. They yearned for the dead spouse but seemed unwilling to display their grief openly and viewed self-control as strength. Widows, on the other hand, viewed their loss as abandonment—being left to fend for themselves—but felt a fierce loyalty to their dead husbands that temporarily inhibited sexual thoughts.

How quickly both men and women in the Harvard study recovered from their bereavement seemed closely related to whether the spouse's death had been antici-pated. If the spouse had died suddenly and unexpectedly, the recovery took longer, and the thought of remarriage was viewed cautiously. The loss of a spouse without warning affected the eventual success of recovery and the length of bereavement for both men and women.

Many men whose wives died suddenly eventually remarried but usually harbored anxiety and personal discomfort at the blow that fate had dealt them. Men who anticipated their wives' death were able to recover fairly rapidly; they wanted to reestablish orderly lives for themselves and their children. They moved more quickly into dating and remarriage than either men whose wives had died suddenly or than widows in general. A few widowers began dating several weeks after the wife's death; by the end of the first year after her death, 50 percent had remarried or were in serious relationships. Those men who had not expected the death were as slow as or slower than widows to recover (Glick, Weiss, and Parkes 1974).

Only about 18 percent of widows were remarried or seriously involved within one year after their husband's death, according to the Harvard study. Nearly one-third would not even consider remarriage at that time, and for most it was three or more years before they could consider "being disloyal to their husband's memory" by contemplating marriage. Willingness to date developed gradually and, often with a considerable sense of guilt, some time after the first year of bereavement. By the end of the fourth year after their husband's death, a good many women were remarried or in serious relationships (about one year later on the average than divorced persons remarried) (U.S. Bureau of the Census 1977b, pp. 13–14). Even so, many widows reported having moments of grief and mourning for their dead husbands for the rest of their lives.

Financial Concerns

Men and women whose spouses die are often in better financial condition than are those whose marriages end in divorce. There are, of course, some widowed persons who face heavy debts due to medical expenses resulting from a spouse's prolonged illness or to strained family finances during the marriage. Medical and life insurance help immeasurably, and Social Security benefits for widows and for minor children allow many families to continue a standard of living that does not change drastically. There is no property to divide as in a divorce, and there are no attorney's fees for battles over custody and support payments. Some states are doing away with inheritance taxes so that death does not place that burden on the survivors in addition to the many others.

Widowers seem to have an easier time financially because most continue in their jobs with steady incomes. Widows know that insurance money usually will not last long and that they must begin to earn an income, if they have not done so previously, but life insurance gives them a period of some financial security while they adjust.

Children

The major adjustments for those who have been widowed seem to involve dealing with their own grief and helping their children deal with theirs. Psychologically, the death of a married man or woman puts a more final end to the relationship for both spouse and children than does a divorce. Some research findings indicate that children from stepfamilies in which the stepfather replaces a deceased father view the stepfather more favorably than do those whose mother remarried after a divorce (Parish and Kappes 1980).

Both adults and children have some tendency to revere the dead person, and children in particular may mourn the loss for a lifetime. This can make the addition of a stepparent to the home difficult if the remarriage takes place too soon after the parent's death. Neither the person nor the role enacted can be the same; it is a mistake on the part of everyone involved to expect or even suggest that the lost one is being replaced.

In a study on bereavement in families it was found that

> the feelings of the child about his dead parent seemed deeply private to him, based on the treasuring of memories. The dead parent, unlike the divorced parent, was no longer in existence in a way in which he could be experienced by others. Strangers who were unable to share the child's perceptions and hadn't known the dead person were, in this context, also often viewed as an intrusion rather than a support. (Tessmann 1978, p. 417)

Even very young children sometimes resist a stepparent and feel angry at what they perceive to be the surviving parent's disloyalty to the dead one. The stepparent is often in the awkward position of being rejected by the spouse's children while feeling compassionate toward them because of their grief.

It is no wonder that the special feelings of bereaved persons often lead widows and widowers to seek each other out for remarriage. They have had similar experiences of grief and have suffered the slow process of recovery accompanied by pangs of sadness and feelings of guilt or disloyalty as they begin to love again. Their children, too, often feel a more kindred spirit with stepparents and stepsiblings who have experienced a similar loss. Although they have many of the same problems in adjusting that other blended families have, they do not have the real pulls of a noncustodial parent. On the other hand, they do not have the advantages of being able to rely on the absent parent as a backup.

Older Couples

Older widows and widowers whose children are grown may also remarry. If a woman is widowed before age 30, there is over a 90 percent chance that she will remarry within five years of her husband's death. If she is between 30 and 40, a 70 percent chance exists, and between 40 and 50, a 40 percent chance. However, if a woman is over 50, she has less than an 8 percent probability of remarriage (U.S. Bureau of the Census 1977b, p. 15).

Research on the remarriages of older couples is scant, but one such study has revealed that these marriages are often quite successful. A widower usually remarries within a year or two of his wife's death, but a widow may wait several years (often until her youngest child leaves home) (McKain 1972). Grown children often resist their parents' remarriages because of concerns over inheritance or out of loyalty to the dead parent. Also, many adult children assume that marriage (and particularly sexual activity) is appropriate only for people much younger than their parents. This may result in part from the typical concealment of parental sexuality from children in earlier years, when many parents have shamed or even punished their children for showing any interest in sex or erotic materials.

Marriage therapist Jerry McKain (1972) reports that older couples who remarry after being widowed are usually only a few years apart in age. They typically come from similar educational, social, economic, and religious backgrounds. This similarity may account for the high success rate of their marriages. Another factor may be that they had long and usually successful first marriages that gave them experience with and insight into the problems of married life. Many of the couples studied had been acquainted for years; some had been friends as couples while they were still married to their now deceased spouses. In general, it has been found that those elderly widowed persons who remarry are in better health and have higher incomes than those who do not remarry. Both good health and adequate finances in turn have a positive effect on marital success.

SUMMARY

1. Four out of five divorced persons eventually remarry—some as soon as the divorce is final, some many years later, with the average interval being about three years. Approximately one-third of all current marriages are remarriages.

2. Although many persons divorce and remarry more than once and are called the "redivorced" and the "multiply married," most people move cautiously from divorce to remarriage. As a result, second marriages are more often successful than not. There is a good chance that the second marriage will last until ended by the death of one spouse.

3. Problems in a remarriage often differ from those of a first marriage. Financial difficulties, conflicts over stepchildren, and involvement with ex-spouses and with former in-laws seem to be the most troublesome issues in remarriages.

4. Financial strains come not only from too little money to go around but also from emotional issues over sending and receiving monies to and from ex-spouses, supporting stepchildren, and having children of their own to support.

5. Integrating children into a "reconstituted" family may be the most difficult task of a remarriage and a source of frequent conflict. How successfully the blending takes place is crucial to the new couple's marital satisfaction.

6. Most stepfamilies involve a mother, her children, and a stepfather. All in all, stepfathers seem to fare better than stepmothers do. The most troublesome area seems to involve discipline. The stepfather who waits to be accepted by the children before he tries to be a disciplinarian usually becomes integrated into the family within two years. The process goes more smoothly if the children are young.

7. Stepmothers get along better with younger children and do better in general if they also are under 40. Most stepmothers report that their roles are stressful, largely because of their greater involvement in daily child care. Stepmothers also usually have their own children living with them; balancing the job of mother and stepmother is often difficult.

8. Binuclear families have become a more commonplace variety of stepfamily as more fathers have taken advantage of the new joint custody laws. In such a family form, children spend more nearly equal time with each parent, thus becoming a member of two households rather than living in one and visiting the other.

9. Stepsiblings often have an easier time adjusting to each other than to a stepparent. Usually, the better the children get along, the better the parents' marriage is.

10. Having a child of their own often has a positive effect that solidifies the reconstituted family. It is not that a new baby improves a bad situation but rather that a child of theirs together makes each person in the family kin in a new way.

11. In-laws, especially grandparents, may interfere with the new marriage and family life either by directly causing problems or by innocently being the source of emotional reactions of the new spouse and stepchildren. Women, who are usually the ones who maintain contact with kin, often want their children and the paternal grandparents to stay in touch. This may have its problems, however.

12. Ex-spouses can be a source of trouble in a remarriage, particularly where there are children. Support, visitation, and continued conflict from the divorce often create trouble in the new marriage. Relationships between former spouses and between former and current ones are poorly defined, and problems often arise over what is acceptable behavior.

13. Friends from the past who may also be friendly with the ex-spouses often are the cause of trouble in a remarriage. When the new spouse moves into the other's "territory" and must daily confront people from the mate's past married life—even the ex-mate—conflict often arises.

14. Remarriages following the death of a spouse differ from those that follow divorce. Widowed persons are usually older and in better financial condition. The previous marriage was more likely a good one than was one that ended in divorce. The dead spouse is physically gone—unlike the divorced one, who may be very much present— although there is a tendency to revere a dead spouse.

15. Those who have been widowed most often seek each other to remarry. They have shared more similar experiences than either has with those who are single or divorced.

16. Young widows and widowers show some differences from each other in how they organize their lives and eventually remarry. Whether the spouse died suddenly or the death was expected influences the length of the bereavement. It takes longer for a spouse to recover from the sudden death of a partner and to reestablish his or her life.

17. Fifty percent of the men studied had remarried or were in a serious relationship by the end of the first anniversary of their wives' deaths. Only about 18 percent of the women were so involved.

18. The children whose parent has died also adjust differently from those whose parents divorce. They have grief over never seeing the parent again and often resist a stepparent because they feel disloyal. If the stepparent and stepsiblings have experienced a parent's death also, however, they usually have more of a kindred spirit.

19. Older widows and widowers who remarry may have problems with acceptance from their grown children over such issues as inheritance or disloyalty to the dead parent. Most such children recognize, however, that companionship is positive for adjustment to old age and that their parents will probably be healthier and happier because of the marriage.

20. Most older couples who marry are similar in age, education, religion, and socio-economic background. This similarity may well account for the high success rate of their marriages.

GLOSSARY

Binuclear family Children of divorced parents with joint custody and the two "new" families of which they are a part. (p. 461)

Blended (reconstituted) families Stepparent homes in which one parent or both have custody of children and a family is formed of his and her children and sometimes children born to them together. (p. 457)

Child snatching The kidnapping of one's own child(ren) from the custodial parent after a divorce. (p. 465)

Redivorced A term used to describe one who is divorced more than once. (p. 452)

Repetition compulsion A term originally used by Freudians to describe a tendency to repeat behavior again and again in a compulsive fashion, even though the results proved negative. (p. 452)

Stepfamily The family formed by the remarriage of a parent following divorce or the death of the children's other parent. (p. 454)

15

To see a young couple loving each other is no wonder; but to see an old couple loving each other is the best sight of all.

n 1990 there will be an estimated 29 million men and women over the age of 65. This represents almost a tenfold increase during this century. In an attempt to understand the needs and coping skills of the elderly population, the field of gerontology has become an important area of research. The prevailing negative view of aging has begun to change recently as people realize that, with luck, old age will come to all of us. Gerontologists have helped people find ways to cope and to make old age satisfying. To understand how we grow old, how to manage aging with grace and satisfaction, and what can be learned from those who are already senior citizens, research has concentrated on middle-age adjustments that are crucial for later adjustments when one is over 65. Research on aging has looked at family relations, marital satisfaction, retirement, widowhood, loneliness, residential requirements, and other adjustment processes. More research is needed; we have just begun to scratch the surface.

POSTPARENTAL LIFE AND AGING

William Makepeace
Thackeray, *Fiery Grains*

*I*n 1949 a survey of twenty marriage and family textbooks revealed that only two devoted more than a brief mention to aging or to how older men and women live and love. Of 10,697 pages of text that were analyzed, only 50 pages related to persons past middle age (Beard 1949). Much of the material in those 50 pages dealt with problems older men and women face and how their grown children must help them cope. Perhaps this was a reflection of the early years of this century, when fewer people lived past middle age than do so today and when those who did may not have been as healthy as today's older citizens. A baby born in 1900 had only a 39 percent chance of reaching age 65. In 1982 the average life expectancy at birth reached a record high of 74.7 years (*World Almanac Book of Facts 1986* 1985, p. 783).

THE GROWING ELDERLY POPULATION

Much has happened in the more than 35 years since the 1949 survey. The older population in the United States has grown rapidly and is expected to continue to increase through the 1990s. Several factors are responsible for this growth—improved diet and health care have increased the chances of living longer; large numbers of children were born from 1900 to 1925 who are now in the aged population; and, perhaps most significantly, the great decrease in infant mortality and death from childhood diseases has allowed more babies to survive to grow old.

In 1900 only 4 percent of the population was 65 or older. In 1980 the fraction was almost three times as great—11.3 percent. Perhaps the growth of the older population can be expressed more impressively by reference to actual numbers since 1900, as seen in Table 15.1.

Textbooks have taken note of the increased numbers and impact of the aged. A survey of marriage and family texts in 1978 found that 50 percent gave good coverage to the issues of aging, although the focus was generally still on problems of retirement, poverty, illness, and widowhood. The other 50 percent gave token attention at best to the older population, and some clearly misrepresented the reality of aging in the United States (Dressel and Avant 1978). Perhaps these omissions or inadequate treatments were carried over from the days when it was believed that college students were not interested in anyone over 30—much less over 50. Not only does this underestimate the awareness and intelligence of young people, but it also ignores the fact that classrooms are not populated solely with young adults. Even if they were, aging is a process that begins when we are conceived and, if we are lucky, will happen to all of us sooner or later. Irish playwright George Bernard Shaw, responding to the question of how it felt to be 80, said that, considering the alternative, it was just fine.

A positive view of aging has unfortunately been missing in our society, and a negative attitude is reflected in our literature. A focus on problems has strongly devalued aging and has usually overlooked the fact that many older persons are leading satisfying and rewarding lives. This omission is reminiscent of the ways racial and ethnic minorities were once portrayed in textbooks and led to the belief that the lives of few, if any, minorities had positive aspects. It is time that our older population

	TABLE 15 • 1		

Year	Population (in millions)
1900	3.1
1920	4.9
1940	9.0
1960	16.7
1970	20.0
1980	25.5
Projections	
1990	29.8
2000	31.8

TABLE 15 • 1
Population of the United States Aged 65 and Over

Sources: U.S. Bureau of the Census, *Current Population Reports,* Series P-23, No. 43 (February 1973), p. 2; Series P-23, No. 78 (January 1979), p. 8; Series P-20, No. 336 (April 1979), p. 15; Series P-20, No. 363 (June 1981), p. 9; and Series P-25, No. 917 (July 1982), p. 1.

becomes represented realistically rather than suffering from the stereotypes that have surrounded aging in our society. Some activist groups have formed among the older population—the Gray Panthers, the National Council of Senior Citizens, the American Association of Retired Persons—and studies in gerontology have proliferated in an attempt to understand the physical, psychological, and social aspects of aging.

As a result, a new picture of the aging population—one that has both positive and negative qualities as well as all the other potentialities and drawbacks that any other age group faces—is beginning to emerge. The view of old age held by the elderly themselves seems to be an ambivalent one, as Shaw intimated.

Older people, of course, have many problems that younger people usually do not have, such as declining physical strength and health problems, but they do not have many others that younger persons must face. They have raised their families and have done their life work. Despite these differences, however, there are remarkable consistencies in life—things that change little over the years. Older persons are still social and sexual. Some are married, some are divorced, some remarry, others are widowed. Topics that are important in other stages of the life cycle are usually just as pertinent in the later stages of life.

Who Is Old?

The objective of this chapter is to look at the roles of older people in families and to explore the influence of the family on aging persons. First, *old* must be defined. Young adults often refer to their 45- or 50-year-old parents as "over the hill" when the parents still think of themselves as young. The parents are seen as old because they belong to another generation and because to a person of 20, even 40 may look ancient. More important, however, their parents have finished their childbearing and child-

Maggie Kuhn founded the Gray Panthers, a group of older persons who have influenced legislation affecting funding for projects for the elderly.

rearing years and soon may become grandparents. When the third generation arrives, even if the grandparents are only 40, they are usually viewed as "growing old."

There is agreement among experts that middle age begins and ends and old age begins at different chronological ages for different persons. The United States Bureau of the Census uses the chronological age of 65 as the end of middle age and the beginning of old age. This choice is tied to the 1935 enactment of Social Security legislation, which up until the present writing has used 65 as the age for maximum retirement benefits to begin. Other countries use other chronological ages. Recently Congress passed a law that mandatory retirement for most employed persons in the United States could not be ordered on grounds of age alone. In accord with this, it is likely that the arbitrary age of 65 as the beginning of old age will eventually be replaced by a later arbitrary age. Also, as the life cycle lengthens and as older people remain healthy, vital, and young looking, the calendar calculation of old age may change. Family sociologist Ethel Shanas (1980) has suggested that we may need to divide our aging population into the "young-old" (65–74) and the "old-old" (75 +). Those who in 1900 might have been considered old may now appear to be "young-old" because at the turn of this century few people lived to be over 80. Currently there are over 2.3 million persons in the United States who are over 85, and the number is growing (U.S. Bureau of the Census 1984i, p. 2).

We all know people who are "young," spry, and alert but who, chronologically, are aged. There are also those in their fifties who look ancient and act for all the world as though life were over. The truth is that people age very differently. Some of the variation is due to genetic differences and some, surely, to physical health. Perhaps more than any other variable, however, gerontologists point to outlook on life (Shanas 1980). A person's self-concept and understanding of relations with others depend on health, of course, and on family and friends, on finances, and on whether he or she views his or her work as meaningful.

Adjusting to Old Age

In a series of interviews with elderly persons, it was determined that patterns of social adjustment established in the earlier stages of their adult lives were related in important ways to their general life satisfaction in later years. Those who had been active in work, in hobbies, and in the community outside the home as younger adults were the most satisfied as they grew older (Maas and Kuypers 1974). This may account, at least in part, for findings from other research that women have a more difficult time in their later years than men do since women who are now over 65 belong to generations in which many middle-class women believed that a woman's "place" was in the home. Perhaps future generations of women will have an easier time adjusting. About half of the women who are currently 45 to 64 have spent some time in the labor force, and the trend seems to be in the direction of increasing participation. Table 15.2 shows the participation of various age cohorts.

Other reasons for greater adjustment problems for older women unfortunately have no such ready solution. One important factor is that there are so many more older women than older men, a discrepancy that increases with each advancing year. In 1981, women had a life expectancy of 77.9 years, whereas men's life expectancy was 70.4 years. For every 100 men who were 65 and older, there were 150 women. After age 80, the ratio soared to 250 women to every 100 men (U.S. Bureau of the Census 1983d, p. 5).

Women are therefore likely to spend their older years single and, as a result, are likely to have fewer economic resources. Half the women over 65 are single and live in poverty, with the bulk of their income coming from Social Security or old-age assistance (Baldwin 1978).

Most pension plans, whose benefits begin at retirement, are tied to full-time employment. Women usually have worked part-time or have had work lives inter-

Age	Percent
All women 16 years and over	51.0
16 to 19	54.5
20 to 24	69.1
25 to 34	63.8
35 to 44	63.6
45 to 54	58.4
55 to 59	48.7
60 to 64	33.9
65 and over	8.3

TABLE 15 • 2
Percent of Women in the Labor Force (by age), 1979

Source: U.S. Bureau of the Census, *Current Population Reports,* Series P-23, No. 111 (June 1981), p. 8.

spersed with periods at home and therefore have contributed less to pension plans. Women's lower salaries (partly due to lower pay scales for the jobs they are most likely to choose but often due to low seniority in equal-opportunity jobs—teaching, for example) also are reflected in lower pension benefits. Also, women not only typically retire earlier but on the average live longer after retirement than men do and thus have more years to survive on what may be smaller benefits than men. Some women have survivor's benefits from a deceased husband's pension, but such benefits may cease if they remarry. However, as today's young and middle-age women spend more years in the labor force and accrue higher pension benefits, the number of retired women with incomes below the poverty line should drop dramatically.

Shanas (1980) believes that another important reason that older women report more difficulties in their later years than men do is that women are judged old by different standards from those used for men. Over twenty years ago Shanas asked a cross section of Americans, "When is a person old?" She reports that the findings still hold today. She found that no matter what a man's actual age, if he was active and energetic, he was not viewed as old. On the other hand, women were judged old according to their chronological ages: "A man, then, is as old as his activities; a woman as old as her birthday."

A definition of old age is incorporated in a description of who is young, middle-aged, and old that gerontology specialist Bernice Neugarten (1968) once gave. She said that when we are young we count our ages by how long it has been since birth. A time comes, however—usually between ages 35 and 40—when we also begin to contemplate how long we have left to live. When we begin to use both measures—time since birth and time left—we have entered middle age. Eventually, she says, another milestone comes, when we no longer want to reckon with birthdays nor to think about how long it has been since the day we were born. Each day is counted as a blessing, but no plans for the future are made. When the focus shifts solely to how long is left, this marks the beginning of old age.

The mother of one of our friends, who is 75, recently bought a very expensive piece of artwork. When her son asked why she had spent so much money this way, she snapped: "For an investment. Just think what I can sell it for in twenty years."

By Neugarten's definition this woman is not old. She is planning for an active future and, we are sure, does not think of herself as old either.

Since one's adjustment to old age seems determined in part by events and experiences in the years preceding retirement, it can be useful to take a look at middle age as the precursor of old age. *Middle age* has been defined in as many different ways as has old age. This postparental stage begins some time around the age of 40 or 45 and coincides roughly with what the Bureau of the Census has for years somewhat arbitrarily designated as midlife (45 to 64 years old). For this reason, for many men and women the realization of their aging process begins in earnest with the launching of children and the onset of the postparental and grandparental years.

THE POSTPARENTAL PERIOD

The departure of the last child from home signals the beginning of the "empty-nest" phase of life. This milestone has been thought to affect women, primarily those whose lives have been devoted to their homes and their children, more than it affects men. Men miss their departed children, too, but they are usually still actively involved in their work. The children's departure changes little of their working life, except to relieve some of the financial burden. However, when children leave home, fathers, as well as mothers, no longer have the distractions of active parenthood to take their attention from their roles as husbands and wives.

The empty-nest stage has recently been postponed by millions of American families. Since 1970, the growing tendency of young adults to delay marriage, along with the high cost of establishing an independent household, has resulted in an 85 percent increase in the fraction of persons aged 18–34 living in the households of their parents (U.S. Bureau of the Census 1983b, p. 5). Many young people move out and then return to the parental home when they have difficulty being independent. Sometimes their divorced offspring bring grandchildren with them, and once again, there is a full house rather than an empty nest.

Some women (and a good many men, for that matter) have a difficult time allowing their children to establish independent lives away from home. We have known parents who became severely depressed and lonely when the last child left. Some have become pregnant again, if they could, or adopted a child or raised their grandchildren in an effort to recreate the years of the filled nest. However, it is not so much that women are upset at the last child's leaving as they are stressed by the question of "Now what do I do?" There is new freedom to fulfill some of their own needs for a change, but often "retired" mothers are uncertain about what they want to do. In addition, women who have been at home for years are often unsure of their abilities to compete in a work world of which they have not been an active part for many years. Going back to school may be attractive—but can they succeed? If they decide on employment, they wonder who will hire them. How will husbands respond if they change their lives? These questions seem to be at the root of much of the turmoil attributed to the empty-nest stage for women.

A study conducted by Japan's National Institute of Health (reported in the *Pomona* [CA] *Progress Bulletin*, October 10, 1983, p. 12) has shown that Japanese homemakers are being affected by the **empty-nest syndrome** in increasing numbers as their lives more closely resemble those of Western wives. In Japan, as in the United

States, **longevity has** increased, family size has decreased, and the extended family pattern is no longer the rule so that women do not spend their later years caring for grandchildren. As a result, Japanese women in their forties and fifties report feeling bored and unfulfilled. They use a derogatory term *san skoku hirunatsuki* ("three meals and an afternoon nap") to describe their day. It is estimated that they average seven hours a day of free time. Most were unable to pursue higher education in order to find acceptable work. Furthermore, Japan's lifetime employment system respects seniority and favors those who stay with the same company for all of their working years. Because the typical retirement age in Japan is 55, women who do not enter the labor force until their children have left home have little chance of achieving seniority or of developing much of a career before retirement.

Reestablishing the Couple Relationship

The departure of the last child from home (who may not necessarily be the youngest child) is a time for husband and wife to be a couple alone again. However, some couples find that they are strangers to each other after their children leave. They have focused so completely on their children's needs that the parental role has totally eclipsed the marital one. They often have almost forgotten that they are husband and wife as they have submerged themselves in parenthood. They may even still refer to each other as "Mom" and "Dad." These emotional strangers, no longer linked together by the family responsibilities, may have serious adjustment problems that are far more complicated than dealing with the departure of children. They may have to relearn how to relate on an intimate level and to direct to each other the love, support, and attention that were given for so many years to the children.

Most men and women, however, report that the postparental period is a time of improvement in their lives. They are still young (by their standards), many financial burdens have been removed, and they have more time to themselves. An overwhelming number of married couples report that their marital satisfaction returns to something resembling the preparenthood level (Feldman and Feldman 1976).

In a series of studies on postparenthood, couples report more shared activities and more companionship. In one particularly thorough research project, family sociologist Norval Glenn (1975) reported that married women's overall happiness was greater when their children left home and that marital happiness was generally higher for both men and women in the postparental stage. Still other studies have indicated that when the children leave home, there is a return to a sharing of wage-earning and domestic tasks similar to that of couples in the period before children were born. Couples over 45 were shown to be twice as likely as younger couples to share earning a living equally, and only one-third of the wives over 45 reported that they did all the housekeeping (Albrecht, Bahr, and Chadwick 1979).

Psychological and Physiological Changes

Most couples also report that they are still in love and still sexually active with each other during their postparental years. Psychologically and physically, men and women

Most married couples report that the postparental period is a time of release from the responsibilities of raising a family and that the saved time, energy, and resources now can be turned to enhancing their lives as a couple.

in midlife undergo some sexual changes, of course, but most couples report that these changes are usually easily accommodated once they understand what to expect. Middle-age men may experience some slowing down of sexual responses as the testosterone level begins to decline between the ages of 40 to 60 (after which it stabilizes for the rest of life) (Huyck 1974).

Some women believe that any depression or anxiety they experience at this stage of life can be attributed to physiological changes accompanying **menopause.** There is no argument about whether physical changes occur during menopause (in the late forties, on the average). Most women notice some uncomfortable effects (hot flashes, dizziness, insomnia, headache, fatigue), but only about 10 percent report severe distress (McKinlay and Jeffreys, 1974, p. 108). A hormonal deficiency may contribute to a woman's depression, but replacement of the hormone estrogen usually relieves the physical causes. Replacement therapy with a combination of estrogen-progesterone also has been proven effective in preventing **osteoporosis,** or weakening of the bones, which causes bone fractures in many older women. Recent research has dispelled most concerns that hormone replacement produces an increased risk of endometrial cancer, a fear that kept many women from seeking help for their menopausal problems (Sarrel and Sarrel 1984). After a few months, most women's bodies make adjustments to their hormonal changes, and the physical symptoms diminish or disappear altogether.

The psychological problems that occur simultaneously with menopause are not thought to be due primarily to the hormonal changes but more to the woman's interpretation of what is happening to her body. It is a forceful reminder that her childbearing years are over and that she is aging. It comes at the same time that her children leave home and that she must redefine her life. So many changes at once may easily be expected to produce psychological stress. As psychologists Janet Hyde and Betty Rosenberg (1980, p. 198) have stated: "Any quirk in a middle-aged woman's behavior is attributed to the 'change.' It simultaneously becomes the cause of, and explanation for, all [her] problems and complaints. Ironically, idiosyncrasies in women of childbearing age are blamed on menstruation, while problems experienced by women who are past that age are blamed on the lack of it."

Women may become more sexually responsive after menopause as a result of losing concern about pregnancy. They experience a rebalance of androgen and estrogen because of the decreased production of the latter. This rebalance may serve to increase female sexual responsiveness. Some experts have suggested that the "out-of-phase" sexual interest on the part of men and women creates sexual problems for middle-age couples. In our experience in counseling such couples, this is sometimes the case; more often, however, it is not a problem. It actually may improve the couple's sex life in cases in which the husband had a higher interest in sex than his wife did previously.

Self-Fulfillment

Middle-age persons seem to sense a renewal of interest in self-fulfillment that may have been almost dormant during the child-rearing years. Men and women seek fulfillment differently during these years, however, and often this difference becomes the source of marital strains. Some men, sensing that their financial burdens have been lifted considerably, may want to relax a bit, enjoy their new freedom, and pull back somewhat from the stresses of the work world. Other men who are less well off may decide that they must work even harder to achieve their goals. Some may acknowledge that they have reached a peak occupationally and that no amount of extra effort will change things. Many men begin to take better care of their bodies—through exercise, diet, and rest—now that they have it made and the family is raised. Others give up and settle into a complacency that may be frustrating to their wives (Levinson et al. 1974).

Women often use their new freedom to seek self-fulfillment in increased activity. They may go to school or begin a serious work commitment. Just when her husband hopes to enjoy the fruits of his years of labor, the woman wants to pursue interests that may block some of his plans. If she is working or going to school, she may want him to help more around the house, whereas he wants to play golf. He may want to travel, but she needs to give extra time to her developing career. Both reactions to middle age reflect a growing awareness of the time left to live and to accomplish the goals not yet met. It is as though the middle-age person is saying, "I'm not old yet but I'm not getting any younger, so I'd better do the things I've had to postpone or it may be too late."

Many men and women make major job changes in their midlives, spend more time on personal pursuits that had previously been postponed, and show certain other changes that are evident to those who know them. For instance, a man who has typically worn three-piece suits and driven a conservative car may buy a sports car and opt for open-necked shirts. One woman lost 50 pounds, bought a youthful wardrobe, and learned to fly an airplane. Childless couples also experience this confrontation with the aging process, but for those who have had children, the transition takes on the added dimension of the end of a great many responsibilities and restrictions to their freedom.

The impact of middle age varies with each individual's reaction to the aging process. For some there are specific stresses and strains that have to do with the realities of aging, with the departure of children, with the push for self-fulfillment, and with the need to take stock of relationships (the marriage in particular) that have changed because of the changed roles that men and women play at this life period.

In general, the so-called "mid-life crisis" period seems to have been considered more negatively than it warrants. Most persons see it instead as a time of increasing freedom, new options for both sexes, and a chance for a more intimate marriage than was possible during the child-rearing years. This is not to say that there are not doubts about aging, some regrets about missed opportunity, and the need for considerable readjustment to changed roles.

All in all, the middle years seem to be rated highly by those in this stage of life as well as by professionals who have studied this age group. From her series of studies of more than 2,000 middle-aged subjects, Neugarten (1968) concluded:

> Despite the new realization of the finiteness of time, one of the most prevailing themes expressed by middle-age respondents is that middle adulthood is the period of maximum capacity and ability to handle a highly complex environment and a highly differentiated self.

THE ROLE OF GRANDPARENT

One of the most significant moments in the life of most middle-age persons is that of becoming a grandparent. Margaret Mead (1972, p. 275) expressed her wonder at this experience when she wrote:

> When the news came that Sevanne Margaret was born, I suddenly realized that through no act of my own I had become biologically related to a new human being. I had never thought how strange it was to be involved at a distance in the birth of a biological descendant. The idea that as a grandparent one was dealing with action at a distance—that somewhere, miles away, a series of events occurred that changed one's status forever—I had not thought of that and I found it very odd.

Until recently, there was little research dealing with grandparenting, and what there was showed clearly that there is little agreement on a grandparent role. One family sociologist some years ago ventured to call grandparenthood a "roleless role" (Burgess 1958). One explanation for the variety of attitudes toward being grandparents lies in the fact that it is an event that occurs in middle age, when most grandparents are still busily engaged in their own pursuits. They do not fit the picture of the retired grandparents who have time to play with the children, go fishing, plant a garden, and feed the birds. The average man or woman in the United States first becomes a grandparent in his or her late forties or very early fifties. It is the "old-old"—the great-grandparents—who may more closely resemble the stereotyped, beloved "gramps."

Early studies on becoming grandparents emphasized how much more significant becoming a grandparent was for women and how men rarely became truly involved with their grandchildren until after retirement (Neugarten and Weinstein 1968). As more and more women enter the labor force, the "new" grandparents may show little difference in involvement between men and women. With jobs claiming their time

"Of course I love you, Alistair. I want to have your
great-grandchildren."

and energy until retirement, it is likely that grandparents will be classified into "young grandparents," who have little time for their grandchildren, and "retired grandparents," who will resemble the stereotype and who may also be great-grandparents. Since more four-generation families exist now than ever before, great-grandparents are increasingly filling the void created by the working grandmother.

Recently, family sociologists have become increasingly interested in the role of grandparents because there are so many more of them in the population. At the turn of the century, only about 3 million Americans lived beyond age 65 compared with 24 million in 1986. Young people today can almost all expect not only to be grandparents in the future but to be great-grandparents as well.

As scientists find ways to extend the life span even longer (some predict to 150–200 years), great-great-grandparents may also be a part of families rather than mere pictures in old photo albums. They will be alive and possibly making new roles for themselves in the ever-increasing number of four- and five-generation families (Cetron and O'Toole 1984).

There is no consensus about what grandparents should do or what meaning the role should have for them. This is due not only to the great variety of grandparent types but to the fact that most of today's grandparents may not have known their own grandparents long enough to have formed a model for their behavior.

In a study of 286 grandparents, ranging in ages from 40 to 90, Kivnick (1983) classified five categories of meaning used by grandparents to define their roles. The categories were not mutually exclusive; there was overlap, and some individuals reported feeling one way with a particular grandchild and a different way with others.

The first type was the grandparent for whom the role was the central one in his or her life. These grandparents often were surrogate parents or regularly tended the children. Other research according to socioeconomic class indicates that in eco-

CHAPTER 15

nomically poorer families grandparents are more likely to take a central position with their grandchildren—especially grandmothers, who often are the primary sources of child care for their grandchildren (Clavan 1979).

The second type, according to Kivnick, consists of grandparents who view themselves as valued elders. They provide advice and resources for their grandchildren. They often serve as teachers and the reservoirs of family wisdom. Grandfathers, who typically get more involved with their grandchildren after retirement, often fill this role of family sage. Grandmothers, too, contribute to a grandchild's knowledge and skills.

The third category found in Kivnick's study centered around the feeling of family heritage and immortality that having a grandchild provided. There was a pride in having the family line carried on by this new generation. Grandparents frequently serve as the family historians, giving the grandchildren a sense of family roots and family strength.

The fourth meaning commonly given to the role of grandparent is that it gives grandparents a chance to relive the past through the life of a grandchild. Finally, many grandparents use their role as a way to give to their grandchildren what they may not have been able to give to their own children. This may include material gifts, time, attention, and patience.

The roles of grandmothers have received more attention in the literature than those of grandfathers have, probably because (since women outlive men) there are *more* grandmothers. Also, women traditionally keep family ties alive and are likely to do more of the actual child care when grandchildren visit or come to live. A study of grandmothers (Robertson 1977) categorized them into four types:

1. Seventeen percent of the grandmothers were somewhat older, usually widowed, and lonely. They saw their grandchildren as sources of company and aid and expected a great deal of contact.
2. About 28 percent of the grandmothers were concerned with doing what was right for the grandchildren and also with wanting to have a good relationship with them. These grandmothers were the most involved with their grandchildren—alternately spoiling them and being concerned with their manners and morals.
3. Another 28 percent of the grandmothers were remote and ritualistic in what little contact they had with their grandchildren (occasional visits and gifts, with most contact on holidays or birthdays).
4. About 26 percent were likely to be working (even more likely than the child's own mother was) and to be more involved in their marriages than any of the other women. They usually had strong ideas about family tradition and appropriate behavior. Their grandchildren were seen as extensions of the family tree and thus were thought to have certain roles to play. These grandmothers were usually busy in the community.

In a recent survey of 600 grandparents in the United States and Canada concerning their relationships with their grandchildren, it was discovered that grandparents spent almost 40 percent more time with their daughter's children than with their son's children. In addition, grandfathers spent more time with their granddaughters than with their grandsons (Smith 1982). The explanation offered is that daughters and granddaughters are seen as a better "kin investment" because females tend to stay more involved with their families of origin than males do.

Research suggests that the roles of grandparents change as both the grandparents and grandchildren grow older (Cherlin and Furstenberg 1985). Small children want grandparents who will play with them and engage in recreational activities. As children and grandparents grow older, the relationship becomes more formal although not less warm. As Sociologists Andrew Cherlin and Frank Furstenberg (1985, p. 100) remind us: "It's easy and natural for grandparents to treat toddlers as sources of leisure-time fun. But no matter how deep and how warm the relationship remains over time, a grandmother doesn't bounce a teenager on her knee."

Most middle-aged parents enjoy becoming grandparents even though they may not always like to think of themselves as old enough for this to happen. Most of them remember their own grandparents as "old-old" and may be reluctant to put themselves in the grandparent category for fear their own aging will miraculously speed up.

Almost all grandparents actively enjoy their roles unless they feel burdened by having to reassume parental duties with their grandchildren. Even some who have this latter responsibility reportedly enjoy it. Some are formal and leave parenting strictly to the parents. Others are informal and playful, totally enjoying the grandchildren. Another type is the distant figure who emerges infrequently and stays distant from the grandchildren. The ways that parents respond to becoming grandparents vary according to their personalities, their other satisfactions, and, of course, the relationships the new grandparents have with their grown children who are now parents (Neugarten and Weinstein 1968).

RETIREMENT

Another fundamental role change that takes place as a part of the aging process is cause for what some experts term an "identity crisis." This change occurs upon retirement, which faces most workers and their spouses, who may or may not be in the labor force themselves.

Retirement usually occurs between ages 60 and 70. For those older persons who are self-employed, there is the option of retiring gradually rather than with an unsettling suddenness. Nonetheless, when the chronological age for "old" is tied to retirement, even those who are still working at 65 or 70 may begin to judge themselves by Social Security standards.

The average life expectancy at age 65 is now 13.9 years for men and 18.3 for women, although it is predicted that by the year 2000, the average number of years following retirement will have risen considerably unless the age of retirement is raised. The difference between blacks and whites in life expectancy at age 65 is small (U.S. Bureau of the Census 1983d, p. 6).

Since women on the average outlive men and also typically marry men older than they, they have a much longer life expectancy than their husbands after both retire. At present there are some 21 million men and women over the age of 65 who are classified as retired (Entine 1976).

Few issues have aroused as much controversy in the field of **gerontology** as the requirement that people who still want to work must retire from their jobs (Streib

Grandparents play many types of roles with their grandchildren. Almost all report enjoying grandparenting, often more than they enjoyed parenting.

and Schneider 1971). Some companies sponsor preretirement workshops to aid in preparation for what usually means a radical change in lifetime habits. Usually, however, men and women are left to deal with the impact on their own. Retirement is a complex phenomenon that can be very stressful because it requires a person to relinquish a meaningful status and, perhaps equally important, to accept a lower income. Of course, not everyone is sorry to retire; many workers look forward to retirement and plan for the enjoyment of more leisure.

Retirement Activities

A recent study of those who retired early (before age 63) found that two out of five had found new jobs for pay, working about 20 hours a week. Many said they needed the money, but most said they also enjoyed it. The other three-fifths who were not employed reported averaging nearly 30 hours a week on volunteer activities and hobbies. Almost half of those gave their volunteer time to religious groups and one-fifth to political groups (Morse and Gray 1980).

Retired persons have found a special place volunteering (sometimes in paid positions) in day-care centers where there is not enough staff help, due in part to government budget cuts. "Everyone benefits," says Meridith Miller, an intergenerational specialist with the National Council on Aging. "There are more hugs and cuddles for the little ones, more intriguing stories and hobby work for the older kids" (*Los Angeles Times*, July 11, 1986, Part V, p. 21).

The Foster Grandparent program, backed by federal and state governments, is a program utilizing retired volunteers to work in institutions giving care to children who are handicapped physically, emotionally, or mentally. The National Council on Aging sponsors a program called Family Friends for in-home care for children and parents who need help. "Latchkey" children also may use a phone-in service to call to talk to a volunteer who is experienced as a grandparent.

There seems to be an increasing desire by older Americans to remain active either as paid workers or as unpaid volunteers. Many retirees report that they have never been so busy, and they often complain of being overcommitted. Early retirement, which at one time was viewed as very desirable, seems to have lost popularity. In 1974 only 57 percent of those surveyed wanted to work to age 65 or older. By 1981, that figure had grown to 67 percent (Sheppard 1981).

Changes Involved in Retirement

Retirement is generally viewed as the milestone that marks the end of middle age and the entry into old age. In a review of studies on factors involved in retirement, the following five areas were identified (Leslie and Leslie 1980):

1. *Loss of finances:* this is perhaps the biggest adjustment that retirement brings. A definite pattern of declining income accompanies retirement. The economic status of the elderly is far more varied than that of any other age group. However, in 1984 the median income of families with heads of household 65 or over was $18,236 compared with $29,292 for households headed by younger people. A fifth of the total elderly population depend solely on Social Security benefits; three-fourths of those over 65 had incomes below $10,000 per year in 1981 (U.S. Bureau of the Census 1983d, p. 7). Only one out of seven elderly persons in 1981 was reported living in poverty—a significant improvement over 1970, when one out of four lived in poverty. The main reason for the decrease in elderly poverty was that increases in Social Security benefits nearly doubled the median income of persons over 65 during this period. Worse off are old people living alone, especially elderly blacks, the very old, and elderly women, who are particularly vulnerable because they are more likely than elderly men to stay single once widowed or divorced.

Of those who are fortunate enough to have adequate income, retirement is often welcomed and enjoyed as a time to travel and to pursue hobbies or other avocations that have been put off until this time. Experts report that, by and large, most people retire just as soon as they have enough financial security to do so. Those who choose to work the longest are either those who cannot afford to retire or those who have absorbing work that they can do as long as they choose.

Current research has shown that responses to old age may be as crucially determined by social class and income as by any other factor. The higher the social class and the more resources the older person has, the more likely he or she is to view old age in terms of leisure, relaxation, and security. The less fortunate tend to regard old age as a time of physical decline, lowered standards of living, and unhappiness (Huyck 1974).

2. *Loss of self-esteem:* the role of productive worker is the equivalent of identity and status for many men and women. When people no longer feel useful and needed, they may lose self-worth. Men and women who are well off financially tend to be exceptions to this generalization, however. Having money may act as a symbol for some that "I was a success"; others may have become accustomed to more leisure

before retirement, possibly gaining recognition from nonemployment skills that they need not give up upon retirement. Research findings are not uniform about the effects of retirement on self-esteem, but most agree that it depends on how comfortable the older person feels about life up to that point. If the retired person believes that he or she has been as successful as anticipated and has something to show for all the effort, self-esteem appears to suffer less.

3. *Loss of work-oriented social contacts:* retirees often report missing the people with whom they interacted daily. Women who retire have been shown to take longer than men do to adjust and to get over their lonely feelings (Atchley 1976). Many retired persons drop out of social organizations because of finances and have trouble finding new avenues to make friends.

4. *Loss of meaningful tasks:* as one observer of retirement puts it, "Marriages which have been stable for years can be shaken by a husband with retirement fidgets. On the simplest level, a great part of a man's adjustment to retirement involves filling the gap provided by the work situation" (Heyman 1970). Women feel this loss, too. Some find homemaking waiting to keep them busy, although our preliminary research on aging couples has shown that women who have had busy careers often are not interested in resuming homemaking. They feel just as much of a sense of loss of meaningful tasks as men do—sometimes more. If both spouses are employed, the chances are great that the husband (who is usually older) will retire sooner than his wife does. In couples whom we have interviewed, there is often a difficult transition as husbands pick up the domestic tasks while wives go to work each day. Should the husbands fail to do so, other kinds of problems result because wives often feel that they are carrying the greater burden. One of the major tasks of retirement seems to be to develop rewarding activities to replace work or to find new work to do. However, the activities need to please both partners rather than just the retired one.

5. *Loss of reference group:* many workers—especially men—identify themselves by their work. It has been a way of life for them for all of their adult years. They now must adjust from having others think of them and refer to them as doctors, lawyers, teachers, contractors, plumbers, or bankers to being identified as retired (or simply old) persons. As more and more women have lifelong work roles, this will become an issue for them as well. A loss of identity with one's occupational status is often mentioned by those who say they would continue working after age 65, if given the opportunity.

A recent study of the effect of retirement on morale of blacks, Mexican-Americans, and whites revealed that although morale is lower generally for all retired persons than for those who are still working, morale is based on so many factors that ceasing to work itself often is not the biggest issue (Adamcik 1980). Fifteen measures of morale were used to discover that there were significant differences in which factors affected morale in each of the three populations. Retired black men differed significantly from working black men in feeling less useful and in having less pep. On thirteen other measures there was very little difference between the two black categories. Neither feeling useful nor loss of pep was significantly related to age or status of the man's health, although lowered income was definitely related to feelings of usefulness (but not related to pep).

Retired white men differed significantly from working white men on three measures of morale: feeling lonely, getting upset easily, and feeling less useful. Mexican-American retired men had significant differences from Mexican-American working men on twelve of the fifteen measures of morale, with both income and health status related to their low morale. They were more likely to feel sad, to feel that life wasn't worth living, to worry so much that they could not sleep, to feel lonely, to get upset easily, to feel that things kept getting worse, to have little pep, to feel less useful, to feel that life was hard, to be unhappy, to believe things were worse than they had expected them to be, and not to foresee that they would be any happier in the future.

Retired black women also generally reported lower morale than did working black women. The primary factors in their low morale were worrying so much they could not sleep and not being happy. White women seemed primarily bothered that life was so hard after retirement. The lower morale expressed by Mexican-American retired women was related to five basic factors. They worried so that they could not sleep, felt afraid, got upset easily, were unhappy, and reported that each of these got progressively worse with age.

In all cases the study revealed that low income (as the result of not working) rather than loss of the worker role seemed to be at the root of the lower morale. Morale had rather different meanings across ethnic and sex groups, as the factors indicate. The feelings expressed by a retired black man, for instance, were not the same as those expressed by a retired Mexican-American man or by a black woman or a white woman.

In an analysis of national data by the University of Michigan Institute of Gerontology, older black women reported that retirement represented a relief from a lifetime of hard, low-paying work. They said they were happier and had more time for family and friends; although most were poor, their suicide rate was lower than those for white men and women who were of comparable financial status (Campbell-Gibson 1984).

Retirement, then, seems to be a matter of morale, of income, of health, and of family support. Not all members of the elderly population have resources in the same areas. Some have better health than others, for instance, but others have more money. The interrelationships between the areas of resources are complex. In his report on older persons in the United States, family expert Gordon Streib (1972) has examined five types of older families in terms of their major resources.

- *Type I:* "the golden sunset family" has all four necessary resources: good physical health, good emotional health, adequate economic resources, and good social resources.
- *Type II:* those who are physically incapacitated but who are emotionally stable, have financial security, and who have family and friends for support make up this category.
- *Type III:* these are older persons who are both physically and emotionally unhealthy, but who have enough money and family resources to take care of themselves.
- *Type IV:* this type includes those who have only family to care for them. They are in poor physical and emotional health and have no money.
- *Type V:* this type is "the totally deprived family," who ends its years in misery. These are the families that present the most serious problems in old age because many of them lack any of the four important resources.

There are many other combinations of resources as well, but these five were found to be the most common for retirement adjustment.

Retirement, which releases men and women from their work roles, causes some older persons to disengage from other roles as well. The **theory of disengagement**, which was developed to explain why some persons withdraw, become preoccupied with themselves, and alter their relationships with others, has given insight into life experiences of the elderly (Cumming and Henry 1961). From this research and that of the theory's critics, it is possible to conclude that for those who do disengage, it is not always a negative experience. For many, in fact, it is not a new or sudden adjustment process at all but, rather, a continuation of a lifestyle that had been one of modified withdrawal in earlier years. Such persons may enjoy a time for reflection and the opportunity to be less invested in others and in life's demands (Rose 1968).

Critics of the disengagement theory believe that on the whole staying active and socially involved is the secret to being happy and well adjusted in old age (Larsen 1978). The **activity theory** has a great deal of support from research indicating that the stimulation and support that comes from socializing and staying active are directly related to higher morale and life satisfaction.

Probably neither the disengagement theory nor the activity theory is sufficient to account for the different successful patterns of aging. Sociologist Robert Havighurst (1968) has postulated that there are two concurrent forces at work—a desire to relax and enjoy leisure and a need for stimulation and social contact.

Perhaps the best explanation lies in the individual older person's personality. If he or she has always been active, slowing down may be difficult; if the older person has been social, withdrawing may make for unhappiness. On the other hand, if the older person likes peace and quiet and was never very outgoing, disengagement may be ideal. Neugarten (1972, p. 13) sums it up well: there is no single way to grow old because "aging is not a leveler of individual differences except, perhaps, at the very end of life."

OLD PEOPLE AND THEIR FAMILIES

Research indicates that most old people have a great deal of contact with family members—particularly their children—and about 8 percent of them have one or more children who provide their most significant social and psychological support. More than half see at least one son or daughter frequently. Furthermore, those children who do not live nearby usually keep in touch by telephone and by mail to keep their family bonds intact. Shanas (1973) has proposed that "socio-emotional distance" is a more significant factor in the closeness of adults and their parents than is geographical distance. Siblings of older men and women also are important, particularly when the older person has no children.

After good health, it appears that the greatest direct effect on the psychological well-being of older men and women is the qualitative nature of their relationships with family members. Affection, good communication, and shared beliefs and activities are the crucial aspects documented in good relationships across generations (Quinn 1983).

In an article discussing the strength of family bonds, it was suggested that family relations are stronger and more durable than friendships because they are characterized by obligation rather than only by shared interests (Troll and Smith 1976). It is interesting to note that although family support has been shown to be one of the most important variables in how well older people adjust, older persons' adjustments toward aging, their health, their finances, and their living environment also influenced how well they got along with their children. It may not be easy, therefore, to distinguish cause and effect—the parents' adjustment causes a better relationship with their children, and a good relationship with their children facilitates the older persons' good adjustment (Johnson and Bursk 1977).

In a study of older married couples in the 1970s, it was found that those who had more extensive interaction with their grown children seemed more satisfied with their lives. However, this did not hold if they lived in the same household with them. It appears that being dependent on children is detrimental to morale of the elderly. Not only do many older persons feel demeaned by dependency on their adult children, but the children also often feel the strain of stretching their energy and income to help their parents. This stress spills over into their feelings for their parents, and many report developing negative feelings about their aging, dependent parents (Swenson, Eskew, and Kohlhepp 1977). Most studies reveal, however, that in general grown children have a sense of obligation that they fulfill when they are needed whether or not there are close emotional ties (Cicirelli 1983).

Help often goes from elderly parent to adult children as well. They may provide child care, care during illness, gifts, and financial assistance. In many instances, they provide shelter and food for a divorced or unemployed child. Obviously, the mutual flow of help, in whatever form, between the generations is influenced by health, finances, and geographical proximity.

Research on the importance of an intact marriage to the adjustment of older persons has indicated that 80 percent of all men and 50 percent of all women over 65 are living with their spouses (U.S. Bureau of the Census 1982a, pp. 45–47). Since the average couple marrying today can expect to live to be over 70 years of age, they have a very good chance to have a marriage that lasts 50 years. We have become particularly interested in couples who have been married for more than 50 years. Of course, most of the couples we have interviewed have had one marriage that has lasted this long. However, we believe that there will be many second marriages that also will last for 50 or more years. Growing numbers of couples are celebrating sixtieth and even seventieth anniversaries. If, as futurists report, the life cycle is someday extended to 150 to 200 years, golden wedding anniversaries will occur at less than half of a couple's married life.

OLDER MARRIAGES

To date the world's record for length of marriage is held by a Bombay, India, couple married 86 years. Death ended their marriage in 1939. They had been betrothed as children. In England a couple were married 78 years; in the United States, the record is 83 years (*Guinness Book of World Records* 1980). In 1980 a California couple celebrated their seventy-first anniversary when they were 94 and 91 years of age, respectively. They celebrated by going out to dinner with their children, who were 70 and 60—themselves "senior citizens." What is their advice to others who want their marriages to last?

"Don't stop on little things," says Mrs. R. "Be satisfied whatever happens. Ben didn't commit adultery, he's not a gambler, not a liar. . . ."

"And not a drunk," adds Ben.

"So what is there to complain about?" she concludes. Mr. R's advice is to "tell the truth. The main thing is to be honest. That way you have nothing to hide." (Elevenstar 1980, p. 2)

Evaluating Long-Term Marital Satisfaction

There has been relatively little research on marriages in the later years—particularly those that have lasted more than 50 years. We have been intrigued by the few studies that have been done, however, because we live in a community that has a large retirement population. Our interest has been piqued by marriage in the later years as we have observed many couples who have been together for over half a century.

From the studies that have been done, we have learned that couples who have been married to each other for longer than 50 years generally report that it has been a very positive experience (Sporakowski and Jughston 1978; Spanier, Lewis, and Cole 1975). In one study of couples who had been married over 50 years and whose average age was 79, all of them described their marriages as happy, and 93 percent said they would marry the same persons if they had to do it over again (Roberts and Roberts 1975). This is not surprising: we might expect that if living together for that long were not generally positive, the marriages would have ended (or at least, that it would be difficult for the couples to admit that they had stayed together so many years unhappily).

The finding that marriages perceived as satisfactory in later years were seen as satisfactory from the beginning is not surprising. Satisfactory marriages should be expected to endure longer than unsatisfactory ones. Also, though not impossible, it is unlikely that a bad marriage in the early years will become a really good marriage in later life.

It may be that when couples are asked to look back over their lives together, there is a tendency to idealize their marriage or to convince themselves that since they had stayed married all those years, it must have been generally positive. **Cognitive dissonance theory** explains this phenomenon as the tendency for one to value something in direct proportion to how much one has invested in it. In a discussion of this theory as it applies to marital satisfaction over the life cycle, it has been proposed that by investing many years of one's life in a relationship—time, emotion, energy, resources—and sharing so many of life's experiences together, an older married person may have a tendency to overemphasize how good it has been and how satisfied he or she is (Spanier, Lewis, and Cole 1975).

There are exceptions to the reports of happiness of over-50-year marriages. One study from interviews with couples who were married before 1930 found that many of the couples did not report satisfaction with their married years. In fact, many spoke of "surviving" but being disappointed that their expectations of marriage had not been met. The researchers reported that by current standards, they probably would have counseled divorce for many of the couples interviewed. The couples, however, reported that divorce was never an option for them since "it was not done" (Friedman and Todd 1979). Since couples who have married more recently do consider divorce an option, perhaps those who celebrate golden wedding anniversaries in the future will report even more satisfaction since they will have stayed in the relationship by choice.

Why the couples in the Friedman-Todd sample seem at odds with the other couples interviewed is an interesting question. The couples were drawn from California and Israel, but we resist the notion that old people in California and Israel are so different from old people in general. Perhaps the explanation lies in the fact that the interviewers drew a different kind of sample or asked for different kinds of information from that requested by others who have done similar research, or that they interpreted the data differently from others.

The Friedman-Todd study began by asking couples who had been married over 45 years for advice about what it takes to be happily married. The couples could not come up with any formula. They did report that they had worked out rules by which to share their lives that helped the marriage to continue. Both power and intimacy were related to their happiness. The spouses with the higher power were significantly happier than those with lower power.

Four patterns of power distribution were identified by Friedman and Todd: (1) *traditional*, in which the husband had more power; (2) *reversed*, in which the wife had more power; (3) *equal-high*, in which both received high power ratings; and (4) *equal-low*, in which both received low ratings. Husbands were happier in the traditional pattern, wives in the reversed pattern. Couples in the equal-high category both reported happiness, and couples in the equal-low category were the least happy.

For those old couples in the Friedman-Todd study who had lower power orientations, intimacy was the most significant factor in happiness. For spouses with high power, the importance of intimacy for happiness was diminished. Being happy, however, was not nearly as important for these couples as surviving in what they saw as a troubled world. It appears that the reports of dissatisfaction may have been more reflective of the older couples' reactions to their lives in general than to their marriages.

A recent study of couples married from 55 to 69 years divided the marriages into types modified from those described by Cuber and Harroff: vital, devitalized, passive-congenial, conflict-habituated, and hostile-accommodating (see Chapter 8). The "vital" marriages had fluctuated throughout their duration, having ups and downs but never losing their vital quality. There were no "devitalized" marriages in the sample, leading to speculation that those who are without vitality at some point during the marriage either terminate or evolve into a different type. The "passive-congenial" marriages had been that way from their beginning and, in a sense, seemed to be marriages "of convenience." "Conflict-habituated" marriages were not found in this sample, although there were clear indications of overt or covert conflict for many of the couples during the first 25 years of their marriages. It was hypothesized that these couples worked out their differences and learned to accommodate to each other. "Hostile-accommodating" couples were found who were held together by religious convictions but made no pretense that they were happy or loved each other (Weishaus and Field 1983).

In a critique of research on marital satisfaction over the life cycle, one of the points made was that marital adjustment may actually be more closely related to individual partners' adjustment to life than to adjustments specific to their marriages (Schram 1979). It may well be, then, that marital adjustment in later years is a reflection of general well-being and life adjustment that allows partners to enjoy each other and to adjust to life together. If, as many experts believe, well-adjusted individuals are more likely to report satisfying marriages, then these same individuals will be likely to be more satisfied than the average person at any time in the marital life cycle. This is not to deny, however, that good marital adjustment contributes significantly to good personal adjustment in old age in a majority of cases, and love and companionship are reported to be valuable as contributors to morale.

A recent study has shown that intimacy and friendship wane as a marriage continues. Two-thirds of couples married more than 50 years did not mention each other when asked to name their three most intimate friends. Part of the reason may have been that they found it difficult to sustain the complex relationship of lover, financial partner, coparent, and intimate friend over such a prolonged period of half a century or more (Rowe and Meredith 1981, p. 3). If intimacy equals happiness for the couples studied (and there is evidence that there is a positive link), this may be one more piece of evidence that not all long-term marriages have been or are currently satisfactory (Stinnett, Carter, and Montgomery 1972). From other research on older persons' marriages we learn that even though most older couples consider their current marriage relationships to be as good as in their early years, lower-income couples report that their marital satisfaction has declined. They also report less satisfaction with life, more loneliness, and more worry. Again we see that low income has a damaging effect on the quality of life for older persons, which seriously affects their morale and their satisfaction in life, including marital satisfaction (Hutchison 1975).

Our own study of couples who have been married for over 50 years has tried to take into consideration the fact that not everything in any long-term marriage can be wonderful and satisfying. After all, these couples have been married through one major world war (perhaps two) and a severe economic depression. They are currently retired at a time when their income has been eaten away by inflation. These couples are special because both have survived (as have their marriages) to a record age for the United States. There are now hundreds of thousands of such couples, so that they are no longer quite the novelty that they were only a generation or two back.

We have been interested primarily in how couples (and their children and grandchildren) assess their marriages now and remember them from the past. This assessment includes satisfaction levels, communication roles, social adjustment as a couple, decision making, and sexual adjustment. We have attempted to adjust for selective recall, which is always a problem in attempting to remember the past. Family sociologist Reuben Hill (1964) has addressed this very point and believes that the longer ago the time period that is being recalled, the less trustworthy the memory.

> Certain behaviors simply may not be elicited back in time for such respondents: marital happiness, marital communication, value consensus, authority patterns and allocation of roles, parent-child and sibling-sibling relationships. On the other hand, from our Minnesota study, we have found residential histories, job histories, automobile and durable goods purchases, and family composition histories not impossible to obtain from our most aged respondents.

It appears that the very issues that are the most relevant in studying long-term marriages are also the ones subject to the most selective recall. We have come to believe that selective recall is one of the major reasons that most studies have found that older couples view their marital histories as positively as they do. To avoid the bias of selective recall as much as possible, studying couples from the beginning to the end of their lives together (a longitudinal study) may seem the only promising solution. However, since such a project would take over 50 years, it is not a practical undertaking for researchers, who may not complete their training until age 30 and who probably will retire at age 65 or 70.

A longitudinal study of long-term marriages was accomplished by use of data collected originally in 1928, updated in 1968, and again in 1982–1983. The data were stored in a computer data bank at the University of California, Berkeley. Couples' memories of the quality of their marriages in earlier years were compared in 1983 with their reports in 1928 and in 1968. The results showed considerable difference, indicating that their recall was often poor and selective (Weishaus and Field 1984).

A number of family sociologists have been interested in methods to correct for selective recall, and various methodologies have been tried (Rodgers 1964). From the possible plans for research, we chose one that involves the children and the grandchildren of the couples we interviewed. Although we recognize that they, too, have selective recall as well as different perspectives from which they view life events, they have provided some checks on facts that we would not have had otherwise. In addition, when there were discrepancies, often one generation helped the others to correct their memories. Another bonus was that more information was made available because what one had forgotten, the others often remembered.

Developing Marital Adjustment Skills

Marriages that last into postretirement years, although clearly not representative of marriages in general, are almost as varied in nature as marriages at any other time in the life cycle. However, there are two intractable facts about the life and marriage situation of older married people that do make them unique. Psychologist Clifford Swensen (1979), who has done extensive research into the lives of retired men and women, says that the two differences are that "they have the time and opportunity to explore the joys and complexities of an intimate relationship with each other; [and] their time is limited." These two factors give an urgency to their lives since they know they cannot live forever, but also give them time to be together as a couple. For some men and women being together seems to be their paramount interest, and they grow closer with each passing day. Such couples have been called "golden sunset" couples as they walk hand in hand into the sunset. On the other hand, some older couples seem preoccupied with the feeling that time is running out. The ways couples cope with both of these factors seem to be important elements in adjustment in later life.

Swensen concludes that when couples readjust their lives in the postparental years, they do so with the same set of skills they have used to face other problems and to cope with other adjustments in the past. Patterns of coping skills are seen to be directly related to the level of personal maturity the partners have reached.

Swensen's research relied heavily on the conceptualization of the stages of **ego development** devised by psychologist Jan Loevinger (1976), who proposed that personality is organized from the simple state of the infant to the highly integrated and complex state of an adult. Loevinger proposed six stages, with transition levels between the fourth, fifth, and sixth levels. The first three stages are not of great

Couples whose marriages last well into postretirement years have the time and opportunity to be a couple again without the competition of children and work pressures. They also know that their time together is limited, so they must make the most of every day.

concern to the study of retired persons because none of Swensen's respondents were still at these levels of maturity [(1) presocial, (2) impulsive, and (3) self-protective]. The last three stages plus the three transition stages, however, are important for understanding the adjustment of older men and women. Those in Swensen's study fell largely between the fourth (conformist) and the fifth (autonomous) states:

- *Stage 4. Conformist:* believed to be the developmental level of most adults. Their concern is with doing what everyone else does, following the rules, and working for the approval of others.
- *Transition level A:* a greater self-awareness begins to take over. People at this stage still are conforming, but they often have reservations about what they are doing.
- *Transition level B:* concern becomes more with personal values than with what others think. Conformity is still the rule, but more behavior is personally motivated.
- *Transition level C:* a much greater emphasis is placed on individuality, and there is a growing awareness of inner conflict between what others expect and what personal needs are.
- *Stage 5. Autonomous state:* those who reach this level have an appreciation for their own and others' individuality. They cope with inner conflicts by recognizing and accepting the fact that everyone is unique and that there are several possible solutions to any given situation.
- *Stage 6. Integrated state:* this is the most complex and highly integrative state, in which one's sense of identity is accepted and consolidated.

Swensen (1979) applies these levels to the adjustment patterns of the aging population. When retirement comes, he says:

For the first time in many years, the couple finds an opportunity to interact with each other as people without the disruption of others and they begin to realize the changes that have taken place within themselves and each other. The husband and wife have been doing different things. Their approach toward autonomy, or post conformity, has been by different paths—each has a job, or the husband has been so engrossed in his job that the wife has had to cope virtually alone with everything else in their lives, or there have been intrusive in-laws. In any case, renewed acquaintance for these intimate strangers may be frightening.

. . . there are several ways people can handle this. The most common way is to avoid the issue. I think this is what the typical conformist level couple does, so there is continued decline. They're stuck in a rut that they can't get out of and it's too disruptive to try. That's what happens in 50 to 60 percent of the cases.

The post conformist people, I think, face it, deal with it, and resolve it. That's where you get an increase in love expression and transcending of sex roles, the development of a relationship that uniquely fits each couple. Disagreements are rather interesting when there is that basic bond underneath for resolving them.

Marital adjustment in later years and level of ego development are thought by Swensen to be closely tied together. None of his couples were more than a one-half level apart in ego development. Had they been, he believes they would have been living in "completely different worlds."

This research points up what may be the basis for differential findings in the quality of marriages of older persons. The 50 to 60 percent who are still at the conformist stage of ego development would be expected to touch on each other's lives in a way that follows the rules for living that they have always followed. Their satisfactions may come largely from interaction with their children, other relatives, and friends. For the other 40 to 50 percent, the postconformist couples, there is the ability to go beyond established roles and to see and appreciate themselves and their partners as individuals. This may well account for the couples who report that marriage is better than ever and who have more intimacy as a couple in their postretirement years.

It is as though roughly half of older married couples see marriage as a given state in their lives that they have made work because it was expected of them or because they felt they had no choice. They are happy enough being married if they have good health, adequate income, and frequent contact with family and friends. If not, they are likely to report disappointment and a belief that marriage was one more ordeal of life that they have survived (as in the Friedman-Todd study).

The other half report greater rewards in their marriages. They seem to appreciate and enjoy life within the partnership increasingly as the years go by. They are very aware of the limited time left to them as a couple and want to make the most of it. One of the couples we interviewed, a retired United States Army general and his wife who have traveled the world, told us that they have never been happier and closer to each other in all their 50 years of marriage than they are now. The general said:

We have been everywhere, seen everything, and now we have time to hold hands and watch a sunset. There is an old story told of natives in India who could retire happily to their villages once they had gone out to see what lay between them and the next village. They often reported that they were happy now that they "had seen the elephant." Well, we have seen the elephant and we are considerably satisfied just to be together at home.

For the couples still in a marriage after 50 years, harmonious relationships seem to be a significant factor in successful aging. They often reminisce about past experiences and reflect on how their lives have progressed. This makes talking to older men and women a rich and rewarding experience. There is the ever-present knowledge that each day is precious since time may be limited. Although worries about one member's surviving the other may be on a couple's minds, for the most part the elderly seem less afraid of death than do younger people (Kalish and Reynolds 1976). Perhaps it follows that if one has had a full and satisfying life, death has a meaning far different from that held by young people who have yet to experience most of the good things they hope life will hold—marriage, children, and satisfying work and friendships.

Remarried Couples

Of the nearly seven million married persons who are over 65 years of age, not all are in first marriages. Many have remarried after a divorce or after being widowed. Because most older people have not accepted divorce easily for themselves, generally their remarriages are the result of one partner's being widowed rather than divorced. Older widowed men have remarriage rates almost seven times higher than those of women. This would be expected because there are so few older men available for marriage compared with the number of older women (U.S. Bureau of the Census 1983d, p. 21). A discussion of those who remarry after the age of 60 gives insight into a special aspect of aging in the United States. The number of older remarried persons has been growing as the aged population increases.

One hundred couples who married after the bride was past 60 years old were studied by McKain (1969) four to six years after their weddings. Certain factors were shown to be closely related to the success of these marriages:

1. The bride and groom had known each other for a long period of time.
2. The marriage was approved by their children and friends.
3. Both partners had adjusted well to other facets of retirement and aging.
4. The couple disposed of previously owned property and bought or rented a home for themselves.
5. There was sufficient income to live without economic hardship.

McKain found a high degree of success in the remarriages. Seventy-four of the 100 were judged to be successful on a five-factor scale (showing respect and affection for each other; enjoying each other's company; no serious complaints from either partner; partners were proud of each other; and they were considerate of each other).

SEX AND THE OLDER PERSON

There is no shortage of literature about the sexual behavior of the older population. There are many times more articles and books on the sex lives of older persons than on marriages of persons over 65. There is not a great deal of scientific research on

The myth persists that older couples are no longer interested in sex. However, older people usually do still enjoy sex, particularly those who reported greater activity and enjoyment in their earlier years.

sexuality in old age, however, possibly because asking older people what they actually do may have been a somewhat sensitive area for younger researchers. The studies that exist report that most couples over 65 are sexually active. There appears to be no fixed cutoff age for sexual desire and ability (Brecher 1984). An enjoyable comment on this topic is reported by social psychologist Carol Tavris (1977), who received this letter:

> I am sixty years old and they say you never get too old to enjoy sex. I know, because once I asked my Grandma when you stop liking it and she was eighty. She said, "child, you'll have to ask someone older than me."

Yet the myth persists that older folks are no longer interested in sex. In our practice we often encounter clients who wonder aloud if they are too old for sex or who feel uneasy admitting their enjoyment of it. However, older persons are often more comfortable about their sexuality than their children and grandchildren are about recognizing that the older couples are still sexually active.

Sexologist Sally Schumacher (1973) told a retirement group that "sexual activity can help keep you young; it is a normal function to be enjoyed at any age, if one is in reasonably good health. In fact, one cause of poor health among the elderly is despondency resulting from a loss of interest in life. They feel that everything of value, including physical love, is over for them. So they let themselves wither away."

Our experience has been that older persons' perceptions of being sexually active may not match what younger men and women use for criteria. We have found much less emphasis on sexual intercourse and orgasms among our older female respondents and far more importance given to other forms of sexual expression. This does not mean that sexual intercourse is not an important part of the sex lives of the elderly but, rather, that other sexual behaviors satisfy many of their needs.

Citing a study sponsored by **Consumers' Union**, Brecher (1984) noted that 75 percent of males over the age of 70 years reported that their interest in sex was "strong" or "moderate," as did 59 percent of females in that age category. Largely because of the difference in available partners, half of the males over the age of 80 reported that they were currently sexually active, whereas only 39 percent of the females over 80 made such a report. Older women may have trouble finding willing partners for sexual intercourse—40 percent of the women past 50 who had no husband but had active sex lives reported that they had sex with men who were married to other women at the time. Forty-three percent of women in their seventies who had no husbands reported that they achieved sexual gratification by masturbating.

Still another study of healthy 80- to 102-year-olds found that 60 percent of the men were sexually active, whereas only 30 percent of the women were. The reason for the smaller percentage of sexually active women was not only that they had no partners but also that they had inhibitions about masturbation (Bretschneider 1983).

For the most part, those couples who reported greater activity and enjoyment in their earlier sex lives were the ones who remained the most active sexually in their older years. Good health, energy, and physical activity are much more evident in the current aged population than they were in previous decades. A man or woman of 75 today may have sexual vigor and interest on a level with that found only in much younger persons in 1900. Although today's older persons may be less sexually active than they were at 35 or even 55, most of them are far from having reached the end of their sexual lives.

ELDERLY SINGLE PEOPLE

There are approximately twelve million persons over 65 who are not married. The bulk of them are divorced or widowed (since less than 6 percent of this population have never married). There are four times as many women as men in this category—a plurality of approximately seven million women. Three out of four American wives can expect to be widowed. The median age at which this event occurs is 56 years of age (Balkwell 1981). It is not surprising, then, that most research on aging single persons has centered on widowed women (Lopata 1973).

Widowhood

The death of a spouse and the ensuing bereavement period are difficult for almost everyone. Most studies have focused on the newly widowed even though it is well documented that the bereavement process usually lasts for some time and moves through distinct phases (Bowlby 1980).

Immediately after the death of a spouse, a widowed person feels helpless and often attempts to deny the loss. Apathy is a common emotional reaction, and the turmoil of making arrangements and rearrangements is so overwhelming that it overshadows feelings of loneliness. In time, however, the grief lightens and the widowed person usually begins to reestablish contact with others on a more social basis as he or she becomes reconciled to a new life as a single person. Loneliness, however, continues to be a very common problem for those who are widowed.

Loneliness

One study of over 400 elderly widows in a rural area of South Carolina found that loneliness was tied more closely to unavailability of friends and "neighboring" than to lack of family involvement. Friends and neighbors provided avenues for daily activities such as meetings, shopping, or visiting (Arling 1976). The importance placed on friends and neighbors has its own problems, however. One of our widowed friends who is 85 remarks frequently that she has outlived most of her friends and that many of those remaining cannot be relied on because of their unpredictable health problems.

Another study of older rural widows also showed that social circumstances weighed heavily in determining whether loneliness was a problem. The basic element of social contact that determined loneliness was the quality rather than the number of such contacts (Kivett 1978).

A recent study of widows in the reconciliation stage showed that what appears to be important in this later stage is not quantity of contact but the intimate quality of companionship (Bankoff 1983). A British study concluded that intimacy was found with friends and family who helped by talking to the bereaved about the loss and his or her new status as a single person (Smith 1975). Some older persons report that having pets helps not only to keep them company but also to force them to be more active physically and to take care of themselves in order to meet their responsibilities to their pets.

The ability to adjust to the role of widow and to adapt relationships accordingly may be closely related to Loevinger's level of ego development. In the case of a widow, adjustment may also hinge on her conception of her role in life. If she has seen herself primarily as a wife, the loss of this status may be more traumatic for her than for a woman who has other sources of identity—such as work—to give continuity and meaning to her life.

For men who are widowed, the stress of being alone seems even more dramatic than it does for widowed women. The overall death rate for men whose wives have recently died is 26 percent higher than for married men of comparable ages. There is less than a 4 percent difference between widowed and married women. Remarriage by widowed men cuts their mortality rate by over 50 percent (Helsing, Szklo, and Comstock 1981).

Other studies point to the impact of physical and mental health on whether or not the elderly are lonely. Several studies have shown that real or perceived poor health is an important factor in emotional and social withdrawal (Weiss 1973).

Research on adjustment and loneliness of elderly single persons has revealed the importance of adequate transportation in facilitating their social involvement. Inability to drive, lack of access to a car, and the general unavailability of public transportation are often cited as major factors contributing to loneliness (Cutler 1975).

Living Arrangements

Loneliness seems to be determined to a large extent by where and with whom the older person lives. It has been estimated that between 80 and 90 percent of an elderly person's time is spent at home. Retired persons seem to like to stay in their own homes even when they must live alone, as widows and widowers often do. Two-thirds of those over 65 own their own residences, and an overwhelming majority like living where they do, even though this may contribute to their loneliness (Hansen 1975). There seems to be something comforting about being in familiar surroundings. In addition, many feel that once they give up their own homes, they will give up their autonomy, and they dislike the thought of being dependent.

Approximately 40 percent of the elderly live in older working-class areas near central cities. nearly 35 percent live in the inner cities, and 25 percent live in rural areas (Hendricks and Hendricks 1977). Mobile homes often are favored by those who choose to leave a larger family home, and a few live in senior citizen apartment houses or hotels. For those who desire to stay in their own homes even after they are unable to care for themselves fully, having some form of home care is one possibility. This option is not without problems, however, because of the difficulty of finding and affording competent help. There are various services available to the elderly, such as visiting nurses, Meals on Wheels, volunteer drivers, and so forth; but coordinating the multiple services may be more than the old person can manage. As aging progresses, living independently in one's own home becomes increasingly problematic. When the decision is made to move, one of three alternatives is open—to live with a grown child or with other relatives or close friends, to move to a retirement community, or to enter a nursing home.

Retirement communities in various forms have attempted to meet the needs of the elderly. They have been particularly successful in dispelling loneliness since they facilitate social involvement. Often they also provide transportation, medical care, and readily accessible services and shopping.

Most elderly persons prefer the retirement community as a residence over a nursing home or a relative's or friend's home. Living with children connotes dependence, and children often cannot be relied on for a variety of reasons. Living with others is of growing interest as a possible solution for those who cannot or do not want to live alone. Sharing a home may meet the needs of many older persons who can help each other and provide needed companionship as well. In a study of a program called Share-a-Home it was reported that older persons form "families" not unlike natural families and that this does provide a viable alternative for the elderly (Streib and Hilker 1980).

Institutional care seems to be a last choice for most older persons. Nonetheless, some 5 percent of the 26 million persons over 65 are in some kind of health care facility, including over 23 percent of those aged 85 and over (U.S. Bureau of the Census 1983d, p. 17). Although many older persons need such care, the **nursing home** is usually viewed as "a place to go to die," as one elderly man told us. In a survey of the elderly in southern California, it was determined that no matter how old, in what fragile health, or how poor they were, nearly all the respondents said they would not consider trading their personal independence for the relative security of a nursing home (Eaton 1974).

A recent study, however, has looked at the positive aspects of institutional living and has soundly criticized the notion that institutional care exists only for the benefit of children who fail to support their elderly parents. The study found, for example, that in many instances the contact and support from adults to their aging parents increased after the parents went to a health care facility. Many stresses and pressures on the grown children were relieved just by knowing that their parents were settled and receiving good care that could not be provided by any other means (Smith and Bengtson 1979).

Research findings are nearly uniform in demonstrating high satisfaction among those who have chosen to live in retirement communities. Their morale is higher, they enjoy more informal social contacts, and there is a decrease in withdrawal from life such as the phenomenon of *disengagement* discussed earlier (Streib 1978). Retirement communities first began in the warm climates of California, Florida, and Arizona; these states continue to be favorites of older persons who want to escape harsh winter weather. Such communities are generally located near stores and transportation, and many older persons enjoy the protected atmosphere with its absence of children, traffic, and crime. Medical care, recreational opportunities, and other services may make life easier for those whose energies may be waning.

Some older men and women dislike the age segregation that a retirement community imposes. A study of black aged persons, for instance, found that twice as many of them as whites lived with relatives. They often helped younger family members with child care and were quite likely to take their children and grandchildren into their own homes (Bourg 1975). There seems to be no one formula that will suit every wish. There is a great need for research on types of living arrangements suitable for those who cannot maintain themselves independently but who do not need 24-hour nursing home care either.

INTEGRITY IN AGING

Much has been written about aging gracefully and about what factors go into the manner in which the crisis of aging is met. Most experts agree that being able to look back over one's life and believe that it was worth all the effort is the key. To feel content and at peace with the meaning of life has been described as a **developmental task** of the later years (Erikson 1963). It may strike some readers as odd to discuss developmental tasks for the end of life, but older people keep changing and growing just as younger people do. Gerontologists have noted the strong tendency most older persons have to be autobiographical as they relive past experiences and do a mental "life review." Even their dreams are often of the past, and they enjoy talking about the good old days (Butler 1975).

To work toward a good feeling about the purpose of one's past life seems as profitable a task as any that comes earlier in the life cycle. Erikson has termed the ability to accept the facts of one's life and to face death without fear the attainment of integrity. Self-evaluation and much thought about one's life in the form of reminiscences go into making peace with the past. Since death is inevitable, one aspect of aging with integrity is to resolve fears of one's death. Studies have indicated that most older persons come to this point. Although they are surrounded by peers who die and they have usually made arrangements for their own funerals, their expressed fear of death is lower than for younger people (Kalish and Reynolds 1976).

Shanas (1980) describes today's senior citizens as the new pioneers who are shaping roles for themselves and carving out patterns for survival, all without the benefit of well-traveled paths to follow. One of the respondents in our study of 50-year marriages told us her formula for making peace with her life and acknowledging that she had left a legacy:

> If you have planted a tree, built a house, written a book, and had a child, you have left the world a different place because you have lived. I have done them all and it feels good.

IMPLICATIONS FOR THE FUTURE

Every 24 hours approximately 1,800 men and women in the United States celebrate their sixty-fifth birthday. Between 1980 and 1983, the population over age 85 grew by nearly 12 percent. There are over two million Americans over 85—1 percent of the population—and this age group is growing faster than any other. (U.S. Bureau of the Census 1984i, p. 2). People are not only living longer, they are also enjoying more of the later years because they do not show the effects of aging as soon as previous generations did. Geriatrics specialists believe that this added vigor is based on improved health habits such as moderate but better diet, less alcohol and tobacco consumption, more exercise, and better preventive medical care. The prediction is that the life cycle will continue to increase, causing an even greater increase in the average age of the population.

Spurred by the knowledge that the elderly will be the most rapidly growing segment of the population for the next half-century, planners are beginning to design communities to house older people. Housing will contain special features for security, mobility, and comfort. Emergency call buttons, safety rails, nonslip floor coverings, electric sliding doors, nearby food stores, restaurants, post office branches, and bus service are all to be provided.

As we have noted, women outlive men to such an extent that there has been increased concern with the "femininization of old age." The future may well see the issues of the "old-old" largely becoming the issues that affect women. Not only may there be colonies of older women looking to each other for support and companionship, but they will increasingly find themselves in the role of care givers during the period of declining health and disability of their husbands. Family care for the elderly often translates to "spouse care," which most often means "wife's care" of her husband (Altergott 1984).

Younger family members will also face new problems as more of their members live to an advanced age. A middle-age married couple frequently has four living parents between them, and a growing number of "young-old" persons have one or two "old-old" parents still living. As a result, families must make major adjustments in living and financial arrangements, as well as availing themselves of outside supplemental services. Typically, these services have been geared toward families who are experiencing severe problems caring for their elderly members. However, it is likely that families will seek aid for more everyday problems in the future. Many family policy planners suggest that reallocation of government resources must be explored so that new programs are made available to support the growing elderly population.

Many other countries already have a much greater proportion of older persons than does the United States. Certain policy alternatives that have led to innovations in housing, gradual retirement from work, health care, and financial aid have been implemented in those societies while only discussed or tested in the United States (Nusberg, Gibson, and Peace 1984). Since the majority of voters can look forward to reaching retirement age, interest in expenditures for "social insurance" for old age both from government sources and from the private sector seems to be gaining in importance. Without reallocation of revenue, it will become more difficult to maintain even existing levels of support, given the growing population of elderly persons.

SUMMARY

1. The older population in the United States has grown rapidly since 1900. Improved diet and health care and the decrease in childhood mortality have allowed more people to survive to old age.

2. A positive view of aging has been missing in our society. Instead, research and literature have concentrated on *problems* of aging such as poor health, poverty, loneliness, and impending death. Problems do exist, of course, but there are also millions of elderly persons living satisfying and productive lives.

3. There are many more elderly women than men. For this reason, much of the research has concentrated on women—particularly widows—who often live at the poverty level and are lonely. Most women over 65 who ever worked for pay at all were in the labor force for too short a time to earn pensions. Today, however, as more women are employed full-time, it is likely that the poverty of elderly women will be eased somewhat.

4. Research indicates that adjustment to old age is determined in important ways by adjustment in middle age. The "empty nest" following the departure of children affects both men and women, but for women who have been homemakers, it raises the question of a mid-life "career" change. Men, on the other hand, usually have a continuous work history and do not face the question of "what to do now" until retirement.

5. The postparental years offer new freedom and allow husbands and wives to recreate the intimacy of their early childless years. Menopause is a landmark for women as they end their childbearing years. Sexually, they are still active, although they undergo some sexual changes. All in all, the middle years are generally given high marks by both family-life experts and those who are middle-aged.

6. Becoming grandparents is a significant milestone marking middle age. Most first-time grandparents are in their forties or fifties and do not match the stereotype of the retired, gray-haired person in a rocking chair. There is no one grandparent role that suits all men and women.

7. Grandmothers have received more attention by family experts because there are more of them as a result of predominance of older women and also because women traditionally have been the ones to keep family ties alive. Grandmothers are not all alike by any means, but most report enjoying their grandchildren.

8. Grandfathers typically get more involved with their grandchildren after retirement and when the grandchildren are older. They, too, have varying styles of grandparenting but are often seen as teachers and as the reservoirs of family wisdom.

9. Retirement has been called an identity crisis. It is usually compulsory between the ages of 65 and 70. Many workers still have good years left (over fifteen on the average) and it is predicted that, by the year 2000, this will increase by ten more years. At present, there are some 24 million retired persons in the United States.

10. The necessary adjustments to retirement seem to be greatest in the areas of income, morale, health, and social contacts. Those who are well off financially seem to fare the best. Many people retire as soon as they have the financial security to do so,

but mandatory retirement unfortunately forces most persons to retire without such security.

11. Aside from finances and health, one of the major problems facing retirees is the need to develop rewarding activities to replace work. Those who stay "engaged" in work, community, and with family and friends seem to make better adjustments than do those who "disengage."

12. As men and women begin their postretirement years, the support they give each other and receive from other family members seems to alleviate much of the stress caused by their transition. Most older persons maintain close relationships with their adult children and grandchildren.

13. Well over half of all men and women over 65 are married—many of them for over 50 years to a first spouse. Most research concludes that these marriages are satisfying and contribute to good adjustment in aging. For the most part, those marriages perceived as good in later years were also perceived as good from the beginning.

14. It is possible that good marital adjustment in later years is a factor of the individual adjustments of the husbands and wives. Those who have adjusted well to circumstances over a lifetime may be better able to use the increased time together during retirement to develop a new level of intimacy.

15. Most of the couples over 65 are still sexually active, although their criteria for satisfying sex may be different from what they were when they were younger. For the most part, those who are sexually active as older men and women report that they were active when they were younger as well.

16. Many older persons are single, and these are predominantly women who have been widowed. Poverty and loneliness seem to be their greatest problems. Loneliness is determined to a large extent by where and with whom the older persons live. Retired persons generally like to stay in their own homes even if they must live alone. However, this often cuts them off from social networks and increases their loneliness.

17. Relocating can be stressful for the older person. Living with their children does not suit many, although, of course, there are those who enjoy such a life. Institutionalization is closely correlated with poor health and inability to cope alone. For this reason, it is low in desirability for most older people. Retirement communities seem to be a favored relocation for many, although some do not like the age segregation that characterizes them.

18. Longer life for most Americans means that the structures of families as well as their needs are changing. The implications for the future are varied, including considerations of retirement income, health care, community services, housing, educational opportunities, and family support.

GLOSSARY

Activity theory A theory of aging that emphasizes that later-life satisfaction is keyed to staying active and retaining social contacts. (p. 495)

Cognitive dissonance theory A social-psychological theory that holds that changes in attitudes or behaviors result from the effort to resolve conflicting perceptions. (p. 497)

Developmental tasks Achievements or abilities that are expected to be accomplished by some given chronological age. (p. 508)

Ego development The degree to which one has achieved a sense of one's unique, unified, and durable personhood, capable of relating effectively to others while attending to one's own needs, of making decisions, and of taking responsibility for their outcomes. (p. 500)

Empty-nest syndrome A term used to describe the emotional problems experienced by some parents, usually mothers, when all their children have grown up and left home. (p. 483)

Gerontology The study of aging and the elderly. (p. 490)

Menopause Cessation of the menstrual cycle as a result of aging. (p. 485)

Nursing home A medical care facility for those who need custodial and maintenance care for an extended period of time. (p. 507)

Osteoporosis A weakening of the bones due to lowered estrogen levels in women after menopause. (p. 485)

Theory of disengagement A theory that postulates that the elderly adjust to aging by withdrawing from activities and relationships. (p. 495)

SEXUAL ANATOMY AND PHYSIOLOGY

By the time they are old enough to start school, nearly all children know what a penis looks like. Those who have not seen one in real life have seen penises in photographs or in works of art of one sort or another. Because small children are likely to comprehend the penis only as an organ for urination, the value attached to its construction by either sex may be that it gives boys more (and sometimes better) options for locations and postures for urinating. This conceptualization may persist for a long time without serious critical review of its validity or implications. It may be years before the distinctive differences in construction between the male and female sex organs are understood as contributing to reproduction of the species by making coitus highly pleasurable.

Young children are much less likely to have seen the female sex organs, either in real life or in art. Sculpture and paintings typically conceal or omit the genital cleft. In fact, at least in contemporary American society, females are likely to see breasts as the sexually attractive features of women's bodies and to view their vulvas first as serving an excretory function and only later as having sexual and reproductive functions. Those women who come to see their vulvas as beautiful and sensual may be in the minority, which speaks poorly of the type of sex education girls receive about their bodies.

This appendix is concerned, first, with the sex organs as they are experienced in real life and, second, with the internal glands, ducts, tubes, and other organs that are involved in sexual reproductive behavior and function but are not readily perceivable in day-to-day experience.

FEMALE SEX ORGANS

All that is likely to be visible of the sex organs of a human female in ordinary postures or activities is the *genital cleft* in the *pubic mound* between her thighs. The cleft appears as a furrow or deep crease running from the pubic mound posteriorly, usually appearing as continuous with the furrow between the buttocks in back.

The pubic mound (Latin: *mons veneris*) is a pad of soft tissue covering the pubic arch, the forward-most part of the pelvis (see Figure A.1). At puberty, pubic hair begins to grow on the pubic mound, often concealing the genital cleft.

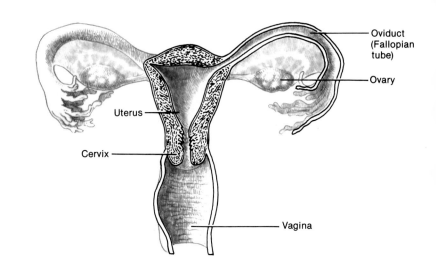

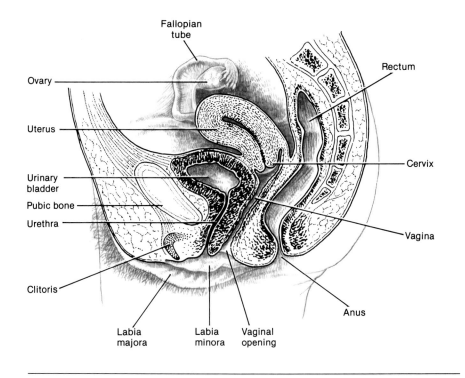

The soft tissue on either side of the genital cleft forms two smooth pillowy structures called the large lips (Latin: *labia majora*). When the large lips are spread apart, the vulva is visible. Women need the aid of a mirror to get an adequate view of their own vulvas.

No two vulvas are quite alike (Delora and Warren 1977, p. 23). Sheila Kitzinger (1983, pp. 41–43) has referred to vulvas as being as distinctive as faces. Betty Dodson (1976) presents representations of the great variety. The coloring of vulvas ranges from pale shell pink to deep plum and is independent of the race of the woman. Parts of the vulva vary in color from time to time in response to both long- and short-term physiological changes. This change is quite normal and should not be cause for alarm (Masters and Johnson 1966, p. 41).

When the large lips of the vulva are parted, the most obvious structure visible is an inner mantle made up of a hood (*prepuce*) over the *clitoris* (the British collo-quialism for which is "the little man in the boat," which seems decorous enough). The hood extends down and merges into the large lips just outside the two little lips (Latin: *labia minora*) that grow directly down from the clitoris.

The tip (*glans*) of the clitoris is usually, but not always, visible. Whether it is or not, its shaft can be felt through the hood as a small stem of erectile tissue. Like nipples or penises, it grows firm in response to gentle massage or erotic thoughts. The diameter of the clitoris when it is excited is usually no greater than that of a small birthday-cake candle. Only the glans can be seen; the shaft is completely covered by the hood. Some women choose to have the opening stretched so that the glans is visible and can be stimulated directly.

There is considerable variation in the reported sensitivity of the clitoris. For a few women, direct contact with the glans is uncomfortable; others report that continued direct stimulation is their most pleasurable erotic sensation. For most there are ranges of pressures, rhythms, and moisture that provide varying degrees of pleasurable feelings. These feelings change with the degree of sexual excitement being experienced at the moment. Because of their changing sensitiv-ities, women who are unable to communicate their feelings and wishes to sexual partners may find that self-stimulation produces orgasms more readily than social sexual activities.

The variation of structure, size, and coloring of the small inner lips of the vulva are responsible for the greatest individual differences in the appearances of vulvas. The lips range from little more than pale pink, semierectile ridges receding from the clitoris into the sides and bottom of the genital cleft to large, fluted, plum-colored, soft "curtains" (called "aprons" in some societies) that may bear a striking resemblance to a cattleya orchid. For some women, the latter configuration may make the small lips protrude visibly from the posterior end of the large lips when they are closed. All these varieties are quite normal, and it should not distress a woman to find that her vulva is quite different from some other woman's, or a man to discover that one woman is remarkably different from another.

At the posterior end of the vulva is the opening to the vagina (Latin: *introitus vagina*). This appears as a small fold or slit since the vagina itself is not actually visible. The entrance must be opened with an instrument (usually a *speculum*) or with the fingers in order to see into the vagina at all. If a woman's vagina has never had anything inserted into it, the entrance has an inner circumference of tissue called a *hymen* (English: maidenhead). This flexible tissue, like the other parts of the vulva, has a variety of possible configurations and thicknesses (Netter 1965, p. 90). Ordi-narily the inner circumference of the hymen is large enough to admit a finger or a tampon; but if it is not, it can usually be gently massaged and stretched until the insertion can be made quite comfortably.

When the inner circumference of the unstretched hymen is smaller than a prospective partner's erect penis (and it almost always is), it can be stretched by gentle massage by first one, then two, and finally perhaps three fingers—ideally, lubricated with vaginal secretions but otherwise with saliva or water-soluble surgical jelly, *not* with oil or petroleum jelly (Van de Velde 1957, p. 169). In those few cases in which a hymen cannot be stretched to a comfortable circumference, a small nick can be made surgically so that it will stretch to the necessary diameter.

The process of stretching a hymen to a comfortable entrance size may take no time at all, or it may take several weeks of frequent genital massage. There should be no great urgency since the stretching process itself ought to be intimate, erotic, and pleasurable. If a partner is involved, knowing him or her well enough to ensure good communication is obviously necessary, as is the willingness and ability of the woman to discuss her sensations and wishes. The period can be a good one for learning to become sexually relaxed together and intimate. If heterosexual intercourse is likely to follow and if pregnancy is not desired, this preparation time is also a good time to discuss contraception.

Between the clitoris and the entrance to the vagina is the tiny slit (Latin: *meatus*) through which urine exits through the *urethra* (urinary duct) from the bladder. It is completely separate from the vagina. Secretions from Skene's gland may come through this passage during sexual excitement, especially if the "Grafenberg Spot" (which lies between the vagina and the urethra) is massaged. These secretions should not be confused with urine. They may constitute much or all of the female ejaculation that has been observed and reported (Ladas, Whipple, and Perry 1982, pp. 56–58).

The part of the vulva that lies between the little lips is called the *vestibule.* It is kept moist by various secretions, some of which come from *Bartholin's glands,* the tiny, barely visible ducts that open near the entrance to the vagina.

The warm, moist vulva may be subject to bacterial infection if it is not kept clean. In the past, unfortunately, confusion of modesty with discretion, and of sexual pleasure with shame, prevented many women from being taught the necessity of, and the techniques for, good hygiene. Van de Velde (1957) recommended frequent washing with clear water, a function best carried out with the use of a bidet. Unfortunately, few North American bathrooms are equipped with bidets, and washing the vulva is likely to be done less conveniently and, perhaps, less hygienically.

Access to air for some part of the day is perhaps more desirable for keeping the vulva healthy or restoring it to health than is frequent washing. Especially if underclothing is not made of natural fibers (cotton, wool, silk, or linen), it is healthful to avoid wearing it all day long and then all night, too. Synthetic materials inhibit air circulation and are less absorbent than natural fibers. A woman who wears tight-fitting polyester pants, all-nylon pantyhose, close-fitting underpants of a synthetic material during the day, and nylon pajamas with close-fitting underpants of a similar material during the night is a prime candidate for vulval infection, which may be difficult to treat (Student Health and Counseling Center 1979).

Although breasts are classed as secondary female sex characteristics, their sexual symbolism and association with erotic sensations in contemporary American society lead many men and women to attach great sexual significance to them. Masters and Johnson (1966, pp. 28–30) reported on the physiological linkage between the breasts, the brain, and the vulvo-vaginal parts. They have observed that women's nipples (and many men's) become erect during the excitement phase of sexual response and that the total volume of the breasts of women who have never nursed a baby increases during the plateau phase. However, only about half of postpubescent females respond to nipple or breast stimulation with definite genital reactions, such as erection of the clitoris and lubrication of the vagina. It is difficult to know the extent to which such responses are affected by the cultural definition of breast play as erotic behavior. A common saying among sexologists is that the most important sex organ in the human body is the brain, suggesting that cognitive and cultural inputs play a powerful part in determining what sensations are perceived as erotic.

MALE SEX ORGANS

The outwardly visible primary sex organs of the human male are the *penis* and the *scrotum*. Penises tend to be more alike in appearance than vulvas, but there are many differences in proportion as well as in size. The smaller the flaccid (soft) penis, the larger proportionately it tends to become when erect (hard) (Katchadourian and Lunde 1972, p. 28). Thus, erect penises tend to be more uniform in size than flaccid penises. For the most men, the size of the flaccid penis changes during each day, responding to such variables as room and body temperatures, fullness of the bladder, degree of sexual excitement, and recency of sexual activity.

The penis is seen as a soft, loose-fitting, elastic tube of skin, covering a structure that somewhat resembles a mushroom with a thick stem and a small cap. In its flaccid state, the body of the penis is quite small, with a consistency roughly similar to that of a relaxed muscle in the forearm. When it is erect, the penile body is larger and has a consistency more like a flexed biceps muscle. The *glans* (Latin for "acorn"; English term: "head") is normally covered by the skin tube when the penis is flaccid but may be partially visible when the penis is erect. The skin covering the glans, called the *foreskin,* can easily be pulled back and caught below the raised ridge (the *corona*) at the base of the glans to expose the entire surface of the glans when the penis is either erect or flaccid (see Figure A.2). In rare cases the foreskin may be tight enough that it needs to be stretched in order to slip easily over the corona.

In the past in the United States, the foreskin has been cut off the majority of the baby boys born in hospitals, in a surgical procedure called *circumcision.* This is classed by the American Academy of Pediatrics as elective surgery for cosmetic, religious, or other personal reasons, although in the past it was believed by many to be hygenic (ICEA *Sharing*, September 10, 1983, p. 3). Masters and Johnson (1966, p. 190) disproved the myth that circumcision had any effect on sexual performance. Because there are many risks (for example, mutilation and septicemia) and no health benefits, many health insurance companies no longer pay for it. It is not covered by the National Health in Great Britain. Among Jews and Moslems, circumcision is practiced for traditional religious reasons. It is not customary in most other advanced societies, with the possible exception of Canada, where it is estimated that as many as half the males born in recent years may have been circumcised, primarily as a result of the influence of customs in the United States (Urion 1977). The physical appearance of a circumcised penis is virtually the same as that of an uncircumcised penis with the foreskin pulled back and caught behind the corona.

The *scrotum* is a thin-skinned pouch that falls behind the penis from a point near its base. The outer skin of the scrotum is typically darker than the skin of the

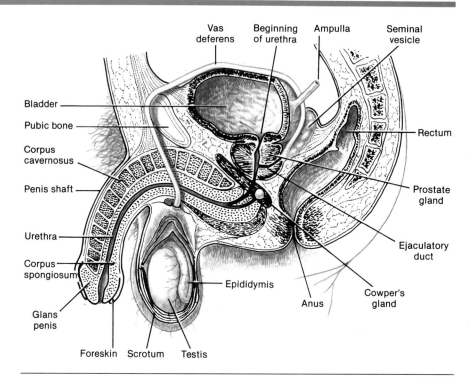

penis, just as the skin of the posterior surface of women's labia is darker than the anterior surface.

The scrotal skin of adult males has sparse, coarse hairs growing from it that are quite different from pubic hair (Katchadourian and Lunde 1972, pp. 27, 66–67). Because a layer of muscles (the *dartos*) just beneath the scrotal skin responds involuntarily to temperature changes, emotions, touches to the skin of the adjacent thighs, and certain stages of sexual excitement, both the volume and the position of the scrotum are in frequent (if not constant) states of change. Fear, anger, cold, stimulation of the inner thigh, or sexual excitement cause the dartos muscles to contract. When that occurs, the pouch shrinks up against the penis and the scrotum takes on a wrinkled appearance. At the other extreme, the skin is smooth, and the testicles may hang as much as three inches below the flaccid penis. When the testicles are drawn up against the penis in sexual excitement, each increases about half again in size; as orgasm becomes inevitable, the testicles rotate within the scrotum (Katchadourian and Lunde 1972, pp. 66–67, 78; Masters and Johnson 1966, pp. 286–293).

Although the two testicles (*testes*) are not directly visible, their shape, size, and position can easily be seen and felt through the scrotum. The testicles are egg shaped, about an inch and a half on the long axis and an inch on the short axis. They contain the tubules in which sperm are produced. One can also feel (but not see the form of) the *spermatic cords* (Latin: *vasa deferentia;* sing., *vas deferens*), which carry sperm out of the scrotum. The testicles and the spermatic cords are extremely sensitive to pressure; anything more than a gentle touch may be very painful.

When the dartos muscles are relaxed, the left testicle hangs lower than the right testicle. This difference in position is normal and is not cause for alarm. The ridge that resembles a seam running from front to back at the center of the scrotum is called the *raphe;* it is a natural formation and should not be mistaken for evidence of injury or vasectomy (Delora and Warren 1977, p. 32). About 30 percent of adult males have nipple erections during sexual excitement, but in the United States, male nipples (unlike female breasts) are not usually considered sex organs, even secondary ones (Masters and Johnson 1966, pp. 286–293).

HIDDEN ANATOMY

Although they may not ordinarily be seen or sensed in other ways, some of the hidden sexual and reproductive organs may affect interpersonal relationships and interactions. Individual experiences with problems in this hidden anatomy should be discussed with a physician on a personal basis, so the discussion here is limited to a few generalizations.

Gonads

Reproductive cells and sexually appropriate hormones are produced by the *gonads.* In women, the gonads are called *ovaries;* in men, they are called *testicles* (Latin: *testes*).

The ovaries are located deep in the abdominal cavity, within the *pelvic girdle,* on either side of the *uterus.* An ovary is about the size and shape of an almond and weighs about one-quarter of an ounce in a young adult woman, although it normally shrinks after menopause. An ovary has perhaps 200,000 tiny capsules (*follicles*), each of which contains an immature egg cell (Latin: *ovum;* plural, *ova*), when a female is born. At puberty the eggs begin to ripen (usually, but not always, one at a time). The egg and its capsule enlarge as it ripens, and at *ovulation* (approximately once every 28 days), a follicle bursts and ejects its egg into the abdominal cavity. The ruptured follicle then changes its form and color and generates the hormones *estrogen* and *progesterone* for a time (Katchadourian and Lunde 1972, pp. 37–38).

The testicles, which are located in the scrotum, have been described briefly above. Cells in the testicles begin to divide and become mature sperm at puberty. Unlike the production of eggs in women, the production of sperm is not cyclic. It is relatively constant, although it may be affected by stress or other factors. Sperm production is estimated at several hundred million per day. The testicles also produce the male hormone *testosterone.*

Female Internal Organs for Conception and Gestation

Humans are born alive (*viviparous*) unlike animals that are hatched from eggs outside of their mothers (*oviparous*); so the period between conception and birth, known as *gestation,* is spent inside the mother rather than in a shell in the outside world.

Even though a newly fertilized ovum is completely separate from the mother, as are the *embryo* and, subsequently, the *fetus* into which it develops, the mother has a protective "nest" that enables her to carry the growing baby within her. It also permits an intimate exchange of hormones, nutrients, chemicals of other sorts, viruses, and some disease germs.

The *uterus* is the nest into which a fertilized ovum is deposited if it is to develop normally. In its nonpregnant state, the uterus is about the size of the woman's fist (perhaps slightly smaller in a woman who has never been pregnant). One may be able to feel the firm, muscular structure of the uterus through the lower abdominal wall, behind the pubic bone, deep inside the pelvis. It also may be felt at the upper end of the vagina, where its neck (Latin: *cervix*) can sometimes be reached deep within. It may feel somewhat like the head of an erect penis.

There is a central opening (Latin: *os*) in the cervix through which a baby emerges during labor. This opening in the cervix is also the passage through which menstrual fluid is expelled. The volume of the uterus usually increases 64-fold or more during a single-fetus pregnancy, and it increases in weight from a couple of ounces to somewhere around two pounds. Immediately following delivery, the process of *involution* begins to return the uterus to near its prepregnant size within remarkably few days.

The flexible passage that connects the cervix to the vulva, the *vagina* (a Latin word meaning "sheath") has both sexual and reproductive functions. Its walls are quite elastic. It is not rigidly structured like the throat or the ear canals but is a soft, stretchable, and (except for its "anchors" at either end) easily movable connector between the cervix and the doughnut-shaped muscle (the forward half of the *pubococcygeus* muscle) that closes it off from the vulva. The sexual function of the vagina is to provide lubrication so that a penis can be inserted comfortably through the muscular entrance. Its reproductive functions are to confine the ejaculated sperm to the vicinity of the cervical opening and to connect the uterus and the outside world and close off the abdominal cavity. During birth, it serves as the passage through which the baby travels between the uterus and the outside world.

The egg released by an ovary is picked up by the *fimbria,* or fingers, of one of the fallopian tubes (Latin: *salpinx;* pl., *salpinges*). These ducts extend from the upper ends of the uterus (one at either side) to the vicinity of the ovaries, sometimes embracing the ovaries but not attached to them. When an egg erupts from an ovarian follicle, it seems to be attracted by a force that is not yet well understood to the fimbria of one or the other of the tubes. (It has been demonstrated that an egg from one ovary can migrate through the abdominal cavity to the tube on the other side (Katchadourian and Lunde 1972, p. 38). The egg travels through the fallopian tube to the uterine cavity. If sperm are present in the tube, fertilization is likely.

Sperm ejaculated into the vagina swim against a current of fluid at the rate of one inch per hour; once they reach the uterus, they may be moved along much more rapidly by contractions of its walls. Sperm deposited directly at the entrance of the uterus can easily fertilize a viable egg within an hour, especially if they are sped on by contractions of the uterus during the woman's orgasm (Katchadourian and Lunde 1972, pp. 101–102).

Once an egg reaches a sperm (or vice versa), fertilization can take place—even outside of the body. Any sperm that have been deposited within the previous three days or so may still be ready and waiting for the egg when ovulation occurs; otherwise, the egg will probably be in a suitable condition and location for newly injected sperm to cause fertilization for the next four days or so (Katchadourian and Lunde 1972, p. 88) (see Figure 10.2). A fertilized egg is called a *zygote*.

If conception occurs, the fertilized ovum enters the uterus and implants on the uterine wall, and pregnancy occurs. At the time of ovulation, the lining of the uterus is in an optimum condition for *implantation* (*nidation*) of the mass of cells, clustered in a spherical shape, that has resulted from fertilization. By the tenth to the twelfth day after ovulation, this mass has burrowed firmly into the *endometrium* (the lining of the uterus) if it is going to be retained, with the result that the menstrual period expected about the fourteenth day after ovulation is unlikely to occur (Katchadourian and Lunde 1972, p. 106). If sperm are not present in the fallopian tube or uterine cavity, fertilization does not normally take place. If implantation of a zygote does not occur, the endometrium sloughs off and is expelled, along with the unfertilized ovum, as menstrual fluid.

Unfortunately, it is possible—although unlikely—for an egg cell to be fertilized and attach itself outside the uterus to create an *ectopic pregnancy* in a tube or even elsewhere in the abdominal cavity. The fetus does not survive in such cases, and the consequences for the mother may be serious (Katchadourian and Lunde 1972, p. 40).

Male Internal Genital Organs

The male genital organs, like those of the female, have both sexual and reproductive functions; unlike those of the female, however, they are inextricably combined from the male's perspective. His reproductive function, in other words, *is* his sexual function.

A female may engage in coitus to orgasm without any reproductive consequences during more than two-thirds of her reproductive life span (usually arbitrarily put at 30 years); a male's coitus can create pregnancy at any time of the month for virtually all of his adolescent and adult life. A female may ovulate without any sexual activity or any sexual sensation at all —indeed, with no awareness of her fertility and without ability on her part to control ovulation. A male can, on the other hand, if he wishes, induce the ejaculation of viable sperm almost any time, and it is unlikely that even an involuntary ejaculation ever goes unnoticed.

Two functions make sex/reproduction possible for males: the erectile function and the ejaculatory function. The erectile function facilitates the delivery of semen to a location that makes fertilization of an egg possible; the ejaculatory function delivers the sperm.

It is possible by means of special techniques or devices for a man to insert his penis into a woman's vagina without his having an erection. However, the natural collapsed state of the vagina and the elasticity of its normally closed entrance muscle make it mechanically more efficient and substantially more pleasurable for both partners if the penis is rigid. Erection makes it possible for the penis to push through the opening far enough that the corona is beyond the pubococcygeus muscle and can massage Skene's gland from inside the vagina and pull the little lips against the clitoris in the vulva.

Although erections may be caused by a variety of kinds of stimuli, the overwhelming majority of them are purely involuntary responses to sexual excitement. A male can voluntarily expose himself to erotic stimuli or intentionally think erotic thoughts that result in an erection, but he cannot simply decide to have an erection (Kogan 1973, p. 38). For that matter, he also cannot decide *not* to have an erection.

Mechanically, erections occur when more arterial blood is being pumped into the three spongy cylinders that make up the body of the penis than the amount of venous blood that is escaping. The result is analogous to the inflation of a football or a device for taking blood pressure. A system of valves (called *polsters*) permitting blood to flow freely from the arteries to the cylinders (two *corpora cavernosa* and one *corpus spongiosum*) are held nearly shut when the penis is flaccid; when the polsters relax in response to a spinal reflex, the penis "inflates" until similar valves controlling the outflow of blood to the veins balance the internal pressure at a degree of erection or flaccidity (Kogan 1973, p. 38).

The ejaculatory function of the male genital organs is to deliver sperm from the testicles to the outside of his body. The sperm, produced by cell division in approximately a mile of tiny tubes coiled within the testicles, are collected within a larger tube (Latin: *epididymis*) at the back of each testicle as they mature. The upward end of this latter tube becomes the *spermatic cord* (Latin: *vas deferens*), which carries the sperm through the lower abdominal cavity to the *seminal vesicles* on either side of the bladder. The spermatic cord can be felt through the thin skin of the scrotum. It is at that point, if a person is sterilized by vasectomy, that the spermatic cord is cut and tied. In the seminal vesicles, fluid is added to the sperm, increasing the volume and diluting it.

The prostate gland completely surrounds the urethra where it leaves the bladder to pass urine through the penis to the outside. A valvelike structure in the urethra between the bladder and the prostate closes off the urethra at a point during sexual excitement so that it is not possible for a male to urinate when he is sexually aroused.

As a man's sexual excitement increases, a clear mucoid secretion is exuded through the urethra. This clear preejaculate neutralizes any acid in the urethra and serves to lubricate the glans penis. Most of it probably comes from *Cowper's glands*, located at the base of the prostate (Masters and Johnson 1966, p. 211).

At orgasm the testicles are drawn up by a contraction of the scrotum, followed by contractions of the various tubes leading to the seminal vesicles; the strong muscles of the prostate begin a series of rhythmic contractions (with eight-tenths of a second between each peak) that draw the semen from the seminal vesicles through ejaculatory ducts into the prostate, and then eject it under considerable pressure, together with more fluid added by the prostate, into the urethra. Once in the urethra, the semen is moved along by a number of muscles that maintain sufficient pressure to expel it with some force at first—the first spurt sometimes being propelled several inches— with the pressure diminishing until the system is empty (Masters and Johnson 1966, pp. 212–213).

THE LOVE PROFILE

We decided to try to find out what people meant when they said, "I love you," or "I don't love you any more." We collected literally hundreds of personal statements about the meaning of love and definitions from literary works, and especially from John Alan Lee's (1976a) scholarly research. By eliminating statements that appeared to be conceptual duplicates, the number of items was reduced to 144 that implied the presence or absence of specific behaviors, thoughts, or feelings of a person with reference to love. Next, we presented 220 subjects with the 144 items arranged as a true-false test. The subjects included a range of ages, religions, social classes, ethnicities, and races; but it cannot be claimed that they were representative of any particular large population. However, we later validated our findings on a much larger population.

By means of a statistical device called *item analysis,* we were able to eliminate 87 items from the scale because they showed no significant relationship to the scoring patterns of the subjects; we later dropped 7 additional items to pare the number down to an even 50. At the suggestion of sociologist Milton Bloombaum at the University of Hawaii, we applied a technique called *smallest space analysis* to the remaining items and discovered that they separated into six quite distinct clusters.

We had confirmed Lee's finding that love means different things to different people, using a population a quarter of the way around the world from his and a different research procedure. We named the clusters of items after Lee's six primary and secondary love styles since they clearly fell into those patterns. It was then a simple step to construct scales for each of the clusters. Each of the six scales became an operational definition of a different kind of understanding of love: storgic, agapic, manic, pragmatic, ludic, and erotic. From the acronym for these scales we named their combined scores "The SAMPLE Profile" (Lasswell and Lasswell 1976).

In a replication of the SAMPLE research, Terry Hatkoff (1978) used a different procedure (called *factor analysis*) to study about 1,200 profiles from several different regions of the United States. She also reached the conclusion that the six dimensions were discrete. We had cooperation from colleagues in the United States, Canada, South America, and Europe so that by the time we completed our research, literally thousands of subjects had contributed to the validation of our scale.

In our research and that of colleagues using "The SAMPLE Profile," the Greek and Latin names used by Lee were retained. For simplicity's sake, however, in 1980, in *Styles of Loving: Why You Love the Way You Do,* the six basic styles of loving were relabeled with popular colloquialisms. Storgic became *best friends;* agapic was translated as *unselfish;* manic was called *possessive;* pragmatic now was *logical;* ludic became *game-playing;* erotic was called *romantic;* and "The SAMPLE Profile" was retitled "The Love Profile" (Lasswell and Lobsenz 1980).

"The SAMPLE Profile," which follows, demonstrates clearly that there are many possible definitions of love. A person responding to these six scales may compare his or her profile with the profiles of others. Such a comparison can help a person know what kinds of behaviors make another feel loved. Not only are the behaviors that are intended to convey love not always perceived as loving by others, but often they may convey an unintended message of "I don't love you."

∎ Instructions for Responding to the Sample Scales

Each of the following questions is to be answered "true" or "false." Answer the questions in consecutive order, and *do not skip or omit any of them.* Some may seem ambiguous or out of your experience, and you may need to let your pencil choose your answer for no special reason. Remember that the test is a research instrument and that the profile was validated by the testing of thousands of men and women. It may help you to answer the questions if you think of your ideal or most memorable love relationship rather than a current one. Finally, complete the questionnaire independently of your classmates or your partner. There are no "correct" or "incorrect" answers to the items. Mark your responses on the answer sheet below or on a facsimile of it.

Answer True or False

	T	F
1. I believe that "love at first sight" is possible.	☐	☐
2. I did not realize that I was in love until I actually had been for some time.	☐	☐
3. When things aren't going right with us, my stomach gets upset.	☐	☐
4. From a practical point of view, I must consider what a person is going to become in life before I commit myself to loving him/her.	☐	☐
5. You cannot have love unless you have first had *caring* for a while.	☐	☐
6. It's always a good idea to keep your lover a little uncertain about how committed you are to him/her.	☐	☐
7. The first time we kissed or rubbed cheeks, I felt a definite genital response (lubrication, erection).	☐	☐
8. I still have good friendships with almost everyone with whom I have ever been involved in a love relationship.	☐	☐
9. It makes good sense to plan your life carefully before you choose a lover.	☐	☐
10. When my love affairs break up, I get so depressed that I have even thought of suicide.	☐	☐

11. Sometimes I get so excited about being in love that I can't sleep. ☐ ☐

12. I try to use my own strength to help my lover through difficult times, even when he/she is behaving foolishly. ☐ ☐

13. I would rather suffer myself than let my lover suffer. ☐ ☐

14. Part of the fun of being in love is testing one's skill at keeping it going and getting what one wants from it at the same time. ☐ ☐

15. As far as my lovers go, what they don't know won't hurt them. ☐ ☐

16. It is best to love someone with a similar background. ☐ ☐

17. We kissed each other soon after we met because we both wanted to. ☐ ☐

18. When my lover doesn't pay attention to me, I feel sick all over. ☐ ☐

19. I cannot be happy unless I place my lover's happiness before my own. ☐ ☐

20. Usually the first thing that attracts my attention to a person is his/her pleasing physical appearance. ☐ ☐

21. The best kind of love grows out of a long friendship. ☐ ☐

22. When I am in love, I have trouble concentrating on anything else. ☐ ☐

23. At the first touch of his/her hand, I knew that love was a real possibility. ☐ ☐

24. When I break up with someone, I go out of my way to see that he/she is OK. ☐ ☐

25. I cannot relax if I suspect that he/she is with someone else. ☐ ☐

26. I have at least once had to plan carefully to keep two of my lovers from finding out about each other. ☐ ☐

27. I can get over love affairs pretty easily and quickly. ☐ ☐

28. A main consideration in choosing a lover is how he/she reflects on my family. ☐ ☐

29. The best part of love is living together, building a home together, and rearing children together. ☐ ☐

30. I am usually willing to sacrifice my own wishes to let my lover achieve his/hers. ☐ ☐

31. A main consideration in choosing a partner is whether or not he/she will be a good parent. ☐ ☐

32. Kissing, cuddling, and sex shouldn't be rushed into; they will happen naturally when one's intimacy has grown enough. ☐ ☐

33. I enjoy flirting with attractive people. ☐ ☐

34. My lover would get upset if he/she knew some of the things I've done with other people. ☐ ☐

35. Before I ever fell in love, I had a pretty clear physical picture of what my true love would be like. ☐ ☐

36. If my lover had a baby by someone else, I would want to raise it, love it, and care for it as if it were my own. ☐ ☐

37. It is hard to say exactly when we fell in love. ☐ ☐

38. I couldn't truly love anyone I would not be willing to marry. ☐ ☐

39. Even though I don't want to be jealous, I can't help it when he/she pays attention to someone else. ☐ ☐

40. I would rather break up with my lover than to stand in his/her way. ☐ ☐

41. I like the idea of my lover and myself having the same kinds of clothes, ☐ ☐
hats, plants, bicycles, cars, etc.

42. I wouldn't date anyone that I wouldn't want to fall in love with. ☐ ☐

43. At least once when I thought a love affair was all over, I saw him/her ☐ ☐
again and knew I couldn't realistically see that person again without loving
him/her.

44. Whatever I own is my lover's to use as he/she chooses. ☐ ☐

45. If my lover ignores me for a while, I sometimes do really stupid things ☐ ☐
to try to get his/her attention back.

46. It's fun to see whether I can get someone to go out with me even if I ☐ ☐
don't want to get involved with that person.

47. A main consideration in choosing a mate is how he/she will reflect on ☐ ☐
my career.

48. When my lover doesn't see me or call for a while, I assume he/she has a ☐ ☐
good reason.

49. Before getting very involved with anyone, I try to figure out how com- ☐ ☐
patible his/her hereditary background is with mine in case we ever have
children.

50. The best love relationships are the ones that last the longest. ☐ ☐

Tally

1. Circle the item number of each T
(true) response on the scales to the
right. Write the number of true responses per column in the space
provided.

S	A	M	P	L	E
2	12	3	4	6	1
5	13	10	9	14	7
8	19	11	16	15	17
21	24	18	28	26	20
29	30	22	31	27	23
32	36	25	38	33	35
37	40	39	42	34	41
50	44	43	47	46	
	48	45	49		

Total circled true
in each column

Sample Profile

2. Now fill in the histogram below by shading in each column up to the number of circles
counted in the corresponding column in item 1, above.*

*We acknowledge the contribution of John and Betty Burnham in designing
"The Love Profile" scoring device. It is reprinted by their permission.

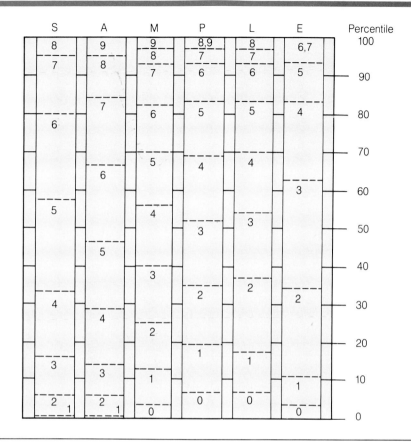

	S	A	M	P	L	E	Percentile
	8	9	9	8,9	8	6,7	100
			8	7	7		
	7	8	7	6	6	5	90
		7	6	5	5	4	80
	6						70
		6	5	4	4	3	60
	5		4	3	3		50
		5	3				40
	4		2	2	2	2	30
		4		1			20
	3	3	1		1	1	10
	2 1	2 1	0	0	0	0	0

3. The percentile reading on the right of the profile shows the proportion of the population that has less of the indicated trait than you have.

$$
\begin{array}{lll}
\textbf{S} & = \text{Storge} & = \text{“Best friends”} \\
\textbf{A} & = \text{Agape} & = \text{“Unselfish”} \\
\textbf{M} & = \text{Mania} & = \text{“Possessive”} \\
\textbf{P} & = \text{Pragma} & = \text{“Logical”} \\
\textbf{L} & = \text{Ludus} & = \text{“Game-playing”} \\
\textbf{E} & = \text{Eros} & = \text{“Romantic”}
\end{array}
$$

EVALUATING YOUR RESPONSE

You will have some "true" answers in several or, probably, all of the scales. Usually, however, two or three scales will have more "true" answers than others. If you have high percentiles in several or all scales, it does not necessarily mean you are a better lover—nor does scoring low in several or all of them mean that your love is in scarce supply. Instead, this is more likely to be a reflection of your test-taking attitude. Some people agree with a statement if it is true only once in a while, but others never answer "true" unless the situation always or almost always exists. The latter person is inclined to be analytical and cautious. Your relative lower and higher percentiles are more significant than your absolute scores.

The percentile numbers at the right side of the profile (page 527) indicate the percentage of respondents whose profiles have been studied who had lower scores than yours. After the first few hundred profiles had been recorded, these percentages became quite precise, and they have shown no tendency to change in subsequent studies.

We have never seen anyone who had "true" responses in only one column and none in the others. In other words, there are probably no "pure" types. Instead, most people define love as some kind of combination of several or all of the six definitions. There is an enormous number of possible combinations.

Your SAMPLE profile shows graphically how your scores on each of the scales blend into your own distinctive definition of love. There is no good or bad combination of scores for a person. Neither is one definition of love more or less mature than another.

Most people automatically assume that their own definitions of love are correct or at least "normal," although they may understand that others disagree with the meaning they give it. Social psychologist Daryl Bem (1970) has termed such unchallenged beliefs *zero-order* ones. He points out that it is unlikely that a fish recognizes that it is wet since it has known nothing else. If you have never been challenged before by the fact that there are as many definitions of love as there are people, you may want to defend the idea that yours is "real love" and someone else's is only infatuation or immature love. However, each person's definition of love is probably as correct to him or her as yours is to you. It is easy to see why, with such zero-order beliefs, partners with quite different styles of loving may have considerable difficulty in communicating their caring to each other.

The following descriptions of the various love styles are in alphabetical order to emphasize that no one style is more important or more popular than another. Further, they do not develop in a sequence from romantic to companionate love, as many believe.

It is important to understand that people do not always *behave* in accordance with their definitions of love, even though they believe that people who are in love *ought* to behave that way (just as persons sometimes tell lies even though they believe firmly that people ought not to lie). Most persons, although their *feelings* tend to overpower their intellectual definitions of whether they are in love, still expect others who are in love to behave according to those intellectual definitions! Such inconsistencies are not uncommon, and most people are able to rationalize their violations of their own rules.

Best Friends

The S (storge) scale on the SAMPLE profile is defined operationally by agreement with items 2, 5, 8, 21, 29, 32, 37, and 50. They indicate a belief that love is slowly growing to care for another person. Building a marriage on a close association over a long period of time together is usually important to those who define love in this way. A relatively high score on this scale (above the seventy-fifth percentile mark) usually indicates a belief that two people who eventually grow to love each other should have begun their relationship by being friends. The initial rapport that Reiss (1980, pp. 126–132) mentions in his wheel theory clearly is seen as an important element by those who share this definition of love. Rapport is based on mutual sharing; thoughtfulness; enjoyment of time spent together; and, particularly, having a great deal in common. Physical attraction and sexual urgency are seldom of paramount importance in "true love" for those with this definition.

Usually, persons whose ideas of love have a strong measure of best-friends meaning believe that sex ought to be deferred until after love is established (whether they defer it themselves or not)—that it should be a natural extension of the deep caring that has grown over time. These persons believe that people in love ought to acknowledge personal decisions of their partners as appropriate even when they do not agree with them. They believe that lovers ought to respect each other's personal dignity and do not see differences of opinion or arguments as threatening to a love relationship. They believe that those in love should not be anxious about a partner's temporary absence on business or on a family visit, for instance, and they also believe that lovers should have a concern about their partner in whatever they do, even if they do not always understand the partner's behaviors.

Those with high best-friends scores usually have difficulty accepting the idea of ending a relationship once it is well established. They expect feelings of caring to continue. In our clinical practice we have observed more than one person with a best-friends definition who after a divorce could not fully accept that the relationship was over and that the ex-spouse could think of marrying someone else. One ex-wife continued to ask for help with her income tax and for aid in choosing a new car. It made no sense to her that even though she and her husband were divorced, they should cease to be close friends.

Those with low scores probably distinguish "being in love" as very different from being "best friends." They may have difficulty accepting that people who feel as those with the best-friends definition do are really in love. They may see such comfortable friendship as "liking" but not as loving, although one with the best-friends orientation clearly knows the difference.

Game-Playing

This conceptualization of love is identified by high scores on the L (ludus) scale (items 6, 14, 15, 26, 27, 33, 34, and 46). The items that cluster together to define this conception of love operationally suggest that true love is viewed as risky, exciting, uncertain, and possibly fleeting. This definition assumes the need for strategies to keep the interaction interesting for both partners. Clinical experience indicates that one who holds this definition believes that "being taken for granted" is one of the worst things that can happen to lovers and might not even believe that one who treated a partner like an old shoe—comfortable and pliable—was truly in love. High scorers often feel that in "true" love partners must be self-sufficient and relatively independent. They do not believe that partners who are "clinging vines" are truly in love. They expect partners to make few demands on each other, not to dwell on one another's "responsibilities." True love is never dull. They expect lovers to provide novelty and adventure for each other. Pleasure in love should come from keeping a partner's interest high by playing the role of lover like a game. To them, a good lover must keep his or her partner somewhat uncertain about the future. As one four-time divorcee said, "When my marriage gets gray, I get out." High scorers on the game-playing scale tend to believe that sex, like love, should be adventuresome if a couple is *really* in love. Sex that is routine is viewed as boring by such persons, and they are more comfortable with the idea of withholding sex on occasion to heighten a partner's anticipation than with keeping to some kind of schedule. If both partners have high scores on game-playing, they usually can keep each other happy. However, if one partner does not define the give-and-take of a good game as being in love, there can be serious difficulties. High-scoring game-players are likely to believe that their partners no longer love them if they are "bored."

Persons with low scores on game-playing may not understand the apparent lack of commitment of game-playing lovers. How can it be love, they reason, if one needs a challenge all the time? A very low scoring woman might be embarrassed or annoyed if a few years after her marriage she received a bouquet of roses from a forgotten lover with a note: "I have missed you too long. Meet me for lunch at noon on Thursday." If she showed up at all (and she most likely would not), she would feel suspicious and probably annoyed. A high-scoring woman, on the other hand, would be excited. If the man turned out to be her husband instead of an old boyfriend, she would feel very much loved.

Logical Love

Relatively high scores on the P (pragma) scale (items 4, 9, 16, 28, 31, 38, 42, 47, and 49) indicate a definition of love that is epitomized in rationality. The items that cluster together here suggest that those who understand love in this way believe that the core of every true love relationship is the practical capability of the partners to satisfy each other's goals, values, and wishes. Relationships that do not enable the partners to solve these practical problems are seen as foolish or are simply "infatuations," "physical attractions," or "immature"—they cannot be "true love."

When a person with a pragma definition thinks about people falling in love, he or she thinks first of the candidates' qualifications. To logical definers, people should not even contemplate "unsuitable" persons as potential lovers. They consider it a waste of time for a person to get involved with anyone who fails to meet their standards. They think it is appropriate to have a series of filters through which a potential partner must pass. The idea of love at first sight makes no sense to those who understand love in this way. They reason that too many questions about the future remain unanswered until two people have done considerable self-revelation. A person with a high score on this definition of love believes that when a partner has failed to live up to his or her promise or has changed in some important ways, there may be a serious question of whether love can still exist.

A young woman we know who had a very high logical score married the "perfect" partner—one of the top students in an Ivy League law school, handsome, a good dancer. He entered a prestigious law firm, and the two of them were delighted at his immediate professional and financial success. But when their first child was born, her expectations of him as a father were unmet. His career absorbed his energy, and he refused to spend as much time with her and their son as she wanted. How could he love her, she thought, if he was unwilling to spend time with her and their child? Deciding he did not, she filed for divorce. Persons with high scores are more likely to weigh problem areas in their relationships against the good that exists. However, if something truly important cannot be worked out to meet their standards, there may be serious difficulty.

Clinical experience with persons who have high logical scores has shown that sex is not necessarily either more or less important than any of their other values. Although they tend to be "sensible," they are often far from calculating sexually. Finding the right partner allows such a person to relax, enjoy the relationship, and care deeply. A warm feeling of contentment comes from thinking about the partner's successes and suitability.

Persons with low logical scores may have difficulty believing that those with high scores can really be in love. Such "love" seems much too calculating and businesslike to them. The idea of measuring love by personal standards is foreign to one whose feelings of love are kindled by very different kinds of stimuli.

Possessive Love

Those with high scores on the possessive or M (mania) scale (items 3, 10, 11, 18, 22, 25, 39, 43, and 45) define being in love as an anxiety-producing relationship. As with the game-playing definition, they believe that a boring relationship is probably not love. In this case, however, uncertainty about the future of the relationship is considered threatening rather than exciting. Those with high possessive scores often expect Tennov's (1979) "limerent" experience for partners. They believe that people in love should alternate between peaks of euphoria and valleys of misery and depression ("The course of true love never runs smoothly"). A person who has a great deal of this quality in his or her definition needs much reassurance from a partner in the form of words, actions, time, and energy devoted to showing love.

A person with a possessive definition of love believes that no one should have to share a partner with anyone or anything else. People who are truly in love are "naturally" jealous. High scorers are likely to be emotional and intense in everything they do; loving is no exception. They see passion as a natural part of being in love and may even believe that the absence of such highs and lows is an indication that one is *not* in love. They usually stress the importance of sexual exclusivity in the relationship, and the thought of a partner's even entertaining the notion that another person might be attractive may be quite unsettling. In fact, such persons may conclude that a relaxed, easygoing partner is not really in love since he or she does not get upset over such matters.

Those with low possessive scores usually do not relate a partner's jealousy to being in love and may even conceptualize it as a "sickness." One woman who scored low on the possessive scale described how the man she had been dating told her at lunch one day that he thought they had been seeing each other too much and should spend some time alone. He said he would call her in a week or so. She was puzzled because he had been very intense in the relationship and had appeared not to want her out of his sight. She agreed to his plan, however, as it seemed reasonable to her. She was awakened at 6:00 A.M. the next morning by her frantic lover asking, "Where were you last night? Who were you with?" He had tried to call and, when she did not answer, had alternated between worrying and feeling unloved because she had so easily agreed to their bargain. In her opinion, however, he was acting "crazy" rather than "in love," as he claimed.

Romantic Love

Eyes meet across a room and love at first sight occurs. For high romantic scorers the event is perfectly understandable. The variables on the E (eros) scale, which cluster to form this definition of love (1, 7, 17, 20, 23, 35, and 41), indicate that love is expected to include a strong physical and sexual component, an urgency, and an enmeshing of the partners.

Our impression of composite traits of persons with high romantic scores is that they expect people who are in love to be "on cloud nine." A total emotional interest is immediately in full bloom. The partner is expected to remember the moment of the first meeting in minute detail. High scorers expect their partners to want to know everything about them and to spend every possible moment with them. Great sexual urgency is expected, although it may not be acted out for various reasons. Sometimes, however, it propels the partners into marriage to legitimize the urgency.

Persons with high romantic scores usually expect their partners—and themselves—to be monogamous. If they become sexually involved with any persons other than their partners, they are likely to decide they have fallen out of love.

One who has a high romantic score expects a lover to commit himself or herself to a relationship quickly from the sheer intensity of the initial attraction. There is a conviction that "love conquers all"—that nothing else is really important as long as love lasts.

Many people believe that most love relationships begin with this definition and either dissolve when the partners' ideals are not met or "mature" into love under a different definition. Although this high level of passion would be difficult to sustain 24 hours a day for 50 years, and ideal images may not always be met, many couples who have been together for decades report that they still retain both their relationship and their romantic definitions. They still have moments between changing diapers and paying bills when smoldering passion and romance are again ablaze. On the other hand, scholars have blamed our high divorce rate on the "romantic fallacy"— the unlikelihood that the illusion about the partner can last more than two or three years. Those with low romantic scores tend to view candlelight and roses, or sentimental cards, as silly or juvenile. They see such things as being unrelated to "real" love, which they, of course, define in their own way. As one woman who scored very low said: "Roses fade, poems on cards are someone else's words. Give me a man who comes home every night, fixes the appliances, and gets along well with my folks. That's love."

Unselfish Love

It is characteristic of unselfish love that a person with high scores believes that true love is shown by caring more for one's partner's welfare than for one's own. The items that cluster to define the A (agape) scale conceptualization of love (12, 13, 19,

24, 30, 36, 40, 44, and 48) are centered about great respect and concern for one's partner's welfare and comfort. Love is not martyrdom but, rather, an unconditional caring, nurturing, giving, forgiving, and understanding of one's partner. One who is in love according to this definition is expected to experience love as a feeling of satisfaction and reward from knowing that the lover's needs are being met.

Clinical impressions show that high scorers enjoy sex to the fullest when the partner is pleased. As surprising as it may seem to some, mainland American men are more likely to incorporate this meaning into their definitions of love than are women (although in Hawaii the reverse was found to be true, and Lee reported that this definition was virtually nonexistent in Canada). The reasoning behind higher scores for men on the mainland may be that culturally, in the United States, men have been taught that loving women involves taking care of them. Perhaps in the future our changing sex roles will lead to a more equal feeling of responsibility for the other's welfare between men and women (Hatkoff 1978).

Those with high unselfish scores usually do not view being in love as an exchange. They neither expect nor particularly want equality. True love for them is giving, forgiving, and doing what is best for one's partner. Benjamin Franklin's wife, Deborah, is someone who acted as we might expect of a person who holds this definition. While her illustrious husband interacted with intellectuals and politicians and charmed the royal courts of Europe, she managed their printing business and raised his illegitimate son. She apparently asked and got little in return for her sacrifices of love.

Persons with low scores on the unselfish scale fail to see behaviors characteristic of high scorers as having much to do with love. Instead, such actions and feelings may be viewed as anything from "parenting" to "being a doormat"—definitely not as a "turn-on." Those with low scores sometimes accuse high scorers of being masochistic. The accusers, of course, are quick to offer their own definitions of love, which typically are devoid of the unselfish quality.

COMPATABILITY OF DEFINITIONS

Whether the partners' definitions of love are similar is less important for the success of their relationship than that each understands what actions the other expects as evidence of being loved. Because many people find it difficult to say what they need to make them feel loved, their partners may be left to guess what to do. Most commonly, what they do is to behave according to their own expectations—doing what would make *them* feel loved. But this is one place where the Golden Rule does not necessarily apply.

In our experience in using "The SAMPLE Profile" in counseling hundreds of couples, whether married or not, partners who define love similarly or whose different definitions are accepted by each other find their relationships more satisfying than do those who are rigid in their different expectations—usually because each assumes there is only one type of "true love"—one that conforms to his or her own definition. Clear communication, respect for each other, and acceptance of the differences among people as a desirable fact are all much more important than demanding that a partner's definition of love be the same as one's own.

In a study carried out in California and Colorado, it was discovered that couples in marital therapy who spent six sessions examining their respective definitions of love showed a greater positive change in their marital adjustment than did a matched control group of couples whose therapy did not include that experience (Underwood 1979).

As Lasswell and Lobsenz (1980, pp. 195–196) state in *Styles of Loving:*

> The most important thing in life is to love someone, the second most important thing in life is to have someone love you, and the third most important thing is for the first two to happen at the same time . . . [and] that each partner understands what makes the other feel truly loved.
>
> Despite the paucity of research into the parameters of love, most studies point to the same single factor as the critical one when a person decides whether or not he or she is in love: the belief that we understand the emotional motivation behind a partner's words and actions and that he or she similarly understands ours.

HANDLING FAMILY FINANCES

Certainly there are lots of things in life that money won't buy, but it's very funny— Have you ever tried to buy them without money?*
Ogden Nash

For many couples, near the top of the list in rating their marital compatability is the matter of how money is earned, how it ought to be spent, and how much (if any) should be saved. Many marital therapists report that money problems are among the most frequently heard complaints in unhappy marriages (Kilgore and Highlander 1976; Feldman 1976). However, disagreements about the management of money are likely to be seen by therapists as most often symptomatic of a couple's problems rather than as an underlying marital difficulty.

Money often provides a concrete focus for the expression of more general conflicts over values, goals, and lifestyles. For some people the accumulation of money may be the only clearly countable measure of their worth to their families or to the world; for others it may be a measure of their self-sufficiency, which in turn may be seen as an index of their freedom.

Couples in every income bracket are represented among those who name finances as an arena for conflict. In fact, for many couples who disagree over how money is managed or who have difficulties in making financial ends meet, real lack of income is not the issue at all. High-income couples are often in as great distress over financial disagreements as are low-income couples. Conflicts about money may surface when credit purchases have exceeded the ability to pay them, creating a real shortage, but even the difference may be symbolic of other problems. The conflict may be about who is in charge or who is to blame that there is too little money.

The welfare system in the United States assures that no one need starve to death or go without shelter. About one family in five (19.2 percent) received some form of welfare in 1984 (U.S. Bureau of the Census 1985k, p. 2). Nearly everyone's dissatisfactions with income have to do with *wishes* rather than *needs;* wishes to drive a car rather than ride a bicycle or take a bus, wishes for more stylish clothing, wishes to eat in expensive restaurants rather than to cook at home, wishes for a landscaped single-family home in the suburbs rather than an apartment near work, wishes to work three days a week rather than six, and so forth ad infinitum.

Financial planning bogs down when one or both partners have strong emotional associations with money or its use. For example, one or both may use money emotionally, either as a weapon with which to control the other or as a way of compensating for inadequacies, guilt, or feelings of being unloved. Such emotional associations are common; most of them probably come from parental responses to the loss, gifts, misuse, finding, or theft of money during the subject's childhood. Psychologists believe that the way an individual handles money is a good indication of how he or she functions in other more general ways (Feldman 1976).

One family-life expert has stated that whatever is wrong with a couple's money management is a direct reflection of what is wrong with their marriage. Conversely, the ways many couples learn to agree on a money plan—taking into consideration their individual idiosyncrasies, goals, values, strengths, and weaknesses in financial affairs—can be a clue to how they manage the other differences in their lives (Bergler 1970).

Messages received from parents about money are often anxiety-ridden. Ideas about who should handle the checkbook and pay the bills often involve deeply entrenched notions of rightness or wrongness learned from the ways such matters were discussed and handled in the parental home. Often the issue in the present is not which partner is the most competent or who has the most time to perform these tasks but whether one's father and/or mother seemed to attach emotional value to one or the other of them doing it.

There appear to be two opposite views about managing finances—"Live for today, it's only money" versus "Save for a rainy day." Both are perfectly good financial philosophies, and each has its loyal adherents. However, when two people who hold opposite views live together in an economic partnership, they often interpret the resulting disagreement as "trouble." If one believes in the short-term philosophy that there will always be more money coming in and hence it is better to buy now before inflation causes prices to go up, but the other is a long-range planner who wants to put money aside and believes in cash-only purchasing, then conflicts and arguments are virtually guaranteed. Couples who differ in their ideas of how money should be handled obviously must come up with a comfortable compromise to bridge their different philosophies if they want to avoid constant bickering.

Since money has such different emotional and practical meanings for each person, it becomes crucial for husbands and wives to explore their meanings together and to be as mutually aware as possible of what money means to them. All the financial planning in the world cannot compensate for poor communication on this score.

Sometimes couples fail to recognize that their differences about saving and spending policies or consumer values may actually be a practical advantage for both of them. If they can reframe their situation, they may come to recognize that, in the long run, the spendthrift is better off married to the person who squirrels away savings than to another spendthrift, even though the two spendthrifts might never argue about money. The squirrel, too, may enjoy some "treats" and valuable experiences as a result of being married to a spendthrift, even though they argue. Complementarity of financial philosophies may mean that both partners will live better lives than they would if their philosophies were identical.

It seems extremely unlikely that any two persons will have precisely the same material values on every count. The extent to which their disagreements are seen as normal and inevitable and not as grounds for assaulting the partner's character or dignity will probably determine their compatibility level.

It is unlikely that anyone can state positively that any two goods are precisely equal; even the courts normally resolve such issues by reducing the value of the goods to money. Is $100 in a safe-deposit box equal to an afternoon spent in a beauty salon? An afternoon on water skis? On snow skis? On a fishing boat? Dinner out at a fancy restaurant? A pair of shoes for one special occasion? A bet on a horse with good odds? It becomes clear that the search for agreement on such questions cannot end with anyone's authoritative answer but depends on the establishing of each partner's rights to accept or violate the other's personal values.

Psychiatrist Edmund Bergler (1970, pp. 18–19) has given these guidelines for what he believes is a normal, healthy approach for couples to use in dealing with money matters:

1. Money is a means to the end of acquiring things one desires; do not make it an end in itself.
2. The fear of being taken advantage of in money matters should not be greatly out of proportion to the actual threat. One does not allow oneself to be taken advantage of, of course, and will be careful to avoid this.
3. One tries to make money as well and as much as one can. However, the process should not sacrifice health, love, hobbies, recreation, or contentment. Money should never become the center of one's life.
4. Spending money for necessities and for some luxuries should be taken for granted; it should not take a surgical operation to get a person to put a dollar in circulation. Hoarding of money, if a predominant motif in one's life, is a neurotic trait.
5. The phrase "I cannot afford it" is a simple statement of an objective fact and should never reflect a defensive way to punish oneself or another.

Sound financial management and planning are necessities in today's world. A financially successful couple operate just as a fiscally sound business does. Both husband and wife should be involved in their finances, just as two business partners would be; marriage is in fact very much a business partnership. It has been estimated that the average older middle-class couple in the United States has passed well over $1 million through their joint hands during their married life (Porter 1975).

Although inflation has slowed down in recent years it is still a concern for American families. Seventy-three percent of those polled cited the high cost of living as the most important problem facing them and the nation. The cost of food alone—which most families agree is an item not easily pared down—has escalated dramatically since 1970 (Gallup Poll 1981).

LIFE-CYCLE CHANGES

Family finances are, of course, a constantly changing phenomenon. Young couples usually have only themselves to take care of and are usually both employed. In fact, it is rare today for a young wife with no children not to work outside the home. Eighty-two percent of childless married women age 25 to 34 are in the labor force (Rawlings 1978, p. 23). Sometimes, of course, young couples have very little money even though both partners are employed because they are in the beginning phases of their occupations. One or both of them may still be going to school, and they may be living in what has been described as "genteel poverty."

Young adult couples often are "broke" but know that things will get better as they accumulate assets and work their way up the occupational ladder. Usually their friends are at the same stage of life, and although they may often wish for the level of living once provided by their parents, they are not pessimistic about their current financial state. Some young couples manage to save money, to buy material items for their homes, and to afford a limited amount of travel and entertainment. Arguments over finances most often arise over how to resolve the earning, spending, and saving patterns brought from their families of origin; over issues of cash flow (income versus outgo); and over how to use credit.

Pay increases average about 8 percent a year for both blue- and white-collar employees and have continued to increase at that rate for 20- to 29-year-olds for almost half a century. This may not seem like a great deal, but it means that a person who earns $16,200 at age 22 will earn $27,764 by age 29 (Stein 1984).

Generally, the longer young couples postpone having children, the better off they become financially. The birth of children changes budgets dramatically. Not only do many women quit their jobs to stay at home with their young children, so that their incomes are lost, but also the expenses of having a child, of increased family needs, and possibly of the need for different housing all combine to change the financial picture.

A Gallup poll reported that a two-person household in 1981 said they needed $200 per week on the average to subsist; a three-person family needed $250; a four-person family needed $277; and a family of five or more could not get along on less than $300 per week. Food for an average couple ran $52 per week, for three persons $64, for four persons $77, and for five or more persons $98 (Gallup Poll 1981). These costs have increased substantially since then.

Very few couples with growing families manage to save much during their child-rearing years. It has been estimated that it takes about three times an average earner's annual salary to provide for a child until he or she is eighteen years old. For most families, this translates to something between $90,000 and $100,000 for each child. The cost of providing college educations for their children is seen as prohibitive by many parents. Others report that they borrow against their homes at this time when they would actually prefer to build their equity in them or to put money away for their own retirements.

One reason that the cost of raising children has escalated so dramatically in recent years is because the cost of housing has risen so high. The single most expensive part of raising a family is providing extra rooms as the family grows. The National Association of Realtors revealed that the average price of homes sold in 1984 was approximately $72,000—an increase of 5 percent from 1983 (*Pomona* [CA] *Progress-Bulletin,* May 8, 1984, p. 6).

Once their children are launched, some couples are able to spend more of their income for their personal needs and wishes unless they have aging parents who are becoming dependent at about the same time. This, unfortunately, is often the case. As a latent effect, this experience sometimes causes middle-aged couples to give increased thought to retirement and to investing wisely so that they will not be financially dependent on their children in their own old age. They may begin to save again instead of using more of their incomes for luxuries, for travel, and for long-postponed projects such as redecorating homes and buying new cars. A couple may even sell the family home and move to smaller or more convenient quarters.

Many women who have been full-time homemakers seek outside employment once their children are grown. The addition of their incomes to their husbands' (usually peak career) earnings means that the average middle-class, middle-aged couple today has more income than at any previous period in their married lives.

Lifelong instruction and encouragement to save money make it imperative that couples with surplus income review very carefully any investments to make certain that the taxes on the income from them do not reduce that income (adjusted for inflation) to a net loss. A clear example of such a misfortune would be the investment of $1,000 at 8 percent simple interest in a year in which the inflation rate is 8 percent or more. Not only is the $1,080 principal at the year's end worth the same as or less than $1,000 at the beginning of the year, but the investor must pay $20 to the Internal Revenue Service (if he or she is in the 25 percent tax bracket) and often about $8 to the state tax collector. The investor is poorer at the end of the year than at the beginning! Passbook savings accounts that pay 5 percent or 5½ percent interest leave the saver unable to buy as much at the end of a year as at the beginning if the inflation rate is 14 percent—the actual loss to the saver is about 9 percent of his or her investment, before taxes, which will increase the loss to 11 percent or more. These realistic figures need to be weighed carefully against sentimental pressures to save money in banks.

Finally, in retirement and old age, couples usually cut back on their spending to habits that resemble those of their newlywed days. Many draw on pension plans provided by their jobs; some have set up their own retirement plans in order to put away income that has not yet been taxed against the day when they believed that their retirement incomes would put them in a much lower tax bracket. They now can draw out this money as income for their retirement years. Unfortunately, as inflation rates continue to be high, many such plans have reduced the purchasing power of the money saved to far below the value of the original investment.

Most retired persons receive Social Security benefits that are paid each month upon retirement and, up to a fixed maximum, are based on the amount paid into the system over the working lifetime.

The average woman will outlive her husband by about ten years (U.S. Bureau of the Census 1979d, p. 11). For this reason, she especially should know about the couple's economic status, be certain that they both have wills, and know the provisions of her husband's will and any estate plans. If they do not have wills, each partner's right to the property held by the other depends on the state in which they have legal residence at the time death occurs.

In community-property states, a married person's property can be either separate or community. If it is separate, it is usually property owned before the marriage or received as a gift or by inheritance during the marriage. Community property includes all other holdings acquired during the marriage or separate property that is commingled (converted into community property, as in a joint home purchase). When a spouse dies, the survivor in such a state automatically retains his or her half of community property. Each can make provisions in a will to leave this half to anyone he or she pleases, including the spouse. If there is no will, some state laws entitle the surviving spouse to the entire estate. In other states, if there are children, they and their surviving parent are awarded specified fixed shares.

In states that have common-law marital property systems, the surviving spouse does not necessarily own a half interest in all property acquired during the marriage by both spouses. In these states all earnings and property accumulated by either spouse during the marriage may be his or her separate property. Often the husband has earned the most, although, as more and more women enter the labor market, this picture is changing somewhat. On the other hand, property or money acquired or inherited by a woman may become a "nest egg" rather than being dissipated in current living costs. This, plus various income and inheritance tax laws, bankruptcy laws, and a distribution of insurance beneficiaries strongly favoring women, results in the majority of inheritable wealth in such states being held by women (Alexander 1975).

If a will is left, most states provide that neither partner can totally exclude the other. What share of the estate is awarded automatically in the absence of a will depends on state law. If no will is left, the surviving spouse's rights to the estate may depend on how many other heirs there are. For instance, in Missouri the surviving spouse is entitled to the entire estate if there are no other heirs but to only half if there are children, grandchildren, parents, brothers, sisters, nieces, or nephews (Alexander 1975).

In Oregon a surviving spouse is entitled to his or her late partner's entire estate if there are no children or grandchildren and to half if there are children and grandchildren. Arkansas adds the qualification that the couple must have been married for more than three years for this to apply, and Oklahoma specifies that a deceased husband's entire estate will be left to his wife only if it has been acquired by their "joint industry" (Alexander 1975).

It is probably safe to say that very few couples at any stage of the life cycle ever believe they have enough money. As income increases and tastes change, what was once considered a luxury easily comes to be viewed as a necessity. It is very difficult to retreat financially and to have to give up what one has become accustomed to having. Since there is nearly always some conflict between what people earn and what they spend (or would like to spend), couples—from the newly married ones to the retired—who have no consensual plan for money management are almost certain to face disagreements.

FINANCIAL PLANNING

Wouldn't it be wonderful to have an intelligent, flexible, workable plan for spending and saving money? Such a plan would calculate the amount available to spend and would keep records of what was spent. By knowing these two basic facts, couples could assess their financial status, plan for the future, and avert mishaps that might plunge them into financial difficulties. They could channel their cash flow into areas that would provide greater benefit to them than their immediate, often impulsive spending patterns might produce.

Budgeting

This sounds good until the name of the plan is mentioned—*budgeting*. The idea seems too restrictive to many, too complicated or boring to others. Yet there are certain things in life that one should do, and a budget seems to be one of them unless both partners are extremely good at managing money without one. Most people are not.

Budgeting can be very simple: what one earns from any source (spendable "take-home" income) should equal or exceed the outlay. This is called the principle of *cash flow*. A budget should be simple and flexible. It will probably need to be revised fairly often to keep up with changes in earnings, unexpected changes in lifestyle, changes in tax laws, and needs to save. Unfortunately for those who abhor such work, budgets do necessitate record keeping. In our experience in working with couples over the years, however, in marriage there is often one record keeper, even if one or both may dislike such a chore.

In a marriage in which both partners like to keep records, they may work cooperatively or take turns; if neither likes to do this job, they may be in trouble. They, too, may need to work cooperatively or to take turns. Some couples use a service that keeps track of their cash flow by computer for a moderate monthly fee. For couples who argue over budgets or who will not keep one at all since neither partner enjoys the record keeping, such a service may easily pay for itself by helping to avoid the pitfalls of emergency borrowing or excess interest charges on credit accounts.

For couples who want to set up a budget for themselves, there are several agreed-on steps to take. (1) It is important to get an accurate reading on fixed expenses based on past records (check stubs and old paid bills can give a good idea of past expenditures). These include those items that come due regularly, such as rent (or house payment), utilities, debt repayments, insurance, transportation costs, food, and household supplies. (2) These may then be subtracted from the fixed income.

Some fixed expenses are *nonnegotiable;* that is, there is nothing one can do to change them because they are set and controlled by someone else. Examples of these are home mortgage payments and property taxes; Social Security, state, and federal income taxes deducted from one's salary; insurance required by law or by lenders; minimum charges for water, power, and garbage collection; business, professional (if necessary for one's work), and driver's licenses; union, trade association, or professional association dues; sewer, street lighting, fire protection, and other assessments by cities or counties; any kind of interest, lien, garnishment, penalty, or fine that can cause one's eviction, imprisonment, or the loss or confiscation of one's property. The only alternatives to paying such minimums, dues, licenses, and taxes are to sell one's home, change one's occupation, declare bankruptcy, or (in some cases) petition for relief from the state legislature.

There is a necessary minimum for survival in some of the expenses called "fixed," such as food, rent, medicine, and medical care. That is, one can survive on a minimum diet, but cutting food expenditures below that minimum could lead to malnutrition. Fortunately, most people have enough income to fix their food budgets within a range that provides for more than a borderline starvation diet. Many can provide a good diet at less cost than they are currently spending, however, simply by planning their grocery shopping and menus more carefully and by paying more attention to nutritional values of foods, seasonal variations in price, and the relative costs of quantity buying (or sometimes of cooperative group purchasing of commodities that store well and are easily divided).

A federal interagency committee of the United States government devised a formula based on the Department of Agriculture's economy food plan that reflects the different consumption requirements of families based on their size and composition, the sex and age of the head of household, and farm or nonfarm residence. It was determined that families of three or more persons spend approximately one-third of their incomes on food. Any income lower than three times the cost of a minimum adequate diet for families of three persons was considered to be at or below the poverty level (U.S. Bureau of the Census 1984j, p. 31).

Persons living below the poverty level are usually eligible for a variety of cash and noncash forms of assistance with their finances. Noncash assistance may be in the form of food stamps, free or reduced-price school lunches, Medicare or Medicaid, public or subsidized housing, and other less common kinds of public assistance. Of the 79,108,000 households in the United States in 1979, 27,190,000 (about 34 percent) received one or more forms of government aid. Of those, 6,925,000 were households living below the poverty level (just under 9 percent of all households). About three-quarters of the households receiving noncash benefits, then, had incomes above the poverty level—for example, 595,000 households receiving food stamps had incomes of over $15,000 in 1979, as did 177,000 households living in publicly owned or subsidized housing (U.S. Bureau of the Census 1981c, pp. 9, 12, 15; see also U.S. Bureau of the Census 1983f).

The number of people living in poverty had risen to 35.3 million persons by 1983, or 15.2 percent of the U.S. population (U.S. Bureau of the Census 1984a, p. 1). An even larger percentage of the population of the United States has need for some form of public assistance. At the same time, government program funding has decreased in proportion to the need. For many families hard decisions have had to be made to cover fixed-cost items on their income.

In 1983, families in which the husband/father was the sole wage earner had a median income of $21,890; if the wife/mother was in the paid labor force part-time or more for any part of the year, their median income was $32,110; single-parent families (no husband present) had a median income of $11,790. If the family had a college-educated householder, its median income was $40,520; if the householder was a high-school dropout, it was $17,469 (U.S. Bureau of the Census 1985j, pp. 1, 35).

The good news is the prediction that the number of families with incomes of at least $30,000 a year in 1980 is expected to double by 1995 so that about half (compared to one-third in 1980) will exceed this figure (Hammond 1984). The bad news is that increase in expendable income has (except in instances when there have been effective price controls) almost invariably been accompanied by increases in the price of consumer goods. The effect of this process is called *inflation*. Persons with fixed incomes lose purchasing power with each rise in prices.

When the fixed-cost items on the budget have been accounted for, any funds remaining can be designated *discretionary expenses*. If no money is left after expenses, then either cuts will have to be made or more income will have to be produced. It is obviously difficult to cut fixed expenses, although sometimes moving to less expensive housing, planning meals more carefully, or trying to cut utility bills (particularly telephone bills) can make the difference between a balanced and an unbalanced budget.

However, no one can live happily for very long without some of the items included in the usual list of discretionary expenses: entertainment, personal allowances, clothing, replacement of household items or furnishings, personal care, cleaning, costs associated with pets, vacations, newspapers, magazines, various contributions—and, for some persons, alcohol and/or tobacco. Each couple and each family will have its own list of items that it considers important to its own health and/or happiness.

Income: Yours/Mine/Ours

Two-paycheck couples divide themselves into three money management approaches. They either (1) pool both incomes and draw from the total for every expense; (2) pool part of their income while reserving some for each partner's separate use; or (3) separate their incomes and contribute individually to joint expenses (Bank of America 1980).

Each option has its advantages and disadvantages. Having one joint checking account is probably simpler; many couples believe that it represents the cooperative and trusting nature that they want their marriage to exhibit. There is a problem of keeping the account straight when two people are writing checks, but, even so, for a large proportion of couples this is the preferred plan.

Pooling part of each partner's income while reserving part for individual needs has the advantage of letting both know who earned how much and from what source; it also allows each partner to provide for his or her joint and separate needs with funds that are designated appropriately. The drawbacks are that three bank accounts are needed, and the responsibility for the joint account can be as complicated as for those who pool all funds.

The third option, separating incomes and contributing individually to joint expenses, is least popular because many couples believe that it implies a lack of trust and commitment. It does, however, have the advantage of preserving each partner's financial identity, which can be important for business reasons (expense accounts or taxes). A considerable amount of bookkeeping can be involved if each partner pays half of each bill or needs to reimburse the other when a bill runs over his or her agreed-on portion. On the other hand, it may provide for a greater awareness of the equitability of personal expenditures.

Personal and Child Allowances

Enough should be included in each family budget (depending on resources) for each person to have some spending money that need not be accounted for. Whether one is an adult or a child, it is unpleasant to have to ask for every penny one needs or to feel guilty each time one spends any money on a personal item. Too often the one who keeps the family books becomes the family "comptroller" who doles out the money on request. This is a situation reminiscent for most of a parent-child relationship in which the child (in this case, the wife, the husband, or a child) must justify money spent. Having an amount of pocket money that is allocated for personal items and does not need an accounting adds to one's feelings of independence and responsibility.

Children can be included in some financial discussions so that they develop responsibility and come to understand the family's cash flow. By the age of five or six a child can understand that a dime or a dollar buys an item; an eight- or nine-year-old can plan ahead, saving today's accumulated dimes for tomorrow's purchases. By middle childhood boys and girls are ready for an allowance—a fixed amount each week determined by their needs, the family's resources, and their peers' allowances (Helms and Turner 1981, p. 234). When children first begin to manage money, they often make mistakes—spend it "foolishly"—just as some adults do. Child psychologists recommend that children not be given advances or gifts unless parents use these extra amounts to teach them about borrowing and credit (Williams and Stith 1980).

Some children earn their spending money. Other families believe that all spendable income is the family's and that children should get their fair share. These are two diametrically opposed points of view, each of which has its adherents. Each produces children with distinct views about money. Children who receive fixed allowances—amounts paid each week that are not connected with working—learn that family resources are shared. Such a child does assigned tasks as a member of the family and may be paid for extra jobs that ordinarily would cost the family extra (such as washing windows, washing the car, or doing yard work). The allowance is not withheld as a disciplinary measure because these parents do not believe it is wise to pay children to be good.

The other philosophy about money is that if children are paid a fixed amount, no matter what they do, they will not learn to work for a living. This approach emphasizes that children have certain tasks that are expected of them (such as keeping their rooms clean and picking up after themselves) but that they must earn any money they need. Tasks are posted with amounts of payment for each; children are expected to work for all amounts they are given. Problems may arise if children choose *not* to do a needed family chore and forgo the income.

Although few studies have been done to determine which method is the best, it is generally agreed that children who share in family resources and do not have to work for their money view money differently from children who earn the money they spend (Williams and Stith 1980). Some parents believe that since the family is the training ground for later life, giving children what they need—rather than making them earn it—is doing the children a disservice. Other families believe that income belongs to all family members and that the proper "work" of children is going to school and growing up: a child should not have to enter the marketplace at such an early age. Since there is no research to back up one side or the other, parents are left to their own sentiments on this issue.

Banking

Most people think of banks, credit unions, and savings and loan associations as safer places to keep their money than storing it at home in cash. That is true, of course, but these institutions also have other important functions. Perhaps the most important for most people is that they facilitate the transfer of money from one person or company to another without the actual cash being carried or sent. Banks always offer checking (sometimes called *commercial*) accounts, as do many credit unions and savings and loan associations.

Writing checks (orders to your financial agent to pay from your account) is not only more convenient and safer than carrying or mailing cash, but also provides a clear record of payment (and, when endorsed, constitutes a receipt by the endorser) and a set of memoranda from which an accounting of expenditures can be readily constructed, provided you use a bank that returns cancelled checks.

Some banks and savings and loan associations pay interest on either the daily amount on deposit in a checking account or on the monthly minimum. Many have several kinds of service charges for maintaining checking accounts, with formulas based on minimum or average balances and/or on the number of checks written. Sometimes it is possible to arrange for a checking account that provides that checks written for more than one's balance are automatically covered by a loan from the financial institution. The interest charged for such an arrangement often runs as high as 21 percent on an annual basis.

Banks, credit unions, and savings and loan associations make their money primarily by lending or investing the money of their depositors. It is obviously important for these institutions to lend the money available to them at interest rates higher than those they pay to the people who have accounts with them and to be sure that the money they lend will be repaid. Loans are *secured* by mortgages or liens on property, by savings accounts, or sometimes by the guarantee of a cosigner that the loan and its interest will be repaid. Since it usually takes a few days to process a loan, anyone who foresees that necessity should apply in advance.

Savings accounts are usually thought of as investments rather than as convenient ways to store money. Savings accounts may be simple passbook accounts to which money may be added or from which it may be withdrawn on demand (an institution may require 30 days notice for withdrawal, although few exercise this in normal times). Passbook accounts draw minimum interest. A higher rate of interest is usually paid on long-term accounts, which sometimes require that the money be kept on deposit for several years if the full interest rate is to be paid, but this is not always true. Investors can choose the kind of account that best serves their personal needs.

Family members must decide whether they want their accounts to be joint or separate. Joint accounts have the advantage that withdrawals can be made or checks written by any of the depositors. This can be particularly advantageous in case of death, disability, or unavailability of the person who might otherwise have all the funds in his or her personal account. In the case of a minimum-balance checking account, a joint account might more often avoid service charges or draw interest than would two or more separate accounts. The chief disadvantage of joint accounts lies in keeping track of the balance in the account, particularly if more than one checkbook is in use.

Banks and savings institutions offer the convenience of safe-deposit boxes, which are useful for storage of valuable papers such as wills, lists of insurance policies or the policies themselves, birth and marriage certificates, military papers, deeds, and an inventory of personal valuables. Some states require that safe-deposit boxes be sealed on the death of any box owner until the decedent's estate has been settled in probate court. In such states it would be wise for a couple to have "his" and "hers" boxes if both have substantial property or valuables (for example, birth certificates, wills, passports, bonds, cash, insurance policies) to which they may need access within a few months.

Savings

There are long-range items that must be planned for in a budget. For instance, families with cars must plan for repairs and for upkeep. The same is true for household appliances and for home and yard maintenance. People sometimes get sick and need medical attention and drugs. There may be emergencies—a needed trip to visit an ailing parent or even to attend a funeral. There may be a layoff at work or an accident that damages the family car. Emergencies, as well as postponed purchases (furniture, cars, vacations, remodeling, children's college educations) all call for advance planning.

For these and other reasons, many families feel an urgency to put part of their income away for a rainy day. When possible, it is wise to plan a budget so that it includes regular savings as a financial cushion and for larger-item purchases. It is usually recommended that 10 percent of spendable income be saved as a ready reserve for emergencies. In addition, many couples put aside another 10 percent for purchases they wish to make in the future (major items, vacations, holiday purchases).

Most couples who manage to save find it easier and more systematic to set aside a fixed amount each pay period. Some employers have payroll deductions to help employees to save regularly. In today's inflationary climate, most couples keep only a minimum of their savings in low-interest accounts—just enough so that they can have ready access to them in an emergency.

Some financial consultants recommend that savings should accumulate until they cover three to six months of expenses. Most suggest that this cash be converted to a money-market (or similar) fund rather than deposited in a simple passbook savings account. Many money-market funds require an initial investment of $1,000, but there are those which accept less. Interest on these accounts fluctuates with the market and, in one particularly unstable year (1981), varied from a high of 16.52 percent to a low of 8.03 percent. The average is, however, almost always above what would have been earned in a passbook account. Money-market funds are usually available to be drawn out at any time so they may have a real advantage over savings certificates (like Treasury bills) that may pay slightly more interest but tie up the money for a period of time with a penalty for early withdrawal. Some people buy U.S. government bonds or municipal bonds. Many of the latter have the advantage of earning tax-free interest.

Investments

In contrast to savings, which put aside spendable income to be used when needed, investments remove income for longer periods, allowing assets to grow into even greater assets. Of course, the money can be removed by selling the investment properties, but the philosophy of investment is that the money will be left to grow on a long-term basis. The stock market is a favorite way to invest, judging by the report that one in seven Americans holds some stock. However, since the stock market fluctuates and is affected by general economic conditions, very few people who invest small amounts of savings make a great deal of profit. Some financial experts warn that it is not advisable to buy stocks if the money used is the only savings held.

In considering an investment, the watchwords are *safety*—if you cannot afford to lose some of what you have put in the market or the investment property, it is not safe enough for you; *growth*—the monies invested should be in investments that will increase in value; and *yield*—there should be some return on money invested (such as interest paid). The investment must be balanced: a safe investment that has no potential for growth or one that has a high yield but is very risky is not thought to be sound for those who have no base of security in other types of savings.

For most families, the biggest investment that they will make—and in inflationary times usually one of the best—is in *buying a home*. The price of housing has risen approximately by a factor of seven since 1946 on a weighted nationwide average (Stein 1984). In a manner of speaking, because regular mortgage payments are required, they amount to enforced savings. Many couples would be tempted to spend their money in other ways, but with the penalty of losing their homes if they default, they easily acquire the habit of "saving" in this manner. Before assessing a home mortgage plan as savings, however, prospective buyers should look carefully at how quickly their equity (the fraction of the home that they actually own) will grow and compare that with the number of years that they intend to retain the property. Many plans do not provide the homeowner much equity for several years, with nearly all of the monthly payments going for interest. However, the fundamental value of a home as an investment is in its value to the family that lives in it.

Unlike monthly rental payments, monthly payments on a house go partially toward an equity in the home, partly toward interest on the loan for the mortgage on the house, sometimes partly toward property taxes, and sometimes partly toward insurance, the last two depending on the mortgage agreement. Since interest and taxes are presently allowable as deductions on income taxes, there is a saving at this level, too. In fact, many financial experts advise that owning a home with a mortgage is one of the best tax shelters available. In the first years of a mortgage, almost all of the payments are applied to the tax-deductible interest and only a small percentage to the principal.

Mortgage payments may be for a fixed amount for the duration of the mortgage so that they do not fluctuate as rent is likely to do. Taxes and insurance, of course, vary with the costs of living and with the increased value of the property. Some banks and loan companies currently offer variable interest rate mortgages that change the rate of interest the borrower pays on the loan according to the current rate of interest. In a graduated payment mortgage, young couples borrow at a low interest rate when their incomes are likely to be lowest, and the interest rate rises as do their incomes, at least theoretically, over the years.

Financial experts suggest a formula for the amount that couples can safely invest in a home. Two to three times the couple's yearly income is considered a reasonable figure. Obviously, other expenditures may make this amount unfeasible for some couples, but some may find that the amount is ridiculously low in relation to the price of property in the locale. For example, the median price for a home in Louisville or Detroit is about one-third the median price in San Francisco or Los Angeles and one-half the price in Washington, D.C., or San Diego. Although salaries are often higher in cities where homes cost more, they are not always two or three times higher.

Most couples buying homes seem to base their decisions on how large a down payment they can afford (the requirement to secure a loan usually is from 10 to 20 percent down) and what monthly payments they can afford. Since most couples spend an average of one week's take-home pay for rent each month, this gives them some idea of what they can afford for a monthly payment on a home. However, since the prices of single-family houses and condominiums are rising much faster than rents, for several years many families will be unable to buy homes, even though currently there are distinct advantages to owning one as an investment.

It is important, of course, to investigate local trends in housing prices and mortgage foreclosures before purchasing a home. The same general rule for all investments holds for real estate: buy low and sell high. When the market for real estate drops in an area, as it did in some localities in 1985, it is possible for the size of one's mortgage to exceed the market value of one's home, so that a homeowner who faces a forced sale may be faced with the alternatives of foreclosure, bankruptcy, or the loss of savings equal to the decline in value, none of which is desirable.

Insurance

There are six major types of insurance: life insurance, property insurance, automobile insurance, medical and hospital insurance, liability insurance, and disability insurance. Insurance is a protection against future needs for money resulting from illness, a death in the family, an accident, a disability, a theft, or a loss of any other kind.

Life insurance is for the purpose of providing dependents with a sufficient amount of money to help them adjust in the event that a major part of their income ceases, as happens with the death of a breadwinner. The purpose of life insurance is to provide a continuing income until the survivors can manage to recuperate and to take care of themselves. It is important that both men and women who have children have such coverage. A wage earner needs to leave his or her family protected, and a homemaker should have coverage to pay someone to take over household and child-care responsibilities. It is generally advised that women take out policies on their husbands and that men take out policies on their wives in keeping with their estimates of needs and of the family budget. If each insures the other's life, neither will have to pay inheritance tax on the amount left as they might if it were left as a part of the estate.

The two major types of life insurance policies are *term insurance* (a policy written for a specified term–usually five years—and then reissued as needed) and *ordinary life insurance*—either that which one pays for throughout one's lifetime and which is collected by survivors, or that which has a specified period for payment. Term policy rates are based on the age of the insured and have the advantage of lower rates for young persons. Ordinary—or whole-life—insurance builds up a cash value that can be tapped by cashing in the policy or borrowing against it. However, the difference in premiums between term and ordinary policies is substantial. For example, Bankers Security Life Insurance Society would sell $100,000 worth of term insurance to a 25-year-old man for approximately $200 per year the first year, rising to approximately $225 the fifth year. The same man would pay over $1,000 for each year for the same coverage with ordinary insurance (*Changing Times,* March 1981, p. 31).

It is advisable to shop for life insurance policies since not all insurance companies give the same coverage for the same rates. In considering employment, it is wise to explore the fringe benefits, which often include various kinds of insurance and usually offer very competitive prices. Some companies pay all the premiums for the employees, but others require a percentage contribution from employees. In many cases, a smaller salary actually is more than compensated for by such fringe benefits, which are not paid directly to the employee (and therefore are not taxable at this writing), but which add immeasurably to the family's security. There are also group insurance plans offered by professional organizations or offered on existing loans, often at very attractive prices. The latter are paid if the insured dies and are used to pay off loans or mortgages that may be left outstanding. Typically, couples with children at home are advised to be insured for three to four times the annual take-home pay of one breadwinner in order to be well covered. For the average family approximately $100,000 of life insurance would be adequate in 1986.

Property insurance usually covers the home against damage or its furnishings against damage or theft. Sometimes families also insure their personal belongings and may take out "rider" or "floater" policies on very expensive items such as jewelry and silver, which are often not covered by homeowner's policies. It is wise to keep an inventory of all belongings and to keep the record in a safe place such as a bank safe-deposit box. A record can be either written or put on tape by going from room to room and describing the property, or it can be made by photographing the property. After a fire or burglary such records, which serve as evidence of ownership before the loss occurred, can make the difference in whether or not many insurance companies will pay some of the claims. Most householders are likely to have trouble recalling details of missing or damaged items or may even fail to remember that certain items were ever owned.

Automobile insurance is essential for the financial security of most car owners. Many states mandate by law that there be minimum coverage for any damages the driver may cause. The two major categories of automobile insurance are *liability insurance* and *collision insurance*. Accident lawsuits can involve large amounts of money; liability coverage to take care of claims for both property damages and personal injuries should be in the hundreds of thousands of dollars to ensure protection. Although laws require a minimum liability coverage, the difference in cost between the minimum amount and larger amounts usually is not great. A capable general insurance agent adviser can find the range of coverage for a family that minimizes the risks without unduly burdening them financially. Collision insurance on one's own car is not mandated by law, although if payments are due on a car loan, the lending agency normally requires it. Most policies are not written to cover the full amount of any damage but have deductible amounts to be paid by the insured with the balance being paid by the insurance company. Many persons choose $100 or $200 deductible policies, although some financial advisors suggest a $500 deductible, which reduces the amount of the yearly premium substantially in most cases.

A serious threat to family security is the cost of a prolonged illness or an accident that could result in hospitalization, large medical bills, and the inability of the sick or injured person to work. For most age groups, serious disability is much more probable than death. In some instances, government sources such as Social Security, state disability insurance, or workers' compensation may help to meet needs of the disabled. However, the definition of disability varies widely, and even though one may be unable to work at all or unable to work at the usual job, these sources may not be available. Among the important fringe benefits of employment is coverage for all these possible events. Such policies may cover a variety of medical, surgical, hospital, and major medical expenses and may provide for some continued income for specified periods of time even though the wage earner cannot work. In addition, should the illness or injury be job related, workers' compensation can provide some income until the employee can return to work.

For those who are self-employed or whose employer provides no medical insurance coverage or only minimal protection, most families carry supplemental or total coverage privately. Disability insurance can be expensive, and most persons who insure privately do not attempt to match their lost income exactly. Experts agree that

70 percent of gross income is probably adequate because benefits are usually tax free or at least partially exempted. It is important to know what the policy will pay for, how much the coverage will be, how often payments will be made, and whether there is any choice of hospital and source of treatment. An insurance broker can be particularly helpful in coordinating comprehensive coverage or coverage supplemental to that provided by employers.

There are a number of kinds of liability insurance besides automobile-related liability. All are designed to protect the insured in the event of claims of damages by another person. Professionals may have malpractice insurance to provide for legal expenses and/or damages should a client or patient sue them; homeowners and businesspeople may have general liability insurance that helps them to deal with claims of injuries by employees, visitors, or customers. As our society becomes more litigious, the need for liability insurance increases, but so does the cost.

Income Taxes

Another consideration in any family budget is money taken from all citizens to run the government. The taxes paid are federal income taxes, state income taxes (which may be an additional 12 percent), municipal income taxes, or, of course, property, sales, or excise taxes.

The tax bite is considerable. Currently, family incomes above the poverty level are taxed at least 25 percent on that amount by the federal government alone; for most persons this is automatically deducted from their paycheck and thus never considered as a part of spendable income. For this reason, the amount paid in income tax is sometimes not as well understood as if couples had to plan for payments (as many persons do who pay a percentage every quarter of a year) or who must pay an additional amount beyond their deductions when they file their yearly reports. Most people are either resigned to the inevitability of these deductions or hope that some of the amount may be returned to them because more was deducted than they owed. Many people are estimated to have overpaid their taxes each year because they do not consult a tax expert, and even more overpay because they file the short income tax form and do not take all their allowable deductions. A government publication entitled "Your Federal Income Tax," available from the Superintendent of Documents, Washington, D.C. 20402, explains how to itemize deductions and how to fill out the more complicated long form. This task, though not easy, should at least be attempted by couples to see whether the effort pays off.

Keeping careful records of expenditures is a prerequisite for filling out the long federal income tax form since taxes already paid for items or for entertainment or certain luxuries may be deducted from taxable income. Interest paid on loans or on credit charges also is deductible. All past tax returns should be kept in a safe place—a fireproof, locked file is recommended. Other records used in preparing the tax return also should be saved for several years, as should any other important papers relating to taxes, for an indefinite period.

For future tax purposes, careful permanent records also should be kept of any expenditures connected with the ownership, improvement, or repair of one's house. Some of these expenses may eventually be deducted from the profit on the sale of the house on which capital gains tax will be levied. A capital gain is a profit made from a change in price of an investment asset. Until recently the price of housing was escalating almost daily. Most persons who invested in property can sell at a profit but will be subjected to capital gains tax (although reinvesting in a home of equal value can delay payment of such a tax). Current law enables homeowners over the age of 55 to take a maximum one-time capital gains exclusion of $125,000, provided they have used the property as their principal residence for at least three of the preceding five years. There is a move in Congress, however, in the wake of budget cuts, to limit the exclusion to only 14 cents on the dollar value of the property sale. Currently, the exclusion amounts to 20 cents on the dollar for those in the 20 percent bracket, 40 cents in the 40 percent and 50 cents in the 50 percent bracket (Bradley-Gephart Tax Proposal 1985).

There are different tax rates for married couples filing jointly, for married couples filing separately, and for single people. Married couples can usually save money by filing joint tax returns rather than individual ones. Joint returns may be more costly, however, if one partner's deductions are large enough to offset the lower rates of a joint return. Medical deductions can be used to illustrate this point. Since only medical expenses over a fixed percent of the adjusted gross income are deductible, it may be that one partner with low income but high medical expenses could take a much larger deduction than would be allowed if the spouse's income was added in.

Credit

With as many places as there are for the family dollar to be spent, it is no wonder that some families decide to buy now and pay later. There are over 300 million retail credit cards, 133 million gasoline credit cards, 93 million bank credit cards, and 6 million general purpose credit cards in circulation in the United States (Kilgore and Highlander 1976, p. 95). It is estimated that half of all retail purchases are made by using credit.

Credit cards are primarily used for convenience because many persons do not like to carry sizable sums of cash with them and because credit card records provide a convenient way to keep track of expenditures. In addition, credit cards have an advantage over writing checks for purchases because they are more easily negotiable (many merchants will not take personal checks, particularly out-of-town checks). In some instances, using a credit card is like borrowing interest-free money for a period of 25 to 30 days. Of course, if the card utilized is from a company that does charge interest immediately, the loan can be an expensive one.

Sometimes, but not always, an item or service has an inflated price to make up for the cost to the vendor of providing credit card service. Some merchants have very competitive prices and do not give discounts to cash-paying customers, so that whether or not one uses credit does not affect the price. Some of the general or single-use credit card companies that do not charge interest if the bill is paid within a specified period (department stores, oil companies, hotels, and car rental firms) also do not charge a membership fee. American Express, Carte Blanche, and Diner's Club charge a small annual fee but require accounts to be kept current and thus do not serve as lending institutions and do not usually charge interest. Bank credit cards such as VISA and MasterCharge now charge for the card and may also charge a service fee each time the card is used. These cards are still convenient but no longer have the economic advantages they once had.

Expensive items such as cars, major household appliances, furniture, and vacations are often paid for in credit installments. Payments include the regular cost of the item or service plus interest charges and any insurance that is deemed necessary. Usually such credit buying involves high interest rates of at least $1\frac{1}{2}$ percent on the unpaid balance each month or 18 percent true annual interest, compounded monthly.

Most couples in the United States believe that at least one automobile is a necessity, not a luxury. Car costs are often a major part of a young couple's budget and remain significant expenditures for all families each time they must be repaired or replaced. Some automobiles cost as much or more than the average home—not that too many people buy a Rolls Royce at over $100,000, but many do buy a Mercedes or a BMW for over $40,000. Financial experts recommend that no more than one in five aftertax dollars be spent on a car and ideally only 16 percent (Stein 1984). A couple earning $20,000 after taxes could spend $300 to $350 per month, including payments, gasoline, insurance, repairs, and incidentals. If this amount must be spread over two or more cars, the picture usually includes one or more used cars or the least costly new models to be found.

Retailers are required to state specifically what their finance charges are, but in most states there is no limit on what they can ultimately charge. There are countless cases in which the fees have run between 30 and 40 percent true annual interest. Some credit issuers have *balloon payments* at the end of the contract, meaning that the customer pays small monthly payments until a specified date, at which time the entire balance must be paid all at once. It is always wise to read any contract very carefully and to get a copy of it. Some contracts have an "add on" clause providing that all items purchased may be repossessed, if any one is not paid for promptly—no matter what the total amount is that has already been collected. If you do not understand a contract, get a qualified person to look it over, and cancel the contract within the three-day limit that is allowed if there are parts that you wish not to agree to.

It is generally recommended that one have some kind of credit established. Using credit wisely and paying all bills when they are due establishes a good credit rating, which may be necessary at some future date for major purchases. There are over 2,000 credit bureaus in the United States that keep files on credit users. A good credit rating is based on past credit history, current capability of paying off what is purchased on credit, and overall capital worth. Buying everything with cash does not establish such a rating; although many couples prefer to remain on a cash basis, most will eventually need an item and want to defer at least part of the payment. Purchase of a car or home, for example, is rarely accomplished without borrowing part of the cost.

When two people enter marriage, they may keep their credit cards in their own names as separate accounts. Frequently, women who marry make the mistake of closing their own credit histories to become a part of their husband's. In most states married persons are, in the long run, responsible for each other's debts, but unless there is a delinquency in payments, credit may be continued on the same terms as when single.

In the mid-1970s the Equal Credit Opportunity Act was passed. This law prohibits creditors from disqualifying credit applicants because of certain sources of personal income (alimony, child support, or part-time wages, for instance). Under this regulation, accounts cannot be closed down because of a divorce if both parties are able to pay the bills they incur. This legislation has been a great boon to families who wish to count the wife's part-time income as evidence that they can pay their bills. It has also allowed divorced women, whose credit previously was closely tied to their husband's income, to establish credit in their own names.

With credit easily established for most adults and with family needs frequently straining the family budget, it is no surprise to find that many couples overextend themselves. Some are impulse spenders to begin with and, with credit cards, can easily become "crediholics." Financial experts recommend that no more than 20 to 25 percent of one's annual take-home income should be charged to future payments. A rule of thumb is that credit card balances should be able to be reduced in no more than 60 days without hurting the family budget. The cash advances or "instant money" offered by some lenders may be so tempting that couples find themselves with runaway debts before they realize what is happening to them.

Some couples turn to a debt consolidation loan from a bank or finance company, which pays off all their outstanding credit bills and requires them to make a payment each month on this loan. Sadly, these loans may carry some of the highest interest rates charged, although these may be justified by the poor credit ratings of the applicants. Couples in this kind of financial difficulty are better advised to see a credit counselor—a nonprofit community service in many areas—to arrange regular payments to creditors while curtailing any further credit purchases—tearing up credit cards, if necessary.

If couples have a good credit rating, they may be able to borrow money at a reasonable rate to pay off high-interest debts. Borrowing against savings, if they have any, or against investments or life insurance, they may be able to negotiate a loan at lower interest rates than the finance charges that creditors charge. Credit unions are excellent sources of low-interest loans for those who qualify, as some 24 million Americans do. Depending on the credit union's financial solvency, members usually can qualify for up to $2,500 at an interest rate well below the rate most banks charge. The problem with borrowing to pay off creditors is that bills are likely to pile up again unless a moratorium is called on using credit.

Some couples get into such financial straits that they are forced to file *bankruptcy*. This is the formal recognition of their inability to pay their debts or other obligations that they owe. The Federal Bankruptcy Reform Act of 1979 liberalized laws and established uniform rules that permit individuals declaring bankruptcy to exempt certain possessions from being claimed by creditors. Formerly many bankruptcy courts ordered debtors to repay as much as possible by selling any personal possessions they had.

The Federal Bankruptcy Reform Act of 1979 allows a person to declare bankruptcy while not being completely insolvent and while retaining considerable equity in a home or other property. The intent of the law, of course, was to permit families to hang on to some assets while getting a fresh start after disastrous financial expenditures or losses. Many families have been helped by these new laws, but it also appears that they have made bankruptcy a more common occurrence. In the first full year following passage of the legislation, personal bankruptcies rose 82 percent. The number of VISA credit card holders who filed bankruptcy was multiplied by five during that period (Clausen 1981).

CONCLUSION

No single budget or financial plan will solve every family's financial problems. Much depends on the ages and sexes of the members, the point in the career cycle of each, the region in which they live, and even the part of town or rural area in which they live. Perhaps most of all, the lifestyle of the family and the habits with which they are comfortable affect their proportionate expenditures.

Every family has extravagances and economies that other families have trouble understanding. One family with two color television sets "can't afford" an encyclopedia; another family can spend several thousand dollars on a wedding or a funeral but "can't afford" to help a child with college expenses. Even advice to keep one's expenditures below one's earnings may not hold at some points in one's family life cycle or one's own career cycle.

The number, sexes, and ages of children affect food, clothing, and housing costs. In cold climates, winter coats, hats, boots, and snowsuits often can be handed down from year to year between children of the same sex who are not too far apart in age, but styles and sizes may limit passing clothing on to children who are much younger or of the opposite sex. A family with two boys or two girls may be adequately housed in a two-bedroom, two-bathroom house, but a comparable family with one boy and one girl may feel inadequately housed unless they have a three-bedroom, three-bathroom house; in cold climates this means two more rooms to heat.

Needs for medical care are high, but fairly predictable, during pregnancy and the early years of child rearing. As the family life cycle progresses, average costs may be lower but also less predictable. Some budgetary strains may be relieved by health insurance programs, which are likely to require more predictable budgeted amounts.

A periodic accounting for expenditures is a necessity in most families. If a record is kept, the items can be categorized (food, clothing, housing, insurance, and so forth) so that the family can at least be aware of how their money has been spent and decide whether the proportional amounts reflect the lifestyle they want. If not, it may be a necessary step to modify the figures in the accounting to make a budget for the coming year and to try to adjust expenditures to match the desired lifestyle as nearly as possible. In most regions of the United States an annual budget is preferable to a monthly one because many expenses vary with the seasons. In the northern and eastern states there are drastic differences in the necessary expenditures for heating, clothing, dry cleaning, and so forth from season to season. Vacations are usually once-a-year expenses. Holiday expenses are often exceptional. Property taxes are usually payable once or twice a year.

Generally speaking, budgeting is better than not budgeting for most families. Budgets fail when they are not comprehensive enough, are unrealistic, or subject the family to an uncomfortable change in lifestyle. A great deal of flexibility is usually necessary to keep family finances stabilized.

REFERENCES

Abarbanel, S. 1979. "Shared Parenting after Separation and Divorce: A Study of Joint Custody." *American Journal of Orthopsychiatry* 49:320–329.

Abramson, Paul R. 1973. "The Relationship of the Frequency of Masturbation to Several Personality Dimensions and Behavior." *Journal of Sex Research* 9:139.

Adamcik, Barbara. 1980. "An Examination of the Comparability of Morale Measures among Working and Retired Blacks, Mexican-Americans and Whites." Unpublished research paper, University of Southern California.

Adams, Bert. 1968. *Kinship in an Urban Setting.* Chicago: Markham.

———. 1970. "Isolation, Function and Beyond." *American Family* 32:575–597.

Adams, Gerald. 1979. "Mate Selection in the United States: A Theoretical Summarization." Pp. 259–267 in *Contemporary Theories about the Family.* Vol. 1, edited by W. Burr, R. Hill, F. I. Nye, and I. Reiss. New York: Free Press.

Adams, Margaret. 1976. *Single Blessedness: Observations on the Single Status in Married Society.* New York: Basic Books.

Ahrons, Constance. 1978. "The Coparental Divorce: Preliminary Research Findings and Policy Implications." Paper presented at the annual meeting of the National Council on Family Relations, Philadelphia, October.

———. 1979. "The Binuclear Family: Two Households, One Family." *Alternative Lifestyles* 2:499–515.

———. 1985. "The Binuclear Family." Paper presented to the Southern California Association for Marriage and Family Therapy, San Diego, February 16.

Ahrons, Constance, and M. Bowman. 1984. "Changes in Family Relationships Following Divorce of Adult Child." Pp. 461–480 in *Family Studies Review Yearbook.* Vol. 2, edited by D. Olson and B. Miller. Beverly Hills, CA: Sage Publications.

Alba, Richard D. 1985. "Marriage across Ethnic Lines." *Marriage and Divorce Today* 10:3.

Albrecht, Sharon. 1979. "Correlates of Marital Happiness among the Remarried." *Journal of Marriage and the Family* (November):857–867.

———. 1980. "Reactions and Adjustments to Divorce: Differences in the Experience of Males and Females." *Family Relations* 29:59–68.

Albrecht, S., H. Bahr, and B. Chadwick. 1979. "Changing Family and Sex Roles: An Assessment of Age Difference." *Journal of Marriage and the Family* 41:41–50.

Aldous, Joan. 1971. "A Framework for the Analysis of Family Problem Solving." P. 266 in *Family Problem Solving: A Symposium on Theoretical, Methodological, and Substantive Concerns,* edited by J. Aldous, T. Condon, R. Hill, M. Straus, and I. Tallman. Hinsdale, IL: Dryden Press.

———. 1975. "The Search for Alternatives: Parental Behaviors and Children's Original Problem Solutions." *Journal of Marriage and the Family* 37:711–722.

———. 1977. *Family Careers: Developmental Change in Families.* New York: Wiley.

———, ed. 1982. *Two Paychecks: Life in Dual-Earner Families.* Sage Focus Editions. Vol. 56. Beverly Hills, CA: Sage Publications.

Alexander, Shana. 1975. *State-by-State Guide to Women's Legal Rights.* Los Angeles: Wollstonecraft.

Altergott, Karen. 1984. "Managing Interdependence: Family Development, Policy and the Care System in an Aging Society. Pp. 479–484 in *Social Change and Family Policies.* Melbourne: Australian Institute of Family Studies.

Altman, Irwin, and Dalmas A. Taylor. 1973. *Social Penetration: The Development of Interpersonal Relationships.* New York: Holt, Rinehart and Winston.

Ammons, P., and Nick Stinnett. 1980. "The Vital Marriage: A Closer Look." *Family Relations* 29:37–42.

Andrews, Lori B. 1984. "Yours, Mine, and Theirs." *Psychology Today* (December 18):20–29.

Apgar, Virginia. 1953. "Proposal for a New Method of Evaluation of Newborn Infants." *Anaesthesia and Analgesia* 32:260–267.

Arehart-Treichel, Joan. 1982. "Program to Prevent Premature Deliveries." *Science News* 121(April 17):262.

Argyle, Michael. 1969. *Social Interaction.* Chicago: Aldine Atherton.

Arkin, W., and L. Dobrofsky. 1978. "Shared Labor and Love: Job Sharing Couples in Academia." *Alternative Lifestyles* 1:492–512.

Arling, Greg. 1976. "The Elderly Widow and Her Family, Neighbors, and Friends." *Journal of Marriage and the Family* 38:757–768.

Arms, Suzanne. 1975. *Immaculate Deception*. San Francisco: San Francisco Book Company.

Arnold, R., R. Bulato, C. Buripakdi, B. Chung, J. Fawcett, T. Iritani, S. Lee, and T. Wu. 1975. *The Value of Children: A Cross-Cultural National Study*. Vol. I, *Introduction and Comparative Analysis*. Honolulu: East-West Population Institute, East-West Center.

Aron, Arthur, et al. 1974. "Relationships with Opposite-Sex Parents and Mate Choice." *Human Relations* 27:17–24.

Aronson, Elliot. 1972. *The Social Animal*. New York: Viking.

———. 1980. *The Social Animal*. 3rd ed. San Francisco: W. H. Freeman.

Ashley, Paul P. 1978. *Oh Promise Me, but Put It in Writing: Living-Together Agreements without, before, during, and after Marriage*. New York: McGraw-Hill.

Atchley, Robert. 1976. "Selected Social and Psychological Differences between Men and Women in Later Life." *Journal of Gerontology* 31:204–211.

Bach, George, and Ronald Deutsch. 1974. *Pairing*. New York: William C. Brown.

Bach, George, and P. Wyden. 1970. *The Intimate Enemy: How to Fight Fair in Love and Marriage*. New York: Avon.

Backman, Carl W., and Paul F. Secord. 1959. "The Effect of Perceived Liking on Interpersonal Attraction." *Human Relations* 12:379–384.

Bacon, Lloyd. 1974. "Early Motherhood, Accelerated Role Transition, and Social Pathologies." *Social Forces* 52.

Bader, E., R. Riddle, and C. Sinclair. 1981. "Do Marriage Preparation Programs Really Work? A Five-Year Study." *Family Therapy News* (July):10–12.

Bagarozzi, D., and R. Rauen. 1983. "Premarital Counseling: Appraisal and Status." Pp. 580–597 in *Family Studies Review Yearbook*. Vol. 1, edited by D. Olson and B. Miller. Beverly Hills, CA: Sage Publications.

Bahr, Howard, and Bruce A. Chadwick. 1985. "Religion and Family in Middletown, U.S.A." *Journal of Marriage and the Family* 47:407–414.

Bahr, Stephen. 1981. "Mediation Is the Answer." *Family Advocate* 3:32–35.

Baldwin, Doris. 1978. "Poverty and the Older Woman: Reflections of a Social Worker." *Family Coordinator* 27:448–450.

Bales, Robert, and Fred L. Srodtbeck. 1951. "Phases in Group Problem Solving." *Journal of Abnormal and Social Psychology* 46:485–495.

Balkwell, Carolyn. 1981. "Transition to Widowhood: A Review of the Literature." *Family Relations* 30:117–127.

Bandura, Albert. 1965. "Influence of Model's Reinforcement Contingencies on the Acquisition of Imitative Responses." *Journal of Personality and Social Psychology* 1:589–595.

———. 1969. "Social-Learning Theory of Identificatory Processes." In *Handbook of Socialization: Theory and Research*, edited by D. Goslin. Chicago: Rand McNally.

———. 1971. *Social Learning Theory*. Morristown, NJ: General Learning Press.

Bandura, Albert, and R. Walters. 1959. *Adolescent Aggression*. New York: Ronald Press.

Bane, Mary Jo. 1976a. *Here to Stay: America—Families in the Twentieth Century*. New York: Basic Books.

———. 1976b. "Marital Disruption and the Lives of Children." *Journal of Social Issues* 32:103–117.

Bank of America. 1980. *Consumer Information Report 7*.

Bankoff, Elizabeth A. 1983. "Social Support and Adaptation to Widowhood." *Journal of Marriage and the Family* 45:827–839.

Bardwick, Judith. 1971. *Psychology of Women: A Study of Biocultural Conflict*. New York: Harper & Row.

Barkas, J. L. 1980. *Single in America*. New York: Atheneum.

Barnhouse, T. 1981. "Marriage: How the 'New' Church Is Helping. *Sexology Today* (April):16–18.

Bartz, Karen W., and Elaine S. Levine. 1978. "Child-Rearing by Black Parents: A Description and Comparison to Anglo and Chicano Parents." *Journal of Marriage and the Family* 40:709–719.

Baruch, Grace, Rosalind Barnett, and Caryl Rivers. 1983. *Life Prints*. New York: McGraw-Hill.

Baumrind, Diana. 1975. "The Contributions of the Family to the Development of Competence in Children." *Schizophrenia Bulletin* 14:12–37.

———. 1977. "Socialization Determinants of Personal Agency." Paper presented to the Society for Research in Child Development, New Orleans, March.

Bayer, Alan E. 1966. "Birth Order and College Attendance." *Journal of Marriage and the Family* 28:480–484.

Bean, Frank D., Margaret P. Clark, Gray Swicegood, and Dorie Williams. 1983. "Husband-Wife Communication, Wife's Employment, and the Decision for Male and Female Sterilization." *Journal of Marriage and the Family* 45:395–410.

Beard, L. 1949. "Are the Aged Ex-Family?" *Social Forces* 27:274–279.

Bebbington, A. C. 1973. "The Function of Stress in the Establishment of the Dual-Career Family." *Journal of Marriage and the Family* (August):530–537.

Becker, Gary S., E. Lanes, and R. Michael. 1977. "An Economic Analysis of Marital Instability." *Journal of Political Economy* 85:1141–1187.

Beckman, Linda J. 1975. "Women Alcoholics: A Review of Social and Psychological Studies." *Journal of Studies on Alcohol* 36:797–824.

Bell, Alan P., and Martin S. Weinberg. 1978. *Homosexualities*. New York: Simon and Schuster.

———. 1979. *Homosexualities*. Bloomington, IN: Institute for Sex Research.

Bell, Robert R. 1964. "The Effect on the Family of a Limitation in Coping Ability in the Child: A Research Approach and Finding." *Merrill-Palmer Quarterly* 10:129–142.

Bell, Robert R., and Kathleen Coughey. 1980. "Premarital Sexual Experience among College Females, 1958, 1968, and 1978." *Family Relations* 29:353–357.

Bell, Robert R., and Norman Lobsenz. 1977. "Marital Sex." In *Human Sexuality in Today's World,* edited by J. Gagnon. Boston: Little, Brown.

Bell, Robert R., Stanley Turner, and Lawrence Rosen. 1975. "A Multi-Variate Analysis of Female Extra-Marital Coitus." *Journal of Marriage and the Family* 37: 375–384.

Bem, Daryl. 1970. *Beliefs, Attitudes and Human Affairs.* Monterey, CA: Brooks/Cole.

Bengis, I. 1973. "Being Alone." *New York* magazine.

Bennett, Dawn D. 1985. "Pelvic Inflammatory Disease: Pill Risk." *Science News* 127 (April 27):263.

Benson, Leonard. 1971. *The Family Bond: Marriage, Love, and Sex in America.* New York: Random House.

Bergler, Edmund. 1970. *Money and Emotional Conflicts.* New York: International Universities Press.

Bernard, Jessie. 1971a. "Jealousy in Marriage." *Medical Aspects of Human Sexuality* 5:200–215.

———. 1971b. *Remarriage: A Study of Marriage.* New York: Russell and Russell.

———. 1973. *The Future of Marriage.* New York: Bantam Books.

Berne, Eric. 1961. *Transactional Analysis Psychotherapy.* New York: Grove Press.

———. 1967. *Games People Play.* New York: Grove Press.

———. 1970. *Sex in Human Loving.* New York: Simon and Schuster.

Bernstein, Anne. 1976. "How Children Learn about Sex and Birth." *Psychology Today* 9:31–36, 66.

Bernstein, Anne, and Philip Cowan. 1975. "Children's Concepts of How People Get Babies." *Child Development* 46:77–92.

Berry, Jon. 1983. "Health and Science File." *Los Angeles Herald Examiner* (January 30):A-2.

Berscheid, Ellen, and Elaine Walster. 1978. *Interpersonal Attraction.* 2nd ed. Reading, MA: Addison-Wesley.

Betcher, W. 1981. "Intimate Play and Marital Adaptation." *Psychiatry* 44:13–33.

Bienvenu, M., Sr. 1978. *A Counselor's Guide to Accompany a Marital Communication Inventory.* Saluda, NC: Family Life.

Biller, Henry. 1970. "Father-Absence and Personality Development of the Male Child." *Developmental Psychology* 2:181–201.

Biller, Henry, and Dennis Meredith. 1974. *Father Power.* New York: David McKay.

Bird, Caroline. 1972. "Women Should Stay Single." In *Marriage: For and Against,* edited by H. Hart. New York: Hart.

Birtchnell, J., and J. Mayhew. 1977. "Toman's Theory: Tested for Mate Selection and Friendship Formation." *Journal of Individual Psychology* 33:18–36.

Blake, Judith. 1979. "Is Zero Preferred? Childlessness in the 1970s." *Journal of Marriage and the Family* 41:245–257.

Blalock, Hubert, and P. Wilken. 1979. *Intergroup Processes: A Micro-Macro Perspective.* New York: Free Press.

Blanche, Ed. 1985. "Ireland Split over Sale of Contraceptives." *Pomona* (CA) *Progress Bulletin* (February 18):6.

Blau, Peter. 1964. *Exchange and Power in Social Life.* New York: Wiley.

Blehar, M. 1980a. "Preparation for Childbirth and Parenting." P. 144 in *Families Today.* Vol. I. *Institute of Mental Health Science Monographs.* Washington, D.C.: U.S. Government Printing Office.

———. 1980b. "Working Couples as Parents." Pp. 299–331 in *Families Today.* Vol. 1. *Institute of Mental Health Science Monographs.* Washington, D.C.: U.S. Government Printing Office.

Blood, Robert O., and Donald M. Wolfe. 1960. *Husbands and Wives: The Dynamics of Married Living.* New York: Free Press.

Bloom, Bernard, Steven R. Asher, and S. White. 1978. "Marital Disruption as a Stressor: A Review and Analysis." *Psychological Bulletin* 85:867–894.

Blumberg, Paul M., and P. W. Paul. 1975. "Continuities and Discontinuities in Upper-Class Marriages." *Journal of Marriage and the Family* 37:63–77.

Blumstein, Philip, and Pepper Schwartz. 1983. *American Couples.* New York: William Morrow.

Bogardus, Emory. 1959. *Social Distance.* Los Angeles: E. S. Bogardus.

Bohannan, Paul. 1970a. *Divorce and After.* New York: Doubleday.

———. 1970b. "Divorce Chains, Households of Remarriage and Multiple Divorces." Pp. 127–139 in *Divorce and After,* edited by P. Bohannan. New York: Doubleday.

———. 1984. *All the Happy Families: Exploring the Varieties of Family Life.* New York: McGraw-Hill.

Bohannan, Paul, and R. Erickson. 1978. "Steppin' In." *Psychology Today* (January):53–59.

Booth, Alan. 1977. "Wife's Employment and Husband's Stress: A Replication and Refutation." *Journal of Marriage and the Family* 39:645–650.

———. 1979. "Does Wives' Employment Cause Stress for Husbands?" *Family Coordinator* 28:445–450.

Booth, Alan, and John Edwards. 1985. "Age at Marriage and Marital Instability." *Journal of Marriage and the Family* 47:67–75.

Boston Women's Health Book Collective. 1976. *Our Bodies, Our Selves.* New York: Simon and Schuster.

Bourg, Carroll J. 1975. "Elderly in a Southern Metropolitan Area." *The Gerontologist* 15:15–22.

Bowen, Gary Lee, and Dennis Orthner. 1983. "Sex-Role Congruency and Marital Quality." *Journal of Marriage and the Family* 45:223–230.

Bowen, Murray. 1978. *Family Therapy in Clinical Practices.* New York: Jason Aronson.

Bower, Bruce. 1984. "Criminal Destiny: Nature Meets Nurture." *Science News* 125 (June 2):342.

Bower, Donald W., and Victor Christopherson. 1977. "University Student Cohabitation: A Regional Comparison of Selected Attitudes and Behavior." *Journal of Marriage and the Family* 39:447–454.

Bowlby, John. 1980. *Attachment and Loss.* Vol. 3. New York: Basic Books.

Bradley, Robert A. 1962. "Fathers' Presence in Delivery Rooms." *Psychosomatics* 3:1–6.

Bradt, Jack O. 1980. "The Family with Young Children." Pp. 121–146 in *The Family Life Cycle: A Framework for Family Therapy,* edited by E. Carter and M. McGoldrick. New York: Gardner Press.

Brayer, F., L. Chiazze, and B. Duffy. 1969. "Calendar Rhythm and Menstrual Cycle Range." *Fertility/Sterility.*

Brazelton, T. Berry. 1980. "The Importance of Mothering the Mother." *Redbook* (October):112–115.

———. 1981. *On Becoming a Family.* New York: Dell.

Brecher, Edward. 1971. *The Sex Researchers.* New York: New American Library.

———. 1984. *Love, Sex and Aging.* Boston: Little, Brown.

Bretschneider, J. 1983. "Sexual Attitudes and Behavior among Healthy 80–102 Year Olds." Unpublished master's thesis, San Francisco State University.

Bringle, Robert T., and Scott Evenback. 1979. "The Study of Jealousy as a Dispositional Characteristic." In *Love and Attraction,* edited by M. Cook and G. Wilson. Oxford: Pergamon Press.

Broderick, Carlfred. 1966a. "Sexual Behavior among Pre-Adolescents." *Journal of Social Issues* 22 (April):6–21.

———. 1966b. "Socio-Sexual Development in a Suburban Community." *Journal of Sex Research* 2:1–24.

———. 1979a. *Couples: How to Confront Problems and Maintain Loving Relationships.* New York: Simon and Schuster.

———. 1979b. *Marriage and the Family.* Englewood Cliffs, NJ: Prentice-Hall.

———. 1983. *The Therapeutic Triangle.* Beverly Hills, CA: Sage Publications.

Broderick, Carlfred, and George P. Rowe. 1968. "A Scale of Pre-Adolescent Heterosexual Development." *Journal of Marriage and the Family* 30:97–101.

Broderick, Carlfred, and James Smith. 1979. "The General Systems Approach to the Family." Pp. 112–129 in *Contemporary Theories about the Family.* Vol. 2, edited by W. Burr, R. Hill, F. I. Nye, and I. Reiss. New York: Free Press.

Bronfenbrenner, Urie. 1977. "Nobody Home: The Erosion of the American Family." *Psychology Today* 10:41–47.

Brown, B. B. 1981. "A Life-Span Approach to Friendship: Age-Related Dimensions of an Ageless Relationship." In *Research on the Interweave of Social Roles.* Vol. 2, *Friendship.* Greenwich, CT: J.A.I. Press.

Budd, L. S. 1976. "Problems, Disclosure, and Commitment of Cohabiting and Married Couples." Ph.D. dissertation, University of Minnesota.

Bullough, Vern L., and Bonnie L. Bullough. 1977. *Sin, Sickness, and Sanity.* New York: New American Library.

Bumpass, Larry, and Ronald R. Rindfuss. 1978. "Children's Experiences of Marital Disruption." *Institute for Research on Poverty Discussion Papers.* No. 512-78. Madison: University of Wisconsin.

Bumpass, Larry, and James A. Sweet. 1972. "Differentials in Marital Instability: 1970." *American Sociological Review* 37:754–766.

Burchinal, Lee G., and Loren E. Chancellor. 1962. "Survival Rates among Religiously Homogamous and Interreligious Marriage." *Iowa Agricultural and Home Economics Station Research Bulletin* 512:743–770.

Burgess, Ernest, and Leonard S. Cottrell, Jr. 1939. *Predicting Success or Failure in a Marriage.* Englewood Cliffs, NJ: Prentice-Hall.

Burgess, Ernest, Harvey Locke, and Mary Margaret Thomes. 1963. *The Family: From Institution to Companionship.* 3rd ed. New York: Van Nostrand Reinhold.

———. 1971. *The Family.* 4th ed. New York: Van Nostrand Reinhold.

Burgess, W. 1958. *Aging in Western Societies.* New York: Thomas Crowell.

Burke, Ronald J., and Tamara Weir. 1976. "Relationship of Wives' Employment Status to Husbands', Wife Pair Satisfaction and Performance." *Journal of Marriage and the Family* 38:279–287.

Burns, Ailsa. 1984. "Perceived Cause of Marriage Breakdown and Conditions of Life." *Journal of Marriage and the Family* 46:551–562.

Burr, Wesley. 1973. *Theory Construction and the Sociology of the Family.* New York: Wiley.

Business Week. 1978. "Commuting: A Solution for Two-Career Couples." (April 3):68.

Buss, David M. 1985. "Human Mate Selection." *American Scientist* 73:47–51.

Butler, J., D. Reisner, and N. Wagner. 1979. "Sexuality: During Pregnancy and Parturition." Pp. 176–190 in *Human Sexuality: A Health Practitioner's Text.* 2nd ed., edited by R. Green. Baltimore, MD: Williams and Wilkins.

Butler, Robert N. 1975. *Why Survive? Being Old in America.* New York: Harper & Row.

Byrd, Richard E. 1938. *Alone.* New York: Putnam.

Cain, Richard, Frank A. Pederson, Martha Zaslow, and Eva Kramer. 1984. "Effects of Father's Presence or Absence during a Cesarean Delivery." *Birth* 11:10–15.

Calhoun, Arthur W. 1960. *A Social History of the American Family.* New York: Barnes and Noble.

California Commission on Crime Control and Violence Prevention. 1981. "An Ounce of Prevention: Toward an Understanding of the Causes of Domestic Violence." Sacramento, CA: California Commission on Crime Control and Violence Prevention.

Campbell, Arthur A. 1968. "The Role of Family Planning in the Reduction of Poverty." *Journal of Marriage and the Family* 30:236–245.

———. 1975. "The American Way of Mating: Marriage, Si; Children, Maybe." *Psychology Today* (May):37–43.

Campbell-Gibson, R. 1984. "The National Survey of Black Americans: An Analysis." *Los Angeles Times* (April 8):Part IV, p. 1.

Cartwright, Dorwin. 1968. "The Nature of Group Cohesiveness." In *Group Dynamics: Research and Theory.* 3rd ed., edited by D. Cartwright and A. Zander. New York: Harper & Row.

Cecre, L. 1982. "Separation Stressful for Commuting Couples." *The Washington Times* magazine (August 16):2.

Centers, Richard. 1975. *Sexual Attraction and Love: An Instrumental Theory.* Springfield, IL: Charles C. Thomas.

Cetron, Marvin, and T. O'Toole. 1984. *Encounters with the Future: A Forecast of Life in the 21st Century.* New York: McGraw-Hill.

Chadwick, Bruce A., Stan L. Albrecht, and Phillip R. Kunz. 1976. "Marital and Family Role Satisfaction." *Journal of Marriage and the Family* 38:431–440.

Chambers, David L. 1979. *Making Fathers Pay: The Enforcement of Child Support.* Chicago: University of Chicago Press.

Charney, Israel. 1974. "Marital Love and Hate." P. 55 in *Violence in the Family,* edited by S. Steinmetz and M. Straus. New York: Dodd, Mead.

Cherlin, Andrew. 1978. "Remarriage as an Incomplete Institution." *American Journal of Sociology* 84:634–650.

Cherlin, Andrew, and Frank F. Furstenberg. 1985. "Styles and Strategies of Grandparenting." Pp. 97–116 in *Grandparenting*, edited by V. Bengtson and J. Robertson. Beverly Hills, CA: Sage Publications.

Cherubin, Jan. 1985. "The Sexual Evolution on Campus." *Los Angeles Herald Examiner* (February 24):E-1.

Chesler, Phyllis. 1986. *Mothers on Trial: The Battle for Children and Custody.* New York: McGraw-Hill.

Chesser, B. 1980. "Analysis of Wedding Rituals: An Attempt to Make Weddings More Meaningful." *Family Relations* 29:204–209.

Chester, Robert. 1977. "The One-Parent Family: Deviant or Variant." In *Equalities and Inequalities in Family Life*, edited by R. Chester and J. Peel. New York: Academic Press.

"Child Custody Project, American Bar Association." 1982. *Marriage and Divorce Today* 7:45.

Christensen, Harold T., ed. 1964. *Handbook of Marriage and the Family.* Chicago: Rand McNally.

Christensen, J. 1979. *The Church of Jesus Christ of Latter-Day Saints: In Support of the Family.* Salt Lake City, Utah: Church Educational System.

Cicirelli, Victor C. 1983. "Adult Children's Attachment and Helping Behavior to Elderly Parents: A Path Model." *Journal of Marriage and the Family* 45:815–825.

Cimons, Marlene. 1985a. "Polls Find Birth Control Pill Risk Highly Overrated." *Los Angeles Times* (March 6):Part I, p. 25.

———. 1985b. "Tripled Infertility Found in U.S. Women Aged 20–24." *Los Angeles Times* (February 11):Part I, p. 4.

———. 1986. "Limited Funds Cited in War on Leading Sexual Disease." *Los Angeles Times* (May 20):Part I, p. 14.

Cipriano, J. 1980. "Childless—Not by Choice: The Poignant Plight of the Infertile Couple." *Sexual Medicine Today* 4:14–17.

Clanton, Gordon, and Lynn Smith, eds. 1977. *Jealousy.* Englewood Cliffs, NJ: Prentice-Hall.

Clarke, F. 1973. "Interpersonal Communication Variables as Predictors of Marital Satisfaction-Attraction." Ph.D. dissertation, University of Denver.

Clarke-Stewart, K. 1978. "And Daddy Makes Three: The Father's Impact on Mother and Young Child." *Child Development* 49:475.

Clausen, A. 1981. Paper presented to the American Bankers Association Installment Credit Conference. Quoted in the *Los Angeles Times* financial section, March.

Clavan, Sylvia. 1979. "The Impact of Social Class and Social Trends on the Role of Grandparent." *Family Coordinator* 27:351–357.

Clayton, Richard R., and Harwin L. Voss. 1977. "Shacking Up: Cohabitation in the 1970s." *Journal of Marriage and the Family* 39:273–284.

Cleveland, W., and D. Gianturco. 1976. "Remarriage Probability after Widowhood: A Retrospective Method." *Journal of Gerontology* 31:99–103.

Cogan, Rosemary, and R. Hinz. 1982. "The Couvade (Fathering) Syndrome." *ICEA Review* 6:1–7.

———. 1984. "Support during Labor." *ICEA Review* 8 (April):1–2.

Cohn, D'Vera. 1982. "Condoms Get New Attention as Means of Birth Control." *Los Angeles Times* (November 19): Part I, p. A-8.

Cole, Charles L. 1977. "Cohabitation in Social Context." Pp. 62–79 in *Marriage and Alternatives: Exploring Intimate Relationships*, edited by R. Libby and R. Whitehurst. Glenview, IL: Scott, Foresman.

———. 1980. "Split-Shift Marriages." Paper presented at the Groves Conference, Gatlinburg, TN, May.

Cole, K. 1982. *Between the Lines: The Search for a Space between Feminism and Femininity . . . and Other Tight Spots.* Garden City, NY: Doubleday.

Coleman, James C. 1979. *Contemporary Psychology and Effective Behavior.* 4th ed. Glenview, IL: Scott, Foresman.

Collins, Randall. 1971. "A Conflict Theory of Sexual Stratification." *Social Problems* 19:3–12.

Commission on Population Growth in America. 1972. *Population and the American Future.* New York: New American Library.

Connecticut Mutual Life Report on American Values in the 80's. 1981. "The Impact of Belief." New York: Research and Forecasts, Inc.

Cooley, Charles Horton. 1902. *Human Nature and the Social Order.* New York: Charles Scribner's Sons.

Corea, Gena. 1977. *The Hidden Malpractice.* New York: Harcourt, Brace, Jovanovich.

Corfman, E. 1979. "Introduction and Overview." P. 1 in *Families Today. National Institute of Mental Health Science Monographs.* Vol. 1. Washington, D.C.: U.S. Government Printing Office.

Corrales, Ramon. 1975. "Power and Satisfaction in Early Marriage." Pp. 197–216 in *Power in Families*, edited by R. Cromwell and D. Olson. New York: Wiley.

Cox, M., and L. Cease. 1978. "Joint Custody." *Family Advocate* (Summer):10–13.

Crane, Tricia. 1986a. "The Pill: 25 Years Later." *Los Angeles Herald Examiner* (January 12):E-1, E-4.

———. 1986b. "Shop around for the Right Pill and the Right Doctor." *Los Angeles Herald Examiner* (January 12):E-5.

Crawley, L., A. Malfetti, E. Stewart, and N. Vas Dass. 1973. *Reproduction, Sex, and Preparation for Marriage.* 2nd ed. Englewood Cliffs, NJ: Prentice-Hall.

Cromwell, Ronald E., and David H. Olson. 1975. *Power in Families.* New York: Wiley.

Crooks, Robert, and Karla Bauer. 1980. *Our Sexuality.* Menlo Park, CA: Benjamin/Cummings.

Cuber, John F., and Peggy Harroff. 1963. "The More Total View: Relationships among Men and Women of the Upper Middle Class." *Marriage and Family Living* 25:140–145.

———. 1965. *The Significant Americans: A Study of Sexual Behavior among the Affluent.* New York: Appleton-Century-Crofts.

Culverwell, Melissa. 1983. "The Odds on Overcoming Infertility." *Los Angeles Times* (March 12):Part VII, p. 17.

Cumming, Elaine, and William E. Henry. 1961. *Growing Old.* New York: Basic Books.

Cutler, Sally. 1975. "Transportation and Changes in Life Satisfaction." *The Gerontologist* 15:155–159.

Cvetkovich, George B. Grote, J. Lieberman, and W. Miller. 1978. "Sex Role Development and Teenage Fertility-Related Behavior." *Adolescence* 13:231–236.

Davenport, William H. 1977. "Sex in Cross-Cultural Perspective." Pp. 115–163 in *Human Sexuality in Four Perspectives,* edited by F. Beach. Baltimore, MD: Johns Hopkins University Press.

Davidson, Bernard, Jack O. Balswick, and Charles Halverson. 1983. "Affective Self-Disclosure and Marital Adjustment: A Test of Equity Theory." *Journal of Marriage and the Family* 45:93–102.

Davis, A., and M. Phillip. 1977. "Working without a Net: The Bachelor as a Social Problem." *Sociological Review* 25:109–129.

Davis, Kingsley. 1947. "Final Note on a Case of Extreme Isolation." *American Journal of Sociology* 52:432–437.

DeFrank-Lynch, B. 1982. "The Developmental Cycle of the Marital Relationship." *Medical Aspects of Human Sexuality* 16, 12:34AA-34JJ.

DeLamater, John, and Patricia MacCorquodale. 1979. *Premarital Sexuality: Attitudes, Relationships, Behavior.* Madison: University of Wisconsin Press.

DeLora, Jo Ann, and Carole Warren. 1977. *Understanding Sexual Interaction.* Boston: Houghton Mifflin.

DeMaris, Alfred, and Gerald R. Leslie. 1984. "Cohabitation with the Future Spouse: Its Influence upon Marital Satisfaction and Communication." *Journal of Marriage and the Family* 46:77–84.

DeMartino, Manfred. 1974. *Sex and the Intelligent Woman.* New York: Springer.

De Young, Alan J. 1979. "Marriage Encounter: A Critical Examination." *Journal of Marital and Family Therapy* 5:27–34.

Deutsch, Morton. 1949. "An Experimental Study of the Effects of Cooperation and Competition upon Group Process." *Human Relations* 2:199–223

———. 1973. *The Resolution of Conflict: Constructive and Destructive Processes.* New Haven, CT: Yale University Press.

Diamond, Milton, and Arno Karlen. 1980. *Sexual Decisions.* Boston: Little, Brown.

Diamond, Milton, Patricia Steinhoff, James Palmore, and Roy G. Smith. 1973. "Sexuality, Birth Control and Abortion: A Decision-Making Sequence." *Biosocial Science* 5:347–361.

Dick-Read, Grantly. 1944. *Childbirth without Fear.* 2nd rev. ed. New York: Harper & Row.

Dicks, H. V. 1967. *Marital Tensions.* Boston and London: Routledge & Kegan Paul.

Dodson, Betty. 1976. *Liberating Masturbation: A Meditation on Self Love.* New York: Betty Dodson.

Doering, S., and D. Entwisle. 1977. *The First Birth.* Final Report, U.S. Public Health Service. Rockville, MD: National Institute of Mental Health.

Doherty, William J., Patricia McCabe, and Robert G. Ryder. 1978. "Marriage Encounter: A Critical Appraisal." *Journal of Marriage and Family Counseling* 4:99–106.

Dorner, G., W. Rohde, F. Stahl, L. Krell, and W. Masius. 1975. "A Neuroendocrine Predisposition for Homosexuality in Men." *Archives of Sexual Behavior* 4:1–8.

Dougherty, Ralph C. 1979. Quoted in *Sexual Medicine Today* (November):14.

Dovidio, J., and W. Morris. 1975. "Effects of Stress and Commonality of Fate on Helping Behaviors." *Journal of Personality and Social Psychology* 31:145–149.

Drapkin, R., and F. Bienenfeld. 1985. "The Power of Including Children in Custody Mediation." Journal of Divorce 8(3/4)(Spring/Summer):63–95.

Draughon, Margaret. 1975. "Stepmother's Model of Identification in Relation to Mourning in the Child." *Psychological Reports* 36:183–189.

Dreifus, C. 1975. "Sterilizing the Poor." *The Progressive* 39:13–19.

Dressel, Paula L., and W. Ray Avant. 1978. "Aging and College Family Textbooks." *Family Coordinator* 27:427–435.

Dryfoos, Joy G. 1985. "Can School-Based Health Clinics Solve the Teen-Pregnancy Problem?" *Los Angeles Herald Examiner* (December 1):1, 4.

Duberman, Lucille. 1975. *The Reconstituted Family: A Study of Remarried Couples and Their Children.* Chicago: Nelson Hall.

———. 1977. *Marriage and Other Alternatives.* 2nd ed. New York: Praeger.

Dudley, Donald, and Elton Welke. 1977. *How to Survive Being Alive.* New York: Doubleday.

Duncan, R. Paul, and Carolyn C. Perrucci. 1976. "Dual Occupational Families and Migration." *American Sociological Review* 41:252–261.

Dunn, Thomas E.. 1984. "Fetal Entrainment and the Implications for a New System of Family Therapy." Unpublished doctoral dissertation.

Eaton, Gerald T. 1974. "Social Functioning and Personal Autonomy in Black and White OAS Recipients." Ph.D. dissertation, University of Southern California.

Edwards, Marie, and Eleanor Hoover. 1974. *The Challenge of Being Single.* New York: New American Library.

Eekelaar, J. M. 1980. "Reforming the English Law Concerning Illegitimate Persons." *Family Law Quarterly* 14:41–58.

Eheart, Brenda K., and Susan K. Martel. 1985. *The Fourth Trimester.* New York: Appleton-Century-Crofts.

Eichler, L. 1924. *The Customs of Mankind.* New York: Doubleday.

Elder, Glen H., Jr. 1977. "Family History and the Life Course." *Journal of Family History* 2:279–304.

———. 1978. "Approaches to Social Change and the Family: A Sociological Perspective." Pp. 1–38 in *Turning Points: Historical and Sociological Essays on the Family,* edited by J. Demos and S. Boocock. Supplement to *American Journal of Sociology.* Chicago: University of Chicago Press.

Elevenstar, D. 1980. "Happy Couple: A Tribute to Old-Fashioned Virtues." *Los Angeles Times* (January 8):2.

Elkin, Meyer. 1976. "Post-Divorce Counseling in a Conciliation Court." Paper presented at the Third Invitational Conference on Marriage Counselors' Education, San Francisco, October 9.

Entine, A. 1976. "Mid-Life Counseling: Prognosis and Potential." *Personnel and Guidance Journal* 55:112–114.

Erikson, Erik. 1963. *Childhood and Society.* New York: Norton.

———. 1968. *Identity, Youth and Crisis.* New York: Norton.

Esfandiary, Fereidoun M. 1977. *Up-Wingers.* New York: Popular Library.

Fagot, Beverly I. 1974. "Sex Differences in Toddlers' Behavior and Parental Reaction." *Developmental Psychology* 10:554–558.

Falek, A., and S. Britton. 1974. "Coping: The Hypothesis and Its Implications." *Social Biology* 2:1–7.

Family Planning Perspectives. 1975. (July-August):147–148.

Farber, Bernard. 1959. "Effects of a Severely Mentally Retarded Child on Family Integration." *Monographs of the Society for Research in Child Development* 24.

Farber, Bernard, and Leonard Gordon. 1982. "Accounting for Jewish Intermarriage: An Assessment of National and Community Studies." *Contemporary Jewry* 6:47–74.

Fechter, Lawrence D. 1984. "Pre-Birth CO Linked to Learning Defects." *Science News* 125 (June 2):342.

Feldman, Frances. 1976. *The Family in Today's Money World.* New York: Family Service Association of America.

Feldman, Harold, and Margaret Feldman. 1976. "Marriage in Later Years: Cohort and Parental Effect." Unpublished paper, Department of Human Development and Family Studies, Cornell University.

Feldman, Saul D., and M. Ingham. 1975. "Attachment Behavior: A Validation Study in Two Age Groups." *Child Development* 46:319–330.

Fendrich, Michael. 1984. "Wives' Employment and Husbands' Distress: A Meta-Analysis and a Replication." *Journal of Marriage and the Family* 46:871–879.

Ferbolt, J., and A. Solnit. 1978. "Counseling Parents of Mentally Retarded and Learning Disordered Children." Pp. 157–173 in *Helping Parents Help Their Children.* New York: Brunner/Mazel.

Field, M. J. 1979. "Determinants of Abortion Policy in Developed Nations." *Policy Studies Journal* 7:771–781.

Finlay, Barbara A. 1981. "Birth Order, Sex and Honors Students' Status in a State University." *Psychological Reports* 49:1000.

Fisher, B., and Douglas H. Sprenkle. 1978. "Therapists' Perceptions of Healing Family Functioning." *International Journal of Family Counseling* 6:9–17.

Fisher, Esther. 1974. *Divorce: The New Freedom.* New York: Harper & Row.

Flanzer, Jerry. 1977–1978. "Family Management in the Treatment of Alcoholism." *British Journal on Alcohol and Alcoholism* (Winter).

"Flurry of Christmas Blizzard Childbirths Expected." 1983. *Denver Post* (September).

Ford, Kathleen. 1978. "Contraceptive Use in the U.S. 1973–1976." *Family Planning Perspectives* 10(September-October): 264–269.

Forer, Lucille, with Henry Still. 1976. *The Birth Order Factor: How Your Personality Is Influenced by Your Place in the Family.* New York: David McKay.

Forisha, Barbara L. 1978. *Sex Roles and Personal Awareness.* Morristown, NJ: General Learning Press.

Forrest, Jacqueline, Christopher Tietze, and Ellen Sullivan. 1978. "Abortion in the United States, 1976–1977." *Family Planning Perspectives* 10:271–279.

"Forum International." 1980. Editorial. *Forum: International Journal of Human Relations* (November):6–7.

———. 1981. Editorial. *Forum: International Journal of Human Relations* 10:10.

Fosburgh, L. 1977. "The Make-Believe World of Teenage Maternity." *The New York Times* magazine (August 7):29–34.

Fox, Greer Litton. 1975. "Love Match and Arranged Marriage in a Modernizing Nation: Mate Selection in Ankara, Turkey." *Journal of Marriage and the Family* 37:180–193.

Fraiberg, Selma. 1977. *Every Child's Birthright: In Defense of Mothering.* New York: Basic Books.

Framo, James L. 1981. "The Integration of Marital Therapy and Sessions with Family of Origin." Pp. 133–158 in *Handbook of Family Therapy,* edited by A. Gurman and D. Kniskern. New York: Brunner/Mazel.

Francoeur, Robert. 1972. *Eve's New Rib.* New York: Delta Press.

Franklin, Deborah. 1984. "Leukemia Virus Variant Fingered as Likely AIDS Cause." *Science News* 125:260.

Freedman, Deborah S., and Arland Thornton. 1979. "The Long-Term Impact of Pregnancy at Marriage on the Family's Economic Circumstances." *Family Planning Perspectives* 11:6–21.

Freeman, M. 1979. *Violence in the Home.* Westmead, England: Saxon House.

Friedan, Betty. 1980. "Their Turn: How Men Are Changing." Redbook (May):23.

Freud, Sigmund. 1927. "Some Psychological Consequences of Anatomical Distinction between the Sexes." *International Journal of Psychological Analysis* 8:133–142.

———. 1949. *An Outline of Psychoanalysis.* New York: Norton.

Friday, Nancy. 1973. *My Secret Garden: Women's Sexual Fantasies.* New York: Trident Press.

———. 1980. *Men in Love.* New York: Delacorte Press.

Friedman, A., and Judy Todd. 1979. "Power, Intimacy, and Happiness in Long Term Marriages." Unpublished paper.

Furstenberg, Frank F. 1976a. "Premarital Pregnancy and Marital Instability." *Journal of Social Issues* 32:67–86.

———. 1976b. Unplanned Parenthood. New York: Free Press.

———. 1978. "Family Support: Helping Teenagers Cope." *Family Planning Perspectives* 10 (November-December):323–333.

Furstenberg, Frank F., Jr., and Graham Spanier. 1984. "The Risk of Dissolution in Remarriage: An Examination of Cherlin's Hypothesis of Incomplete Institutionalization." *Family Relations* 33:433–441.

Gadpaille, Warren. 1975. *The Cycles of Sex.* New York: Scribner's.

Gagnon, John. 1977. *Human Sexualities.* Glenview, IL: Scott, Foresman.

Gagnon, John, and Cathy Greenblat. 1978. *Life Designs: Individuals, Marriages and Families.* Glenview, IL: Scott, Foresman.

Gagnon, John, and Bruce Henderson. 1985. "The Social Psychology of Sexual Development." Pp. 145–151 in *Marriage and Family in a Changing Society,* edited by J. Henslin. New York: Free Press.

Gagnon, John, and William Simon. 1968. "Sexual Deviance in Contemporary America." *Annals of the American Academy of Political and Social Science* (March).

Gallup Poll. 1981. "1981 Cost of Living Audit."

Ganong, Lawrence, and Marilyn Coleman. 1984. "The Effects of Remarriage on Children: A Review of the Empirical Literature." *Family Relations* 33:389–406.

Gebhard, Paul. 1965. *Sex Offenders*. New York: Harper & Row.

———. 1971. "Postmarital Coitus among Widows and Divorcees." Pp. 81–96 in *Divorce and After*, edited by P. Bohannan. Garden City, NY: Doubleday.

Gelles, Richard. 1984. "Parental Child Snatching: A Preliminary Estimate of the National Incidence." *Journal of Marriage and the Family* 46:735–739.

Gelles, Richard, and Murray A. Straus. 1979. "Violence in the American Family." *Journal of Social Issues* 35:15–39.

Gernstein, M., and M. Papen-Daniel. 1981. *Understanding Adulthood*. Fullerton, CA: California Personnel and Guidance Association, Monograph No. 15.

Gerson, Menachem. 1978. "Motivation for Motherhood." Ph.D. dissertation No. 7818420, New York University.

Gilbert, S. 1976. "Self-Disclosure, Intimacy and Communication in Families." *Family Coordinator* 25:221–230.

Gillespie, Dair. 1971. "Who Has the Power? The Marital Struggle." *Journal of Marriage and the Family* 33:455–458.

Gitchel, Sam, and Lorri Foster. 1985. *Let's Talk about SEX: For People 9 to 12 and Their Parents*. Los Angeles: Planned Parenthood.

Glenn, Norval. 1975. "Psychological Well-Being in the Post-Parental Stage: Some Evidence from National Surveys." *Journal of Marriage and the Family* 37:105–110.

———. 1982. "Interreligious Marriage in the United States: Patterns and Recent Trends." *Journal of Marriage and the Family* 44:555–556.

Glenn, Norval D., Adreain A. Ross, and Judy Corder Tully. 1974. "Patterns of Intergenerational Mobility of Females through Marriage." *American Sociological Review* 39:683–699.

Glenn, Norval, and Charles Weaver. 1977. "The Marital Happiness of Remarried Divorced Persons." *Journal of Marriage and the Family* 39:331–337.

———. 1979. "Attitudes toward Premarital, Extramarital, and Homosexual Relations in the U.S. in the 1970s." *Journal of Sex Research* 15:108–118.

Glick, Ira, Robert Weiss, and C. Parkes. 1974. *The First Four Years of Bereavement*. New York: Wiley.

Glick, Paul. 1979. "Children of Divorced Parents in Demographic Perspective." *Journal of Social Issues* 35:170–182.

———. 1980. "Remarriage: Some Recent Changes and Variations." *Journal of Family Issues* 1:455–478.

———. 1985. As reported in *Marriage and Divorce Today* 10:1.

Glick, Paul, and Arthur Norton. 1971. "Frequency, Duration, and Probability of Marriage and Divorce." *Journal of Marriage and the Family* 33:307–317.

———. 1977. "Marrying, Divorcing and Living Together in the U.S. Today." *Population Bulletin* 32:1–41.

Glick, Paul, and Graham Spanier. 1980. "Married and Unmarried Cohabitation in the United States." *Journal of Marriage and the Family* 42:19–30.

Glueck, Sheldon, and Eleanor Glueck. 1968. *Delinquents and Nondelinquents in Perspective*. Cambridge, MA: Harvard University Press.

Goetting, Ann. 1980. "Former Spouse-Current Spouse Relationships." *Journal of Family Issues* 1:58–80.

———. 1982. "The Six Stations of Remarriage: Developmental Tasks of Remarriage after Divorce." *Family Relations* 31:213–222.

Goldstein, H. 1974. "Reconstituted Families: The Second Marriage and Its Children." *Psychiatric Quarterly* 48:433–440.

Goleman, Daniel. 1984. "News Focus." *Los Angeles Herald Examiner* (February 29):A-1.

Goode, William J. 1956. *After Divorce*. New York: Free Press.

———. 1959. "The Theoretical Importance of Love." *American Sociological Review* 24:38–47.

———. 1963. *World Revolution and Family Patterns*. New York: Free Press.

Goodman, Ellen. 1986. "Sex and the Single Teen-Ager." *Los Angeles Times* (March 11):Part II, p. 5.

Gottlieb, David, and Janet Chafetz. 1977. "Dynamics of Familial, Generational Conflict and Reconciliation: A Research Note." *Youth and Society* 9:213–224.

Gottman, John. 1979. *Marital Interaction: Experimental Investigations*. New York: Academic Press.

Gottman, John, H. Markman, and C. Notarius. 1977. "The Topography of Marital Conflict: A Sequential Analysis of Verbal and Nonverbal Behavior." *Journal of Marriage and the Family* 39:461–477.

Gould, Roger L. 1978. *Transformations, Growth, and Change in Adult Life*. New York: Simon and Schuster.

Goulder, Lois. 1985. "The Dilemma of 'Concealed' Conception." *Family Weekly* (May 26):8.

Gove, Walter. 1972. "The Relationship between Sex Roles, Marital Status and Mental Illness." *Social Forces* 51:34–44.

Gove, Walter, and M. Greerken. 1977. "The Effect of Children and Employment on the Mental Health of Married Men and Women." *Social Forces* 56:66–76.

Gove, Walter, Michael Hughes, and Carolyn Briggs Style. 1983. "Does Marriage Have Positive Effects on the Psychological Well-Being of the Individual?" *Journal of Health and Social Behavior* 24:122–131.

Gove, Walter, and J. Tudor. 1973. "Adult Sex Roles and Mental Illness." *American Journal of Sociology* 78:50–73.

Grace, Gloria, and M. Steiner. 1978. "Wives' Attitudes and the Retention of Navy Enlisted Personnel." Pp. 42–54 in *Military Families*, edited by E. Hunter and E. Nice. New York: Praeger.

Greenblatt, Robert B., and Virginia P. McNamara. 1976. "Endocrinology of Human Sexuality." Pp. 104–118 in *The Sexual Experience*, edited by B. Sadock, H. Kaplan, and A. Freedman. Baltimore, MD: Williams and Wilkins.

Greif, Geoffrey. 1984. "Custodial Dads." *Single Parent* (January/February).

———. 1985a. *Single Fathers*. Lexington, MA: Lexington Books.

———. 1985b. "Single Fathers Rearing Children." *Journal of Marriage and Family* 47(1)(February):185–191.

Group for the Advancement of Psychiatry. 1973. *Joys and Sorrows of Parenthood*. New York: Charles Scribner's Sons.

———. 1985b. "Single Fathers Rearing Children." *Journal of Marriage and the Family* 47:185–191.

Grusky, Oscar, Philip Bonacich, and M. Peyrot. 1984. "Physical Contact in the Family." *Journal of Marriage and the Family* 46:715–723.

Guinness Book of World Records. 1980. New York: Sterling.

Hager, P. 1985. "Medical Gains Stir Debate on Abortion Ruling." *Los Angeles Times* (September 9):Part I, pp. 1, 12–13.

Hale, W. 1970. *Ancient Greece*. New York: American Heritage Press.

Hall, Francine S., and Douglas T. Hall. 1979. *The Two-Career Couple*. Reading, MA: Addison-Wesley.

Halliday, T. 1980. "Remarriage: The More Complete Institution?" *American Journal of Sociology* 86:630–635.

Hammond, J. 1984. "Consumer Economics." *American Demographics* (May).

Hansen, G. 1975. "Meeting Housing Challenges: Involvement—the Elderly." In *Housing Issues, Proceedings of the Fifth Annual Meeting, American Association of Housing Educators*. Lincoln: University of Nebraska Press.

Harlow, Harry. 1958. "The Nature of Love." *American Psychologist* 13:673–685.

———. 1962. "The Heterosexual Affectional System in Monkeys." *American Psychologist* 17:1–9.

Harriman, L. 1986. "Marital Adjustment as Related to Personal and Marital Changes Accompanying Parenthood." *Family Relations* 35:233–239.

Hatcher, R., G. Stewart, F. Stewart, F. Guest, P. Stratton, and A. Wright. 1978. *Contraceptive Technology: 1978–79*. 9th ed. New York: Irvington.

Hatkoff, Terry. 1978. "Cultural and Demographic Differences in Persons' Cognitive Referents of Love." Ph.D. dissertation, University of Southern California.

Hatkoff, Terry, and Thomas E. Lasswell. 1977. "Love and Age, Sex, and Life Course Experiences." Paper presented at the meeting of the National Council on Family Relations (October).

Haun, D., and Nick Stinnett. 1974. "Does Psychological Comfortableness between Engaged Couples Affect Their Probability of Successful Marriage Adjustment?" *Family Perspective* 9:11–18.

Haverstein, L. 1980. "Married Women: Work and Family." *Family Today* 1:365–386.

Havighurst, Robert. 1968. "Personality and Patterns of Aging." *The Gerontologist* 8:20–23.

Hawkins, James L., Carol Weisberg, and Dixie L. Ray. 1977. "Marital Communication Style and Social Class." *Journal of Marriage and the Family* 39:479–490.

Hayes, Mary. 1981. "Family Ordinal Position of Status Offenders." Unpublished monograph, Department of Sociology, University of California.

Heckman, Norma A., Rebecca Bryson, and Jeff B. Bryson. 1977. "Problems of Professional Couples: A Content Analysis." *Journal of Marriage and the Family* 39:323–330.

Heer, David, and Amyra Grossbard-Schectman. 1981. "The Impact of the Female Marriage Squeeze and the Contraceptive Revolution on Sex Roles and the Women's Liberation Movement in the United States, 1960 to 1975." *Journal of Marriage and the Family* 43:49–55.

Heider, Fritz. 1958. *The Psychology of Interpersonal Relations*. New York: Wiley.

Heinowitz, Jack R. 1982. *Pregnant Fathers*. Englewood Cliffs, NJ: Prentice-Hall.

Heiss, Jerold. 1980. "Family Theory—20 Years Later." *Contemporary Sociology* 8:201–204.

Helms, D., and J. Turner. 1981. *Exploring Child Behavior*. 2nd ed. New York: Holt, Rinehart and Winston.

Helsing, S., M. Szklo, and G. Comstock. 1981. "Factors Associated with Mortality after Widowhood." *American Journal of Public Health* 71:802–809.

Hendricks, John, and C. Davis Hendricks. 1977. *Aging in Mass Society: Myths and Realities*. Cambridge, MA: Winthrop Publishers.

Henslin, James M. 1985. "Sex Roles." Pp. 142–144 in *Marriage and Family in a Changing Society*, edited by J. Henslin. New York: Free Press.

Henze, Lura F., and John Hudson. 1974. "Personal and Family Characteristics of Cohabiting and Noncohabiting College Students." *Journal of Marriage and the Family* 36:722–726.

Hess, Beth, Elizabeth Markson, and Peter Stein. 1985. *Sociology*. New York: Macmillan.

Hess, E. 1965. "Attitude and Pupil Size." *Scientific American* 212:46–54.

Hess, R. 1970. "Social Class and Ethnic Influence upon Socialization." In *Carmichael's Manual of Child Psychology*. Vol. 2, edited by P.H. Mussen. New York: Wiley.

Hess, R., and K. Camara. 1979. "Postdivorce Family Relationships as Mediating Factors in the Consequences of Divorce for Children." *Journal of Social Issues* 35:79–96.

Hetherington, E. Mavis. 1972. "Effects of Father Absence on Personality Development in Adolescent Daughters." *Developmental Psychology* 7:313–326.

Hetherington, E. Mavis, Martha Cox, and Roger Cox. 1976. "Divorced Fathers." *Family Coordinator* 25:417–428.

———. 1978. "The Aftermath of Divorce." In *Mother-Child, Father-Child Relations*, edited by J. Stevens and M. Matthew. Washington, D.C.: National Association for the Education of Young Children.

Hetherington, E. Mavis, and G. Frankie. 1967. "Effects of Parental Dominance, Warmth, and Conflict on Imitation in Children." *Journal of Personality and Social Psychology* 6:119–125.

Heyman, D. 1970. "Does a Wife Retire?" *The Gerontologist* 10:54–56.

Hicks, Mary, and Marilyn Platt. 1970. "Marital Happiness and Stability: A Review of the Research in the Sixties." *Journal of Marriage and the Family* 32:553–574.

Hill, Charles T., Zick Rubin, and Letitia Anne Peplau. 1976. "Breakups before Marriage: The End of 103 Affairs." *Journal of Social Issues* 32:147–168.

Hill, Reuben. 1949. *Families under Stress*. New York: Harper & Row.

———. 1964. "Methodological Problems with the Developmental Approach to Family Study." *Family Process* 3:186–206.

———. 1966. "Contemporary Developments in Family Theory." *Journal of Marriage and the Family* 28:10–25.

Hiller, Dana V. 1984. "Power Dependence and Division of Family Work." *Sex Roles* 10:1003–1019.

Himes, Norman. 1963. *Medical History of Contraception*. New York: Gamut Press.

Hinkle, Dennis E., and Michael J. Sporakowski. 1975. "Attitudes toward Love: A Reexamination." *Journal of Marriage and the Family* 37:764–767.

Hipgrave, T. 1981. "Child Rearing by Lone Fathers." Pp. 149–166 in *Changing Patterns of Childbearing and Child*

Rearing, edited by R. Chester, P. Diggory, and M. Sutherland. London: Academic Press.

Hitchens, D. 1979–1980. "Social Attitudes, Legal Standards, and Personal Trauma in Child Custody Cases." *Journal of Homosexuality* 5:89–95.

Hobbs, Daniel, and Sue Peck Cole. 1976. "Transition to Parenthood: A Decade Replication." *Journal of Marriage and the Family* 38:723–731.

Hoffenstein, S. 1978. "Poems in Praise of Practically Nothing." P. 2 in The *Crown Treasury of Relevant Quotations*, edited by E. Murphy. New York: Crown.

Hoffman, Lois W. 1974. "Effects on Children: Summary and Discussion." Pp. 190–212 in *Working Mothers*, edited by L. W. Hoffman and F. I. Nye. San Francisco: Jossey-Bass.

Hoffman, Lois, and Martin Hoffman. 1973. "The Value of Children to Parents." In *Psychological Perspectives on Population*, edited by J. Fawcett. New York: Basic Books.

Hoffman, Lois, and Jerome G. Manis. 1978. "Influences of Children on Marital Interaction and Parental Satisfactions and Dissatisfactions." Pp. 165–214 in *Child Influences on Marital and Family Interactions*, edited by R. Lerner and G. Spanier. New York: Academic Press.

Hoffman, Lois W., and F. Ivan Nye, eds. 1974. *Working Mothers*. San Francisco: Jossey-Bass.

Hoffman, Lynn. 1980. "The Family Life Cycle and Discontinuous Change." Pp. 53–68 in *The Family Life Cycle: A Framework for Family Therapy*, edited by E. Carter and M. McGoldrick. New York: Gardner Press.

Holman, Thomas B., and Wesley R. Burr. 1980. "Beyond the Beyond: The Growth of Family Theories in the 1970's." *Journal of Marriage and the Family* 42: 729–741.

Holmstrom, Lynda L. 1972. *The Two-Career Family*. Cambridge, MA: Schenkman.

Hopkins, J., and P. White. 1978. "The Dual-Career Couple: Constraints and Supports." *Family Coordinator* 27:253–259.

Horn, Jack C. 1984. "Maculate Contraception." *Psychology Today* 18:14.

Hoult, Thomas F. 1969. *Dictionary of Modern Sociology*. Totowa, NJ: Littlefield, Adams.

Horney, Karen. 1950. "The Tyranny of the Should." Pp. 64–85 in *Neurosis and Human Growth*. New York: W. W. Norton.

Hoult, Thomas F., Lura Henze, and John W. Hudson. 1978. *Courtship and Marriage in America*. Boston: Little, Brown.

Houseknecht, Sharon. 1977. "Reference Group Support for Voluntary Childlessness: Evidence for Conformity." *Journal of Marriage and the Family* 39:285–292.

———. 1979a. "Childlessness and Marital Adjustment." *Journal of Marriage and the Family* 41:259–265.

———. 1979b. "Timing of the Decision to Remain Voluntarily Childless: Evidence for Continuing Socialization." *Psychology of Women Quarterly* 4:81–96.

Huber, W. 1977. "Marriage Encounter Evaluated by CRI." San Diego, CA: Research and Development.

Humphreys, Laud 1972. *Out of the Closet: The Sociology of Homosexual Liberation*. Englewood Cliffs, NJ.: Prentice-Hall.

Hunt, Janet G., and Larry L. Hunt. 1982. "The Dualities of Careers and Families: New Integrations or New Polarizations?" *Social Problems* 29:499–510.

Hunt, Morton. 1966. *The World of the Formerly Married*. New York: McGraw-Hill.

———. 1974a. *Sexual Behavior in the 1970s*. New York: Dell.

———. 1974b. *Sexual Behavior of the 1970s*. Chicago: Playboy Press.

Hunt, Morton, and Bernice Hunt. 1977. *The Divorce Experience*. New York: McGraw-Hill.

Hunt, R., and M. King. 1978. "Religiosity and Marriage." *Journal for the Scientific Study of Religion* 17:399–406.

Hurlock, Elizabeth. 1972. *Child Development*. New York: McGraw-Hill.

Hutchison, Ira W. 1975. "The Significance of Marital Status for Morale and Life Satisfaction among Lower Income Elderly." *Journal of Marriage and the Family* 37:287–293.

Huyck, Margaret H. 1974. *Growing Older*. Englewood Cliffs, NJ: Prentice-Hall.

Hyde, Janet S., and Betty Rosenberg. 1980. *Half the Human Experience: The Psychology of Women*. Lexington, MA: D.C. Heath.

Iliffe, A. H. 1960. "A Study of Preferences in Feminine Beauty." *British Journal of Psychology* 51:267–273.

Indvik, J., and M. Fitzpatrick. 1982. "If You Could Read My Mind: Love . . . Understanding and Misunderstanding in the Marital Dyad." *Family Relations* 31:43–57.

Jackson, Don. 1967. "The Eternal Triangle." Pp. 174–264 in *Techniques of Family Therapy*, edited by J. Haley and L. Hoffman. New York: Basic Books.

———. 1977. "Family Rules: Marital Quid pro Quo." In *The Interactional View*, edited by P. Watzlawick and J. Weakland. New York: Norton.

Jackson, Patrick G. 1983. "On Living Together Unmarried." *Journal of Family Issues* 4, 1:35–59.

Jacobsen, Neil, and Gayla Margolin. 1979. *Marital Therapy: Strategies Based on Social Learning and Behavior Exchange Principles*. New York: Brunner/Mazel.

Jacobsen, Paul H. 1959. *American Marriage and Divorce*. New York: Rinehart.

Jacoby, Susan. 1975. "Forty-Nine Million Singles Can't Be All Right." Pp. 115–123 in *Life Styles: Diversity in American Society*. 2nd ed., edited by S. Feldman and G. Thieller. Boston: Little, Brown.

Jacques, Jeffrey M., and Karen M. Chason. 1979. "Cohabitation: Its Impact on Marital Success." *Family Coordinator* (January):35–39.

Jessel, Camilla. 1983. *The Joy of Birth: A Book for Parents and Children*. New York: E.P. Dutton (Hillside Books).

Jewson, Ruth. 1980. "The National Council of Family Relations: Decade of the Seventies." *Journal of Marriage and the Family* 42:1017–1028.

Johnson, E., and B. Bursk. 1977. "Relationships between the Elderly and Their Adult Children." *The Gerontologist* 17:90–96.

Jones, C., and J. Else. 1979. "Racial and Cultural Issues in Adoption." *Child Welfare* 58:373–382.

Jones, R., and J. Bates. 1978. "Satisfaction in Male Homosexual Couples." *Journal of Homosexuality* 3:217–224.

Jordan, T. 1962. "Research on the Handicapped Child and the Family." *Merrill-Palmer Quarterly* 8:354–360.

Julty, Sam. 1979. *Men's Bodies, Men's Selves.* New York: Dell.

Kagan, Jerome. 1964. "Acquisition and Significance of Sex Typing and Sex Role Identity." In *Review of Child Development Research.* Vol. 2, edited by M. Hoffman and L. Hoffman. New York: Russell Sage.

Kalish, Richard, and D. Reynolds. 1976. *Death and Ethnicity: A Psychocultural Study.* Los Angeles: University of Southern California Press.

Kalter, Constance. 1983. "The Post-Partum Adjustment of First-Time Fathers." Unpublished doctoral dissertation, University of Southern California.

Kalter, N. 1977. "Children of Divorce in an Outpatient Psychiatric Population." *American Journal of Orthopsychiatry* 47:40–51.

Kantor, David. 1980. "Critical Identity Image: A Concept Linking Individual, Couple, and Family Development." In *Family Therapy: Combining Psychodynamic and Family Systems Approaches,* edited by J. Pearce and L. Friedman. New York: Grune and Stratton.

Kaplan, Helen Singer. 1979. *Disorders of Sexual Desire: And Other New Concepts and Techniques in Sex Therapy.* New York: Brunner/Mazel.

Katchadourian, H., and D. Lunde. 1972. *Fundamentals of Human Sexuality.* New York: Holt, Rinehart and Winston.

Katz, S., and U. Gallagher. 1976. "Subsidized Adoption in America." *Family Law Quarterly* 10:3.

Keith, Pat M. 1983. "A Comparison of the Resource of Parents and Childless Men and Women in Very Old Age." *Family Relations* 32:403–409.

Kelley, Harold H., and John W. Thibaut. 1978. *Interpersonal Relations: A Theory of Independence.* New York: Wiley.

Kelly, C. 1977. "Empathic Listening." In *Bridges, Not Walls,* edited by J. Steward. Reading, MA: Addison-Wesley.

Kemp, Ruth. 1986. "Breastfeeding and the Expectant Father." *International Journal of Childbirth Education* 1:8.

Kephart, William. 1967. "Some Correlates of Romantic Love." *Journal of Marriage and the Family* 29:470–474.

Kerckhoff, Alan C. 1972. *Socialization and Social Class.* Englewood Cliffs, NJ: Prentice-Hall.

Kerpelman, Leonard. 1985. *Divorce: A Guide for Men.* New York: Icarus.

Keshet, H., and K. Rosenthal. 1978. "Fathering after Marital Separation." *Social Work* 23:11–18.

Kessler, Ronald C., and James A. McRae, Jr. 1984. "The Effects of Wives' Employment on the Mental Health of Married Men and Women." Pp. 349–360 in *Family Studies Review Yearbook.* Vol. 2, edited by D. Olson and B. Miller. Beverly Hills, CA.: Sage Publications.

Kessler, Sheila. 1975. *The American Way of Divorce: Prescriptions for Change.* Chicago: Nelson-Hall.

Kilgore, James, and Don Highlander. 1976. *Getting More Family out of Your Dollar.* Irvine, CA: Harvest House.

Kimmel, D. 1976. "Adult Development: Challenges for Counseling." *Personnel and Guidance Journal* 55:103–105.

Kinard, E. 1979. "The Psychological Consequences of Abuse for the Child." *Journal of Social Issues* 35:82–100.

King, Nick. 1982. "The Struggle for Fathers' Rights." *Los Angeles Times* (December 16):Part V, p. 8.

Kinsey, Alfred, Wardell Pomeroy, Clyde Martin, and Paul Gebhard. 1953. *Sexual Behavior in the Human Female.* Philadelphia: W.B. Saunders.

———. 1969. *Sexual Behavior in the Human Female.* New York: Pocket Books.

Kinsey, Alfred, Wardell Pomeroy, and Clyde Martin. 1948. *Sexual Behavior in the Human Male.* Philadelphia: W.B. Saunders.

Kitzinger, Sheila. 1972. *The Experience of Childbirth.* New York: Taplinger.

———. 1983. *Women's Experience of Sex.* New York: G.P. Putnam's Sons.

Kivett, Vera R. 1978. "Loneliness and the Rural Widow." *Family Coordinator* 27:389–394.

Kivnick, H. 1983. "Dimensions of Grandparenthood Meaning: Deductive Conceptualization and Empirical Deviation." *Journal of Personality and Social Psychology* 44:1056–1058.

Klaus, Marshall, and John Kennell. 1976. *Maternal Infant Bonding.* St. Louis, MO: C.V. Mosby.

———. 1983a. *Bonding.* St. Louis, Mo.: C.V. Mosby

———. 1983b. *Maternal Infant Bonding.* Rev. ed. St. Louis, MO: C.V. Mosby.

Klein, David. 1979. "A Social History of a Grass-Roots Institution: The Case of the NCFR Workshop on Theory Construction and Research Methodology." Paper presented to the NCFR Workshop on Theory Construction and Research Methodology, Boston.

Klein, David, and Reuben Hill. 1979. "Determinants of Family Problem Solving Effectiveness." Pp. 493–548 in *Contemporary Theories about the Family.* Vol. 1, edited by W. Burr, R. Hill, F. I. Nye, and I. Reiss. New York: Free Press.

Klein, David, Jay D. Schvaneveldt, and Brent Miller. 1977. "The Attitudes and Activities of Contemporary Family Theorists." *Journal of Comparative Family Studies* 8:5–27.

Klimek, David. 1979. *Beneath Mate Selection and Marriage.* New York: Van Nostrand Reinhold.

Klinman, Debra, and Rhiana Kohl. 1984. *Fatherhood, U.S.A.* New York: Garland.

Knapp, J., and Robert Whitehurst. 1977. "Sexually Open Marriage and Relationships: Issues and Propects." Pp. 147–160 in *Marriage and Alternatives: Exploring Intimate Relationships,* edited by R. Libby and R. Whitehurst. Glenview, IL: Scott, Foresman.

Knaub, Patricia Kain, and Suzanne Hanna. 1984. "Children of Remarriage: Perceptions of Family Strengths." *Journal of Divorce* 7:73–90.

Knox, David. 1979. *Exploring Marriage and the Family.* Glenview, IL: Scott, Foresman.

Knupfer, Genevieve, W. Clark, and R. Room. 1966. "The Mental Health of the Unmarried." *American Journal of Psychiatry* 122:841–851.

Kogan, Bernard. 1973. *Human Sexual Expression.* New York: Harcourt Brace Jovanovich.

Kohlberg, L. 1969. "Stage and Sequence: The Cognitive Developmental Approach to Socialization." In *Handbook of Socialization Theory and Research,* edited by D.A. Goslin. Chicago: Rand McNally.

Kohn, Melvin L. 1959. "Social Class and Parental Values." *American Journal of Sociology* 64:337–351.

———. 1977. *Class and Conformity: A Study in Values.* 2nd ed. Chicago: University of Chicago Press.

Kolb, Trudy M., and Murray A. Straus. 1974. "Marital Power and Marital Happiness in Relation to Problem-Solving Ability." *Journal of Marriage and the Family* 36:757–766.

Komarovsky, Mirra. 1964. *Blue-Collar Marriage*. New York: Random House.

Kopkind, A. 1973. "Gay Rock: The Boys in the Band." *Ramparts* 11:49–50.

Korner, A. 1974. "Methodological Considerations in Studying Sex Differences in the Behavioral Functioning of Newborns." In *Sex Differences in Behavior*, edited by R.C. Friedman, R.M. Richart, and R.L. Van de Wiele. New York: Wiley.

Kressel, K. 1980. "Patterns of Coping in Divorce and Some Implications for Clinical Practice." *Family Relations* 29:234–240.

Kressel, K., and M. Deutsch. 1977. "Divorce Therapy: An In-Depth Survey of Therapists' Views." *Family Process* 16:413–443.

Kretzschmar, Robert. 1978. "Smoking during Pregnancy." *ACOG Newsletter* (December 6).

Kulka, R., and H. Weingarter. 1979. "The Long-Term Effects of Parental Divorce in Childhood on Adult Adjustment." *Journal of Social Issues* 35:50–78.

Kunz, Phillip R., and E. Peterson. 1975. "Parental Control over Adolescents According to Family Size." *Adolescence* 10:419–427.

L'Abate, Luciano. 1977. "Intimacy Is Sharing Hurt Feelings: A Reply to David Mace." *Journal of Marriage and Family Counseling* 3:13–16.

Lacey, P. 1969. *The Wedding*. New York: Grosset & Dunlap.

Ladas, Alice Kahn, Beverly Whipple, and John D. Perry. 1982. *The G Spot: And Other Recent Discoveries about Human Sexuality*. New York: Holt, Rinehart and Winston.

Lamaze, Fernand. 1970. *Painless Childbirth*. L. Celestin, trans. Chicago: Regnery.

Lamb, Michael. 1977. "The Role of the Father: An Overview." Pp. 1–63 in *The Role of the Father in Child Development*, edited by M. Lamb. New York: Wiley.

Landis, Judson. 1956. "The Pattern of Divorce in Three Generations." *Social Forces* 34: 213–216.

Landis, Paul. 1955. *Making the Most of Marriage*. New York: Appleton-Century-Crofts.

LaRossa, Ralph. 1977. *Conflict and Power in Marriage*. Beverly Hills, CA: Sage Publications.

Larsen, R. 1978. "Thirty Years of Research on the Subjective Well-Being of Older Americans." *Journal of Gerontology* 33:109–129.

Larson, J. 1984. "The Effect of Husband's Unemployment on Marital and Family Relations in Blue-Collar Families." *Family Relations* 33:503–510.

Lasswell, Marcia. 1974. "Is There a Best Age to Marry? An Interpretation." *Family Coordinator* 23: 237–242.

———. 1983. "Marrying Too Early." *Medical Aspects of Human Sexuality* 17(7):20–41.

———. 1984. "Turbulent Periods in a Marriage." *Medical Aspects of Human Sexuality* 18:120–140.

Lasswell, Marcia, and Norman Lobsenz. 1976. *No-Fault Marriage*. New York: Doubleday.

———. 1978a. "The 'Little Things' That Can Destroy a Marriage." *McCall's* (February):66–70.

———. 1978b. "When Someone You Love Suddenly Changes." *McCall's* (May):120–124.

———. 1979a. "Can You Really Change the One You Love?" *McCall's* (June):78–81.

———. 1979b. "The Right (and Wrong) Way to Make Decisions." *McCall's* (August):70–74.

———. 1979c. "When and How to Be Honest." *McCall's* (July):69–74, 149.

———. 1980. *Styles of Loving: Why You Love the Way You Do*. Garden City, NY: Doubleday.

———. 1983. *Equal Time: The New Way of Living, Loving, and Working Together*. New York: Doubleday.

Lasswell, Thomas E., and Marcia Lasswell. 1976. "I Love You but I'm Not in Love with You." *Journal of Marriage and the Family* 2:211–224.

Lasswell, Thomas E., Marcia Lasswell, and Larry Goodman. 1976. "What Biofeedback Can Tell Us about Love." Paper presented at meeting of American Association of Marriage and Family Counselors, Las Vegas, Nevada.

Lavori, Nora. 1976. *Living Together, Married or Single: Your Legal Rights*. New York: Harper & Row.

Lax, Ruth, Sheldon Bach, and J. Alexis Burland, eds. 1980. *Rapprochement: The Critical Subphase of Separation-Individuation*. New York: Jason Aronson.

Le Boyer, Frederick. 1975. *Birth without Violence*. New York: Alfred A. Knopf.

Lee, John. 1973. *Colours of Love*. Toronto: New Press.

Lee, John. 1976a. *The Colors of Love*. Englewood Cliffs, NJ: Prentice-Hall.

———. 1976b. "Forbidden Colors of Love: Patterns of Gay Love and Gay Liberation." *Journal of Homosexuality* 4:401–418.

LeMasters, E.E. 1957. "Parenthood as Crisis." *Marriage and Family Living* 19:352–355.

———. 1974. *Parents in Modern America*. Homewood, IL: Dorsey.

Leslie, Gerald, and Elizabeth Leslie. 1980. *Marriage in a Changing World*. 2nd ed. New York: Wiley.

Leveno, Kenneth J., F. Gary Cunningham, and Jack A. Pritchard. 1985. "Cesarean Section: An Answer to the House of Horne." *American Journal of Obstetrics and Gynecology* 152(December 15):838–844.

Lever, Janet. 1978. "Sex Differences in the Complexity of Children's Play." *American Sociological Review* 43:471–483.

Levin, M. 1976. "Let George Do It: Male Contraceptives." *Ms.* (January):91–94.

Levinger, George, and D. J. Senn. 1967. "Disclosure of Feelings in Marriage." *Merrill-Palmer Quarterly* 13:237–249.

Levinson, Daniel, C. Darrow, E. Klein, M. Levinson, and B. McKee. 1974. "The Psychosocial Development of Men in Early Adulthood and Mid-Life Transition." In *Life History Research in Psychotherapy*. Vol. 3, edited by D. Ricks, A. Thomas, and M. Roff. Minneapolis: University of Minnesota Press.

———. 1978. *The Seasons of a Man's Life*. New York: Alfred A. Knopf.

Levy, Marion. 1966. *Modernization and the Structure of Societies*. Princeton, NJ: Princeton University Press.

Lewis, Jerry M. 1979. *How's Your Family?* New York: Brunner/Mazel.

Lewis, J., W. Robert Beavers, J. Gossett, and V. Phillips. 1976. *No Single Thread: Psychological Health in Family Systems.* New York: Brunner/Mazel.

Lewis, Robert A. 1972. "A Developmental Framework for the Analysis of Premarital Dyadic Formation." *Family Process* 11:17–48.

———. 1984. "Some Changes in Men's Values, Meanings, Roles and Attitudes toward Marrriage and Family in the USA." Pp. 59–80 in *Social Change and Family Policies.* Part I. Melbourne: Australian Institute of Family Studies.

Lewis, Robert A., and Joseph P. Pleck, eds. 1979. "Men's Roles in the Family." *Family Coordinator* 28:4.

Lewis, Robert A., and Graham B. Spanier. 1979. "Theorizing about the Quality and Stability of Marriage." Pp. 268–294 in *Contemporary Theories about the Family.* Vol 2, edited by W. Burr, R. Hill, I. Nye, and I. Reiss. New York: Free Press.

Lewis, Robert A., Graham B. Spanier, V. Atkinson, and C. LeHecks. 1977. "Commitment in Married and Unmarried Cohabitation." *Sociological Focus* 10:367, 373.

Lichtendorf, Susan, and Phyllis Gillis. 1979. *The New Pregnancy.* New York: Random House.

Liebowitz, Michael R., and Donald F. Klein. 1979. "Hysteroid Dysphoria." *Psychiatric Clinics of North America* 2, 3:555–575.

Lindsey, Ben. 1927. *The Companionate Marriage.* Garden City, NY: Garden City Publishers.

Linner, Birgitta. 1976. *Sex and Society in Sweden.* New York: Pantheon.

Little, M. 1983. *Status Report of the Denver Divorce Mediation Research Project.* San Diego: Association of Family Conciliation Courts Mediators Institute.

Locke, Harvey J. 1951. *Predicting Adjustment in Marriage: A Comparison of a Divorced and a Happily Married Group.* New York: Henry Holt.

Locke, Harvey J., and Karl Wallace. 1959. "Short Marital Adjustment and Prediction Tests: Their Reliability and Validity." *Marriage and Family Living* 21:251–255.

Loevinger, Jan. 1976. *Ego Development: Conceptions and Theories.* San Francisco: Jossey-Bass.

Lopata, Helen. 1973. *Widowhood in an American City.* Cambridge, MA: Schenkman.

Lott, A., and B. Lott. 1965. "Group Cohesiveness as Interpersonal Attraction: A Review of Relationships with Antecedent and Consequent Variables." *Psychological Bulletin* 64:259–309.

Luckey, Eleanor B., and J. Bain. 1970. "Children: A Factor in Marital Satisfaction." *Journal of Marriage and the Family* 32:43–44.

Lund, Dale. 1978. "Junior Officer Retention in the Modern Volunteer Army: Who Leaves and Who Stays?" Pp. 32–41 in *Military Families,* edited by E. Hunter and E. Nice. New York: Praeger.

Lundberg, Margaret J. 1974. *The Incomplete Adult: Social Class Constraints on Personality Development.* Westport, CT: Greenwood Press.

Lynch, J. 1977. *The Broken Heart: The Medical Consequences of Loneliness in America.* New York: Basic Books.

Lynn, David B. 1969. *Parental and Sex-Role Identification: A Theoretical Formulation.* Berkeley, CA: McCutchan.

———. 1974. *The Father: His Role in Child Development.* Belmont, CA: Brooks/Cole.

Maas, Henry S., and Joseph A. Kuypers. 1974. *From Thirty to Seventy.* San Francisco: Jossey-Bass.

Maccoby, Eleanor E., and Carol N. Jacklin. 1974. *Psychology of Sex Differences.* Stanford, CA: Stanford University Press.

MacCorquodale, Patricia L. 1984. "Gender Roles and Premarital Contraception." *Journal of Marriage and the Family* 46:57–63.

Macke, Ann S., George W. Bohrnstedt, and Ilene N. Bernstein. 1979. "Housewives' Self-Esteem and Their Husbands Success: The Myth of Vicarious Involvement." *Journal of Marriage and the Family* 41:51–57.

Mackey, W., and R. Day. 1979. "Some Indicators of Fathering Behaviors in the United States: A Cross-Cultural Examination of Adult Male–Child Interaction." *Journal of Marriage and the Family* 41:287–298.

Macklin, Eleanor. 1978. "Review of Research on Nonmarital Cohabitation in the United States." Pp. 197–243 in *Exploring Intimate Lifestyles,* edited by Bernard Murstein. New York: Springer.

———. 1980. "Nontraditional Family Forms: A Decade of Research." *Journal of Marriage and the Family* 42:905–922.

Macovsky, S. 1979. "Coping with Cohabitation." *Money Magazine* (May).

Maddox, Brenda. 1975. *The Half Parent.* New York: Evans.

Magoun, F. 1948. *Love and Marriage.* New York: Harper and Brothers.

Mahler, Martha, F. Pine, and A. Bergman. 1975. *The Psychological Birth of the Human Infant: Symbiosis and Individuation.* New York: Basic Books.

Mahoney, Michael J. 1974. *Cognition and Behavior Modification.* Cambridge, MA: Ballinger.

Makepeace, James M. 1975. "The Birth Control Revolution: Consequences for College Student Life Styles." Ph.D. dissertation, Washington State University.

Mall, Janice. 1985. "A Study of U.S. Teen Pregnancy Rate." *Los Angeles Times* (March 17):Part VII, p. 27.

Maret, E., and Barbara Finlay. 1983. "The Distribution of Household Labor among Women in Dual-Earner Families." Unpublished paper, Department of Sociology, Texas A&M University, College Station.

Marini, Margaret M. 1984. "Women's Educational Attainment and the Timing of Entry into Parenthood." *American Sociological Review* 49:491–511.

Markowski, E., J. Croake, and J. Keller. 1978. "Sexual History and Present Sexual Behavior of Cohabiting and Married Couples." *Journal of Sex Research* 14:27–39.

Marriage and Divorce Today. 1980. Survey. 6(3)(August 25).

Marshall, B., and C. Marshall. 1980. *The Marriage Secret.* Maplewood, NJ: Hammond.

Marshall, Donald S. 1971. *Human Sexual Behavior: Variations in the Ethnographic Spectrum.* New York: Basic Books.

Martin, Elmer P., and Joanne Mitchell Martin. 1978. *The Black Extended Family.* Chicago: University of Chicago Press.

Martin, Thomas W., Kenneth J. Berry, and R. Brooke Jacobsen. 1975. "The Impact of Dual-Career Marriages on Female Professional Careers: An Empirical Test of a Parsonian Hypothesis." *Journal of Marriage and the Family* 37:734–742.

"Marvin v. Marvin." 1979. *Family Law Reporter* 5:3109.

Maslow, Abraham. 1971. *The Farther Reaches of Human Nature.* New York: Viking Press.

Mason, Karen O., and Larry Bumpass. 1975. "U.S. Women's Sex Role Ideology, 1970." *American Journal of Sociology* 80:1212–1220.

Masters, William H. 1976. "Sex Therapy in a Clinical Setting." Paper presented to the International Congress of Sexology, Philadelphia.

Masters, William H., and Virginia Johnson. 1966. *Human Sexual Response.* Boston: Little, Brown.

———. 1970. *Human Sexual Inadequacy.* Boston: Little, Brown.

May, Lee. 1983. "IUD Use Doubles Risk of Infertility, Researchers Say." *Los Angeles Times* (April 11):Part I, pp. 1, 26.

Mayfield, Mark. 1982. "New Birth Control Devices Described." *Los Angeles Times* (October 7):Part V, p. 17.

Maykovich, Minako K. 1976. "Attitudes versus Behavior in Extramarital Sexual Relations." *Journal of Marriage and the Family* 38:693–699.

McCarthy, J. 1978. "A Comparison of the Probability of Dissolution of First and Second Marriages." *Demography* 15:345–359.

McCary, James L. 1978. *Human Sexuality.* 3rd ed. New York: Van Nostrand Reinhold.

McCary, Stephen P. 1978. "Ages and Sources of Information for Learning About and Experiencing Sexual Concepts as Reported by 43 University Students." *Journal of Sex Education and Therapy* 4:50–53.

McCary, Stephen P., and James L. McCary. 1977. "A Measure of Level of Sex Information." *Journal of Sex Education and Therapy* 3:26–28.

McCubbin, Hamilton, Constance B. Joy, A. Elizabeth Cauble, Joan K. Comeau, Joan M. Patterson, and Richard H. Needle. 1980. "Family Stress and Coping: A Decade Review." *Journal of Marriage and the Family* 42:865.

McCubbin, Hamilton, and David H. Olson. 1980. "Beyond Family Crisis: Family Adaptation." Paper presented at the Families in Disaster Conference, Uppsala, Sweden, June.

McDermott, John F., Wen-Shing Tseng, W. Char, and C. Fukunaga. 1978. "Child Custody Decision Making: The Search for Improvement." *Journal of the American Academy of Child Psychiatry* 17:104–116.

McDonald, Gerald W. 1977. "Family Power: Reflections and Direction." *Pacific Sociological Review* 20:607–621.

———. 1980. "Family Power: The Assessment of a Decade of Theory and Research, 1970–1979." *Journal of Marriage and the Family* 42:841–854.

McGoldrick, Monica. 1980. "The Joining of Families through Marriage: The New Couple." Pp. 95–96 in *The Family Life Cycle: A Framework for Family Therapy,* edited by E. Carter and M. McGoldrick. New York: Gardner Press.

McGuinness, D., and K. Pribram. 1979. "The Origins of Sensory Bias in the Development of Gender Differences in Perception and Cognition." Pp. 3–56 in *Cognitive Growth and Development: Essay in Honor of Herbert G. Birch,* edited by M. Bortner. New York: Brunner/Mazel.

McKain, Jerry 1969. *Retirement Marriages.* Storrs, CT: Agricultural Experiment Station, Monograph 3.

———. 1972. "A New Look at Older Marriages." *Family Coordinator* 21:61–69.

McKinlay, S., and Jeffreys, M. 1974. "The Menopausal Syndrome." *British Journal of Preventive and Social Medicine* 28:108.

Mead, Margaret. 1928. *Coming of Age in Samoa.* New York: William Morrow.

———. 1961. *Sex and Temperament in Three Primitive Societies.* New York: William Morrow.

———. 1966. "Marriage in Two Steps." *Redbook* (July):48–49.

———. 1972. *Blackberry Winter.* New York: William Morrow.

Mecklenburg, Marjory E., and Patricia G. Thompson. 1983. "The Adolescent Family Life Program as a Prevention Measure." *Public Health Reports* 98:21–29.

Meigs, A. 1976. "Male Pregnancy and the Reduction of Sexual Opposition in a New Guinea Highlands Society." *Ethnology* 15:393–407.

Meisner, William. 1978. "The Conceptualization of Marriage and Family Dynamics from a Psychoanalytic Perspective." P. 47 in *Marriage and Family Therapy,* edited by T. Paolino and B. McCrady. New York: Brunner/Mazel.

Menaghan, E. 1983. "Marital Stress and Family Transitions: A Panel Analysis." *Journal of Marriage and the Family* 45:371–386.

Menning, Barbara E. 1977. *Infertility: A Guide for the Childless Couple.* Englewood Cliffs, NJ: Prentice-Hall.

Meshorer, Marc, and Judith Meshorer. 1986. *Ultimate Pleasure: The Secrets of Easily Orgasmic Women.* New York: St. Martin's Press.

Messinger, Lillian. 1976. "Remarriage between Divorced People with Children from Previous Marriage." *Journal of Marriage and Family Counseling* 2:193–200.

Meyers, L. 1978. "Battered Wives, Dead Husbands." *Student Lawyer* 6:46–51.

Miller, Brent, and Diana Gerard. 1979. "Family Influences on the Development of Creativity in Children: An Integrative Review." *Family Coordinator* 28:295–321.

Miller, Julie Ann. 1983. "Alcohol Damage at Time of Conception." *Science News* 123 (April 2):215.

———. 1985. "Making Babies Bigger before Birth." *Science News* 127 (March 2):134.

Miller, Stuart. 1983. *Men and Friendship.* Boston: Houghton Mifflin.

Miller, S., R. Corrales, and D. Wackman. 1975. "Recent Progress in Understanding and Facilitating Marital Communication." *Family Coordinator* 24:143–152.

Mills, David. 1984. "A Model for Stepfamily Development." *Family Relations* 33:365–372.

Mills, James L., Barry I. Graubard, Ernest E. Harley, George G. Rhoads, and Heinz W. Barendes. 1984. "Maternal Alcohol Consumption and Birth Weight." *Journal of the American Medical Association* 252:1875–1879.

Mitchell, W. 1978. *Mishpokhe: A Study of New York City Jewish Family Clubs.* New York: Mouton.

Moen, Phyllis. 1979. "Family Impacts of the 1975 Recession: Duration of Unemployment." *Journal of Marriage and the Family* 41:561–573.

Money, John. 1980. *Love and Love Sickness: The Science of Sex, Gender Difference and Pair-Bonding.* Baltimore, MD: Johns Hopkins University Press.

———. 1983. "Pairbonding and Limerence." P. 314 in *International Encyclopedia of Psychiatry, Psychology, Psychoanalysis, and Neurology.* Vol. 1, Progress, edited by B. Wolman. New York: Aesculapius.

Money, John, and P. Rucker. 1975. *Sexual Signatures: On Being a Man or a Woman.* Boston: Little, Brown.

Money, John, P. Rucker, and R. Weideking. 1980. "Gender Identity Roles: Normal Differentiation and Its Transpositions." In *Handbook of Human Sexuality,* edited by B. Wolman and J. Money. Englewood Cliffs, NJ: Prentice-Hall.

Montemayor, Raymond. 1982. "The Relationship between Parent-Adolescent Conflict and the Amount of Time Adolescents Spend Alone and with Parents and Peers." *Child Development* 53:1512–1519.

Montgomery, Barbara. 1981. "The Form and Function of Quality Communication in Marriage." *Family Relations* 30:21–30.

Moore, Keith. 1977. *The Developing Human.* 2nd ed. Philadelphia: W.B. Saunders.

Moore, Kristin A., and Isabel V. Sawhill. 1976. "Implications of Women's Employment for Home and Family Life." Pp. 102–122 in *Women and the American Economy: A Look to the 1980's,* edited by J. Knaps. Englewood Cliffs, NJ: Prentice-Hall.

"More Bad News about Sex." 1986. *Newsweek* (April 21):70–71.

Moroney, R. 1979. "The Issue of Family Policy: Do We Know Enough to Take Action?" *Journal of Marriage and the Family* 41:461–463.

Morris, Desmond. 1971. *Intimate Behavior.* New York: Random House.

Morse, D., and S. Gray. 1980. *Early Retirement: Boon or Bane?* New York: Allanheld, Osmun & Co.

Morse, Gardiner. 1984a. "Herpes Virus Suspect in Nearly a Third of Miscarriages." *Science News* 125 (June 30):404.

———. 1984b. "Sperm Antibodies Frustrate Fertility." *Science News* 126 (July 21).

Mott, Frank L., and Sylvia F. Moore. 1983. "The Tempos of Remarriage among Young American Women." *Journal of Marriage and the Family* (May):427–436.

Mueller, Charles W., and Hallowell Pope. 1977. "Marital Instability: The Study of Its Transmission between Generations." *Journal of Marriage and the Family* 39:83–92.

Murdock, George P. 1957. "World Ethnographic Sample." *American Anthropologist* 59:664–687.

Murguia, Edward, and E. Cazares. 1982. "Intermarriage of Mexican-Americans." *Marriage and Family Review* 5:91–100.

Murstein, Bernard. 1971a. "Self–Ideal-Self Discrepancy and the Choice of Marital Partner." *Journal of Consulting and Clinical Psychology* 37:47–52.

———. 1971b. *Theories of Attraction and Love.* New York: Springer.

———. 1980. "Mate Selection in the 1970s." *Journal of Marriage and the Family* 42:777–792.

Murstein, Bernard, M. Cerreto, and M. McDonald. 1977. "A Theory and Investigation of the Effects of

Exchange-Orientation on Marriage and Friendships." *Journal of Marriage and the Family* 39:543–548.

Mutryn, Cynthia S. 1984. "Psychosocial Impact of Cesarean Section on the Family." *ICEA News* 23:4, 12.

———. 1986. "Research Concerning the Cesarean Father." *International Journal of Childbirth Education* 1:8, 37.

Myricks, N. 1980. "Palimony: The Impact of Marvin v. Marvin." *Family Coordinator* (April):210–215.

Nadelson, T., and Leon Eisenberg. 1977. "The Successful Professional Woman: on Being Married to One." *American Journal of Psychiatry* 134:1071–1076.

Nason, Ellen M., and Margeret M. Poloma. 1976. *Voluntary Childless Couples: The Emergence of Variant Lifestyles.* Beverly Hills, CA: Sage Publications.

National Academy of Sciences. 1982. "Families That Work: Children in a Changing World."

National Center for Health Statistics. 1976. *Vital Statistics Report. Annual Summary for the United States.* Vol. 24, No. 13. Washington, D.C.: U.S. Government Printing Office.

———. 1978. "Divorce and Divorce Rates." *Vital and Health Statistics.* Washington, D.C.: U.S. Government Printing Office, Series 21, No. 29.

———. 1979a. *Monthly Vital Statistics Report.* Vol. 27, No 11. Washington, D.C.: U.S. Government Printing Office.

———. 1979b. "Final Marriage Statistics, 1977." *Monthly Vital Statistics Report.* Vol. 28, No. 4. Washington, D.C.: U.S. Government Printing Office.

———. 1980. "Births, Marriages, Divorces, and Deaths for 1979." In *Monthly Vital Statistics Report.* Vol. 28, No. 12. Washington, D.C.: U.S. Government Printing Office.

———. 1983. *Monthly Vital Statistics Report.* Vol. 31, No. 12. Washington, D.C.: U.S. Government Printing Office.

———. 1984a. *Monthly Vital Statistics Report.* Vol. 32, No. 9. Washington, D.C.: U.S. Government Printing Office.

———. 1984b. *Monthly Vital Statistics Report.* Vol. 32, No. 13. Washington, D.C.: U.S. Government Printing Office.

———. 1985. "Marriages and Divorces: 1960–1981." *Monthly Vital Statistics Report,* p. 2. Washington, D.C.: U.S. Government Printing Office.

———. 1986. *Monthly Vital Statistics Report.* Vol. 35, No. 2. Washington, D.C.: U.S. Government Printing Office.

National Centers for Disease Control. 1985. Cited in *Los Angeles Herald Examiner* (May 17):A-11.

National Institutes of Health. 1980. *Consensus Development Summary. Caesarean Childbirth.* Washington D.C.: U.S. Government Printing Office.

Navron, L. 1967. "Communication and Adjustment in Marriage." *Family Process* 6: 173–184.

Nelson, Waldo E., V. Vaughn, and Robert J. McKay. 1969. *Textbook of Pediatrics.* 9th ed. Philadelphia: W.B. Saunders.

Netter, F. 1965. "Reproductive System." In *Ciba Collection of Medical Illustrations.* Vol. 2. Summit, NJ: Ciba.

Neugarten, Bernice. 1968. "The Awareness of Middle Age." In *Middle Age and Aging: A Reader in Social Psychology,* edited by B. Neugarten. Chicago: University of Chicago Press.

———. 1972. "Personality and the Aging Process." *The Gerontologist* 12:9–15.

Neugarten, Bernice, and Karol K. Weinstein. 1968. "The Changing American Grandparent." In *Middle Age and Aging: A Reader in Social Psychology*, edited by B. Neugarten. Chicago: University of Chicago Press. New York: McGraw-Hill.

Newhaus, R. 1977. "A Study of the Effects of the Marriage Encounter Experience of Being on Personal Interaction of Married Couples." *Dissertation Abstracts International* 37:6793.

Newman, Philip, and Barbara Newman. 1984. "Parenthood and Adult Development." Unpublished paper presented to the Midwestern Society for Research in Life-Span Development, May.

Newsweek. 1986. "More Bad News about Sex." (April 21):70–71.

Norton, Arthur, and Paul Glick. 1976. "Marital Instability: Past, Present, and Future." *Journal of Social Issues* 32(June):5–20.

Nordwind, Richard. 1983. "Cucumber May Be Male Contraceptive." *Los Angeles Herald Examiner* (August 19):A-1, A-8.

Norwood, Christopher. 1978. "A Humanizing Way to Have a Baby." *Ms.* (May):89–91.

Nusberg, C., M. Gibson, and S. Peace. 1984. "Innovative Aging Programs Abroad: Implications for the United States." In *Contributions to the Study of Aging*, No. 2. Westport, CT: Greenwood Press.

Nye, F. Ivan. 1976. "School-Age Parenthood: Consequences for Babies, Mothers, Fathers, Grandparents, and Others." *Washington State University Extension Bulletin* 667 (April).

———. 1978. "Is Choice aand Exchange Theory the Key?" *Journal of Marriage and the Family* 40:219–233.

———. 1979. "Choice, Exchange, and the Family." Pp. 1–41 in *Contemporary Theories about the Family*. Vol. 2, edited by W. Burr, R. Hill, F. I. Nye, and I. Reiss. New York: Free Press.

Nye, F. Ivan, and S. McLaughlin. 1976. "Role Competence and Marital Satisfaction." In *Role Structure and Analysis of the Family*, edited by F. I. Nye et al. Beverly Hills, CA: Sage Publications.

O'Kelley, Charlotte, and Larry S. Carney. 1986. *Women and Men in Society.* 2nd ed. Belmont, CA: Wadsworth.

Olson, David H., D. Fourier, and J. Druckerman. 1982. *Counselor's Manual for PREPARE, ENRICH.* Rev. ed. Minneapolis, MN: PREPARE, ENRICH, Inc.

Olson, David H., Douglas Sprenkle, and Candyce Russell. 1979. "Circumplex Model of Marital and Family Systems: I. Cohesion and Adaptability Dimensions, Family Types, and Clinical Application." *Family Process* 18:3–28.

Oppong, Christine. 1981. *Middle Class African Marriage.* London: George Allen & Unwin.

"Oral Contraceptives: OC's Update on Usage, Safety, and Side Effects." 1979. *Population Reports.* Series A, No. 5. Washington, D.C.: George Washington University.

Orden, Susan, and Norman Bradburn. 1969. "Working Wives and Marital Happiness." *American Journal of Sociology* 74:392–407.

Orthner, Dennis. 1976. "Patterns of Leisure and Marital Interaction." *Journal of Leisure Research* 9:98–111.

Osmond, Marie. 1978. "Reciprocity: A Dynamic Model and a Method to Study Family Power." *Journal of Marriage and the Family* 40:49–61.

Osofsky, J., H. Osofsky, and R. Rajan. 1973. "Psychological Effects of Abortion." Pp. 188–205 in *The Abortion Experience: Psychological and Medical Impact*, edited by H. Osofsky and J. Osofsky. New York: Harper & Row.

Packard, Vance. 1972. *A Nation of Strangers.* New York: David McKay.

Parachini, Allan. 1983. "High Hopes Held for New Test on Unborn Infants." *Los Angeles Times* (October 4):Part V, pp. 1, 3.

———. 1984. "Study Refutes Claim That Vasectomy Is Health Hazard." *Los Angeles Times* (February 17):Part V, pp. 1, 6.

———. 1986. "Home Pregnancy Tests Questioned." *Los Angeles Times* (May 20):Part V, pp. 1, 4.

Pardes, H. 1979. "Foreword." In *Families Today. National Institute of Mental Health Science Monographs.* Vol. 1. Washington, D.C.: U.S. Government Printing Office.

Parish, Thomas S., and T. Copeland. 1979. "The Relationship between Self-Concepts and Evaluations of Parents and Stepfathers." *Journal of Psychology* 101:135–138.

Parish, Thomas S., and Bruno Kappes. 1980. "Impact of Father Loss on the Family." *Social Behavior and Personality* 8:107–112.

Parke, Ross D., and S. O'Leary. 1975. "Father-Mother-Infant Interaction in the Newborn Period: Some Findings, Some Observations, and Some Unresolved Issues." Pp. 653–663 in *Developing Individual in a Changing World.* Vol. II, *Social and Environmental Issues.* Chicago: Aldine.

Parke, Ross D., and Douglas B. Sawin. 1976. "The Father's Role in Infancy: A Reevaluation." *Family Coordinator* (October).

Parks, A. Lee 1977. "Children and Youth of Divorce in Parents without Partners, Inc." *Journal of Clinical Child Psychology* 6:44–48.

Parsons, Talcott P. 1951. *The Social System.* New York: Macmillan.

Parsons, Talcott P., and Robert F. Bales. 1955. *Family Socialization and Interaction Process.* Glencoe, IL: Free Press.

Pear, T. H. 1955. *English Social Differences.* London: George Allen & Unwin.

Pearce, John, and Leonard Friedman. 1980. *Family Therapy.* New York: Grune and Stratton.

Pearlin, Leonard I., and J. S. Johnson. 1977. "Marital Status, Life Strains and Depression." *American Sociological Review* 42:704–715.

Pearson, J., and N. Thoennes. 1982. "The Medication and Adjudication of Divorces Disputes: Some Costs and Benefits." *Family Advocate* 4:3.

Pearson, W., Jr., and L. Hendrix. 1979. "Divorce and the Status of Women." *Journal of Marriage and the Family* 41:375–385.

Peele, Stanton, with Archie Brodsky. 1975. *Love and Addiction.* New York: New American Library.

Pepitone-Rockwell, Fran, ed. 1980. *Dual-Career Couples.* Beverly Hills, CA: Sage Publications.

Peterman, Don J., Carl A. Ridley, and Scott M. Anderson. 1974. "A Comparison of Cohabiting and Noncohabiting College Students." *Journal of Marriage and the Family* 36:344–354.

Peterson, James L., and Nicholas Zill. 1986. "Marital Disruption, Parent-Child Relationships, and Behavior Problems in Children." *Journal of Marriage and the Family* 48:295–307.

Pietropinto, Anthony, and Jacqueline Simenauer. 1977. *Beyond the Male Myth.* New York: Quadrangle/New York Times.

Pinsker, M., and K. Geoffroy. 1981. "A Comparison of Parent Effectiveness Training and Behavior Modification Parent Training." *Family Relations* 30:61–68.

Pleck, Joseph H. 1975a. "Man to Man: Is Brotherhood Possible?" Pp. 229–244 in *Old Family/New Family*, edited by N. Glazer-Malbin. New York: Van Nostrand Reinhold.

———. 1975b. "Men's Roles in the Family: A New Look." Paper presented to Sex Roles in Sociology Conference, Merrill-Palmer Institute, Detroit, Michigan, November.

———. 1977. "The Work-Family Role System." *Social Problems* 24:417–427.

———. 1981. *The Myth of Masculinity.* Cambridge, MA: MIT Press.

Pleck, Joseph H., and Robert Brannon. 1978. "Male Roles and the Male Experience." *Journal of Social Issues* 34:1–4.

Podolski, Alfred L. 1975. "Abolishing Baby Buying: Limiting Independent Adoption Placement." *Family Law Quarterly* 9:547–554.

Pogrebin, Letty. 1978. "There's More Than One Way to Slice the Pie . . . and Clean Up Afterward." *Ms.* (October).

———. 1980. *Growing Up Free: Raising Your Child in the 80's.* New York: McGraw-Hill.

Polikoff, N. 1982. "Why Are Mothers Losing? A Brief Analysis of Criteria Used in Child Custody Determination." *Women's Rights Law Reporter* 7:235–243.

Pollie, Robert. 1982. "Gossypol: All-Purpose Antimicrobial." *Science News* 122 (October 16):245.

Poloma, Margaret, B. Pendleton, and T. Garland. 1971. "The Married Professional Woman: A Study of the Tolerance of Domestication." *Journal of Marriage and the Family* 33:531–540.

———. 1982. "Reconsidering the Dual-Career Marriage." Pp. 173–192 in *Two Paychecks: Life in Dual-Earner Families*, edited by J. Aldous. Beverly Hills, CA: Sage Publications.

Porter, Sylvia. 1975. *Sylvia Porter's Money Book.* New York: Doubleday.

Pratt, Lois. 1972. "Conjugal Organization and Health." *Journal of Marriage and the Family* 34:85–95.

———. 1976. *Family Structure and Effective Health Behavior: The Energized Family.* Boston: Houghton Mifflin.

Price, Ann, and Nancy Bamford. 1983. *The Breastfeeding Guide for the Working Woman.* New York: Simon and Schuster.

Price-Bonham, Sharon, and Jack Balswick. 1980. "The Noninstitutions: Divorce, Desertion, and Remarriage." *Journal of Marriage and the Family* 42:959–972.

Queen, Stuart A., and Robert W. Habenstein. 1974. *The Family in Various Cultures.* 4th ed. Philadelphia: Lippincott.

Quinn, William. 1983. "Personal and Family Adjustments in Later Life." *Journal of Marriage and the Family* 45:57–73.

Rank, Mark A. 1982. "Determinants of Conjugal Influences in Wives' Employment Decision Making." *Journal of Marriage and the Family* 44:591–603.

Rapoport, Robert, and Rhona Rapoport. 1976. *Dual-Career Families Re-Examined.* New York: Harper & Row.

———. 1978. "Dual-Career Families: Progress Prospects." *Marriage and Family Review* 1:3–12.

Rapoport, Robert, Rhona Rapoport, and Ziona Strelitz, with Stephen Kew. 1980. *Fathers, Mothers and Society: Perspectives on Parenting.* New York: Vintage Books.

Raschke, Helen. 1976. "Sex Differences in Voluntary Post Marital Dissolution Adjustment." Paper presented at the American Sociological Association annual meeting, New York, August.

———. 1977. "The Role of Social Participation in Postseparation and Postdivorce Adjustment." *Journal of Divorce* 1:129–139.

Raschke, Helen, and Vern Raschke. 1979. "Family Conflict and Children's Self-Concept: A Comparison of Intact and Single-Parent Families." *Journal of Marriage and the Family* 41:367–374.

Raven, Bertram H., and Jeffrey Z. Rubin. 1976. *Social Psychology: People in Groups.* New York: Wiley.

Rawlings, Steve W. 1978. *Perspectives on American Husbands and Wives.* Washington, D.C.: U.S. Department of Commerce, Bureau of the Census, Special Studies, Series P-23, No. 77.

Reamy, Kenneth, Susan E. White, Walter Daniell, and Elaine Levine. 1982. "Sexuality and Pregnancy." *Journal of Reproductive Medicine* 27: 321–327.

Redbook. 1980. "The Redbook Poll on In-Laws." (June):62.

Reevy, William K. 1973. "Adolescent Sexuality." Pp. 52–68 in *Encyclopedia of Sexual Behavior*, edited by A. Ellis and A. Abarbanel. New York: Jason Aronson.

Reiss, Ira L. 1967. *The Social Context of Premarital Permissiveness.* New York: Holt, Rinehart and Winston.

———. 1980. *Family Systems in America.* 3rd ed. New York: Holt, Rinehart and Winston.

Report of the Commission on Obscenity and Pornography, 1970. New York: Bantam Books.

Research and Forecasts, Inc. 1981. *Survey for Connecticut Mutual Life Insurance Company.* New York: Connecticut Mutual Life Insurance Company.

Rettig, Kathryn D., and Margaret M. Bubolz. 1983. "Interpersonal Resource Exchanges as Indicators of Quality of Marriage." *Journal of Marriage and the Family* 45:497–509.

Rice, D. 1979. *Dual-Career Marriage: Conflict and Treatment.* New York: Free Press.

Richardson, J. 1979. "Wife Occupational Superiority and Marital Troubles: An Examination of the Hypothesis." *Journal of Marriage and the Family* 41:63–72.

Richmond, Marie L. 1976. "Beyond Resource Theory: Another Look at Factors Enabling Woment to Affect Family Interaction." *Journal of Marriage and the Family* 38:257–266.

Ridley, Carl A. 1973. "Exploring the Impact of Work Satisfaction and Involvement on Marital Interactions

When Both Partners Are Employed." *Journal of Marriage and the Family* 35:229–237.

Riegel, Klaus. 1976. "The Dialectics of Human Development." *American Psychologist* 31:679–700.

Riley, E., et al. 1984. "Relationship Enhancement with Premarital Couples: An Assessment of Effects on Relationship Quality." Pp. 547–554 in *Family Studies Review Yearbook*. Vol. 2, edited by D. Olson and B. Miller. Beverly Hills, CA: Sage Publications.

Rindfuss, Ronald, and Larry Bumpass. 1977. "Fertility during Marital Disruptions." *Journal of Marriage and the Family* 39:517–528.

Rindfuss, Ronald, P. Morgan, and C. Gray Swicegood. 1984. "The Transition to Motherhood." *American Sociological Review* 49:359–372.

"Rise of the Singles—40 Million Free Spenders." 1974. *U.S. News and World Report* (October 7):54ff.

Risman, Barbara, Charles T. Hill, Zick Rubin, and Letitia Anne Peplau. 1981. "Living Together in College: Implications for Courtship." *Journal of Marriage and the Family* 43:77–83.

Robertiello, Robert. 1979. *A Man in the Making: Grandfathers, Fathers, Sons*. New York: R. Marek.

Roberts, A., and W. Roberts. 1975. "Factors in Life-Styles of Couples Married over Fifty Years." Paper presented at annual meeting of National Council on Family Relations, Salt Lake City, August.

Robertson, Joan. 1977. "Grandmotherhood: A Study of Role Conceptions." *Journal of Marriage and the Family* 39:165–174.

Rodes, T. 1976. *National Child Care Consumer Study: 1975*. Vols. I–II, *Basic Tabulation, Current Pattern of Child Use in the United States, American Consumer Attitudes and Opinion on Child Care*. Prepared by U.S. Department of Health, Education, and Welfare, Washington, D.C.

Rodgers, J. 1980. "Special Report on the Third International Congress on Twin Studies." *Los Angeles Herald Examiner* (June 22):A-7.

Rodgers, Roy. 1964. "Toward a Theory of Family Development." *Journal of Marriage and the Family* 26:262–270.

Rogers, Rita. 1982. "Commentary." *Medical Aspects of Human Sexuality* 16:92BB-92FF.

Rollins, Boyd C., and Kenneth L. Cannon. 1974. "Marital Satisfaction over the Family Life Cycle: A Reevaluation." *Journal of Marriage and the Family* 36:271–283.

Rollins, Boyd C., and Harold Feldman. 1970. "Marital Satisfaction over the Family Life Cycle." *Journal of Marriage and the Family* 32:20–28.

Rollins, Boyd C., and Richard J. Galligan. 1978. "The Developing Child and Marital Satisfaction of Parents." Pp. 71–105 in *Child Influences on Marital and Family Interaction*, edited by R. Lerner and G. Spanier. New York: Academic Press.

Rollins, Boyd C., and Darwin L. Thomas. 1979. "Parental Support, Power and Control Techniques in the Socialization of Children." In *Contemporary Theories about the Family*. Vol. 1, edited by W. Burr, R. Hill, F. I. Nye, and I. Reiss. New York: Free Press.

Roof, W., and D. Hage. 1980. "Church Involvement in America: Social Factors Affecting Membership and Participation." *Review of Religious Research* 21:405–426.

Roosevelt, Ruth, and Jeanette Lofas. 1976. *Living in Step*. New York: Stein and Day.

Roper Organization. 1974. *The Virginia Slims' American Women's Opinion Poll*. New York: Roper Organization.

Rose, Arnold. 1968. "A Current Theoretical Issue in Social Gerontology." In *Middle Age and Aging: A Reader in Social Psychology*, edited by B. Neugarten. Chicago: University of Chicago Press.

Rosenberg, Michael. 1965. *Society and the Adolescent Self-Image*. Princeton, NJ: Princeton University Press.

Rosenthal, K., and H. Keshet. 1978. "The Impact of Child Care Responsibilities on Part-Time or Single Fathers." *Alternative Lifestyles* 1:465–491.

Ross, C., and J. Mirowsky. 1984. "The Social Construction of Reality in Marriage." *Sociological Perspectives* 27, 3:281–300.

Rossi, Alice. 1964. "Equality between the Sexes: An Immodest Proposal." *Daedalus* 93:607–652.

———. 1968. "Transition to Parenthood." *Journal of Marriage and the Family* 30:26–39.

Roth, R. 1981. "Alcoholism and the Family: Putting the Pieces Together." *Alcoholism* 1:19–22.

Rovner, Sandy. 1984. "The Year of the Chorionic Villi Biopsy." *Los Angeles Times* (February 10):Part V, pp. 34–35.

Rowand, Andrea. 1984a. "The (Anti-Cancer?) Pill." *Science News* 125 (June 30):404.

———. 1984b. "Used Fumes Pollute Non-Smokers, Too." *Science News* 125 (June 2):342.

Rowe, George, and B. Meredith. 1981. Research note reported in *Marriage and Divorce Today* 7:3.

Rowe, M. 1978. "Choosing Child Care: Many Options." Pp. 89–99 in *Working Couples*, edited by R. Rapoport and R. Rapoport. New York: Harper & Row.

Rubin, Lillian. 1985. *Just Friends: The Role of Friendship in Our Lives*. New York: Harper & Row.

Rubin, Zick. 1973. *Liking and Loving: An Invitation to Social Psychology*. New York: Holt, Rinehart and Winston.

Russell, Candyce. 1974. "Transition to Parenthood: Problems and Gratifications." *Journal of Marriage and the Family* 36:294–302.

Rutter, M. 1975. *Helping Troubled Children*. New York: Plenum Press.

Ryder, Robert G. 1973. "Longitudinal Data Relating to Marriage Satisfaction and Having a Child." *Journal of Marriage and the Family* 35:604–606.

Ryne, D. 1981. "Bases of Marital Satisfaction among Men and Women." *Journal of Marriage and the Family* 43:941–955.

Rytina, N., and Bianchi, S. 1984. "Occupational Reclassification and Changes in Distribution by Gender." *Monthly Labor Review* (March).

Sabagh, Georges. 1980. "Fertility Planning Status of Chicano Couples in Los Angeles." *American Journal of Public Health* 70:56–61.

Saegert, S., W. Swap, and R. Zajonc. 1973. "Exposure, Context, and Interpersonal Attraction." *Journal of Personality and Social Psychology* 25:234–242.

Safilios-Rothschild, Constantina. 1967. "A Comparison of Power Structure and Marital Satisfaction in Urban Greek and French Families." *Journal of Marriage and the Family* 29:345–359.

————. 1970. "The Influence of the Wife's Degree of Work Commitment upon Some Aspects of Family Organization and Dynamics." *Journal of Marriage and the Family* 32:681–691.

————. 1976. "A Macro- and Micro-Examination of Family Power and Love: An Exchange Model." *Journal of Marriage and the Family* 37:355–362.

————. 1977. *Love, Sex, and Sex Roles*. Englewood Cliffs, NJ: Prentice-Hall.

Saghir, Marcel T., and E. Robins. 1973. *Male and Female Homosexuals*. Baltimore, MD: Williams and Wilkins.

Saluter, Arlene. 1983. *Current Population Reports*. Washington, D.C.: U.S. Government Printing Office, Series P-20., No. 380.

Sandberg, Eugene C. 1976. "Psychological Aspects of Contraception." Pp. 335–347 in *The Sexual Experience*, edited by B. Sadock, H. Kaplan, and A. Freedman. Baltimore, MD: Williams and Wilkins.

Sandler, Judith, J. Myerson, and L. Kinder. 1980. *Human Sexuality: Current Perspectives*. Tampa, FL: Mariner.

Santrock, John W., and Richard A. Warshak. 1979. "Father Custody and Social Development in Boys and Girls." *Journal of Social Issues* 35:112–125.

Sardanis-Zimmerman, Irene. 1977. "The Stepmother: Mythology and Self-Perception." Ph.D. dissertation. Reported in E. Visher and J. Visher, *Step-Families: A Guide to Working with Stepparents and Stepchildren*. New York: Brunner/Mazel, 1979, p. 81.

Sarnoff, Suzanne, and Irving Sarnoff. 1979. *Sexual Excitement/Sexual Peace*. New York: M. Evans.

Sarrel, Lorna, and Phillip Sarrel. 1984. *Sexual Turning Points*. New York: Atcom.

Sarrel, Phillip. 1984. Cited by Patricia McCormick in "Campus Sexual Mores Are in Flux." *Los Angeles Times* (June 5):Part V, p. 17.

Satir, Virginia. 1964. *Conjoint Family Therapy*. Palo Alto, CA: Science and Behavior Books.

————. 1967. "A Family of Angels." Pp. 97–173 in *Techniques of Family Therapy*, edited by J. Haley and L. Hoffman. New York: Basic Books.

Sawin, Douglas B., and Ross D. Parke. 1979. "Fathers' Affectional Stimulation and Caregiving Behaviors with Newborn Infants." *Family Coordinator* 28(October):509–513.

Scanlon, J. 1974. "Obstetric Anesthesia as a Neonatal Risk Factor in Normal Labor and Delivery." *Clinics in Perinatology* 1:465–482.

Scanzoni, John. 1975. *Sex Roles, Life Styles, and Childbearing*. New York: Free Press.

————. 1979a. "Social Exchange and Behavioral Interdependence." In *Social Exchange in Developing Relationships*, edited by R. Burgess and T. Houston. New York: Academic Press.

————. 1979b. "Social Processes and Power in Families." Pp. 295–316 in *Contemporary Theories about the Family*. Vol. 1, *Research Based Theories*, edited by W. Burr, R. Hill, I. Nye, and I. Reiss. New York: Free Press.

Scanzoni, John, and Karen Polonko. 1980. "A Conceptual Approach to Explicit Marital Negotiation." *Journal of Marriage and the Family* 42:31–44.

Schachter, Stanley. 1964. "The Interaction of Cognitive and Physiological Determinants of Emotional State." Pp. 49–80 in *Advances in Experimental Social Psychology*. Vol. I, edited by L. Berkowitz. New York: Academic Press.

Schauble, P., and C. Hill. 1976. "A Laboratory Approach to Treatment in Marriage Counseling: Training in Communication Skills." *Family Coordinator* 25:227–284.

Scheff, Thomas. 1967. "Toward a Sociological Model of Consensus." *American Sociological Review* 32:32–46.

Schoeninger, D., and W. Wood. 1969. "Comparison of Married and Ad Hoc Mixed-Sex Dyads Negotiating the Division of a Reward." *Journal of Experimental Social Psychology* 5:483–499.

Schrader, Sandra. 1980. "Commitment: A Conceptualization and an Empirical Demonstration in the Courtship Process." Ph.D. dissertation, University of Southern California.

Schram, Rosalyn W. 1979. "Marital Satisfaction over the Family Life Cycle." *Journal of Marriage and the Family* 41:7–12.

Schulman, G. 1972. "Myths That Intrude on the Adaptation of the Stepfamily." *Social Casework* 49:131–139.

Schulman, Marion. 1970. "Communication between Engaged Couples." Ph.D. dissertation, University of Southern California.

————. 1974. "Idealization in Engaged Couples." *Journal of Marriage and the Family* 36:139–147.

Schumacher, Sally. 1973. Report from a symposium on Sex for the Mature Adult, Miami, FL.

Schumm, W., J. Benigas, M. McCutcheon, C. Griffen, S. Anderson, J. Morris, and G. Race. 1983. "Measuring Empathy, Regard, and Congruence in the Marital Relationship." *Journal of Social Psychology* 119:141–142.

Schwartz, Mark A. 1976. "Career Strategies of the Never Married." Paper presented at the 71st annual meeting of the American Sociological Association, New York (September).

Schwartz, Mark, and William Masters. 1984. Cited in *Los Angeles Herald Examiner* (February 29).

Scoresby, A. L. 1977. *The Marriage Dialogue*. Reading, MA: Addison-Wesley.

Scott, Rebecca Lovell. 1984. "Alcohol and Pregnancy." *ICEA Review* (August 2):1–2.

Seaman, Barbara, and G. Seaman. 1977. *Women and the Crisis in Sex Hormones*. New York: Rawson and Associates.

Sears, Robert, L. Rau, and R. Alpert. 1965. *Identification and Child Rearing*. Palo Alto, CA: Stanford University Press.

Seligson, Marcia. 1973. *The Eternal Bliss Machine: America's Way of Wedding*. New York: William Morrow.

Shah, Farida, and Melvin Zelnik. 1981. "Parent and Peer Influence on Sexual Behavior, Contraceptive Use, and Pregnancy Experience of Young Women." *Journal of Marriage and the Family* 43:339–348.

Shanas, Ethel. 1973. "Family-Kin Networks and Aging in Cross-Cultural Perspective." *Journal of Marriage and the Family* 35:505–511.

————. 1980. "Older People and Their Families." *Journal of Marriage and the Family* 42:9–15.

Shaw, George Bernard. 1960. *Dear Liar: A Comedy of Letters*. Adapted from the correspondence of George Bernard Shaw and Mrs. Patrick Campbell. London: M. Reinhardt.

Shaw, M. 1976. *Group Dynamics: The Psychology of Small Group Behavior*. 2nd ed. New York: McGraw-Hill.

Sheppard, H. 1981. "National Council on the Aging Survey." *Aging and Work* 4:221–223.

Shertzer, B. 1981. *Career Planning: Freedom to Choose.* Boston: Houghton Mifflin.

Shoen, R., V. Nelson, and M. Collins. 1978. "Intermarriage among Spanish Surnamed Californians, 1962–1974." *International Migration Review* 12:359–369.

Shostak, M. 1981. *Nisa: The Life and Words of a !King Woman.* Cambridge, MA: Harvard University Press.

Silberner, Joanne. 1985a. "IUD-Infertility Link." *Science News* 127 (April 13):229.

———. 1985b. "Why Doesn't the Body Reject the Fetus?" *Science News* 128 (August 3):69.

Silka, Linda, and Sara Kiesler. 1977. "Couples Who Choose to Remain Childless." *Family Planning Perspectives* 9(January-February):16–25.

Silverstein, C. 1977. *A Family Matter: A Parent's Guide to Homosexuality.* New York: McGraw-Hill.

Simenauer, Jacqueline, and D. Carroll. 1982. *Singles: The New Americans.* New York: Simon and Schuster.

Simon, A. 1964. *Stepchild in the Family: A View of Children in Remarriage.* New York: Odyssey Press.

Simon, William, and John Gagnon. 1967. "Selected Aspects of Adult Socialization." Unpublished paper.

Sims, L., and B. Paolucci. 1975. "An Empirical Reexamination of the Parent Attitude Research Instrument, Part I." *Journal of Marriage and the Family* 37: 724–732.

Singer, Laura, and B. Stern. 1980. *Stages: The Crises That Shape Your Marriage.* New York: Grosset and Dunlap.

Skolnick, Arlene. 1973. *The Intimate Environment: Exploring Marriage and the Family.* Boston: Little, Brown.

———. 1980. "The Paradox of Perfection." *The Wilson Quarterly* (Summer):113–121.

Skovholt, T., J. Gormally, P. Schauble, and R. Davis, eds. 1978. "Counseling Men." *The Counseling Psychologist* 7:4.

Smith, C. 1975. "Bereavement: The Contribution of Phenomenological and Existential Analysis to a Greater Understanding of the Problem." *British Journal of Social Work* 5:75–92.

Smith, J., and M. Ward. 1984. *Rand Corporation Study.* Bethesda, MD: National Institute of Child Health and Human Development.

Smith, K. and Vern Bengtson. 1979. "Positive Consequences of Institutionalization: Solidarity between Elderly Patients and Their Middle-Aged Children." *The Gerontologist* 19:438–447.

Smith, Roy G. 1979. *Women in the Labor Force in 1990.* The Urban Institute.

Snyder, Douglas K. 1981. *Manual for the Marital Satisfaction Inventory.* Los Angeles: Western Psychological Service.

Snyder, M., E. Tanke, and Ellen Berscheid. 1981. "Social Perception and Interpersonal Behavior: On the Self-Fulfilling Nature of Social Stereotypes." Pp. 391–406 in *Readings about the Social Animal,* edited by E. Aronson. San Francisco: W.H. Freeman.

Sollie, Donna L., and Brent C. Miller. 1980. "The Transition to Parenthood as a Critical Time for Building Family Strengths." Pp. 149–169 in *Family Strengths: Positive Models for Family Life,* edited by N. Stinnett, B. Chesser, J. Defrain, and P. Knaub. Lincoln: University of Nebraska Press.

Sorenson, Robert. 1973. *Adolescent Sexuality in Contemporary America.* New York: World.

Spake, A. 1984. "The Choices That Brought Me Here." *Ms.* (November).

Spanier, Graham. 1976. "Measuring Dyadic Adjustment: New Scales for Assessing the Quality of Marriage and Similar Dyads." *Journal of Marriage and the Family* 38:15–28.

———. 1983. "Married and Unmarried Cohabitation in the United States: 1980." *Journal of Marriage and the Family* 45:277–288.

Spanier, Graham, and R. Casto. 1979. "Adjustment to Separation and Divorce: An Analysis of 50 Case Studies." *Journal of Divorce* 2:241–253.

Spanier, Graham, and Robert Lewis. 1980. "Marital Quality: A Review of the Seventies." *Journal of Marriage and the Family* 42:825–839.

Spanier, Graham, Robert Lewis, and Charles Cole. 1975. "Marital Adjustment over the Family Life Cycle: The Issue of Curvilinearity." *Journal of Marriage and the Family* 37:263–375.

Spezzano, C., and J. Waterman. 1977. "The First Day of Life." *Psychology Today* (December 11):110.

Spicer, J., and G. Hampe. 1975. "Kinship Interaction after Divorce." *Journal of Marriage and the Family* 37:113–119.

Spitz, René. 1975. "Hospitalism: the Genesis of Psychiatric Conditions in Early Childhood." Pp. 29–43 in *Human Life Cycle,* edited by W. Sze. New York: Jason Aronson.

Spock, Benjamin. 1976. *Baby and Child Care.* New York: Pocket Books.

Sporakowski, Michael, and G. Jughston. 1978. "Prescriptions for Happy Marriage: Adjustments and Satisfaction of Couple Married for 50 or More Years." *Family Coordinator* 27:321–327.

Spreitzer, R., and L. Riley. 1974. "Factors Associated with Singlehood." *Journal of Marriage and the Family* 36:533–542.

Sprenkle, Douglas H., and David H. Olson. 1978. "Circumplex Model of Marital Systems: An Empirical Study of Clinic and Nonclinic Couples." *Journal of Marriage and Family Counseling* 4:59–74.

Sprey, Jetse. 1972a. "Extramarital Relationships." *Sexual Behavior* 2:34–36.

———. 1972b. "Family Power Structure: A Critical Comment." *Journal of Marriage and the Family* 33:722–733.

———. 1979. "Conflict Theory and the Study of Marriage and the Family." Pp. 130–159 in *Contemporary Theories about the Family.* Vol. 2, edited by W. Burr, R. Hill, I. Nye, and I. Reiss. New York: Free Press.

St. John, Craig, and D. Parsons. 1978. "Continuous Dual-Career Families: A Case Study." In *Dual-Career Couples,* edited by J. Bryson and R. Bryson. New York: Human Sciences.

Stacey, W., and A. Shupe. 1983. *The Family Secret: Violence in America.* New York: Atcom.

Stafford, Rebecca, Elaine Backman, and Pamela V. DiBona. 1977. "The Division of Labor among

Cohabiting and Married Couples." *Journal of Marriage and the Family* 39:43–57.

Stannard, Una. 1970. "The Male Maternal Instinct." *Transaction* 8:24–35.

Staples, Robert. 1981. *The World of Black Singles.* Westport, CT: Greenwood Press.

Stein, B. 1984. *Financial Passages.* Garden City, NY: Doubleday.

Stein, Martha L. 1974. *Lovers, Friends, Slaves . . . The Nine Male Sexual Types: Their Psycho-Sexual Transactions with Call Girls.* New York: G.P. Putnam's Sons.

Stein, Peter. 1976. *Single.* Englewood Cliffs, NJ: Prentice-Hall.

———. 1978. "The Lifestyles and Life Chances of the Never-Married." *Marriage and Family Review* 1–14.

Steinberg, Sarah. 1983. "Male Contraceptive in Stomach Salve." *Science News* 124 (August 20):117.

Steinhoff, Patricia, et al. 1979. "Women Who Obtain Repeat Abortions: A Study Based on Record Linkage." *Family Planning Perspectives* 10:30–38.

Steinmetz, Suzanne. 1977a. *The Cycle of Violence: Assertive, Aggressive, and Abusive Family Interaction.* New York: Praeger.

———. 1977b. "Violence Between Siblings." Paper presented at the Second World Conference of the International Society of Family Law, Montreal, June.

———. 1978. "Battered Parents." *Society* 15:54–55.

Stern, P. 1978. "Stepfather Families: Integration around Child Discipline." *Issues in Mental Health Nursing* 1:50–56.

Sternberg, R. 1985. "The Measure of Love." *Science Digest* (April):60, 78–79.

Stewart, D. W., and J. B. Nicholson. 1979. "Abortion Policy in 1978: A Follow-Up Analysis." *Publius* 9:61–167.

Stewart, F., F. Guest, G. Stewart, and R. Hatcher. 1979. *My Body, My Health: The Concerned Woman's Guide to Gynecology.* New York: Wiley.

Stinnett, Nick. 1978. "Strengthening Families." Paper presented at the National Symposium on Building Family Strengths. University of Nebraska, Lincoln.

———. 1983. "Strong Families: A Portrait." In *Toward Family Wellness,* edited by D. Mace. Beverly Hills, CA: Sage Publications.

Stinnett, Nick, L. Carter, and J. Montgomery. 1972. "Older Persons' Perceptions of Their Marriages." *Journal of Marriage and the Family* 32:665–670.

Stolk, Y. 1981. "The Spinster Stereotype: A Demographic Refutation." *Australian Journal of Social Issues* 16:187–199.

Stoller, Robert. 1968. *Sex and Gender: On the Development of Masculinity and Femininity.* New York: Science House.

Storms, Michael. 1982. Cited in *Science News* (September 4):151.

Straus, Murray A., Richard J. Gelles, and Suzanne K. Steinmetz. 1978. *Behind Closed Doors: Violence in the American Family.* Garden City, NY: Anchor Books.

Strean, Herbert S. 1980. *The Extramarital Affair.* New York: Free Press.

Streib, Gordon. 1972. "Older Families and Their Troubles: Familial and Social Responses." *Family Coordinator* 21:5–19.

———. 1978. "An Alternative Family Form for Older Persons: Need and Social Context." *Family Coordinator* 27 (October):413–420.

Streib, Gordon F., and Rubye Wilkerson Beck. 1980. "Older Families: A Decade Review." *Journal of Marriage and the Family* 42:937–956.

Streib, Gordon F., and M. Hilker. 1980. "The Cooperative 'Family': An Alternative Lifestyle for the Elderly." *Alternative Lifestyles* 3:167–184.

Streib, Gordon F., and C. Schneider. 1971. *Retirement in American Society: Impact and Process.* Ithaca, NY: Cornell University Press.

Stuart, Richard. 1976. "An Operant Interpersonal Program for Couples." Pp. 119–132 in *Treating Relationships,* edited by D. Olson. Lake Mills, IA: Graphic.

———. 1980. *Helping Couples Change.* New York: Guilford Press.

Stuckert, Robert P. 1963. "Role Perception and Marital Satisfaction—A Configurational Approach." *Marriage and Family Living* 25:415–419.

Student Health and Counseling Center. 1979. *Herpes II.* Bulletin Number HEC 055 (January). University of Southern California, Los Angeles.

Sullivan, Harry Stack. 1953. *The Interpersonal Theory of Psychiatry.* New York: Norton.

Sussman, Marvin B. 1965. "Relations of Adult Children with Their Parents." Pp. 62–92 in *Social Structure and the Family: Generational Relations,* edited by E. Shanas and G. Streib. Englewood Cliffs, NJ: Prentice-Hall.

Sutherland, Edwin H., and Donald R. Cressey. 1960. *Principles of Criminology.* Philadelphia: Lippincott.

Suzuki, B. 1980. "Asian-American Families." Pp. 74–102 in *Parenting in a Multicultural Society,* edited by M. Fantini and R. Cardenas. New York: Longmans.

Swenson, Clifford. 1979. "Marriage Relationship and Problems of Retired Married Couples." Unpublished manuscript, Purdue University. Reported in *Families Today, National Institute of Mental Health Monographs* 1:249–286.

Swenson, Clifford, R. Eskew, and K. Kohlhepp. 1977. "Factors in the Marriages of Older Couples." Unpublished paper, Purdue University.

Sze, William. 1975. "Social Variables and Their Effect on Psychiatric Emergency Situations among Children." Pp. 207–215 in *Human Life Cycle,* edited by W. Sze. New York: Jason Aronson.

Takas, M. 1986. "Divorce: Who Gets the Blame in 'No-Fault.'" *Ms.* (February).

Tallman, I. 1970. "The Family as a Small Problem Solving Group." *Journal of Marriage and the Family* 32:94–104.

Tanfer, Koray, and M. Horn. 1985. *Family Planning Perspectives.* New York: Alan Guttmacher Institute.

Tanner, D. 1978. *The Lesbian Couple.* Lexington, MA: Lexington Books, D. C. Heath.

Taulbee, Pamela. 1983. "New Clues Link Leukemia Virus to AIDS." *Science News* 123:324.

Tavris, Carol T. 1978. *The Longest War: Understanding Sex Differences.* New York: Harcourt Brace Jovanovich.

———. 1977. "The Sexual Lives of Women over Sixty." *Ms.* (July):62–65.

Tennov, Dorothy. 1979. *Love and Limerence: The Experience of Being in Love.* New York: Stein and Day.

Terkelson, Kenneth G. 1980. "Toward a Theory of the Family Life Cycle." Pp. 21–52 in *The Family Life Cycle: A Framework for Family Therapy*, edited by E. Carter and M. McGoldrick. New York: Gardner Press.

Tessman, L. 1978. *Children of Parting Parents*. New York: Jason Aronson.

Thibaut, J., and Harold Kelley. 1959. *The Social Psychology of Groups*. New York: Wiley.

Thomas, Darwin, Victor Gecas, Andrew Weigert, and Elizabeth Rooney. 1974. *Family Socialization and the Adolescent*. Lexington, MA: D.C. Heath.

Thomas, Sandra, Kay Albrecht, and Priscilla White. 1984. "Determinants of Marital Quality in Dual-Career Couples." *Family Relations* 33:513–521.

Thompson, C. 1932. *The Hand of Destiny*. London: Rider.

Thornburg, H. 1970. "Age and First Sources of Sex Information as Reported by 88 College Women." *Journal of School Health* 40:156–158.

Thornton, Arland, and Deborah S. Freedman. 1982. "Changing Attitudes toward Marriage and Single Life." *Family Planning Perspectives* 14.

Tietze, Christopher. 1977. "Induced Abortion: 1977 Supplement." *Reports on Population and Family Planning* 14.

"The Times Poll." 1984. *Los Angeles Times* (September 10):1.

Titus, S. S. 1980. "A Function of Friendship: Social Comparisons as a Frame of Reference for Marriage." *Human Relations* 33:409–431.

Toman, Walter. 1961. *Family Constellation*. New York: Springer.

———. 1969. *Family Constellation: Its Effect on Personality and Social Behavior*. New York: Springer.

Trattner, W. 1979. *From Poor Law to Welfare State*. New York: Free Press.

Trause, Mary Anne, John Kennell, and Marshall Klaus. 1978. "Parental Attachment Behavior." In *Handbook of Sexology, Procreation and Parenting*. Vol. 3, edited by J. Money and H. Mustaph. New York: Elsevier.

Treas, Judy, and Anneke Van Hilst. 1976. "Marriage and Remarriage Rates among Older Americans." *The Gerontologist* 16:136–143.

Troll, Lillian, and J. Smith. 1976. "Attachment through the Life Span: Some Questions About Dyadic Relationships in Later Life." *Human Development* 19:156–171.

Trost, Jan. 1967. "Some Data on Mate Selection: Homogamy and Perceived Homogamy." *Journal of Marriage and the Family* 29:739–755.

———. 1975. "Married and Unmarried Cohabitation: The Case of Sweden with Some Comparisons." *Journal of Marriage and the Family* 37:677–682.

———. 1979. *Unmarried Cohabitation*. Vasteras, Sweden: International Library.

Tumulty, K. 1984. "Wage Gap: Women Still the Second Sex." *Los Angeles Times* (September 13):1, 12.

Turner, Ralph. 1976. "The Real Self: from Institution to Impulse." *American Journal of Sociology* 81:989–1016.

Twain, Mark. 1962. *Letters from the Earth*. New York: Harper & Row.

Udry, J. Richard. 1971. *The Social Context of Marriage*. Philadelphia: Lippincott.

Udry, J. Richard, Karl E. Bauman, and Naomi M. Morris. 1975. "Changes in Premarital Experience of Recent Decades of Birth Cohorts of Urban American Women." *Journal of Marriage and the Family* 37:783–787.

Underwood, Donna. 1979. "The Use of the Lasswell Profile in Marital Therapy: A Study of Re-Defining Dissimilarities in Relationship Treatment." Ph.D. dissertation, Fielding Institute, Santa Barbara, CA.

Urion, Carl. 1977. "Circumcision and Sexual Conduct: A Cross-Cultural Comparison." Paper presented at the International Conference on Love and Attraction, Swansea, Wales, September 7.

U.S. Bureau of the Census. 1976. *Current Population Reports*. Washington, D.C.: U.S. Government Printing Office, Series P-20, No. 297.

———. 1977a. *Current Population Reports*. Washington, D.C.: U.S. Government Printing Office, Series P-20, No. 308.

———. 1977b. *Current Population Reports*. Washington, D.C.: U.S. Government Printing Office, Series P-20, No. 312.

———. 1977c. *Current Population Reports*. Washington, D.C.: U.S. Government Printing Office, Series P-25, No. 704.

———. 1978a. *Current Population Reports*. Washington, D.C.: U.S. Government Printing Office, Series P-20, No. 324.

———. 1978b. *Current Population Reports*. Washington, D.C.: U.S. Government Printing Office, Series P-23, No. 77.

———. 1979a. *Current Population Reports*. Washington, D.C.: U.S. Government Printing Office, Series P-20, No. 336.

———. 1979b. *Current Population Reports*. Washington, D.C.: U.S. Government Printing Office, Series P-20, No. 338.

———. 1979c. *Current Population Reports*. Washington, D.C.: U.S. Government Printing Office, Series P-20, No. 341.

———. 1979d. *Current Population Reports*. Washington, D.C.: U.S. Government Printing Office, Series P-23, No. 78.

———. 1980a. "Marital Status and Living Arrangements: March, 1979." Pp. 3–5 in *Current Population Reports*. Washington, D.C.: U.S. Government Printing Office, Series P-20, No. 349.

———. 1980b. *Current Population Reports*. Washington, D.C.: U.S. Government Printing Office, Series P-20, No. 352.

———. 1980c. *Current Population Reports*. Washington, D.C.: U.S. Government Printing Office, Series P-23, No. 106.

———. 1980d. *Current Population Reports*. Washington, D.C.: U.S. Government Printing Office, Series P-23, No. 107.

———. 1981a. *Current Population Reports*. Washington, D.C.: U.S. Government Printing Office, Series P-20, No. 363.

———. 1981b. *Current Population Reports*. Washington, D.C.: U.S. Government Printing Office, Series P-20, No. 365.

———. 1981c. *Current Population Reports*. Washington, D.C.: U.S. Government Printing Office, Series P-23, No. 110.

———. 1981d. *Current Population Reports*. Washington, D.C.: U.S. Government Printing Office, Series P-23, No. 111.

———. 1982a. *Current Population Reports*. Washington, D.C.: U.S. Government Printing Office, Series P-23, No. 59.

———. 1982b. *Current Population Reports*. Washington, D.C.: U.S. Government Printing Office, Series P-23, No. 141.

———. 1983a. *Current Population Reports*. Washington, D.C.: U.S. Government Printing Office, Series P-20, No. 380.

———. 1983b. *Current Population Reports*. Washington, D.C.: U.S. Government Printing Office, Series P-20, No. 389.

———. 1983c. *Current Population Reports*. Washington, D.C.: U.S. Government Printing Office, Series P-23, No. 123.

———. 1983d. *Current Population Reports*. Washington, D.C.: U.S. Government Printing Office, Series P-23, No. 128.

———. 1983e. *Current Population Reports*. Washington, D.C.: U.S. Government Printing Office, Series P-23, No. 130.

———. 1983f. *Technical Paper No. 52*. Washington, D.C.: U.S. Government Printing Office.

———. 1984a. *Current Population Reports*. Washington, D.C.: U.S. Government Printing Office, Series P-16, No. 145.

———. 1984b. *Current Population Reports*. Washington, D.C.: U.S. Government Printing Office, Series P-20, No. 358.

———. 1984c. *Current Population Reports*. Washington, D.C.: U.S. Government Printing Office, Series P-20, No. 385.

———. 1984d. *Current Population Reports*. Washington, D.C.: U.S. Government Printing Office, Series P-20, No. 386.

———. 1984e. *Current Population Reports*. Washington, D.C.: U.S. Government Printing Office, Series P-20, No. 387.

———. 1984f. *Current Population Reports*. Washington, D.C.: U.S. Government Printing Office, Series P-20, No. 388.

———. 1984g. "Earnings in 1981 of Married Couple Families." *Current Population Reports*. Washington, D.C.: U.S. Government Printing Office, Series P-23, No. 133.

———. 1984h. "Lifetime Work Experience and Its Effects on Earnings." *Current Population Reports*. Washington, D.C.: U.S. Government Printing Office, Series P-23, No. 136.

———. 1984i. *Current Population Reports*. Washington, D.C.: U.S. Government Printing Office, Series P-25, No. 949.

———. 1984j. *Current Population Reports*. Washington, D.C.: U.S. Government Printing Office, Series P-60, No. 145.

———. 1985a. *Current Population Reports*. Washington, D.C.: U.S. Government Printing Office, Series P-20, No. 398.

———. 1985b. *Current Population Reports*. Washington, D.C.: U.S. Government Printing Office, Series P-20, No. 399.

———. 1985c. *Current Population Reports*. Washington, D.C.: U.S. Government Printing Office, Series P-20, No. 401.

———. 1985d. *Current Population Reports*. Washington, D.C.: U.S. Government Printing Office, Series P-20, No. 402.

———. 1985e. *Current Population Reports*. Washington, D.C.: U.S. Government Printing Office, Series P-23, No. 124.

———. 1985f. *Current Population Reports*. Washington, D.C.: U.S. Government Printing Office, Series P-23, No. 140.

———. 1985g. *Current Population Reports*. Washington, D.C.: U.S. Government Printing Office, Series P-23, No. 142.

———. 1985h. *Current Population Reports*. Washington, D.C.: U.S. Government Printing Office, Series P-23, No. 145.

———. 1985i. *Current Population Reports*. Washington, D.C.: U.S. Government Printing Office, Series P-25, No. 965.

———. 1985j. *Current Population Reports*. Washington, D.C.: U.S. Government Printing Office, Series P-60, No. 146.

———. 1985k. *Current Population Reports*. Washington, D.C.: U.S. Government Printing Office, Series P-70, No. 3.

———. 1986a. *Current Population Reports*. Washington, D.C.: U.S. Government Printing Office, Series P-25, No. 186.

———. 1986b. *Current Population Reports*. Washington, D.C.: U.S. Government Printing Office, Series P-60, No. 153.

U.S. Department of Labor, Bureau of Labor Standards. 1985, January. *Employment and Earnings*. Washington, D.C.: U.S. Government Printing Office.

US News & World Report. 1974. "Rise of the Singles—40 Million Free Spenders. (October 7):54ff.

Van de Velde, Theodor Hendrik. 1957. *Ideal Marriage: Its Physiology and Technique*. New York: Random House.

Van Sell, M., A. Brief, and R. Addag. 1979. "Job Satisfaction among Married Working Women." *Journal of Employment Counseling* 16:38–42.

Vaughn, Barbara, James Trusell, Jane Menken, and Elise F. Jones. 1977. "Contraceptive Failure among Married Women in the United States, 1970–1973." *Family Planning Perspectives* 9(November-December):251–258.

Veevers, Jean E. 1979. "Voluntary Childlessness: A Review of Issues and Evidence." *Marriage and Family Review* 2:1, 3–24.

Venture. 1985. "The Venture Survey." (January):24.

Vihko, Reijo, and Dan Apter. 1983. Cited in "Early Menarche, More Sex Hormone." *Science News* 124 (July 30):74.

Vincent, Clark. 1973. *Sexual and Marital Health: The Physician as a Consultant*. New York: McGraw-Hill.

Visher, Emily, and John Visher. 1979. Stepfamilies: A Guide to Working with Stepparents and Stepchildren. New York: Brunner/Mazel.

Voeller, B., and J. Walters. 1978. "Gay Fathers." *Family Coordinator* 27:149–157.

Voissem, N., and F. Sistrunk. 1971. "Communication Schedule and Cooperative Game Behavior." *Journal of Personality and Social Psychology* 19:160–167.

Wachtel, S. 1978. "Genes and Gender." *The Sciences* (May-June):16–17, 32–33.

Waite, Linda J., G. Haggstrom, and D. Kanouse. 1985. "The Consequences of Parenthood for Marital Stability of Young Adults." *American Sociological Review* 50:850–857.

Wallerstein, Judith, and Joan Kelly. 1974. "The Effects of Parental Divorce: The Adolescent Experience." In *The Child in His Family: Children at Psychiatric Risk*, edited by E. Anthony and C. Koupernik. New York: Wiley.

———. 1975. "The Effects of Parental Divorce: Experiences of the Preschool Child." *Journal of the American Academy of Child Psychiatry* 14:600–616.

———. 1976. "The Effects of Parental Divorce: Experiences of the Child in Later Latency." *American Journal of Orthopsychiatry* 46:256–269.

Wallum L. 1977. *The Dynamics of Sex and Gender: A Sociological Perspective*. Chicago: Rand McNally.

Walster, Elaine, and G. William Walster. 1978. *A New Look at Love*. Reading, MA: Addison-Wesley.

Walster, Elaine, G. William Walster, and J. Traupmann. 1978. "Equity and Premarital Sex." *Journal of Personality and Social Psychology* 36:82–92.

Walters, James, and Lynda Walters. 1980. "Parent-Child Relationships: A Review, 1970–1979." *Journal of Marriage and the Family* 42:807–822.

Walters, William, and Peter Singer, eds. 1982. *Test-Tube Babies: A Guide to Moral Questions, Present Techniques, and Future Possibilities*. New York: Oxford University Press.

Ward, R. 1978. "Limitations of the Family as a Supportive Institution in the Lives of the Aged." *Family Coordinator* 47:365–373.

Warren, Carol A. B., and Barbara Ponse. 1979. "The Existential Self and the Gay World." In *Existential Sociology*, edited by J. Douglas. Cambridge, MA: Harvard University Press.

Warren, D. 1972. "How to Use Transactional Analysis in Counseling." Pp. 101–103 in *Techniques of Marriage and Family Counseling*, edited by P. Popenoe. Los Angeles, CA: American Institute of Family Relations.

Watson, Roy E. 1983. "Pre-Marital Cohabitation vs. Traditional Courtship: Their Effects on Subsequent Marital Adjustment." *Family Relations* 32:139.

Watzlawick, Paul, J. Beavin, and D. Jackson. 1967. *Pragmatics of Human Communication: A Study of Interactional Patterns, Pathologies, and Paradoxes*. New York: Norton.

Watzlawick, Paul, J. Weakland, and R. Fisch. 1974. *Change: Principles of Problem Formation and Problem Resolution*. New York: Norton.

Webster, M., and Driskell, J., Jr. 1983. "Beauty as Status." *American Journal of Sociology* 89:140–165.

Weintraub, P. 1981. "The Brain: His and Hers." *Discover* 2:14–20.

Weishaus, Sylvia, and D. Field. 1983. "Fifty-Year Marriages: A Longitudinal Study." Paper presented at the annual meeting of the American Association for Marriage and Family Therapy, Washington, D.C., October.

———. 1984. "Continuity and Change in Half-Century Marriages: A Longitudinal Study." Paper presented at annual meeting of American Orthopsychiatry Association, Toronto, April.

Weiss, Robert, ed. 1973. *Loneliness: The Experience of Emotional and Social Isolation*. Cambridge, MA: MIT Press.

———. 1975. *Marital Separation: Managing after a Marriage Ends*. New York: Basic Books.

Weitzman, Lenore J. 1986. *The Divorce Revolution: The Unexpected Social and Economic Consequences for Women and Children in America*. New York: Free Press.

Weitzman, Lenore J., and Ruth B. Dixon. 1980. "The Alimony Myth: Does No-Fault Divorce Make a Difference?" *Family Law Quarterly* 14:141–186.

West, Donald J. 1968. *Homosexuality*. Chicago: Aldine.

Westhoff, Charles F., and Elise Jones. 1977. "Contraception and Sterilization in the United States, 1965–1975." *Family Planning Perspectives* 9 (September-October):52–157.

Westoff, Leslie Aldridge. 1977. *The Second Time Around: Remarriage in America*. New York: Viking Press.

Whelan, E. 1975. *A Baby . . . Maybe?* New York: Bobbs-Merrill.

White, B., J. Watts, and I. Barnett. 1973. *Experiences and Environment: Major Influences on the Development of the Young Child*. Vol. I. Englewood Cliffs, NJ: Prentice-Hall.

White, Lynn K. 1979. "Sex Differentials in the Effect of Remarriage on Global Happiness." *Journal of Marriage and the Family* 41:869–876.

———. 1983. "Determinants of Spousal Interaction: Marital Structure or Marital Happiness." *Journal of Marriage and the Family* 45:511–519.

White, Lynn K., and Alan Booth. 1985. "The Quality and Stability of Remarriages: The Role of Stepchildren." *American Sociological Review* 50:689–698.

Whitehurst, Robert N. 1975. "Alternate Life-Styles." *The Humanist* (May-June):23–26.

"Wife Beating: The Silent Crime." 1983. *Time* (September 5):24.

Wilder, C. 1978. "From the Interactional View—A Conversation with Paul Watzlawick." *Journal of Communication* 28:41.

Williams, C. 1977. "The New Morality." *Time* (November 21):111–116.

Williams, J., and M. Stith. 1980. *Middle Childhood*. 2nd ed. New York: Macmillan.

Willie, Charles V., and Susan L. Greenblatt. 1978. "Four 'Classic' Studies of Power Relationships in Black Families: A Review and Look to the Future." *Journal of Marriage and the Family* 40:691–694.

Willis, J., J. Crowder, and J. Willis. 1975. *Guiding the Psychological and Educational Growth of Children*. Springfield, IL: Charles C Thomas.

Wilson, B. 1982. *Religion in Sociological Perspective*. Oxford: Oxford University Press.

Wilson, Glenn, and David Nias. 1976. *The Mystery of Love*. New York: Quadrangle/New York Times.

Wilson, S. 1978. *Informal Groups*. Englewood Cliffs, NJ: Prentice-Hall.

Winch, Robert. 1958. *Mate Selection: A Study of Complementary Needs*. New York: Harper and Brothers.

Wisconsin Association on Alcoholism and Other Drug Abuse. 1984. "Questions People Ask about Drinking Alcohol during Pregnancy." *ICEA Review* 8:2.

Witkin, Stanley, and S. Rose. 1978. "Group Training in Communication Skills for Couples: A Preliminary Report." *International Journal of Family Counseling* 6:45–56.

Wood, Leland Foster, and Robert Latou Dickinson. 1948. *Harmony in Marriage.* New York: Round Table Press.

Wood, S., R. Bishop, and D. Cohen. 1978. *Parenting.* New York: Hart.

World Almanac Book of Facts 1986. 1985. New York: Newspaper Enterprise Association, Inc.

Wright, James D. 1978. "Are Working Women Really More Satisfied? Evidence from Several National Surveys." *Journal of Marriage and the Family* 40:301–313.

Wrightsman, Leonard, Jr. 1966. "Personality and Attitudinal Correlates of Trusting and Trustworthy Behaviors in a Two-Person Game." *Journal of Personality and Social Psychology* 4:328–332.

Yablonsky, Louis. 1979. *The Extra-Sex Factor: Why Over Half of America's Married Men Play Around.* New York: New York Times Book Company.

Yahraes, H., and Diana Baumrind. 1980. "Parents as Leaders: The Role of Control and Discipline." Pp. 289–297 in *National Institute of Mental Health Science Monographs.* Vol. 1. Washington, D.C.: U.S. Government Printing Office.

Yankelovich, Skelly, and White, Inc. 1977. *The General Mills American Family Report 1976–1977.* Minneapolis, MN: General Mills.

Young, Diony, and Charles Mahan. 1980. *Unnecessary Cesarians: Ways to Avoid Them.* Minneapolis, MN: ICEA.

Zelnik, Melvin. 1979. "Sex Education and Knowledge of Pregnancy Risk among U.S. Teenage Women." *Family Planning Perspectives* 11(November):355–357.

Zelnik, Melvin, and John F. Kantner. 1977. "Sexual and Contraceptive Experience of Young Unmarried Women in the United States, 1976 and 1971." *Family Planning Perspectives* 9:55–71.

———. 1978. "First Pregnancies to Women Aged 15–19 in 1976." *Family Planning Perspectives* 10 (May-June):135–142.

———. 1979. "Reasons for Non-Use of Contraception by Sexually Active Women Aged 15–19." *Family Planning Perspectives* 11 (September-October):289–298.

Zerin, Edward, and Marjory Zerin. 1980. "Four Styles of Communication." Unpublished paper.

Zerof, H. 1978. *Finding Intimacy: The Art of Happiness in Living Together.* New York: Random House.

Zimberg, S., J. Wallace, and S. Blume, eds. 1978. *Practical Approaches to Alcoholism Psychotherapy.* New York: Plenum Press.

Zimmerman, Don, and Candace West. 1975. "Sex Roles, Interruptions, and Silences in Conversations." Pp. 105–129 in *Language and Sex, Difference and Domination,* edited by B. Thoma and Nancy Henley. Rowley, MA: Newbury House.

Zimring, F. 1983. "Inter-spousal Homicide Patterns." In *University of Chicago's Center for Studies in Criminal Justice.* Chicago: University of Chicago Press.

Zuckerman, M., R. Albright, C. Marks, and G. Miller. 1962. "Stress and Hallucinatory Effects of Perceptual Isolation and Confinement." *Psychology Monographs* 76.

Zusman, Jack. 1978. "Relationship of Demographic Factors to Parental Discipline Techniques." *Developmental Psychology* 14:685–686.

NAME INDEX

Abarbanel, S., 430
Abramson, Paul, 94
Adamcik, Barbara, 493
Adams, Bert, 395
Adams, Gerald, 18, 147
Adams, Margaret, 120
Addag, R., 373
Ahrons, Constance, 421, 433, 435, 466
Alba, Richard D., 150
Albrecht, Kay, 382
Albrecht, Sharon, 451, 453
Albrecht, Stan L., 220, 484
Albright, R., 59
Aldous, Joan, 220, 234, 352, 378
Alexander, Shana, 540
Alpert, R., 36
Altergott, Karen, 509
Altman, Irwin, 184
Ammons, P., 223
Anderson, Scott, 131, 132, 133
Andrews, Lori B., 283
Apgar, Virginia, 316
Apter, Dan, 297
Arehart–Treichel, Joan, 304
Argyle, Michael, 194
Arkin, W., 390
Arling, Greg, 506
Arms, Suzanne, 313, 314
Arnold, R., 355
Aron, Arthur, 156
Aronson, Elliot, 64, 158
Asher, Steven R., 421
Ashley, Paul, 140
Atchley, Robert, 493
Avant, W. Ray, 478

Bach, George, 208
Bach, Sheldon, 75
Backman, Carl W., 8
Backman, Elaine, 134
Bacon, Lloyd, 360
Bader, E., 173

Bagarozzi, D., 172–173
Bahr, Howard, 400
Bahr, Stephen, 484
Bain, J., 354
Baldwin, Doris, 481
Bales, Robert, 47, 234
Balkwell, Carolyn, 505
Balswick, Jack O., 189, 421, 448
Bamford, Nancy, 318
Bandura, Albert, 35, 37
Bane, Mary Jo, 5, 6
Bank of America, 543
Bankoff, Elizabeth E., 506
Bardwick, Judith, 41
Barkas, J. L., 117
Barnett, I., 342
Barnett, Rosalind, 48
Barnhouse, T., 400
Bartz, Karen W., 344
Baruch, Grace, 48
Bates, J., 135
Bauman, Karl E., 127
Baumrind, Diana, 342, 343, 347
Baur, Karla, 271
Bayer, Alan E., 337
Bean, Frank D., 266
Beard, L., 478
Beavers, W. Robert, 460
Beavin, J., 183, 188, 189
Bebbington, A. C., 368
Beck, Rubye Wilkerson, 14
Becker, Gary S., 453
Beckman, Linda J., 417
Behrman, Richard E., 304
Bell, Alan P., 45, 135
Bell, Robert R., 92, 109, 199, 356
Bem, Daryl, 528
Bengis, I., 125
Bengtson, Vern, 508
Bennett, Dawn D., 261
Benson, Leonard, 174
Bergler, Edmund, 536–537
Bergman, A., 74

Bernard, Jessie, 125, 225, 463
Berne, Eric, 58, 59, 60, 207, 214
Bernstein, Anne, 82, 83, 293, 294
Bernstein, Ilene, 379
Berry, Jon, 268
Berry, Kenneth, 384
Berscheid, Ellen, 63, 65
Betcher, W., 238
Bianchi, S., 382
Bienenfeld, F., 423
Bienvenu, M., Sr., 195
Biller, Henry, 36, 350
Bird, Caroline, 118
Bishop, R., 346
Blake, Judith, 255
Blalock, Hubert, 230
Blanche, Ed, 245
Blau, Peter, 23, 154
Blehar, M., 290, 320, 323
Blood, Robert, 225, 227
Bloom, Bernard, 421
Bloombaum, Milton, 523
Blumberg, Paul M., 174
Blume, S., 418
Blumstein, Philip, 134, 232, 235
Bogardus, Emory, 58
Bohannan, Paul, 223, 422, 458, 466
Bohrnstedt, George W., 379
Bonacich, Philip, 353
Booth, Alan, 162, 377, 378, 452
Boston Women's Health Book
    Collective, 261
Bourg, Carroll J., 508
Bowen, Gary Lee, 225
Bowen, Murray, 322–323
Bower, Bruce, 285
Bower, Donald W., 130, 131, 165
Bowlby, John, 505
Bowman, M., 435
Bradburn, Norman, 378
Bradley, Robert A., 315
Brannon, Robert, 49
Brayer, F., 269

Brazelton, T. Berry, 298, 324
Brecher, Edward, 61, 504, 505
Bretschneider, J., 505
Brief, A., 373
Bringle, Robert T., 392
Britton, S., 422
Broderick, Carlfred, 24, 77, 91, 157,
    203, 213, 214, 221, 321, 333
Brofenbrenner, Urie, 5
Brown, B. B., 393
Bryson, Jeff B., 384, 386
Bryson, Rebecca, 384, 386
Bubolz, Margaret M., 223
Budd, L. S., 136
Bulato, R., 355
Bullough, Bonnie L., 245
Bullough, Vern L., 245
Bumpass, Larry, 162, 249, 376, 408,
    443
Burchinal, Lee G., 409
Burgess, Ernest, 7, 11, 164, 225, 487
Buripaki, C., 355
Burke, R., 378
Burland, J. Alexis, 75
Burns, Aisla, 411
Burr, Wesley, 22, 23, 24, 212, 367
Bursk, E., 496
Business Week, 386
Buss, David M., 153
Butler, Robert N., 307, 508
Byrd, Admiral Richard E., 59

Cain, Richard, 298, 311
Calhoun, Arthur W., 171
California Commission on Crime
    Control, 347
Camara, K, 433
Campbell, Arthur A., 124, 125, 251
Campbell-Gibson, R., 494
Cannon, Kenneth, 25
Carroll, D., 120
Carney, Larry S., 12
Carter, L., 499
Cartwright, Dorwin, 217
Casto, R., 439
Cazares, E., 150
Cease, L., 429
Cecre, L., 386
Centers, Richard, 152, 157
Cerreto, M., 24
Cetron, Marvin, 488
Chadwick, Bruce A., 220, 400, 484
Chafetz, Janet, 334
Chambers, David L., 434
Chancellor, Loren E., 409
Changing Times, 548
Charney, Israel, 202
Chason, Karen M., 132, 136
Cherlin, Andrew, 408, 453, 490
Chesler, Phyllis, 432
Chester, Robert, 360
Chiazze, L., 269
Christensen, Harold T., 7
Christensen, J., 275

Christopherson, Victor, 130, 131, 165
Chung, B., 355
Cicirelli, Victor C., 496
Cimons, Marlene, 260, 280
Cipriano, J., 284
Clanton, Gordon, 391
Clark, Margaret P., 266
Clark, W., 118
Clarke, F., 189
Clark-Stewart, K., 351, 353
Clausen, A., 553
Clavan, Sylvia, 489
Clayton, Richard R., 129, 130, 132
Cleveland, W., 468
Cogan, Rosemary, 298, 316
Cohen, D., 346
Cohn, D'Vera, 263, 264
Cole, Charles L., 129, 390, 497
Cole, K., 238
Cole, Sue Peck, 24, 319
Coleman, James C., 206
Coleman, Marilyn, 463
Collins, M., 150
Collins, Randall, 25
Commission on Population Growth in
    America, 254
Comstock, G., 506
*Connecticut Mutual Life Report on
    American Values in the 80's*, 232
Cooley, Charles Horton, 167
Copeland, T., 443
Corea, Gena, 314
Corfman, E., 22
Corrales, Ramon, 182, 232
Cottrell, Leonard S., 225
Coughey, Kathleen, 92
Cowan, Philip, 83, 294
Cox, Martha, 420, 421, 429, 441
Cox, Roger, 429, 441
Crane, Tricia, 260, 261
Crawley, L., 280
Cressey, Donald, 58
Croake, J., 133
Cromwell, Ronald E., 234
Crooks, Robert, 271
Crowder, J., 342
Cuber, John F., 202, 224, 498
Culverwell, Melissa, 279
Cumming, Elaine, 495
Cunningham, F. Gary, 311
Cutler, Sally, 506
Cvetkovich, George, 252

Davenport, William H., 298
Davidson, Bernard, 188
Davis, A., 125
Davis, Keith, 70
Davis, Kingsley, 59
Davis, R., 49
Day, R., 352
DeFrank-Lynch, B., 222
DeLamater, John, 107, 130
Delora, Jo Ann, 515, 519
DeMaris, Alfred, 136

DeMartino, Manfred, 94
Deutsch, Morton, 425
Deutsch, Ronald, 208, 217, 218, 219
Diamond, Milton, 87, 91, 259, 268,
    276, 294
DiBona, Pamela V., 134
Dickinson, Robert Latou, 290
Dick-Read, Grantly, 314
Dicks, H. V., 238
Dixon, R., 439
Dobrofsky, L., 390
Dodson, Betty, 515
Doering, S., 299, 309, 311, 318, 319
Dorner, G., 45
Dougherty, Ralph C., 281
Dovidio, J., 467
Drapkin, R., 423
Draughon, Margaret, 460
Dreifus, C., 265
Dressel, Paula, 478
Driskell, J. Jr., 61
Druckerman, J., 173, 226
Dryfoos, Joy, 252
Duberman, Lucille, 5, 454, 459, 461,
    462
Dudley, Donald, 369, 370
Duffy, B., 269
Duncan, R. Paul, 386
Dunn, Thomas E., 299

Eaton, Gerald T., 507
Edwards, Marie, 127, 128, 162
Eekelaar, J. M., 248
Eheart, Brenda K., 320
Eichler, L., 174
Eisenberg, Leon, 378
Elder, Glen H., Jr., 4, 7
Elkin, Meyer, 420, 426, 465
Ellis, Havelock, 61
Elevenstar, D., 497
Entine, A., 490
Entwisle, D., 299, 309, 311, 318, 319
Erickson, R., 458
Erikson, Erik, 75, 185, 334, 338, 341,
    508
Esfandiary, F. M., 6
Eskew, R., 496
Evenback, Scott, 392

Fagot, Beverly I., 37
Falek, A., 422
Family Planning Perspectives, 258
Family Therapy News, 465, 466
Farber, Bernard, 150, 356
Fawcett, J., 355
Fechter, Lawrence, 302
Feldman, Frances, 332
Feldman, Harold, 221, 222, 484, 535,
    536
Feldman, Margaret, 484, 535, 536
Feldman, Saul D., 332
Fendrich, Michael, 386
Ferbolt, J., 356
Field, D., 498

Finlay, Barbara A., 337, 381
Fisch, R., 202
Fisher, B., 191
Fisher, Esther, 440
Fitzpatrick, M., 190
Flanzer, Jerry, 417
Ford, Kathleen, 260
Forer, Lucille, 156, 157, 337
Forisha, Barbara L., 224
Forrest, Jacqueline, 274, 275
"Forum International," 263, 268
Fosburgh, L., 252
Foster, Lorri, 89
Fourier, D., 173, 226
Fox, Greer Litton, 146
Fraiberg, Selma, 388
Framo, James, 333
Francoeur, Robert, 126
Frankie, G., 35
Franklin, Deborah, 107
Freedman, Deborah S., 121, 360
Freeman, M., 416
Freidman, A., 497–498, 502
Freud, Sigmund, 37, 156
Friday, Nancy, 99
Friedan, Betty, 50
Friedman, Leonard, 215
Furstenberg, Frank, 253, 360, 408, 453, 490

Gadpaille, Warren, 87, 93, 108
Gagnon, John, 34, 44, 78, 94, 96, 174
Gallagher, U., 284
Galligan, Richard, 354
Gallup Poll, 537, 538
Ganong, Lawrence, 463
Garland, T., 384
Gebhard, Paul, 86, 126
Gelles, Richard, 415, 416, 465
Geoffroy, K., 342
Gerard, Diana, 337–338
Gernstein, M., 187
Gerson, Menachem, 291
Gianturco, D., 468
Gibson, M., 509
Gilbert, S., 196
Gillespie, Dair, 234
Gillis, Phyllis, 292
Gitchel, Sam, 89
Glenn, Norval, 130, 150, 153, 451, 484
Glick, Ira, 469, 470
Glick, Paul, 163, 440, 451, 452, 455, 468
Glueck, Eleanor, 344
Glueck, Sheldon, 344
Goetting, Ann, 451, 467
Goldstein, H., 458, 459
Goleman, Daniel, 99
Goode, William J., 5, 147, 449
Goodman, Ellen, 251
Goodman, Larry, 74
Gordon, Leonard, 150, 494
Gormally, J., 49

Gossett, J., 460
Gottlieb, David, 334
Gottman, John, 202, 207
Gould, Roger L., 221, 410
Goulder, Lois, 283
Gove, Walter, 6, 124, 125, 385, 389
Grace, Gloria, 368
Gray, S., 491
Greenblatt, Cathy, 174
Greenblatt, Robert, 96
Greenblatt, Susan, 230
Greerken, M., 385, 389
Greif, Geoffrey, 432, 434
Grossbard-Schectman, Amyra, 119
Grote, B., 252
Group for the Advancement of
    Psychiatry, 354, 355
Grusky, Oscar, 353
Guest, F., 263, 267, 275
Guinness Book of World Records,
    496

Habenstein, Robert W., 127
Hage, D., 399
Haggstrom, G., 336
Hale, W., 44
Hall, Douglas T., 155, 234, 384
Hall, Francine S., 155, 234, 384
Halliday, T., 453
Halverson, Charles, 189
Hammond, J., 542
Hampe, G., 464
Hanna, Suzanne, 463
Hansen, G., 507
Harlow, Harry, 59, 68
Harriman, L., 336
Harroff, Peggy, 202, 224, 498
Hatcher, R., 263, 267, 275
Hatkoff, Terry, 78, 523, 533
Haun, D., 225
Haverstein, L., 376
Havighurst, Robert, 495
Hawkins, James, 196
Hayes, Mary, 156
Heckman, Norma A., 384, 386
Heer, David, 119
Heider, Fritz, 152, 153
Heinowitz, Jack R., 298
Heiss, Jerold, 25
Helms, D., 544
Helsing, S., 506
Henderson, B., 34
Hendricks, C. Davis, 507
Hendricks, John, 507
Hendrix, L., 232
Henry, William E., 495
Henslin, James, 32
Henze, Lura, 133, 246
Hess, Beth, 17–18
Hess, E., 63
Hess, R., 36, 433
Hetherington, E. Mavis, 35, 36, 420, 421, 429, 441
Heyman, D., 493

Hicks, Mary, 354
Highlander, Don, 535, 551
Hilker, M., 507
Hill, Charles T., 136, 168
Hill, Reuben, 22, 193, 207, 367, 499
Hiller, Dana V., 227
Himes, Norman, 244, 263
Hinkle, Dennis E., 68
Hinz, R., 298, 316
Hipgrave, T., 432
Hitchens, D., 135
Hobbs, Daniel, 24, 319
Hoffman, Lois, 204, 254, 388
Hoffman, Martin, 254
Holman, Thomas, 22, 23, 24
Holmstrom, Lynda L., 384
Hoover, Eleanor, 127, 128
Hopkins, J., 380
Horn, Jack C., 274
Horn, M., 126
Horney, Karen, 384
Hoult, Thomas F., 19, 246
Houseknecht, Sharon, 257
Hudson, John, 133, 246
Hughes, Michael, 6
Humphreys, Laud, 105
Hunt, Bernice, 439
Hunt, Janet, 385, 450, 452
Hunt, Larry L., 385, 450, 452
Hunt, Morton, 105, 107, 108, 126, 439
Hunt, R., 399
Hurlock, Elizabeth, 311–312
Hutchinson, I., 499
Huyck, Margaret H., 485, 492
Hyde, Janet S., 485

ICEA Review, 302, 303
ICEA *Sharing*, 517
Iliffe, A. H., 60
Indvik, J., 190
Ingham, M., 332
*International Journal of Childbirth
    Education*, 302
Iritani, T., 355

Jacklin, Carol N., 191
Jackson, Don, 183, 188, 189, 194, 349
Jackson, Patrick G., 134
Jacobsen, Neil, 204
Jacobsen, Paul H., 11, 13
Jacobsen, R. Brooke, 384
Jacoby, Susan, 122
Jacques, Jeffrey M., 132, 136
Jeffreys, M., 485
Johnson, E., 496
Johnson, J. S., 422
Johnson, Virginia, 86, 96, 97, 98, 268, 317, 515, 516, 517, 518, 519, 522
Jones, Elise, 266
Jones, R., 135
Jordan, T., 356

Meredith, B., 499
Meredith, Dennis, 350
Messinger, Lillian, 455
Meyers, L., 414
Michael, R., 453
Miller, Brent, 336, 337–338
Miller, G., 59
Miller, Julie Ann, 302, 304
Miller, S., 76
Miller, Stuart, 182
Miller, W., 252
Mills, James, 302
Mills, David, 457, 463
Mirowsky, J., 227
Mitchell, W., 397
Moen, Phyllis, 367
Money, John, 42, 46, 66, 71, 77, 170, 171
Montemayor, Raymond, 337
Montgomery, Barbara, 182, 189, 193, 197
Montgomery, J., 499
Moore, Kristin, 379
Moore, Sylvia F., 455
Morgan, Paul, 253, 290
Moroney, R., 5
Morris, Desmond, 62, 127
Morris, W., 467
Morse, Gardiner, 264, 267, 272, 491
Mott, Frank L., 455
Mueller, Charles W., 409
Murdock, George, 20
Murguia, Edward, 150
Murstein, Bernard, 24, 56, 65, 72, 73, 147, 152, 153, 154
Mutryn, Cynthia S., 311
Myerson, J., 127, 269, 275
Myricks, N., 138, 139

Nadelson, T., 378
Nason, Ellen, 256
National Academy of Sciences, 388
National Center for Health Statistics, 14, 16, 168, 249, 407, 410, 414, 448, 456
National Opinion Research Center, 6
Navron, L., 183
Nelson, V., 150
Nelson, Waldo E., 317
Netter, F., 515
Neugarten, Bernice, 482, 487, 490, 495
Newman, Barbara, 332, 336, 337, 354, 355
Newman, Philip, 332, 336, 337, 354, 355
Newsweek, 128
Nias, David, 57, 60, 61, 72, 73
Nordwind, Richard, 272
Norton, Arthur, 451, 452
Norwood, Christopher, 314
Notarius, C., 207
Nusberg, C., 509
Nye, F. Ivan, 23, 154, 225, 360, 361, 388

O'Kelley, Charlotte, 12
O'Leary, S., 352, 353
Olson, David H., 24, 173, 189, 212, 226, 234, 366
Oppong, Christine, 146
"Oral Contraceptives," 259
Orden, Susan, 378
Orthner, Dennis, 183, 225
Osmond, Marie, 24
Osofsky, H., 276
Osofsky, J., 276
Ota, Paula, 320
O'Toole, T., 488

Packard, Vance, 6
Paolucci, B., 346
Papen-Daniel, M., 187
Parachini, Allan, 276, 277, 300
Pardes, H., 4
Parish, Thomas S., 443, 471
Parke, Ross D., 319, 349, 352, 353
Parkes, C., 469, 470
Parks, A. Lee, 441
Parsons, D., 385
Parsons, Talcott P., 47, 394
Paul, P. W., 174
Peace, S., 509
Pear, T. H., 61
Pearce, John, 215
Pearlin, Leonard, 422
Pearson, J., 423
Pearson, W., Jr., 232
Peele, Stanton, 72
Pendleton, B., 384
Pepitone-Rockwell, Fran, 235
Peplau, Letitia Anne, 136, 168
Perrucci, Carolyn C., 386
Perry, John D., 516
Peterman, Don, 131, 132, 133
Peterson, E., 337
Peterson, James L., 442
Peyrot, M., 353
Phillip, M., 125
Phillips, V., 460
Pietropinto, Anthony, 109
Pine, F., 74
Pinsker, M., 342
Platt, Marilyn, 354
Pleck, Joseph P., 49, 125, 350, 385, 386
Podolski, Alfred L., 284
Pogrebin, Letty, 352, 381
Polikoff, N., 427
Pollie, Robert, 272
Poloma, Margaret M., 256, 384, 385
Polonko, Karen, 230
Pomeroy, Wardell, 44, 94
Pomona (CA) *Progress Bulletin*, 138, 483, 538
Ponse, Barbara, 106
Pope, Hallowell, 409
Porter, Sylvia, 537
Pratt, Lois, 7, 224, 368
Pribram, K., 191

Price, Ann, 318
Price-Bonham, Sharon, 421, 448
Pritchard, Jack A., 311

Queen, Stuart, 127
Quinn, William, 495

Rajan, R., 276
Rank, Mark A., 227
Rapoport, Rhona, 354, 355, 376, 380, 381, 392
Rapoport, Robert, 354, 355, 376, 380, 381, 392
Raschke, Helen, 427, 443, 467
Raschke, Vern, 443
Rau, L., 36
Rauen, R., 172–173
Raven, Bertram H., 218
Rawlings, Steve W., 15, 16, 537
Ray, Dixie L., 196
Reamy, Kenneth, 304, 305
Redbook, 394, 395, 398
Reevy, William K., 90
Reisner, D., 307
Reiss, Ira L., 66, 70, 71, 107, 126, 127, 132, 258, 378, 408, 529
Research and Forecasts, Inc., 5
Rettig, Kathryn D., 223
Reynolds, D., 503, 508
Rhode, W., 45
Rhodes, 391
Rice, D., 382
Richardson, J., 379
Richmond, Marie L., 232
Riddle, R., 173
Ridley, Carl A., 131, 132, 133, 383
Riegel, Klaus, 355
Riley, E., 132, 173
Riley, L., 117
Rindfuss, Ronald R., 249, 253, 290, 443
Risman, Barbara, 134, 170
Rivers, Caryl, 48
Robins, E., 46
Robertiello, Robert, 438
Roberts, A., 497
Roberts, W., 497
Robertson, Joan, 489
Rodgers, J., 281
Rodgers, Roy, 500
Rogers, Rita, 86
Rollins, Boyd, 25, 221, 222, 347, 354
Roof, W., 399
Room, R., 118
Roosevelt, Ruth, 460
Roper Organization, 341
Rose, Arnold, 495
Rose, S., 184
Rosen, Lawrence, 109
Rosenberg, Betty, 485
Rosenberg, Michael, 344
Rosenthal, K., 134, 432
Ross, Adreain A., 153
Ross, C., 227

Rossi, Alice, 320, 373
Roth, R., 417
Rovner, Sandy, 276
Rowand, Andrea, 302
Rowe, George, 77, 499
Rowe, M., 387
Rubin, Jeffrey Z., 218
Rubin, Lillian, 67, 75, 76, 393
Rubin, Zick, 61, 63, 69, 70, 136, 168
Rucker, P., 42, 46
Russell, Candyce, 24, 212, 319
Rutter, M., 358
Ryder, Robert G., 257
Ryne, D., 222
Rytina, N., 382

Saegert, S., 148
Safilios-Rothschild, Constantina, 129, 231
Saghir, Marcel, 46
Saluter, Arlene, 16
Sandberg, Eugene, 279
Sandler, Judith, 127, 269, 275
San Fernando Valley News, 415
Santrock, John, 432
Sardanis-Zimmerman, Irene, 459
Sarrel, Lorna, 94, 485
Sarrel, Phillip, 94, 485
Satir, Virginia, 182, 349
Sawhill, Isabel V., 379
Sawin, Douglas B., 319, 349
Scanlon, J., 313
Scanzoni, John, 154, 230, 232
Schacter, Stanley, 73
Schauble, P., 49, 193
Scheff, Thomas, 194
Schneider, C., 491
Schrader, Sandra, 168–170
Schram, Rosalyn W., 498
Schulman, G., 459
Schulman, Marion, 167, 168, 194
Schumacher, Sally, 504
Schumm, W., 195
Schvaneveldt, Jay D., 23
Schwartz, Mark A., 99, 123
Schwartz, Pepper, 134, 232, 235
Science News, 264, 265, 268, 272, 276, 279, 280, 303, 310, 352
Scoresby, A. L., 195, 200
Scott, Rebecca Lovell, 302
Seaman, Barbara, 269
Seaman, G., 269
Sears, R., 36
Secord, Paul F., 8
Seligson, Marcia, 174
Senn, D. J., 189
Sexual Medicine Today, 281
Shah, Farida, 252
Shanas, Ethel, 394, 480, 482, 495, 508
Shaw, George Bernard, 56
Shaw, M., 8, 217
Sheppard, H., 492
Shertzer, B., 382

Shoen, R., 150
Shostak, M., 46
Shupe, A., 416
Silberner, Joanne, 265, 300
Silka, Linda, 257
Silverstein, C., 135
Simenauer, Jacqueline, 109, 120
Simon, A., 459
Simon, William, 44, 78
Sims, L., 346
Sinclair, C., 173
Singapore Straits Times, 146
Singer, Laura, 186, 216, 283
Sistrunk, F., 219
Skolnick, Arlene, 6, 236
Skovholt, T., 49
Smith, C., 506
Smith, J., 24, 203, 333, 373, 375, 496
Smith, K., 508
Smith, Lynn, 391
Smith, M., 489
Smith, Roy G., 389
Snyder, Douglas K., 226
Snyder, M., 65
Sollie, Donna, 336
Solnit, A., 356
Sorensen, Robert, 90
Spake, A., 120
Spanier, Graham, 25, 133, 150, 166, 225, 439, 453, 497
Spezzano, C., 315
Spicer, J., 464
Spitz, René, 339
Spock, Benjamin, 341
Sporakowski, Michael, 68, 497
Spreitzer, R., 117
Sprenkle, Douglas H., 24, 189, 191, 212
Sprey, Jetse, 25, 109, 202, 230
St. John, Craig, 385
Stacey, W., 416
Stafford, Rebecca, 134
Stahl, F., 45
Stannard, Una, 244
Stein, B., 121, 538, 547, 552
Stein, Martha L., 99
Stein, Peter, 17–18, 117, 118, 120, 122
Steinberg, Sarah, 272
Steiner, M., 368
Steinhoff, Patricia, 276
Steinmetz, Suzanne, 414–415, 416
Stern, B., 186, 216
Stern, P., 457, 458
Sternberg, Robert, 69
Stewart, E., 262
Stewart, F., 263, 267, 275, 279
Stewart, G., 263, 267, 275
Still, Henry, 156, 157
Stinnett, Nick, 8, 223, 225, 399, 499
Stith, M., 544
Stolk, Y., 116
Stoller, Robert, 41
Storms, Michael, 104

Stratton, P., 263, 267, 275
Straus, Murray A., 232, 415, 416
Strean, Herbert, 108
Streib, Gordon, 14, 490–491, 494, 507, 508
Strelitz, Ziona, 354, 355
Strodtbeck, Fred L., 234
Stuart, Richard, 24, 188, 215, 218
Stuckert, Robert P., 224
Student Health Counseling Center, 516
Style, Carolyn Briggs, 6
Sullivan, Ellen, 274, 275
Sullivan, Harry Stack, 77
Sussman, Marvin B., 394
Sutherland, Edwin, 58
Suzuki, B., 10
Swap, W., 148
Sweet, J., 162, 408
Swenson, Clifford, 496
Swicegood, C. Gray, 253, 266, 290
Sydney Sunday Telegraph, 267
Sze, William, 60, 341
Szklo, M., 506

Takas, M., 429
Tallman, I., 234
Tanfer, Koray, 126
Tanke, E., 65
Tanner, D., 135
Taulbee, Pamela, 107
Tavris, Carol, 504
Taylor, Alexander, 394
Taylor, Dalmas A., 184
Tennov, Dorothy, 70, 531
Terkelson, Kenneth G., 203
Tessman, L., 471
Thibaut, John, 62, 154
Thoennes, N., 423
Thomas, Darwin, 340, 347
Thomas, Sandra, 382
Thomes, Mary Margaret, 7, 11, 164
Thompson, C., 174, 175
Thompson, Patricia G., 250
Thornburg, H., 83
Thornton, Arland, 121, 360
Tietze, Christopher, 274, 275
Time, 280, 284, 415
Titus, S. S., 393
Todd, Judy, 497–498, 502
Todd, Michael, 70
Toman, Walter, 156, 157, 337
Trattner, W., 428
Traupmann, J., 133, 154, 155
Trause, Mary Anne, 298
Treas, Judy, 468
Troll, Lillian, 496
Trost, Jan, 132, 136, 153
Tudor, J., 124
Tully, Judy Corder, 153
Tumulty, K., 373
Turner, J., 544
Turner, Ralph, 185
Turner, Stanley, 109
Twain, Mark, 82

Udry, J. Richard, 60, 127
Underwood, Donna, 534
Urion, Carl, 517
U.S. Bureau of the Census, 6, 11, 13,
    15, 16, 17, 19, 116, 118, 124,
    129, 130, 133, 134, 151, 165,
    166, 216, 246, 247, 249, 250,
    251, 253, 255, 257, 258, 266,
    290, 334, 350, 351, 358, 360,
    371, 373, 374, 375, 409, 428,
    434, 443, 448, 449–450, 454,
    470, 471, 479, 480, 481, 483,
    490, 496, 503, 507, 509, 535,
    539, 542
U.S. Department of Labor, Bureau of
    Labor Standards, 13
U.S. News & World Report, 120

Van de Velde, Theodor Hendrik, 61,
    516
Van Hilst, Anneke, 468
Van Sell, M., 373
Vas Dass, N., 280
Vaughn, Barbara, 259
Vaughn, V., 317
Veevers, Jean, 256
Venture, 384
Vihko, Reijo, 297
Visher, Emily, 457, 458
Visher, John, 457, 458
Voeller, B., 135
Voissem, N., 219
Voss, Harwin L., 129, 130, 132

Wachtel, S., 41
Wackman, D., 182
Wagner, N., 307
Waite, Linda J., 336
Wallace, J., 418
Wallace, Karl, 173
Wallerstein, Judith, 442
Wallum, L., 377
Walster, Elaine, 56, 63, 65, 133, 154,
    155

Walster, William, 56, 133, 154, 155
Walters, J., 135
Walters, James, 353, 354
Walters, Lynda, 353, 354
Walters, R., 37
Ward, M., 373, 375
Ward, R., 396
Warren, Carole, 106, 515, 519
Warren, D., 214
Warshak, Richard, 432
Waterman, J., 315
Watson, R., 136
Watts, J., 342
Watzlawick, Paul, 183, 188, 189, 202
Weakland, J., 202
Weaver, Charles, 130, 451
Webber, Leon, 368
Webster, M., 61
Weideking, R., 42
Weinberg, Martin S., 45, 135
Weingarter, H., 443
Weinstein, Karol K., 487, 490
Weintraub, P., 41
Weir, Tamara, 378
Weisberg, Carol, 196
Weishaus, Sylvia, 498
Weiss, Robert, 126, 235, 435, 450,
    452, 469, 470, 506
Weitzman, L., 431, 439
Welke, Elton, 369, 370
West, Candace, 190
West, D., 91
Westhoff, Charles F., 266
Westoff, L., 450, 464
Whelan, E., 248
Whipple, Beverly, 516
Whitaker, Carl, 413
White, B., 342
White, L., 223, 452, 455
White, Priscilla, 380, 382
White, S., 421
Whitehurst, Robert, 6, 109
Wilder, C., 188
Wilken, P., 230

Williams, C., 126
Williams, Dorie, 266
Williams, J., 544
Willie, Charles, 230
Willis, J., 342
Wilson, B., 400
Wilson, Glenn, 57, 60, 61, 72, 73
Wilson, S., 232
Winch, Robert, 147, 155
Wisconsin Association on Alcoholism
    and Other Drug Abuse, 302
Witkin, Stanley, 184
Wolfe, Donald M., 225, 227
Wood, Leland Foster, 290
Wood, S., 346
Working Woman, 385
World Almanac Book of Facts, 478
Wright, A., 263, 267, 275
Wright, James D., 378
Wrightsman, Leonard, Jr., 219
Wu, T., 355
Wyden, P., 208

Yablonsky, Louis, 108
Yahraes, H., 342
Yankelovich, Skelly, White Inc., 40
Young, Diony, 311

Zajonc, R., 148
Zelnik, Melvin, 126, 127, 129, 251,
    252
Zerin, Edward, 196
Zerin, Marjory, 196
Zerof, H., 186
Zill, Nicholas, 442
Zimberg, S., 418
Zimmerman, Don, 190
Zimmerman, J. A., 269
Zimring, F., 414
Zuckerman, M., 59
Zusman, J., 337

SUBJECT INDEX

Boldfaced page numbers indicate text page on which terms are defined in glossary.

Confusion in communication, 183
Consummation, 20, **27**
Contactful style of communication, 197
Contact hunger, 60. *See also* Touching
Contraception, 83, **111**
   history of methods, 244–246
   teenage, 250–253
   usage in sexually active women, 253
Contraceptives
   barrier, 262–265
   chemical, 259–262
   experimental, 271–274
Contract
   cohabitation, 139–140
   marital, 175–176
Controlling style of communication, 196
Convenience, of cohabitation, 133
Conventional style of communication, 196–197
Cooperation, 346–349
   in family, 348
   vs. competition, 218–220
Coparental divorce, 427–435
Coping, in family system, 335
Core symbols, 215, **240**
Corona, 96, **111**, 517
Corpora cavernosa, 522
Corpus spongiosum, 522
Cost-reward ratio, 366, **402**
Counseling, marital, 420–421
Couples
   cohabitating, 129–134
   decision to start family, 325
   dual-worker, 371–380
   friends, 392
   reestablishing relationship in postparental stage, 484
   remarried older, 471–472, 503
Courtship, 132, 168
Couvade, 298, **327**
Cowper's glands, 522
Credit, 551–553
Crises, dealing positively with, 8
Critical-hostility, in marital relationship, 225
Criticism, 188, 204
Crying, neonatal, 324
Cultural, **27**
   definitions in decision-making patterns, 227, 230
   differences in family and marriage, 8–10
   forms of marriage, 21–22
Cunnilingus, 96, **111**
Curettage, 277
Custody, child, 423–424, 427–431

Dalkon Shield, 265
Dartos muscles, 518, 519
Day-care centers, 391
Decidophobia, 227

Decision making
   challenges in marriage, 226–235
   influence of wife's employment on, 379–380
   power in, 227, 230–232
De facto marriage, 123
Defense-oriented, 206–207, **209**
Denial, 206
   of infertility, 284
Dependence, 213
Depo Provera, 272
Depression
   childhood, 441
   in infertility syndrome, 284
   menopausal, 485
   postpartum, 320–321
Developmental level, 338–339, **363**
Developmental tasks, 508, **511**
Developmental theory, 25
Devitalized marriage style, 223
Diabetes, 303
Diaphragm, 262–263
Diethylstilbestrol (DES), 262
Differences. *See* Conflicts; Disagreements
Differential association, 147–148, **178**
Dilation and evacuation surgery, 278
Dilation of cervix, 307
Disability insurance, 549–550
Disagreements. *See also* Conflicts
   relationship to stage of marriage, 207–208
   resolving, 201–202
Discipline, 346–349
   effective, 340
   stepfathers and, 458
Disconfirmation, 188, 189, **209**
Disengagement, 508
Disillusionment, 168
Dissolution, 411, **445**
Dissonance reduction, 355, **363**
Divorce
   adjustments to new lifestyles, 436–437
   age at marriage and, 164
   changing patterns in, 16–17
   child custody, 433–434
   conversation of, 413
   coparental, 427–435
   economic, 425–427
   emotional, 422
   extramarital affairs and, 413–414
   family violence and, 414–417
   happiness and, 6
   increase of singlehood and, 118
   legal, 423–425
   marital life cycle and, 409–411
   marital power and, 232
   professional help, 419–421
   psychic, 437
   public, 435–436
   rates, 16, 406–407
   ratio, 408
   from remarriage, 448–450
   social factors contributing to, 407–409

   stages in process, 421–422
   substance abuse and, 417–419
   of teenage couples with children, 360
   unfulfilled expectations and, 216
   in United States, 406–411
"Divorce chain," 466
Divorce mediation, 423–424
Dizygotic, 312, **327**
Douching, 262, 294–295
Down's syndrome, 247–248, 356
Drug abuse, 418–419
Dual-career marriage, 382–387
   job relocation, 385–387
   marital adjustment, 384
   parenting, 384–385
   stresses, 382–384
Dual-career marriages, earnings, 539
Duration
   of commitment, 169
   length of marriage, 6, 164
Dyadic adjustment scale, 226, 228–229

Earnings. *See* Income
Ecbelatericin, 272
Economic factors
   in divorce, 17, 425–427
   effect on marriage, 222, 366–367
   in reduction of birthrate, 16
Ectopic pregnancy, 521
Education
   childlessness and, 255–256
   divorce and, 408
   of teenage parents, 360
Effacement, 307
Egalitarian model of marriage, 224
Egg cell, 295
Ego development, 500–502, **512**
Ego strength, 340–341, **363**
Ejaculation, 89, **111**
Elderly
   divorce among, 412
   financial aspects, 539
   growing population of, 478–483
   integrity in aging, 508–509
   older achievers, 481
   parents, abuse of, 416
   remarriage after widowhood, 471–472
   retirement of, 490–495
   sex and, 503–505
   single people, 505–508
   and their families, 495–503
Emancipation, cohabitation and, 132
Embryo, 300, **327**, 520
Emotional divorce, 422
Emotional space, 213
Emotions
   aspects of family finances in remarriage and, 455
   communication about, 192
Empathy, **178**
   in communication, 190–193
   listening with, 194

Genitalia, **51**
  male, 521–522
  sex determination and, 41
German measles, 303
Gerontology, 477, **512**
Gestation, 299–300, **327**
  female internal organs for, 519–521
  multiple, 312–313
Glans
  of clitoris, 515
  of penis, 517
Goals
  individual vs. mutual, 217–218
  mutual, setting of, 217–220
Gonads, 519
Gonorrhea, 128, **142**
Gossypol, 272
Grafenberg spot, 516
Grandmothers, 489
Grandparent, role of, 487–490
Grandparents' Visitation Act, 436
Gray Panthers, 479, 480

Handfasting, 171, **178**
Handicapped children, 356
Happenings, 60
Heart disease, risk and birth control pills, 260–261
Herpes simplex II, 128, **142**, 264, 310
Heterosexual, 21, **27**
Heterosexuality, **52**
  preference, 44, 45, 104
  sexual fantasies, 99–100
Hispanic-Americans
  living arrangements of children, 359
  morale after retirement, 493–494
  physical abuse and, 414
  single-parent household incomes, 375
Home, purchasing, 547–548
Home pregnancy tests, 277, 300
Homicides, spousal, 414
Homogamy, 149, 153, **178**
Homosexual cohabitation, 135
Homosexuality, **52**
  adolescent experimentation, 90–91
  preference, 44–45, 104–105
  sexual fantasies, 99–100
Homosexual love, 66
Honesty, in communication, 188–189
Hormones, sexual preference and, 45
Households, changing size, 17
Housekeeping. See Housework
Housewives, marital satisfaction of, 377–378
Housework
  division of responsibilities in dual-worker family, 381
  participation by men, 350–351
  standards, work overload and, 380–381

Human chorionic gonadotropin, 272, 277, 279
Human hunger, 58–62
Human interaction, need for, 59
Humor, in marriage, 238
Husband, presence during childbirth, 316
Husband-dominated marriages, 232
Hymen, 515–516
Hyperthermia, 270–271
Hyperthermic contraceptive procedures, 271–272
Hysterectomy, 268, **286**

Ideal images, 56
Idealization, 202, 216
  of parenthood, 332
  of sexual and marital partners, 167–168
Ideal self, 56
Ideation, 91, **111**
Identification, 36–37, **52**
Idiosyncrasies, 62
Illegitimacy, 248–250, **286**
Imitation, 34–36
Implantation, 521
Implementation power, 231, **240**
Imprinting, 157, **178**
Incest, **27**
Incest laws, 151–152
Incestuous marriages, 21
Incident hunger, 60
Income
  adjustment to divorce and, 442
  balance of power and, 231–232
  of dual-working couples, 372, 373–375
  family, 358, 360
  loss in retirement, 492
  related to work experience, 372
  remarriage and, 454–455
  yours/mine/ours, 543
Income taxes, 550–551
Individualistic lifestyle, 123
Induced abortion, 274–279
Infants. See also Children; Neonates
  feeding of, 40
Infatuation, 65, 68
Infertility
  adoption and, 284–285
  causes, 279
  emotional reactions to, 283–284
  legal and moral issues, 282–283
  in men, 280–281
  treatment for, 281–282
  in women, 279–280
"Infertility syndrome," 284
Inflation, 367, 542
Influence, over another person's feelings and behavior, 58
Inheritance tax laws, 540
In-laws. See also Kinship; Relatives
  influence on marriage, 395–396
  remarriage and, 463–464
Insecurity, 184

Insurance, 292–293, 548–550
Intellectualization, 206
Intensity, of commitment, 169
Interactional disqualification, 152, **178**
Interdependence
  by developing mutual goals, 218
  in marriage, 212–213
  mutual, 217
Interest-care, in marital relationship, 225
Intergenerational patterns of divorce, 409
Interlocutory period, 163, **178**
Interracial marriage, 150
Intimacy, 67
  dishonesty and, 200
  establishing, 186–187
  fear of, 413
  in long-term marriage, 499
  trust and, 189–190
Intrauterine device (IUD), 264–265
Intrinsic marriages, 223–224
Introitus vagina, 515
In vitro fertilization, 280, **286**
Involution, 311, **327**, 520
Irritations, minor, 207
Isolated nuclear unit, 394, **402**
Isolation, 59
Item analysis, 523

Jealousy, marital, 391–392
Job sharing, 389–390, **402**
Judgment, negative, 190

Kinship. See also In-laws; Relatives
  characteristics of system, 17–19
  indirect influence from, 397–398
  influences on marriage, 394–398
  mate selection and, 151–152

Labia majora, 514
Labia minora, 515
Labor, 307–311
  first state, 307–310
  fourth stage, 311
  second stage, 310–311·
  third stage, 311
Lactation, 317, **327**
La Leche League, 318–319
Laminaria digitate, 277
Language
  behavior, attractiveness and, 61–62
  between couple, 183–184
Laparoscope, 267
Laparotomy, 267
"Latchkey" children, 390, 492
Law enforcement agencies, sexual behavior and, 95
Laws
  age of consent, 151, 159–162
  cohabitation and, 136–140
  incest, 151–152, 159–162
  minimum age for marriage, 159–164

Mate selection (*continued*)
  by parents, 18
  positive factors, 152–153
  sex and age considerations, 164–165
  social maturity, 165–166
  theories, 154–158
  transition from choice to commitment, 166–168
Matrilineal, 18, **27**
Matrilocal family, 18
Meanings, in sexual communication, 199–200
Medical insurance, 549–550
Men
  feminization of, 43–44
  ideal, 33
  postdivorce adjustment problems, 438–439
  roles of, 32
Menopause, 485, **512**
"Men's liberation," 49
Menstruation, 83, **111**
Messages
  meaning and intent of, 183
  sending and receiving, 182–184
Metacommunication, 183, **209**
Mexican-Americans. *See* Hispanic-Americans
Microculture, 10, **27**
"Mid-life crisis," 221–222, 487
Minilaparotomy, 267
"Minipill," 261
Misinterpretation, 194
Misunderstanding, of message, 183
Mittelschmerz, 269
Monitrice, 310
Monogamy, 18, 20, 21, **27**, 107–108
Monozygotic, 312, **327**
Mons veneris, 513
Moral issues
  implications for future, 271
  of infertility treatment, 282–283
Morning-after injection, 272
Morning-after pill, 262
Mortgage rates and payments, 367, 547
Mothers
  differences with father, 349–353
  divorced, child custody and, 428
  reasons for becoming, 291
  reliability to reduce stress, 60
  stepmothers, 459–461
  unmarried, 358
  working, 13
Mutual dependence, 70
Mutual validation, 189, **209**

Name change, marriage and, 176
National Association of Social Workers, 419
National Council of Senior Citizens, 479
National Council on Family Relations, 419

"Natural" childbirth, 314–315
Natural disasters, 366
Natural family planning, 269–270
Need fulfillment, 70
Needs
  distinguishing from wants, 214
  individual, coordinating of, 213–214
Neo-Freudian, 77, **79**
Neolocal family, 18–19
Neonate, 311, **328**
  bonding, 315–317
  crying, 324
Neural, **52**
Neurotransmitters, love sickness and, 72
Nicotine, 301–302
Nidation, 521
Nipples, male, 519
Nonceremonial marriage, 20, **28**, 132
Nuclear family, 18–19, **28**
Nursing home, 507, **512**

Observation, of others, 57–58
Odor, attractiveness and, 62
Old. *See also* Elderly
  definition of, 479–480
Oogonia, 295, **328**
Open-couple, 123
"Open" marriage, 109
Openness, in communication, 184–187
Oral contraceptives, 259–262
Orchestration power, 231, **240**
Orgasm, 87, **111**
  male vs. female, 97
  process of, 96–98
Os, 520
Osteoporosis, 485, **512**
Ovabloc, 267–268
Ovaries, 519
Overprotectiveness, 75, 345, 356
Oviparous, 519
Ovix Fertility Computer, 269
Ovulation, 295, 519
  rhythm method and, 269
  stoppage, 280
Ovum (ova), 294, **328**, 519
  fertilization, 520–521

Palimony, 138–139, **142**
Parallel communication, 196
Parental abuse, 416
Parental Attitude Research Instrument, 345–346
Parental coalition, 348
Parent-child roles, changing, 334–338
Parent effectiveness training, 342, **363**
Parenthood
  adjustments to, 319–325, 321–323, 336
  advantages, 354
  guidelines, 323–325
  postpartum depression, 320–321

reasons for, 290–291
  roles and responses to child development, 338–341
Parenting
  discipline, cooperation and communication, 346–349
  in dual-career marriages, 384–385
  models, 344–345
  social class and, 343–344
  styles, 341–346
Parents
  athletic coach type, 345
  attitudes, 345–346
  authoritarian, 343
  authoritative, 343
  bonding process, 315–317
  buddy or pal type, 345
  elderly, abuse of, 416
  gay, 135
  gender-role models of, 37
  influence on teenage contraceptive usage, 252
  learning to live separately from, 186
  living with 20–24 year-old child, 335
  love between, 76–77
  as marital script models, 214–215
  martyr type, 344–345
  permissive, 343
  police or drill sergeant, 345
  responsibility, 320
  responsiveness of, 352–353
  role change, 320
  satisfaction, 350
  teacher-counselor type, 345
  teenage, 360–361
Parents Anonymous, 348
Parents Helping Parents, 356
Parents without Partners, 439
Partrilineal family form, 18
Passive-congenial marriage style, 223
Passive lifestyle, 123
Patriarchy, 18, **28**
Patrilineal, **28**
Patrilocal family, 18
Payments
  balloon, 552–553
  mortgage, 367, 547
Peers, **111**
  gender-role models of, 37
  influence in teenage contraceptive usage, 252
  influence on love, 77–78
  role in sex education, 83–84
  sexual activity with cross-sex, 91–94
  sexual activity with same-sex, 90–91
Pelvic girdle, 519
Pelvic inflammatory disease (PID), 260–261, 265, 280, **287**
Penis, **111**, 513, 517
  erection, 96, 521–522

Subcortical, 95, **112**
Substance abuse, 417–419
Supportive lifestyle, 123
Suppression, 206
Surrender, 187
Swinging singles, 122
Symbiotic relationship, 21
Symbolic interaction theory, 23
Symmetrical communication, 195–196
"Sympto-thermal" methods, 269
Systems theory
    behavior change and, 203–204
    of family member
        interrelationships, 333

Taboo, 82, **112**
    on discussion of sexual and erotic
        behavior, 84, 86
    mate selection, 151–152
    social, 83
    terms, 84
Tasks, loss of meaningful, 493
TATUM-T, 265
Taxes, 539
    income, 550–551
Teenage parents, 360–361
Tension. See Stress
Term insurance, 548
Testes, 518
Testicles (testes), 519
Testosterone, 519
Theory, **28**
    of attraction, 56–57, 62–63
    of disengagement, 495, **512**
    exchange, 23–24
    general systems, 24
    marriage and family, 24–26
    of marriage and family, 22–23
    of symbolic interaction, 23
Time, for family togetherness, 8
Time management, in marriage, 235–238
Total marriage style, 223
Touching, 57, 59, 60, 353
Toys, sex-role stereotypes and, 42
Traditional model of marriage, 224
Transition, 309

Transsexual, 42–44, **52**
Transvestism, 44, **52**
Trial marriage. **28**, 132, 133, 165, 172. See also Cohabitation.
"Triphasic pill," 261
Triplets, 312
"True self," 185
Trust, 189–190
    cooperation and, 219–220
    in marital relationship, 225
Tubal ligation, 267, **287**
Twins, 295, 312–313

Ultraertia, 72
Ultrasound, diagnostic, 303
Umbilical cord, 300, **328**
Unemployment, 375
Unmarried adults. See Singlehood
Urbanization, of marriage and family, 11–13
Uterus, 83, 520
    involution, 311, **327**, 520
    natural preparation for labor, 307
Utilitarian marriages, 223

Vacuum aspiration, 277
Vagina, 96, **112**, 520
Value comparison, in attraction, 56
Vas deferens, 518
Vasectomy, 265–268, **287**
Vasocongestion, 305, **328**
Venereal disease, singlehood and, 128
Verbal dominance, 190
Vernix caseosa, 307, **328**
Vestibule, 516
Violence, prevention and treatment, 417
Visitation, 433–434
Vital marriage style, 223
Viviparous, 519
Voice, attractiveness and, 61
Volunteering, during retirement, 491–492
Vulnerability
    fears of, 187
    trust and, 189–190
Vulva, 96, **112**, 514–515

Wages, 372, 373–374
Wants, acknowledging, 214–217
Wedding, 173–176
Welfare, 535
"Wet dreams," 98
Wheel theory of love, 70, 71
Widowhood
    elderly, 505
    remarriage after, 468–472
Will, 540
Withdrawal, 270
Women
    changing roles of, 48–49
    ideal, 33
    in labor force, 482
    postdivorce adjustment problems, 438
    roles of, 32
Women's liberation, 128
Work
    marital relationship and, 370–371
    marriage and family life, 375–377
    overload, 380–382
    stress and, 369–371
Workaholic, 383–384, **402**
Work force
    changes in, 371–373
    participation for married women, 375–376
    women in. See Working women
Working women, 49
    acceptance of, 40
    divorced, child custody and, 428
    dual responsibilities, 373–377
    inflation and, 367
    marital satisfaction of, 377–380
    pregnancy and, 306
    return to work after childbirth, 318
    wages and income, 372, 373–374
Writing, men vs. women, 191–192

X chromosome, 296–297

Y chromosome, 296–297

Zero population growth, 246, **287**
Zygote, 296, **328**, 521